X. J. KENNEDY ◆ DOROTHY M. KENNEDY
MARCIA F. MUTH

THE BEDFORD GUIDE

for COLLEGE WRITERS

EIGHTH EDITION

with Reader

BEDFORD / ST. MARTIN'S   Boston ◆ New York

KH

FOR BEDFORD/ST. MARTIN'S

Developmental Editors: Beth Castrodale, Christina Gerogiannis
Senior Production Editor: Deborah Baker
Senior Production Supervisor: Joe Ford
Senior Marketing Manager: Karita dos Santos
Editorial Assistant: Stephanie Naudin
Copyeditor: Mary Lou Wilshaw-Watts
Text Design: Claire Seng-Niemoeller
Cover Design and Art: Hannus Design Associates
Composition: Monotype, LLC
Printing and Binding: R.R. Donnelley & Sons Company

President: Joan E. Feinberg
Editorial Director: Denise B. Wydra
Editor in Chief: Karen S. Henry
Director of Marketing: Karen Melton Soeltz
Director of Editing, Design, and Production: Marcia Cohen
Managing Editor: Elizabeth M. Schaaf

Library of Congress Control Number: 2007927475

For information, write: Bedford/St. Martin's, 75 Arlington Street, Boston, MA 02116
(617-399-4000)

ISBN-13: 978–0–312–46929–0
ISBN-10: 0–312–46929–2

ACKNOWLEDGMENTS

Michael Abernethy, "Male Bashing on TV." First published on *PopMatters.com,* January 9, 2003. Copyright © 2003 by PopMatters.com. Reprinted with permission of PopMatters Media, Inc.

Russell Baker, "The Art of Eating Spaghetti" from pp. 186–89 of *Growing Up* by Russell Baker. Copyright © 1982 by Russell Baker. Published by Congdon and Weed/Contemporary Publishing. Reprinted by permission of Don Congdon Associates, Inc.

John Barbieri, "Save Hydrogen for Later; Ethanol Power Is the Viable Option for Now" from the *Amherst Student,* April 19, 2006. Copyright © 2006. Reprinted with the permission of the *Amherst Student.*

Dave Barry, "From Now On, Let Women Kill Their Own Spiders." First published in the *Miami Herald,* February 12, 1999. Copyright © 1999 by Dave Barry. Reprinted with the permission of the author.

Sam Benen, "A Royal Mess: How Online Poker Has Enraptured Today's College Student" from *Business Today Online Journal,* November 13, 2006. Reprinted with the permission of the Federation for Student Communication.

Linn Bourgeau, from "Crucial Choices: Who Will Save the Wetlands If Everyone Is at the Mall?" Reprinted with the permission of the author.

Judy Brady, "I Want a Wife." First published in *Ms.* magazine, December 1971. Copyright © 1970 by Judy Brady. Reprinted with the permission of the author.

Suzanne Britt, "Neat People vs. Sloppy People" from *Show and Tell* (Raleigh, North Carolina: Morning Owl Press, 1982). Copyright © 1982 by Suzanne Britt. Reprinted with the permission of the author.

Acknowledgments and copyrights are continued at the back of the book on pages A-54–57, which constitute an extension of the copyright page. It is a violation of the law to reproduce these selections by any means whatsoever without the written permission of the copyright holder.

11/26/08

Preface: To the Instructor

When it was first published twenty years ago, *The Bedford Guide for College Writers* brought a lively and innovative approach to the teaching of writing. Since that time, authors X. J. and Dorothy M. Kennedy have won praise for their friendly, engaging writing style and their remarkable sense of what students need to know to succeed in the composition course. More recently, experienced teacher and writer Marcia F. Muth joined the author team, adding more practical advice to help all students, even those underprepared for college, become successful academic writers. The result is an unusually thorough and accessible book that continues to evolve to meet the needs of both students and instructors.

With its process-oriented rhetoric and provocative thematic reader *The Bedford Guide* gives students essential tools to succeed as writers. And now this new edition does even more to build essential academic writing skills, with expanded coverage of source-based writing, audience analysis, argumentation and reasoning, and more. Additionally, an expanded array of innovative student and instructor resources ensures that you and your students are supported every step of the way.

Overview of The Bedford Guide

This version of *The Bedford Guide for College Writers* offers a writing guide and thematic reader, both of them now even better resources for students. *The Bedford Guide* is available in two other versions as well: as four books in one, with the writing guide and reader, as well as a research manual and handbook, and as three books in one (without the handbook). An e-book version is also available. (For more details on the e-book and other exciting new resources accompanying *The Bedford Guide*, see pp. ix–xiii.)

BOOK ONE: *A Writer's Guide*

This uniquely accessible — yet thorough — process-oriented rhetoric with readings helps students become better writers, regardless of their skill level. Addressing all the assignments and topics typically covered in the first-year writing course, it is divided into four parts.

Part One, "A College Writer's Processes," introduces students to the interconnected processes of writing (Chapter 1), reading (Chapter 2), and critical thinking (Chapter 3). In Chapter 3, coverage of logic and reasoning, expanded in this edition, helps students become better thinkers and writers.

In Part Two, "A Writer's Situations," nine core chapters — each including two sample readings (one by a student) — guide students step-by-step through a full range of common first-year writing assignments. If followed sequentially, these chapters lead students gradually into the rigorous analytical writing that will comprise most of their college writing. The rhetorical situations in Part Two include recalling an experience (Chapter 4), observing a scene (Chapter 5), interviewing a subject (Chapter 6), comparing and contrasting (Chapter 7), explaining causes and effects (Chapter 8), taking a stand (Chapter 9), proposing a solution (Chapter 10), evaluating (Chapter 11), and supporting a position with sources (Chapter 12). Chapter 12, new to this edition, helps students write position papers that draw on a few sources — an increasingly common academic writing assignment.

Part Three, "Special Writing Situations," offers helpful strategies and plenty of examples to support students' efforts in three additional situations: responding to literature (Chapter 13), writing in the workplace (Chapter 14), and writing for assessment (Chapter 15).

Part Four, "A Writer's Strategies," is a convenient resource for approaching all aspects of writing, and each chapter in this part has been updated with new examples. The first five chapters explain and illustrate the stages of the writing process: generating ideas (Chapter 16), stating a thesis and planning (Chapter 17), drafting (Chapter 18), developing (Chapter 19), and revising and editing (Chapter 20). Marginal annotations in the earlier parts of the book guide students to these chapters, which collectively serve as a writer's toolbox. Part Four also includes two chapters on using and analyzing visuals: "Strategies for Designing Your Document" (Chapter 21) and "Strategies for Understanding Visual Representations" (Chapter 22). Both chapters, which are the basis of the popular Bedford/St. Martin's supplement *Getting the Picture*, have been updated to include even more visuals.

BOOK TWO: *A Writer's Reader*

A Writer's Reader is a thematic reader, unique in a book of this kind. The reader offers 32 selections — 19 of them new — arranged around five engaging themes that provide a meaningful context for students, giving them something to write about. The themes are families (Chapter 23), men and women (Chapter 24), popular culture (Chapter 25), electronic technology (Chapter 26), and education (Chapter 27). Electronic technology, a new chapter, was added in response to reviewer requests, and it explores possibilities and implications from online learning communities to free speech and privacy issues in the age of MySpace. Each reading is accompanied by apparatus that moves students smoothly from reading and thinking to writing. The selections are coordinated with *A Writer's Guide* and serve as models of the writing situations assigned there; a rhetorical table of contents (p. xxxviii) helps students see these connections.

Each reading is introduced by a biographical headnote and a brief reading tip. Each is followed by questions on meaning, writing strategies, critical reading, vocabulary, and connections to other selections; journal prompts; and suggested writing assignments, one personal and the other analytical. These questions move students from reading carefully for both thematic and rhetorical elements to applying new strategies and insights in their own writing.

USEFUL APPENDICES

All versions of the book also include a Quick Research Guide and a Quick Editing Guide. The Quick Research Guide conveniently and briefly reviews how to find, evaluate, integrate, cite, and document sources. The Quick Editing Guide gives special attention to the most troublesome grammar and editing problems.

New to the Eighth Edition

The revisions in this new edition reflect trends in composition courses and incorporate the suggestions of a host of reviewers. The changes have resulted in an even more practical book that helps students become better academic writers.

A NEW CHAPTER ON POSITION PAPERS

Reviewers have pointed out that while full research papers remain important components of the composition class, students increasingly are being asked to write papers that use a few sources, especially to support a position. We've responded to this trend with a new chapter (Chapter 12) that shows students how to marshal evidence to support a stance while maintaining their own strong voice — a common academic writing challenge. It also shows, through text and graphics, how to cite and document this material fairly.

Information Captured from Your Source

Sample Working Thesis

A clear thesis statement establishes a framework for selecting source material as useful evidence and for explaining its relevance to readers.

> WORKING THESIS: In order to counter national and worldwide trends toward obesity, agricultural communities like Grand Junction need to apply their expertise as food producers to the promotion of healthy food products.

Quotation from an Indirect Source

A quotation from an indirect source captures the exact words of an author quoted within the source.

An 1894 action by Congress created a holiday to recognize workers who "delved and carved" to produce what Americans enjoy (qtd. in Salcian par. 1).

If possible, go to the original source to be sure that the quotation is accurate and that you are using it appropriately. (See the bottom lefthand page.)

Credit, though disputed, has gone to labor leader Peter McGuire for promoting the recognition of those who "delved and carved all the grandeur we behold" (US Dept. of Labor par. 4).

UNIQUE SELF-ASSESSMENT CHARTS — DRAFT DOCTORS

These innovative charts are designed to make students stronger writers, regardless of their skill level. Specifically, the charts help students reflect on their own writing, identify its weaknesses, and then use relevant strategies for strengthening their papers. Draft Doctors address such important issues as supporting a stand, integrating and synthesizing sources, and strengthening thesis statements.

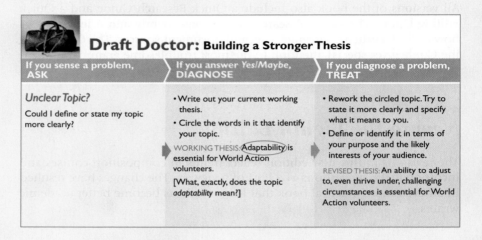

Draft Doctor: Building a Stronger Thesis		
If you sense a problem, ASK	**If you answer Yes/Maybe, DIAGNOSE**	**If you diagnose a problem, TREAT**
Unclear Topic? Could I define or state my topic more clearly?	• Write out your current working thesis. • Circle the words in it that identify your topic. WORKING THESIS: (Adaptability) is essential for World Action volunteers. [What, exactly, does the topic *adaptability* mean?]	• Rework the circled topic. Try to state it more clearly and specify what it means to you. • Define or identify it in terms of your purpose and the likely interests of your audience. REVISED THESIS: An ability to adjust to, even thrive under, challenging circumstances is essential for World Action volunteers.

EXPANDED COVERAGE OF AUDIENCE

Even students who realize that the language they use chatting with friends might be inappropriate for addressing instructors or work supervisors may not know how to adjust their writing for different audiences. Expanded cov-

Audience Characteristics and Expectations	GENERAL AUDIENCE	COLLEGE INSTRUCTOR	WORK SUPERVISOR	CAMPUS FRIEND	PARENT OR GRANDPARENT
READER'S RELATIONSHIP TO YOU	Imagined but not known personally	Known briefly in a class context	Known for some time in a job context	Known in campus and social contexts	Known all of your life in family contexts
REASON FOR READING YOUR WRITING	Curious attitude and interest in your topic assumed	Professional responsibility for your knowledge and skills	Managerial interest in and reliance on your job performance	Personal interest based on shared circumstances	Family bond and lifelong concern about you
KNOWLEDGE ABOUT TOPIC	Level of awareness assumed and gaps addressed with logical presentation	Well informed about college topics but wants to see what you know	Informed about the business and expects reliable information from you	Friendly but may or may not be informed beyond social interests	Loving but may or may not be informed beyond family concerns

erage helps students understand how to address various audiences effectively and respectfully in writing. Additionally, new coverage helps students meet the expectations of academic audiences in particular.

IMPROVED COVERAGE OF CRITICAL THINKING, REASONING, AND ARGUMENT

Chapter 3 ("Critical Thinking Processes") now provides advice on applying critical thinking to academic problems through analysis, synthesis, and evaluation. It also offers new coverage of inductive versus deductive reasoning and of sound versus weak reasoning. And Chapter 9 ("Taking a Stand") provides more support for making logical arguments, with new coverage of the Toulmin method, clearer advice on supporting claims effectively, and more.

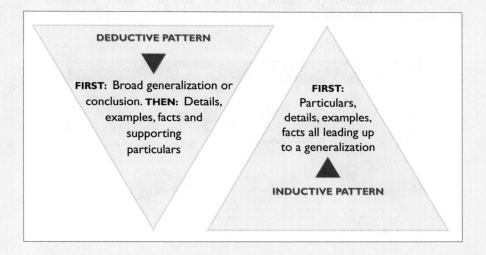

AN IMPROVED SUITE OF ELECTRONIC RESOURCES

Never before have *Bedford Guide* users had access to a more extensive and innovative array of electronic resources, helping students with everything from strategies for planning and drafting to revising based on the comments of peers.

A Redesigned and Expanded Companion Web Site.   The companion Web site (at <bedfordstmartins.com/bedguide>) has a cleaner, less cluttered look while offering multiple routes of access to important information (by topic or keyword search). The site includes the following features:

- Interactive writing, research, and grammar practices, with new ESL exercises
- Readings and model papers
- New "Ask the Draft Doctor" feature: students pick a writing concern they have and then get suggestions for improving their papers, as well as links to related resources on the Web site.
- New links for authors featured in *The Bedford Guide*
- Research and documentation advice
- New peer review worksheets
- Classroom activities, syllabi, and other instructor tools, including new PowerPoint presentations on writing, research, and grammar

Premium Web content (including an e-book and peer review resources) is also available. These resources are described in the following sections.

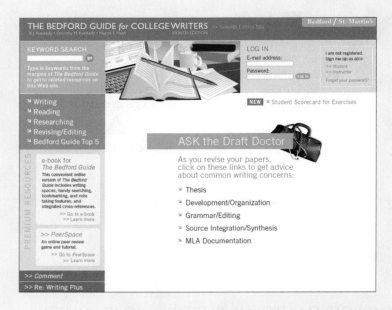

A New E-Book.   The e-book offers the complete text of the print book, with state-of-the-art tools and multimedia from the book's Web site built in. Students can highlight and annotate the readings, respond to writing prompts directly in the book, jump to interactive exercises, and bookmark sections to be used for reference. Instructors can add their own materials — models, notes, assignments, course guidelines — and even reorganize chapters.

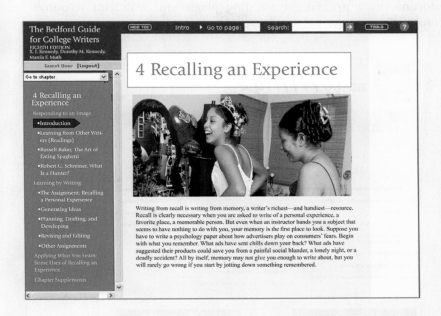

A New Peer Review Resource: *PeerSpace*. *PeerSpace* is a collection of confidence-building activities that teach best practices for peer review. Resources include an interactive simulation game, models, exercises, and assignments. When students are ready to put what they've learned into practice, there's *Comment* (see below), which is integrated into *PeerSpace*.

Other Electronic Resources

Comment for THE BEDFORD GUIDE FOR COLLEGE WRITERS (<comment .bedfordstmartins.com>). This Web-based peer-review software lets students share and comment on their writing. Instructors can create comments that link directly to specific passages in *The Bedford Guide e-Book.* Students who need more peer review help will find it in *PeerSpace*, integrated into *Comment.*

Re: Writing (at <bedfordstmartins.com/rewriting>). This free and open Web site collects Bedford/St. Martin's most popular and widely used online resources at a single address. It includes *Exercise Central* (more than 7,000 interactive online exercises), research and documentation advice, model documents, a tutorial on avoiding plagiarism, instructor resources, and more.

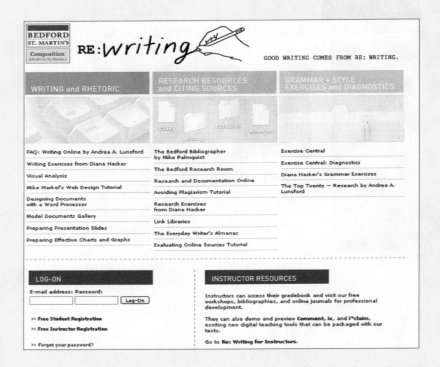

An Innovative New Online Course Space: *CompClass.* This easy-to-use online course space integrates all the innovative media supporting *The Bedford Guide*—the e-book, *Comment*, the book companion site, and more—with course tools designed specifically for the reading, writing, practice, and discussion that writing instructors and students do. *CompClass* also lets you add spaces designed for writing—blogs, journals, and discussion forums—and mix in your own course materials, customizing the site so that it reflects the way you teach. *CompClass* is *your* composition course space—whether you teach online, face-to-face, or a little of each.

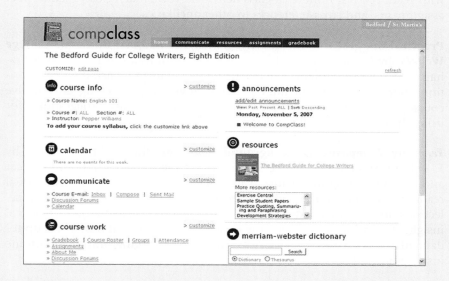

Exercise Central to Go.   This CD-ROM offers hundreds of practice items to improve students' writing and editing skills. Drawn from the popular *Exercise Central* Web site, the exercises cover a wide variety of topics, from identifying effective main points and support to integrating and documenting sources to fixing grammar errors. No Internet connection is necessary.

Testing Tool Kit: A Writing and Grammar Test Bank.   This CD-ROM allows instructors to create secure, customized tests and quizzes to assess students' writing and grammar competency and gauge their progress during the course. The CD includes nearly 2,000 test items on 47 writing and grammar topics, at two levels of difficulty. Also, ten pre-built diagnostic tests are included. Scoring is instantaneous when tests and quizzes are administered online.

Print Resources

Instructor's Annotated Edition of *The Bedford Guide for College Writers* puts information right where busy instructors need it: on the pages of the book itself. The marginal annotations offer teaching tips, analysis tips with readings, last-minute in-class activities, vocabulary glosses, additional assignments, and cross-references to other ancillaries.

Practical Suggestions for Teaching with *The Bedford Guide for College Writers*, by Dana Waters of Dodge City Community College, Shirley Morahan, and Sylvia A. Holladay, helps instructors plan and teach their composition course. This text includes practical advice on designing an effective course, sample syllabi, chapter-by-chapter support, and suggestions for using the electronic media package.

Teaching Composition: Background Readings, third edition, edited by T. R. Johnson of Tulane University, addresses the concerns of both first-year and veteran writing instructors. This collection includes thirty professional readings on composition and rhetoric written by leaders in the field. The selections are accompanied by helpful introductions, activities, and practical insights for inside and outside the classroom. The new edition offers up-to-date advice on avoiding plagiarism, classroom blogging, improving online instruction, and more.

Study Skills for College Writers, by Laurie Walker of Eastern Michigan University, is a handy booklet full of activities designed to help underprepared students improve their study skills. It offers many practical tips and strategies for managing time, taking notes, taking tests, and accessing college resources.

Ordering Information

To order any of the ancillaries, please contact your Bedford/St. Martin's sales representative, e-mail sales support at sales_support@bfwpub.com, or visit our Web site at <bedfordstmartins.com>. Note that activation codes are required for the e-book, *PeerSpace*, *Comment*, and *CompClass*. Codes can be purchased separately or packaged with the print book at a significant discount.

When ordering an access card for premium Web site content (the e-book and *PeerSpace*) packaged with the book, use these ISBNs:

- with Reader, Research Manual, and Handbook (hardcover):
  ISBN-13: 978-0-312-47756-1; ISBN-10: 0-312-47756-2

- with Reader, Research Manual, and Handbook (paperback): ISBN-13: 978-0-312-47759-2; ISBN-10: 0-312-47759-7
- with Reader and Research Manual (paperback only): ISBN-13: 978-0-312-47753-0; ISBN-10: 0-312-47753-8
- with Reader (paperback only): ISBN-13: 978-0-312-47744-8; ISBN-10: 0-312-47744-9

When ordering an access card for *Comment* packaged with the book, use these ISBNs:

- with Reader, Research Manual, and Handbook (hardcover): ISBN-13: 978-0-312-47755-4; ISBN-10: 0-312-47755-4
- with Reader, Research Manual, and Handbook (paperback): ISBN-13: 978-0-312-47758-5; ISBN-10: 0-312-47758-9
- with Reader and Research Manual (paperback only): ISBN-13: 978-0-312-47752-3; ISBN-10: 0-312-47752-X
- with Reader (paperback only): ISBN-13: 978-0-312-47743-1; ISBN-10: 0-312-47743-0

When ordering an access card for *CompClass* packaged with the book, use these ISBNs:

- with Reader, Research Manual, and Handbook (hardcover): ISBN-13: 978-0-312-47754-7; ISBN-10: 0-312-47754-6
- with Reader, Research Manual, and Handbook (paperback): ISBN-13: 978-0-312-47757-8; ISBN-10: 0-312-47757-0
- with Reader and Research Manual (paperback only): ISBN-13: 978-0-312-47751-6; ISBN-10: 0-312-47751-1
- with Reader (paperback only): ISBN-13: 978-0-312-47742-4; ISBN-10: 0-312-47742-2

When ordering *Study Skills for College Writers* packaged with your students' books, use these ISBNs:

- with Reader, Research Manual, and Handbook (hardcover): ISBN-13: 978-0-312-47696-0; ISBN-10: 0-312-47696-5
- with Reader, Research Manual, and Handbook (paperback): ISBN-13: 978-0-312-47691-5; ISBN-10: 0-312-47691-4
- with Reader and Research Manual (paperback only): ISBN-13: 978-0-312-47686-1; ISBN-10: 0-312-47686-8
- with Reader (paperback only): ISBN-13: 978-0-312-47680-9; ISBN-10: 0-312-47680-9

Thanks and Appreciation

Many individuals contributed significantly to the eighth edition of *The Bedford Guide for College Writers*, and we extend our sincerest thanks to all of them.

EDITORIAL ADVISORY BOARD

As we began to prepare the eighth edition, we assembled an Editorial Advisory Board to respond to the many significant changes we planned and to share ideas about how to make the book more useful to both students and teachers. These dedicated instructors responded thoroughly and insightfully to just about every new feature of the text, and we are extremely grateful to each and every one of them:

- Kathleen Beauchene, Community College of Rhode Island
- Jan Bone, Roosevelt University and Harper College
- Rita Buscher-Weeks, Spartanburg Technical College
- Helen Duclos, Arkansas State University
- Julie Freeman, Indiana University–Purdue University Indianapolis
- Leigh A. Martin, Community College of Rhode Island
- Terry Novak, Johnson & Wales University
- Brit Osgood-Treston, Riverside Community College
- Mark Reynolds, Jefferson Davis Community College
- Patrick Smith, Axia College of University of Phoenix
- Dana Waters, Dodge City Community College

OTHER COLLEAGUES

We also extend our gratitude to instructors across the country who took time and care to review this and previous editions, to participate in a focus group, and to send us their suggestions gleaned from experience with students. For this we thank Alice B. Adams, Prestonsburg Community College; Rosemary R. Adams, Eastern Connecticut State University; Ted Allder, University of Arkansas Community College at Batesville; Patricia Allen, Cape Cod Community College; Steve Amidon, University of Rhode Island; David Auchter, San Jacinto Junior College; Renee Bangerter, Fullerton College; Stuart Barbier, Delta College; Marci Bartolotta, Nova Southeastern University; Barry Batorsky, DeVry University; Shannon Beasley, Arkansas State University; Randolph A. Beckham, Germanna Community College; Pamela J. Behrens, Alabama A&M University; Carmine J. Bell, Pasco Hernando Community College; Kay Berg, Sinclair Community College; Tanya Boler, East Central Community College; Jeannie Boniecki, Naugatuck Valley Community College; Debbie Boyd, East Central Community College; Barbara Brown, San Jacinto College Central; Ty Buckman, Wittenberg University; Joan Campbell, Wellesley College; Tom Casey, El Paso Community College; Steve Cirrone, Tidewater Community College; Susan Romayne Clark, Central Michigan University; Ted Contreras, Long Beach City College; Nancy Cook, Sierra College; Jane Corbly, George Peabody College for Teachers; Monica Cox, Community College of Rhode Island; Carolyn Craft, Longwood College; Sheilah Craft, Marian College; Mary Cullen, Middlesex Community College; P. R. Dansby, San Jacinto Community College; Fred D'Astoli, Ventura College; Ed Davis, Sinclair Community College; Patricia Ann Delamar, University of Dayton; Irene Duprey-Gutierrez, University of Massachusetts, Dartmouth; Corinna Evett, Fullerton and Santa Ana Colleges; Carol Luers Eyman, St. Joseph School of Practical Nursing; Leora Freedman, Modesto Junior College; Sandy Fuhr, Gustavus Adolphus College; Jan Fulwiler, Lethbridge Community College; Pamela Garvey, St. Louis Community College–Meramec; Mary Ann Gauthier, St. Joseph College; Michael Gavin, Prince George's Community College; Olga Geissler, San Joaquin Delta College; Robert Gmerlin, Sierra College; Aaron Goldweber, Heald College; Daniel Gonzales, Louisiana State University; Sherry F. Gott, Danville Community College; Daniel V. Gribbin, University of Central Florida; Robert Grindy, Richland Community College; Joyce Hall, Border Institute of Technology; Jefferson Hancock, San Jose State University; Alyssa Harad, University of Texas at Austin; Johnnie Hargrove, Alabama A&M University; Judy Hatcher, San Jacinto College Central; Elaine Hays, University of Rhode Island; Diana Hicks, American River College; Marita Hinton, Alabama A&M University; Tom Hodges, Amarillo College; Jane Holwerda, Dodge City Community College; Patricia Hunt, Catonsville Community College; Elizabeth Jarok, Middlesex Community College; Barbara Jensen, Modesto Junior College; Greg Jewell, Madisonville Community College; Jean L. Johnson, University of North Alabama; Ted Johnston, El Paso Community College; Andrew Jones, University of California at Davis; Anne D. Jordan, Eastern Connecticut State University; M. L. Kayser, Heald College; Cynthia Kellogg, Yuba College; Dimitri Keriotis, Modesto Junior College; Kate Kiefer, Colorado State University; Yoon Sik Kim, Langston University; Kaye Kolkmann, Modesto Junior College; Fred A. Koslowski III, Delaware Valley College; Brandy Kreisler, Axia College of University of Phoenix; Sandra Lakey, Pennsylvania College of Technology; Norman Lanquist, Eastern Arizona College; Colleen Lloyd, Cuyahoga Community College; Stephen Ma, University of Alberta; Susan Peck MacDonald, California State University at Long Beach; Jennifer Madej, Milwaukee Area Technical College; Janice Mandile, Front Range Community College; Phil Martin, Minneapolis Community and Technical College; Gerald McCarthy, San Antonio College; Miles S. McCrimmon, J. Sargeant Reynolds Community College; Jackie McGrath, College of DuPage; Jenna Merritt, Eastern Michigan University; Elizabeth Metzger, University of South Florida; Eric Meyer, St. Louis Community College–Meramec; Libby Miles, University of Rhode Island; Sandra Moore,

Mississippi Delta Community College; Cleatta Morris, Louisiana State University at Shreveport; Robert Morse, Western International University; Sheryl A. Mylan, Stephen F. Austin State University; Clement Ndulute, Mississippi Valley State University; Jerry Nelson, Lincoln University; Peggy J. Oliver, San Jacinto College South; Laura Osborne, New River Community College; Mike Palmquist, Colorado State University; Geraldine C. Pelegano, Naugatuck Valley Community College; Laurel S. Peterson, Norwalk Community Technical College; Mary F. Pflugshaupt, Indiana State University; John F. Pleimann, Jefferson College; Kenneth E. Poitras, Antelope Valley College; Michael Punches, Oklahoma City Community College; Patrice Quarg, Cantonsville Community College; Jeanie Page Randall, Austin Peay State University; Betty Ray, Jones College; Joan Reteshka, Sewickley Academy; Kira Roark, University of Denver; Peggy Roche, California University of Pennsylvania; Dawn Rodrigues, University of Texas at Brownsville; Ann Westmoreland Runsick, Gateway Technical College; Karin Russell, Keiser University; Joyce Russo, Lakeland Community College; Wendy Schmidt, Axia College of University of Phoenix; Nancy J. Schneider, University of Maine at Augusta; Janis Schulte, Colby Community College; Susan Schurman, Ventura College; Patricia C. Schwindt, Mesa Community College; Herbert Shapiro, SUNY Empire State College; Andrea Shaw, Nova Southeastern University; Elizabeth Smart, Utah State University; Ognjen Smiljanic, Eastern Michigan University; Allison Smith, Middle Tennessee State University; David Sorrells, Lamar State College–Port Arthur; Ann Spencer-Livingstone, SUNY Morrisville Norwich Campus; Lori Spillane, Indiana University–Purdue University Indianapolis; Scott R. Stankey, Anoka-Ramsey Community College; Leroy Sterling, Alabama A&M University; Dean Stover, Gateway Community College; Ellen Straw, Mt. San Antonio College; Monnette Sturgill, Prestonsburg Community College; Ronald Sudol, Oakland University; Darlene Summers, Montgomery College; David Tammer, Eastern Arizona College; William G. Thomas, Saddleback College; Daphne Thompson, Johnson & Wales; Janice M. Vierk, Metropolitan Community College; Dave Waddell, California State University at Chico; Christopher Walker, Prince George's Community College; Laurie Walker, Eastern Michigan University; Carol Westcamp, University of Arkansas–Fort Smith; Patricia South White, Norwich University; Susan Whitlow, University of Arkansas–Fort Smith; Jim Wilcox, Southern Nazarene University; Carmiele Wilkerson, Wittenberg University; Mary Zacharias, San Jacinto Community College Central; and Valerie P. Zimbaro, Valencia Community College.

CONTRIBUTORS

The eighth edition could not have been completed without the help of numerous individuals. Mark Gallaher wrote excellent apparatus for the new reading selections as well as tips for the *Instructor's Annotated Edition*. Julie Nichols (Okaloosa-Walton College) wrote engaging new ESL exercises for *Exercise Central*. A special thanks to Dana Waters (Dodge City Community

College) for once again revising *Practical Suggestions* and for suggesting many excellent student essays, some of which we have included in the book. Kathleen Beauchene (Community College of Rhode Island) also contributed to *Practical Suggestions,* adding advice on teaching with new reader selections. Once again, T. R. Johnson (Tulane University) edited *Teaching Composition: Background Readings* with energy and insight. Art researcher Linda Finigan helped us take the book in an even more visually rich direction, finding new photographs and other images. She also cleared permissions for the art, while Fred Courtright efficiently cleared text permissions under the able guidance of Sandy Schechter. Grace Talusan contributed engaging activities to *The Bedford Guide*'s companion Web site and also compiled links on authors featured in the reader. Jan Bone created PowerPoints for the book to spark class discussion and learning.

We are grateful as well for Mary Lou Wilshaw-Watts's thoughtful copyediting and, last but not least, for Claire Seng-Niemoeller's attractive and accessible designs of new visual elements.

STUDENT WRITERS

We offer sincere thanks to all the students who have challenged us over the years to find better ways to help them learn. In particular we would like to thank those who granted us permission to use their essays in the eighth edition. Focused as this textbook is on student writing, we consider it essential to provide effective model essays by students. The writings of Anne Cahill, Jonathan Burns, Tim Chabot, Yun Yung Choi, David Ian Cohn, Michael Coil, Heather Colbenson, Geoffrey Fallon, Sarah Goers, Heidi Kessler, Dawn Kortz, Lindsey Schendel, Robert G. Schreiner, Lillian Tsu, and Carrie Williamson were included in earlier editions as well as this one. New to the eighth edition are the writings of John Barbieri, Sam Benen, Linn Bourgeau, Cindy Keeler, Melissa Lamberth, Daniel Matthews, Angela Mendy, Susanna Olsen, and Dennis O'Neil.

EDITORIAL

At Bedford/St. Martin's three individuals merit special recognition. President Joan E. Feinberg and Editorial Director Denise B. Wydra (also a former editor of *The Bedford Guide*) continue to contribute invaluable suggestions for improving the book for both students and instructors. We also greatly value the guidance of Editor in Chief Karen S. Henry, who has helped sustain the direction of the book throughout many editions and who has provided perceptive advice at crucial points in the development of the current edition.

The editorial effort behind this edition was truly a team endeavor. Marcia F. Muth assumed a major authorial role in the seventh edition, answering needs expressed by users with many exciting new features. She has continued in that role in the eighth edition, bringing innovation to every part of the book and making it an even stronger resource for all students, regardless of their skill level. Beth Castrodale skillfully managed all aspects of the eighth edition, keeping the team on track and on schedule. She once again brought to the project her sharp eye for textual and visual elements alike and her remarkable creative energy, cheerfully and patiently solving problems large and small. Karin Halbert, a gifted writer and editor, oversaw development of the book in its early stages and later helped with a variety of other tasks. This book could not have been completed without her. Christina Gerogiannis and Stephanie Naudin energetically developed *A Writer's Reader*, finding many excellent selections, and Christina helped with a host of other tasks as the development of this new edition got off the ground. Stephanie also took on many other responsibilities, from overseeing an extensive and ongoing review program to developing *Teaching Composition: Background Readings*. Kimberly White, succeeded by Daniel Cole, guided the development and production of the electronic resources, bringing incredible creativity and energy to the development of the e-book and other parts of the package. Anne Leung, a constant source of smart ideas, also helped develop the electronic resources, especially the book's companion Web site. Her insights and extensive contact with Web site users were invaluable in improving what was already a comprehensive resource. Other members of the Bedford/St. Martin's staff contributed greatly to the eighth edition. Many thanks and heartfelt appreciation go to Deborah Baker, whose exacting eye, careful hand, and great patience once again shepherded the book through production. We especially appreciate her care in overseeing the design updates and the production of the book's growing art program. Marcia Cohen, Elizabeth Schaaf, and John Amburg were immensely helpful in overseeing production. Donna Dennison and Billy Boardman oversaw the redesign of the book's cover, giving us a fresh look that still preserves the integrity of *The Bedford Guide*. Karita dos Santos skillfully coordinated the marketing of the book and offered much good advice based on feedback from the field. Karen Melton Soeltz and Jane Helms also offered valuable marketing advice. The book's promotion was ably handled by Shelby Disario and Pelle Cass, and Pelle created a colorful and appealing brochure.

Marcia Muth is especially grateful to the School of Education at the University of Colorado at Denver and Health Sciences Center for sponsoring her writing workshops. Finally, we once again thank our friends and families for their unwavering patience, understanding, and encouragement.

How to Use The Bedford Guide for College Writers

Just as you may be unsure of what to expect from your writing course, you may also be unsure of what to expect from your writing textbook. You may even be wondering how any textbook can improve your writing. In fact, a book alone can't make you a better writer, but practice can, and *The Bedford Guide for College Writers* guides your practice. This text offers help — easy to find and easy to use — for writing the essays most commonly assigned in the first-year composition course.

Underlying *The Bedford Guide* is the idea that writing is a necessary and useful skill in and beyond the writing course. For this reason, the book provides help with writing for other college courses, writing on the job, and writing as a member of a community. In other words, the skills you will learn throughout this book are transferable to other areas of your life, making *The Bedford Guide* both a time-saver and a money-saver.

The following sections describe how you can get the most out of this text. *The Bedford Guide* is designed so that you can move quickly and easily to the section you need. And once you are there, several key features can help you improve your writing by guiding your practice. Let us show you what we mean.

Finding Information in The Bedford Guide

It's easy to find what you need when you need it in *The Bedford Guide*. Each of the tools described here will direct you to useful information — fast.

Brief List of Contents.   Open the book to the inside front cover. At a glance you can see a list of the topics within *The Bedford Guide*. If you are looking for a specific chapter, this brief list of contents is the quickest way to find it.

Detailed List of Contents.   Beginning on p. xxxi, the longer, more detailed list of contents breaks down the topics covered within each chapter of the book. Use this list to find a specific part of a chapter. For example, if you have been assigned to read Russell Baker's "The Art of Eating Spaghetti," a quick scan of the detailed contents will show you that it begins on page 56.

Rhetorical List of Contents.   This list, which begins on page xxxviii, includes all of the readings in *The Bedford Guide,* organized by writing strategy. You can use this list to help you locate additional examples of a particular kind of writing such as comparing and contrasting or explaining causes and effects.

Resource Charts.   If you open the book to the inside back cover and its facing page, you'll find a chart showing where you can get help in the text or its companion Web site, no matter where you are in the writing process. If you find yourself stuck at a particular stage, consider turning here for help.

A Writer's Resources

Major stages	Help in this book	Web help*
Generate Ideas • Find a topic and something to say. • Brainstorm, freewrite, doodle, map, imagine, question, seek motives, or keep a journal. • Read, talk, observe, and think.	▪ "Generating Ideas" section in Part Two, including Discovery Checklists ▪ "Strategies for Generating Ideas," Chapter 16 ▪ "Reading Processes" in Chapter 2 and	🔍 activities 🔍 reading ▪ TopLinks

This chart is much like the three charts in Part One, which show you how to find resources specifically for writing (p. 20), reading (p. 32), and critical thinking (p. 50).

Index. An index is a complete list of a book's contents in alphabetical order. Turn to page I-1 when you want to find all of the information available in the book for a particular topic. This example shows you all the places to look for help with your thesis.

List of Features for College Writers. At the back of the book is a list of resources in *The Bedford Guide* that will help you become more adept at activities — such as thinking critically, supporting an argument or position, and using outside sources — that are essential for effective academic writing.

List of Visuals. At the back of the book, you'll also find a list of different types of visuals in the book (organized by genre). Refer to this for ideas about how to use or analyze images effectively.

Marginal Cross-References. You can find additional information quickly by using the references in the margins — notes on the sides of each page that tell you exactly where to turn in the book or on the Web site for more help or for other activities related to what you are reading. Many of the Web

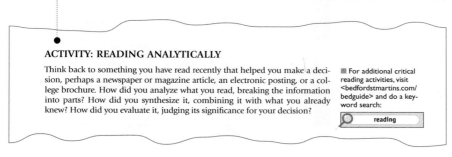

ACTIVITY: READING ANALYTICALLY

Think back to something you have read recently that helped you make a decision, perhaps a newspaper or magazine article, an electronic posting, or a college brochure. How did you analyze what you read, breaking the information into parts? How did you synthesize it, combining it with what you already knew? How did you evaluate it, judging its significance for your decision?

▪ For additional critical reading activities, visit <bedfordstmartins.com/bedguide> and do a keyword search:

🔍 reading

references include keywords. Simply type these words into a search box at <bedfordstmartins.com/bedguide> to get to the relevant information.

Colored Edges. If you need fast help with research, turn to the Quick Research Guide on the pages with the dark red edge. If you need help as you edit your essay, turn to the Quick Editing Guide on the pages with the dark blue edge. Frequent references in the margin note when you might want to turn to these resources.

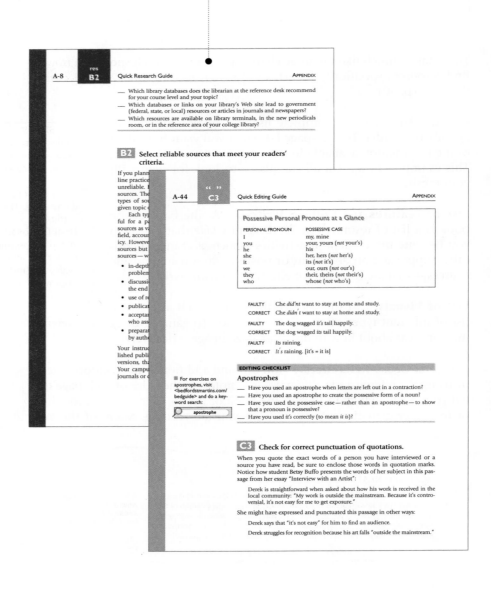

A-8 · res · B2 · Quick Research Guide · APPENDIX

___ Which library databases does the librarian at the reference desk recommend for your course level and your topic?
___ Which databases or links on your library's Web site lead to government (federal, state, or local) resources or articles in journals and newspapers?
___ Which resources are available on library terminals, in the new periodicals room, or in the reference area of your college library?

B2 Select reliable sources that meet your readers' criteria.

A-44 · " " · C3 · Quick Editing Guide · APPENDIX

Possessive Personal Pronouns at a Glance

PERSONAL PRONOUN	POSSESSIVE CASE
I	my, mine
you	your, yours (*not* your's)
he	his
she	her, hers (*not* her's)
it	its (*not* it's)
we	our, ours (*not* our's)
they	their, theirs (*not* their's)
who	whose (*not* who's)

FAULTY Che *did'nt* want to stay at home and study.
CORRECT Che *didn't* want to stay at home and study.

FAULTY The dog wagged *it's* tail happily.
CORRECT The dog wagged *its* tail happily.

FAULTY *Its* raining.
CORRECT *It's* raining. [it's = it is]

EDITING CHECKLIST

Apostrophes
___ Have you used an apostrophe when letters are left out in a contraction?
___ Have you used an apostrophe to create the possessive form of a noun?
___ Have you used the possessive case—rather than an apostrophe—to show that a pronoun is possessive?
___ Have you used *it's* correctly (to mean *it is*)?

■ For exercises on apostrophes, visit <bedfordstmartins.com/bedguide> and do a key-word search:

🔍 apostrophe

C3 Check for correct punctuation of quotations.

When you quote the exact words of a person you have interviewed or a source you have read, be sure to enclose those words in quotation marks. Notice how student Betsy Buffo presents the words of her subject in this passage from her essay "Interview with an Artist":

Derek is straightforward when asked about how his work is received in the local community: "My work is outside the mainstream. Because it's controversial, it's not easy for me to get exposure."

She might have expressed and punctuated this passage in other ways:

Derek says that "it's not easy" for him to find an audience.

Derek struggles for recognition because his art falls "outside the mainstream."

Becoming a Better Writer by Using The Bedford Guide

The Bedford Guide includes readings, checklists, tips for writing on a computer, and other help you can use to complete each writing assignment.

Model Readings.   *The Bedford Guide* is filled with examples of both professional and student essays to help you as you write your own. These essays are located on the blue-shaded pages in *A Writer's Guide* and in *A Writer's Reader*. All the essays in the book include informative notes about the author, helpful prereading questions, definitions of difficult words, questions for thinking more deeply about the reading, and suggestions for writing.

Reading Annotations.   The professional essays in *A Writer's Guide* begin with some annotations to point out notable features, such as the thesis and the first of the points supporting it. The student essays include a few intriguing questions in the margins to spark your imagination as you read.

> **THESIS**
> stating dominant
> impression

The idea of the rocker rebel is sorely tarnished° in these days of pop lite,   1
but there's nothing sugarcoated about the intensity Bono brings to the
world. Consider these few events from the past year in the life of U2's
charismatic° front man: a sold-out tour; an album (*All That You Can't Leave
Behind*) that went to number one in thirty-two countries; the birth of his
fourth child in May; talks with the leaders of the world's strongest

tarnished: Dulled, diminished.   **charismatic:** Powerfully appealing.

88

Part of the danger of online poker is that it is unregulated. Casinos in the United   2
States are not allowed to accept wagers online because of federal interstate commerce
laws, so all online casinos are offshore operations. PartyPoker.com, the largest online
poker room, states on its Web site that it is "licensed and regulated by the Government
of Gibraltar."° Its servers and business operations are offshore and, as a result, not

> *Do you agree that
> online poker playing is
> a serious problem? Why
> or why not?*

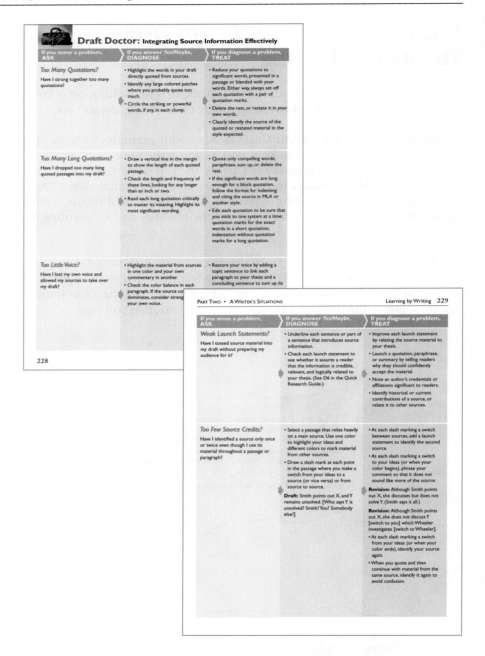

Draft Doctors.   In chapters 9, 12, and 17, and in the Quick Editing Guide, you'll find Draft Doctors to help you treat common writing problems. These special features help you figure out what you need to revise in a draft and then decide how to do so. You can also get help from the Draft Doctor on this book's companion Web site, at <bedfordstmartins.com/bedguide>.

Learning by Writing

THE ASSIGNMENT: WRITING AN EVALUATION

■ For writing activities for evaluating, visit <bedfordstmartins.com/bedguide> and do a keyword search:

Pick a subject to evaluate—one you have personal experience with and feel competent to evaluate. This might be a movie, a TV program, a piece of music, an artwork, a new product, a government agency, a campus facility or policy, an essay or a reading, or anything else you can think of. Then in a thoughtful essay, analyze your subject and evaluate it. You will need to determine specific criteria for evaluation and make them clear to your readers. In writing your evaluation, you will have a twofold purpose: (1) to set forth your assessment of the quality of your subject and (2) to convince your readers that your judgment is reasonable.

Among the lively student-written evaluations we've seen are these:

> A music major evaluated several works by American composer Aaron Copland, finding him trivial and imitative, "without a tenth of the talent or inventiveness that George Gershwin or Duke Ellington had in his little finger."

> A student planning a career in business management evaluated a computer firm in which he had worked one summer. His criteria were efficiency, productivity, appeal to new customers, and employee satisfaction.

> A student from Brazil, who had seen firsthand the effects of industrial development in the Amazon rain forest, evaluated the efforts of the U.S. government to protect forests and wetlands, comparing them with the efforts of environmentalists in her own country.

GENERATING IDEAS

Find Something to Evaluate.   Try using *brainstorming* or *mapping* to identify as many possible topics as you can think of. Select the ones with most potential—the ones that are most familiar or easiest to find out about. Spend enough time investigating these possibilities that you can comfortably choose one subject for your essay.

Consider Sources of Support.   You'll want to spend time finding material to help you develop a judgment. You may recall a program on television or hunt for an article to read. You might observe a performance or a sports team. An interview or conversation could reveal what others think. Perhaps you'll want to review several examples of your subject: watching several films, listening to several CDs, examining several works of art, or testing several

College production of Romeo and Juliet

Developing a Consensus

Meet with your writing group to discuss the subject you plan to evaluate, and see whether the group can help you arrive at a sound judgment. The others will need to see or hear your detailed report about what you're evaluating. If possible, pass around a product, show a photograph of artwork, play a song on a CD, or read aloud a short literary work or an idea expressed in a reading. Ask your listeners to explain the reasons for their own evaluations. Maybe they'll suggest criteria or evidence that hadn't occurred to you.

FOR GROUP LEARNING

products. You might also browse for information about your subject at several Web sites or attend a campus concert or play.

Establish Your Criteria.   Jot down criteria, standards to apply to your subject based on the features of the subject worth considering. How well, for example, does a popular entertainer score on musicianship, onstage manner, rapport with the audience, selection of material, originality? In evaluating the desirability of Portland as a home for a young careerist, you might ask: Does it provide an ample choice of decent-paying entry-level positions in growth firms? Any criterion you use to evaluate has to fit your subject, your audience, and your purpose. After all, ample entry-level jobs might not matter to an audience of retirees.

■ For more strategies for generating ideas, see Ch. 16.

Try Comparing and Contrasting.   Often you can readily size up the worth of a thing by setting it next to another of its kind. (When you *compare*, you point to similarities; when you *contrast*, you note differences.) To be comparable, of course, your two subjects need to have plenty in common. The quality of a Harley Davidson motorcycle might be judged by contrasting it with a Honda but not with a Hummer.

■ For more on comparing and contrasting, see Ch. 7.

For example, if you are writing a paper for a film-history course, you might compare and contrast the classic German horror movie *The Cabinet of Dr. Caligari* with the classic Hollywood movie *Frankenstein*, concluding that *Caligari* is more artistic. In planning the paper, you might make two columns in which you list the characteristics of each film, point by point:

	CALIGARI	FRANKENSTEIN
SETS	Dreamlike and impressionistic	Realistic, but with heavy Gothic atmosphere
	Sets deliberately angular and distorted	Gothic sets
LIGHTING	Deep shadows that throw figures into relief	Torches highlighting monster's face in night scene

---

Clear Assignments.   The "Learning by Writing" section in Chapters 4 to 12 presents the assignment for the chapter and guides you through the process of writing that type of essay. The "Facing the Challenge" box in each of these sections helps you through the most complicated step in the assignment.

Computer Advice.   Each "For E-Writers" box offers handy tips for using technology wisely as you write your paper.

FOR E-WRITERS

Checking Your Source Citations

Use your software's search capacity to help you check your source credits. For example, search for all the quotation marks in your paper. As you find each one, make sure that it is one of a pair surrounding every quotation in your paper. Also check that the source and the page (or other location, if available) are identified for each quotation. Use color highlighting to help you spot and refine the details in your list of sources. For instance, if you tend to forget periods or other conventional punctuation after authors' names or titles, go through your list of sources, and highlight those marks in color, adding any that are missing. After all the entries are checked and corrected, restore the passage to the usual black color.

120   Chapter 7 • Comparing and Contrasting   A WRITER'S GUIDE

Applying What You Learn:
Some Uses of Comparing and Contrasting

In College Courses.   College instructors know that distinguishing subtle similarities and differences between two subjects requires close attention, so they frequently ask students to demonstrate that understanding.

- You would compare and contrast to "evaluate" the relative merits of Norman Rockwell and N. C. Wyeth in an art history course.
- An assignment to "consider" doing business as a small corporation and as a partnership calls for comparison and contrast.
- When you are asked to "describe" a subject, such as medieval funeral customs, comparing or contrasting it with a similar familiar subject, modern traditions, might be the best way to set up a frame of reference.

In the Workplace.   At work, you will constantly compare and contrast products or services of one company with those of another, merits of one proposal with those of another, or benefits of option A with those of option B.

- Analysts compare employment data and projections to inform employers and workers about labor trends and help them plan for the future.
- When you recommend a new procedure, you can emphasize its strong points by comparing and contrasting it with the existing procedure.
- When hiring, organizations compare and contrast management style, work experience, education, and personal attributes of applicants.

In Your Community.   Comparing and contrasting is an effective method of analyzing alternatives in your community life as well.

- The advantages of one option over another quickly become apparent when you compare or contrast them, whether you want to choose a childcare provider, a fitness center, or backup aid cameras for your car.
- Your pamphlet urging voters to approve bonds for building a new elementary school can contrast costs and benefits of building with those of renovation.
- If you were to recommend a resort for your organization's annual conference, your report would compare and contrast accommodations, meeting facilities, food services, and dates of availability.

Employment by class of worker, 2004 and projected 2014
Source: Occupational Outlook Quarterly

Source: From "Driving Blind," Consumer Reports

Useful Visuals.   Watch for images, figures, charts, tables, visual examples, and other graphics throughout the text. Although we hope that these visuals contribute to an attractive book, they have been selected or designed to help you learn more effectively. Some may suggest ideas for writing or expand your thinking about a topic; others present information so that it's easy to absorb.

Helpful Checklists.   Easy-to-use checklists help you to discover something to write about, get feedback from a peer, revise your draft, and edit using references to the Quick Editing Guide (the dark-blue-edged pages).

EDITING CHECKLIST

Common and Serious Problems in College Writing

For more help, turn to the dark-blue-edged pages, and find the Quick Editing Guide sections noted there.

Grammar Problems
— Have you avoided writing sentence fragments?   A1
— Have you avoided writing comma splices or fused sentences?   A2
— Have you used the correct form for all verbs in the past tense? A3
— Do all verbs agree with their subjects?   A4
— Have you used the correct case for all pronouns?   A5
— Do all pronouns agree with their antecedents?   A6
— Have you used adjectives and adverbs correctly?   A7

For help documenting any sources in your paper, turn to the dark-red-edged pages, and find D6 and E1–E2 in the Quick Research Guide there.

Sentence Problems
— Does each modifier clearly modify the appropriate sentence element?   B1
— Have you used parallel structure where necessary?   B2

Punctuation Problems
— Have you used commas correctly?   C1
— Have you used apostrophes correctly?   C2
— Have you punctuated quotations correctly?   C3

Mechanics and Format Problems
— Have you used capital letters correctly?   D1
— Have you spelled all words correctly?   D2
— Have you used correct manuscript form?   D3

Research Advice.   The Quick Research Guide (the dark-red-edged pages) helps you find, evaluate, and capture information from sources by quoting, paraphrasing, and summarizing. It also briefly illustrates how to credit those sources.

Editing Advice.   Editing advice in the Quick Editing Guide (the dark-blue-edged pages) helps you write correctly and concisely.

Applying What You Learn.   You can apply the writing skills that you learn using *The Bedford Guide* to writing in other college courses, at your job, in your community, and in your everyday life. The "Applying What You Learn" section that ends Chapters 4 through 12 shows how you might use different kinds of writing — for example, using observation to write a case study on the job or using evaluation to assess a public service in your community.

Contents

A
WRITER'S
READER

Introduction: Reading to Write   439

Rhetorical Contents

(Essays listed in order of appearance)

THE
BEDFORD
GUIDE

for COLLEGE WRITERS

A Writer's Guide

A Writer's Guide Contents

Introduction: Writing in College 3

Introduction:
Writing in College

As a college writer you probably wrestle with the question, What should I write? You may feel you have nothing to say or nothing worth saying. Sometimes your difficulty lies in understanding the requirements of your writing situation, sometimes in finding a topic, and sometimes in uncovering information about it. Perhaps you, like many other college writers, have convinced yourself that professional writers have some special way of discovering ideas for writing. But they have no magic. In reality, what they have is experience and confidence, the products of lots of practice writing.

In *The Bedford Guide for College Writers*, we want you to become a better writer by actually writing. To help you do so, we'll give you a lot of practice as well as useful advice about writing to help you build your skills and confidence. Because writing and learning to write are many-faceted tasks, each part of *A Writer's Guide* is devoted to a different aspect of writing.

Part One, "A College Writer's Processes."   This part introduces writing, reading, and thinking critically — essential processes for meeting college expectations.

Part Two, "A Writer's Situations."   The nine chapters in Part Two form the core of *The Bedford Guide*. Each presents a writing situation and then guides you as you write a paper in response. You'll develop skills in recalling, observing, interviewing, comparing and contrasting, explaining causes and effects, taking a stand, proposing a solution, evaluating, and supporting a position with sources.

Part Three, "Special Writing Situations."   This part leads you through three special situations that most students encounter at some point — writing about literature, writing in the workplace, and writing for assessment.

Part Four, "A Writer's Strategies."   Part Four is packed with tips and activities that you can use to generate ideas, plan, draft, develop, revise, and edit. You'll also find strategies for designing documents and analyzing images.

Together, these four parts contribute to a seamless whole, much like the writing process itself. Read them at a leisurely pace, study them for helpful information, browse through them for ideas, or turn to them in a pinch. They will guide you as you write — and as you become a more skillful and confident writer.

PART ONE

A
College Writer's
Processes

Introduction

Your composition course may be one of your first college classes. For this reason, the course will both introduce you to college expectations and equip you with the skills that you need to meet these expectations. You may already feel confident that your past education and experiences have prepared you well for higher education. On the other hand, like many students, you may feel worried about your skills or uncertain about what will be expected and how you will fare in the academic world. In either case, *The Bedford Guide for College Writers* will give you concrete advice to help you succeed.

You already know a good deal about what college instructors expect. Like other teachers you've had, they'll require you to come to class, contribute to discussions, and hand in assignments. But they hope and expect that you'll do far more than this — that you'll engage fully in what's sometimes called "the college experience." The richness of this experience depends on your active response to the intellectual exchanges, resources, and opportunities that surround you in college. Sometimes this environment seems intimidating, and you may feel that you are simply drifting with the current, passively absorbing ideas as they flow through your classrooms. But you can learn how to ask questions about your writing, reading, and thinking — and how to navigate your own voyage of discovery.

As you undertake the process of becoming a well-educated person, your college instructors will expect you to show how you have grown as a writer, a reader, and a thinker. More specifically, they will want you to write thoughtful, purposeful papers, appropriately directed to your audience. They will want you not only to rely on your own ideas but also to read the writings of others, to ask questions about what you read, and to conduct research in complex disciplines, sometimes using and documenting many sources. And they will expect you to think critically and to state your points clearly as you write, integrating and supporting your own ideas with those drawn from your reading. The first three chapters in this book briefly introduce the processes — writing, reading, and thinking critically — that will help you meet these essential academic expectations.

Chapter 1

Writing Processes

You are already a writer with long experience. In school you have taken notes, written book reports and term papers, answered exam questions, perhaps kept a journal. In community meetings you have recorded minutes, and on the job you've composed memos. You've sent e-mails or instant messages to friends, made shopping lists, maybe even tried your hand at writing songs or poetry. All this experience is about to pay off for you.

Unlike parachute jumping, writing in college is something you go ahead and try without first learning all there is to know. In truth, nothing anyone can tell you will help as much as learning by doing. In this book our purpose is to help you to write better, deeper, clearer, and more satisfying papers than you have ever written before and to learn to do so by actually writing. Throughout the book we'll give you a lot of practice — in writing processes, patterns, and strategies — to build confidence. And we'll pose various writing situations and say, "Go to it!"

Writing, Reading, and Critical Thinking

In college you will add new techniques and perform challenging tasks that expand what you already know about writing. You may be asked not only to recall an experience but also to reflect upon its significance. Or you may be asked to go beyond summarizing varied positions about an issue by presenting your own position or proposing a solution. Above all, you will be reading and thinking critically — not just stacking up facts but analyzing what you discover, deciding what it means, and weighing its value.

In your composition course, you can view each writing task as a problem to solve, often through careful reading and objective thinking. You will

For more on reading critically, see Ch. 2. For more on thinking critically, see Ch. 3.

need to read — and write — actively, engaging with the ideas of others. At the same time, you will need to think critically, analyzing and judging those ideas. To help you assess your own achievement, you will use criteria — models, conventions, principles, standards. As you write and rewrite, you can evaluate what you are doing by considering specific questions:

- Have you achieved your purpose?
- Have you considered your audience?
- Have you made your point clear by stating it as a thesis or unmistakably implying it?
- Have you supported your point with enough reliable evidence to persuade your audience?
- Have you arranged your ideas logically so that each follows from, supports, or adds to the one before it?
- Have you made the connections among ideas clear to a reader?
- Have you established an appropriate tone?

In large measure, learning to write well is learning what questions to ask as you write. Throughout *A Writer's Guide*, we include questions and suggestions designed to help you accomplish your writing tasks and reflect on your own processes as you write, read, and think critically.

A Process of Writing

Writing can seem at times an overwhelming drudgery, worse than scrubbing floors; at other moments, it's a sport full of thrills — like whizzing downhill on skis, not knowing what you'll meet around a bend. Surprising and unpredictable as the process may seem, nearly all writers do similar things:

- They generate ideas.
- They plan, draft, and develop their papers.
- They revise and edit.

These three activities form the basis of most effective writing processes, and they lie at the heart of each chapter in Part Two, "A Writer's Situations."

■ For more help with every stage of the writing process, visit <bedfordstmartins.com/ bedguide>.

GETTING STARTED

As you begin writing, two considerations — what you want to accomplish as a writer and how you want to appeal to your audience — will shape your direction. As you clarify your purpose and consider your audience, you are likely to gain confidence as a writer. Even so, your writing process may take you in unexpected directions. After all, your writing activities aren't lockstep stages: you don't always proceed in a straight line. You can skip around, taking up parts of the process in whatever order you like, work on several parts at a time, or circle back over what's already done. For example, while gathering material, you may feel an urge to play with a sentence until it clicks. Or while writing a draft, you may decide to look for more material. You may leap ahead, cross out, backtrack, adjust, question, test a fresh approach, tinker, polish — and then, at the end, spell-check the tricky words.

GENERATING IDEAS

■ For strategies for generating ideas, see Ch. 16.

The first activity in writing — finding a topic and something to say about it — is often the most challenging and least predictable. Each chapter in Part Two includes a section called "Generating Ideas," which is filled with examples, questions, checklists, and visuals designed to trigger ideas and associations that will help you begin the chapter's writing assignment.

Discovering What to Write About.   Finding a topic is not always easy, but you may discover an idea while talking with friends, riding your bike, or staring out the window. Sometimes a topic lies near home, in a conversation or an everyday event you recall. Often, your reading will raise questions that call for investigation. Even if a particular writing assignment doesn't appeal to you, your challenge is to find a slant that does interest you. Find it, and words will flow — words that can engage readers as you accomplish your purpose.

Discovering Material.   You'll need information to shape and support your ideas — facts and figures, reports and opinions, examples and illustrations. How do you find supporting material that makes your slant on a topic clear and convincing to your audience? Luckily you have numerous sources at your fingertips. You can recall your experience and knowledge, observe things around you, converse with others who are knowledgeable, read enlightening materials that draw you to new approaches, and think critically about all these sources around you.

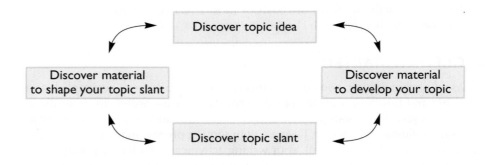

PLANNING, DRAFTING, AND DEVELOPING

After discovering a topic and beginning to gather material about it, you will plan your paper, write a draft, and then develop your ideas further. Each chapter in Part Two has a section titled "Planning, Drafting, and Developing," designed to help you through these stages of the writing process for the assignment in that chapter.

Planning.   Having discovered a burning idea to write about (or at least a smoldering one) and some supporting material (but maybe not enough yet), you will sort out what matters most. If right away you see one main point, or thesis, for your paper, test various ways of stating it, given your purpose and audience:

> MAYBE   Parking in the morning before class is annoying.
>
> OR   Campus parking is a big problem.

Next arrange your ideas and material in a sensible order that will clarify your point. For example, you might group and label the ideas you have generated, make an outline, or analyze the main point, breaking it down into its parts:

> Parking on campus is a problem for students because of the long lines, inefficient entrances, and poorly marked spaces.

But if no clear thesis emerges quickly, don't worry. You may find one while you draft—that is, while you write an early version of your paper.

For thesis and planning strategies, see Ch. 17.

For practice choosing a main point, visit <bedfordstmartins.com/ bedguide> and do a key-word search:

> 🔍 **thesis**

Drafting.   When your ideas first start to flow, you want to welcome them— lure them forth, not tear them apart—or they might go back into hiding. Don't be afraid to take risks at this stage: you'll probably be surprised and pleased at what happens, even though your first version will be rough. Writing takes time; a paper usually needs several drafts and may need a clearer introduction, stronger conclusion, more convincing evidence, or a revised plan. Especially when your subject is unfamiliar or complicated, you may throw out your first attempt and start over if a stronger idea hits you.

For drafting strategies, see Ch. 18.

Developing.   As you draft, you'll weave in explanations, definitions, examples, details, and varied evidence to make your ideas clear and persuasive. For example, you may define an at-risk student, illustrate the problems faced by a single parent, or supply statistics about hit-and-run accidents. If you lack specific support for your main point, you can use strategies for developing ideas—or return to strategies for generating ideas. You'll keep gaining insights and drawing conclusions while you draft. By all means, welcome these ideas, and work them in if they fit.

For strategies for developing ideas, see Ch. 19. For strategies for generating ideas, see Ch. 16. For advice on using a few sources, see the Quick Research Guide (the dark-red-edged pages).

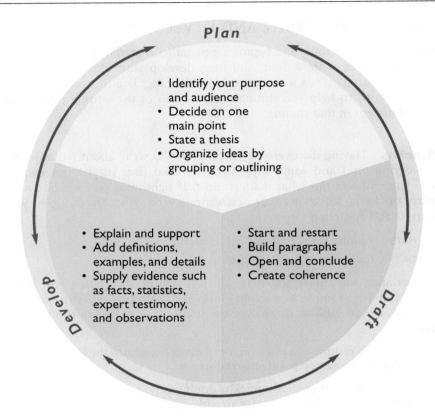

Plan

- Identify your purpose and audience
- Decide on one main point
- State a thesis
- Organize ideas by grouping or outlining

Develop

- Explain and support
- Add definitions, examples, and details
- Supply evidence such as facts, statistics, expert testimony, and observations

Draft

- Start and restart
- Build paragraphs
- Open and conclude
- Create coherence

Processes for Planning, Drafting, and Developing

REVISING AND EDITING

For revising and editing strategies, see Ch. 20.

You might want to relax once you have a draft, but for most writers, revising begins the work in earnest. Revising means both reseeing and rewriting, making major changes so that your paper accomplishes what you want it to. After you have a well-developed and well-organized revision, you are ready to edit: to correct errors and improve wording. Each chapter in Part Two has a "Revising and Editing" section where you will find revision and editing checklists with a suggestion for working with a peer.

Revising.   Revision is more than just changing words: in fact, you may revise what you know and what you think while you're writing or when you pause to reread. You can then reconsider your purpose and audience, rework your thesis, shift your plans, decide what to put in or leave out, rearrange for clarity, move sentences or paragraphs around, connect ideas differently, or express them better. Perhaps you'll add costs to a paper on parking problems or switch attention to fathers instead of mothers as you consider teen parenthood.

If you put aside your draft for a few hours or a day, you can reread it with fresh eyes and a clear mind. As humorist Leo Rosten has said, "You have to put yourself in the position of the negative reader, the resistant reader, the reader who doesn't surrender easily, the reader who is alien to you as a type, even the reader who doesn't like what you are writing." Other students can also help you — sometimes more than a textbook or an instructor can — by responding to your drafts as engaged readers.

Editing.   Editing means refining details and correcting flaws that may stand in the way of your readers' understanding and enjoyment. Don't edit too early, though, because you may waste time on some part that you later revise out. In editing, you usually make these repairs:

For editing advice, see the Quick Editing Guide (the dark-blue-edged pages).

- Get rid of unnecessary words.
- Choose livelier and more precise words.
- Replace incorrect or inappropriate wording.
- Rearrange words in a clearer, more emphatic order.
- Combine short, choppy sentences, or break up long, confusing sentences.
- Refine transitions for continuity of thought.
- Check grammar, usage, punctuation, and mechanics.

Proofreading.   Finally you'll proofread your paper, taking a last look, checking correctness, and catching doubtful spellings or word-processing errors.

For more on proofreading, see pp. 386–87.

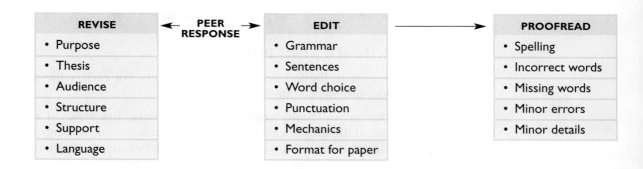

REVISE	← PEER → RESPONSE	EDIT		PROOFREAD
• Purpose		• Grammar		• Spelling
• Thesis		• Sentences		• Incorrect words
• Audience		• Word choice		• Missing words
• Structure		• Punctuation		• Minor errors
• Support		• Mechanics		• Minor details
• Language		• Format for paper		

ACTIVITY: DESCRIBING YOUR WRITING PROCESS

Describe your writing process. How do you get started? How do you keep writing? What process do you go through to reach a final draft? Do your steps ever vary depending upon the type of writing you're doing? What step or strategy in your writing process would you most like to change?

Purpose and Audience

At any moment in the writing process, two questions are worth asking:

Why am I writing?   **Who is my audience?**

WRITING FOR A REASON

■ For more on planning with your purpose in mind, see pp. 310–11. For more on revising for purpose, see pp. 372–73.

Like most college writing assignments, every assignment in this book asks you to write for a definite reason. For example, in Chapter 4 you'll be asked to recall a memorable experience in order to explain its importance for you; in Chapter 9, you'll take a stand on a controversy in order to convey your position and persuade readers to respect it. Be careful not to confuse the sources and strategies you are asked to apply in these assignments with your ultimate purpose for writing. "To compare and contrast two things" is not a very interesting purpose; "to compare and contrast two Web sites *in order to explain their differences*" implies a real reason for writing. In most college writing, your ultimate purpose will be to explain something to your readers or to convince them of something.

To sharpen your concentration on your purpose, ask yourself from the start: What do I want to do? And, in revising, Did I do what I meant to do? You'll find that these practical questions will help you slice out irrelevant information and remove other barriers to getting your paper where you want it to go.

ACTIVITY: CONSIDERING PURPOSE

Imagine that you are in the following writing situations. For each, write a sentence or two summing up your purpose as a writer.

1. The instructor in your introductory psychology course has assigned a paragraph about the meanings of three essential terms in your readings.
2. You're very upset about a change in financial-aid procedures and plan to write a letter asking the registrar to remedy the problem.
3. You're going to start a blog about your first year at college so that all of your extended family can envision the campus environment and share your experiences during the year.
4. Your supervisor wants you to write an article about the benefits of a new company service for the customer newsletter.
5. Your MySpace profile seemed appropriate when you were in high school, but you want to revise it now that you're attending college and have a job with future prospects.

WRITING FOR YOUR AUDIENCE

Your audience, or your readers, may or may not be defined in your assignment. Consider the following examples:

For more on planning for your readers, see pp. 310–11.

> ASSIGNMENT 1 Discuss the advantages and disadvantages of homeschooling.
>
> ASSIGNMENT 2 In a letter to parents of school-aged children, discuss the advantages and disadvantages of homeschooling.

If your assignment defines an audience, as the second example does, you will need to think about how to approach those readers and what to assume about their relationship to your topic. For example, what points would you include in a discussion aimed at parents? How would you organize your ideas? Would you discuss advantages or disadvantages first? On the other hand, how might your approach differ if the assignment read this way?

> ASSIGNMENT 3 In a newsletter article for teachers, discuss the advantages and disadvantages of homeschooling.

Audiences may be identified by characteristics, such as occupation (teachers) or role (parents), that suggest values to which a writer might appeal. For example, most teachers and parents share the desire to help a student succeed. Even so, while a teacher might see a quiet classroom loner, a parent might see a shy animal lover who volunteers at the zoo. As the chart on page 16 suggests, you can analyze the preferences, biases, and concerns of your audience in order to engage and influence readers more successfully.

When you analyze what readers know, believe, and value, you can aim your writing toward them with a better chance of hitting your mark. Use these questions to help you write and revise for your audience:

AUDIENCE CHECKLIST

____ Who are your readers? What is their relationship to you?

____ What do your readers already know about this topic? What do you want them to learn?

____ How much detail will they want to read about this topic?

____ What objections are they likely to raise as they read? How can you anticipate and overcome their objections?

____ What's likely to convince them?

____ What's likely to offend them?

For more on revising for audience, see p. 374.

Audience Characteristics and Expectations	GENERAL AUDIENCE	COLLEGE INSTRUCTOR	WORK SUPERVISOR	CAMPUS FRIEND	PARENT OR GRANDPARENT
READER'S RELATIONSHIP TO YOU	Imagined but not known personally	Known briefly in a class context	Known for some time in a job context	Known in campus and social contexts	Known all of your life in family contexts
REASON FOR READING YOUR WRITING	Curious attitude and interest in your topic assumed	Professional responsibility for your knowledge and skills	Managerial interest in and reliance on your job performance	Personal interest based on shared circumstances	Family bond and lifelong concern about you
KNOWLEDGE ABOUT TOPIC	Level of awareness assumed and gaps addressed with logical presentation	Well informed about college topics but wants to see what you know	Informed about the business and expects reliable information from you	Friendly but may or may not be informed beyond social interests	Loving but may or may not be informed beyond family concerns
EXPECTED FORMS AND FORMATS	Essay, article, letter, report, or other format	Essay, report, or research paper using academic format	Memo, report, or letter using company format	Chats, notes, blog entries, sociable IMs, or other informal messages	Family e-mails, chats, letters, notes, or cards
EXPECTED LANGUAGE AND STYLE	Formal, using clear words and sentences	Formal, following academic conventions	Appropriate for advancing you and the company	Informal, using abbreviations, phrases, and slang	Informal, but showing your maturity
EXPECTED ATTITUDE AND TONE	Interested and thoughtful about the topic	Serious and thoughtful about the topic and course	Respectful, showing reliability and work ethic	Friendly and interested in shared experiences	Concerned about home and family despite new experiences
EXPECTED AMOUNT OF DETAIL	Sufficient detail to inform or persuade the reader envisioned	Enough sound or research-based evidence to support your thesis	General or technical information as needed	Much detail or little, depending on the topic	Enough to be reassured about your welfare and success

ACTIVITY: CONSIDERING AUDIENCE

Read the following renewal notices sent to subscribers of two magazines, *Zapped!* and the *Atlantic*. Examine the style, tone, language, sequence of topics, or other features of each letter. Write two short paragraphs — one about each letter — explaining what you can conclude about the letter's target audience and its appeal to that audience.

Zapped! misses you.

Dear Dan Morrison,

All last year, *Zapped!* magazine made the trek to 5 Snowden Lane and it was always a great experience. You took great care of *Zapped!*, and *Zapped!* gave you hours of entertainment, with news and interviews from the latest indie bands, honest-as-your-momma reviews of musical equipment, and your first glimpse of some of the finest graphic serials being published today.

But, Dan, we haven't heard from you and are starting to wonder what's up. Don't you miss *Zapped!*? One thing's for sure: *Zapped!* misses you.

We'd like to re-establish the relationship: if you renew your subscription by March 1, you'll get 20% off last year's subscription price. That's only $24 for another year of great entertainment. Just fill out the other side of this card and send it back to us; we'll bill you later.

Come on, Dan. Why wait?

Thanks,

Carly Bevins

Carly Bevins
Director of Sales

Figure 1.1   Letter from Zapped!

Figure 1.2   Letter from The Atlantic

TARGETING A COLLEGE AUDIENCE

In college, many of your assignments may resemble Assignment 1 on page 15. They may assume that you are addressing general college readers, represented by your instructor and possibly your classmates. Such readers typically expect clear, logical writing with lots of supporting evidence to explain or persuade. Of course, the format, approach, or evidence may differ by field. For example, biologists might expect the findings from your experiment while literature specialists might look for plenty of relevant quotations from the novel you're analyzing. Use these questions to help you pinpoint what your college audience expects:

COLLEGE AUDIENCE CHECKLIST

___ How has your instructor advised you to write for readers? What criteria related to audience will be used for grading your papers?

___ What do the assigned readings in your course assume about the expectations of an audience? Has your instructor recommended useful models or sample readings?

___ What topics and issues concern readers in the course area? What puzzles do they want to solve? How do they want to solve them?

___ How is writing in the course area commonly organized? For example, do writers tend to follow a persuasive pattern — introducing the issue, stating an assertion or a claim, backing the claim with logical points and supporting evidence, acknowledging other views, and concluding? Or do they use conventional headings — perhaps *Abstract, Introduction to the Problem, Methodology, Findings,* and *Discussion*?

___ What evidence is typically gathered to support ideas or interpretations — facts and statistics, quotations from texts, summaries of research, references to authorities or prior studies, results from experimental research, field notes from observations, or interviews?

___ What style, tone, and level of formality do writers in the course area tend to use?

ACTIVITY: CONSIDERING A COLLEGE AUDIENCE

1. Use the checklist above to examine reading or writing assignments for one of your courses. What are some prominent features of writing in the area, and which of these might be expected in student papers? How would your college paper differ from writing on the same topic for another audience (such as a letter to the editor, a newspaper article, a consumer brochure, an explanation for young students, or a Web page)?

2. Select a typical passage from a textbook or a reading assigned in a course. Rewrite the passage for a specific nonacademic audience (such as readers of a particular magazine or newspaper, visitors to a certain Web site, or amateurs interested in the area).

3. Find a nonacademic article, pamphlet, or Web page. Try your hand at rewriting a passage from it to present the material as a college textbook or reading in the field might. Then write an informal paragraph explaining why this task was easy, challenging, or impossible.

What Matters Most

Like a hard game of basketball, writing a college paper is strenuous. As the following chart shows, you can find help throughout the writing process in this book and on its Web site. Without getting in your way, we want to lend you all possible support and guidance. So, no doubt, does your instructor, someone closer to you than any textbook writers. Still, like even the best coaches, instructors and textbook writers can improve your game only so far. Advice on how to write won't make you a better writer. You'll learn more and have more fun when you take a few sentences to the hoop and make points yourself. After you sink a few baskets, you'll gain confidence in your ability and find the process of writing easier.

A Writer's Resources

Major stages	Help in this book	Web help*
Generate Ideas • Find a topic and something to say. • Brainstorm, freewrite, doodle, map, imagine, question, seek motives, or keep a journal. • Read, talk, observe, and think.	☐ "Generating Ideas" section in Part Two, including Discovery Checklists ☐ "Strategies for Generating Ideas," Chapter 16 ☐ "Reading Processes" in Chapter 2 and A Writer's Reader	🔍 activities 🔍 reading ■ TopLinks
Plan • Think about your purpose and audience. • Convert a topic idea to a working thesis. • Organize by grouping or outlining.	☐ "Planning, Drafting, and Developing" sections in Part Two ☐ "Strategies for Stating a Thesis and Planning," Chapter 17	🔍 thesis 🔍 organize
Draft • Start and restart. • Write paragraphs and topic sentences. • Write openings and conclusions. • Create coherence with transitions, repetitions, and pronouns.	☐ "Planning, Drafting, and Developing" sections in Part Two ☐ "Strategies for Drafting," Chapter 18 ☐ Advice on using graphics in Chapter 21	🔍 activities 🔍 open_end 🔍 coherence
Develop • Weave in supporting examples, details, and definitions. • Analyze, divide and classify, compare and contrast, or identify cause and effect. • Supply evidence—facts, statistics, expert testimony, and firsthand observation.	☐ "Planning, Drafting, and Developing" sections in Part Two ☐ "Strategies for Developing," Chapter 19 ☐ Advice on sources and citation style in Quick Research Guide	🔍 examples 🔍 development 🔍 support ■ Ask the Draft Doctor
Revise • Reconsider purpose, thesis, and audience. • Rework structure, support, and connections. • Stress what counts; whittle what doesn't. • Work with a peer editor.	☐ "Revising and Editing" sections in Part Two ☐ "Strategies for Revising and Editing," Chapter 20	🔍 process 🔍 peer ■ Ask the Draft Doctor
Edit • Refine grammar, sentences, and word choice. • Correct punctuation and mechanics. • Check the paper's format.	☐ "Revising and Editing" sections in Part Two ☐ "Strategies for Revising and Editing," Chapter 20 ☐ Format for academic papers in Chapter 21 ☐ Quick Editing Guide	🔍 process ■ Exercise Central ■ Ask the Draft Doctor
Proofread • Check for misspelled, incorrect, or missing words. • Check for minor errors and details.	☐ "Revising and Editing" sections in Part Two ☐ "Strategies for Revising and Editing," Chapter 20	🔍 process ■ Exercise Central

*At <bedfordstmartins.com/bedguide>, use the search box shown to find writing resources or exercises by keyword.

Chapter 2
Reading Processes

What's so special about college reading? Don't you pick up the book, start on the first page, and keep going, just as you have ever since you met *The Cat in the Hat*? Reading from beginning to end works especially well when you are eager to find out what happens next, as in a thriller, or what to do next, as in a cookbook. On the other hand, much of what you read in college — textbooks, scholarly articles, research reports, or the papers of your peers — is complicated and challenging. Dense material like this often requires closer reading and deeper thinking — in short, a process for reading critically.

Reading critically is a useful skill. For assignments in this course alone, you will need to evaluate the strengths and weaknesses of essays by professionals and students. If you research any topic, you will need to figure out what your sources say, how you might use their information, and whether they are reliable. Critical reading is important in other courses, too. For example, you might analyze a sociology report on violent children for its assumptions and implications as well as the soundness of its argument. On the job, you may be required to verify that your product meets technical specifications, while in the community, you may want to respond to a proposal for a tax hike. Whenever your writing relies on critical reading, you need to explain what is going on in the text and then go further, making your own point based on what you have read.

A Process of Critical Reading

Reading critically means approaching whatever you read in an active, questioning manner. This essential college-level skill changes reading from a spectator sport to a contact sport. You no longer sit in the stands, watching graceful skaters glide by. Instead, you charge right into a rough-and-tumble hockey game, gripping your stick and watching out for your teeth.

■ For more on critical thinking, see Ch. 3.

Critical reading, like critical thinking, is not a specialized, isolated activity. It is a continuum of strategies that thoughtful people use every day to grapple with new information, to integrate it with existing knowledge, and to apply it to problems in daily life and in academic courses. Many readers do similar things:

- They get ready to do their reading.
- They respond as they read.
- They read on literal and analytical levels.

Building your critical reading skills can bring many benefits, especially if you aren't a regular reader. You'll open the door to new possibilities, information you've never encountered, and ideas unlikely to come up talking with friends. As you absorb and challenge what you read, you also deepen your resources as a writer.

ACTIVITY: DESCRIBING YOUR OWN READING PROCESS

How do you read a magazine, newspaper, or popular novel? What are your goals when you do this kind of reading? What's different about reading the material assigned in college? What techniques do you use for reading assignments? How might you read more effectively? Which of your strategies might help your classmates, especially in classes with a lot of reading?

Getting Started

College reading is active reading. Before you read, think ahead about how to approach the reading process — how to make the most of the time you spend reading.

PREPARING TO READ

Thinking about Your Purpose.   Naturally enough, your overall goal for doing most college reading is to be successful in your courses. When you begin to read, ask questions like these about your immediate purpose:

- What are you reading?
- Why are you reading?
- What do you want to do with the reading?
- What does your instructor expect you to learn from the reading?
- Do you need to memorize details, find main points, or connect ideas?
- How does this reading build on, add to, contrast with, or otherwise relate to other reading assignments in the course?

Planning Your Follow-Up.   When you are assigned a specific essay, chapter, or article or are required to choose a reading about a certain topic, ask yourself what your instructor probably expects to follow the reading:

- Do you need to be ready to discuss the reading during class?
- Will you need to mention it or analyze it during an examination?
- Will you need to write about it or its topic?
- Do you need to find its main points? Sum it up? Compare it? Question it? Spot its strengths and weaknesses? Draw useful details from it?

Skimming the Text.   Before you actively read a text, begin by skimming it — quickly reading only enough to introduce yourself to its content and organization. If the reading has a table of contents or subheadings, read those first to figure out what the material covers and how it is organized. Read the first paragraph and then the first (or first and last) sentence of each paragraph that follows. If the material has any illustrations or diagrams, read the captions.

RESPONDING TO READING

Reading Deeply.   The books, articles, and essays assigned in college often require more concentration from you as a reader than other readings do. Use the following questions to help you understand the complexities below the surface of a reading:

- Are difficult or technical terms defined in specific ways? How might you highlight, list, or record such terms so that you master them?
- How might you record or recall the details in the reading? How could you track or diagram interrelated ideas to grasp their connections?
- How do word choice, tone, and style alert you to the complex purpose of a reading that is layered or indirect rather than straightforward?
- How might you trace the progression of ideas in the reading? How do headings, previews of what's coming up, summaries of what's gone before, and transitions signal the organization?
- Does the reading include figurative or descriptive language, references to other works, or recurring themes? How do these elements enrich the reading?

■ For more on figurative language, see p. 248.

- Can you answer any reading questions supplied in your textbook, assignment, study guide, or syllabus? Can you restate headings in question form to create your own questions and then supply the answers? For example, change "Major Types of X" to "What are the major types of X?"

Keeping a Reading Journal.   A reading journal is an excellent place to record not just what you read but how you respond to it. It helps you read

■ For advice on keeping a writer's journal, see Ch. 16.

actively and build a reservoir of ideas for follow-up writing. You can use a special notebook or computer file to address questions like these:

- What is the subject of the reading? What is the writer's stand?
- What does the writer take for granted? What assumptions does he or she begin with? Where are these stated or suggested?
- What evidence supports the writer's main points?
- Do you agree with what the writer has said? Do his or her ideas clash with your ideas or question something you take for granted?
- Has the writer told you more than you wanted to know or failed to tell you something you wish you knew?
- What conclusions can you draw from the reading?
- Has the reading opened your eyes to new ways of viewing the subject?

■ For more on evaluating what you read, see section C in the Quick Research Guide (the dark-red-edged pages).

Annotating the Text.   Writing notes on the page (or on a photocopy if the material is not your own) is a useful way to trace the author's points, question them, and add your own comments as they pop up. You can underline key points, mark checks and stars by ideas when you agree or disagree, and jot questions in the margins.

The following passage ends the introduction of "The New Science of Siblings," written by Jeffrey Kluger (with reporting by Jessica Carsen, Wendy Cole, and Sonja Steptoe) and featured as the cover story in the July 10, 2006, *Time* (pp. 47–48). Notice how one writer annotated this passage:

■ For a Critical Reading Checklist, see pp. 28–29.

Key point — will this be a pain? Or a help?

Good quote — from UC Davis authority

Sums up past studies but new to me

Not exactly! My sister's definitely a striver, but I'm no rebel

Wow — global research!

Have to go for the drama — competition and favorites!!

Our spouses arrive comparatively late in our lives; our parents eventually leave us. Our siblings may be the only people we'll ever know who truly qualify as partners for life. "Siblings," says family sociologist Katherine Conger of the University of California, Davis, "are with us for the whole journey."

Within the scientific community, siblings have not been wholly ignored, but research has been limited mostly to discussions of birth order. Older sibs were said to be strivers; younger ones rebels; middle kids the lost souls. The stereotypes were broad, if not entirely untrue, and there the discussion mostly ended.

But all that's changing. At research centers in the United States, Canada, Europe, and elsewhere, investigators are launching a wealth of new studies into the sibling dynamic, looking at ways brothers and sisters steer one another into — or away from — risky behavior; how they form a protective buffer against family upheaval; how they educate one another about the opposite sex; how all siblings compete for family recognition and come to terms — or blows — over such impossibly charged issues as parental favoritism.

Scary — I never thought of my sister this way!

Cousins- example — pulled together when parents split

ACTIVITY: ANNOTATING A PASSAGE

Annotate the following passage on a recent trend.

For a sample annotated passage, see p. 24.

Every woman's dream is to find the perfect spouse and settle down for life, right? Although this may be the dream of some, it doesn't reflect reality, according to a recent analysis of census data. Based on this analysis, the *New York Times* reported that, for the first time in history, most U.S. women are single ("51% of Women Are Now Living without Spouse," 16 Jan. 2007; reported by Sam Roberts). Specifically, in 2005, 51 percent of women reported being unmarried, up from 49 percent in 2000 and 35 percent in 1950.

The *Times* and other media sources have pointed to several factors behind the shift, including the fact that women are waiting longer to get married. "We don't need men anymore," said twenty-nine-year-old New York City resident Jessica Cohen, in an interview with CBS News ("More Women Saying, 'I Don't,'" 16 Jan. 2007; reported by Kelly Wallace). As Cohen explained, "I mean, we want men, we want someone to share everything with, but I don't think we need to rush."

Other women are choosing to live with partners instead of marrying. Many divorced women are staying single or delaying remarriage. As divorced Baltimore attorney Catherine Flynn told MSNBC, "I get to make the choices myself about where I live, how I live, how I decorate my house" ("Watch Out, Men! More Women Opt to Live Alone," 16 Jan. 2007; reported by Dawn Fratangelo). And in another trend behind the shift, women are living longer as widows.

Social commentators who have studied marriage trends say that women today simply have more choices than were available in past generations. Many are financially independent and are even willing to raise children on their own. Freed from the need to find someone to support them as soon as possible, these women can take more time to find a partner with whom they are emotionally, intellectually, and spiritually compatible. But even then, they might not marry such a man, as the *Times* story shows.

Reading on Literal and Analytical Levels

Educational expert Benjamin S. Bloom identified six levels of cognitive activity: knowledge, comprehension, application, analysis, synthesis, and evaluation.[1] Each level acts as a foundation for the next. Each also becomes more complex and demands higher thinking skills than the previous one.

[1]Benjamin S. Bloom et al., *Taxonomy of Educational Objectives, Handbook 1: Cognitive Domain* (New York: McKay, 1956).

Experienced readers, however, jump among these levels, gathering information and insight as they occur. (See the reading skills figure below.)

The first three levels are literal skills. When you show that you know a fact, comprehend its meaning, and can apply it to a new situation, you demonstrate your mastery over the building blocks of thought. The last three levels — analysis, synthesis, and evaluation — are critical skills. These skills take you beyond the literal level: you break apart the building blocks to see how they work, recombine them in new and useful ways, and judge their worth or significance. To read critically, you must engage with a reading on both literal and analytical levels.

As you first tackle an unfamiliar reading, you may struggle simply to discover what — exactly — it presents to readers. For example, suppose you read in your history book a passage about Franklin Delano Roosevelt (FDR), the only American president elected to four consecutive terms of office.

Knowing.   Once you read the passage, even if you have little background in American history, you can decode and recall the information it presents about FDR and his four terms in office.

Comprehending.   To understand the passage, you need to know that a term for a U.S. president is four years and that *consecutive* means "continuous." Thus, FDR was elected to serve for sixteen years.

Applying.   To connect this knowledge to what you already know, you think of other presidents — George Washington, who served two terms; Grover Cleveland, who served two terms but not consecutively; Jimmy Carter, who served one term; and Bill Clinton, who served two terms. Then you realize that being elected to four terms is quite unusual. In fact, the Twenty-second Amendment to the Constitution, ratified in 1951, now limits a president to two terms.

Analyzing.   You can scrutinize FDR's four terms as president from various angles, selecting a principle for analysis that suits your purpose. Then you

Literal and Analytical Reading Skills
The information in this figure is adapted from Benjamin S. Bloom et al., Taxonomy of Educational Objectives, Handbook 1: Cognitive Domain *(New York: McKay, 1956).*

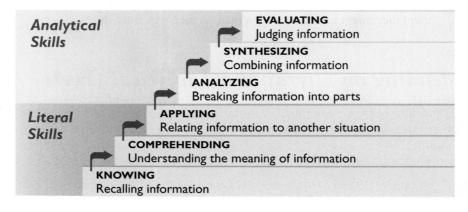

can use this principle to break the information into its components or parts. For example, you might analyze FDR's tenure in office in relation to the political longevity of other presidents. Why has FDR been the only president elected to serve four terms? What circumstances during his terms contributed to three reelections?

Synthesizing.   To answer your questions, you may have to read more or review material you have read in the past. Then you begin synthesizing — recombining information, pulling together facts and opinions, identifying evidence accepted by all or most sources, examining any controversial evidence, and drawing whatever conclusions reliable evidence seems to support. For example, it would be logical to conclude that the special circumstances of the Great Depression and World War II contributed to FDR's four terms. On the other hand, it would not be logical to conclude that Americans reelected him out of pity because he had polio.

Evaluating.   Finally, you evaluate your new knowledge to determine its significance, both to your understanding of Depression-era politics and to your assessment of your history book's approach. For instance, you might ask yourself, Why has the book's author chosen to make this point? How does it affect the rest of the discussion? Does this author seem reliable? And you may also have formed your own opinion about FDR's reelections, perhaps concluding that FDR's four-term presidency is understandable in light of the events of the 1930s and 1940s, that the author has mentioned this fact to highlight the unique political atmosphere of that era, and that, in your opinion, it is evidence neither for nor against FDR's excellence as a president.

ACTIVITY: READING ANALYTICALLY

Think back to something you have read recently that helped you make a decision, perhaps a newspaper or magazine article, an electronic posting, or a college brochure. How did you analyze what you read, breaking the information into parts? How did you synthesize it, combining it with what you already knew? How did you evaluate it, judging its significance for your decision?

■ For additional critical reading activities, visit \<bedfordstmartins.com/ bedguide> and do a keyword search:

reading

GENERATING IDEAS FROM READING

Like flints that strike each other and cause sparks, readers and writers provoke one another. For example, when your class discusses an essay, you may be surprised by the range of insights your classmates report. If you missed some of their insights during your reading, remember that they may be equally surprised by what you see.

■ For more on generating ideas, see Ch. 16.

Often you look to other writers — in books or magazines — to suggest a topic, provide information about it, or help you explain it or back it up with evidence. You may read because you want to understand ideas, test them, or debate with the writer, but reading is a dynamic process. It may change your ideas instead of support them. Here are suggestions for unlocking the potential hidden in a good text.

Looking for Meaty Pieces.   Spur your thinking about intriguing current topics by browsing through essay collections or magazines in the library or online. Try *Atlantic, Harper's, New Republic, Commentary,* or special-interest magazines such as *Architectural Digest* or *Scientific American.* Check the editorials and op-ed columns in your local newspaper, the *New York Times,* or the *Wall Street Journal.* Also search the Internet on interesting subjects that challenge you to think seriously (such as film classics or the effects of poverty on children). Look for articles that are meaty, not superficial, and that are written to inform and convince, not to entertain or amuse.

Logging Your Reading.   For several days keep a log of the articles that you find. Record the author, title, and source for each promising piece so that you can easily find it again. Briefly note the subject and point of view as well, so you identify a range of possibilities.

Recalling Something You Have Already Read.   What have you read lately that started you thinking? Return to a recent reading — a chapter in a humanities textbook, an article assigned in a sociology course, a research study for a biology course.

■ For more on para-
phrase and summary,
see Ch. 12 and D4–D5 in
the Quick Research
Guide (the dark-red-
edged pages).

Capturing Complex Ideas.   When you find a challenging reading, do you sometimes feel too overwhelmed to develop ideas from it? If so, read slowly and carefully. Then consider two common methods of recording and integrating ideas from sources into papers. First try *paraphrasing:* restating an author's ideas fully but in your own words. Then try *summarizing:* reducing an author's main point to essentials. Accurately recording what a reading says can help you grasp its ideas, especially on literal levels. Once you understand what it says, you are equipped to agree, disagree, or raise questions.

Reading Critically.   Read a thought-provoking piece, slowly and carefully, both literally and analytically. Instead of just soaking up what the reading says, engage in a dialogue or conversation with the writer. Criticize. Wonder. Argue back. Demand convincing evidence. Use the following checklist to get you started as a critical reader:

CRITICAL READING CHECKLIST

____ What problems and issues does the author raise?

____ What is the author's purpose? Is it to explain or inform? To persuade? To amuse? In addition to this overall purpose, is the author trying to accomplish some other agenda?

___ How does the author appeal to you as a reader? Where do you agree, and where do you disagree? Where do you want to say "Yeah, right!" or "I don't think so!"?

___ How does this piece relate to your own experiences or thoughts? Have you encountered anything similar? Does the topic or approach intrigue you?

___ Are there any important words or ideas that you don't understand? If so, do you need to reread or turn to a dictionary or reference book?

___ What is the author's point of view? What does the author assume or take for granted? Where does the author reveal these assumptions? Do they make the selection seem weak or biased?

For more on facts and opinions, see pp. 37–38.

___ Which statements are facts that can be verified by observation, firsthand testimony, or research? Which are opinions? Does one or the other dominate the piece?

___ Is the writer's evidence accurate, relevant, and sufficient? Do you find it persuasive?

For more on evaluating evidence, see C1–C3 in the Quick Research Guide (the dark-red-edged pages).

Analyzing Writing Strategies.   Reading widely and deeply can reveal not only what others say but also how they shape it and state it. For some readings in this book, notes in the margin illustrate how to identify key features such as the introduction, thesis statement or main idea, major points, and supporting evidence. Ask questions such as these to help you identify writing strategies:

WRITING STRATEGIES CHECKLIST

___ How does the author introduce the reading and try to engage the audience?

___ Where does the author state or imply the main idea or thesis?

___ How is the text organized? What main points develop the thesis?

___ How does the author supply support — facts, data, statistics, expert opinions, personal experiences, observations, explanations, examples, or other information?

___ How does the author connect or emphasize ideas for readers?

___ How does the author conclude the reading?

___ What is the author's tone? How do the words and examples reveal the author's attitude, biases, or assumptions?

ACTIVITY: READING CRITICALLY

Using the advice in this chapter, critically read the following essay from the *Chicago Tribune Online*. First, add your own notes and comments in the margin, responding on both literal and analytical levels. Second, add notes about the writer's writing strategies. (Sample annotations are supplied to help you get started.) Finally, write out your own well-reasoned conclusions about the reading.

For a sample annotated passage, see p. 24.

For more practice reading critically, read and annotate "Guys Just Want to Have Fun" (pp. 482–84) or "Male Bashing on TV" (pp. 515–19) from A Writer's Reader.

Jeffery M. Leving and Glenn Sacks
Women Don't Want Men? Ha!

The recent census data finding that for the first time the majority of American women are unmarried is being greeted in a largely celebratory tone. One newspaper explains, "Who needs a man? Not most women." MSNBC warns, "Watch out, men! More women opt to live alone." CBS says, "More women saying 'I don't.'" One newspaper cartoon depicts a happily divorced woman remembering her ex-husband bellowing, "Where's my dinner?! Iron my shirts!! Lose weight!!!" Several others depict women pondering the single life as their fat, lazy husbands drink beer and watch TV sports. One female blogger summed up the female blogosphere's reaction — "Hurray for all single women! You go girls!"

The message is clear — men don't measure up and are no longer needed nor often even wanted. Since women have careers now, we are told, men's traditional contribution — financial support — has become largely irrelevant, and men do not now nor did they ever contribute much more than that.

In reality, men give a lot to their families — as much as women do. The current trend away from marriage and toward divorce and/or remaining single has more to do with overcritical women and their excessive expectations than it does with unsuitable men.

The most common charge leveled at men is that they don't hold up their end in the home. Men do work, many critics say, but women work too, and also do most of the childcare and housework — the "second shift."

Research contradicts this. Census data show that only 40 percent of married women with children under eighteen work full-time, and more than a quarter do not hold a job outside the home. According to the Bureau of Labor Statistics' 2004 Time Use Survey, men spend $1 \frac{1}{2}$ times as many hours working as women do, and full-time employed men still work significantly more hours than full-time employed women. When work outside the home and inside the home are properly considered, it is clear that men do at least as much as women. A 2002 University of Michigan Institute for Social Research survey found that women do eleven more hours of housework a week than men, but men work at their jobs fourteen hours a week more than women. According to the Bureau of Labor Statistics, men's total time at leisure, sleeping, doing personal-care activities, or socializing is a statistically meaningless 1 percent higher than women's. The Families and Work Institute in New York City found that fathers, despite their greater market labor load, provide three-fourths as much childcare as mothers do. And these studies do not account for the fact, strongly supported by federal Department of Labor data, that men's jobs tend to be more dangerous and physically straining than women's.

To what, then, do we attribute women's discontent with marriage and relationships and the fact that they initiate the vast majority of divorces? A

Writers quote from media sources

Writers sum up sources, but not all women would agree

Thesis challenges sources

Seems true in my family!

Writers cite data

1

2

3

4

5

6

new *Woman's Day* magazine poll found that 56 percent of married women would not or might not marry their husbands if they could choose again.

Nobody would dispute that, in selecting a mate, women are more dis- 7 cerning than men. This is an evolutionary necessity — a woman must carefully evaluate who is likely to remain loyal to her and protect and provide for her and her children. If a man and a woman go on a blind date and don't hit it off, the man will shrug and say "It went OK." The woman will give five reasons why he's not right for her.

A woman's discerning, critical nature doesn't disappear on her wedding 8 day. Most marital problems and marriage counseling sessions revolve around why the wife is unhappy with her husband, even though they could just as easily be about why the husband is unhappy with the wife. In this common predivorce scenario there are only two possibilities — either she's a great wife and he's a lousy husband, or she's far more critical of him than he is of her. Usually it's the latter.

Despite last week's media homilies, it's doubtful that many men or 9 women are truly happy alone. Much of women's cheerful "I don't need a man/I love my cats" reaction has a hollow ring to it and sounds a lot more like whistling in the dark than a celebration.

Yes, there are some men who make poor mates but not nearly enough 10 to account for the divorce epidemic and the decline of marriage. While it's easy to blame men, many of the wounds women bear from failed relationships and loneliness are self-inflicted.

A Reader's Resources

Major stages	Help in this book	Web help*
Get Started • Prepare to read purposefully. • Plan your follow-up in discussions, exams, or essays. • Skim the text.	▦ Information about a writer's purposes in Chapters 1 and 17 ▦ Common academic and other writing situations in Parts Two and Three ▦ "Getting Started" as a reader (pp. 22–25) and "Getting Ready" as a writer (pp. 308–09)	🔍 reading 🔍 examples ▦ TopLinks
Respond to Reading • Read deeply. • Keep a reading journal. • Annotate the text.	▦ Advice on journals in Chapter 16 ▦ Annotated readings in Part Two and *A Writer's Reader* ▦ Reading questions in Part Two and *A Writer's Reader*	🔍 reading ▦ TopLinks
Read on a Literal Level • Know and recall what you read. • Comprehend the information. • Apply the information to other situations.	▦ "Questions to Start You Thinking" about meaning after each reading ▦ "As You Read" questions before the readings in Part Two and *A Writer's Reader* ▦ "Responding to an Image" prompts in *A Writer's Reader* and "Observing the Characteristics of an Image" in Chapter 22 for advice about "reading" images	🔍 reading 🔍 visual ▦ TopLinks
Read on an Analytical Level • Analyze by breaking into parts or components. • Synthesize by combining with other materials. • Evaluate and assess.	▦ "Questions to Start You Thinking" about reading critically and making connections after each reading in *A Writer's Reader* ▦ Advice in Chapters 12, 13, and 19 and the Quick Research Guide on summarizing, analyzing, and evaluating ▦ Advice on interpreting the meaning of an image in Chapter 22	🔍 reading 🔍 evaluate 🔍 visual ▦ TopLinks
Generate Ideas from Reading • Look for meaty pieces. • Log your reading. • Recall previous reading. • Capture complex ideas. • Read critically. • Analyze writing strategies.	▦ Advice on finding and evaluating sources in the Quick Research Guide ▦ Specialized advice about reading literature in Chapter 13 ▦ Paired and related readings in *A Writer's Reader* ▦ Sample annotations and reading questions in Part Two and *A Writer's Reader* ▦ "Questions to Start You Thinking" about writing strategies after each reading	🔍 reading 🔍 evaluate ▦ TopLinks

*At <bedfordstmartins.com/bedguide>, use the search box shown to find writing resources or exercises by keyword.

Chapter 3
Critical Thinking Processes

*C*ritic, from the Greek word *kritikos*, means "one who can judge and discern"—in short, someone who thinks critically. College will have given you your money's worth if it leaves you better able to judge and discern—to determine what is more and less important, to make distinctions and recognize differences, to generalize from specifics, to draw conclusions from evidence, to grasp complex concepts, to choose wisely. The effective thinking that you will need in college, on the job, and in your daily life is active and purposeful, not passive and ambling. It is critical thinking.

A Process of Critical Thinking

You use critical thinking every day to solve problems and make decisions. Suppose you don't have enough money both to pay your tuition and to buy the car you need. First, you might pin down the causes of your financial problem. Next, you might examine your options to find the best solution, as shown in the graphic on page 34.

ACTIVITY: THINKING CRITICALLY TO SOLVE A CAMPUS PROBLEM

With classmates, identify a common problem for students at your college—juggling a busy schedule, parking on campus, making a class change, joining a social group, or some other issue. Working together, use critical thinking to explore the problem and identify possible solutions.

Critical Thinking
Processes in Action

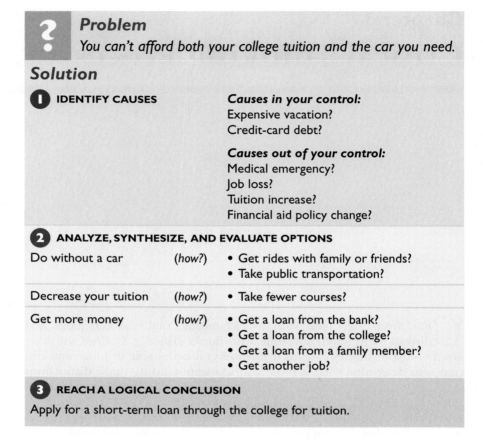

? Problem

You can't afford both your college tuition and the car you need.

Solution

1 IDENTIFY CAUSES

Causes in your control:
Expensive vacation?
Credit-card debt?

Causes out of your control:
Medical emergency?
Job loss?
Tuition increase?
Financial aid policy change?

2 ANALYZE, SYNTHESIZE, AND EVALUATE OPTIONS

Do without a car	(*how?*)	• Get rides with family or friends? • Take public transportation?
Decrease your tuition	(*how?*)	• Take fewer courses?
Get more money	(*how?*)	• Get a loan from the bank? • Get a loan from the college? • Get a loan from a family member? • Get another job?

3 REACH A LOGICAL CONCLUSION

Apply for a short-term loan through the college for tuition.

Getting Started

For more on critical
reading, see Ch. 2.

Using critical thinking, you can explore many problems step by step and reach reasonable solutions. Critical thinking, like critical reading, draws on a cluster of intellectual strategies and skills.

CRITICAL THINKING SKILL	DEFINITION	APPLICATIONS FOR READERS	APPLICATIONS FOR WRITERS
Analysis	Breaking down information into its parts and elements	Analyzing the information in articles, reports, and books to grasp the facts and concepts they contain	Analyzing events, ideas, processes, and structures to understand them and explain them to readers

(*continued on next page*)

CRITICAL THINKING SKILL	DEFINITION	APPLICATIONS FOR READERS	APPLICATIONS FOR WRITERS
Synthesis	Putting together elements and parts to form new wholes	Synthesizing information from several sources, examining implications, and drawing conclusions supported by reliable evidence	Synthesizing source materials with your own thoughts in order to convey the unique combination to others
Evaluation	Judging according to standards or criteria	Evaluating a reading by determining standards for judging, applying them to the reading, and arriving at a conclusion about its significance or value	Evaluating something in writing by convincing readers that your standards are reasonable and that the subject either does or does not meet those standards

These three activities — analysis, synthesis, and evaluation — are the core of critical thinking. They are not new to you, but applying them rigorously in college-level reading and writing may be. When you approach college reading and writing tasks, instructors will expect you (and you should expect yourself) to think, read, write, and think some more.

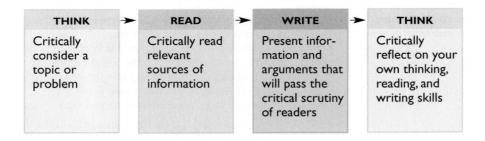

THINK	**READ**	**WRITE**	**THINK**
Critically consider a topic or problem	Critically read relevant sources of information	Present information and arguments that will pass the critical scrutiny of readers	Critically reflect on your own thinking, reading, and writing skills

ACTIVITY: THINKING CRITICALLY TO EXPLORE AN ISSUE

You have worked hard on a group presentation that will be a major part of your grade — and each member of the group will get the same grade. Two days before the project is due, you discover that one group member has plagiarized heavily from sources well known to your instructor. Working together with classmates, use critical thinking to explore your problem and determine what you might do.

APPLYING CRITICAL THINKING TO ACADEMIC PROBLEMS

As you write your college papers, you'll gain experience grappling with academic problems. You'll be expected to use your critical thinking skills — analyzing, synthesizing, and evaluating—as you read and write. Although you may simply dive in, using each skill as needed, sometimes the very wording of an assignment or examination question will alert you to a skill that your instructor expects you to use. What an instructor might expect is illustrated for the first sample assignment in each set in the chart below.

Using Critical Thinking for College Assignments	CRITICAL THINKING SKILL	SAMPLE COLLEGE WRITING ASSIGNMENTS
	Analysis: breaking into parts and elements based on a principle	• Describe the immediate causes of the 1929 stock market crash. (Analyze by using the principle of immediate causes to identify and explain the reasons for the 1929 crash.) • Trace the stages through which a bill becomes federal law. • Explain and illustrate the three dominant styles of parenting. • Define *romanticism,* identifying and illustrating its major characteristics.
	Synthesis: combining parts and elements to form new wholes	• Discuss the following statement: high-minded opposition to slavery was only one cause, and not a very important one, of the animosity between North and South that in 1861 escalated into civil war. (Synthesize by combining the causes or elements of the North-South animosity, going beyond the opposition to slavery, to form a new whole: your conclusion that accounts for the escalation into civil war.) • Imagine that you are a trial lawyer in 1921, charged with defending Nicola Sacco and Bartolomeo Vanzetti, two anarchists accused of murder. Argue for their acquittal on whatever grounds you can justify.
	Evaluation: judging according to standards or criteria	• Present and evaluate the most widely accepted theories that account for the disappearance of the dinosaurs. (Evaluate, based on standards such as scientific merit, the credibility of each theory.) • Defend or challenge the idea that houses and public buildings should be constructed to last no longer than twenty years. • Contrast the models of the solar system advanced by Copernicus and by Kepler, showing how the latter improved on the former.

ACTIVITY: THINKING CRITICALLY TO RESPOND TO AN ACADEMIC PROBLEM

Working with a classmate or a small group, select a sample assignment (not already explained) from the table on page 36 or from one of your classes. Explain how you would approach the assignment in order to demonstrate your critical thinking. Share your strategies for figuring out how to tackle college assignments.

Supporting Critical Thinking with Evidence

As you write a college paper, you try to figure out your purpose, the position you want to take, and ways to get readers to follow your logic and accept your points. Your challenge, of course, is not just to think clearly but to demonstrate your thinking to others, to persuade them to pay attention to what you say. And sound evidence is what critical readers want to see.

Sound evidence supports your main idea or thesis, substantiating your points for readers. It also bolsters your credibility as a writer, demonstrating the merit of your position. When you write, you need to marshal enough appropriate evidence to clarify, explain, and support your ideas. You need to weave claims, evidence, and your own interpretations together into a clearly reasoned explanation or argument. And as you do so, you need to select and test your evidence so that it will convince your readers.

■ For advice on using a few sources, see the Quick Research Guide (the dark-red-edged pages).

TYPES OF EVIDENCE

What is evidence? It is anything that demonstrates the soundness of a claim. Facts, statistics, firsthand observations, and expert testimony are four reliable forms of evidence. Other evidence might include examples, illustrations, details, and opinions. Depending on the purpose of your assignment, some kinds of evidence weigh more heavily than others. For example, readers might appreciate your memories of livestock care on the farm in an essay recalling your childhood summers. However, they would probably discount your memories in an argumentative paper about agricultural methods unless you could show that your memories are representative or that you are an expert on the subject. Personal experience may strengthen an argument but generally is not sufficient as its sole support. If you are in doubt about the type of evidence an assignment requires, ask your instructor whether you should use sources or rely on personal experience and examples.

■ For more on using evidence in a paper that takes a stand, see pp. 152–56.

Facts.   Facts are statements that can be verified objectively, by observation or by reading a reliable account. They are usually stated dispassionately: "If you pump the air out of a five-gallon varnish can, it will collapse." Of course, we accept many of our facts based on the testimony of others. For example, we believe that the Great Wall of China exists although we may never have seen it with our own eyes.

Sometimes people say facts are true statements, but truth and sound evidence may be confused. Consider the truth of these statements:

The tree in my yard is an oak.	*True* because it can be verified
A kilometer is 1,000 meters.	*True* using the metric system
The speed limit on the highway is 65 miles per hour.	*True* according to law
Fewer fatal highway accidents have occurred since the new exit ramp was built.	*True* according to research studies
My favorite food is pizza.	*True* as an opinion
More violent criminals should receive the death penalty.	*True* as a belief
Murder is wrong.	*True* as a value judgment

Some would claim that each statement is true, but when you think critically, you should avoid treating opinions, beliefs, judgments, or personal experience as true in the same sense that verifiable facts and events are true.

Statistics.   Statistics are facts expressed in numbers. What portion of American children are poor? According to statistics from the U.S. Census Bureau, 13.4 million children (or 18.5 percent of all children) lived in poverty in 2005 compared with 11.7 million (or 16.3 percent) in 2001. Clear as such figures seem, they may raise complex questions. For example, how significant is the increase in the poverty rate over four years? What percentage of children were poor over longer terms such as ten years or twenty?

Most writers, without trying to be dishonest, interpret statistics to help their causes. The statement "Fifty percent of the populace have incomes above the poverty level" might substantiate the fine job done by the government of a developing nation. Putting the statement another way — "Fifty percent of the populace have incomes below the poverty level" — might use the same statistic to show the inadequacy of the government's efforts.

Even though a writer is free to interpret a statistic, statistics should not be used to mislead. On the wrapper of a peanut candy bar, we read that a one-ounce serving contains only 150 calories. The claim is true, but the bar weighs 1.6 ounces. Gobble it all — more likely than eating 62 percent of it — and you'll ingest 240 calories, a heftier snack than the innocent statistic on the wrapper suggests. Because abuses make some readers automatically distrustful, use figures fairly when you write, and make sure they are accurate. If you doubt a statistic, compare it with figures reported by several other sources. Distrust a statistical report that differs from every other report unless it is backed by further evidence.

Expert Testimony.   By "experts," we mean people with knowledge gained from study and experience of a particular field. The test of an expert is whether his or her expertise stands up to the scrutiny of others who are knowledgeable in that field. The views of Michael Jordan on how to play offense in basketball carry authority. So do the views of economist and former Federal Reserve chairman Alan Greenspan on what causes inflation. However, Jordan's take on the economy or Greenspan's thoughts on basketball might not be authoritative. Also consider whether the expert has any bias or special interest that would affect reliability. Statistics on cases of lung cancer attributed to smoking might be better taken from government sources than from the tobacco industry.

░ Should you want to contact a campus expert, turn to Ch. 6 for advice about interviews.

Firsthand Observation.   Firsthand observation is persuasive. It can add concrete reality to abstract or complex points. You might support the claim "The Meadowfield waste recycling plant fails to meet state guidelines" by recalling your own observations: "When I visited the plant last January, I was struck by the number of open waste canisters and by the lack of protective gear for the workers who handle these toxic materials daily."

░ For more on observation, see Ch. 5.

As readers, most of us tend to trust the writer who declares, "I was there. This is what I saw." Sometimes that trust is misplaced, however, so always be wary of a writer's claim to have seen something that no other evidence supports. Ask yourself, Is this writer biased? Might the writer have (intentionally or unintentionally) misinterpreted what he or she saw? Of course, your readers will scrutinize your firsthand observations, too; take care to reassure them that your observations are unbiased and accurate.

ACTIVITY: LOOKING FOR EVIDENCE

Using the issue you explored with classmates for the activity on page 33, what would you need to support your identification, explanation, or solution of the problem? Working with classmates, identify the kinds of evidence that would be most useful. Where or how might you find such evidence?

░ For more on selecting evidence to persuade readers, see pp. 155–156.

Testing Evidence

As both a reader and a writer, you should always critically test and question evidence to see whether it is strong enough to carry the weight of the writer's claims. Use these questions to determine whether evidence is useful and trustworthy:

░ For advice on evaluating sources of evidence, see C in the Quick Research Guide (the dark-red-edged pages).

EVIDENCE CHECKLIST

___ Is it accurate?
- Do the facts and figures seem accurate based on what you have found in published sources, reports by others, or reference works?
- Are figures or quoted facts copied correctly?

___ Is it reliable?
- Is the source trustworthy and well regarded?
- Does the source acknowledge any commercial, political, advocacy, or other bias that might affect the quality of its information?
- Does the writer supplying the evidence have appropriate credentials or experience? Is the writer respected as an expert in the field?
- Do other sources agree with the information?

___ Is it up-to-date?
- Are facts and statistics — such as population figures — current?
- Is the information from the latest sources?

___ Is it to the point?
- Does the evidence back the exact claim made?
- Is the evidence all pertinent? Does any of it drift from the point to interesting but irrelevant evidence?

___ Is it representative?
- Are examples typical of all the things included in the writer's position?
- Are examples balanced? Do they present the topic or issue fairly?
- Are contrary examples acknowledged?

■ For information on mistakes in thinking, see pp. 46–47 and pp. 162–63.

___ Is it appropriately complex?
- Is the evidence sufficient to account for the claim made?
- Does it avoid treating complex things superficially?
- Does it avoid needlessly complicating simple things?

___ Is it sufficient and strong enough to back the claim and persuade readers?
- Are the amount and quality of the evidence appropriate for the claim and for the readers?
- Is the evidence aligned with the existing knowledge of readers?
- Does the evidence answer the questions readers are likely to ask?
- Is the evidence vivid and significant?

Using Evidence to Appeal to Your Audience

■ For more on appeals, see pp. 157–58.

One way to select evidence and to judge whether it is appropriate and sufficient is to consider the types of appeal — logical, emotional, and ethical. Most effective arguments work on all three levels, using all three types of appeals with evidence that supports all three.

LOGICAL APPEAL (LOGOS)

When writers use a logical appeal (*logos* or "word" in Greek), they appeal to the reader's mind or intellect. This appeal relies on evidence that is factual, objective, clear, and relevant. Critical readers expect to find logical evidence that supports major claims and statements. For example, if a writer were arguing for term limits for legislators, she wouldn't want to base her argument on the evidence that some long-term legislators weren't reelected last term (irrelevant) or that the current system is unfair to young people who want to get into politics (not logical). Instead, she might argue that the absence of term limits encourages corruption, using evidence of legislators who repaid lobbyists for campaign contributions with key votes.

EMOTIONAL APPEAL (PATHOS)

When writers use an emotional appeal (*pathos* or "suffering" in Greek), they appeal to the reader's heart. They choose language, facts, quotations, examples, and images that evoke emotional responses. Of course, convincing writing does touch readers' hearts as well as their minds. Without this heartfelt tug, a strict logical appeal may seem cold and dehumanized. If a writer opposed hunting seals for their fur, he might combine statistics about the number of seals killed each year and the overall population decrease with a vivid description of baby seals being slaughtered. Some writers use emotional words and sentimental examples to manipulate readers — to arouse their sympathy, pity, or anger in order to convert them without much logical evidence — but dishonest emotional appeals may alienate readers. Instead of basing an argument against a political candidate on pitiful images of scrawny children living in roach-infested squalor, a good writer would report the candidate's voting record on issues that affect children.

ETHICAL APPEAL (ETHOS)

When writers use an ethical appeal (*ethos* or "character" in Greek), they call on the reader's sense of fairness and trust. They select and present evidence in a way that will make the audience trust them, respect their judgment, and believe what they have to say. The best logical argument in the world falls flat when readers don't take the writer seriously. How can you use an ethical appeal to establish your credibility as a writer? First you need to establish your credentials in the field through experience, reading, or interviews that helped you learn about the subject. If you are writing about environmental pollution, tell your readers that your allergies have been irritated by chemicals in the air. Identify medical or environmental experts you have contacted or whose publications you have read. Demonstrate your knowledge through the information you present, the experts and sources you cite, and the depth of understanding you convey. Establish a rapport with readers by indicating values and attitudes that you share with them and by responding seriously to opposing arguments. Finally, use language that is precise, clear, and appropriate in tone.

ACTIVITY: IDENTIFYING TYPES OF APPEALS

Bring to class the editorial or opinion page from a newspaper or news-magazine. Read some of the letters or articles. Identify the types of appeals used by each author to support his or her point.

Presenting Your Critical Thinking

■ For more on taking a stand, see Ch. 9; on proposals, see Ch. 10; on evaluation, see Ch. 11; and on supporting a position, see Ch. 12.

Why do you have to worry about critical thinking? Isn't it enough just to tell everybody else what you think? That tactic probably works fine when you casually debate with your friends. After all, they already know you, your opinions, and your typical ways of thinking. They may even find your occasional rant entertaining. Whether they agree or disagree, they probably tolerate your ideas because they are your friends.

When you write a paper in college, however, you face a different type of audience, one that expects you to explain what you assume, what you advocate, and why you hold that position. That audience also wants to learn the specifics — the reasons you find compelling, the evidence that supports your view, and the connections that relate each point to your position. Finally, your college audience expects reasoning, not emotional pleading or bullying or preaching.

How you reason and how you present your reasoning are important parts of gaining the confidence of college readers. College papers typically develop their points based on logic, not personal opinions or beliefs. Most are organized logically, often as a series of reasons, each making a claim, a statement, or an assertion that is backed up with persuasive supporting evidence. Your assignment or your instructor may recommend ways such as the following for showing your critical thinking.

■ For more about the statement-support pattern, see A3 in the Quick Research Guide (the dark-red-edged pages).

Reasoning Deductively or Inductively.   When you state a *generalization,* you present your broad, general point, viewpoint, or conclusion.

> The admissions requirements at Gerard College are unfair.

On the other hand, when you supply a *particular,* you present an instance, a detail, an example, an item, a case, or other specific evidence to demonstrate that a general statement is reasonable.

> A Gerard College application form shows the information collected by the admissions office. According to the admissions policies, standardized test scores are weighted more heavily than better predictors of performance, such as high school grades. Qualified students who do not test well often face a frustrating admissions process, as Irma Lang's situation illustrates.

Your particulars consist of details that back up your broader point; your generalizations connect the particulars so that you can move beyond isolated, individual cases.

Most college papers are organized *deductively*. They begin with a general statement (often a thesis) and then present particular cases to support or apply it. Readers like this pattern because it reduces mystery; they learn right away what the writer wants to show. Writers like this pattern because it helps them state up front what they want to accomplish (even if they have to figure some of that out as they write and state it more directly as they revise). Papers organized deductively sacrifice suspense but gain directness and clarity.

On the other hand, some papers are organized *inductively*. They begin with the particulars—a persuasive number of instances, examples, or details—and lead up to the larger generalization that they support. Because readers have to wait for the generalization, this pattern allows them time to adjust to an unexpected conclusion that they might initially reject. For this reason, writers favor this pattern when they anticipate resistance from their audience and want to move gradually toward the broader point.

For more about thesis statements, see Ch. 17.

For more on inductive and deductive reasoning, see pp. 357–59.

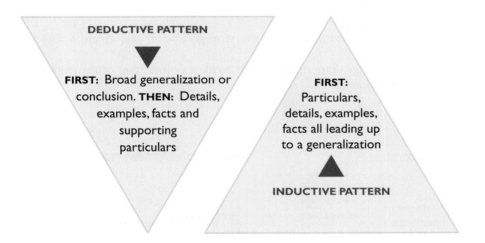

Building Sequences and Scaffolds.   You may use several strategies for presenting your reasoning, depending on what you want to show and how you think you can show it most persuasively. You may develop a line of reasoning, a series of points and evidence, running one after another in a sequence or building on one another to support a persuasive scaffold (see p. 44).

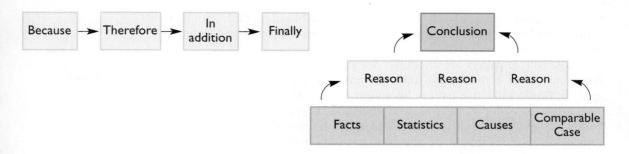

■ For more strategies
for developing, see Ch. 19.
Developing Logical Patterns.   The following patterns are often used to organize reasoning in college papers. Although they can help you show relationships, they don't automatically prove them. In fact, each has advantages but may also have disadvantages, as the sample strengths and weaknesses illustrate.

> *Pattern:* Least to Most
> *Advantage:* Building up to the best points can produce a strong finish.
> *Disadvantage:* Holding back on the strongest points makes readers wait.

> *Pattern:* Most to Least
> *Advantage:* Beginning with the strongest point can create a forceful opening.
> *Disadvantage:* Tapering off with weaker points may cause readers to lose interest.

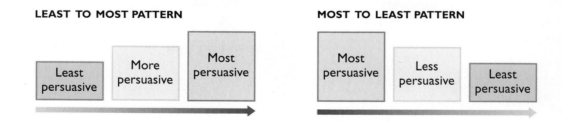

■ For more on comparison and contrast, see Ch. 7.
> *Pattern*: Comparison and Contrast
> *Advantage*: Readers can easily relate comparable points about things of like kind.
> *Disadvantage*: Some similarities or differences don't guarantee or prove others.

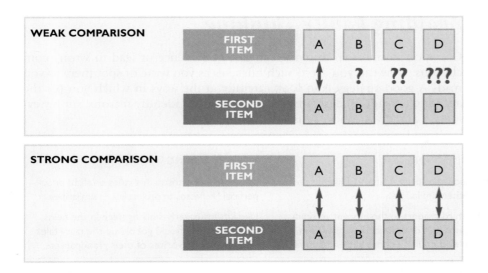

Pattern: Cause and Effect

Advantage: Tracing causes or effects can tightly relate and perhaps predict events.

Disadvantage: Weak links can call into question all relationships in a series of events.

For more on cause and effect, see Ch. 8.

WEAK CAUSAL CONNECTIONS

STRONG CAUSAL CHAIN

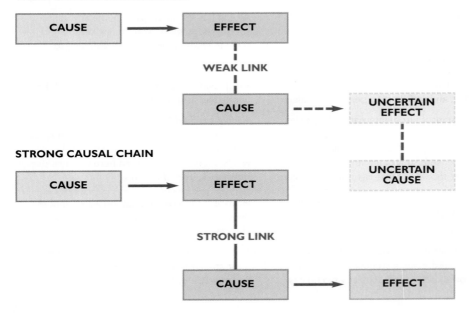

Avoiding Faulty Thinking

For specific logical fallacies, see pp. 162–63.

Common mistakes in thinking can distort evidence or lead to wrong conclusions. How can you avoid such mistakes as you write or spot them as you read? A good strategy is to look carefully at the ways in which you (or the author of a reading) describe events, relate ideas, identify reasons, supply evidence, and draw conclusions.

	SOUND REASONING	WEAK REASONING
Comparisons	Comparison that uses substantial likeness to project other similarities: Like the third graders in the innovative reading programs just described, the children in this town also could become better readers.	Inaccurate comparison that relies on slight or superficial likenesses to project other similarities: Like kittens eagerly stalking mice in the fields, young readers should gobble up the tasty tales that were the favorites of their grandparents.
Causes and Effects	Causal analysis that relies on well-substantiated connections relating events and outcomes: City water reserves have suffered from below-average rainfall, above-average heat, and steadily increasing consumer demand.	Faulty reasoning that oversimplifies causal relationships, confuses coincidences with causes, or assumes that a first event must cause a second: One cause—and one alone—accounts for the ten-year drought that has dried up local water supplies.
Reasons	Logical reasons that are supported by relevant evidence and presented with fair and thoughtful consideration: As the recent audit indicates, all campus groups that spend student activity fees should prepare budgets, keep clear financial records, and substantiate expenses.	Faulty reasons that rely on bias, emotion, or unrelated personal traits or that accuse, flatter, threaten, or inspire fear: All campus groups, especially the arrogant social groups, must stop ripping off the average student's fees and threatening to run college costs sky high.
Evidence	Evidence that is accurate, reliable, current, relevant, fair, and sufficient to persuade readers: Both the statistics from international agencies and the accounts of Sudanese refugees summarized earlier suggest that, while a fair immigration policy needs to account for many complexities, it should not lose sight of compassion.	Weak evidence that is insufficient, out of date, unreliable, slanted, or emotional: As five-year-old Lannie's frantic flight across the Canadian border in 1988 proves, refugees from all the war-torn regions around the world should be welcomed here because this is America, land of the free.
Conclusions	Solid conclusions that are based on factual evidence and recognize multiple options or complications: As the recent campus wellness study has demonstrated, college students need education about healthy food and activity choices.	Hasty conclusions that rely on insufficient evidence, assumptions, or simplistic two-option choices: The campus health facility should refuse to treat students who don't eat healthy foods and exercise daily.

Use the following questions to help you refine your reasoning as you plan, draft, or revise a college paper:

LOGICAL REASONING CHECKLIST

___ Have you reviewed your assignment or syllabus, looking for advice or requirements about the kind of reasoning or evidence expected?

___ Have you developed your reasoning on a solid foundation? Are your initial assumptions sound? Do you need to identify, explain, or justify them?

___ Is your thesis or position stated clearly? Are its terms explained or defined?

___ Have you presented your reasons for thinking that your thesis is sound? Have you arranged them in a sequence that will make sense to your audience? Have you used transitions to introduce and connect them so readers can't miss them?

___ Have you used evidence that your audience will respect to support each reason you present? Have you favored objective, research-based evidence (facts, statistics, and expert testimony that others can substantiate) rather than personal experiences or beliefs that others cannot or may not share?

___ Have you explained your evidence so that your audience can see how it supports your points and applies to your thesis? Have you used transitions to specify relationships for readers?

___ Have you enhanced your own credibility by acknowledging, rather than ignoring, other points of view? Have you integrated or countered these views?

___ Have you adjusted your tone and style so that you come across as reasonable and fair-minded? Have you avoided arrogant claims about proving (rather than showing) points?

___ If you have used any sources, have you credited them as expected by academic readers?

ACTIVITY: ANALYZING REASONING

Analyze the newspaper column and the letter on pages 48–49, looking for clear reasoning as well as flaws in logic. For each, identify its position, its sequence of reasons or points, its supporting evidence, and its methods of appealing to readers. The column by Al Knight appeared in the *Denver Post* on November 22, 2006.

Al Knight

Perhaps We Should Move to Save Dogs from Their Owners

The election earlier this month settled a lot of the state's big issues, like 1 who will sit in the governor's office, but there are plenty of little problems that were left for another day. One of them is whether Colorado should join a handful of other states and prohibit pickup owners from plying the state's major highways with one or several dogs loose in the truck bed.

Colorado is a big state with lots of open road. Anyone who has traveled 2 those roads will have seen a truck owner speeding down the highway with his pet or pets running from side to side in the open bed, seemingly inches from certain disaster. There is, alas, more than the prospect of disaster. According to one estimate, 100,000 dogs are killed each year by either falling out of or being intentionally tossed out of careening pickup trucks.

Some states — including Virginia, Florida, New Hampshire, California, 3 Rhode Island, Massachusetts, and Oregon — have passed legislation regulating the practice. Some localities and counties also have local ordinances on the subject. In all of these locations, proponents advanced arguments dealing with public as well as animal safety. A frolicking dog in the back of a pickup is an obvious distraction and hazard, not only for the truck owner and the dog but for anybody else on or near that road or highway.

As to animal safety, as far back as 1988, the Society for the Prevention of 4 Cruelty to Animals did a study in Massachusetts that was based on interviews with 141 veterinarians. The organization found that those vets had treated 592 dogs that year for injuries received when tossed from the bed of a pickup. The Humane Society, in an article titled "Why Dogs and Pickup Trucks Don't Mix," stated the obvious quite nicely: "If your truck hits a bump, or if you step on the brakes suddenly or swerve to avoid an obstacle, your dog can easily be thrown from the truck bed and onto the road. Chances are, this will injure or kill your dog. But even if it doesn't, being struck by another vehicle probably will. Also, other drivers may cause an accident by swerving to avoid hitting your dog."

The question remains whether the plainly unwise practice of transport- 5 ing loose dogs in pickup beds should be regulated. Would such a law, for example, interfere with the rights of farmers, ranchers, hunters, and others who might have a reason to transport dogs in this fashion? Well, the handful of states that have addressed that concern have carved out narrow exceptions to cover those situations. Oregon, for example, has an exception for ranching and farming which is limited to noninterstate highways and population centers with less than 5,000 people. In Tennessee, where a bill was considered and later defeated, the measure had a narrow exception for licensed hunters. In Texas, where there has been a petition drive urging the legislature to act, a proposed law has exceptions for hunters and ranchers.

These exceptions haven't satisfied everyone. During the Tennessee debate, one lawmaker complained that the proposed statute would "absolutely destroy the way people live with these animals."

Hysteria aside, there are good arguments to be made in favor of a state 6 statute requiring the use of carriers or restraints:

- The current system doesn't work. While many dogs can survive a ride in the back of a pickup, many will not.

- Public education doesn't seem to be a good option. The typical pickup/dog owner surely knows the risks but has chosen to ignore them. More education is unlikely to change that fact.

- Enforcement of a statute would be a breeze. The dog is typically in plain sight. A safety officer need not listen to the kind of stories offered when someone is stopped for speeding or a seat-belt violation. It would be hard for a driver to claim the officer was mistaken and that "the dog wasn't really in the bed of the pickup in the first place."

If one of the new legislators in Colorado wants to take on the task of 7 passing such a law, next year would be a good time to start.

Letter from an Irate Dog Owner

Dear Editor:

Even a city slicker should be able to see why dogs belong in pickup trucks. All dogs love riding out in the air. They need room to jump around. And you'd better just zip your lip if you see me driving down I-25 with my dog.

Who would want Colorado to turn into one of those wimpy states that amends its constitution whenever some bleeding heart starts feeling sorrowful about wolves or dolphins? Maybe we should bring fur coats back here instead of trying to force hard-working citizens to take their dogs out of their trucks. This whole issue stinks!

Dog owners have the right to do whatever they want with their animals. This is the kind of law that only busybodies would support. If you're thinking of supporting this issue, you'd better think again. Besides, if my dog had any complaints, he'd have to take them up with me!

An Irate Dog Owner

A Critical Thinker's Resources

Major stages	Help in this book	Web help*
Get Started • Analyze by breaking into parts or components. • Synthesize by combining with other materials. • Evaluate and assess.	▪ Summarizing, analyzing, synthesizing, and evaluating advice in Chapters 12 and 19 and the Quick Research Guide ▪ Criteria for evaluating sources in the Quick Research Guide ▪ Advice on interpreting images in Chapter 22	🔍 development 🔍 evaluate 🔍 visual
Apply Critical Thinking Skills • Think through topics, problems, and assignments. • Think critically as a reader. • Think critically as a writer.	▪ Logical thinking advice in Chapter 9, "Taking a Stand" ▪ *A Writer's Reader* and Part Two (for applying your critical thinking skills as a reader) ▪ Writing situations in Parts Two and Three (for applying your critical thinking skills)	🔍 reading 🔍 examples
Supply Evidence to Support Thinking • Find facts. • Add statistics. • Look for expert testimony. • Observe.	▪ Tips for finding and evaluating sources in the Quick Research Guide ▪ "Using Visuals to Reinforce Your Content" section in Chapter 21 ▪ Observing and interviewing advice in Chapters 5 and 6	🔍 support 🔍 visual 🔍 evaluate
Test Evidence • Read to confirm accuracy, reliability, and currency. • Select what is pertinent and representative. • Monitor complexity. • Supply enough strong evidence to persuade readers.	▪ Advice on critical reading in Chapter 2; questions and annotations with readings ▪ "Strategies for Developing," in Chapter 19 ▪ Critical thinking skills for researchers in the Quick Research Guide ▪ Part Two, especially Chapters 7 to 12 (for applying these skills)	🔍 reading 🔍 development 🔍 support
Use Evidence to Support Appeals • Appeal to logic. • Appeal to emotions. • Appeal to ethical issues of fairness and trust.	▪ Advice on making compelling appeals to readers in Chapters 9, 10, and 11 ▪ Advice on purpose and audience in Chapters 1 (pp. 14–19) and 17 (pp. 310–12)	🔍 support 🔍 examples
Present Your Critical Thinking • Develop logical reasoning. • Build sequences and scaffolds. • Watch out for faulty thinking.	▪ Advice on logical reasoning in Chapters 3, 9, 10, and 11 ▪ Advice on development in Chapter 19 ▪ Advice on avoiding faulty thinking (p. 46) and logical fallacies (pp. 162–63)	🔍 development

*At <bedfordstmartins.com/bedguide>, use the search box shown to find writing resources or exercises by keyword.

PART TWO

A Writer's Situations

Introduction

In Part Two, we present a sequence of writing situations that require you to use processes for writing, reading, and thinking critically. The nine writing assignments — recalling an experience, observing a scene, interviewing a subject, comparing and contrasting, explaining causes and effects, taking a stand, proposing a solution, evaluating, and supporting a position with sources — are arranged roughly in order of increasing complexity — that is, according to the level of critical reading and thinking required. Some require analysis — breaking something down into its components to understand it better. Others require synthesis — combining information from various sources with your own ideas in order to achieve a new perspective. Still others call for evaluation, using criteria to judge. Let's look at these writing situations in more detail.

Recalling an Experience.   Recalling an event depends on your richest resource as a writer — your memory. Chapter 4 guides you in focusing and shaping your writing from memory so that you can present recollections effectively and convey their importance to your readers.

Observing a Scene.   Observation relies on using your senses to see, hear, smell, touch, and taste what's around you. Chapter 5 helps you select and arrange compelling details in order to convey your insights about what you have observed.

Interviewing a Subject.   Interviewing adds to your writing the freshness of conversation and the liveliness of exchange with someone else. Chapter 6 encourages you to bring the subject of an interview to life as you distill the impression and information gained during your interview.

Comparing and Contrasting.   Comparing and contrasting focuses on the similarities and differences of two (or more) items or groups. Chapter 7 guides you first in analyzing each item and then in lining up the characteristics of each, side by side, to determine how they are alike and how they are different. Most important, because effective comparison and contrast has some significant purpose, you will convey your conclusion about how each alternative operates or which alternative is preferable.

Explaining Causes and Effects.   As you focus on an action, event, or situation, identifying causes means ferreting out roots and origins. Determining effects means figuring out results. Sometimes as you analyze, you will find a chain of causes and effects: a situation causes specific effects, which in turn cause other effects. Chapter 8 helps you to analyze and explain causes, effects, or both in order to support an overall point.

Taking a Stand.   When you take a stand, you argue for one side or another of an issue. Chapter 9 helps you develop your position in a controversy and present your opinion so that readers will respect it even if they do not agree with you. You may come to a debate with strong views or develop a position while looking into the matter. Once you reach a clear position, you will present your case persuasively to readers using solid, pertinent evidence — facts, statistics, expert opinion, and direct observation.

Proposing a Solution.   Proposing a solution requires not only taking a stand but also presenting a feasible solution to the problem at hand. Chapter 10 helps you identify a problem and then propose a convincing, workable solution. You will use two main methods of persuading readers to accept your recommendation: showing readers why the problem matters to them and supplying evidence to support your solution.

Evaluating.   Evaluating means judging: deciding whether an idea, a product, a work of art, or some other thing is good or bad, effective or ineffective. As Chapter 11 explains, you will identify specific criteria for judging your subject. Once your standards are clear, based on your personal preferences or the views of experts in the field, you can analyze your subject to see how well it meets your criteria. As you explain your judgment, you will also try to persuade readers that your view is reasonable.

Supporting a Position with Sources.   Especially in college papers, you often need to state and support a position with evidence from a few sources. Chapter 12 guides you through the process of reading a cluster of sources and capturing information from them in quotations, paraphrases, and summaries. You will launch such information with a suitable introduction, cite the source as you mention it, and list the source at the end of your paper. Finally, you will learn strategies for keeping sources in their proper supporting role by developing your own voice as a credible college writer.

Taken together, these nine chapters present many of the writing situations you will encounter in other college courses and in your career. Use the processes outlined in these chapters as resources when you meet unfamiliar writing situations or need to marshal appropriate evidence for essays.

Chapter 4
Recalling an Experience

Responding to an Image

Look carefully at one of the photographs in the grid. In your view, when was this photograph taken? Who might the person or people be? Where are they, and why are they there? What are they doing? What relationships and emotions does the picture suggest with its focal point and arrangement? Write about an experience the image helps you recall or about a possible explanation of events in this picture. Use vivid detail to convey what happened to you or what might have happened to the people in the picture.

Writing from recall is writing from memory, a writer's richest — and handiest — resource. Recall is clearly necessary when you are asked to write of a personal experience, a favorite place, a memorable person. But even when an instructor hands you a subject that seems to have nothing to do with you, your memory is the first place to look. Suppose you have to write a psychology paper about how advertisers prey on consumers' fears. Begin with what you remember. What ads have sent chills down your back? What ads have suggested that their products could save you from a painful social blunder, a lonely night, or a deadly accident? All by itself, memory may not give you enough to write about, but you will rarely go wrong if you start by jotting down something remembered.

Learning from Other Writers

■ For more on thesis and support, see Chs. 17 and 19.

Here are two samples of good writing from recall — one by a professional writer, one by a college student. To help you begin to analyze the first reading, look for the notes in the margin. They identify features such as the main idea, or thesis, and the first of the main events that support it in a paper written from recall.

As You Read These Recollections

As you read these essays, ask yourself the following questions:

■ For more examples of writing from recall, visit <bedfordstmartins.com/ bedguide> and do a key- word search:

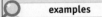

examples

1. Is the perspective of the essay primarily that of a child or an adult? Why do you think so?

2. What does the author realize after reflecting on the events recalled? Does the realization come soon after the experience or later, when the writer examines the events from a more mature perspective?

3. How does the realization change the individual?

In this essay from his autobiography Growing Up *(1982), columnist Russell Baker recalls being sixteen in urban Baltimore and wondering what to do with his life.*

Russell Baker
The Art of Eating Spaghetti

The only thing that truly interested me was writing, and I knew that sixteen-year-olds did not come out of high school and become writers. I thought of writing as something to be done only by the rich. It was so obviously not real work, not a job at which you could earn a living. Still, I had begun to think of myself as a writer. It was the only thing for which I seemed to have the smallest talent, and, silly though it sounded when I told people I'd like to be a writer, it gave me a way of thinking about myself which satisfied my need to have an identity.

Introduction

56

The notion of becoming a writer had flickered off and on in my head 2
since the Belleville days, but it wasn't until my third year in high school that
the possibility took hold. Until then I'd been bored by everything associated
with English courses. I found English grammar dull and baffling. I hated the
assignments to turn out "compositions," and went at them like heavy labor,
turning out leaden, lackluster paragraphs that were agonies for teachers to
read and for me to write. The classics thrust on me to read seemed as dead-
ening as chloroform.

 When our class was assigned to Mr. Fleagle for third-year English I antici- 3
pated another grim year in that dreariest of subjects. Mr. Fleagle was notorious among City students for dullness and inability to inspire. He was said to
be stuffy, dull, and hopelessly out of date. To me he looked to be sixty or seventy and prim to a fault. He wore primly severe eyeglasses, his wavy hair was
primly cut and primly combed. He wore prim vested suits with neckties
blocked primly against the collar buttons of his primly starched white shirts.
He had a primly pointed jaw, a primly straight nose, and a prim manner of
speaking that was so correct, so gentlemanly, that he seemed a comic antique.

 I anticipated a listless,° unfruitful year with Mr. Fleagle and for a long 4
time was not disappointed. We read *Macbeth*. Mr. Fleagle loved *Macbeth* and
wanted us to love it too, but he lacked the gift of infecting others with his
own passion. He tried to convey the murderous ferocity of Lady Macbeth
one day by reading aloud the passage that concludes

 . . . I have given suck, and know
How tender 'tis to love the babe that milks me.
I would, while it was smiling in my face,
Have plucked my nipple from his boneless gums. . . .

The idea of prim Mr. Fleagle plucking his nipple from boneless gums was
too much for the class. We burst into gasps of irrepressible snickering. Mr.
Fleagle stopped.

 "There is nothing funny, boys, about giving suck to a babe. It is the— 5
the very essence of motherhood, don't you see."

 He constantly sprinkled his sentences with "don't you see." It wasn't a 6
question but an exclamation of mild surprise at our ignorance. "Your pronoun needs an antecedent, don't you see," he would say, very primly. "The
purpose of the Porter's scene, boys, is to provide comic relief from the horror, don't you see."

 Late in the year we tackled the informal essay. "The essay, don't you see, 7
is the . . ." My mind went numb. Of all forms of writing, none seemed so
boring as the essay. Naturally we would have to write informal essays. Mr.
Fleagle distributed a homework sheet offering us a choice of topics. None
was quite so simpleminded as "What I Did on My Summer Vacation," but
most seemed to be almost as dull. I took the list home and dawdled until
the night before the essay was due. Sprawled on the sofa, I finally faced up

THESIS
stating main idea

Major event I

Support for
major event I

---

listless: Lacking energy or enthusiasm.

to the grim task, took the list out of my notebook, and scanned it. The topic on which my eye stopped was "The Art of Eating Spaghetti."

This title produced an extraordinary sequence of mental images. Surging   8
up out of the depths of memory came a vivid recollection of a night in Belleville when all of us were seated around the supper table — Uncle Allen, my mother, Uncle Charlie, Doris, Uncle Hal — and Aunt Pat served spaghetti for supper. Spaghetti was an exotic treat in those days. Neither Doris nor I had ever eaten spaghetti, and none of the adults had enough experience to be good at it. All the good humor of Uncle Allen's house reawoke in my mind as I recalled the laughing arguments we had that night about the socially respectable method for moving spaghetti from plate to mouth.

Suddenly I wanted to write about that, about the warmth and good feel-   9
ing of it, but I wanted to put it down simply for my own joy, not for Mr. Fleagle. It was a moment I wanted to recapture and hold for myself. I wanted to relive the pleasure of an evening at New Street. To write it as I wanted, how-ever, would violate all the rules of formal composition I'd learned in school, and Mr. Fleagle would surely give it a failing grade. Never mind. I would write something else for Mr. Fleagle after I had written this thing for myself.

When I finished it the night was half gone and there was no time left to   10
compose a proper, respectable essay for Mr. Fleagle. There was no choice next morning but to turn in my private reminiscence° of Belleville. Two days passed before Mr. Fleagle returned the graded papers, and he returned everyone's but mine. I was bracing myself for a command to report to Mr. Fleagle immediately after school for discipline when I saw him lift my paper from his desk and rap for the class's attention.

"Now, boys," he said, "I want to read you an essay. This is titled 'The Art   11
of Eating Spaghetti.'"

And he started to read. My words! He was reading *my words* out loud to   12
the entire class. What's more, the entire class was listening. Listening atten-tively. Then somebody laughed, then the entire class was laughing, and not in contempt and ridicule, but with openhearted enjoyment. Even Mr. Fleagle stopped two or three times to repress a small prim smile.

I did my best to avoid showing pleasure, but what I was feeling was pure   13
ecstasy at this startling demonstration that my words had the power to make people laugh. In the eleventh grade, at the eleventh hour as it were, I had discovered a calling. It was the happiest moment of my entire school career. When Mr. Fleagle finished he put the final seal on my happiness by saying, "Now that, boys, is an essay, don't you see. It's — don't you see — it's of the very essence of the essay, don't you see. Congratulations, Mr. Baker."

Conclusion restating thesis — For the first time, light shone on a possibility. It wasn't a very heartening   14
possibility, to be sure. Writing couldn't lead to a job after high school, and it was hardly honest work, but Mr. Fleagle had opened a door for me. After that I ranked Mr. Fleagle among the finest teachers in the school.

reminiscence: Memory.

Questions to Start You Thinking

Meaning

1. In your own words, state what Baker believes he learned in the eleventh grade about the art of writing. What incidents or statements help identify this lesson for readers? What lesson, if any, did you learn from the essay?

2. Why do you think Baker included this event in his autobiography?

3. Have you ever changed your mind about something you had to do, as Baker did about writing? Or about a person, as he did about Mr. Fleagle?

Writing Strategies

4. What is the effect, in paragraph 3, of Baker's repetitions of the words *prim* and *primly*? What other devices does he use to characterize Mr. Fleagle vividly? Why do you think Baker uses so much space to portray his teacher?

5. What does the quotation from *Macbeth* add to Baker's account? Had the quotation been omitted, what would have been lost?

6. How does Baker organize the essay? Why does he use this order?

STUDENT ESSAY

Robert G. Schreiner

What Is a Hunter?

What is a hunter? This is a simple question with a relatively straightforward answer. A hunter is, according to <u>Webster's New Collegiate Dictionary</u>, a person who hunts game (game being various types of animals hunted or pursued for various reasons). However, a second question is just as simple but without such a straightforward answer: What characteristics make up a hunter? As a child, I had always considered the most important aspect of the hunter's person to be his ability to use a rifle, bow, or whatever weapon was appropriate to the type of hunting being done. Having many relatives in rural areas of Virginia and Kansas, I had been exposed to rifles a great deal. I had done extensive target shooting and considered myself to be quite proficient in the use of firearms. I had never been hunting, but I had always thought that since I could fire a rifle accurately I would make a good hunter.

One Christmas holiday, while we were visiting our grandparents in Kansas, my grandfather asked me if I wanted to go jackrabbit hunting with him. I eagerly accepted, anxious to show off my prowess° with a rifle. A younger cousin of mine also wanted to come, so we all went out into the garage, loaded two .22 caliber rifles and a 20-gauge shotgun, hopped into the pickup truck, and drove out of town. It

1   *In this college essay, Robert G. Schreiner uses vivid details to bring to life a significant childhood event.*

2

prowess: Superior skill.

had snowed the night before, and to either side of the narrow road swept six-foot-deep powdery drifts. The wind twirled the fine crystalline snow into whirling vor-texes° that bounced along the icy road and sprayed snow into the open windows of the pickup. As we drove, my grandfather gave us some pointers about both spotting and shooting jackrabbits. He told us that when it snows, jackrabbits like to dig out a hollow in the top of a snowdrift, usually near a fencepost, and lie there soaking up the sunshine. He told us that even though jackrabbits are a grayish brown, this coloration is excellent camouflage in the snow, for the curled-up rabbits resemble rocks. He then pointed out a few rabbits in such positions as we drove along, show-ing us how to distinguish them from exposed rocks and dirt. He then explained that the only way to be sure that we killed the rabbit was to shoot for the head and, in particular, the eye, for this was on a direct line with the rabbit's brain. Since we were using solid point bullets, which deform into a ball upon impact, a hit anywhere but the head would most likely only wound the rabbit.

How does the writer convey his grandfather's definition of hunting?

My grandfather then slowed down the pickup and told us to look out for the   3
rabbits hidden in the snowdrifts. We eventually spotted one about thirty feet from the road in a snow-filled gully. My cousin wished to shoot the first one, so he hopped out of the truck, balanced the .22 on the hood, and fired. A spray of snow erupted about a foot to the left of the rabbit's hollow. My cousin fired again, and again, and again, the shots pockmarking the slope of the drift. He fired once more and the rabbit bounced out of its hollow, its head rocking from side to side. He was hit. My cousin eagerly gamboled into the snow to claim his quarry.° He brought it back holding it by the hind legs, proudly displaying it as would a warrior the severed head of his enemy. The bullet had entered the rabbit's right shoulder and exited through the neck. In both places a thin trickle of crimson marred the gray sheen of the rabbit's pelt. It quivered slightly and its rib cage pulsed with its labored breath-ing. My cousin was about to toss it into the back of the pickup when my grandfather pointed out that it would be cruel to allow the rabbit to bleed slowly to death and instructed my cousin to bang its head against the side of the pickup to kill it. My cousin then proceeded to bang the rabbit's head against the yellow metal. Thump, thump, thump, thump; after a minute or so my cousin loudly proclaimed that it was dead and hopped back into the truck.

Why do you think that the writer reacts as he does?

The whole episode sickened me to some degree, and at the time I did not know   4
why. We continued to hunt throughout the afternoon, and feigning boredom, I al-lowed my cousin and grandfather to shoot all of the rabbits. Often, the shots didn't kill the rabbits outright so they had to be killed against the pickup. The thump, thump, thump of the rabbits' skulls against the metal began to irritate me, and I was

vortex: Rotation around an axis, as in a whirlwind.   **quarry:** Prey.

strangely glad when we turned around and headed back toward home. We were a few miles from the city limits when my grandfather slowed the truck to a stop, then backed up a few yards. My grandfather said he spotted two huge "jacks" sitting in the sun in a field just off the road. He pointed them out and handed me the .22, saying that if I didn't shoot something the whole afternoon would have been a wasted trip for me. I hesitated and then reluctantly accepted the rifle. I stepped out onto the road, my feet crunching on the ice. The two rabbits were about seventy feet away, both sitting upright in the sun. I cocked and leveled the rifle, my elbow held almost horizontal in the military fashion I had learned to employ. I brought the sights to bear on the right eye of the first rabbit, compensated° for distance, and fired. There was a harsh snap like the crack of a whip and a small jolt to my shoulder. The first rabbit was gone, presumably knocked over the side of the snowdrift. The second rabbit hadn't moved a muscle; it just sat there staring with that black eye. I cocked the rifle once more and sighted a second time, the bead of the rifle just barely above the glassy black orb that regarded me so passively. I squeezed the trigger. Again the crack, again the jolt, and again the rabbit disappeared over the top of the drift. I handed the rifle to my cousin and began making my way toward the rabbits. I sank into powdery snow up to my waist as I clambered to the top of the drift and looked over.

On the other side of the drift was a sight that I doubt I will ever forget. There   5
was a shallow, snow-covered ditch on the leeward side of the drift and it was into this ditch that the rabbits had fallen, at least what was left of the rabbits. The entire ditch, in an area about ten feet wide, was spattered with splashes of crimson blood, pink gobbets of brain, and splintered fragments of bone. The twisted corpses of the rabbits lay in the bottom of the ditch in small pools of streaming blood. Of both the rabbits, only the bodies remained, the heads being completely gone. Stumps of vertebrae protruded obscenely from the mangled bodies, and one rabbit's hind legs twitched spasmodically. I realized that my cousin must have made a mistake and loaded the rifle with hollowpoint explosive bullets instead of solid ones.

I shouted back to the pickup, explaining the situation, and asked if I should   6
bring them back anyway. My grandfather shouted back, "No, don't worry about it, just leave them there. I'm gonna toss these jacks by the side of the road anyway; jackrabbits aren't any good for eatin'."

Looking at the dead, twitching bodies I thought only of the incredible waste of   7
life that the afternoon had been, and I realized that there was much more to being a hunter than knowing how to use a rifle. I turned and walked back to the pickup, riding the rest of the way home in silence.

⏾ Why do you think the writer returns in silence?

compensate: Counterbalance.

Questions to Start You Thinking

Meaning

1. Where in the essay do you first begin to suspect the writer's feelings about hunting? What in the essay or in your experience led you to this perception?

2. How would you characterize the writer's grandfather? How would you characterize his cousin?

3. How did the writer's understanding of himself change as a result of this hunting experience?

Writing Strategies

4. How might the essay be strengthened or weakened if the opening paragraph were cut out? Without this paragraph, how would your understanding of the author and his change be different?

5. Would Schreiner's essay be more or less effective if he explained in the last paragraph what he means by "much more to being a hunter"?

6. What are some of Schreiner's memorable images?

7. Using highlighters or marginal notes, identify the essay's introduction, thesis, major events, support for each event, and conclusion. How effective is the organization of this essay?

Learning by Writing

THE ASSIGNMENT: RECALLING A PERSONAL EXPERIENCE

■ For writing activities for recalling an experience, visit <bedfordstmartins.com/bedguide> and do a keyword search:

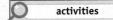
activities

Write about one specific experience that changed how you acted, thought, or felt. Use your experience as a springboard for reflection. Your purpose is not merely to tell an interesting story but to show your readers — your instructor and your classmates — the importance of that experience for you.

We suggest you pick an event that is not too personal or too subjective. Something that happened to you or that you observed, an encounter with a person who greatly influenced you, a decision that you made, or a challenge or an obstacle that you faced will be easier to recall (and to make vivid for your readers) than an interior experience like a religious conversion or falling in love.

Memorable student papers have recalled experiences heavy and light:

One writer recalled guitar lessons with a teacher who at first seemed harsh but who turned out to be a true friend.

Another student recalled a childhood trip when everything went wrong and she discovered the complexities of change.

Another recalled competing with a classmate who taught him a deeper understanding of success.

Facing the Challenge: Writing from Recall

The major challenge writers confront when writing from recall is to focus their essays on a main idea. When writing about a familiar — and often powerful — experience, it is tempting to include every detail that comes to mind and equally easy to overlook familiar details that would make the story's relevance clearer to the reader.

Once you are certain of your *purpose* in writing about a particular event — what you want to show readers about your experience — you can transform a laundry list of details into a narrative that connects events clearly around a main idea. You can select details that work together to convey the significance of your experience. To help you decide what to show your readers, respond to each of the following questions in a few sentences:

- What was important to you about the experience?
- What did you learn from it?
- How did it change you?
- How would you reply to a reader who asked "So what?"

Once you have decided on your main point about the experience, you should select the details that best illustrate that point and show readers why the experience was important to you.

GENERATING IDEAS

You may find that the minute you are asked to write about a significant experience, the very incident will flash to mind. Most writers, though, will need a little time for their memories to surface. Often, when you are busy doing something else — observing the scene around you, talking with someone, reading about someone else's experience — the activity can trigger a recollection. When a promising one emerges, write it down. Perhaps, like Russell Baker, you found success when you ignored what you thought you were supposed to do in favor of what you really wanted to do. Perhaps, like Robert Schreiner, you learned from a painful experience.

For more strategies for generating ideas, see Ch. 16.

Try Brainstorming.   When you brainstorm, you just jot down as many ideas as you can. You can start with a suggestive idea — *disobedience, painful lesson, childhood, peer pressure* — and list under it whatever occurs through free association. You can also use the questions in the following checklist:

For more on brainstorming, see pp. 296–98.

DISCOVERY CHECKLIST

___ Did you ever break an important rule or rebel against authority? Did you learn anything from your actions?

___ Did you ever succumb to peer pressure? What were the results of going along with the crowd? What did you learn?

___ Did you ever regard a person in a certain way and then have to change your opinion of him or her?

___ Did you ever have to choose between two equally attractive alternatives? How might your life have been different if you had chosen differently?

___ Have you ever been appalled by witnessing an act of prejudice or insensitivity? What did you do? Do you wish you had done something different?

For more on freewriting, see pp. 298–99.

Try Freewriting.   Devote ten minutes to freewriting—simply writing without stopping. If you get stuck, write "I have nothing to say" over and over, until ideas come. They will come. After you finish, you can circle or draw lines between related items, considering what main idea connects events.

For more on doodling or sketching, see pp. 299–300.

Try Doodling or Sketching.   As you remember an experience such as breaking your arm during a soccer tournament, try sketching or doodling whatever helps you recollect the event and its significance. Begin turning your doodles into words by adding comments on main events, notable details, and their impact on you.

For more on mapping, see p. 301.

Try Mapping Your Recollections.   Identify a specific time period such as your birthday last year, the week when you decided to enroll in college, or a time when you changed in some way. On a blank page, on movable sticky notes, or in a computer file, record all the details you can recall about that time—people, statements, events, locations, and related physical descriptions.

For more on using a reporter's questions, see pp. 303–04.

Try a Reporter's Questions.   Once you recall an experience you want to write about, ask "the five W's and an H" that journalists find useful.

- Who was involved?
- What happened?
- Where did it take place?
- When did it happen?
- Why did it happen?
- How did the events unfold?

FOR E-WRITERS

Creating Your Writing Space

As you keyboard words onto a screen and use the Edit menu to copy, cut, or paste, you can manipulate your writing to answer the writing task. You may start generating ideas by brainstorming, freewriting, answering reporter's questions, outlining a chronology, or writing directly about the experience you recall. Some students write out notes or guidelines in bold type to remind themselves about their tasks and their assignment's challenges. As you find and develop your own writing processes, you should actively create your own electronic writing space to support these processes.

Any question might lead to further questions — and to further discovery.

- **Who** was involved? → What did the others look like?
  - What did they say or do?
  - Would their words supply any lively quotations?

- **What** happened? → What did you think as the event unfolded?
  - When did you see the importance of the experience?

Consider Sources of Support. Because your memory drops as well as retains, you may want to check your recollections against those of a friend or family member who was there. Did you keep a journal at the time? Was the experience a turning point (big game, graduation) that your family would have documented with photos? Was it sufficiently public (such as a demonstration) or universal (such as a campus orientation) to have been recorded in a newspaper? If so, these resources can refresh your memory so that you rediscover forgotten details or angles.

Family photograph

PLANNING, DRAFTING, AND DEVELOPING

Now, how will you tell your story? If the experience is still fresh in your mind, you may be able simply to write a draft, following the order of events and shaping your story as you go along. If you want to plan before you write, here are some suggestions.

Start with a Main Idea, or Thesis. As you think about the experience, jot down a few words that identify it and express its importance to you. Next, begin to shape these words into a sentence that states the significance of the experience — the main idea that you want to convey to a reader. If you aren't certain yet about what that idea is or how to put it into words, just begin writing. You can work again on your thesis as you revise.

TOPIC IDEA + SLANT   reunion in Georgia + really liked meeting family

WORKING THESIS   When I went to Georgia for a family reunion, I enjoyed meeting many relatives.

Establish a Chronology. Retelling an experience is called *narration*, and the simplest way to organize is chronologically — relating the essential

For more strategies for planning, drafting, and developing papers, see Chs. 17, 18, and 19.

For more on stating a thesis, see pp. 312–19.

For exercises on choosing effective thesis statements, visit <bedfordstmartins.com/bedguide> and do a keyword search:

thesis

For examples of time markers and other transitions, see pp. 346–49.

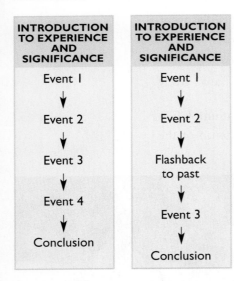

events in the order in which they occurred. On the other hand, sometimes you can start an account of an experience in the middle and then, through *flashback,* fill in whatever background a reader needs to know.

Richard Rodriguez, for instance, begins *Hunger of Memory* (Boston: David R. Godine, 1982), a memoir of his bilingual childhood, with an arresting sentence:

> I remember, to start with, that day in Sacramento, in a California now nearly thirty years past — when I first entered a classroom, able to understand about fifty stray English words.

The opening hooks our attention. In the rest of his essay, Rodriguez fills us in on his family history, on the gulf he came to perceive between the public language (English) and the language of his home (Spanish).

For more on providing details, see pp. 353–55.

For exercises on supporting a thesis, visit <bedfordstmartins.com/bedguide> and do a keyword search:

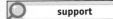

support

For more on the placement of visuals, see pp. 410–16.

Show Your Audience What Happened.   How can you make your recollections come alive for your readers? Look again at Russell Baker's account of Mr. Fleagle teaching *Macbeth* and at the way Robert G. Schreiner depicts his cousin putting the wounded rabbits out of their misery. These two writers have not merely told us what happened; they have *shown* us, by creating scenes that we can see in our mind's eye.

As you tell your story, zoom in on at least two or three such specific scenes. Show your readers exactly what happened, where it occurred, what was said, who said it. Use details and words that appeal to all five senses — sight, sound, touch, taste, and smell. Because photographs and illustrations can clarify visual details for readers, carefully position any images you decide to include. (Be sure that your instructor approves such additions.)

REVISING AND EDITING

For more revising and editing strategies, see Ch. 20.

After you have written an early draft, put it aside for a day or two — or a few hours if your deadline is looming. Then read it over carefully. Try to see it through the eyes of one of your readers, noting both the pleasing parts and the confusing spots. Revise to ensure that you've expressed your thoughts and feelings clearly and strongly in a way that will reach your readers; edit to repair any distracting weaknesses in grammar or expression.

Focus on a Main Idea, or Thesis.   As you read over the essay, return to your purpose: What was so important about this experience? Why is it so memorable? Will readers be able to see why this experience was a crucial one in your life? Will they understand how your life has been different ever since? Be sure that you specify a genuine difference, reflecting the incident's

Learning to Be a Peer Editor

To practice peer response before trying your skills on a classmate's paper, select any student-written paper from this book's table of contents. Write a short but detailed letter to the student writer. Tell the writer what is effective and ineffective about the essay, and explain why. Compare comments with others in your class who chose the same paper. What did you notice in the essay? Is its main idea or thesis clear to you? What did you miss that others noticed? As you will see, several people can notice far more than one individual can.

FOR GROUP LEARNING

real impact on you. In other words, revise to keep your essay focused on a single main idea or thesis.

> WORKING THESIS   When I went to Georgia for a family reunion, I enjoyed meeting many relatives.
>
> REVISED THESIS   Meeting my Georgia relatives showed me how powerfully two values — generosity and resilience — unite my family.

■ For more on stating a thesis, see pp. 312–19.

Add Concrete Detail.   Ask whether you have made events come alive for your audience by recalling them in sufficient concrete detail. Be specific enough that your readers can see, smell, taste, hear, and feel what you experienced. Make sure that all your details support your main idea or thesis. Notice again Robert Schreiner's focus in his second paragraph on the world outside his own skin: his close recall of the snow, of his grandfather's pointers about the habits of jackrabbits and the way to shoot them. As you revise, you may well recall more vivid details to include.

■ For more about providing details, see pp. 353–55.

Follow a Clear Sequence.   Reconsider the order of events in terms of your audience, looking for changes that might make your essay easier for readers to follow. For example, if a classmate seems puzzled about the sequence of your draft, you might make a rough outline or list of the main events to check the clarity of your arrangement. Or you might add more transitions to connect events so that readers can tell exactly where your account is going.

■ For more on outlining, see pp. 325–33.

■ For more on transitions, see pp. 346–49.

Revise and rewrite until you've related your experience and its impact as well as you can. Here are some useful questions about revising your paper:

REVISION CHECKLIST

___ Where have you shown why this experience was important and how it changed your life?

___ How have you engaged readers so that they will want to keep reading? Will they find your paper dramatic, instructive, or revealing? Will they see and feel what you experienced?

— Why do you begin your narration as you do? Is there another place in the draft that would make a better beginning?

— If the events are not in chronological order, how have you made the organization easy for readers to follow?

— In what ways does the ending provide a sense of finality?

— Do you stick to a point? Is everything relevant to your main idea or thesis?

— If you portray any people, how have you made their importance clear? Which details make them seem real, not just shadowy figures?

— Does any dialogue have the ring of real speech? Read it aloud. Try it on a friend.

For more editing and proofreading strategies, see pp. 384–87.

After you have revised your recall essay, edit and proofread it. Carefully check the grammar, word choice, punctuation, and mechanics—and then correct any problems you find. Here are some questions to get you started:

EDITING CHECKLIST

For more help, turn to the dark-blue-edged pages, and find the sections of the Quick Editing Guide noted here.

— Is your sentence structure correct? Have you avoided writing fragments, comma splices, or fused sentences?	A1, A2
— Have you used correct verb tenses and forms throughout? When you present a sequence of past events, is it clear what happened first and what happened next?	A3
— When you use transitions and other introductory elements to connect events, have you placed any needed commas after them?	C1
— In your dialogue, have you placed commas and periods before (inside) the closing quotation mark?	C3
— Have you spelled everything correctly, especially the names of people and places? Have you capitalized names correctly?	D1, D2

When you have made all the changes you need to make, save your file, print out a clean copy of your paper—and hand it in.

OTHER ASSIGNMENTS

1. Choose a person outside your immediate family who had a marked effect on your life, either good or bad. Jot down ten details that might help a reader understand what that person was like. Consider the person's physical appearance, way of talking, and habits as well as any memorable incidents. When your list is finished, look back at "The Art of Eating Spaghetti" to identify the kinds of detail Baker uses in his portrait of Mr. Fleagle, noting any you might add to your list. Then write a paper in which you portray that person, including details to help your audience understand his or her impact on you.

2. Recall a place you were once fond of—your grandmother's kitchen, a tree house, a library, a locker room, a vacation retreat. If you have a pho-

Have a classmate or friend read your draft and suggest how you might present the main idea about your experience more clearly and vividly. Ask your peer editor questions such as these about writing from recall:

- What do you think the writer's main idea or thesis is? Where is it stated or clearly implied? Why was this experience significant?

- What emotions do the people in the essay feel? How did *you* feel while reading the essay?

- Where does the essay come alive? Underline images, descriptions, and dialogue that seem especially vivid.

- If this were your paper, what is the one thing you would be sure to work on before handing it in?

FOR PEER RESPONSE

For general questions for a peer editor, see p. 377.

tograph of the place, looking at it may help to jog your memory. Write a paper that explains to your audience why this place was memorable. What made it different from other places? Why was it important to you? What do you feel when you remember it?

3. Write a paper or the text for a podcast in which you recall some familiar ceremony, ritual, or observation. Such a tradition can pertain to a holiday, a rite of passage (confirmation, bar or bat mitzvah, college orientation, graduation), a sporting event, a family custom. Explain to your audience the importance of the tradition to you, using whatever information you recall. How did the tradition originate? Who takes part? How has it changed through the years? What does it add to the lives of those who observe it?

Applying What You Learn: Some Uses of Recalling Experience

In College Courses.   Virtually every paper, no matter what it sets out to accomplish, can benefit from vivid examples that you recall.

- Recalling a relevant personal experience can engage your readers' interest and provide a springboard for your investigation, analysis, explanation, or argument. For example, your recollections of visiting or living in another country might introduce a sociology paper on cultural differences.

- Your recollection of events may provide the foundation for the reflective journal you keep during an internship or clinical experience.

- Your personal experience can add authority to the judgments and conclusions you offer in your academic writing assignments. In a paper for an anthropology course, you might recall your impressions of visiting the Anasazi ruins at Mesa Verde.

In the Workplace.   Recall is useful as you write on the job.

- Recalling your past jobs and workplace skills might help you identify opportunities at the next campus career day.

- Detailed data that help you recall past successes, failures, or customer comments can provide compelling reasons for adopting your proposals for changing a product or service.

- Recalling past contacts with customers or clients can remind them of your company's valuable product or service and help to personalize your letters, e-mail messages, or other contacts with them.

Career day, Iowa State University

Reunion Memories

Brown Family Gathering
September 6-7, 2003
Marion, Virginia

In Your Community.   In your private life, your memory is a source not only for personal journals, diaries, or correspondence, but also for your writing as an involved member of your community.

- Your personal experiences can lend enormous impact to an appeal for changes in city plans, school policies, or government funding. If your child has been upset by her school's use of standardized tests, recalling her frustration could alert the school board to problems with the testing policies.

- Recalling and recording how you have organized or implemented plans can save time and improve an event the next time around.

- Recalling events from your childhood or from your happiest or most difficult days with your family can make your next reunion or holiday gathering even more meaningful for you.

Chapter 5
Observing a Scene

Responding to an Image

A scene like this one might look and feel very different to different observers, depending on their vantage points, emotions, background, and experience. In this image, what prominent element attracts your attention? Who is the observer? What details might be important for this observer? Although visual details are obviously central, feel free to describe sound, smell, and touch, as well as any emotions that might come into play. Next, identify a second person who might be observing this scene. Which details might matter most to this other observer? In what ways are your two lists of details similar or different?

Most writers begin to write by recalling what they know. Then they look around and add what they observe. Some writing consists almost entirely of observation — a reporter's eyewitness account of a fire, an anthropologist's field notes, a clinical report by a nurse detailing a patient's condition, a scientist's account of a laboratory experiment. So does any writing that describes a person, place, or thing. In other instances, observation provides support, details to make a point clear or convincing.

If you need more to write about, open your eyes — and your other senses. Take in not only what you can see but also what you can hear, smell, touch, and taste. Then when you write, report your observations in concrete detail. Of course, you can't record everything your senses bring you. You must be selective based on what's important and relevant for your purpose and your audience. To make a football game come alive for readers of your college newspaper, you might mention the overcast cold weather and the buttery smell of popcorn. But if your purpose is primarily to explain which team won and why, you might stress the muddy playing field, the most spectacular plays, and the players who scored.

Learning from Other Writers

■ For more on thesis and support, see Chs. 17 and 19.

Here are two essays by writers who observe their surroundings and reflect on their observations. As you begin to analyze the first reading, look for the notes in the margin. They identify features such as the main impression created in the observation and stated in the thesis, the first of the locations observed, and the supporting details that describe the location.

■ For more examples of writing from observation, visit <bedfordstmartins.com/bedguide> and do a keyword search:

As You Read These Observations

As you read these essays, ask yourself the following questions:

1. Specifically, what does the writer observe? Places? People? Behavior? Nature? Things?

2. What senses does the writer rely on? What sensory images does each writer develop? Find some striking passages in which the writer reports his or her observations. What makes these passages memorable to you?

3. Why does the writer use observation? What conclusion does the writer draw from reflecting on the observations?

Eric Liu
The Chinatown Idea

In this selection from The Accidental Asian *(1998), Eric Liu describes a childhood visit to Chinatown in New York City.*

Another family outing, one of our occasional excursions to the city. It was a Saturday. I was twelve. I remember only vaguely what we did during the day — Fifth Avenue, perhaps, the museums, Central Park, Carnegie Hall. But I recall with precision going to Chinatown as night fell.

Introduction

We parked on a side street, a dim, winding way cluttered with Chinese placards° and congested with slumbering Buicks and Chevys. The license

Vantage point 1

plates — NEW YORK, EMPIRE STATE — seemed incongruous here, foreign. We walked a few blocks to East Broadway. Soon we were wading through thick crowds on the sidewalk, passing through belts of aroma: sweat and breath, old perfume, spareribs. It was late autumn and chilly enough to numb my cheeks, but the bustle all around gave the place an electric warmth. Though it was evening, the scene was lit like a stage, thanks to the aluminum lamps hanging from every produce stand. Peddlers lined the street, selling steamed buns and chicken feet and imitation Gucci bags. Some shoppers moved along slowly. Others stopped at each stall, inspecting the greens, negotiating the price of fish, talking loudly. I strained to make sense of the chopped-off twangs of Cantonese coming from every direction, but there were more tones than I knew: my ear was inadequate; nothing was intelligible.

Supporting detail

This was the first time I had been in Chinatown after dark. Mom held Andrea's hand as we walked and asked me to stay close. People bumped us, brushed past, as if we were invisible. I felt on guard, alert. I craned my neck as we walked past a kiosk° carrying a Chinese edition of *Playboy*. I glanced sidelong at the teenage ruffians on the corner. They affected an air of menace with their smokes and leather jackets, but their feathery almost-mustaches and overpermed hair made them look a bit ridiculous. Nevertheless, I kept my distance. I kept an eye on the sidewalk, too, so that I wouldn't soil my shoes in the streams of putrid° water that trickled down from the alleyways and into the parapet° of trash bags piled up on the curb.

I remember going into two stores that night. One was the Far Eastern Bookstore. It was on the second floor of an old building. As we entered, the sounds of the street fell away. The room was spare and fluorescent. It looked like an earnest community library, crowded with rows of chest-high shelves. In the narrow aisles between shelves, patrons sat cross-legged on the floor, reading intently. If they spoke at all it was in a murmur. Mom and Dad each found an absorbing book. They read standing up. My sister and I, meanwhile, wandered restlessly through the stacks, scanning the spines for stray English words or Chinese phrases we might recognize. I ended up in children's books and leafed through an illustrated story about the three tigers. I couldn't read it. Before long, I was tugging on Dad's coat to take us somewhere else.

placards: Posters, signs.   **kiosk:** Booth.   **putrid:** Rotten; decaying.   **parapet:** Wall; suggesting a castle.

The other shop, a market called Golden Gate, I liked much more. It was 5
noisy. The shoppers swarmed about in a frenzy. On the ground level was an
emporium° of Chinese nonperishables: dried mushrooms, spiced beef, sea-
weed, shredded pork. Open crates of hoisin sauce° and sesame chili paste.
Sweets, like milky White Rabbit chews, coconut candies, rolls of sour "haw
flakes." Bags of Chinese peanuts, watermelon seeds. Down a narrow flight of
stairs was a storehouse of rice cookers, ivory chopsticks, crockery, woks that
hung from the wall. My mother carefully picked out a set of rice bowls and
serving platters. I followed her to the long checkout line, carrying a basket
full of groceries we wouldn't find in Poughkeepsie. I watched with wonder
as the cashier tallied up totals with an abacus.

THESIS —
stating main impression

We had come to this store, and to Chinatown itself, to replenish our 6
supply of things Chinese: food and wares, and something else as well. We
had ventured here from the colorless outer suburbs to touch the source, to
dip into a pool of undiluted Chineseness. It was easier for my parents, of
course, since they could decode the signs and communicate. But even I,
whose bond to his ancestral culture had frayed down to the inner cord of
appetite — even I could feel somehow fortified by a trip to Chinatown.

Conclusion drawn
from observation

Yet we knew that we couldn't stay long — and that we didn't really want 7
to. We were Chinese, but we were still outsiders. When any peddler addressed us in Cantonese, that became obvious enough. They seemed so familiar and so different, these Chinatown Chinese. Like a reflection distorted
just so. Their faces were another brand of Chinese, rougher-hewn. I was fascinated by them. I liked being connected to them. But was it because of
what we shared — or what we did not? I began that night to distinguish between my world and theirs.

It was that night, too, as we were making our way down East Broadway, 8
that out of the blur of Chinese faces emerged one that we knew. It was Po-
Po's° face. We saw her just an instant before she saw us. There was surprise
in her eyes, then hurt, when she peered up from her parka. Everyone hugged
and smiled, but this was embarrassing. Mom began to explain: we'd been
uptown, had come to Chinatown on a whim, hadn't wanted to barge in on
her unannounced. Po-Po nodded. We made some small talk. But the realization that her daily routine was our tourist's jaunt,° that there was more
than just a hundred miles between us, consumed the backs of our minds
like a flame to paper. We lingered for a minute, standing still as the human
current flowed past, and then we went our separate ways.

Afterward, during the endless drive home, we didn't talk about bump- 9
ing into Po-Po. We didn't talk about much of anything. I looked intently
through the window as we drove out of Chinatown and sped up the FDR
Drive, then over the bridge. Manhattan turned into the Bronx, the Bronx
into Yonkers, and the seams of the parkway clicked along in soothing inter-
vals as we cruised northward to Dutchess County. I slipped into a deep,

emporium: Marketplace.   **hoisin sauce:** A sweet brown sauce that is a popular Chinese condiment.   **Po-Po:** The narrator's grandmother.   **jaunt:** trip, outing.

open-mouthed slumber, not awakening until we were back in Merrywood, our development, our own safe enclave. I remember the comforting sensation of being home: the sky was clear and starry, the lawn a moon-bathed carpet. We pulled into our smooth blacktop driveway. Silence. It was late, perhaps later than I'd ever stayed up. Still, before I went to bed, I made myself take a shower.

Questions to Start You Thinking

Meaning

1. Why do Liu and his family go to Chinatown?
2. How do Liu and his family feel when they encounter Po-Po? What observations and descriptions lead you to that conclusion?
3. What is the significance of the last sentence? How does it capture the essence of Liu's Chinatown experience?

Writing Strategies

4. In which paragraphs or sections does the writer's use of sensory details capture the look, feel, or smell of Chinatown? In general, how successfully has Liu included various types of observations and details?
5. How does Liu organize his observations? Is this organization effective? Why or why not?
6. Which of the observations and events in this essay most clearly reveal that Liu considers himself to be a "tourist"?

STUDENT ESSAY

Michael Coil
Communications

Walking into the county government building, a visitor would not imagine what goes on in the basement twenty-four hours a day, seven days a week. The building is so quiet, and nobody is in sight. I make my way down the stairs and into the basement. A long hallway and an inconspicuous,° unmarked brown wooden door lead me to the communications center, where the radio traffic for all of Dodge City and Ford County is handled. Nothing along the way even hints at the amount of emotion that is felt in this small space.

Inside the center a kitchen is connected to a workspace with a large glass window that looks in on the main room. An office for the supervisor sits closed and locked, and a bathroom hides around the corner. The smell of constantly brewing coffee is thick, as though permanently tattooed on the air. I step through the

inconspicuous: Not noticeable.

1 *For his first-year composition class, Michael Coil took a fresh look at a familiar location.*

? *What kinds of places does this building bring to mind?*

2

② *When have you had
a similar change in
perception?*

kitchen and past the long window into the Dispatch Room. As a police officer for
the city, I have been in the Dispatch Room many times, but I have never sat and
thought of everything that goes on there. I begin to see things through new eyes.

The first thing to attract my attention is the number of computers at the work-   3
stations. I see three individual stations, each with a tall leather chair and a computer keyboard. At each station is a line of computer screens of various shapes and
sizes, all brightly lit and streaming with information. A large green digital clock on
the wall keeps the time, and a stack of printers taller than I am decorates the wall
beside me. I notice a quiet hum from the many hard drives and printer fans. It is
cold outside, but still the heat of the machines makes it necessary to run the air
conditioner.

A television hangs from the ceiling in the corner. I can tell it's muted because   4
it makes no sound though lines streaming with information slide off the screen. The
reporters on the screen appear to be talking about Iraq. The anchorman looks angry,
but nobody in the room pays him any attention. The only real noise is from the three
911 dispatchers talking happily. The mood is light, and conversation seems to come
very easily.

A phone rings, and one of the dispatchers answers. She enters something on her   5
screen and then hangs up. She tells me that the hospital was calling to ask them to
page one of the on-call doctors. The dispatchers resume their conversation. They are
casual and friendly, and their conversation ranges from what they ate today to the
personalities of their dogs at home. I find it easy to talk with them, and I can tell
that spending so much time side by side in this room brings the three dispatchers
together like close friends.

After a few minutes the phone rings again. The situation is different this time.   6
The first phone that rang was a normal ring without unusual volume or tone, but this

② *How can a ring be
"obnoxious"?*

one makes my blood churn. It is loud, obnoxious,° and ugly. It's like combining the
screech of a vulture and the wail of a dying animal. The air becomes thick and tense.
The conversation stops in mid-sentence, and I can feel all of the dispatchers tense
up in anticipation of what they are about to hear. The three of them pick up the
phone, and one begins to talk. Another begins to type on the computer screen, and
the third gets on the radio and dispatches the call to the police. From where I am
sitting at the rear of the workspace, I can hear the woman on the phone screaming.
I can't quite decipher° what she is saying, but by the dispatcher's rising tone, I can
tell it is not good. Repeatedly the caller is told to calm down and tell what's going
on. With each command the dispatcher's voice gets more edgy. Hearts are racing
now, and the room fills with dread. "Somebody is breaking into my house," the voice
on the line finally pushes out. I read the screen and see that she lives not far from

obnoxious: Offensive, intolerable.   **decipher:** Interpret.

where we are sitting. It only takes a minute or two for the first unit to arrive, but sitting and listening to that poor woman's plea for help makes that short time feel like an eternity. The officers inform the dispatcher that they are in front of the house, and they don't see anybody. The person must have left just moments before they got there. The dispatcher speaking with the woman leans back slowly in her chair, causing it to groan softly. She rubs her hands on her face as though she were sweating and suddenly goes back into her casual mode. She politely tells the woman to answer the door because the police are standing out front, then pauses a moment and says goodbye.

How have you responded to the sounds that the writer has described?

Several minutes pass before I can collect myself and begin to process every-thing I just saw and heard. I feel as though I had been sitting in the house with that distraught woman watching helplessly. I feel suddenly tired, stressed, and still my nerves are shaking from the adrenaline. The dispatchers, however, return to their conversation without missing a beat. The tension filters silently away, and the mood becomes friendly again. Only a unique and brave person could willingly face chal-lenges like that one on a day-to-day basis.   7

As I walk out of the communications room, I see multiple cartoons cut out of   8 the newspaper and taped to the doorway. I think to myself, What a difficult task it must be to come back down after eight hours on the emotional rollercoaster. It would be so easy for the dispatchers to become bitter, angry people, but they are quite the opposite. They are inviting and friendly, and though they will always deny it, they are modern-day heroes waiting to come to our rescue. Day and night they sit, behind the brown unmarked wooden door, at the end of the long marble hallway, always ready to help.

Questions to Start You Thinking

Meaning

1. Is the Dispatch Room as "quiet" as Coil originally suspects as he enters the building? Which paragraph best supports your answer?

2. In paragraph 8, Coil uses the term "modern-day heroes" to describe the dis-patchers. What details in his account support that description?

3. What does Coil learn about himself from his visit to the Dispatch Room?

Writing Strategies

4. How does comparing and contrasting the dispatchers' behavior before a call and during a call help Coil create a vivid impression of the room?

5. Which sense does Coil use most effectively? Point to a few examples that support your choice.

6. Paragraph 6 includes the only dialogue in the essay. What is its effect?

7. Using highlighters or marginal notes, identify the essay's introduction, thesis, major vantage points for observation, details supporting each part of the observation, and conclusion. How effective is this organization?

Learning by Writing

THE ASSIGNMENT: OBSERVING A SCENE

■ For writing activities for observing a scene, visit <bedfordstmartins.com/ bedguide> and do a key-word search:

Observe a place near your campus, home, or job and the people who frequent this place. Then write a paper in which you describe the place, the people, and their actions so as to convey the spirit of the place and offer some insight into the impact of the place on the people.

This assignment is meant to start you observing closely enough that you go beyond the obvious. Go somewhere nearby, and station yourself where you can mingle with the people there. Open your senses — all of them, so that you see, smell, taste, hear, and feel. Jot down what you immediately notice, especially the atmosphere and its effect on the people there. Take notes describing the location, people, and actions and events you see. Then use your observations to convey the spirit of the scene. What is your main impression of the place? Of the people there? Of the relationship between the people and

---

Facing the Challenge: Observing a Scene

The major challenge writers face when writing from observation is to select compelling details that fully convey an engaging main impression of a scene. As we experience the world, we are bombarded by sensory details, but our task as writers is to choose those that bring a subject alive for readers. For example, describing an oak as "a big tree with green leaves" is too vague to help readers envision the tree or grasp what is unique about it. Use these questions to help you notice sensory details:

- What colors, shapes, and sizes do you see?
- What tones, pitches, and rhythms do you hear?
- What textures, grains, and physical features do you feel?
- What fragrances and odors do you smell?
- What sweet, spicy, or other flavors do you taste?

After recording the details that define the scene, ask two more questions:

- What overall main impression do these details establish?
- Which specific details will best show the spirit of this scene to a reader?

Your answers will help you decide which details to include in your paper and which to leave out.

the place? Remember, your purpose is not only to describe the scene but also to express thoughts and feelings connected with what you observe.

Three student writers wrote about these observations:

One student, who works nights in the emergency room, observed the scene and the community that abruptly forms when an accident victim arrives: doctors, nurses, orderlies, the patient, and friends or relatives.

Another observed a bar mitzvah celebration that reunited a family for the first time in many years.

Another observed the activity in the bleachers in a baseball stadium before, during, and after a game.

GENERATING IDEAS

Although setting down observations might seem a cut-and-dried task, to many writers it is true discovery. Here are some ways to generate such observations.

For more strategies for generating ideas, see Ch. 16.

Brainstorm.   First, you need to find a scene to observe. What places interest you? Which are memorable? Start brainstorming—listing rapidly any ideas that come to mind. Here are a few questions to help you start your list:

For more on brainstorming, see pp. 296–97.

DISCOVERY CHECKLIST

___ Where do people gather for some event or performance (a stadium, a church, a theater, an auditorium)?

___ Where do people get together for some activity (a gym, a classroom)?

___ Where do crowds form while people are getting things or services (a shopping mall, a dining hall or student union, a dentist's waiting room)?

___ Where do people go for recreation or relaxation (an arcade, a ballpark)?

___ Where do people gather (a fire, a party, a wedding, a graduation)?

Get Out and Look.   If nothing on your list strikes you as compelling, plunge into the world to see what you see. Visit a city street or a country hillside, a campus building or a practice field, a lively scene — a mall, an airport, a fast-food restaurant, a student hangout — or one with only a few people sunbathing, walking dogs, or tossing Frisbees. Stand off in a corner for a while, and then mix with the group to gain different views of the scene.

Band practice at University of California, Berkeley

Record Your Observations.   Michael Coil's essay "Communications" began with

For more on journal
keeping, see pp. 306–07.

some notes Coil made about his county communications center and the phone traffic it receives. He was able to mine those notes for details to bring his subject to life.

Your notes on a subject — or tentative subject — can be taken in any old order or methodically. To draw up an "observation sheet," fold a sheet of paper in half lengthwise. Label the left column "Objective," and impartially list what you see, like a zoologist looking at a new species of moth. Label the right column "Subjective," and list your thoughts and feelings about what you observe. If possible, keep looking at your subject while you write.

Objective	Subjective
The ticket holders form a line outside the old brick hall, standing two or three deep all the way down the block.	This place has seen concerts of all kinds — you can feel the history as you wait, as if the hall protects the crowds and the music.
Groups of friends talk, a few couples hug, and some guys laugh as they tell jokes.	The crowd seems relaxed and friendly, all waiting to hear their favorite group.
Everyone shuffles forward when the doors finally open, looking around at the crowd and edging toward the entrance.	The excitement and energy grow with the wait, but it's just the concert ritual — the prelude to a perfect night.

The quality of your paper will depend in large part on the truthfulness and accuracy of your observations. Your objective notes on an observation sheet will trigger more subjective notes. As your list grows, write on one side of your paper only: later you can spread out your notes and look at them all at once. Even in the sample observation sheet made at the concert venue, a main impression is starting to take shape. The old hall shelters concertgoers and musicians alike, channeling their enthusiasm into the music.

Include a Range of Images.   Have you captured not just sights but sounds, touches, odors? Have you observed from several vantage points or on several occasions to deepen your impressions? Have you added sketches or doodles to your notes, perhaps drawing the features or mapping the shape of the place? Can you begin writing as you continue to observe your subject? Have you noticed how other writers use *images*, evoking sensory experience, to record what they sense? In the memoir *Northern Farm* (New York: Rinehart, 1948), naturalist Henry Beston describes a remarkable sound: "the voice of ice," the midwinter sound of a whole frozen pond settling and expanding in its bed.

Sometimes there was a sort of hollow oboe sound, and sometimes a groan with a delicate undertone of thunder.... Just as I turned to go, there came from below one curious and sinister crack which ran off into a sound like the whine of a giant whip of steel lashed through the moonlit air.

PLANNING, DRAFTING, AND DEVELOPING

After recording your observations, look over your notes or your observation sheet, circling whatever looks useful. Maybe you can rewrite your notes into a draft, throwing out details that don't matter, leaving those that do. Maybe you'll need a plan to help you organize all the observations, laying them out graphically or in a simple scratch outline.

■ For more strategies for planning, drafting, and developing, see Chs. 17, 18, and 19.

Start with a Main Impression or Thesis.   What main insight or impression do you want to get across? Answering this question will help you decide which details to include and which to omit. It will also help you avoid a dry recitation of observed facts.

■ For more on stating a thesis, see pp. 312–19.

PLACE OBSERVED	Smalley Green after lunch
MAIN IMPRESSION	relaxing activity is good after a morning of classes
WORKING THESIS	After their morning classes, students have fun relaxing on Smalley Green with their dogs and Frisbees.

■ For exercises on choosing effective thesis statements, visit <bedfordstmartins.com/bedguide> and do a keyword search:

🔍   thesis

Organize to Show Your Audience Your Point.   How do you map out a series of observations? Your choice will depend on your purpose in writing and the main impression that you want to create. Whatever your choice, be sure to add transitions—words or phrases that guide the reader from one vantage point, location, or idea to the next. Experiment with options such as the ones at the top of the next page.

■ For more organization strategies, see pp. 319–33.

■ For transitions that mark place or direction, see p. 347.

As you create your "picture," you bring a place to life using the details that capture its spirit. If your instructor approves, consider whether adding a photograph, sketch, diagram, or other illustration would enhance your written observation.

REVISING AND EDITING

Your revising, editing, and proofreading will all be easier if you have taken accurate notes on your observations. But what if, when you look over your draft, you find that you don't have enough detail? If you have any doubts, go back to the scene, and take more notes to flesh out your draft.

■ For more revising and editing strategies, see Ch. 20.

Focus on a Main Impression or Thesis.   As you begin to revise, ask a friend to read your observation, or read it yourself as if you had never visited the place you observed. While reading, you might notice gaps that would

Sequential Organization

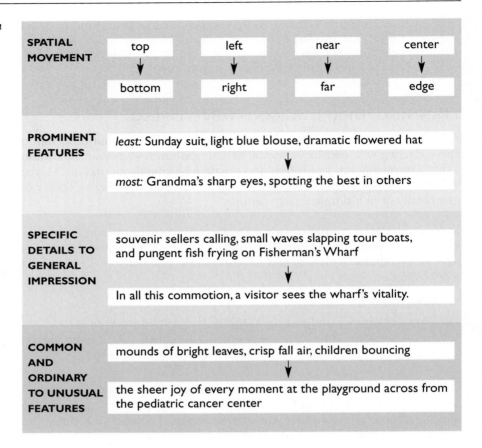

SPATIAL MOVEMENT

top	left	near	center
↓	↓	↓	↓
bottom	right	far	edge

PROMINENT FEATURES

least: Sunday suit, light blue blouse, dramatic flowered hat
↓
most: Grandma's sharp eyes, spotting the best in others

SPECIFIC DETAILS TO GENERAL IMPRESSION

souvenir sellers calling, small waves slapping tour boats, and pungent fish frying on Fisherman's Wharf
↓
In all this commotion, a visitor sees the wharf's vitality.

COMMON AND ORDINARY TO UNUSUAL FEATURES

mounds of bright leaves, crisp fall air, children bouncing
↓
the sheer joy of every moment at the playground across from the pediatric cancer center

puzzle a reader or decide that the spirit of the place seems understated. Consider whether the main impression you want to convey would be clearer if you sharpened its description in your thesis.

For more on stating a thesis, see pp. 312–19.

WORKING THESIS   After their morning classes, students have fun relaxing on Smalley Green with their dogs and Frisbees.

REVISED THESIS   When students, dogs, and Frisbees accumulate on Smalley Green after lunch, they show how much campus learning takes place outside of class.

For exercises on supporting a thesis, visit <bedfordstmartins.com/bedguide> and do a keyword search:

Add Relevant and Powerful Details.   Next, check your selection of details. Does each detail contribute to your main impression? Should any details be dropped or added? Should any be rearranged so that your organization, moving from point to point, is clearer? Could any observations be described more vividly or powerfully? Could more precise or more concrete wording strengthen the way you present the details?

Let a classmate or friend respond to your draft, suggesting how to use detail to convey your main impression more powerfully. Ask your peer editor to answer questions such as these about writing from observation:

- What is the main insight or impression you carry away from this writing?

- Which sense does the writer use particularly well? Are any senses neglected that could be used?

- Can you see and feel what the writer experienced? Would more details make this writing more compelling? Put check marks wherever you want more detail.

- How well has the writer used evidence from the senses to build a main impression? Which sensory impressions contribute most strongly to the overall picture? Which seem superfluous?

- If this were your paper, what is the one thing you would be sure to work on before handing it in?

FOR PEER RESPONSE

For general questions for a peer editor, see p. 377.

To see where your draft could need work, you might consider these questions:

REVISION CHECKLIST

____ Have you accomplished your purpose — to convey to readers your overall impression of your subject and to share some telling insight about it?

____ What can you assume your readers know? What do they need to be told?

____ Have you gathered enough observations to describe your subject? Have you observed with *all* your senses when possible — even smell and taste?

____ Have you been selective, including details that effectively support your overall impression?

____ Which observations might need to be checked for accuracy? Which might need to be checked for richness or fullness?

____ Is your organizational pattern the most effective for your subject? Is it easy for readers to follow? Would another pattern work better?

After you have revised your observation essay, edit and proofread it. Carefully check the grammar, word choice, punctuation, and mechanics — and then correct any problems you find. If you have added more details while revising, consider whether they have been sufficiently blended with the ideas already there.

Here are some questions to get you started when editing and proofreading your observation paper:

For more editing and proofreading strategies, see pp. 384–87.

■ For more help, turn to the dark-blue-edged pages, and find the sections of the Quick Editing Guide noted here.

EDITING CHECKLIST

___ Is your sentence structure correct? Have you avoided writing fragments, comma splices, and fused sentences?   A1, A2

___ Have you used an adjective whenever describing a noun or pronoun? Have you used an adverb whenever describing a verb, adjective, or adverb? Have you used the correct form when comparing two or more things?   A7

___ Is it clear what each modifier in a sentence modifies? Have you created any dangling or misplaced modifiers?   B1

___ Have you used parallel structure wherever needed, especially in lists or comparisons?   B2

FOR GROUP LEARNING

Reading Your Writing Aloud

Try reading your draft aloud to your group. Rehearse your reading beforehand, and deliver it with feeling. Ask your audience to stop you when something isn't clear. Have a pencil in hand to mark such problems, or ask someone else to note them for you. After you've finished reading aloud, ask for reactions. (Or ask your listeners any of the questions in the peer response checklist on page 83.) Have someone record the most vital suggestions and reactions that your draft provokes. If possible, audiotape your reading and the reactions. Review both the notes and the tape when you revise.

FOR E-WRITERS

Strengthening Descriptive Words

When you write an observation, you will use modifiers (adjectives or adverbs) to qualify other words so that your observations are clear. However, adverbs like *very* and *really* or adjectives like *beautiful* and *great* are vague rather than concrete and precise. Read your draft aloud, and note any vague or imprecise modifiers. Then, use the Find function in your word processor's Edit menu to help you locate each place in your paper where you have used *really,* for example, or another vague modifier. As you find each modifier, ask, "Is it specific enough?" "Will it guide my reader through my way of seeing?" Delete any weak modifiers, or replace them with more specific words.

OTHER ASSIGNMENTS

1. To develop your powers of observation, go for a walk, recording your observations in two or three detailed paragraphs. Let your walk take you through either an unfamiliar scene or a familiar scene worth a closer look than you normally give it (such as a supermarket, a city street, an

open field). Avoid a subject so familiar that you would struggle to see it from a fresh perspective (such as a dormitory corridor or a parking lot). Sum up your impression of the place, including any opinion you form through your close observations.

2. Try this short, spontaneous writing exercise. Begin the assignment immediately after class, and turn it in the same afternoon.

> Go to a nearby public place — a café, library, copy center, art gallery — and select a person who catches your eye, who somehow intrigues you. Try to choose someone who looks as if she or he will stay put for a while. Settle yourself where you can observe your subject unobtrusively. Take notes, if you can do so without being observed.
>
> Now, carefully and tactfully (we don't want any fistfights or lawsuits) notice everything you can about this person. Start with physical characteristics, but focus on other things too. How does the person talk? Move? What does the person's body language tell you?
>
> Write a paragraph describing the person. Pretend that the person is going to hold up a bank ten minutes from now, and the police will expect you to supply a full and accurate description.

3. The perspective of a tourist, an outsider alert to details, often reveals the distinctive character of places and people. Think of some place you have visited as an outsider in the past year, and jot down any notable details you recall. Or spend a few minutes as a tourist right now. Go to a busy spot on or off campus, and record your observations of anything you find amusing, surprising, puzzling, or intriguing. Then write an essay on the unique character of the place.

Applying What You Learn: Some Uses of Observing a Scene

In College Courses.   Observing and accurately recording observations are critical to your success in many courses besides English, especially those with labs, field trips, or practica that prepare you for your career.

- Students in the social sciences — sociology, criminal justice, psychology, anthropology — often take field trips requiring them to observe behavior closely and report their observations. Similarly, students in the humanities or fine arts may be expected to observe and record their impressions of a play, a concert, an exhibit, or a historical site.

- Classes in health, education, or other professional fields may include clinical or field observations.

- Science classes — biology, anatomy, physics, or chemistry — may call for lab reports, recording observations of experiments, or field reports on animal life within a habitat.

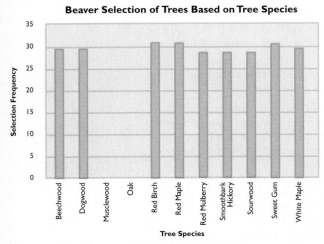

Beaver Selection of Trees Based on Tree Species

From a research report on beaver foraging behavior

In the Workplace. In many careers and professions, observation and analysis provide valuable information and lend credibility to your writing.

- If you choose a career in nursing, teaching, or social work, you will probably write case studies based on observation, sometimes for publication, sometimes for reference.

- Journalists draw on what they observe to report news events or write feature articles. During interviews, body language, tone of voice, and surroundings may be as revealing as a subject's words.

- Many careers will require you to make field observations and report your findings to your superiors. Architects and engineers observe at a building site; biologists and conservationists observe animals in the wild; astronomers observe movement in the night sky.

In Your Community. Observation is a primary resource for your writing as an active member of your community.

- Vivid observations in an editorial or proposal calling for resolution of a neighborhood problem — a dangerous intersection, a poorly lighted park, a run-down building — will make the hazards real for readers.

- Joining the planning group for a community project, such as a sports arena or a performing arts center, may require you to observe facilities in other communities and report your findings. Observing another community's festival also can provide ideas and identify logistical details for planning an event in your own community.

- You may need to report to authorities and to insurance agents what you've observed at the site of an accident, a natural disaster, or a crime. Photos of the scene can be useful support.

A fraternity house destroyed during a three-day party

Chapter 6
Interviewing a Subject

Responding to an Image

Suppose that you had an opportunity to interview media personality Oprah Winfrey, political leader Barack Obama, figure skater Michelle Kwan, or musician and advocate Bono. What two or three questions would you most like to ask the interviewee? Based on the person's public image and his or her personality as revealed in these photos, what kind of response would you expect to receive? How do you think the photographer has tried to bring the person to life or suggest something about the person?

Don't know what to write about? Go talk with someone. Meet for half an hour with an anthropology professor, and you probably will have plenty of material for a paper. Just as likely, you can get a paper's worth of information from a ten-minute exchange with a mechanic who relines brakes. Both the mechanic and the professor are experts. But even people who aren't usually considered experts may tell you things you didn't know and provide you with material.

As this chapter suggests, you can direct a conversation by asking questions to elicit what you want to find out. You do so in an *interview* — a special kind of conversation with a purpose — usually to help you understand the other person or to find out what that person knows.

Learning from Other Writers

▮ For more on thesis and support, see Chs. 17 and 19.

Here are two essays whose writers talked to someone and reported the conversations, using direct quotations and telling details to reveal engaging personalities. To help you begin to analyze the first reading, look for the notes in the margin. They identify features such as the main idea, or thesis, and the quotations providing support.

▮ For more examples of writing based on interviews, visit <bedfordstmartins.com/ bedguide> and do a key-word search:

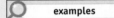

examples

As You Read These Interview Essays

As you read these essays, ask yourself the following questions:

1. Was the conversation reported from an informal discussion or planned as an interview? Does the writer report the conversation directly or indirectly?

2. What does the interview show about the character and personality of the individual speaking? What does it show about the author who is listening?

3. Why do you think the writer draws on conversation?

Elaina Richardson interviewed Bono, lead singer of the rock band U2, for this article, which was originally published in O, The Oprah Magazine, *in February 2002.*

THESIS
stating dominant impression

Elaina Richardson

Bono-Fire: U2's Brilliant Front Man Rocks Convention

The idea of the rocker rebel is sorely tarnished° in these days of pop lite, but there's nothing sugarcoated about the intensity Bono brings to the world. Consider these few events from the past year in the life of U2's charismatic° front man: a sold-out tour; an album (*All That You Can't Leave Behind*) that went to number one in thirty-two countries; the birth of his fourth child in May; talks with the leaders of the world's strongest

tarnished: Dulled, diminished.   **charismatic:** Powerfully appealing.

88

economies — the G8 — in Genoa, Italy, in July; the death of his father in August; countless one-on-ones about AIDS relief and trade with cabinet officials from Colin Powell° to Condoleezza Rice.° Where does his stamina° come from? "God made me stubborn," Bono says with a throaty laugh that tells you something about the state of his vocal cords. . . . "Stubbornness and Catholic guilt," he continues. "That'll work for you every time. And I've had the best life that a man's ever had: I don't just mean with U2, I mean with my family and even my father, whose loss I feel every day, he lived a long and colorful life, and he left me with a sense of moral outrage."

Elaboration of dominant impression

Quotations showing subject's personality

Description added to bring subject to life

This is how Bono talks, long strings of run-on sentences that can encompass° pub life, the AIDS pandemic° in Africa, blues guitar, and a healthy dose of self-deprecation.° The bottom line of all this speechifying° is that it's time for a major initiative that would combine debt cancellation for the world's poorest nations with trade reform and a commitment from pharmaceutical companies to give free HIV drugs to African countries. Bono spouts numbers effortlessly and accurately, noting that sub-Saharan Africa° spends around $13.5 billion a year repaying debts to rich countries, which is more than double what it spends on health care.   2

His charm lies in the fact that, whether he's at an audience with Pope John Paul II or singing "Beautiful Day" for 20,000, his need to communicate is palpable.° There was a time when Bono harangued° the world — "Am I bugging you?" he would spit at U2 fans, all the while making it clear that he didn't give a damn if he was. A decade later he has learned a more effective path: "Sometimes instead of climbing over the barricades you've got to walk around them, and sometimes you discover that the real enemy is not what you think it is," he says. That attitude has led to some strange-seeming bedfellows,° chief among them Senator Jesse Helms, the eighty-year-old archconservative° from North Carolina, who became Bono's champion in the struggle to get a debt-relief plan through Congress. According to Bono, "When I first started going to Washington for meetings on Capitol Hill, I'm sure I looked like a very exotic creature, but eventually they didn't see me, they just saw the argument. And the thing about the pictures of me the rock star with, say, Jesse Helms the politican is — it's really unhip for both of us, you know, it's a bad look for the two of us!"   3

While the other guys in U2 may find it incredibly unsexy to have the likes of Orrin Hatch° or Paul Volcker° hanging backstage, Bono knows that   4

Colin Powell: Former secretary of state under President George W. Bush.   **Condoleezza Rice:** National Security advisor and then secretary of state under President George W. Bush.   **stamina:** Endurance.   **encompass:** Include.   **pandemic:** Illness affecting many people across a large geographic area.   **self-deprecation:** Playing down one's own accomplishments.   **speechifying:** Speechlike talk.   **sub-Saharan Africa:** The part of Africa south of the Sahara Desert.   **palpable:** Obvious.   **harangued:** Lectured; taunted.   **bedfellows:** Friends or allies.   **archconservative:** Someone who is very conservative.   **Orrin Hatch:** Republican senator from Utah.   **Paul Volcker:** Former chairman of the Federal Reserve, the central U.S. banking system.

power is not always pretty. ("Just the sight of Orrin Hatch in the mosh pit° . . . it's exciting," Bono says, and you can't tell if he means it or not.) "I think that politicians are attracted at first by the celebrity," says Harvard economics professor Jeffrey Sachs, "but once they meet him they find that he is outstandingly capable." Along with producer Bobby Shriver, Sachs became part of Bono's American kitchen cabinet in 1999 in the quest to get debt relief on the agenda. In his Class Day address at Harvard in June, Bono summed up the trio: "Sachs and I, with Bobby Shriver, hit the road like some kind of surreal° crossover act.° A Rock Star, a Kennedy, and a Noted Economist crisscrossing the globe like the Partridge family° on psychotropic° drugs."

Quotation from another person providing insight marks the first portion.

The results have already been impressive: in November of 2000, Congress 5 passed legislation authorizing $435 million in debt relief. Last July President Bush and the G8 countries focused the debate on issuing grants rather than loans to developing nations, and Bono is sure a lot more is about to happen. "I'm confident that President Bush has a real feeling for the AIDS pandemic. Essentially, what we're asking for is a kind of Marshall Plan° for Africa. A few months ago that didn't look like a possibility, but post–September 11 the comparisons are striking. When you have nothing, you are easy prey to terrorists and to groups who keep alive the lie that the West is not interested in your calamity.° We've just seen what happens when one country, Afghanistan, implodes.° God knows what will happen if the entire continent of Africa is left on its current trajectory,° which is disaster."

Provocative quotation marks this portion.

Born in Ballymun, Dublin, in 1960 (he was Paul Hewson then) to a 6 Protestant mother and a Catholic father, Bono is no stranger to the links between economic depression, bigotry, and terrorism. But he has an idealist's faith that all three can be overcome. The Sandinistas° and the Troubles° in Ireland were Bono's issues when the band came on the scene in 1978, and by 1983 U2 had released the first of many anthems° in "Sunday, Bloody Sunday": "I can't believe the news today, I can't close my eyes and make it go away." Bono was married by the time this record came out, to his high school girlfriend, Ali Stewart, and neither one of them was interested in closing their eyes. Bob Geldof's Live Aid° work "woke them up to what was happening in Africa," and, Bono recalls, "Ali and I got quite caught up in it. We went to work in Ethiopia for a month. We worked in an orphanage, in one of those awful camps, and we'd wake up in the morning to the sight of

Background and influences marks this portion.

mosh pit: Place in front of rock or punk performers where people jump around or slam into each other.   surreal: Strange or dreamlike.   crossover act: Something that appeals to diverse audiences (for example, both jazz and rock fans).   Partridge family: A fictional family rock band from a 1970s sitcom of the same name.   psychotropic: Affecting the mind.   Marshall Plan: A post–World War II program to rebuild European countries.   calamity: Catastrophe or disaster.   implodes: Breaks down.   trajectory: Course; path.   Sandinistas: Left-wing group that led a 1979 revolution in Nicaragua. the Troubles: The violent struggles from 1968 to 1998 between Catholic and Protestant factions in Northern Ireland.   anthems: Songs with special political or cultural significance.   Live Aid: A series of concerts in 1985 to raise money for famine relief in Ethiopia.

thousands of people walking through the mist in the hopes of getting some food. My experience there was very hard to forget. . . . We went back to our daily life in Ireland and me being in a band, but we'd always hoped we might be able to look at the structure of the problem. There's a certain kind of poverty that is structural, not just misfortune, and so when I heard about this plan to use the millennium as an opportunity to give the poorest countries a chance to start again, I thought, 'This is major, and it's the right thing to do.'"

Four children and twenty-one years into life with Bono, Ali hasn't lost 7 any of her ability to roll up her sleeves either. She is deeply involved with the Chernobyl° Children's Project (one of six campaigns highlighted on U2's Web site and on their albums), even getting behind the wheel of a truck to drive from Dublin to Belarus° with food and emergency supplies. "Irish women are very informed and very vocal," Bono says, before releasing his chesty laugh again. "And I should know because I'm living with one, and it's hard to keep up."

Yeats° has a famous line about the sound and fury of politics: "The best 8 lack all conviction, while the worst / Are full of passionate intensity." But Bono, the self-conscious rebel-rocker, with his mop of lank° hair and his sunglasses and his tireless talk, gives that line the lie, transforming passionate intensity into action that just might change the world.

> Literary quotation and observation lead into restatement of thesis

Questions to Start You Thinking

Meaning

1. What makes Bono a "rocker rebel," according to Richardson? What evidence does she use to support this view?

2. In paragraph 2, Bono outlines changes that are needed to solve serious world problems. What are these changes? What results have been achieved?

3. Over the years, how has Bono changed the ways in which he communicates his views to people?

Writing Strategies

4. Richardson gives some of Bono's personal history in paragraph 6. How does this add to the article and the impression of Bono?

5. What seem to be Richardson's feelings about her dominant impression of Bono? What observations and details does she include to affect your impression of him?

6. Throughout this essay, Richardson uses quotations from Bono to reveal his personality and philosophy. Would this essay be as effective if she paraphrased rather than quoted? Why or why not?

Chernobyl: Ukrainian city that was the site of a 1986 nuclear disaster.   **Belarus:** Eastern European nation that borders Ukraine, where the 1986 Chernobyl nuclear disaster occurred.   **Yeats:** Irish poet and dramatist William Butler Yeats (1865–1939).   **lank:** Straight.

STUDENT ESSAY

Dawn Kortz

Listen

Dawn Kortz, who wrote this as a student at Dodge City Community College, creates a lively portrait of an elderly man.

Mic-Leo's Café--named after the two sisters that own it, Mickey and Lee--is   1
tucked into a corner of the Eckles Building, a former department store located in
downtown Dodge City, Kansas. The first time I saw the café, I fell in love. It is
decorated in warm tones of green and burgundy, with plants in almost every corner.
The tables are of every shape, size, and color imaginable, giving the room a cozy,
comfortable feeling. Warm sunlight wafts through the café during business hours
from the large plate windows that make up the front of the café. The people that
come to Mic-Leo's Café are, for the most part, regulars--folks we all know by name.
In the mornings the local businessmen and farmers can be seen gathering around
the tables, drinking coffee, and sharing stories of grandchildren, politics, and golf.
Among these regulars is Emmett Sherwood, who taught me how to appreciate the past.

Can you identify with Kortz's relationship with Emmett? In what way?

I first met Emmett when I began working at Mic-Leo's Café as a part-time wait-   2
ress trying to earn some extra money for college. Emmett, a grandfatherly man, has a
gift for making everyone around him laugh with his colorful personality and stories.
Interested in Emmett and how much of Dodge City's history he has lived through, I
arrange to meet with him at the café early one afternoon. As we settle ourselves
into a quiet corner, I take notice of the deliberate, professional way that Emmett is
dressed. It is obvious from his clothing that he is from another generation. Unlike
my generation, which believes comfort is the most important quality in clothing,
Emmett dresses for style. Today, like every other day, he is wearing dress slacks and
a starched white shirt and tie. When I ask him about his clothing and why he wears
a tie every day, he replies, "Going to town requires dignity." The only casual thing
Emmett is wearing is his signature bright red beret. The red color matches Emmett's
bright personality. Everyone who knows Emmett recognizes him by his hat.

I can tell that Emmett is excited to have a captive audience listen to his stories   3
by the eagerness with which he accepts my invitation for this interview. As we begin
to talk, I notice the far-off look in his eyes, as if he is trying to remember the old
days, his youth, and how the city he loves looked when he first arrived. After each
of us is served a cup of steaming coffee, Emmett begins by telling me he was born in
Oklahoma but grew up in St. Johns, Kansas. As a young man of fourteen, he became
attracted to the big city and in 1920 moved to Dodge City, Kansas, where he was
married, raised a family, and continues to live.

Emmett points out the window and shows me where, on Saturdays, the farmers   4
would come to town and set up open-air markets for the town folks to trade for

baked goods, produce, and eggs. "For me," he says, "going shopping at Wal-Mart can't compare to the feeling I got when I dressed up to go to town, see friendly folks, and help my neighbor." Emmett fondly remembers the 1920s as a time of growth for the nation and for Dodge City and as a happy, carefree time. With a smile and a mischievous twinkle, Emmett remembers the saloons and harlot houses--and especially the popular Harvey House restaurant where the waitresses wore black and white outfits which "sported the shortest skirts anyone in Dodge had seen until then." He blushes and his voice drops to a hush as he recalls this detail. He recovers and goes on to describe Front Street, the only street at the time to be paved with the distinctive red brick that now covers most of downtown. Front Street was the center of business for Dodge City; the Eckles Building, too, is located here. Emmett explains that all of the most prominent establishments were located in the down-town square, including the famous O'Neal Hotel. Emmett glows as he remembers the dances and shows he saw there, but his eyes glaze over as he recounts the fire that destroyed the beautiful, majestic building.

I ask Emmett what Dodge City was like during the Great Depression. Emmett re-   5
calls with sadness families and children that he knew then. Many went hungry while the men went to look for jobs, sometimes even leaving the state in search of an op-portunity. Other men, who before the Depression worked in stores, were forced to work fields for local farmers for enough food to feed their families. "I am lucky to have always had a decent job and a place to sleep," Emmett says reflectively. "People these days think they need so much; they're wrong." Emmett's words are especially meaningful in today's material world.

How are Emmett's words "especially mean-ingful" today?

The time after World War II was important for Dodge City. Emmett remembers it   6
as a period of economic boom when everyone had a renewed sense of pride in the United States. After the war ended, the communities came together to celebrate the return of their fathers, sons, and husbands. For the first time in history, it was com-mon for women to work outside of the home, and Emmett remarks, "We never could get them back home!" I know he is teasing by his smile.

As we wind down our interview, coffee cups sitting cold and empty, I thank   7
Emmett for taking the time to talk. The café has emptied, and the sun has started going down--leaving a chill in the air. As Emmett slowly rises to leave, stretching his weak back from the long period of inactivity, I appreciate his age for the first time. As he walks down the sidewalk toward his car, he turns and with a tip of his head waves good-bye.

Today, when I look around the city in which I live, I realize that what I see is   8
not what Dodge City has always been. Emmett has given me a new appreciation of the past. He has instilled in me the importance of history--my family history, my town's history, my country's history, and my world's history. Every day when he

Do you agree with Kortz's conclusion about the importance of history?

comes into Mic-Leo's and I serve him coffee, I remember our talk, and I can only hope that there are others like Emmett sharing their life stories with people of another generation. I also hope that there are more people of my generation willing to take the time to listen.

Questions to Start You Thinking

Meaning

1. What is the main point of Kortz's essay?

2. What kind of man is Emmett Sherwood? How does Kortz feel about him?

3. How is Emmett's history the history of Dodge City? Is an interview an effective method of relating the history of a place? Why or why not?

Writing Strategies

4. Why does Kortz begin her essay with a description of Mic-Leo's Café? What sensory details does she use to create the scene for a reader? How does Kortz's description serve as a frame for her conversation with Emmett?

5. What details does Kortz use to describe Emmett? What senses does she draw on? Does she provide enough detail for you to form a clear image of him?

6. How much of what Emmett says does Kortz quote directly? Why does she choose to quote directly rather than paraphrase in these places? Would her essay be stronger if she used more of Emmett's own words?

7. Using highlighters or marginal notes, identify the essay's introduction, thesis, major emphases, supporting quotation and description for each emphasis, and conclusion. How effective is the organization of this essay?

Learning by Writing

THE ASSIGNMENT: INTERVIEWING

■ For writing activities for interview-based writing, visit <bedfordstmartins.com/ bedguide> and do a keyword search:

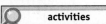

■ To interview someone for information about something, see Other Assignments on p. 102.

Write a paper about someone who interests you and base the paper primarily on a conversation with that person. Select any acquaintance, friend, relative, or person you have heard about whose traits, interests, activities, background, or outlook on life might intrigue your readers. Your purpose is to show this person's character and personality — to bring your subject to life for your readers — through his or her conversation.

Notable student papers from a similar assignment included these:

One student wrote about a high school science teacher who had quit teaching for a higher-paying job in the computer industry, only to return three years later to the classroom.

One writer recorded the thoughts and feelings of a discouraged farmer she had known since childhood.

Another learned about adjustment to life in a new country by talking to his neighbor from Somalia.

GENERATING IDEAS

If an image of the perfect subject has flashed into your mind, consider yourself lucky, and set up an appointment with that person at once. If you have drawn a blank, you'll need to cast about for a likely interview subject.

For strategies for generating ideas, see Ch. 16.

Brainstorm for Possible Subjects.   Try brainstorming for a few minutes, seeing what pops into mind. Your subject need not be spectacular or unusual; ordinary lives can make fascinating reading. As you begin examining the possibilities, you may find the following questions helpful:

For more on brainstorming, see pp. 296–97.

DISCOVERY CHECKLIST

___ Are you acquainted with anyone whose life has been unusually eventful, stressful, or successful?

___ Are you curious about why someone you know made a certain decision or how that person got to his or her current point in life?

___ Is there an expert or a leader whom you admire or are puzzled by?

___ Do you know someone whose job or hobby interests you?

___ What older person could tell you about life thirty or even fifty years ago?

___ Who has passionate convictions about society, politics, sex, or childrearing?

___ Whose background and life history would you like to know more about?

___ Whose lifestyle, values, or attitudes are utterly different from your own and from those of most people you know?

Tap Local Interview Resources.   Investigate campus resources such as the directory, student guide, Web page, departmental faculty lists, student activity officers and sponsors, recent yearbook photographs, stories from the newspaper archives, or facilities such as the theater, media, or sports centers. Look for students, staff, or faculty with intriguing backgrounds or experiences. Campuses and libraries often maintain lists or databases of local authorities, researchers, and authors available for press contacts or expert advice. Identify several prospects in case your first choice isn't available.

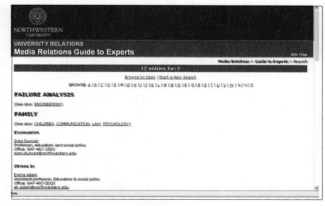

Experts' database on a university Web site

Set Up an Interview.   Find out whether your prospect will grant an interview, talk at length — an hour, say — and agree to appear in your paper. If you sense reluctance, your wisest course is to find another subject.

Don't be timid about asking for an interview. After all, your request is flattering, acknowledging that person as someone with valuable things to say. Try to schedule the interview on your subject's own ground — his or her home or workplace. The details you observe in those surroundings can make your essay more vivid.

■ For more on asking a reporter's questions, see pp. 303–04.

Prepare Questions.   The interview will go better if you have prepared questions in advance. Ask about the person's background, everyday tasks, favorite activities, and hopes to encourage your subject to open up. Asking for a little imagining may elicit a revealing response. (If your house were on fire, what would you try to save? If you had your life to live over, what would you do differently?)

You can't find out everything about someone, but you can focus on whatever aspects best reveal his or her personality. Good questions will help

---

Facing the Challenge: Writing from an Interview

The major challenge writers face when writing from an interview is to find a clear focus for the paper. They must first sift through the huge amount of information generated in an interview and then decide what dominant impression of the subject to present in an essay. Distilling the material you have gathered into a focused, overall impression may seem overwhelming. As a writer, however, you have the responsibility to select and organize your material for your readers, not simply transcribe your notes.

To identify possible angles, jot down answers to these questions:

• What did you find most interesting about the interview?

• What topics did your subject talk about the most?

• What did he or she become most excited or animated about?

• What topics generated the most interesting quotations?

Your answers should help you to determine a dominant impression — the aspect of your interviewee's character or personality that you want to emphasize for your readers. Once you have this focus, you can pick the details and direct quotations from the interview that best illustrate the points you want to make. Use direct quotations strategically and sparingly to reveal the character traits that you wish to emphasize. Select colorful quotations that allow readers to "hear" your subject's distinctive voice. Make sure that all quotations — long or short — are accurate. To capture the dynamic of conversation, include your own observations as well as actual quotations.

Ask a classmate to read the questions you plan to use in your interview and then to respond to the following:

- Are the questions appropriate for the person who will be interviewed?
- Will the questions help gather the information you are seeking?
- Are any of the questions unclear? How could you rephrase them?
- Do any of the questions seem redundant? Irrelevant?
- What additional questions might you ask?

FOR PEER RESPONSE

you lead the conversation where you want it to go, get it back on track when it strays, and avoid awkward silences. For example, to interview someone with an unusual job or hobby, you might ask questions like these:

- How long have you been a park ranger?
- How did you get involved in this work?
- How have you learned about the physical features and ecological balance in your park?
- What happens in a typical day on the job?
- Has this job changed your life or your concerns in any way?
- What are your plans and hopes for the future?

One good question can get some people talking for hours, and four or five may be enough for any interview, but it's better to prepare too many than too few. You can easily skip any that seem irrelevant during the interview.

Be Flexible and Observant.   Sometimes a question won't interest your subject as much as you'd hoped it would. Or the person may seem reluctant to answer, especially if you're unwittingly trespassing into private territory, such as someone's love life. Don't badger. If you wait silently for a bit, you might be rewarded. But if the silence persists, just go on to the next question. Anytime the conversation heads toward a dead end, you can always steer it back: "But to get back to what you were saying about . . ."

Sometimes the most rewarding question simply grows out of what the subject says or an item you note in the environment. Observing your subject's clothing, expressions, mannerisms, and equipment may also suggest unexpected facets of personality. For example, Kortz describes both the café and Emmett's clothing as she introduces his character.

For more on using observation, see Ch. 5.

Decide How to Record the Interview.   Many interviewers use only paper and pen or pencil to take notes unobtrusively. Even though they can't write down everything the person says, they want to look the subject in the eye

FOR E-WRITERS

Transcribing Your Interview Notes

After your interview, follow the lead of reporters who routinely transcribe conversations into computer files. Try to type in the exact conversation from your tape or as much of the interview as possible from your notes. If you have used both tape and notes, combine them in a single computer file, but use bold to distinguish your notes. Save the complete, unedited conversation transcript and original notes with a descriptive name.

Open a new file to begin your draft. As you quote and summarize your subject's ideas, you can return to your transcript and notes to copy or check the wording. In this way you can refine your draft while preserving your original research in the first file. Use the menu in your word processor to go back and forth between the two files as you copy and paste quotations into your draft. Add quotation marks to show exact words from the interview.

and keep the conversation lively. As you take notes, be sure to record or sketch details on the scene—names and dates, numbers, addresses, surroundings, physical appearance. Also jot down memorable words just as the speaker says them. Put quotation marks around them so that when you transcribe your notes later, you will know that they are quoted directly.

A telephone or an e-mail interview sounds easy but lacks the lively interplay you can achieve face-to-face. You'll miss observing the subject's possessions and environment, which so often reveal personality, or seeing your subject's smiles, frowns, or other body language. Meet with your subject if possible.

Many professionals advise against using a tape recorder because it may inhibit the subject and make the interviewer lazy about concentrating on the subject's responses. Too often, the objections go, it tempts the interviewer simply to quote the rambling conversation from the tape without shaping it into good writing. If you do bring a tape recorder to your interview, be sure that the person you're talking with has no objections. Arm yourself with a pad of paper and a pen or pencil just in case the recorder malfunctions. Perhaps the best practice is to tape-record the interview but at the same time take notes. Write down the main points, and use your tape as a backup to check for accuracy or to expand an idea or a quotation.

As soon as the interview ends, rush to the nearest desk, and write down everything you remember but couldn't record. The questions you prepared for the interview will guide your memory, as will notes you took while talking.

PLANNING, DRAFTING, AND DEVELOPING

For more strategies for planning, drafting, and developing, see Chs. 17, 18, and 19.

After your interview, you may have a good notion of what to include in your first draft, what to emphasize, what to quote directly, what to summarize. But if your notes seem a confused jumble, what should you do?

Evaluate Your Material.   Remember that your purpose in this assignment is to reveal your subject's character and personality through his or her conversation. Start by listing the details you're already likely to include. As you sift your material, you may find these questions useful:

For strategies for using examples and details, see Ch. 19.

> What part of the conversation gave you the most insight into your subject's character and circumstances?

> Which direct quotations reveal the most about your subject? Which are the most amusing, pithy, witty, surprising, or outrageous?

> Which objects in the subject's environment provide you with valuable clues about his or her interests?

> What, if anything, did your subject's body language reveal? Did it suggest discomfort, pride, self-confidence, shyness, pomposity?

> What did tone or gestures tell you about the person's state of mind?

> How can you summarize your subject's character or personality?

> Does one theme run through your material? If so, what is it?

Photographs, sketches, or your own doodles also may help you clarify the dominant impression and main emphases for your paper.

Focus Your Thesis on a Dominant Impression.   Most successful portraits focus on a single dominant impression of the interview subject. How would you characterize your subject in one sentence? Try to state a single main impression that you want to convey about your subject. Then eliminate anything that doesn't contribute to this view.

For more on stating a thesis, see pp. 312–19.

For exercises on choosing effective thesis statements, visit <bedfordstmartins.com/bedguide> and do a keyword search:

| DOMINANT IMPRESSION | Del talked a lot about the freedom of the press. |
| WORKING THESIS | Del Sampat is a true believer in the freedom of the press. |

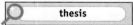

If you have lots of material and if, as often happens, your conversation rambled, you may want to develop the dominant impression by emphasizing just a few things about your subject — personality traits, views on particular topics, or shaping influences. To find such a focus, try grouping your details in three layers of notes, following the pattern in the graphic below.

For more on grouping ideas, see Ch. 17.

1. Dominant Impression   ☐
2. Main Emphases   ☐   ☐
     points about traits, views, influences
3. Supporting Details   ☐   ☐   ☐   ☐   ☐
     quotations, reported words, description

Bring Your Subject to Life for Your Audience.   At the beginning of your paper, can you immediately frame the person you interviewed? A quotation, a bit of physical description, a portrait of your subject at home or at work

TOURO COLLEGE LIBRARY

FOR PEER RESPONSE

For general questions for a peer editor, see p. 377. For peer response worksheets, visit <bedfordstmartins.com/bedguide> and do a keyword search:

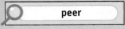
peer

Have a classmate or friend read your draft and suggest how to make the portrait more vivid, complete, and clear. Ask your peer editor to answer questions such as these about writing from an interview:

- Does the essay opening make you want to know the person portrayed? If so, how has the writer interested you? If not, what gets in your way?
- What seems to make the person interviewed interesting to the writer?
- What is the writer's dominant impression of the person interviewed?
- Does the writer include any details that contradict or are unrelated to the dominant impression or insight?
- Do the quoted words or reported speech "sound" real to you? Do any quotations seem at odds with the dominant impression of the person?
- Would you leave out any of the conversation the writer used? Mark anything you would omit.
- Do you have questions about the subject that aren't answered?
- If this were your paper, what is the one thing you would be sure to work on before handing it in?

can bring the person instantly to life in your reader's mind. If your instructor approves adding an image, consider where to place it so that it supplements your text but does not overshadow your essay.

For more on using visuals, see p. 410–16.

When you quote directly, be as accurate as possible, and don't put into quotation marks anything your subject didn't say. Sometimes you may want to quote a whole sentence or more, sometimes just a phrase. Keep evaluating your quotations until they all convey the essence of your subject.

For more on selecting and presenting quotations, see D3 and D6 in the Quick Research Guide (the dark-red-edged pages). For more on punctuating quotations, see C3 in the Quick Editing Guide (the dark-blue-edged pages).

Double-Check Important Information.   You may find that you can't read your hasty handwriting or that some crucial bit of information escaped when you were taking notes. In such a case, telephone the person you interviewed to ask specific questions so that you will not take much time. You may also want to read back to your subject any direct quotations you intend to use, so that he or she can confirm their accuracy.

For more revising and editing strategies, see Ch. 20.

REVISING AND EDITING

As you read over your first draft, keep in mind that your purpose was to make the person you interviewed come alive for your reader.

Conducting a Collective Interview

With your whole class or your writing group, interview someone with special knowledge or expertise. Public figures often visit schools and are used to facing class questions. Or someone on campus might visit to discuss a problem that interests your group. Plan the interview in advance:

FOR GROUP LEARNING

- What do you want to find out?

- What lines of questioning will you pursue?

- What topic will each student ask about?

- How much time will each group member have to ask a series of questions?

- Who will take notes?

Preview each other's questions to avoid duplication. Ask open-ended, rather than yes/no, questions to encourage discussion. Your group's product can be many individual papers or one collaborative paper.

Focus on Your Main Idea or Thesis.   Once you have finished a draft, you may realize that you still feel swamped by too much information. Will your readers feel that your essay is overloaded? Will they understand the dominant impression you want to convey about the person you have interviewed? To be certain that they will, first polish and refine your thesis.

For more on stating a thesis, see pp. 312–19.

WORKING THESIS   Del Sampat is a true believer in the freedom of the press.

REVISED THESIS   Del Sampat, news editor for the *Campus Times,* sees every story he writes as an opportunity to exercise and defend the freedom of the press.

Screen Your Details.   Using your revised thesis as a guide, look again at the quotations and other details you have included. Will readers see how each of these strengthens the dominant impression expressed in your thesis? Keep only those that support your thesis and enhance the dominant impression. Drop all the others, even if they are vivid or catchy.

For exercises on supporting a thesis, visit <bedfordstmartins.com/ bedguide> and do a keyword search:

support

Remember, readers will be interested in your observations and insights. This checklist may help you revise your work to strengthen them:

REVISION CHECKLIST

____ Are the details focused on a dominant impression you want to emphasize? Are all of them relevant? How do you convey the impression to readers?

____ How do the parts of the conversation you've reported reveal the subject's unique personality, character, mood, or concerns?

___ Should your paper have a stronger beginning? Is your ending satisfactory?

___ Should some quotations be summarized or indirectly quoted? Should some explanation be enlivened by adding specific quotations?

___ When the direct quotations are read out loud, do they sound as if they're from the mouth of the person you're portraying?

___ Where might you need to add revealing details about the person's surroundings, personal appearance, or mannerisms?

___ Have you included your own pertinent observations and insights?

___ Does any of your material strike you now as irrelevant or dull?

■ For more editing and proofreading strategies, see pp. 384–87.

After you have revised your essay, edit and proofread it. Carefully check the grammar, word choice, punctuation, and mechanics—and then correct any problems you find. Here are some questions to get you started when editing and proofreading your paper:

■ For more help, turn to the dark-blue-edged pages, and find the sections of the Quick Editing Guide noted here.

EDITING CHECKLIST

___ Is it clear what each pronoun refers to so that the *he*'s and *she*'s are not confusing? Does each pronoun agree with (match) its antecedent?	A6
___ Have you used the correct case (*he* or *him*) for all your pronouns?	A5
___ Is your sentence structure correct? Have you avoided writing fragments, comma splices, or fused sentences?	A1, A2
___ Have you used quotation marks, ellipses (to show the omission of words), and other punctuation correctly in all your quotations?	C3

OTHER ASSIGNMENTS

1. Interview someone from whom you can learn, possibly someone whose profession interests you or whose advice can help you solve a problem or make a decision. Your purpose will be to communicate what you have learned, not to characterize the person you interview.

2. Write a paper based on an interview with at least two members of your extended family about some incident that is part of your family lore. Direct your paper to younger relatives. If accounts of the event don't always agree, combine them into one vivid account, noting that some details may be more trustworthy than others. Give credit to your sources.

3. After briefly talking with fifteen or twenty students on your campus to find out what careers they are preparing for, write a short essay summing up what you find out. What are their reasons for their choices? Are most intent on earning money or on other pursuits? How many have to pay back college loans? Provide some quotations to flesh out your survey. From the information you have gathered, characterize your classmates. Are they materialists? Idealists? Practical people?

Applying What You Learn:
Some Uses of Writing from an Interview

In College Courses. Often you will find yourself interviewing people who can contribute valuable insights into what you are studying.

- In a human development course, you might interview people at various stages of the life cycle — asking about the transition from student life to the working world, about parenthood, or about widowhood or retirement.

- History students may interview people who have firsthand knowledge of an event or era they are studying — a veteran of the Vietnam War, a farmer who remembers a major drought, a woman who participated in the famous Selma to Montgomery civil rights march.

- Education students may interview classroom teachers to gain an understanding of the demands and rewards of teaching.

In the Workplace.   Interviewing is a useful tool, too, for writing on the job.

- Journalists interview "informed sources" to give readers the complete story; conversely, political figures, authors, or actors often use interviews to air their opinions.

- Businesses interview customers to gain feedback on a product or service so they can meet consumer demands.

- Professional investigators conduct interviews to gather evidence — insurance adjusters settling a claim, lawyers preparing a case, medical researchers tracking a disease.

In Your Community.   As a citizen of the larger community, you will find conversation can provide the support you need in many writing tasks.

- Interviewing experts can help you make informed evaluations of community proposals. If county commissioners propose raising taxes to build a new sewage treatment center, you might talk to a waste water management expert about the merits of the plan.

- Information from experts or citizens can support your position on civic issues, such as the need for a traffic light or more transit police.

- Interviewing the missionary group speaking at your church is a good way to create a flyer or pamphlet seeking support for the group's work.

Survey about an issue

Chapter 7
Comparing and Contrasting

Responding to an Image

Examine the buildings in this photograph. List some of the ways that they are similar and different. What do their similarities and differences suggest to you? Although the residents and neighbors of these buildings are not visible in the photograph, what do you suppose the similarities and differences mean to them? What broader issues and changes might these buildings suggest or represent? Why do you suppose that the photographer shot the photograph from the location and angle that he did?

W hich city—Dallas or Atlanta—has more advantages and more drawbacks for a young single person thinking of settling down to a career? As singers and songwriters, how are Beyoncé Knowles and Shakira similar and dissimilar? Such questions invite answers that set two subjects side by side.

When you compare, you point out similarities; when you contrast, you discuss differences. When you write about two complicated subjects, usually you will need to do both. Considering Mozart and Bach, you might find that each has traits the other has—or lacks. Instead of concluding that one is great and the other inferior, you might conclude that they're two distinct composers, each with an individual style. On the other hand, if your main purpose is to judge between two subjects (as when you'd recommend moving either to Dallas or to Atlanta), you would look especially for positive and negative features, weigh the attractions and faults of each city, and then stick your neck out and make your choice.

Learning from Other Writers

In this chapter you will be asked to write a paper setting two subjects side by side, comparing and contrasting them. Let's see how two other writers have used these familiar habits of thought in writing. To help you begin to analyze the first reading, look for the notes in the margin. They identify features such as the thesis, or main idea, the sequence of the broad subjects considered, and the specific points of comparison and contrast.

For more on thesis and support, see Chs. 17 and 19.

As You Read These Comparisons and Contrasts

As you read these essays, ask yourself the following questions:

1. What two (or more) items are compared and contrasted? Does the writer use comparison only? Contrast only? A combination of the two? Why?
2. What is the purpose of the comparison and contrast? What idea does the information support or refute?
3. How does the writer organize the essay? Why?

For more examples of writing based on comparing and contrasting, visit <bedfordstmartins.com/bedguide> and do a keyword search:

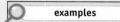

examples

Suzanne Britt
Neat People vs. Sloppy People

Suzanne Britt takes a lighthearted look at neat and sloppy people in this selection from her essay collection Show and Tell *(1983).*

I 've finally figured out the difference between neat people and sloppy people. The distinction is, as always, moral. Neat people are lazier and meaner than sloppy people.

Sloppy people, you see, are not really sloppy. Their sloppiness is merely the unfortunate consequence of their extreme moral rectitude.° Sloppy people

Introduction

THESIS
Setting up subjects
Subject A

rectitude: Correctness, decency.

105

Point 1— carry in their mind's eye a heavenly vision, a precise plan, that is so stupendous, so perfect, it can't be achieved in this world or the next.

Point 2— Sloppy people live in Never-Never Land. Someday is their métier.° 3 Someday they are planning to alphabetize all their books and set up home catalogs. Someday they will go through their wardrobes and mark certain items for tentative mending and certain items for passing on to relatives of similar shape and size. Someday sloppy people will make family scrapbooks into which they will put newspaper clippings, postcards, locks of hair, and the dried corsage from their senior prom. Someday they will file everything on the surface of their desks, including the cash receipts from coffee purchases at the snack shop. Someday they will sit down and read all the back issues of *The New Yorker*.

For all these noble reasons and more, sloppy people never get neat. They 4 aim too high and wide. They save everything, planning someday to file, order, and straighten out the world. But while these ambitious plans take clearer and clearer shape in their heads, the books spill from the shelves onto the floor, the clothes pile up in the hamper and closet, the family mementos accumulate in every drawer, the surface of the desk is buried under mounds of paper, and the unread magazines threaten to reach the ceiling.

Sloppy people can't bear to part with anything. They give loving atten- 5 tion to every detail. When sloppy people say they're going to tackle the surface of a desk, they really mean it. Not a paper will go unturned; not a rubber band will go unboxed. Four hours or two weeks into the excavation, the desk looks exactly the same, primarily because the sloppy person is meticulously creating new piles of papers with new headings and scrupulously stopping to read all the old book catalogs before he throws them away. A neat person would just bulldoze the desk.

Exaggeration to make a
point and add humor—

Neat people are bums and clods at heart. They have cavalier° attitudes 6 toward possessions, including family heirlooms. Everything is just another dust-catcher to them. If anything collects dust, it's got to go and that's that. Neat people will toy with the idea of throwing the children out of the house just to cut down on the clutter.

Neat people don't care about process. They like results. What they want 7 to do is get the whole thing over with so they can sit down and watch the rasslin' on TV. Neat people operate on two unvarying principles: Never handle any item twice, and throw everything away.

The only thing messy in a neat person's house is the trash can. The 8 minute something comes to a neat person's hand, he will look at it, try to decide if it has immediate use and, finding none, throw it in the trash.

Neat people are especially vicious with mail. They never go through 9 their mail unless they are standing directly over a trash can. If the trash can is beside the mailbox, even better. All ads, catalogs, pleas for charitable contributions, church bulletins, and money-saving coupons go straight into the trash can without being opened. All letters from home, postcards from

métier: Trade, specialty.   **cavalier:** Dismissive.

Europe, bills, and paychecks are opened, immediately responded to, then dropped in the trash can. Neat people keep their receipts only for tax purposes. That's it. No sentimental salvaging of birthday cards or the last letter a dying relative ever wrote. Into the trash it goes.

Neat people place neatness above everything, even economics. They are 10 incredibly wasteful. Neat people throw away several toys every time they walk through the den. I knew a neat person once who threw away a perfectly good dish drainer because it had mold on it. The drainer was too much trouble to wash. And neat people sell their furniture when they move. They will sell a La-Z-Boy recliner while you are reclining in it. ———————— Another exaggeration for effect

Neat people are no good to borrow from. Neat people buy everything in 11 expensive little single portions. They get their flour and sugar in two-pound bags. They wouldn't consider clipping a coupon, saving a leftover, reusing plastic nondairy whipped cream containers, or rinsing off tin foil and draping it over the unmoldy dish drainer. You can never borrow a neat person's newspaper to see what's playing at the movies. Neat people have the paper all wadded up and in the trash by 7:05 A.M.

Neat people cut a clean swath° through the organic as well as the inor- 12 ganic world. People, animals, and things are all one to them. They are so insensitive. After they've finished with the pantry, the medicine cabinet, and the attic, they will throw out the red geranium (too many leaves), sell the dog (too many fleas), and send the children off to boarding school (too many scuff marks on the hardwood floors). — Concluding exaggeration for effect

Questions to Start You Thinking

Meaning

1. Does Britt favor one group over the other? Which details or statements support your response?

2. Based on the details presented here, to which group do you belong? What specific details describe you most accurately?

3. What is Britt's purpose in contrasting neat people and sloppy people? Is her goal to explain or to convince? Or is it something else?

Writing Strategies

4. In the introductory paragraph, Britt jumps right into the essay. Is that technique effective? How else might she have begun her essay?

5. Which method of organization does Britt use to arrange her essay? How effectively does she switch between her two subjects of "sloppy" and "neat"?

6. From reading this essay, are readers to assume that "sloppy" and "neat" people have nothing in common? Why?

swath: Path.

STUDENT ESSAY

Tim Chabot
Take Me Out to the Ball Game, but Which One?

Student Tim Chabot compares and contrasts baseball and basketball, asking which deserves the title of America's national pastime.

For much of the twentieth century, baseball has been considered the national pastime of the United States. Hank Aaron, home runs, and hot dogs seem as American as Thanksgiving. Many American presidents, from Eisenhower to Bush, have participated in the tradition of a celebrity throwing out the first ball on opening day of a new baseball season. But beginning in the 1990s, baseball stars were being eclipsed by the stars of another game invented in America--basketball. Some argue that Michael Jordan and Shaquille O'Neal, basketball greats and household names, are more famous than any current pitcher or home run king. This shift has raised a question in the minds of many: Should baseball continue to be considered our national pastime, or should basketball take its place?

❓ Why do you think the writer raises this question here?

Both sports are very popular with American sports fans. In addition, both games attract fans of all races--white, African American, Asian American, Hispanic--and all classes, rich and poor, educated and uneducated. Baseball has become a national treasure through its appeal to a wide, wide audience. At a Saturday afternoon game, men, women, grandparents, and kids of all ages wait to catch a fly ball. The appeal of basketball is growing, the sport having become popular in urban and rural areas, on high school and college campuses. Both sports are played in quite a variety of locations. Baseball games occur on neighborhood sandlots as well as official diamonds. Basketball requires little space and equipment, so pickup basketball games occur in almost every neighborhood park and virtually anywhere that a hoop can be rigged up.

❓ Do you agree with the analogy between baseball and an "open-air carnival"?

Although both sports are popular with American fans, attending a baseball game is quite different from attending a basketball game. Baseball is a family-oriented spectator sport. Because of the widely diverse baseball fans with varied attention spans, attending a baseball game is like going to an open-air carnival, and the game itself is only one of the many spectacles. If fans are bored with the game, they can listen to the vendors hawking ice cream, watch a fight brewing in the bleacher seats, stand in line to buy peanuts or hot dogs, participate in "the wave," or just bask in the sun. Only diehard fans keep a constant eye on the game itself because there are frequent breaks in the play.

In contrast, the central spectacle of any basketball arena is definitely the game itself. Few distractions to entertain a casual fan occur, except for cheerleaders for college teams. Basketball arenas are always indoors, and the games are usually at night, creating an atmosphere that is urban and adult. The constant motion of the

1

2

3

4

sport rivets° attention to the game itself. Attending a basketball game can be compared to an exciting night on the town, while watching a baseball game is like relaxing with the family in the backyard.

What other differences in attending the games come to mind?

The pace of the two games is also quite different. The leisurely pace of a baseball game contributes to its popularity because it offers relaxation to harried Americans. Each batter may spend several minutes at the plate, hit a few foul balls, and reach a full count of three balls and two strikes before getting on base, hitting a routine pop fly, or striking out. While batters slow things down by stepping out of the box to practice their swing, pitchers stall the play by "holding the runners on" to prevent stolen bases. The substitution of relief pitchers suspends the game and gives spectators an opportunity to purchase junk food or memorabilia. In games in which star pitchers duel, the audience may see only a few men on base in nine innings and a very low score. Also, the tradition of the seventh-inning stretch underscores baseball's appeal to a person who wants to take it easy and relax.   5

On the other hand, the quick pace of basketball has contributed to its popularity in our fast-paced society. Players run down the court at sometimes exhausting speed for a "fast break," successful baskets can occur merely seconds apart, each team may score as many as one hundred points a game, and the ball changes sides hundreds of times, as opposed to every half-inning in baseball. Games can be won or lost in the few seconds before the final buzzer. Basketball players are always in motion, much like American society. The pounding excitement of basketball appeals to people who play hard as well as work hard.   6

These two sports require different athletic abilities from the players. Although baseball games are slow-paced, the sport places a premium on athletic precision and therefore showcases strategy and skill rather than brute physical strength. The choice of a pitch, the decision to bunt or to steal a base, and the order of batters are all careful strategic moves that could affect the outcome of the whole game. Baseball has been called the "thinking person's game" because of its emphasis on statistics and probabilities. Although mental strategy and dexterity° are emphasized, physical strength is important, too. A strong arm obviously increases the power of a player's throw or of his swing, and speed is essential in running bases. But intimidating physical ability is not necessarily a required element to become a major league player, and even out-of-shape players can become stars if their bats are hot. The importance of skill over brawn has contributed to baseball's popularity not merely as a spectator sport but also as a sport in which millions of Americans participate, from Little League to neighborhood leagues for adults.   7

Do you agree that baseball requires "skill" and basketball "brawn"?

Unlike baseball, basketball emphasizes physical power, stamina, and size since jumping high, running fast, and just being tall with long legs and big hands usually   8

rivets: Commands or fixes attention to.   **dexterity:** Skill in using the hands or body.

contribute to a player's success. Skill and dexterity are certainly necessary in executing a slam dunk or dribbling past a double team, but these skills are usually combined with physical strength. In order to be a successful rebounder, a player needs to be extremely aggressive and occasionally commit fouls. Many more injuries occur on basketball courts than on baseball fields. Perhaps the physical power and intimidation required in basketball have led to the media's focus on individual players' star qualities. Magic, Bird, Jordan, Shaq, and Le Bron James are icons° who have taken the place of baseball stars of previous generations like Joe DiMaggio, Ted Williams, and Babe Ruth. Furthermore, in the international arena of the Olympics, basketball came to be seen as a symbol of American strength and power, as the 1992 Dream Team demolished all of its opponents.

If the rest of the world now equates basketball with America, should we consider it to be our true national pastime? The increasing popularity of basketball seems to reflect the change in American society in the past few decades, a change to a more fast-paced and aggressive culture. But basketball doesn't yet appeal to as diverse an audience as does baseball, and thus it doesn't seem to deserve to be called a national phenomenon--yet. Until kids, women, and grandparents are as prevalent at a Lakers game as are young males, baseball will retain its title as the national pastime. But the exciting speed of basketball may soon have more appeal than the leisurely pace of baseball.

Why do you agree or disagree with this conclusion?

9

Questions to Start You Thinking

Meaning

1. In what specific ways does Chabot claim that baseball and basketball are similar? In what ways are these two sports different? Do the similarities outweigh the differences, or vice versa?

2. Can you think of other ways these two sports are similar and different?

3. Would you nominate another sport, say soccer or ice hockey, for the national pastime? If so, why?

Writing Strategies

4. Is Chabot's support for his comparison and contrast sufficient and balanced? Explain.

5. What transitional devices does Chabot use to indicate when he is comparing and when he is contrasting?

6. What is Chabot's thesis? Why does Chabot state it where he does?

7. Using highlighters or marginal notes, identify the essay's introduction, thesis, contrasting subjects, points of comparison and contrast, and conclusion. How effective is the organization of this essay?

icons: Images or symbols.

Learning by Writing

THE ASSIGNMENT: COMPARING AND CONTRASTING

Write a paper in which you compare and contrast two items to enlighten readers about both subjects. The specific points of similarity and difference will be important, but you will go beyond them to draw a conclusion from your analysis. This conclusion, your thesis, needs to be more than "point A is different from point B" or "I prefer subject B to subject A." You will need to explain why you have drawn your conclusion. You'll also need to provide specific supporting evidence to explain your position and to convince your readers of its soundness. You may choose two people, two kinds of people, two places, two objects, two activities, or two ideas, but be sure to choose two you care about. You might write an impartial paper that distinctly portrays both subjects, or you might show why you favor one over the other.

■ For writing activities for comparing and contrasting, visit <bedfordstmartins.com/bedguide> and do a keyword search:

🔍 activities

Engaging student papers from similar assignments include these:

An American student compared and contrasted her home life with that of her roommate, a student from Nigeria. Her goal was to deepen her understanding of Nigerian society and her own.

A student who was interested in history compared and contrasted civilian responses to the Vietnam and Iraq wars, considering how popular attitudes about military service had changed.

Another writer compared and contrasted conditions at two city facilities, making a case for a revised funding formula.

GENERATING IDEAS

Find Two Subjects.   Pick subjects you can compare and contrast purposefully. An examination question may give them to you, ready-made: "Compare and contrast ancient Roman sculpture with that of the ancient Greeks." But suppose you have to find your subjects for yourself. You'll need to choose things that have a sensible basis for comparison, a common element.

■ For strategies for generating ideas, see Ch. 16.

moon rocks + stars = no common element

Dallas + Atlanta = cities to consider settling in

Montel Williams + Oprah Winfrey = television talk-show hosts

Besides having a common element, the subjects should have enough in common to compare but differ enough to throw each other into sharp relief.

sports cars + racing cars = common element + telling differences

sports cars + oil tankers = limited common element + unpromising differences

Try generating a list or brainstorming. Recall what you've recently read, discussed, or spotted on the Web. Let your mind skitter around in search of pairs that go together, or play the game of *free association*, jotting down a

■ For more on brainstorming, see pp. 296–97.

word and whatever it brings to mind: *Democrats? Republicans. New York? Los Angeles. MySpace? Friendster.* Or try the following questions:

DISCOVERY CHECKLIST

___ Do you know two people who are strikingly different in attitude or behavior (perhaps your parents or two brothers, two friends, two teachers)?

___ Can you think of two groups of people who are both alike and different (perhaps two teams or two clubs)?

___ Have you taken two courses that were quite different but both valuable?

___ Do you prefer one of two places where you have lived or visited?

___ Can you recall two events in your life that shared similar aspects but turned out to be quite different (perhaps two sporting events or two romances or the births of two children)?

___ Can you compare and contrast two holidays or two family customs?

___ Are you familiar with two writers, two artists, or two musicians who seem to have similar goals but quite different accomplishments?

Once you have a list of pairs, put a star by those that seem promising. Ask yourself what similarities immediately come to mind. What differences? Can you jot down several of each? Are these striking, significant similarities and differences? If not, move on until you discover a workable pair.

Limit the Scope of Your Paper.   If you propose to compare and contrast Japanese literature and American literature in 750 words, your task is probably impossible. But to cut down the size of this subject, you might compare and

---

Facing the Challenge: Comparing and Contrasting

The major challenge that writers face when comparing and contrasting two subjects is to determine their purpose. Writers who skip this step run the risk of having readers ask, "So, what's the point?" Suppose you develop brilliant points of similarity and difference between the films of Oliver Stone and those of Stanley Kubrick. Do you want to argue that one director is more skilled than the other? Or perhaps you want to show how they treat love or war differently in their films? Consider the following questions as you determine your primary purpose for comparing and contrasting:

• Do you want to inform your readers about these two subjects in order to provide a better understanding of the two?

• Do you want to persuade your readers that one of the two subjects is preferable to the other?

Asking what you want to demonstrate, discover, or prove *before* you begin to draft will help you to write a more effective comparison-and-contrast essay.

Making a Comparison-and-Contrast Table

After deciding what to compare, open a file and record what you know about subject A and then subject B. (Separate them with a page break if you wish.) Next, use your word processor menu to create a table with three columns (up and down) and at least half a dozen rows (across). Use the first row to label the columns: Categories (left), subject A (middle), and subject B (right).

Now read over your notes on subject A. When you spot related details, identify a logical category that encompasses them. Enter the category name in the left column of the second row of your table, and copy the related details for subject A into the middle column. Repeat this process, labeling more rows as categories and moving corresponding details into the subject A column for each row. (Insert new rows at the end of your table as needed.)

Next review your notes on subject B. If some details fall into categories already listed in your table, copy those details into the subject B column for each category. If new categories emerge, add them in new rows along with the subject B details. After you finish categorizing your notes, round out the table — adding details to fill in empty cells, combining similar categories, or adding entirely new categories. Select the most promising categories from your table as common features for logical comparison and contrast in your essay.

FOR E-WRITERS

For more on tables, see pp. 414–15.

contrast, say, a haiku of Bashō about a snake with a short poem about a snake by Emily Dickinson. This topic you could cover adequately in 750 words.

Explore Each Member of Your Pair to Build Support.   As you examine your two subjects, your goal is twofold. You want to analyze each using a similar approach so that you have a reasonable basis for comparison and contrast. You also want to find the details and examples that you'll need to support your points. Consider these sources of support:

• Two events, processes, procedures	Ask a reporter's questions — 5 W's (who, what, where, when, why) and an H (how).
• Two events from the past	Using the same questions, interview someone present at each event, or read news or other accounts.
• Two perceptions (public and private)	Interview someone behind the scenes; read or listen to contrasting views.
• Two approaches or viewpoints	Browse online for Web sites or pages that supply different examples.
• Two subject ideas	Read a few articles for options.
• Two policies or options	Look for studies or government statistics like those on page 113.

For more on using a reporter's questions, see pp. 303–05.

For more on interviewing, see Ch. 6.

For advice on finding a few useful sources, turn to B1–B2 in the Quick Research Guide (the dark-red-edged pages). For more on using sources for support, see Ch. 12.

Per Capita Personal Income in
Great Lakes States, 2005
Sources: Personal income data from U.S. Bu-
reau of Economic Analysis <www.bea.gov>
and population data from U.S. Census Bureau
<www.census.gov>.

State	2005 Personal Income (in millions)	2005 Population (in thousands)	2005 Per Capita Personal Income
Illinois	$462,857	12,763	$36,266
Indiana	$195,372	6,272	$31,150
Michigan	$331,304	10,121	$32,734
Ohio	$365,319	11,464	$31,867
Wisconsin	$184,087	5,536	$33,253

PLANNING, DRAFTING, AND DEVELOPING

As you start planning your paper, be prepared to cover both subjects in a similar fashion. If you use two columns (one for each subject), a table, or a scratch outline to record ideas, you can easily identify promising points of comparison or contrast, consolidate supporting details, and spot gaps in your information. Remind yourself of your goal in comparing and contrasting the two subjects. What is it you want to show, argue, or find out?

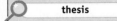
For more on planning, drafting, and developing, see Chs. 17, 18, and 19. For more on outlines, see pp. 325–33.

For more on stating a thesis, see pp. 312–19.

State Your Purpose in a Thesis.   You need a reason to place two subjects side by side — a reason that you and your audience will find compelling and worthwhile. Ask yourself if you prefer one subject in the pair over the other. What reasons can you give for your preference? It's also all right not to have a preference; you can try instead to understand both subjects more clearly, making a point about each or both. Comparing and contrasting need not be a meaningless exercise. Try instead to think clearly and pointedly in order to explain an idea about which you care.

For exercises on choosing effective thesis statements, visit <bedfordstmartins.com/bedguide> and do a keyword search:

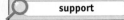
🔍   **thesis**

TWO SUBJECTS	two teaching styles in required biology courses
REASON	to show why one is better
WORKING THESIS	Although students learn a lot in both of the required introductory biology courses, one class teaches information and the other teaches how to be a good learner.

For exercises on supporting a thesis, visit <bedfordstmartins.com/bedguide> and do a keyword search:

🔍   **support**

Select a Pattern to Help Your Audience Follow Your Evidence.   Besides understanding your purpose and thesis, readers also need to follow your supporting evidence — the clusters of details that reveal the nature of each subject you consider. They're likely to expect you to follow one of two ways to organize a comparison-and-contrast essay.

OPPOSING PATTERN, SUBJECT BY SUBJECT

Subject A
   Point 1
   Point 2
   Point 3

ALTERNATING PATTERN, POINT BY POINT

Point 1
   Subject A
   Subject B

	Point 2
Subject B	Subject A
Point 1	Subject B
Point 2	Point 3
Point 3	Subject A
	Subject B

Although both patterns present the same information, each has its own advantages and disadvantages.

Use the Opposing Pattern of Organization.   When you use the *opposing pattern* of *subject by subject,* you state all your observations about subject A and then do the same for subject B. In the following paragraph from *Whole Brain Thinking* (New York: William Morrow, 1984), Jacquelyn Wonder and Priscilla Donovan, management consultants, use the opposing pattern of organization to explain the differences in the brains of females and males.

For other examples, see pp. 367–68.

> At birth there are basic differences between male and female brains. The female cortex is more fully developed. The sound of the human voice elicits more left-brain activity in infant girls than in infant boys, accounting in part for the earlier development in females of language. Baby girls have larger connectors between the brain's hemispheres and thus integrate information more skillfully. This flexibility bestows greater verbal and intuitive skills. Male infants lack this ready communication between the brain's lobes; therefore, messages are routed and rerouted to the right brain, producing larger right hemispheres. The size advantage accounts for males having greater spatial and physical abilities and explains why they may become more highly lateralized and skilled in specific areas.

Subject A: Female brain

Point 1: Development

Point 2: Consequences
Shift to subject B: Male brain
Point 1: Development
Point 2: Consequences

For a single paragraph or a short essay, the opposing pattern can effectively unify all the details about each subject, like neat versus sloppy people in Suzanne Britt's essay. For a long essay or a complicated subject, it has a drawback: readers might find it difficult to remember all the separate information about subject A while reading about subject B.

Use the Alternating Pattern of Organization.   There's a better way to organize most longer papers: the *alternating pattern* of *point by point.* Using this method, you take up one point at a time, applying it first to one subject and then the other. If your paper will have headings, you can use them to identify these points as well, thus helping readers preview the structure at a glance and anticipate what's covered in each section. Tim Chabot uses this pattern to lead the reader along clearly and carefully, looking at each subject before moving on to the next point. His outline might have looked like this:

For more on headings, see pp. 405–09.

THESIS: The exciting speed of basketball may soon have more appeal than the leisurely pace of baseball.

FOR PEER RESPONSE

For general questions for a peer editor, see p. 377.

You may want a classmate or friend to respond to your draft, suggesting how to present your two subjects more clearly. Ask your peer editor to answer questions like these about comparison and contrast:

- How does the introduction motivate you to read the entire essay?
- What is the point of the comparison and contrast of the two subjects? Is the thesis stated in the essay, or is it implied?
- Is the essay organized by the opposing pattern or by the alternating pattern? Is the pattern appropriate, or would the other one work better?
- Are the same categories discussed for each item? If not, should they be?
- Are there enough details for you to understand the comparison and contrast? Put a check where more details or examples would be useful.
- If this were your paper, what is the one thing you would be sure to work on before handing it in?

   I. Similarities of fans
      A. Appeal to diverse groups
         1. Baseball
         2. Basketball
      B. Varied locations
         1. Baseball
         2. Basketball

  II. Difference in atmosphere at game
      A. Baseball as a diverse family-oriented spectator sport
         1. Many distractions
         2. Frequent breaks in play
      B. Basketball as game-focused sport
         1. Few distractions
         2. Constant game activity

 III. Difference in pace of game
      A. Leisurely pace of baseball
         1. Slow batters
         2. Stalling pitchers
         3. Substitution of relief pitchers
         4. Low score
         5. Seventh-inning stretch
      B. Quick pace of basketball
         1. Fast players
         2. High scores
         3. Frequent changes of sides
         4. Constant motion

Comparing and Contrasting Yourself with a Partner

Using assignment 3 on page 119 as a guide, compare and contrast yourself with a classmate in a collaborative essay. Decide together what your focus will be: Your backgrounds? Your hobbies? Your career goals? Your study habits? Your taste in music or clothes? Your politics? Then each partner should work alone on a detailed analysis of himself or herself, given this focus. Together again, compare your analyses, decide how to shape the essay, and draft, revise, and edit the paper. If your instructor approves, consider a mixed-media presentation.

FOR GROUP LEARNING

IV. Different athletic abilities of players
   A. Baseball as a mental game
      1. Emphasis on athletic precision
         a. Strategy
         b. Skill
         c. Decision making
      2. Physical strength less important
   B. Basketball as a physical game
      1. Emphasis on physical power
         a. Jumping high
         b. Running fast
         c. Being tall and big
         d. Being aggressive
      2. Importance of skill and dexterity

For more on outlines, see pp. 325–33. For Tim Chabot's full paper, see pp. 108–10.

Add Transitions. Once your essay is organized, you can bring cohesion to it through effective transitional words and phrases — *on the other hand, in contrast, also, both, yet, although, finally, unlike.* Your choice of wording will depend on the content, but keep it varied and smooth. Jarring, choppy transitions distract attention instead of contributing to a unified essay, each part working to support a meaningful thesis.

For more on transitions, see pp. 346–49.

REVISING AND EDITING

Focus on Your Thesis. Reconsider your purpose when you review your draft. If your purpose is to illuminate two subjects impartially, ask whether you have given readers a balanced view. Obviously it would be unfair to set forth all the advantages of Oklahoma City and all the disadvantages of Honolulu and then conclude that Oklahoma City is superior on every count.

For more on revising and editing strategies, see Ch. 20.

Of course, if you love Oklahoma City and can't stand Honolulu, or vice versa, go ahead: don't be balanced; take a stand. Even so, you will want to include the same points about each city and to admit, in all honesty, that Oklahoma City has its faults. One useful way to check for balance or thoroughness is to outline your draft and give the outline a critical look.

For more on outlines, see pp. 325–33.

■ For more on stating a thesis, see pp. 312–19.

If classmates have made suggestions, perhaps about clearer wording to sharpen distinctions, use their ideas as you rework your thesis.

> WORKING THESIS   Although students learn a lot in both of the required introductory biology courses, one class teaches information and the other teaches how to be a good learner.

> REVISED THESIS   Although students learn the basics of biology in both of the required introductory courses, one class teaches how to memorize information and the other teaches an invaluable lesson: how to be an active learner.

Vary Your Wording.   Make sure, as you go over your draft, that you have escaped a monotonous drone: A does this, B does that; A has these advantages, B has those. Comparison and contrast needn't result in a paper as symmetrical as a pair of sneakers. Revising and editing give you a chance to add lively details, transitions, dashes of color, and especially variety:

■ For strategies for increasing coherence, see pp. 346–49.

The menu is another major difference between the Cozy Cafe and the Wilton

Inn. For lunch, the Cozy Cafe offers sandwiches, hamburgers, and chili. ~~For lunch,~~ _L_ _at_

features

the Wilton Inn ~~offers~~ dishes such as fajitas, shrimp salads, and onion soup topped

with Swiss cheese. ~~For dinner, the Cozy Cafe continues to serve the lunch menu and~~

adding

~~adds~~ home-style comfort foods such as meatloaf, stew, macaroni and cheese, and

after five o'clock

barbecued ribs. ~~By dinner,~~ the Wilton's specialties for the day are posted--perhaps

marinated buffalo steak or orange-pecan salmon.

In critiquing your draft as you rewrite, this checklist may prove handy:

REVISION CHECKLIST

___ Does your introduction present your topic and main point clearly? Is it interesting enough to make a reader want to read the whole essay?

___ Is your reason for doing all the comparing and contrasting unmistakably clear? What do you want to demonstrate, argue for, or find out? Do you need to reexamine your goal?

___ Have you used the same categories for each item so that you treat them fairly? In discussing each feature, do you always look at the same thing?

___ What have you concluded about the two? Do you prefer one to the other? If so, is this preference (and your rationale for it) clear?

___ Does your draft look thin at any point for lack of evidence? If so, how might you develop your ideas?

___ Are there any spots where you need to revise a boringly mechanical, monotonous style ("On one hand, . . . now on the other hand")?

After you have revised your comparison-and-contrast essay, edit and proofread it. Carefully check the grammar, word choice, punctuation, and mechanics — and then correct any problems you may find. Here are some questions to get you started editing and proofreading your paper:

■ For more editing and proofreading strategies, see pp. 384–87.

EDITING CHECKLIST

—— Have you used the correct comparative forms (for two things) and superlative forms (for three or more) for adjectives and adverbs?	A7
—— Is your sentence structure correct? Have you avoided writing fragments, comma splices, or fused sentences?	A1, A2
—— Have you used parallel structure in your comparisons and contrasts? Are your sentences as balanced as your ideas?	B2
—— Have you used commas correctly after introductory phrases and other transitions?	C1

■ For more help, turn to the dark-blue-edged pages and find the sections of the Quick Editing Guide noted here.

OTHER ASSIGNMENTS

1. Listen to two different recordings of the same piece of music as performed by two different groups, orchestras, or singers. What elements of the music does each stress? What contrasting attitudes toward the music do you detect? In an essay, compare and contrast these versions.

2. Write an essay in which you compare and contrast the subjects in any of the following pairs for the purpose of throwing light on both. In a short paper, you can trace only a few similarities and differences, but don't hesitate to observe, go to the library, or interview a friendly expert.

■ For more on using sources to support a position, see Ch. 12 and the Quick Research Guide (the dark-red-edged pages).

>Women and men as single parents
>Living at home and living away from home
>The coverage of a world event on television and in a newspaper
>The experience of watching a film on a DVD and in a theater
>The styles of two athletes playing in the same position (two pitchers, two quarterbacks, two goalies)
>English and another language
>Your college and a rival college
>Two differing views of a current controversy
>Northern and southern California (or two other regions)
>Two similar works of architecture (two churches, two skyscrapers, two city halls, two museums, two campus buildings)
>Two articles, essays, or Web sites about the same topic

3. In a serious or nonserious way, introduce yourself to your class by comparing and contrasting yourself with someone else. You might choose either a real person or a character in a film, a TV series, a novel, or a comic strip, but you and this other person should have much in common. Choose a few points of comparison (an attitude, a habit, or a way of life), and deal with each in an essay or, if your instructor approves, a mixed-media format.

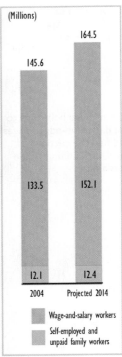

(Millions)

Employment by class of worker, 2004 and projected 2014
Source: Occupational Outlook Quarterly

Applying What You Learn: Some Uses of Comparing and Contrasting

In College Courses.   College instructors know that distinguishing subtle similarities and differences between two subjects requires close attention, so they frequently ask students to demonstrate that understanding.

- You would compare and contrast to "evaluate" the relative merits of Norman Rockwell and N. C. Wyeth in an art history course.
- An assignment to "consider" doing business as a small corporation and as a partnership calls for comparison and contrast.
- When you are asked to "describe" a subject, such as medieval funeral customs, comparing or contrasting it with a similar familiar subject, modern traditions, might be the best way to set up a frame of reference.

In the Workplace.   At work, you will constantly compare and contrast products or services of one company with those of another, merits of one proposal with those of another, or benefits of option A with those of option B.

- Analysts compare employment data and projections to inform employers and workers about labor trends and help them plan for the future.
- When you recommend a new procedure, you can emphasize its strong points by comparing and contrasting it with the existing procedure.
- When hiring, organizations compare and contrast management style, work experience, education, and personal attributes of applicants.

In Your Community.   Comparing and contrasting is an effective method of analyzing alternatives in your community life as well.

- The advantages of one option over another quickly become apparent when you compare or contrast them, whether you want to choose a childcare provider, a fitness center, or backup aid cameras for your car.
- Your pamphlet urging voters to approve bonds for building a new elementary school can contrast costs and benefits of building with those of renovation.
- If you were to recommend a resort for your organization's annual conference, your report would compare and contrast accommodations, meeting facilities, food services, and dates of availability.

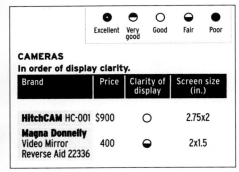

Brand	Price	Clarity of display	Screen size (in.)
HitchCAM HC-001	$900	○	2.75x2
Magna Donnelly Video Mirror Reverse Aid 22336	400	◕	2x1.5

CAMERAS
In order of display clarity.

● Excellent   ◕ Very good   ○ Good   ◔ Fair   ● Poor

Source: From "Driving Blind," Consumer Reports

Chapter 8
Explaining Causes and Effects

Responding to an Image

This image shows both causes and effects. What causes can you identify? What effects? Also consider artistic choice—the selection of the scene and the vantage point from which it was photographed. What mood does the photograph create? How does it affect you personally?

When a house burns down, an insurance company assigns a claims adjuster to look into the disaster and ask, Why? He or she investigates to find the answer—the *cause* of the fire, whether lightning, a cooking mishap, or a match that someone deliberately struck—and presents it in a written report. The adjuster also details the *effects* of the fire—what was destroyed or damaged, what repairs will be needed, how much they will cost.

Often in college you are asked to investigate and think like the insurance adjuster, tracing causes or identifying effects. To do so, you have to gather information to marshal evidence. Effects, by the way, are usually easier to identify than causes. Results of a fire are apparent to an onlooker the next day, although its cause may be obscure. For this reason, seeking causes and effects may be an uncertain pursuit, and you are unlikely to set forth definitive explanations with absolute certainty.

Learning from Other Writers

■ For more on thesis and support, see Chs. 17 and 19.

The following essays explore causes and effects, each examining a different environment. To help you begin to analyze the first reading, look for the notes in the margin. They identify features such as the thesis, or main idea, and the first of the causes or effects that develop it in a paper analyzing cause and effect.

As You Read These Cause-and-Effect Essays

■ For more examples of writing that explains causes and effects, visit <bedfordstmartins.com/bedguide> and do a keyword search:

examples

As you read these essays, ask yourself the following questions:

1. Does the writer explain causes? Or effects? Or both? Why?
2. Does the writer perceive and explain a chain or series of causal relationships? If so, how are the various causes and effects connected?
3. What evidence does the writer supply? Is the evidence sufficient to clarify the causal relationships and to provide credibility to the essay?

William Severini Kowinski examines some of the underlying reasons for "mall culture" in this excerpt from his book The Malling of America *(1985).*

Quotation used to preview writer's focus

William Severini Kowinski
Kids in the Mall: Growing Up Controlled

Butch heaved himself up and loomed over the group. "Like it was different for me," he piped. "My folks used to drop me off at the shopping mall every morning and leave me all day. It was like a big free baby-sitter, you know? One night they never came back for me. Maybe they moved away. Maybe there's some kind of a Bureau of Missing Parents I could check with."

–Richard Peck, *Secrets of the Shopping Mall*, a novel for teenagers

From his sister at Swarthmore, I'd heard about a kid in Florida whose | 1
mother picked him up after school every day, drove him straight to the
mall, and left him there until it closed — all at his insistence. I'd heard about
a boy in Washington who, when his family moved from one suburb to another, pedaled his bicycle five miles every day to get back to his old mall,
where he once belonged.

    Introduction

Their stories aren't unusual. The mall is a common experience for the | 2
majority of American youth; they have probably been going there all their
lives. Some ran within their first large open space, saw their first fountain,
bought their first toy, and read their first book in a mall. They may have
smoked their first cigarette or first joint or turned them down, had their first
kiss or lost their virginity in the mall parking lot. Teenagers in America now
spend more time in the mall than anywhere else but home and school.
Mostly it is their choice, but some of that mall time is put in as the result of
two-paycheck and single-parent households, and the lack of other viable°
alternatives. But are these kids being harmed by the mall?

    Situation described in transitional paragraph

    Question raised about effects

I wondered first of all what difference it makes for adolescents to experi- | 3
ence so many important moments in the mall. They are, after all, at play in
the fields of its little world and they learn its ways; they adapt to it and make
it adapt to them. It's here that these kids get their street sense, only it's mall
sense. They are learning the ways of a large-scale artificial environment: its
subtleties and flexibilities, its particular pleasures and resonances,° and the
attitudes it fosters.

    THESIS *specifying effects*

The presence of so many teenagers for so much time was not something | 4
mall developers planned on. In fact, it came as a big surprise. But kids became
a fact of mall life very early, and the International Council of Shopping Centers
found it necessary to commission a study, which they published along with a
guide to mall managers on how to handle the teenage incursion.°

The study found that "teenagers in suburban centers are bored and | 5
come to the shopping centers mainly as a place to go. Teenagers in suburban centers spent more time fighting, drinking, littering, and walking than
did their urban counterparts, but presented fewer overall problems." The report observed that "adolescents congregated in groups of two to four and
predominantly at locations selected by them rather than management." This
probably had something to do with the decision to install game arcades,
which allow management to channel these restless adolescents into naturally contained areas away from major traffic points of adult shoppers.

The guide concluded that mall management should tolerate and even | 6
encourage the teenage presence because, in the words of the report, "The
vast majority support the same set of values as does shopping center management." *The same set of values* means simply that mall kids are already pre-
programmed to be consumers and that the mall can put the finishing

viable: Effective or practical.   **resonances:** Profound and lasting impacts.   **incursion:**
Invasion.

touches to them as hard-core, lifelong shoppers just like everybody else. That, after all, is what the mall is about. So it shouldn't be surprising that in spending a lot of time there, adolescents find little that challenges the assumption that the goal of life is to make money and buy products, or that just about everything else in life is to be used to serve those ends.

Growing up in a high-consumption society already adds inestimable 7 pressure to kids' lives. Clothes consciousness has invaded the grade schools, and popularity is linked with having the best, newest clothes in the cur-

Use of contrast — rently acceptable styles. Even what they read has been affected. "Miss [Nancy] Drew wasn't obsessed with her wardrobe," noted the *Wall Street Journal*. "But today the mystery in teen fiction for girls is what outfit the heroine will wear next." Shopping has become a survival skill and there is certainly no better place to learn it than the mall, where its importance is powerfully reinforced and certainly never questioned.

Education comparison: negative — The mall as a university of suburban materialism, where Valley Girls 8 and Boys from coast to coast are educated in consumption, has its other lessons in this era of change in family life and sexual mores° and their economic and social ramifications.° The plethora° of products in the mall, plus the pressure on teens to buy them, may contribute to the phenomenon that psychologist David Elkind calls "the hurried child": kids who are exposed to too much of the adult world too quickly, and must respond with a sophistication that belies their still-tender emotional development. Certainly the adult products marketed for children — form-fitting designer jeans, sexy tops for preteen girls — add to the social pressure to look like an adult, along with the home-grown need to understand adult finances (why mothers must work) and adult emotions (when parents divorce).

Kids spend so much time at the mall partly because their parents allow 9 it and even encourage it. The mall is safe, it doesn't seem to harbor any unsavory activities, and there is adult supervision; it is, after all, a controlled environment. So the temptation, especially for working parents, is to let the mall be their babysitter. At least the kids aren't watching TV. But the mall's role as a surrogate mother may be more extensive and more profound.

Karen Lansky, a writer living in Los Angeles, has looked into the subject 10 and she told me some of her conclusions about the effects on its teenaged denizens of the mall's controlled and controlling environment. "Structure is the dominant idea, since true 'mall rats' lack just that in their homelives," she said, "and adolescents about to make the big leap into growing up crave more structure than our modern society cares to acknowledge." Karen pointed out some of the elements malls supply that kids used to get from their families, like warmth (Strawberry Shortcake dolls and similar cute and cuddly merchandise), old-fashioned mothering ("We do it all for you," the fast-food slogan), and even home cooking (the "homemade" treats at the food court).

---

mores: Moral principles or codes of conduct.   **ramifications:** Consequences stemming from an initial plan, act, or process.   **plethora:** Abundance.

    The problem in all this, as Karen Lansky sees it, is that while families 11
nurture children by encouraging growth through the assumption of responsibility and then by letting them rest in the bosom of the family from the
rigors° of growing up, the mall as a structural mother encourages passivity
and consumption, as long as the kid doesn't make trouble. Therefore all
they learn about becoming adults is how to act and how to consume.

    Kids are in the mall not only in the passive role of shoppers — they also 12
work there, especially as fast-food outlets infiltrate the mall's enclosure. There
they learn how to hold a job and take responsibility, but still within the same
value context. When *CBS Reports* went to Oak Park Mall in suburban Kansas
City, Kansas, to tape part of their hour-long consideration of malls, "After the
Dream Comes True," they interviewed a teenaged girl who worked in a fast-
food outlet there. In a sequence that didn't make the final program, she described the major goal of her present life, which was to perfect the curl on
top of the ice-cream cones that were her store's specialty. If she could do that,
she would be moved from the lowly soft-drink dispenser to the more prestigious ice-cream division, the curl on top of the status ladder at her restaurant.
These are the achievements that are important at the mall.

    Other benefits of such jobs may also be overrated, according to Lau- 13
rence D. Steinberg of the University of California at Irvine's social ecology
department, who did a study on teenage employment. Their jobs, he found,
are generally simple, mindlessly repetitive, and boring. They don't really
learn anything, and the jobs don't lead anywhere. Teenagers also work primarily with other teenagers; even their supervisors are often just a little
older than they are. "Kids need to spend time with adults," Steinberg told
me. "Although they get benefits from peer relationships, without parents
and other adults it's one-sided socialization. They hang out with each other,
have age-segregated jobs, and watch TV."

    Perhaps much of this is not so terrible or even so terribly different. Now 14
that they have so much more to contend with in their lives, adolescents
probably need more time to spend with other adolescents without adult im-
positions, just to sort things out. Though it is more concentrated in the mall
(and therefore perhaps a clearer target), the value system there is really the
dominant one of the whole society. Attitudes about curiosity, initiative, self-
expression, empathy, and disinterested learning aren't necessarily made in
the mall; they are mirrored there, perhaps a bit more intensely — as through
a glass brightly.

    Besides, the mall is not without its educational opportunities. There are ⌉ 15
bookstores, where there is at least a short shelf of classics at great prices, and │
other books from which it is possible to learn more than how to do sit-ups. │
There are tools, from hammers to VCRs, and products, from clothes to ├ Education comparison:
records, that can help the young find and express themselves. There are │ positive
older people with stories, and places to be alone or to talk one-on-one with │
a kindred spirit. And there is always the passing show. ⌋

rigors: Harsh difficulties.

The mall itself may very well be an education about the future. I was 16 struck with the realization, as early as my first forays into Greengate,[1] that the mall is only one of a number of enclosed and controlled environments that are part of the lives of today's young. The mall is just an extension, say, of those large suburban schools—only there's Karmelkorn instead of chem lab, the ice rink instead of the gym: It's high school without the impertinence of classes.

Conclusion; writer ends with another quotation —

Growing up, moving from home to school to the mall—from enclosure 17 to enclosure, transported in cars—is a curiously continuous process, without much in the way of contrast or contact with unenclosed reality. Places must tend to blur into one another. But whatever differences and dangers there are in this, the skills these adolescents are learning may turn out to be useful in their later lives. For we seem to be moving inexorably° into an age of pre-planned and regulated environments, and this is the world they will inherit.

Still, it might be better if they had more of a choice. One teenaged girl 18 confessed to *CBS Reports* that she sometimes felt she was missing something by hanging out at the mall so much. "But I'm here," she said, "and this is what I have."

Questions to Start You Thinking

Meaning

1. According to Kowinski, what do teenagers seek at the mall?

2. In paragraph 6, Kowinski quotes a study concluding that mall management and teens share "the same set of values." What are the values they share? What is the effect of these values on teenagers?

3. How do mall experiences shape the kinds of adults these teens become?

4. Kowinski compares the mall experience to high school. In what ways is it similar to high school? How is it different?

Writing Strategies

5. Kowinski examines both negative and positive effects of mall life on teens. In which paragraphs do you find negative effects? Where does he include positive effects? How well does this organization work?

6. Does Kowinski's essay deal predominantly with causes or effects? Where and to what degree does he examine each of these? How would his essay change if he limited his focus to only causes or only effects?

7. Kowinski begins his essay with a quotation from Richard Peck's *Secrets of the Shopping Mall*. Is this an effective beginning? Why or why not? In what other ways might he have begun his essay?

---

inexorably: Incapable of being stopped or deterred.

[1] Greengate Mall in Greensburg, Pennsylvania, where Kowinski began his research on malls. [Eds.]

STUDENT ESSAY

Yun Yung Choi
Invisible Women

Yun Yung Choi examines the adoption of a new state religion in her native Korea and the effects of that adoption on Korean women.

For me, growing up in a small suburb on the outskirts of Seoul, the adults' pref- 1 erence for boys seemed quite natural. All the important people that I knew--doctors, lawyers, policemen, and soldiers--were men. On the other hand, most of the women that I knew were either housekeepers or housewives whose duty seemed to be to obey and please the men of the family. When my teachers at school asked me what I wanted to be when I grew up, I would answer, "I want to be the wife of the president." Because all women must become wives and mothers, I thought, becoming the wife of the president would be the highest achievement for a woman. I knew that the birth of a boy was a greatly desired and celebrated event, whereas the birth of a girl was a disappointing one, accompanied by the frequent words of consolation for the sad parents: "A daughter is her mother's chief help in keeping house."

How would you have answered this question?

These attitudes toward women, widely considered the continuation of an unbro- 2 ken chain of tradition, are, in fact, only a few hundred years old, a relatively short period considering Korea's long history. During the first half of the Yi dynasty, which lasted from 1392 to 1910, and during the Koryo period, which preceded the Yi dynasty, women were treated almost as equals with many privileges that were denied them during the latter half of the Yi dynasty. This turnabout in women's place in Korean society was brought about by one of the greatest influences that shaped the government, literature, and thoughts of the Korean people--Confucianism.°

Throughout the Koryo period, which lasted from 918 to 1392, and throughout 3 the first half of the Yi dynasty, according to Laurel Kendall in her book View from the Inner Room, women were important and contributing members of the society and not marginal and dependent as they later became. Women were, to a large extent, in command of their own lives. They were permitted to own property and receive inheritances from their fathers. Wedding ceremonies were held in the bride's house, where the couple lived, and the wife retained her surname. Women were also allowed freedom of movement--that is, they were able to go outside the house without any feelings of shame or embarrassment.

With the introduction of Confucianism, however, the rights and privileges that 4 women enjoyed were confiscated. The government of the Yi dynasty made great efforts to incorporate into society the Confucian ideologies, including the principle of agnation. This principle, according to Kendall, made men the important members of

Confucianism: Ethical system based on the teachings of Chinese philosopher Confucius (551–479 B.C.).

How do you respond to this historical background?

society and relegated° women to a dependent position. The government succeeded in Confucianizing the country and encouraging the acceptance of Confucian proverbs such as the following: "Men are honored, but women are abased." "A daughter is a 'robber woman' who carries household wealth away when she marries."

The unfortunate effects of this Confucianization in the lives of women were numerous. The most noticeable was the virtual confinement of women. They were forced to remain unseen in the anbang, the inner room of the house. This room was the women's domain, or, rather, the women's prison. Outside, a woman was carried through the streets in a closed sedan chair. Walking outside, she had to wear a veil that covered her face and could travel abroad only after nightfall. Thus, it is no wonder that Westerners traveling through Korea in the late nineteenth century expressed surprise at the apparent absence of women in the country.   5

Women received no formal education. Their only schooling came from government textbooks. By giving instruction on the virtuous° conduct of women, these books attempted to fit women into the Confucian stereotype--meek, quiet, and obedient. Thus, this Confucian society acclaimed particular women not for their talent or achievement but for the degree of perfection with which they were able to mimic the stereotype.   6

A woman even lost her identity in such a society. Once married, she became a stranger to her natal° family, becoming a member of her husband's family. Her name was omitted from the family chokpo, or genealogy book, and was entered in the chokpo of her in-laws as a mere "wife" next to her husband's name.   7

Even a desirable marriage, the ultimate hope for a woman, failed to provide financial and emotional security for her. Failure to produce a son was legal grounds for sending the wife back to her natal home, thereby subjecting the woman to the greatest humiliation and to a life of continued shame. And because the Confucian ideology stressed a wife's devotion to her husband as the greatest of womanly virtues, widows were forced to avoid social disgrace by remaining faithfully unmarried, no matter how young they were. As women lost their rights to own or inherit property, these widows, with no means to support themselves, suffered great hardships. Thus, as Sandra Martielle says in Virtues in Conflict, what the government considered "the ugly custom of remarriage" was slowly eliminated at the expense of women's happiness.   8

This male-dominated system of Confucianism is one of the surviving traditions from the Yi dynasty. Although the Constitution of the Republic of Korea proclaimed on July 17, 1948, guarantees individual freedom and sexual equality, these ideals failed to have any immediate effect on the Korean mentality that stubbornly adheres   9

relegated: Reduced to a less important position.   **virtuous:** Moral, honorable.   **natal:** Relating to one's birth.

to its belief in the superiority of men. Women still regard marriage as their prime objective in life, and little girls still wish to become the doctor's wife, the lawyer's wife, and even the president's wife. But as the system of Confucianism is slowly being forced out of existence by new legal and social standards, perhaps a day will come, after all, when a little girl will stand up in class and answer, "I want to be the president."

Why do you think the writer ends with this quotation?

Questions to Start You Thinking

Meaning

1. What effect does Choi observe? What cause does she attribute it to?
2. What specific changes in Korean culture does Choi attribute to the introduction of Confucianism?
3. What evidence do you find of the writer's critically rethinking an earlier belief and then revising it? What do you think may have influenced her to change her belief?

Writing Strategies

4. What does Choi gain by beginning and ending with her personal experience?
5. Where does Choi use the strategy of comparing and contrasting? Do you think this is effective?
6. How does Choi consider readers for whom her culture might be foreign?
7. Using highlighters or marginal notes, identify the essay's introduction, thesis, major causes or effects, supporting explanations and details for each of these, and conclusion. How effective is the organization of this essay?

Learning by Writing

THE ASSIGNMENT: EXPLAINING CAUSES AND EFFECTS

Pick a disturbing fact or situation that you have observed, and seek out the causes and effects to help you and your readers understand the issue better. You may limit your essay to the causes *or* the effects, or you may include both but emphasize one more than the other. Yun Yung Choi uses the last approach when she briefly identifies the cause of the status of Korean women (Confucianism) but spends most of her essay detailing effects of this cause.

The situation you choose may have affected you and people you know well, such as student loan policies, the difficulty of working while going to school, or divorce in the family. It might have affected people in your city or region—a small voter turnout in an election, decaying bridge supports, or

■ For writing activities for cause and effect, visit <bedfordstmartins.com/ bedguide> and do a keyword search:

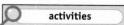
activities

pet owners not using pooper-scoopers. It may affect society at large — identity theft, immigration laws, or the high cost of health care. It might be gender or racial stereotypes on television, binge drinking at parties, spouse abuse, teenage suicide, global warming, student debt, or the use of dragnets for ocean fishing. Don't think you must choose an earthshaking topic to write a good paper. On the contrary, you will do a better job if you are personally familiar with the situation you choose.

Papers written in response to this assignment have included the following:

One student cited her observations of the hardships faced by Indians in rural Mexico as one cause of the recent rebellions there.

Another analyzed the negative attitudes of men toward women at her workplace and the resulting tension, inefficiency, and low production.

A third contended that buildings in Miami are not constructed to withstand hurricanes due, for one reason, to an inadequate inspection system.

GENERATING IDEAS

■ For more strategies for generating ideas, see Ch. 16.

Find a Topic.   What familiar situation would be informative or instructive to explore? This assignment leaves you the option of writing from personal experience, from what you know, what you can find out, or a combination of the two. Begin by letting your thoughts wander over the results of an undesirable situation. Has the situation always been this way? Or has it changed in the last few years? Have things gotten better or worse?

The ideas in the following list may help you search your memory:

DISCOVERY CHECKLIST

___ Has a difficult situation resulted from a change in your life (a new job; a fluctuation in income; personal or family upheaval following death, divorce, accident, illness, or good fortune; a new school)?

___ Has the environment changed (due to air pollution, a flood or a storm, a new industry, the failure of an old industry)?

___ Has a disturbing situation been caused by an invention (the computer, the DVD player, the television, the ATM, the cell phone)?

___ Do certain employment trends cause you concern (for women in management, for blacks in the military, for white males in nursing)?

___ Is a situation on campus or in your neighborhood, city, or state causing problems for you (traffic, housing costs, population, health care)?

■ For more on brainstorming, see pp. 296–97.

When your thoughts begin to percolate, jot down likely topics. Then choose the idea that you care most about and that promises to be neither too large nor too small. A paper confined to the causes of a family's move from New Jersey to Montana might be only one sentence long: "My father's company transferred him." But the subsequent effects of the move on the family might become an interesting essay. On the other hand, you might need hundreds of pages to study all the effects of gangs in urban high schools. Instead, you might consider just one unusual effect, such as gang members staking out territory in the parking lot of a local school.

List Causes and Effects.   Your choice tentatively made, write for ten or fifteen minutes, identifying likely causes and effects. After noting those you see, consider which are immediate (evident and close at hand), which are remote (underlying, more basic, or earlier), and how you might arrange them in a logical sequence or causal chain.

FOCUS ON CAUSAL CHAIN

Remote Causes	→	Immediate Causes	→	SITUATION		→	Immediate Effects	→	Remote Effects
Foreign competition	→	Sales, profits drop	→	**Clothing factory closing**	→	Jobs vanish		→	Town flounders

Once you have figured out the basic causal relationships, focus on complexities or implications. Probe more deeply for contributing, related, or even hidden factors. When you begin to draft your paper, these ideas will be a rich resource, allowing you to concentrate on the causes or effects you find most important and skip any that are minor.

For more on thinking critically, see Ch. 3.

FOCUS ON IMMEDIATE EFFECTS			FOCUS ON REMOTE EFFECTS
Factory workers lose jobs	→	Households curtail spending	Town economy undermined
Grocery and other stores suffer	→	Businesses fold	Food pantry, social services overwhelmed
Workers lose health coverage	→	Health needs ignored	Hospital limits services and doctors leave
Retirees fear benefits lost	→	Confidence erodes	Unemployed and young people leave

Try Mapping the Situation.   If a visual technique might help you analyze the situation, try mapping. Using a blank page, movable sticky notes, or a computer file, identify and position causes and effects in order to show their relationships or relative importance.

For more on mapping, see p. 301.

Consider Sources of Support.   After identifying causes and effects, note your evidence next to each item. You can then see at a glance exactly where you need more material. Star or underline any causes and effects that stand

For advice on finding a few pertinent sources, turn to the Quick Research Guide (the dark-red-edged pages).

Facing the Challenge: Causes and Effects

The major challenge writers face when exploring causal relationships is how to limit the subject. When you explore a given phenomenon—from teenage drug use to the success of your favorite band—devoting equal space to all possible causes and effects will either overwhelm your readers or put them to sleep. Instead, you need to decide what you want to show your readers—and then emphasize the causal relationships that help achieve this purpose.

Rely on your purpose to help you decide which part of the relationship—cause or effect—to stress and how to limit your ideas to strengthen your overall point. If you are writing about your parents' divorce, for example, you may be tempted to discuss all the possible *causes* for their separation and then analyze all the *effects* it has had on you. Your readers, however, won't want to know about every single argument your parents had. Both you and your readers will have a much easier time if you make some decisions about your focus:

- Do you want to concentrate on *causes* or *effects*?
- Which of your explanations are most and least effective?
- How can you emphasize the points that are most important to you?
- Which relatively insignificant or irrelevant ideas can you omit?

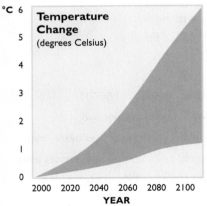

Projected global temperature change. Source: Intergovernmental Panel on Climate Change.

For Choi's complete essay, see pp. 127–29.

out as major ones. A way to rate the items on your list is to ask, How significant is this cause? Would the situation not exist without it? (This major cause deserves a big star.) Or would the situation have arisen without it, for some other reason? (This minor cause might still matter but be less important.) Has this effect had a resounding impact? Is it necessary to explain the results adequately?

As you set priorities—identifying major causes or effects and noting missing information—you may wish to talk with others, use a search engine, or browse the library Web site for sources of supporting ideas, concrete details, and reliable statistics. For example, you might look for illustrations of the problem, accounts of comparable situations, or charts showing current data and projections.

PLANNING, DRAFTING, AND DEVELOPING

Start with a Scratch Outline and Thesis.   Yun Yung Choi's "Invisible Women" follows a clear plan. The essay was written from a brief scratch outline that simply lists the effects of the change:

Intro—Personal anecdote

—Tie with Korean history

—Then add working thesis: The turnabout for women resulted from the influence of Confucianism in all aspects of society.

Comparison and contrast of status of women before and after Confucianism

Effects of Confucianism on women

1. *Confinement*
2. *Little education*
3. *Loss of identity in marriage*
4. *No property rights*

Conclusion: Impact still evident in Korea today but some hints of change

■ For more about informal outlines, see pp. 326–28.

■ For exercises on choosing effective thesis statements, visit <bedfordstmartins.com/bedguide> and do a keyword search:

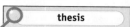

thesis

The paper makes its point: it identifies Confucianism as the reason for the status of Korean women and details four specific effects of Confucianism on women in Korean society. And it shows that cause and effect are closely related: Confucianism is the cause of the change in the status of Korean women, and Confucianism has had specific effects on Korean women.

■ For more about stating your main point in a thesis, see pp. 312–19.

Organize to Show Causes and Effects to Your Audience. The main part of your paper — showing how the situation came about (the causes) or what followed as a result (the effects) or both — more than likely will follow one of these patterns:

I. The situation	I. The situation	I. The situation
II. Its causes	II. Its effects	II. Its causes
		III. Its effects

You can begin planning your paper by grouping the causes and effects and then classifying them as major or minor. If, for example, you are writing about the reasons more college students accumulate credit-card debt now than they did a generation ago, you might list the following:

■ For more planning strategies, see Ch. 17.

1. easy credit
2. high credit limits
3. compulsive buying

On reflection you might decide that compulsive buying — especially of CDs, DVDs, games, and electronic equipment — is a major cause and that the availability of credit actually is a minor one. You could then organize the causes from least to most important, giving the major one more space and the final place in your essay. When your plan seems logical to you, discuss it or share your draft with a classmate, a friend, or your instructor. Ask whether your organization will make sense to someone else.

Introduce the Situation. When you draft the first part of your paper, describe the situation you want to explain in no more than two or three paragraphs. Make clear to your readers your task — explaining causes, explaining effects, or explaining both. Instead of doing this in a flat, mechanical fashion ("Now I am going to explain the causes"), announce your task casually, naturally, as if you were talking to someone: "At first, I didn't realize that keeping six pet cheetahs in our backyard would bother the neighbors." Or, tantalize your readers as one writer did in a paper about her father's sudden move to a Trappist monastery: "The real reason for Father's decision didn't become clear to me for a long while."

■ For more on using sources for support, see Ch. 12 or the Quick Research Guide (the dark-red-edged pages).

■ For exercises on supporting a thesis, visit <bedfordstmartins.com/bedguide> and do a keyword search:

Work in Your Evidence.   Some writers want to rough out a cause-and-effect draft, positioning all the major points first and then circling back to pull in supporting explanations and details. Others want to plunge deeply into each section — stating the main point, elaborating, and working in the evidence all at once. Tables, charts, and graphs can often consolidate information that substantiates or illustrates causes or effects. If such additions would strengthen your essay, place your graphics near the related text discussion, supporting but not duplicating it.

REVISING AND EDITING

■ For more revising and editing strategies, see Ch. 20.

■ For more on stating a thesis, see pp. 312–19.

Because explaining causes and effects takes hard thought, set aside plenty of time for rewriting. As Yun Yung Choi approached her paper's final version, she wanted to rework her thesis with greater precision and more detail.

WORKING THESIS   The turnabout for women resulted from the influence of Confucianism in all aspects of society.

REVISED THESIS   This turnabout in women's place in Korean society was brought about by one of the greatest influences that shaped the government, literature, and thoughts of the Korean people — Confucianism.

She also faced a problem pointed out by classmates who had read her draft: how to make a smooth transition from recalling her own experience to probing causes.

(emphasize that everyone thinks that) ——> *widely*

, a relatively short time, considering Korea's long history

These attitudes toward women, ~~which I once~~ believed to be the continuation of an unbroken chain of tradition, are, in fact, only a few hundred years old. During the *[tell when]* first half of the Yi dynasty, which lasted from 1392 to 1910, and during [the Koryo period,] women were treated almost as equals, with many privileges that were denied them during the latter half of the Yi dynasty. This upheaval in women's place in Korean society was brought about by one of the greatest influences that shaped the government, literature, and thoughts of the Korean people: Confucianism. Because of Confucianism, my birth was not greeted with joy and celebration but rather with these words of consolation: "A daughter is her mother's chief help in keeping house."

(Belongs in opening paragraph)

In revising a paper that traces causes, effects, or both, you might consider questions like these:

REVISION CHECKLIST

___ Have you shown your readers your purpose in presenting causes or effects?

___ Is your explanation thoughtful, searching, and reasonable?

___ Where might you need to reorganize or add transitions so your paper is easy for readers to follow?

If you are tracing causes,

___ Have you made it clear that you are explaining causes?

___ Do you need to add any significant causes?

___ At what points might you need to add more evidence to convince readers that the causal relationships are valid, not just guesses?

___ Do you need to drop any remote causes you can't begin to prove? Or any assertions made without proof?

___ Have you oversimplified by assuming only one small cause accounts for a large phenomenon or that one thing caused another just because the one preceded the other?

If you are determining effects,

___ Have you made it clear that you are explaining effects?

___ What possible effects have you left out? Are any of them worth adding?

___ At what points might you need to supply more evidence that these effects have occurred?

___ Could any effect have resulted not from the cause you describe but from some other cause?

For more on evidence, see pp. 37–42. For more on mistakes in thinking called logical fallacies, see pp. 162–63.

Making a Cause-and-Effect Table

Use the Table menu in your word processor to help you assess the importance of causes and effects. Set up a table with four columns; label them "Major Cause," "Minor Cause," "Major Effect," and "Minor Effect." Divide up your causes and effects accordingly, making entries under each heading. Refine your table as you relate, order, or limit your points.

FOR E-WRITERS

■ For more editing and proofreading strategies, see pp. 384–87.

After you have revised your cause-and-effect essay, edit and proofread it. Carefully check the grammar, word choice, punctuation, and mechanics — and then correct any problems you find. Here are some questions to get you started when editing and proofreading your paper:

■ For more help, turn to the dark-blue-edged pages and find the sections of the Quick Editing Guide noted here.

EDITING CHECKLIST

___ Have you used correct verb tenses and forms throughout? When you describe events in the past, is it clear what happened first and what happened next?	A3
___ Have you avoided creating fragments when adding causes or effects? (Check revisions carefully, especially those beginning "*Because . . .*" or "*Causing . . . .*") Have you avoided comma splices or fused sentences when trying to integrate ideas smoothly?	A1, A2
___ Do your transitions and other introductory elements have commas after them, if these are needed?	C1

FOR PEER RESPONSE

For general questions for a peer editor, see p. 377. For peer response worksheets, visit <bedfordstmartins.com/bedguide> and do a keyword search:

peer

For more on evidence, see pp. 37–42. For mistakes in thinking called logical fallacies, see pp. 162–63.

Let a classmate or friend read your draft, considering how you've analyzed causes or effects. Ask your peer editor to answer questions such as the following: If the writer explains causes,

- Does the writer explain, rather than merely list, causes?

- Do the causes seem logical and possible?

- Are there other causes that the writer might consider? If so, list them.

If the writer explains effects,

- Do all the effects seem to be results of the situation the writer describes?

- Are there other effects that the writer might consider? If so, list them.

For all cause-and-effect papers,

- What is the writer's thesis? Does the explanation of causes or effects help the writer accomplish the purpose of the essay?

- Is the order of supporting ideas clear? Can you suggest a better organization?

- Are you convinced by the writer's logic? Do you see any logical fallacies?

- Are any causes or effects hard to accept?

- Do the writer's evidence and detail convince you? Put stars where more or better evidence is needed.

- If this were your paper, what is the one thing you would be sure to work on before handing it in?

Explaining the News

In class or in your writing group, tell aloud a two-minute story that you invent to explain the causes behind any surprising event in the morning's news. Either realistic explanations or tall tales are acceptable. Prepare some brief notes about your story in advance. Invite the others to comment on it, and, with their reactions in mind, write it down to turn in at the next class, embellished and improved as you wish. If your group wants to tape or podcast its version of the news, select an anchor, decide on the order of your stories, and rehearse first. Invite your class to enjoy and evaluate your presentation.

FOR GROUP LEARNING

OTHER ASSIGNMENTS

1. Pick a change that has taken place during your lifetime — a noticeable, lasting transformation produced by an event or a series of events. Explore its causes and effects to help you and your audience understand that change better. The change might have affected only you, such as a move, a decision, or an alteration in a strong personal opinion or belief. It might have also affected others in your community (a new zoning law), in a region (the growth of a new industry), or in society at large (general access to the Internet). Or it might be a new invention, medical breakthrough, or deep-down shift in the structure or attitudes of society.

2. Explore your own motives and explain your reasons for taking some step or for doing something in a routine way.

3. Read a newspaper or magazine article that probes the causes of some contemporary problem: the shortage of certain types of jobs, for instance, or tuition increases in your state. Can you suggest causes that the article writer ignored? Write an essay in which you argue that the author has or has not done a good job of explaining the causes of this problem.

   For more on supporting a position with sources, see Ch. 12.

Applying What You Learn: Some Uses of Explaining Causes and Effects

In College Courses.   Both writing assignments and examination questions often pose problems in causality.

- One or two paragraphs that explore the causes of a phenomenon or its effects might add depth to a paper on almost any subject — a sociology paper about teenage parenthood or a literature paper on romanticism in American fiction.

- Exam questions may call for you to identify causes ("Trace the causes of the decline of automobile sales in America") or survey effects ("What economic effects were immediately evident when Prohibition was repealed in 1933?").

- Instructors in many courses will ask you to write about causal relationships. In a speech pathology course, you might investigate effects of head trauma, fetal alcohol syndrome, or learning disabilities.

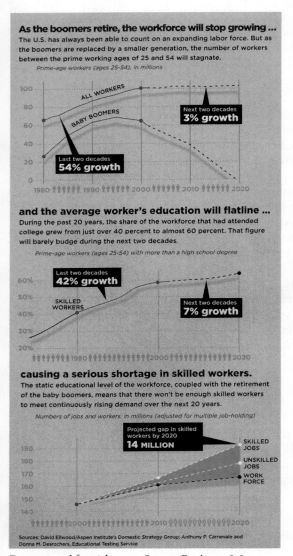

As the boomers retire, the workforce will stop growing ...
The U.S. has always been able to count on an expanding labor force. But as the boomers are replaced by a smaller generation, the number of workers between the prime working ages of 25 and 54 will stagnate.

Prime-age workers (ages 25-54), in millions

ALL WORKERS

BABY BOOMERS

Next two decades
3% growth

Last two decades
54% growth

1980 1990 2000 2010 2020

and the average worker's education will flatline ...
During the past 20 years, the share of the workforce that had attended college grew from just over 40 percent to almost 60 percent. That figure will barely budge during the next two decades.

Prime-age workers (ages 25-54) with more than a high school degree

Last two decades
42% growth

SKILLED
WORKERS

Next two decades
7% growth

1980   2000   2020

causing a serious shortage in skilled workers.
The static educational level of the workforce, coupled with the retirement of the baby boomers, means that there won't be enough skilled workers to meet continuously rising demand over the next 20 years.

Numbers of jobs and workers, in millions (adjusted for multiple job-holding)

Projected gap in skilled
workers by 2020
14 MILLION

SKILLED
JOBS

UNSKILLED
JOBS

WORK
FORCE

2000   2010   2020

Sources: David Ellwood/Aspen Institute's Domestic Strategy Group; Anthony P. Carnevale and Donna M. Desrochers, Educational Testing Service

Data on workforce changes. Source: Business 2.0

In the Workplace.   Understanding causal relationships, often driving issues of the workplace, can make the difference between success or failure.

- Advertising agencies and marketing departments examine causes and effects to determine how to convince consumers to buy.

- State Department officials and military officers analyze international relations and issue reports — the possible consequences of an impending war between Pakistan and India, the effects of instability in the Middle East, or the causes of genocide in Darfur.

- Economic analysts look at circumstances that will produce changes in the workforce.

In Your Community.   Understanding why a problem exists or what might result from a proposed action allows you to add your voice to those who favor the status quo or who support change.

- Your professional or civic organization may outline likely consequences of a proposed practice, making clear the group's stance.

- Images of the long-term effects of dumping in your city's landfill can help build a persuasive poster campaign for recycling.

- A letter sharing evidence of the effects of a dress code on student behavior in other schools can assist school-board members in making a decision beneficial to your child.

Chapter 9
Taking a Stand

Responding to an Image

The banner in this image identifies a group and its position. What is the stance being taken? What issues and concerns might have led to this position? Based on the image, what event do you think it portrays? What might the photographer have wanted to convey?

Both in and outside of class, you'll hear controversial issues discussed — immigration policy, the use of standardized testing, disaster preparedness, global outsourcing of jobs, copyright issues, health care. Even in academic fields, experts don't always agree, and issues may remain controversies for years. Taking a stand in response to such issues will help you understand the controversy and clarify what you believe.

Writing of this kind has a twofold purpose — to state an opinion and to win your readers' respect for it. What you say might or might not change a reader's opinion. But if you fulfill your purpose, a reader at least will see good reasons for your views. In taking a stand, you do these things:

- You state your opinion or stand.
- You give reasons with evidence to support your position.
- You enlist your readers' trust.
- You consider and respect what your readers probably think and feel.

Learning from Other Writers

■ For more on thesis and support, see Chs. 17 and 19.

In the following two essays, the writers take a stand on issues of importance to them. To help you begin to analyze the first reading, look for the notes in the margin. They identify features such as the thesis, or main idea, and the first of the points that support it in a paper that takes a stand.

■ For more such writings, visit <bedfordstmartins.com/bedguide> and do a keyword search:

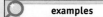

examples

As You Read These Essays That Take a Stand

As you read these essays, ask yourself the following questions:

1. What stand does the writer take? Is it a popular opinion, or does it break from commonly accepted beliefs?
2. How does the writer appeal to readers?
3. How does the writer support his or her position? Is the evidence sufficient to gain your respect? Why or why not?

As a result of persuasive efforts such as Suzan Shown Harjo's essay, the Native American Graves Protection and Repatriation Act was passed in 1990.

Introduction appeals to readers

Suzan Shown Harjo
Last Rites for Indian Dead

What if museums, universities, and government agencies could put your dead relatives on display or keep them in boxes to be cut up and otherwise studied? What if you believed that the spirits of the dead could not rest until their human remains were placed in a sacred area?

THESIS

The ordinary American would say there ought to be a law — and there is, for ordinary Americans. The problem for American Indians is that there

140

are too many laws of the kind that make us the archaeological property of
the United States and too few of the kind that protect us from such insults.

THESIS
taking a stand

Some of my own Cheyenne relatives' skulls are in the Smithsonian Institution today, along with those of at least 4,500 other Indian people who
were violated in the 1800s by the U.S. Army for an "Indian Crania Study." It
wasn't enough that these unarmed Cheyenne people were mowed down by
the cavalry at the infamous Sand Creek massacre; many were decapitated
and their heads shipped to Washington as freight. (The Army Medical Museum's collection is now in the Smithsonian.) Some had been exhumed°
only hours after being buried. Imagine their grieving families' reaction on
finding their loved ones disinterred° and headless.

Point I

Some targets of the army's study were killed in noncombat situations
and beheaded immediately. The officer's account of the decapitation of the
Apache chief Mangas Coloradas in 1863 shows the pseudoscientific nature
of the exercise. "I weighed the brain and measured the skull," the good doctor wrote, "and found that while the skull was smaller, the brain was larger
than that of Daniel Webster."

Supporting evidence

These journal accounts exist in excruciating detail, yet missing are any
records of overall comparisons, conclusions, or final reports of the army
study. Since it is unlike the army not to leave a paper trail, one must wonder
about the motive for its collection.

The total Indian body count in the Smithsonian collection is more than
19,000, and it is not the largest in the country. It is not inconceivable that the
1.5 million of us living today are outnumbered by our dead stored in museums, educational institutions, federal agencies, state historical societies, and
private collections. The Indian people are further dehumanized by being exhibited alongside the mastodons and dinosaurs and other extinct creatures.

Where we have buried our dead in peace, more often than not the sites
have been desecrated. For more than two hundred years, relic-hunting has
been a popular pursuit. Lately, the market in Indian artifacts has brought
this abhorrent activity to a fever pitch in some areas. And when scavengers
come upon Indian burial sites, everything found becomes fair game, including sacred burial offerings, teeth, and skeletal remains.

One unusually well-publicized example of Indian grave desecration occurred two years ago in a western Kentucky field known as Slack Farm, the site
of an Indian village five centuries ago. Ten men — one with a business card
stating "Have Shovel, Will Travel" — paid the landowner $10,000 to lease dig-
ging rights between planting seasons. They dug extensively on the forty-acre
farm, rummaging through an estimated 650 graves, collecting burial goods,
tools, and ceremonial items. Skeletons were strewn about like litter.

What motivates people to do something like this? Financial gain is
the first answer. Indian relic-collecting has become a multimillion-dollar
industry. The price tag on a bead necklace can easily top $1,000; rare pieces
fetch tens of thousands.

Question used as
transition

---

exhumed: Dug up out of the earth.   **disinterred:** Taken out of a place of burial.

And it is not just collectors of the macabre° who pay for skeletal re- 10 mains. Scientists say that these deceased Indians are needed for research that someday could benefit the health and welfare of living Indians. But just how many dead Indians must they examine? Nineteen thousand?

There is doubt as to whether permanent curation of our dead really 11 benefits Indians. Dr. Emery A. Johnson, former assistant Surgeon General, recently observed, "I am not aware of any current medical diagnostic or treatment procedure that has been derived from research on such skeletal remains. Nor am I aware of any during the thirty-four years that I have been involved in American Indian . . . health care."

Indian remains are still being collected for racial biological studies. 12 While the intentions may be honorable, the ethics of using human remains this way without the full consent of relatives must be questioned.

Some relief for Indian people has come on the state level. Almost half 13 of the states, including California, have passed laws protecting Indian burial sites and restricting the sale of Indian bones, burial offerings, and other sacred items. Representative Charles E. Bennett (D-Fla.) and Senator John McCain (R-Ariz.) have introduced bills that are a good start in invoking the federal government's protection. However, no legislation has attacked the problem head-on by imposing stiff penalties at the marketplace, or by changing laws that make dead Indians the nation's property.

Some universities — notably Stanford, Nebraska, Minnesota, and Seattle — 14 have returned, or agreed to return, Indian human remains; it is fitting that institutions of higher education should lead the way.

Congress is now deciding what to do with the government's extensive 15 collection of Indian human remains and associated funerary objects. The secretary of the Smithsonian, Robert McC. Adams, has been valiantly° attempting to apply modern ethics to yesterday's excesses. This week, he announced that the Smithsonian would conduct an inventory and return all Indian skeletal remains that could be identified with specific tribes or living kin.

Transition to concluding proposal — But there remains a reluctance generally among collectors of Indian re- 16 mains to take action of a scope that would have a quantitative impact and a healing quality. If they will not act on their own — and it is highly unlikely that they will — then Congress must act.

Conclusion proposes action — The country must recognize that the bodies of dead American Indian 17 people are not artifacts to be bought and sold as collector's items. It is not appropriate to store tens of thousands of our ancestors for possible future research. They are our family. They deserve to be returned to their sacred burial grounds and given a chance to rest.

The plunder of our people's graves has gone on too long. Let us rebury 18 our dead and remove this shameful past from America's future.

macabre: Gruesome, ghastly.   **valiantly:** Bravely.

Questions to Start You Thinking

Meaning

1. What is the issue Harjo identifies? How extensive does she show it to be?

2. What is Harjo's position on this issue? Where does she first state it?

3. What evidence does Harjo present to refute the claim that housing skeletal remains of Native Americans in museums is necessary for medical research and may benefit living Indians?

Writing Strategies

4. What assumptions do you think Harjo makes about her audience?

5. What types of evidence does Harjo use to support her argument? How convincing is the evidence to you?

6. How does Harjo use her status as a Native American to enhance her position? Would her argument be as credible if it were written by someone of another background?

7. How does she appeal to the emotions of the readers in the essay? In what ways do these strategies strengthen or detract from her logical reasons?

8. Why does Harjo discuss what legislatures and universities are doing in response to the situation?

STUDENT ESSAY

Sam Benen
A Royal Mess

The poker boom has come home to roost. Once an edgy and provocative novelty,° televised poker is now the norm. Go to any college campus at any time and you can find a group of guys playing a no-limit Texas hold'em° game. On the one hand, reasonable people ought not to be alarmed by poker on TV and $20 games amongst friends. On the other hand, a shocking state of affairs has arisen among college students who play online poker. As someone who is highly familiar with the online poker scene at college, I posit° that there are serious hazards associated with college students gambling online.

Part of the danger of online poker is that it is unregulated. Casinos in the United States are not allowed to accept wagers online because of federal interstate commerce laws, so all online casinos are offshore operations. PartyPoker.com, the largest online poker room, states on its Web site that it is "licensed and regulated by the Government of Gibraltar."° Its servers and business operations are offshore and, as a result, not

Sam Benen's opinion piece originally appeared in Business Today, *an online student journal at Princeton University.*

❓ *Do you agree that online poker playing is a serious problem? Why or why not?*

novelty: Something new and exciting.   **Texas hold'em:** A popular variety of poker.   **posit:** State an opinion.   **Gibraltar:** A British colony on a landmass connected to Spain.

subject to any United States laws or taxes. Online poker is also unregulated in the sense that one can play poker online 24 hours a day, 7 days a week, 365 days a year, without exception, and there is no restriction on the amount of money a player can win or lose in a given session. That means a college student could stay up all night and gamble away thousands of dollars. I recall two specific instances on this campus when people I know suffered five-digit losses in online poker. Some time ago, I was talking to a Princeton student (I choose to keep him anonymous) who had recently lost $15,000 in a night. When I asked him how he intended to cope with such a striking downswing, I recall him saying very stoically,° "Yeah, I should probably cool it for a while and focus on other things in life." There is no reason to believe that such horror stories are restricted to Princeton or the Ivy League. Based on the inherent° lack of regulation in online poker, it is easy to imagine students across the nation doing the same.

Since online gambling remains unchecked by our government, a glaring question 3 is whether online poker is legal. The PartyPoker.com "Terms and Conditions of Use" state that you may only play real money games (as opposed to playing money games also offered that do not involve betting of real money) if you are at least eighteen years of age "or such other minimum legal age in the jurisdiction° where you are connecting." The agreement, which one must acknowledge and sign before activating a real money account, also states that it is the player's sole responsibility to abide by° "the laws that apply in the jurisdiction from where you are connecting." In other words, if you are situated somewhere where gambling is illegal, then you are not allowed to play online poker. Even if gambling is legal in your state, you still need to be at least twenty-one to gamble just about everywhere in the United States. If you are gambling online and are underage, then you are breaking the law; not to mention you have falsely signed a contractual agreement stating that you are legally allowed to play (I won't even touch upon kids under eighteen who are playing online poker).

Why is it, then, that so many underage college students play online poker? Part 4 of it is the same reason that so many drink underage: because seemingly everyone does so, and the punishment for getting caught is a slap on the wrists. There is such a low risk of getting caught, and the penalties are lenient° enough that there are effectively no legal ramifications.° [Making it harder to buy] into online poker games is not a significant deterrent to students, either. Despite a recent initiative in which the lion's share° of banks that issue credit and debit cards blocked all online gaming transactions, depositing into online poker is remarkably hassle free. In order to buy in, one can set up an account with a foreign online cash intermediary,° i.e. an equivalent of PayPal operated outside of the United States (the most common are

stoically: Without emotion.   **inherent:** Part of something's nature.   **jurisdiction:** A territory or an area of control.   **abide by:** Follow.   **lenient:** Mild or forgiving.   **ramifications:** Consequences.   **lion's share:** Greatest share; majority.   **intermediary:** Someone or something that comes between (and may aid interaction between) two people or entities.

Firepay.com and Neteller.com), and then use this middleman to channel in the funds. PartyPoker offers an even easier method of depositing, where a player can costlessly write electronic checks from his checking account just by supplying his account number and ABA° routing number. In either case, a player has 24/7/365 real-time access to every dollar in his or her checking account. So much for the idea that it's somehow difficult or complicated to start playing for real, big money online.

Moreover, using a combination of basic poker strategy, common sense, and discipline, a student can earn thousands of dollars a year playing poker online (compare that to a campus job that pays under $10 an hour). Indeed the house always makes money, but an online poker player is not playing against the casino. Rather, players wager against other players who are simultaneously° logged into the game interface° through the server, and the house takes a small percentage of all the money in play as a fee for hosting the game. Most people who play online are impulsive,° irrational,° and sometimes plain stupid; it is very easy for a savvy° individual to capitalize on the weaknesses of others and make money. Many college students who play semiprofessionally try to compute their hourly rate (and other personal statistics), as though playing poker online were some kind of job with a predictable wage over time. With the kind of morons on the Internet throwing away their money the way they do, thinking of poker as a job in which one methodically takes money from less intelligent people is not all that far-fetched.

5

Because it can be fun and easy to make money playing poker online, students often overlook one of the main hazards associated with playing—how to legally handle all the money they make. To clarify, "making money" by playing poker online involves a few steps. Once your account is funded, it functions as a poker wallet where you keep a virtual bankroll. You take money from this wallet to buy chips for the various games. All gains (and losses) from the games are credited to (or deducted from) your account. If the amount of money in your account increases because you win at the tables, you must withdraw against the virtual dollars in your poker wallet if you want to realize the gains. The money flows out of the poker account via the same financial intermediary through which you funded the account, and the profit appears on your bank statement within a few business days. Now, the quagmire:° every citizen is bound to report all sources of income to the IRS, but how would a college student claim online poker gains? If you are nineteen years old, then you don't want to admit that you made the money gambling underage, but the only alternative is to defraud the IRS. The people I know who make a substantial amount of money gambling online are split down the middle between those who don't claim it at

6   *Do colleges have any responsibility to address student gambling? If so, what actions might they take?*

ABA: American Bankers Association.   **simultaneously:** At the same time.   **interface:** Means of accessing a computer program or Web site.   **impulsive:** Acting with little or no thought or reflection.   **irrational:** Without reason or logic.   **savvy:** Knowledgeable. **quagmire:** A messy situation (literally, a swamp).

all (which, to my mind, is a blatant° evasion of income tax) and those who claim it as miscellaneous income. I wonder what an IRS agent would think if he were auditing someone who had $10,000 in "miscellaneous income" at age nineteen. By the way, in the event of an audit, all poker cash-outs are completely traceable.

Do you agree that online casinos should take more responsibility for screening users? Why or why not?

It strikes me as particularly scary that so much of online poker playing by   7
college students is illegal. It also disturbs me that online casinos do not perform any kind of background check on the accounts they are opening to see whether the players are underage in their jurisdiction. I won't even expound° upon the addictive element of online poker that is potentially destructive to a student's grades and so-cial life. Nevertheless, there is something intrinsically° wrong with college students having access to unlimited gambling for unlimited amounts of money. In reality, thankfully, most students I know who play poker online play for low stakes and treat it as an innocent waste of time. I don't find any fault with students who keep up to a few hundred dollars in their poker account to play an occasional game. But even if online poker is a relatively harmless vice° most of the time, it has the capacity, albeit° seldom, to devastate a student. Even if a student is profiting financially, there is the murky° issue of income tax. From personal experience, I can say that online poker is a lot of fun and potentially very profitable with proper play, but the whole world of online poker is laden with legal risks, gray areas, and very real detriments.°

Questions to Start You Thinking

Meaning

1. What points does Benen make to support his position that online poker playing among students has serious consequences?
2. Why, according to Benen, do so many students play online poker despite the risks?
3. What kind of gambling, according to the author, is not a cause for concern?

Writing Strategies

4. What kind of support does Benen use to back up his claims about the dan-gers of online poker? Do you find his argument effective? Why or why not?
5. To what extent does Benen account for other points of view? How does the inclusion (or absence) of opposing views affect your opinion on the issue?
6. This article was written for a student business journal. How might Benen change the article if he were writing for a parenting magazine?
7. Using highlighters or marginal notes, identify the essay's introduction, the-sis, major points or reasons, supporting evidence for each point, and con-clusion. How effective is the organization of this essay?

blatant: Clear or obvious.   **expound:** To state in detail.   **intrinsically:** By nature. **vice:** An immoral deed or activity.   **albeit:** Although.   **murky:** Unclear or uncertain. **detriments:** Negative consequences.

Learning by Writing

THE ASSIGNMENT: TAKING A STAND

Find a controversy that rouses your interest. It might be a current issue, a long-standing one, or a matter of personal concern: military benefits for national guard troops sent to war zones, the contribution of sports to a school's educational mission, or the need for menu changes at the cafeteria to accommodate ethnic, religious, and personal preferences. Your purpose isn't to solve a social or moral problem but to make clear exactly where you stand on an issue and to persuade your readers to respect your position, perhaps even to accept it. As you reflect on your topic, you may change your position, but don't shift positions in the middle of your essay.

Assume that your readers are people who may or may not be familiar with the controversy, so provide some background or an overview to help them understand the situation. Furthermore, your readers may not have taken sides yet or may hold a position different from yours. You'll need to consider their views and choose strategies that will enlist their support.

Here are brief summaries of a few good papers that take a stand:

A writer who pays her own college costs disputed the opinion that working during the school year provides a student with valuable knowledge. Citing

■ For writing activities for taking a stand, visit <bedfordstmartins.com/ bedguide> and do a keyword search:

🔍   **activities**

Facing the Challenge: Taking a Stand

The major challenge writers face when taking a stand is to gather enough relevant evidence to support their position. Without such evidence, you'll convince only those who agreed with you in the first place. You also won't persuade readers by ranting emotionally about an issue or insulting as ignorant those who hold different opinions. Moreover, few readers respect an evasive writer who avoids taking a stand.

What does work is respect — yours for the views of readers who will, in turn, respect your opinion, even if they don't agree with it. You convey — and gain — respect when you anticipate readers' objections or counterarguments, demonstrate knowledge of these alternate views, and present evidence that addresses others' concerns as it strengthens your argument.

To anticipate and find evidence that acknowledges other views, list groups that might have strong opinions on your topic. Then try putting yourself in the shoes of a member of each group by writing a paragraph on the issue from *her* point of view.

• What would her opinion be?

• On what grounds might she object to your argument?

• How can you best address her concerns and overcome her objections?

Your paragraph will suggest additional evidence to support your claims.

her painful experience, she maintained that devoting full time to studies is far better than juggling school and work.

Another writer challenged his history textbook's portrayal of Joan of Arc as "an ignorant farm girl subject to religious hysteria."

A member of the wrestling team argued that the number of weight categories in wrestling should be increased because athletes who overtrain to qualify for the existing categories often damage their health.

GENERATING IDEAS

For this assignment, you will need to select an issue, take a stand, develop a clear position, and assemble evidence that supports your view.

■ For more strategies for generating ideas, see Ch. 16.

■ For more on brainstorming, see pp. 296–97. For more on keeping a journal, see pp. 306–07.

Find an Issue.   The topic for this paper should be an issue or controversy that interests both you and your audience. Try brainstorming a list of possible topics. To get started, look at the headlines of a newspaper or newsmagazine, review the letters to the editor, check the political cartoons on the opinion page, or watch for stories or photos on civic demonstrations or protests. You might also consult the indexes to *CQ Researcher* or *Opposing Viewpoints* in the library, watch a news broadcast, use a search engine to browse news or opinion Web sites, talk with friends, or consider topics raised in class. If you keep a journal, look over your entries to see what has perplexed or angered you. If you need to understand the issue better or aren't sure you want to take a stand on it, investigate by freewriting, reading, or turning to other sources.

Student war protest

■ For advice on finding a few sources, see B1–B2 in the Quick Research Guide (the dark-red-edged pages).

Once you have a list of possible topics, drop those that seem too broad or complex or that you don't know much about. Weed out anything that might not hold your interest or that of your readers. From your new, shorter list, pick the issue or controversy for which you can make the strongest argument.

Start with a Question and a Thesis.   At this stage, many writers find it useful to pose the issue as a question — a question that will be answered through the position they take. Skip vague questions that most readers wouldn't debate or convert them to questions that allow different stands.

VAGUE QUESTION   Is stereotyping bad?

CLEARLY DEBATABLE   Should we fight gender stereotypes in advertising?

You can help focus your position by stating it in a sentence—a thesis, or statement of your stand. Your statement can answer your question:

■ For more on stating a thesis, see pp. 312–19.

WORKING THESIS   We should expect advertisers to fight rather than reinforce gender stereotypes.

OR   Most people who object to gender stereotypes in advertising need to get a sense of humor.

Your thesis should invite continued debate, not state a fact, by taking a strong position that could be argued.

FACT   Hispanics constitute 16 percent of the community but only 3 percent of our school population.

WORKING THESIS   Our school should increase its outreach to the Hispanic community, which is underrepresented on campus.

Use Formal Reasoning to Refine Your Position.   When you take a position about a debatable matter, you are likely to use reasoning as well as specific evidence to support your position. A *syllogism* is a series of statements, or premises, used in traditional formal logic to lead deductively to a logical conclusion.

MAJOR STATEMENT   All students must pay tuition.

MINOR STATEMENT   You are a student.

CONCLUSION   Therefore, you must pay tuition.

You

All students must pay tuition

Nonstudents

For a syllogism to be logical, ensuring that its conclusion always applies, its major and minor statements must be true, its definitions of terms must remain stable, and its classification of specific persons or items must be accurate. In real-life arguments, such tidiness may be hard to achieve.

For example, maybe we all agree with the major statement on page 149: all students must pay tuition. However, some students owe tuition, but it is paid for them through a loan or scholarship. Others are admitted under special programs, such as a free-tuition benefit for families of college employees or a back-to-college program for retirees. Further, the word *student* is general; it might apply to students at public high schools who pay no tuition. Next, everyone might agree that you are a student, but maybe you haven't completed registration or the computer has mysteriously dropped you from the class list. Such complications can threaten the success of your conclusion, especially if your audience doesn't accept it. In fact, many civic and social arguments revolve around questions such as these: What — exactly — is the category or group affected? Is its definition or consequence stable — or does it vary? Who falls in or out of the category?

Use Informal Toulmin Reasoning to Refine Your Position.   A contemporary approach to logic is presented by the philosopher Stephen Toulmin in *The Uses of Argument*. He describes an informal way of arguing that acknowledges the power of assumptions in our day-to-day reasoning. This approach starts with a concise statement — the essence of an argument — that makes a claim and supplies a reason to support it.

                              ┌──────── CLAIM ────────┐ ┌────── REASON ──────┐
          Students should boycott the campus cafeteria <u>because</u> the food costs too much.

You develop a claim by supporting your reasons with evidence — your *data* or grounds. For example, your evidence might include facts about the cost of lunches on campus, especially in contrast to local fast-food options, and statistics about the limited resources of most students enrolled at your campus.

However, most practical arguments rely on a *warrant*, your thinking about the connection or relationship between your claim and your supporting data. Because you accept this connection and assume that it applies, you generally assume that others also take it for granted. For instance, nearly all students probably would accept your assumption that a campus cafeteria should serve the needs of its customers. Many might also agree that students should take action rather than allow a campus cafeteria to take advantage of them by charging high prices. Even so, you could state your warrant directly if you thought that your readers would not see the same connection that you do. You also could back up your warrant, if necessary, in various ways:

- using facts, perhaps based on quality and cost comparisons with food service operations on other campuses

- using logic, perhaps based on research findings about the relationship between cost and nutrition for institutional food as well as the importance of good nutrition for brain function and learning

■ For more on appeals, see pp. 40–41.

- making emotional appeals, perhaps based on happy memories of the cafeteria or irritation with its options

- making ethical appeals, perhaps based on the college mission statement or other expressions of the school's commitment to students

As you develop your reasoning, you might adjust your claim or your data to suit your audience, your issue, or your refined thinking. For instance, you might *qualify* your argument (perhaps limiting your objections to most, but not all, of the cafeteria prices). You might also add a *rebuttal* by identifying an *exception* to it (perhaps excluding the fortunate, but few, students without financial worries due to good jobs or family support). Or you might simply reconsider your claim, concluding that the campus cafeteria is, after all, convenient for students and that the manager might be willing to offer more inexpensive options without a student boycott.

> ─────────── REVISED CLAIM ───────────── ┐ ┌─ REASON ─
> The campus cafeteria should offer less expensive options <u>because</u> most
>
> students can't afford a well-rounded meal at current prices.

Toulmin reasoning is especially effective for making claims like these:

- Fact—*Loss of polar ice can accelerate ocean warming.*

- Cause—*The software company went bankrupt because of its excessive borrowing and poor management.*

- Value—*Cell phone plan A is a better deal than cell phone plan B.*

- Policy—*Admissions policies at Triborough University should be less restrictive.*

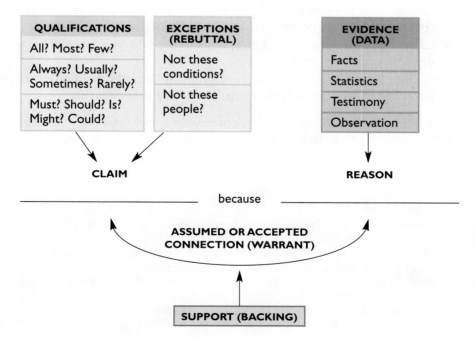

Use these questions to develop or clarify your reasoning as you take a stand:

___ What issue or controversy concerns you? What current debate engages you?

___ What position do you want to take? How can you state your stand? What evidence might you need to support it?

___ How might you refine your working thesis? How could you make your statements more accurate, your definitions clearer, or your categories more exact?

___ What assumptions are you making? What clarification of or support for these assumptions might your audience need?

___ How might you qualify your thesis? What exceptions should you note? What other views might you want to recognize?

Select Evidence to Support Your Position.　As you begin to look for evidence to support your position or claim, consider the issue in terms of the three general types of claims — claims that require substantiation, claims that provide evaluation, and claims that endorse policy.

1. Claims of substantiation require examining and interpreting information in order to resolve disputes about facts, circumstances, causes or effects, definitions, or the extent of a problem, as in these examples:

- Certain types of cigarette ads, such as the once-popular Joe Camel ads, significantly encourage smoking among teenagers.

- Despite a few well-publicized exceptions to the rule, police brutality in this country is not a major problem.

- On the whole, bilingual education programs actually help students learn English more quickly than total immersion programs do.

2. Claims of evaluation consider right or wrong, appropriateness or inappropriateness, worth or lack of worth involved in issues, as in these instances:

FOR GROUP LEARNING

Making a Claim

Have each member of your writing group write out, in one complete sentence, the core claim or position he or she will support. Drop all these "position statements" into a hat, with no names attached. Then, draw and read each aloud in turn. For each position, invite the group to suggest useful supporting evidence, counterevidence, and possible sources for both. Ask the group's recorder to list suggestions on a separate page for each claim. Finally, match up writers with claims, and share reactions. If this activity causes you to alter your stand, be thankful: it will be easier to revise now than later.

- Research using fetal tissue is unethical in a civilized society.
- English-only legislation promotes cultural intolerance in our society.
- Keeping children in foster care for years, instead of releasing them for adoption, is wrong.

3. Claims of policy challenge or defend approaches for achieving generally accepted goals, as in the following:

- The federal government should support the distribution of clean needles to reduce the rate of HIV infection among intravenous drug users.
- Denying illegal immigrant children enrollment in public schools will reduce the problem of illegal immigration.
- All teenagers accused of murder should be tried as adults.

To help you decide how to support your claim, try to reduce it to its core question. Then brainstorm or use other planning strategies to figure out what reliable and persuasive evidence might answer the question.

For more on planning, see Ch. 17.

TYPE OF CLAIM	CORE QUESTION	POSSIBLE SUPPORTING EVIDENCE
Substantiation	What happened?	• Facts and information (parties involved, dates, times, places) and clear definitions of terms (such as *police brutality* or *total immersion*)
		• Logical, well-supported reasoning patterns such as comparison and contrast (using statistics to contrast "a few well-publicized exceptions" with a majority of instances that are "not a problem") or cause-and-effect analysis (using information from authorities or investigative reports to demonstrate how actions of tobacco companies "significantly encourage smoking" or bilingual programs "help students learn English faster")
Evaluation	What is right?	• Explanations or definitions of appropriate criteria for judging or assessing (deciding what's "unethical in a civilized society")
		• Corresponding details and reasons showing how the topic does or does not meet the criteria (details or applications of English-only legislation that meet the criteria for "cultural intolerance" or reasons with supporting details that show why years of foster care meet the criteria for being "wrong")
Policy	What should be done?	• Explanations and definition of the policy goal (assuming that most in your audience agree that it is desirable to reduce "the rate of HIV infection" or "the problem of illegal immigration" or to try murderers in the same way regardless of age)
		• Corresponding details and reasons showing how your policy recommendation would meet the goal (such as results of "clean needle" trials or examples of crime statistics and cases involving teen murderers) and, if needed, explanations or definitions of the policy's limits or applications (such as why some teens should not be tried as adults because of their situations)

Consider Your Audience as You Develop Your Claim.   The nature of your audience might influence the type of claim you choose to make. For example, suppose you wish to promote the distribution of free condoms in high school. The following table illustrates how the responses of your audience might vary with your claim.

These three types of claims may also be used as support for a position. Stating supporting claims as supporting points can provide topic sentences to help your reader follow your reasoning. Each topic sentence can establish one of your points as it introduces supporting examples, statistics, or other evidence.

■ For more about forms of evidence, see pp. 37–42.

■ For more about using sources, see Ch. 12 and the Quick Research Guide (the dark-red-edged pages).

Assemble Supporting Evidence.   Your claim stated, you'll need evidence to support it. What is evidence? It is anything that demonstrates the soundness of your position and the points you make in your argument—facts, statistics, observations, expert testimony, illustrations, examples, and case studies.

The three most important sources of evidence are these:

1. *Facts, including statistics.*   Facts are statements that can be verified by objective means; statistics are facts expressed in numbers. Facts usually form the basis of a successful argument.
2. *Expert testimony.*   Experts are people with knowledge of a particular field gained from study and experience.
3. *Firsthand observation.*   Your own observations can be persuasive if you can assure your readers that your account is accurate.

AUDIENCE	TYPE OF CLAIM	POSSIBLE EFFECT ON AUDIENCE
Conservative parents who believe that free condoms would promote immoral sexual behavior	*Evaluation:* In order to save lives and prevent unwanted pregnancies, distributing free condoms in high school is our moral duty.	Counterproductive if the parents feel that you are accusing them of immorality for not agreeing with you
Conservative parents who believe that free condoms would promote immoral sexual behavior	*Substantiation:* Distributing free condoms in high school can effectively reduce pregnancy rates and the spread of STDs, especially AIDS, without substantially increasing the rate of sexual activity among teenagers.	Possibly persuasive, based on effectiveness, if parents feel that you recognize their desire to protect their children from harm, no matter what, and your evidence deflates their main fear (promoting sexual activity)
School administrators who want to do what's right but don't want hordes of angry parents pounding down the school doors	*Policy:* Distributing free condoms in high school to prevent unwanted pregnancies and the spread of STDs, including AIDS, is best accomplished as part of a voluntary sex education program that strongly emphasizes abstinence as the primary preventative.	Possibly persuasive if administrators see that you address health and pregnancy issues without setting off parental outrage (by proposing a voluntary program that would promote abstinence, thus addressing a primary concern of parents)

Of course, evidence must be used carefully to avoid defending logical fallacies — common mistakes in thinking — and making statements that lead to wrong conclusions. Examples are easy to misuse (claiming proof by example or using too few examples). Because two professors you know are dissatisfied with state-mandated testing programs, you can't claim that all or even most professors are. Even if you surveyed more professors at your school, you could speak only generally of "many professors." To claim more, you might need to conduct scientific surveys, access reliable statistics in the library or on the Internet, or solicit the views of a respected expert in the area.

For more on logical fallacies, see pp. 162–63.

Record Evidence.   For this assignment, you will need to record your evidence in written form. Take notes in a notebook, on index cards, or in a computer file. Be sure to note exactly where each piece of information comes from. Keep the form of your notes flexible so that you can easily rearrange them as you plan your draft.

Test and Select Evidence to Persuade Your Audience.   Now that you've collected some evidence, you need to sift through it to decide which pieces of information to use. Evidence is useful and trustworthy when it is accurate, reliable, up-to-date, to the point, representative, appropriately complex, and sufficient and strong enough to back the claim and persuade your readers. You may find that your evidence supports a stand different from the one you intended to take. Might you find some facts, testimony, and observations that would support your original position after all? Or should you rethink your position? If so, revise your working thesis. Does your evidence cluster around several points or reasons? If so, use your evidence to help plan the sequence of your essay.

For more on testing evidence, see pp. 39–40.

In addition, consider whether information presented visually would strengthen your case or make your evidence easier for readers to grasp. For example, graphs can effectively show facts or figures, tables can convey terms or comparisons, and photographs or other illustrations can substantiate situations. Test each visual as you would test other evidence for accuracy, reliability, and relevance. Mention each visual in your text, and place the visual close to that reference. Cite the source of any visual you use and of any data you consolidate in your own graph or table.

For more on the use of visuals and their placement, see pp. 410–16.

Most effective arguments take opposing viewpoints into consideration whenever possible. Use these questions to help you assess your evidence from this standpoint.

ANALYZE YOUR READERS' POINTS OF VIEW

- What are their attitudes? Interests? Priorities?
- What do they already know about the issue?
- What do they expect you to say?
- Do you have enough appropriate evidence that they'll find convincing?

FOCUS ON THOSE WITH DIFFERENT OR OPPOSING OPINIONS

- What are their opinions or claims?
- What is their evidence?
- Who supports their positions?
- Do you have enough appropriate evidence to show why their claims are weak, only partially true, misguided, or just plain wrong?

ACKNOWLEDGE AND REBUT THE COUNTERARGUMENTS

- What are the strengths of other positions? What might you want to concede or grant to be accurate or relevant?
- What are the limitations of other positions? What might you want to question or challenge?
- What facts, statistics, testimony, observations, or other evidence would support questioning, qualifying, challenging, or countering other views?

PLANNING, DRAFTING, AND DEVELOPING

■ For more on stating a thesis, see pp. 312–19.

Reassess Your Position and Your Thesis.   Now that you have looked into the issue, what is your current position? If necessary, revise the thesis that you formulated earlier. Then summarize your reasons for holding this view, and list your supporting evidence.

WORKING THESIS   We should expect advertisers to fight rather than reinforce gender stereotypes.

REFINED THESIS   Consumers should spend their shopping dollars thoughtfully in order to hold advertisers accountable for reinforcing rather than resisting gender stereotypes.

■ For exercises on choosing effective thesis statements, visit <bedfordstmartins.com/ bedguide> and do a keyword search:

thesis

■ For more on outlines, see pp. 325–33.

Organize Your Material to Persuade Your Audience.   Arrange your notes into the order you think you'll follow, perhaps making an outline. One useful pattern is the classical form of argument:

1. Introduce the subject to gain the readers' interest.
2. State your main point or thesis.
3. If useful, supply the historical background or an overview of the situation.
4. Present your points or reasons and provide evidence to support them.
5. Refute the opposition.
6. Reaffirm your main point.

■ For exercises on supporting a thesis, visit <bedfordstmartins.com/ bedguide> and do a keyword search:

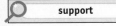
support

Especially when you expect readers to be hostile to your position, you may want to take the opposite approach: refute the opposition first, then replace those views by building a logical chain of evidence that leads to your main point, and finally state your position. If you state your position too early, you might alienate resistant readers or make them defensive. Of course, you can always try both approaches to see which one works better. Note also that some papers will be mostly based on refutation (countering

Making Columns of Appeals

Try making three columns to write about your logical, emotional, and ethical appeals. Using the Format menu, select "Columns," and click on the number "3." Label the first column "Logical Appeals." Here write the claims and support that rely on reasoning and sound evidence. Create the next column, generally by going to the Insert menu, clicking on "Break," selecting "Column break," and clicking "OK." Label your second column "Emotional Appeals," and note the claims and support that may affect readers' emotions. Now create a third column, headed "Ethical Appeals." Record here your claims and support based on values and your understanding of the values of opposing points of view. To move back and forth between columns, simply move your cursor. As you reread each column, consider how to relate your claims and support across columns, how to organize your ideas persuasively, and how best to merge or separate your logical, emotional, and ethical appeals. Try color coding if you want to identify related ideas.

FOR E-WRITERS

opposing views) and some mostly on confirmation (directly supporting your position). Others might even alternate refutation and confirmation rather than separate them.

Define Your Terms.   To prevent misunderstanding, make clear any unfamiliar or questionable terms used in your thesis. If your position is "Humanists are dangerous," give a short definition of what you mean by *humanists* and by *dangerous* early in the paper.

Attend to Logical, Emotional, and Ethical Appeals.   The logical appeal engages readers' intellect; the emotional appeal touches their hearts; the ethical appeal draws on their sense of fairness and reasonableness. A persuasive argument usually operates on all three levels. For example, you might use all three appeals to support a thesis about the need to curb accidental gunshot deaths, as the following table illustrates.

▨ For more on appeals, see pp. 40–41.

TYPE OF APPEAL	WAYS OF MAKING THE APPEAL	POSSIBLE SUPPORTING EVIDENCE
Logical (logos)	• Rely on clear reasoning and sound evidence to influence a reader's thinking. • Demonstrate what you claim, and don't claim what you can't demonstrate. • Test and select your evidence.	• Supply current and reliable statistics about gun ownership and accidental shootings. • Prepare a bar graph that shows the number of incidents each year in Lion Valley during the past ten years, using data from the county records. • Describe the immediate and long-term consequences of a typical shooting accident.

(*continued on next page*)

TYPE OF APPEAL	WAYS OF MAKING THE APPEAL	POSSIBLE SUPPORTING EVIDENCE
Emotional (pathos)	• Choose examples and language that will influence a reader's feelings. • Include effective images, but don't overdo them. • Complement logical appeals, but don't replace them.	• Describe the wrenching scenario of a father whose college-age son unexpectedly returns home at 3 A.M. The father mistakes his son for an intruder and shoots him, throwing the family into turmoil. • Use quotations and descriptions from newspaper accounts to show reactions of family members and neighbors.
Ethical (ethos)	• Use a tone and approach that appeal to your reader's sense of fairness and reasonableness. • Spell out your values and beliefs, and acknowledge values and beliefs of others with different opinions. • Establish your credentials, if any, and the credentials of experts you cite. • Instill confidence in your readers so that they see you as a caring, trustworthy person with reliable views.	• Establish your reasonable approach by acknowledging the views of hunters and others who store guns at home and follow recommended safety procedures. • Supply the credentials or affiliation of experts ("Raymond Fontaine, public safety director for the town of Lion Valley"). • Note ways in which experts have established their authority ("During my interview with Ms. Dutton, she related recent incidents involving gun accidents in the home, testifying to her extensive knowledge of this issue in our community.")

■ For pointers on integrating and documenting sources, see Ch. 12 and D6 and E1–E2 in the Quick Research Guide (the dark-red-edged pages).

■ For more revising and editing strategies, see Ch. 20.

Credit Your Sources.   As you write, make your sources of evidence clear. One simple way to do so is to incorporate your source into the text: "According to an article in the October 15, 2007, issue of *Time*" or "According to my history professor, Dr. Harry Cleghorn..."

REVISING AND EDITING

When you're writing a paper taking a stand, you may be tempted to fall in love with the evidence you've gone to such trouble to collect. Taking out information is hard to do, but if it is irrelevant, redundant, or weak, the evidence won't help your case. Play the crusty critic as you reread your paper. Consider outlining what it actually includes so that you can check for missing or unnecessary points or evidence. Pay special attention to the suggestions of friends or classmates who read your draft for you. Apply their advice by ruthlessly cutting unneeded material, as in the following passage:

> The school boundary system requires children who are homeless or whose
> families move frequently to change schools repeatedly. ~~They often lack clean
> clothes, winter coats, and required school supplies.~~ As a result, these children

Enlist several other students to read your draft critically and tell you whether they accept your arguments. For a paper in which you take a stand, ask your peer editors to answer questions such as these:

- Can you state the writer's claim?

- Do you have any problems following or accepting the reasons for the writer's position? Would you make any changes in the reasoning?

- How persuasive is the writer's evidence? What questions do you have about it? Can you suggest good evidence the writer has overlooked?

- Has the writer provided enough transitions to guide you through the argument?

- Has the writer made a strong case? Are you persuaded to his or her point of view? If not, is there any point or objection that the writer could address to make the argument more compelling?

- If this were your paper, what is the one thing you would be sure to work on before handing it in?

FOR PEER RESPONSE

For general questions for a peer editor, see pp. 377.

struggle to establish strong relationships with teachers, to find caring advocates at school, and even to make friends to join for recess or lunch.

Use the Draft Doctor (pp. 160–61) to help you figure out how to improve your draft. Skim down the left column to identify questions you might ask about problems in your draft. When you answer a question with "Yes" or "Maybe," move straight across the row to the Diagnose column next to that question. Use the diagnostic activities to identify gaps or weaknesses, and then move across the row again to the Treat column on the right. Use the advice that suits your problem as you revise.

As you continue to revise, here are some questions to consider:

For online help from the Draft Doctor, visit <bedfordstmartins.com/bedguide>.

REVISION CHECKLIST

___ Is your main point, or thesis, clear? Do you stick to it rather than drifting into contradictions?

___ Where might you need better reasons or more evidence?

___ Have you tried to keep in mind your readers and what would appeal to them? Where have you answered their likely objections?

___ Have you defined all necessary terms and explained your points clearly?

___ Is your tone suitable for your readers? Are you likely at any places to alienate them, or, at the other extreme, to sound weak or apologetic?

___ Might your points seem stronger if arranged in a different sequence?

___ Have you unfairly omitted any evidence that would hurt your case?

___ In rereading your paper, do you have any excellent, fresh thoughts? If so, where might you make room for them?

Draft Doctor: Strengthening Support for a Stand

If you sense a problem, ASK	If you answer *Yes/Maybe*, DIAGNOSE	If you diagnose a problem, TREAT
Missing Points? Did I leave out some of the main points that I planned to include or that I promised in my thesis?	• List the main points you meant to include. • List the main points that your thesis states or suggests. • Check both lists against your draft by highlighting each point in your draft.	• Add any missing point. • Express any assumptions—points, main ideas, reasons—that are in your head but not in your draft. • Revise your thesis, adding or dropping points, until it makes a promise you can deliver to readers.
Missing Supporting Evidence? Did I leave out evidence—facts, statistics, expert testimony, firsthand observations, details, or examples—needed to support my points?	• Highlight or color code each bit of supporting evidence in your draft. • Put a check by any passages that lack supporting evidence. • Jot reminders to yourself about where to add more evidence.	• Add any missing evidence that you meant to include. • For each checked passage, brainstorm or ask questions (who, what, where, when, why, how) to decide what support readers might expect. • Add the facts, statistics, expert testimony, observations, details, or examples needed to support each main point.
Vague Support? Would any of the support in my draft seem unclear to my audience?	• Read your draft aloud, listening to it as a reader would. • Mark any vague or imprecise patches. **Draft:** A new student parking lot should be constructed now because delaying is *a bad idea*. [What is "a bad idea"?]	• State each point plainly and directly enough that it will be clear to your audience. • Use simple, direct words to replace any vague language. **Revision:** A new student parking lot should be constructed now because any delay will frustrate current students and might reduce future enrollment.
Inappropriate Support? Would my instructor (or others) find any of my supporting evidence unsuitable for this type of paper?	• Reread the assignment (or the criteria in your syllabus) to figure out what support is expected. • Mark any support that might not meet expectations.	• Drop anything that ignores what's required. For example, if you are asked to explain the point made in a reading, don't tell a personal story instead.

If you sense a problem, ASK	If you answer *Yes/Maybe*, DIAGNOSE	If you diagnose a problem, TREAT
Irrelevant Support? Would readers find any of my support unrelated or off-topic?	• Reread your thesis statement. Use an *X* to mark anything that doesn't directly support it.	• Return to each mark, and rework or drop any supporting evidence that strays from your thesis, or revise your thesis to align it accurately with your support. • Decide whether you need to add more relevant information.
Disconnected Support? Does my support seem disconnected from the sequence of my draft? Does my draft seem to jump from point to point?	• Underline your thesis for easy reference. • Place a check by any support that isn't clearly connected to your thesis in your draft, not just in your mind. • Highlight your transitions so you can see where they are sparse or missing.	• Connect your thesis and your support by previewing or explaining how they relate (*The primary reasons why ..., The four stages ..., Several traditional explanations ..., This event triggered ...*). • Add transitions to show the sequence of ideas (*first, second, next, then, finally*) or set priorities (*a minor point, despite, most importantly*).
One-Sided Support? Have I skipped mentioning opposing or alternative perspectives? Have I mentioned them but treated them disrespectfully?	• Highlight passages in which you recognize other points of view (or copy them into a separate file) so that you can look at them on their own. • Read these passages to see whether they sound fair.	• Identify other points of view if they are expected and you have left them out. • Acknowledge credible alternative views, agreeing or explaining your differences. • Reasonably challenge or counter questionable views. • Edit your wording so your tone is respectful of others.
Any Other Weak Support? After a final look at the supporting points and evidence in my draft, should I revise anything else?	• Read your draft out loud, marking any support that sounds weak or awkward. • Ask your peer editors how to improve support for your stand.	• Return to each mark to add facts, statistics, expert testimony, observations, or examples. • Consider the useful suggestions of your peers. • Revise until your draft does what you want it to do.

■ For more editing and
proofreading strategies,
see pp. 384–87.

After you have revised your argument, edit and proofread it. Carefully check the grammar, word choice, punctuation, and mechanics — and then correct any problems you find. Wherever you have given facts and figures as evidence, check for errors in names and numbers. Here are some questions to get you started editing and proofreading:

EDITING CHECKLIST

■ For more help, turn
to the dark-blue-edged
pages and find the
sections of the Quick
Editing Guide noted here.

___ Is it clear what each pronoun refers to? Does each pronoun agree   A6
with (match) its antecedent? Do pronouns used as subjects agree
with their verbs? Carefully check sentences making broad claims
about *everyone, no one, some, a few,* or some other group identified
by an indefinite pronoun.

___ Have you used an adjective whenever describing a noun or   A7
pronoun? Have you used an adverb whenever describing a verb,
adjective, or adverb? Have you used the correct form when
comparing two or more things?

___ Have you set off your transitions, other introductory elements,   C1
and interrupters with commas, if these are needed?

___ Have you spelled and capitalized everything correctly, espe-   D1, D2
cially names of people and organizations?

___ Have you correctly punctuated quotations from sources and   C3
experts?

RECOGNIZING LOGICAL FALLACIES

■ For more on faulty
thinking, see pp. 46–47.

Logical fallacies are common mistakes in thinking that may lead to wrong conclusions or distort evidence. Here are a few familiar logical fallacies.

TERM	EXPLANATION	EXAMPLE
Non Sequitur	Stating a claim that doesn't follow from your first premise or statement; Latin for "It does not follow"	Jenn should marry Mateo. In college he got all A's.
Oversimplification	Offering easy solutions for complicated problems	If we want to end substance abuse, let's send every drug user to prison for life. (Even aspirin users?)
Post Hoc Ergo Propter Hoc	Assuming a cause-and-effect relationship where none exists even though one event preceded another; Latin for "after this, therefore because of this"	After Jenny's black cat crossed my path, everything went wrong, and I failed my midterm.

(continued on next page)

TERM	EXPLANATION	EXAMPLE
Allness	Stating or implying that something is true of an entire class of things, often using *all, everyone, no one, always,* or *never*	Students enjoy studying. (All students? All subjects? All the time?)
Proof by Example or Too Few Examples	Presenting an example as proof rather than as illustration or clarification; overgeneralizing (the basis of much prejudice)	Armenians are great chefs. My neighbor is Armenian, and can he cook!
Begging the Question	Proving a statement already taken for granted, often by repeating it in different words or by defining a word in terms of itself	Rapists are dangerous because they are menaces. Happiness is the state of being happy.
Circular Reasoning	Supporting a statement with itself; a form of begging the question	He is a liar because he simply isn't telling the truth.
Either/Or Reasoning	Oversimplifying by assuming that an issue has only two sides, a statement must be true or false, a question demands a yes or no answer, or a problem has only two possible solutions (and one that's acceptable)	What are we going to do about global warming? Either we stop using all of the energy-consuming vehicles and products that cause it, or we just learn to live with it.
Argument from Dubious Authority	Using an unidentified authority to shore up a weak argument or an authority whose expertise lies outside the issue, such as a television personality selling insurance	According to some of the most knowing scientists in America, smoking two packs a day is as harmless as eating oatmeal cookies.
Argument *ad Hominem*	Attacking an individual's opinion by attacking his or her character, thus deflecting attention from the merit of a proposal; Latin for "against the man"	Diaz may argue that we need to save the whales, but he's the type who gets emotional over nothing.
Argument from Ignorance	Maintaining that a claim has to be accepted because it hasn't been disproved or that it has to be rejected because it has not been proved	Despite years of effort, no one has proved that ghosts don't exist; therefore, we should expect to see them at any time. No one has ever shown that life exists on any other planet; clearly the notion of other living things in the universe is absurd.
Argument by Analogy	Treating an extended comparison between familiar and unfamiliar items, based on similarities and ignoring differences, as evidence rather than as a useful way of explaining	People were born free as the birds; it's cruel to expect them to work.
Bandwagon Argument	Suggesting that everyone is joining the group and readers who don't may miss out on happiness, success, or a reward	Purchasing the new Swallowtail admits you to the nation's most elite group of drivers.

OTHER ASSIGNMENTS

1. Write a letter to the editor of your newspaper or a newsmagazine in which you agree or disagree with the publication's editorial stand on a current question or with the recent words or actions of some public figure. Make clear your reasons for holding your view.

2. Write one claim each of substantiation, of evaluation, and of policy for or against censoring pornographic Web sites. Indicate an audience each claim might address effectively. Then list reasons and types of evidence you might need to support one of these claims. Finally, for the same claim, indicate what opposing viewpoints you would need to consider and how you could best do so.

3. Write a short paper, blog entry, or class posting expressing your view on one of these topics or another that comes to mind. Make clear your reasons for believing as you do.

> For more on supporting a position with sources, see Ch. 12.

Bilingual education	Raising the minimum wage
Nonsmokers' rights	Protecting the rain forests
Dealing with date rape	Controlling terrorism
Salaries of professional athletes	Prayer in public schools

Applying What You Learn: Some Uses of Taking a Stand

Percent Increase in Public Two-Year Tuition and Fees
(2001–02 to 2002–03)

0–5%
6–10%
11–26%

In College Courses.   When assignments and examination questions ask you to take a stand on a controversy, your responses indicate clearly to your instructor how firmly you grasp the material.

- In a health-care course, you might be asked to criticize this statement: "There's too much science and not enough caring in modern medicine."

- In a criminal justice course, you might be asked to state and defend your opinion on juvenile sentencing.

- In your research paper for an economics course, you might be asked to take a stand on the state budget allocations in terms of their effects on college tuition.

In the Workplace.   In nearly every professional position — lawyer, teacher, nurse, business manager, journalist — you will be invited to state and support your views for others in your profession or the public.

- Scientists must persuade the scientific community that their research findings are valid, publishing their work in journals for evaluation by their peers.

- Social workers write documents to persuade courts and other agencies that certain actions or services are best for the welfare of their clients.

- Facing fierce competition, executives must convince their CEO that their ideas will result in impressive benefits for the company.

In Your Community.   As an active citizen, you may feel compelled to inform and influence the public on matters of concern to all.

- You may want to write a letter to the editor of your newspaper or to your political representative about a controversial issue faced by your community — controlling violence in your schools, funding a new drainage system, enforcing the leash law.

- You may represent the tenants in your apartment building by writing a letter of protest to a landlord who wants to raise rents.

- You may write a letter and design a poster to protest a company's operating and marketing policies.

Chapter 10

Proposing a Solution

If you polluted the air in the 80's,
here's your chance to redeem yourself

Riders wanted.

Responding to an Image

This advertisement appeared as a "spoof ad" on Adbusters, a Web site that advocates a critical eye toward advertisements of all kinds (<www.adbusters.org>). What is the problem posed by the ad? What techniques are used to help viewers understand the problem? What solution does the ad propose? Is this solution realistic and workable? What is the significance of the "Riders wanted" logo, and how does it affect the credibility of the ad's message? Compare this ad to the Volkswagen ad that appears on page 425, noting the similarities and differences between the two images. How does awareness of Volkswagen's advertising help to make this a more effective spoof?

$\mathcal{S}$ometimes when you learn of a problem such as the destruction of the rain forest, homelessness, or famine, you say to yourself, "Something should be done about that." You can do something constructive yourself—through the powerful and persuasive activity of writing.

Your purpose in such writing, as political leaders and advertisers well know, is to rouse your audience to action. Even in your daily life at college, you can write a letter to your college newspaper or to someone in authority and try to stir your readers to action. Does some college policy irk you? Would you urge students to attend a rally for a cause or a charity?

The uses of such writing go far beyond these immediate applications. In Chapter 9, you took a stand and backed it up with evidence. Now go a step further, writing a *proposal*—a recommendation for taking action. If, for instance, you have made the claim "Our national parks are in sorry condition," you might urge readers to act—to write to their representatives in Congress or to visit a national park and pick up trash. On the other hand, you might suggest that the Department of the Interior be given a budget increase to hire more park rangers, purchase additional park land to accommodate more visitors, and buy more cleanup equipment. You might also suggest that the department could raise funds through sales of park DVDs as well as increased revenues from visitors attracted by the DVDs. The first paper would be a call to immediate action on the part of your readers; the second, an attempt to forge a consensus about what needs to be done.

Learning from Other Writers

The writers of the following two essays propose sensible solutions for pressing problems. To help you begin to analyze the first reading, look for the notes in the margin. They identify features such as the introduction of the problem, the thesis, or main idea, and the introduction of the proposed solution.

■ For more on thesis and support, see Chs. 17 and 19.

As You Read These Proposals

As you read these essays, ask yourself the following questions:

1. What problem does the writer identify? Does the writer rouse you to want to do something about the problem?

2. What solution does the writer propose? What evidence supports the solution? Does the writer convince you to agree with this solution?

3. How is the writer qualified to write on this subject?

■ For more examples of writing that proposes a solution, visit <bedfordstmartins.com/bedguide> and do a keyword search:

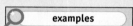
examples

Wilbert Rideau, editor of the Angolite, *the Louisiana State Penitentiary newsmagazine, offers a voice seldom heard in the debate over crime control — that of the criminal.*

Wilbert Rideau
Why Prisons Don't Work

I was among thirty-one murderers sent to the Louisiana State Penitentiary in 1962 to be executed or imprisoned for life. We weren't much different from those we found here, or those who had preceded us. We were unskilled, impulsive, and uneducated misfits, mostly black, who had done dumb, impulsive things — failures, rejects from the larger society. Now a generation has come of age and gone since I've been here, and everything is much the same as I found it. The faces of the prisoners are different, but behind them are the same impulsive, uneducated, unskilled minds that made dumb, impulsive choices that got them into more trouble than they ever thought existed. The vast majority of us are consigned to suffer and die here so politicians can sell the illusion that permanently exiling people to prison will make society safe.

Getting tough has always been a "silver bullet," a quick fix for the crime and violence that society fears. Each year in Louisiana — where excess is a way of life — lawmakers have tried to outdo each other in legislating harsher mandatory penalties and in reducing avenues of release. The only thing to do with criminals, they say, is get tougher. They have. In the process, the purpose of prison began to change. The state boasts one of the highest lockup rates in the country, imposes the most severe penalties in the nation, and vies to execute more criminals per capita than anywhere else. This state is so tough that last year, when prison authorities here wanted to punish an inmate in solitary confinement for an infraction,° the most they could inflict on him was to deprive him of his underwear. It was all he had left.

If getting tough resulted in public safety, Louisiana citizens would be the safest in the nation. They're not. Louisiana has the highest murder rate among states. Prison, like the police and the courts, has a minimal impact on crime because it is a response after the fact, a mop-up operation. It doesn't work. The idea of punishing the few to deter the many is counterfeit because potential criminals either think they're not going to get caught or they're so emotionally desperate or psychologically distressed that they don't care about the consequences of their actions. The threatened punishment, regardless of its severity, is never a factor in the equation. But society, like the incorrigible° criminal it abhors, is unable to learn from its mistakes.

Prison has a role in public safety, but it is not a cure-all. Its value is limited, and its use should also be limited to what it does best: isolating young criminals long enough to give them a chance to grow up and get a grip on their impulses. It is a traumatic experience, certainly, but it should be only a temporary one, not a way of life. Prisoners kept too long tend to embrace the criminal culture, its distorted values and beliefs; they have little choice — prison is their life. There are some prisoners who cannot be returned to society — serial killers, serial rapists, professional hit men, and the like — but

infraction: Violation.   **incorrigible:** Incapable of reform.

the monsters who need to die in prison are rare exceptions in the criminal landscape.

Crime is a young man's game. Most of the nation's random violence is committed by young urban terrorists. But because of long, mandatory sentences, most prisoners here are much older, having spent fifteen, twenty, thirty, or more years behind bars, long past necessity. Rather than pay for new prisons, society would be well served by releasing some of its older prisoners who pose no threat and using the money to catch young street thugs. Warden John Whitley agrees that many older prisoners here could be freed tomorrow with little or no danger to society. Release, however, is governed by law or by politicians, not by penal professionals. Even murderers, those most feared by society, pose little risk. Historically, for example, the domestic staff at Louisiana's Governor's mansion has been made up of murderers, hand-picked to work among the chief-of-state and his family. Penologists° have long known that murder is almost always a once-in-a-lifetime act. The most dangerous criminal is the one who has not yet killed but has a history of escalating offenses. He's the one to watch.

Transitions (underlined) for coherence

5

Rehabilitation can work. Everyone changes in time. The trick is to influence the direction that change takes. The problem with prisons is that they don't do more to rehabilitate those confined in them. The convict who enters prison illiterate will probably leave the same way. Most convicts want to be better than they are, but education is not a priority. This prison houses 4,600 men and offers academic training to 240, vocational training to a like number. Perhaps it doesn't matter. About 90 percent of the men here may never leave this prison alive.

6

The only effective way to curb crime is for society to work to prevent the criminal act in the first place, to come between the perpetrator° and crime. Our youngsters must be taught to respect the humanity of others and to handle disputes without violence. It is essential to educate and equip them with the skills to pursue their life ambitions in a meaningful way. As a community, we must address the adverse life circumstances that spawn criminality. These things are not quick, and they're not easy, but they're effective. Politicians think that's too hard a sell. They want to be on record for doing something now, something they can point to at reelection time. So the drumbeat goes on for more police, more prisons, more of the same failed policies.

Conclusion summing up solution

7

Ever see a dog chase its tail?

8

Questions to Start You Thinking

Meaning

1. Does Rideau convince you that the belief that "permanently exiling people to prison will make society safe" is an "illusion" (paragraph 1)?

2. According to Rideau, why don't prisons work?

3. What does he propose as solutions to the problem of escalating crime? What other solutions can you think of?

Penologists: Those who study prison management and criminal justice.   **perpetrator:** One who is responsible for an action or a crime.

Writing Strategies

4. What justifications, if any, for the prison system has Rideau left out of his essay? Do these omissions help or hurt his essay? Why or why not?

5. What evidence does the author provide to support his assertion that Louisiana's "getting tough" policy has not worked? Does he provide sufficient evidence to convince you? Does he persuade you that action is necessary?

6. What would make Rideau's argument for his proposals more persuasive?

7. Other than himself, what authorities does Rideau cite? Why do you think he does this?

8. Does the fact that the author is a convicted criminal strengthen or weaken his argument? Why do you think he mentions this in his first sentence?

9. How do you interpret the last line, "Ever see a dog chase its tail?" Is this line an effective way for Rideau to end his essay? Explain.

STUDENT ESSAY

John Barbieri's opinion piece appeared in the Amherst Student, *the newspaper of Amherst College, in April 2006.*

❓ *Do you have any experience with, or views about, alternative energy?*

John Barbieri
Save Hydrogen for Later; Ethanol Power Is the Viable Option for Now

Face it. Hydrogen power is not going to happen anytime soon. It's too costly   1
and underdeveloped to provide a replacement for gasoline-powered cars. And even if the costly infrastructure° and technology needed for hydrogen cars are developed, hydrogen cars will have a negligible° impact on the environment because hydrogen is produced using electricity, and in the United States, electricity is produced primarily by fossil fuels. As a result, switching over to hydrogen cars will not actually reduce greenhouse emissions;° it will only shift where they are produced. It's time to stop waiting for a solution that isn't going to help or happen and implement° one that already is here. It's time to look toward ethanol.

Ethanol is an alternative fuel option that can be made by fermenting° and   2
distilling° starch that has been converted into simple sugars. Anything from corn and wheat to biomass, which is basically waste plant material, can be used to produce ethanol. Since ethanol can be produced entirely from plant sources, it is a renewable energy source. Ethanol can also be combined with gasoline to make E85,

---

infrastructure: Physical foundation or resources needed for a system to work.   **negligible:** Small.   **greenhouse emissions:** Pollutants, including carbon dioxide, that trap heat in the atmosphere, much as a greenhouse holds heat. Fossil fuels like gasoline are a major source of greenhouse-gas emissions.   **implement:** Carry out; put into place.   **fermenting:** Using enzymes to turn complex organic substances into their component parts.   **distilling:** Extracting the essence from something; concentrating.

which is 85 percent ethanol, or E95, which is 95 percent ethanol. Both of these fuels are considered to be alternative fuels under the Energy Policy Act of 1992.

Ethanol-powered vehicles have many advantages over gasoline-powered vehicles. Since ethanol has a higher hydrogen-to-carbon ratio than gasoline, it produces fewer greenhouse gases than gasoline. Furthermore, where gasoline must for the most part be imported from abroad, ethanol can be produced from corn and biomass, which are abundant in the United States. As a result, by switching over to ethanol the United States can finally reduce its dependence on overseas oil. Between 1978 and 2005, Brazil was able to reduce its dependence on oil from about 85 percent to nearly 0 percent by switching over to ethanol-powered vehicles, according to Brazilian officials. Following the precedent set by Brazil, the United States could easily reduce its oil consumption and finally become energy independent. Ethanol costs about the same amount as gasoline per gallon, and as gasoline prices continue to rise, ethanol could soon become cheaper than gasoline.

3

Why is dependence on foreign oil a problem?

Ethanol offers many distinct advantages over hydrogen power as well. First, the production of ethanol creates much less pollution than the production of hydrogen in a country where a large percentage of power is produced by fossil fuels. In the United States, nearly 90 percent of electricity is produced by fossil-fuel-burning power plants. Furthermore, many of the nuclear power plants in the United States will soon be out of commission; as a result, it is likely that the reliance on fossil fuels in the United States will increase even further. Making ethanol from plant sources creates about 200 times less pollution than producing an equivalent amount of electricity in a fossil-fuel power plant. Moreover, the production of hydrogen using electricity is only 70 percent efficient. As a result, in the United States making ethanol creates much less pollution as a by-product than making hydrogen. While ethanol may not be a perfectly "clean" energy source, it certainly creates less pollution than either gasoline or hydrogen would, given our current electricity production capacities.

4

Second, Ethanol can be stored and transported much more efficiently than hydrogen. Ethanol exists naturally as a liquid, while hydrogen exists naturally as a gas. Consequently, more ethanol can be stored in a smaller space than hydrogen. In fact, trying to store hydrogen effectively has been a significant hurdle for those trying to develop hydrogen cars. Even those who have tried to store hydrogen as a compressed gas, metal hydride, have had limited success. This problem does not exist for ethanol-powered cars because ethanol can be stored in the exact same way as gasoline. Unlike hydrogen, which would most likely need to be produced on site due to its lack of transportability, ethanol could be mass produced at another site more efficiently and then be transported to fuel stations.

5

Third, it is less costly to implement ethanol as an alternative power source than it would be to implement hydrogen power. To create a hydrogen economy, hydrogen cars would have to be researched further, hydrogen fuel stations and production

6

plants would have to be built, and more effective hydrogen storage systems would have to be created. All of this infrastructure would cost billions of dollars and would take a significant amount of time to implement. Current gas stations could easily be converted to supply ethanol or could supply ethanol in addition to gasoline just as many gas stations have diesel pumps along with gasoline pumps. There are also already many "flex-fuel" cars on the road that can run on either gasoline or ethanol. GM and Ford have been producing these cars since the 1980s to get a government subsidy° but have not advertised the flex-fuel capability because they did not believe it would affect consumer decisions on whether or not to buy the cars. Today, there are over 1.5 million flex-fuel cars on the road, and GM and Ford have plants that could easily produce more if the demand for flex-fuel cars increased.

What images or messages might ads for flex-fuel cars include?

Ethanol is an excellent alternative energy source for the United States to look toward in the coming years. It is cleaner than gasoline and costs the same amount per gallon. Ethanol can be produced from corn and biomass produced in the United States and can consequently reduce American dependence on foreign oil for energy. Less pollution is created producing ethanol than producing hydrogen, given the high percentage of electricity produced by fossil fuels in the United States. Furthermore, an ethanol infrastructure would be much easier to implement than a hydrogen one, especially as GM and Ford have already produced millions of flex-fuel cars that can run on either ethanol or gasoline and could easily produce many more. And ethanol doesn't just have to power our cars. It can heat our homes, power our lights, and much more. Hydrogen may be the alternative fuel of the future, but ethanol is the alternative fuel of today.

7

Questions to Start You Thinking

Meaning

1. What problem would the use of ethanol address? Does Barbieri provide enough background on this problem?

2. How is ethanol produced, and what is the benefit of this means of production?

3. In what ways, according to Barbieri, is ethanol superior to gasoline and hydrogen as a fuel source? Do you find these arguments convincing? Why or why not?

Writing Strategies

4. What kinds of transitions does Barbieri use to lead readers through his points? How effective do you find them?

5. Is Barbieri's evidence specific and sufficient? Explain.

6. Do you find Barbieri's conclusion to be effective? Why or why not?

7. Using highlighters or marginal notes, identify the essay's introduction, explanation of the problem, thesis, proposal to solve the problem, and conclusion. How effective is the organization of this essay?

subsidy: Monetary support or assistance.

Learning by Writing

THE ASSIGNMENT: PROPOSING A SOLUTION

In this essay you'll first carefully analyze and explain a specific social, economic, political, civic, or environmental problem — a problem you care about and strongly wish to see resolved. The problem may be large or small, but it shouldn't be trivial. It may affect the whole country or mainly people in your city, campus, or classroom. Show your readers that this problem really exists and that it matters to you and to them. After setting forth the problem, you also may want to explain why it exists. Write for an audience who, once aware of the problem, may be expected to help do something about it.

■ For writing activities for proposing a solution, visit <bedfordstmartins.com/bedguide> and do a keyword search:

🔍   **activities**

The second thing you are to accomplish in the essay is to propose one or more ways to solve the problem or at least alleviate it. In making a proposal, you urge action by using words like *should, ought,* and *must*: "This city ought to have a Bureau of Missing Persons"; "Small private aircraft should be banned from flying close to a major commercial airport." Lay out the reasons why your proposal deserves to be implemented; supply evidence that your solution is reasonable and can work. Remember that your purpose is to convince readers that something should be done about the problem.

Students cogently argued for action in the following papers:

Based on research studies and statistics, one student argued that using standardized test scores from the SAT or the ACT as criteria for college admissions is a problem because it favors aggressive students from affluent families. His proposal was to abolish this use of the scores.

Another argued that one solution to vacation frustration is to turn everything — planning, choosing a location, arranging transportation, reserving lodging — over to a travel agent.

A third argued that the best solution to the problem of her children's poor education is homeschooling.

GENERATING IDEAS

Identify a Problem.   Brainstorm by writing down all the possible topics that come to mind. Observe events around you to identify irritating campus or community problems you would like to solve. Watch for ideas as you read the newspaper or listen to the news. Browse through issue-oriented Web sites. Look for sites sponsored by large nonprofit foundations that accept grant proposals and fund innovative solutions to societal issues. Then star the ideas that seem to have the most potential. Here are a few questions to help ideas start flowing:

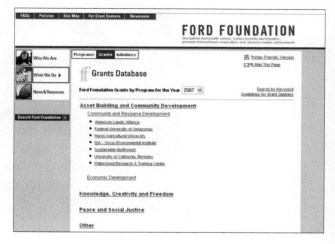

DISCOVERY CHECKLIST

___ Can you recall any problem that needs a solution? What problems do you meet every day or occasionally? What problems concern people near you?

___ What conditions in need of improvement have you observed on television or in your daily activities? What action is called for?

___ What problems have been discussed recently on campus or in class?

___ What problems are discussed in blogs, chat rooms, newspapers, or news-magazines such as *Time, Newsweek,* or *U.S. News & World Report?*

Consider Your Audience.   Readers need to believe that your problem is real and your solution is feasible. If you are addressing your classmates, maybe they haven't thought about the problem before. Try to discover ways to make it personal for them, to show that it affects them and deserves their attention. Here are some questions to ask yourself about your readers:

• Who are your readers? How would you describe them?

• Why should your readers care about this problem? Does it affect their health, welfare, conscience, or pocketbook?

• Have they ever expressed any interest in the problem? If so, what has triggered their interest?

• Do they belong to any organization or segment of society that makes them especially susceptible to — or uninterested in — this problem?

Facing the Challenge: Proposing a Solution

The major challenge writers face when writing a proposal is to develop a detailed and convincing solution. Finding solutions is much harder than finding problems. Convincing readers that you have found a reasonable, workable solution is harder still. For example, suppose you propose the combination of a rigorous exercise program and a low-fat diet as a solution for obesity. While these solutions seem reasonable and workable to you, readers who have lost weight and then gained it back might point out that their main problem is not losing weight but maintaining weight loss over time. To account for their concerns and enhance your credibility, you might revise your solution to focus on realistic long-term goals and strategies for sticking to an exercise program. For instance, you might recommend that friends walk together two or three times a week or that employees lobby for a fitness center at work.

To develop a realistic solution that fully addresses a problem and satisfies the concerns of readers, consider questions such as these:

• How might the problem affect different groups of people?

• What range of concerns are your readers likely to have?

• What realistic solution addresses the concerns of readers about *all* aspects of the problem?

- What attitudes about the problem do you share with your readers? Which of their assumptions or values that differ from yours will affect how they view your proposal?

Think about Solutions.   Once you've chosen a problem, brainstorm — alone or with classmates — for possible solutions, or use your imagination. Some problems, such as reducing international tensions, present no easy solutions. Still, give some thought to any problem that seriously concerns you, even if it has thwarted teams of experts. Sometimes a solution will reveal itself to a novice thinker, and even a small contribution to a partial solution is worth offering. You can use several strategies to think about problems and solutions:

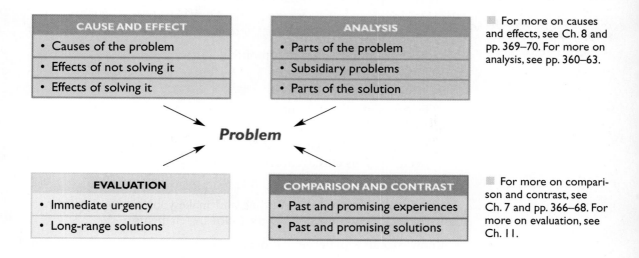

> For more on brainstorming, see pp. 296–97. For more on imagining, see pp. 302–03.

CAUSE AND EFFECT
- Causes of the problem
- Effects of not solving it
- Effects of solving it

ANALYSIS
- Parts of the problem
- Subsidiary problems
- Parts of the solution

Problem

EVALUATION
- Immediate urgency
- Long-range solutions

COMPARISON AND CONTRAST
- Past and promising experiences
- Past and promising solutions

> For more on causes and effects, see Ch. 8 and pp. 369–70. For more on analysis, see pp. 360–63.

> For more on comparison and contrast, see Ch. 7 and pp. 366–68. For more on evaluation, see Ch. 11.

Consider Sources of Support.   To show that the problem really exists, you'll need evidence and examples. If you feel that further research in the library will help you know more about the problem, now is the time to do it. In addition, previous efforts to solve the problem may help you develop your solution. Consider whether local history archives, past newspaper stories or photographs, accounts of public meetings, interviews with others, or Web sites sponsored by interested organizations might identify concerns of readers or practical limitations of solutions.

> For more on evidence, see Ch. 3. For more on using evidence to support an argument, see pp. 152–56.

> For advice on finding a few sources, see A and B in the Quick Research Guide (the dark-red-edged pages).

PLANNING, DRAFTING, AND DEVELOPING

Start with Your Proposal and Your Thesis.   A basic approach is to state your proposal in a sentence that can act as your thesis.

For more on stating a thesis, see pp. 312–19. For strategies for planning, drafting, and developing, see Chs. 17, 18, and 19.

For exercises on choosing effective thesis statements, visit <bedfordstmartins.com/ bedguide> and do a keyword search:

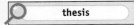

For more on outlines, see pp. 325–33.

PROPOSAL   Let people get divorced without going to court.

WORKING THESIS   The legislature should pass a law allowing couples to divorce without having to go to court.

From such a statement, the rest of the argument may start to unfold, often falling naturally into a simple two-part shape:

1. *A claim that a problem exists.* This part explains the problem and supplies evidence of its significance — for example, the costs, adversarial process, and stress of divorce court for a couple and their family.
2. *A claim that something ought to be done about it.* This part proposes a solution to the problem — for example, legislative action to authorize other options such as mediation.

These two parts can grow naturally into an informal outline.

1. Introduction

   Overview of the situation
   Working thesis stating your proposal

2. Problem

   Explanation of its nature
   Evidence of its significance

3. Solution

   Explanation of its nature
   Evidence of its effectiveness and practicality

4. Conclusion

You can then expand your outline and make your proposal more persuasive by including some or all of the following elements:

- Knowledge or experience that qualifies you to propose a solution (your experience as a player or a coach, for example, that establishes your credibility as an authority on Little League)
- Values, beliefs, or assumptions that have caused you to feel strongly about the need for action
- An estimate of the resources — money, people, skills, material — and the time required to implement the solution (perhaps including what is available now and what needs to be obtained)
- Step-by-step actions needed to achieve your solution
- Controls or quality checks to monitor implementation
- Possible obstacles or difficulties that may need to be overcome
- Reasons your solution is better than others proposed or tried already
- Any other evidence that shows that your suggestion is practical, reasonable in cost, and likely to be effective

For exercises on supporting a thesis, visit <bedfordstmartins.com/ bedguide> and do a keyword search:

Making Problem-Solution Columns

To propose a solution persuasively, you must show that you understand a problem well enough to suggest solutions while addressing specific audience needs. Considering these ideas in columns can help you see them differently than you do as you write. After drafting your ideas in one file, open a new file, go to the Format menu and choose "Columns," and then click on "3." Label the first column "Problems," the second "Solutions," and the third "Readers' Objections." Use your draft file to copy and paste your ideas into the appropriate column in your new file. Add points as needed so that you move logically from problem to solution and answer readers' objections point by point.

FOR E-WRITERS

Imagine Possible Objections of Your Audience.   You can increase the likelihood that readers will accept your proposal in two ways. First, start your proposal by showing that a problem exists. Then, when you turn to your claim that something should be done, begin with a simple and inviting suggestion. For example, a claim that national parks need better care might begin by suggesting that readers head for such a park and personally size up the situation. Besides drawing readers into the problem and the solution, you may think of objections they might raise — reservations about the high cost, the complexity, or the workability of your plan, for instance. You can persuade your readers by anticipating an objection that might occur to them and laying it to rest.

Cite Sources Carefully.   When you collect ideas and evidence from outside sources, you need to document your evidence — that is, tell where you found everything. Check with your instructor on the documentation method he or she wants you to use. You may also want to identify sources as you introduce them to assure a reader that they are authoritative.

For pointers on integrating and documenting sources, see Ch. 12 and D6 and E1–E2 in the Quick Research Guide (the dark-red-edged pages).

> According to Newsweek correspondent Josie Fair, . . .

> In his biography FDR: The New Deal Years, Davis reports . . .

> While working as a Senate page in the summer of 2007, I observed . . .

You can introduce a table, graph, drawing, map, photograph, or other visual evidence in much the same way.

For more advice about integrating visuals, see pp. 410–16.

> As the 2000 census figures in Table 1 indicate, . . .

> The photograph illustrating the run-down condition of the dog park (see Fig. 2) . . .

REVISING AND EDITING

■ For more revising and editing strategies, see Ch. 20.

As you revise, concentrate on a clear explanation of the problem and solid supporting evidence for the solution. Make your essay coherent and its parts clear to help achieve your purpose of convincing your readers.

Clarify Your Thesis.   Your readers are likely to rely on your thesis to identify the problem and possibly to preview your solution. Look again at your thesis from a reader's point of view.

> WORKING THESIS   The legislature should pass a law allowing couples to divorce without having to go to court.
>
> REVISED THESIS   Because divorce court can be expensive, adversarial, and stressful, passing a law that allows couples to divorce without a trip to court would encourage simpler and more harmonious ways of ending a marriage.

Reorganize for Unity and Coherence.   When Heather Colbenson revised her first draft, she wanted to clarify the presentation of her problem.

Why would high schools in farming communities drop agriculture classes and the

The main reason that   *is that*

FFA program? Small schools are cutting ag programs ~~because~~ the state has not pro-

vided significant funding for the schools to operate. The small schools have to make

Move main reason last for emphasis

cuts, and some small schools are deciding that the agriculture classes are not as im-

portant as other courses. Some small schools are consolidating to receive more aid.

Why did I put a solution here? Move to end!

Many of these schools have been able to save their ag programs.

One reason is that m

Rewrite this!
Not really college requirements but college-prep courses vs. others when budget is tight

Many colleges are demanding that students have two years of foreign language.

In small schools, like my own, the students could take either foreign language or ag

classes. Therefore, students choose language classes to fill the college requirement.

When the students leave the ag classes to take foreign language, the number of stu-

dents declines, which makes it easier for school administrators to cut ag classes.

■ For strategies for achieving coherence see pp. 346–49.

Her revised paper was more forcefully organized and more coherent, making it easier for readers to follow. The bridges between ideas were now on paper, not just in her mind.

■ For more on errors in reasoning, see pp. 46–47 and 162–63.

Be Reasonable.   Exaggerated claims for your solution will not persuade your readers. Neither will oversimplifying the problem so that the solution

Exchanging Written Reactions

Exchange proposals with another student, and read each other's draft. Then take turns sharing first reactions — positive as well as negative. After this exchange, take your partner's draft home for a day or two. Before your next meeting, write a review letter to your partner in which you thoughtfully critique the draft and suggest revisions. (To help the writer, mark the draft as you comment on the organization, thesis, support, and so forth.) Exchange letters during your next meeting, and discuss your experiences. What did you learn about proposing solutions? About writing? About peer editing?

FOR GROUP LEARNING

seems more likely to apply. Don't be afraid to express your own reasonable doubts about the completeness of your solution. If necessary, rethink both the problem and the solution.

In looking back over your draft once more, consider these questions:

REVISION CHECKLIST

____ Does your introduction invite the reader into the discussion?

____ Is your problem clear? How have you made it relevant to readers?

____ Have you clearly outlined the steps necessary to solve the problem?

____ Where have you demonstrated the benefits of your solution?

____ Have you considered other solutions before rejecting them for your own?

____ Have you anticipated the doubts readers may have about your solution?

____ Do you come across as a well-meaning, reasonable writer willing to admit that you don't know everything? If you sound preachy, have you overused *should* and *must*?

____ Have you avoided promising that your solution will do more than it can possibly do? Have you made believable predictions for its success?

After you have revised your proposal, edit and proofread it. Carefully check the grammar, word choice, punctuation, and mechanics — and then correct any problems you find. If you have used sources, be sure that you have cited them correctly in your text and added a list of works cited.

Make sure your sentence structure helps you make your points clearly and directly. Don't let yourself slip into the passive voice, a grammatical construction that represents things as happening without any obvious agent: "The problem should be remedied by spending more money on prevention." Instead, every sentence should specify who should take action: "The dean of students should remedy the problem by spending more money on prevention."

For more editing and proofreading strategies, see pp. 348–87. For more on documenting sources, see E1–E2 in the Quick Research Guide (the dark-red-edged pages).

FOR PEER RESPONSE

For general questions for a peer editor, see p. 377. For peer response worksheets, visit <bedfordstmartins.com/bedguide> and do a keyword search:

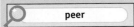

peer

Ask several classmates or friends to review your proposal and solution, answering questions such as these:

- What is your overall reaction to this proposal? Does it make you want to go out and do something about the problem?
- Are you convinced that the problem is of concern to you? If not, why not?
- Are you persuaded that the writer's solution is workable?
- Has the writer paid enough attention to readers and their concerns?
- Restate what you understand to be the proposal's major points:
  - Problem
  - Explanation of problem and why it matters
  - Proposed solution
  - Explanation of proposal and its practicality
  - Reasons and procedure to implement proposal
  - Proposal's advantages, disadvantages, and responses to other solutions
  - Final recommendation
- If this were your paper, what is the one thing you would be sure to work on before handing it in?

Here are some questions to get you started editing and proofreading:

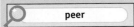

EDITING CHECKLIST

___ Is it clear what each pronoun refers to? Is any *this* or *that* ambiguous? Does each pronoun agree with (match) its antecedent?	A6
___ Is your sentence structure correct? Have you avoided writing fragments, comma splices, or fused sentences?	A1, A2
___ Do your transitions and other introductory elements have commas after them, if these are needed?	C1
___ Have you spelled and capitalized everything correctly, especially names of people and organizations?	D1, D2

For more help, turn to the dark-blue-edged pages, and find the sections of the Quick Editing Guide noted here.

OTHER ASSIGNMENTS

1. If you followed the assignment in Chapter 9 and took a stand, now write a few paragraphs extending that paper to propose a solution that argues for action. To gather ideas, brainstorm with classmates first.
2. Write a memo to your supervisor at work in which you propose an innovation (related to procedures, schedules, policies, or similar matters) that could benefit your department or company.

3. Choose from the following list a practice that you find inefficient, unethical, unfair, or morally wrong as a solution to a problem. In a few paragraphs, give reasons for your objections. Then propose a better solution in an essay, letter to the editor, blog entry, or class posting.

Censorship	Genetic engineering
Corporal punishment for children	Outsourcing jobs
Laboratory experiments on animals	Dumping wastes in the ocean

Applying What You Learn: Some Uses of Proposals

In College Courses.   Many courses will require writing a proposal, often a plan to be approved before implementation.

- Students embarking on a research project may be required to submit to an adviser or a committee a proposal that sets forth what they will investigate and how they will conduct their study.

- In social science courses, you may examine a current issue and propose a solution to the disclosure of adoption records, the rising costs of prescription drugs, prison overcrowding, or racial profiling.

- Students who object to a grade can file a grievance proposing a grade change. Like writers of persuasive essays, they state a claim and supply evidence in support of it.

In the Workplace.   Proposals often suggest new projects, recommend purchases or changes in procedure, and solve personnel problems.

- After gathering comments from workers and financial analyses, the human resources office prepares proposals outlining benefits such as medical and dental insurance.

- When a company builds or renovates a building, the architect submits a proposal outlining the plans, and then contractors submit bids, proposing to complete the work for a certain cost.

- Every job application is a proposal. Applicants propose that an employer hire them and support that proposal by selecting the best evidence for their résumés and letters or applications.

In Your Community.   Every day we encounter proposals for solutions — in editorials, in books, in public-service announcements, in political debate.

- You might write to the board proposing that your congregation begin a building fund to expand your overcrowded fellowship hall. Your proposal would include evidence of the need for more space, the cost of the addition, ways of raising the money, and a time frame for completion.
- In a speech to your local service club, you might inform them about the drop-out rate at your local high school and propose that members donate their time to work with at-risk teens.
- Alarmed by the low literacy rate of many adults in your community, you propose a tutoring program to the library and design posters to promote it.

Chapter 11

Evaluating

Responding to an Image

This image originally appeared on the cover of an issue of *Utne,* next to these lines promoting a featured article: "Clear your head. Too many choices? How to make up your mind without losing it." What does this image suggest about decision making, a critical step in evaluation? How does the image guide a viewer's eye to its focal point? What details contribute to the overall impression it conveys? In what ways does it reflect the feelings of writers and others who must repeatedly make and present thoughtful choices? In your journal, notebook, or laptop, record your responses—as a writer—to this image.

Evaluating means judging. You do it when you decide what candidate to vote for, pick which camera to buy, or recommend a new restaurant to your friends. All of us pass judgments—often snap judgments—as we move through a day's routine. A friend asks, "How was that movie you saw last night?" and you reply, "Terrific—don't miss it" or maybe "Pretty good, but it had too much blood and gore for me."

But to *write* an evaluation calls for you to think more critically. As a writer you first decide on *criteria*, or standards for judging, and then come up with evidence to back up your judgment. Your evaluation zeroes in on a definite subject that you inspect carefully in order to reach a considered opinion. The subject might be a film, a book, a sports team, a group of performers, a product, a body of research: the possibilities are endless.

Learning from Other Writers

For more on thesis and support, see Chs. 17 and 19.

Here are evaluations by a professional writer and by a student. To help you begin to analyze the first reading, look for the notes in the margin. They identify features such as the thesis, or main idea, the criteria for evaluation, and the evidence supporting the writer's judgment, all typical of essays that evaluate.

As You Read These Evaluations

For more examples of evaluative writing, visit <bedfordstmartins.com/bedguide> and do a key-word search:

🔍 examples

As you read these essays, ask yourself the following questions:

1. Do you consider the writer qualified to evaluate the subject he or she chose? What biases and prejudices might the writer bring to the evaluation?

2. What criteria for evaluation does the writer establish? Are these reasonable standards for evaluating the subject?

3. What is the writer's assessment of the subject? Does the writer provide sufficient evidence to convince you of his or her evaluation?

Seth Stevenson regularly evaluates advertising for Slate.com. In this particular Ad Report Card, published in May 2006, Stevenson discusses a startling television spot for the Volkswagen Jetta.

Seth Stevenson
Wham! Bam! Buy a VW, Ma'am!

The spot: Four young people are riding in a Volkswagen Jetta. They're engaged in some lighthearted banter° when BLAM! An SUV runs a red light and smashes into their driver's side door. Air bags deploy. Glass shatters. We fade out, and then fade back in on the Jetta's passengers, unharmed,

banter: Casual talk; chitchat.

standing next to the badly damaged car as police sirens wail. "Holy sh-," says one of the passengers, with the profanity° cut off before she can finish pronouncing it. "Safe happens," reads the on-screen slogan,° and then some text tells us that the Jetta has received the "highest government side impact rating."

This Volkswagen spot — along with another one just like it — has prompted massive amounts of reader mail. Some of you are terrified, some of you are appalled,° and some of you think the ads are absolutely brilliant. Personally, I don't find these to be works of surpassing° genius, but I do think they're pretty sharp.

> **THESIS**
> presenting judgment

For one, the execution° is remarkable. I'm not sure I've seen a more realistic depiction of a car crash. The spots capture that out-of-nowhere moment at the heart of all accidents, when everyday mundanity° flashes into a hyperintense freak-out explosion. The ads also hint at an accident's aftermath: hours of jittery° detachment.° Anyone who's been in a car crash will recognize this mood triptych.°

> Introduction to first criterion: execution

Visually, I love that they've avoided clichéd° slow-mo° footage of headlights exploding, glass shards floating through the crisp night air, and so forth. This choice reminds me of my other favorite car-crash scene, from Steven Soderbergh's *Erin Brockovich:* in a single, unadorned, middle-distance shot (with no foreshadowing° whatsoever), we see Julia Roberts's car get violently crunched as it rolls through an intersection. The Volkswagen spot is similarly stripped-down. It's a brutally frank look at the physical chaos° that results when an SUV enters your sedan without an invitation.

> Supporting evidence

So, the execution is fantastic, but what about the concept? Why a campaign that centers on safety? It seems particularly odd given that a recent VW campaign was all about aggressive, high-speed driving, and finding your inner "fast." Now we're asked to contemplate° air bags and government safety ratings? Granted, the "Make Friends with Your Fast" campaign was for the pocket-rocket GTI, while this "Safe Happens" campaign is for the slightly more grown-up Jetta. But still, I'm feeling some . . . whiplash.

> Introduction to second criterion: concept

According to Kurt Schneider, general manager for creative content at Volkswagen, the idea was to find a fresh way to pitch safety. "Safety has mostly been portrayed in a more rational, family-oriented way," he says. "This was an attempt to reach eighteen- to thirty-four-year-olds [the target market for the Jetta] by presenting safety in a more emotional and dramatic light. We show young people out with friends, and the message is about protecting the people who are close to you."

> Supporting evidence

---

profanity: Swearword.   **slogan:** Headline; advertising claim.   **appalled:** Shocked. **surpassing:** Exceptional; extraordinary.   **execution:** The way in which something is carried out or achieved.   **mundanity:** Ordinariness.   **jittery:** Nervous.   **detachment:** Lack of emotional involvement.   **triptych:** Series of three.   **clichéd:** Something that has been repeated so often that it is no longer fresh.   **slow-mo:** Slow motion.   **foreshadowing:** Hinting at what is to come.   **chaos:** Disorder; disarray.   **contemplate:** To think about or seriously consider.

I like this argument. But there's a reason that safety traditionally gets 7 pitched at families and not at the childless. Most parents are obsessively fixated° on their kids' well-being, while most fancy-free° young folks don't give safety much thought. In urging young people to take heed,° Volkswagen seems to be fighting human nature.

Supporting evidence (continued)

Their plan, obviously, is to get us totally freaked about car crashes. And, 8 judging by the posttraumatic° e-mails I'm getting from readers, that plan appears to be working. Since these spots are filmed mostly from inside the cars and feature likable, attractive but not-too-attractive characters, the viewer is led to feel like part of the gang. When the accidents hit, we feel like victims, too. If being drawn into these violent clips doesn't get you thinking about auto fatalities, nothing will.

The question is whether this will translate into Volkswagen sales. Will 9 young people (1) actually start prioritizing° safety in their car shopping, and (2) if so, will those people looking for safety now decide that VW is the answer? I've always found safety an oddly slippery brand attribute. Every carmaker throws its safety claims out there, and they all seem to wash right over me. Blah blah front-impact blah blah stars blah side curtain blah government rating. Volvo has its safety rep all sewn up, but I've no idea whether Volvos are in fact any safer than other cars. And, despite these ads, I've no idea whether Volkswagens are, either.

Conclusion underscoring thesis, with a final grade

Grade: B. I'm not sure Jetta's target demo° can be convinced to care 10 about safety. But I'm thoroughly convinced that these ads will haunt their dreams and keep the Volkswagen brand at the front of their thoughts. That's half the battle.

As for the appropriateness of the ads and all the outraged reaction: they 11 don't really bother me much. Volkswagen says it's trying to keep the spots from airing before 9 P.M., so little kids are less likely to see them. And part of me thinks it's healthy for us to contemplate our mortality° during the breaks in our sitcoms.°

Questions to Start You Thinking

Meaning

1. Why, based on Stevenson's description, might viewers find the Jetta ads shocking?

fixated: Focused.　　**fancy-free:** Without cares or concerns.　　**take heed:** Pay attention to.　　**posttraumatic:** A reference to posttraumatic stress disorder, in which a past trauma haunts the victim over an extended period.　　**prioritizing:** In this sense, giving a high rank or importance to something.　　**demo:** Short for *demographic,* the age group that Volkswagen is aiming for with the Jetta ads (eighteen- to thirty-four-year-olds).　　**mortality:** Death.　　**sitcoms:** Short for *situation comedies,* television comedies that take place in certain situations or settings.

2. Why, according to the author, do car advertisers tend to direct claims about safety to parents more than to young people? Why did Volkswagen do the reverse with the Jetta ad?

3. What is Stevenson's personal view of ads that make claims about safety?

Writing Strategies

4. What is Stevenson's overall judgment of the Jetta ads, and what criteria does he use to make this judgment?

5. In your view, how well does he support his judgment? Point to some specific examples in making your case.

6. Stevenson quotes an ad executive at Volkswagen in paragraph 6. How does this quotation contribute to Stevenson's evaluation? What other outside sources might Stevenson have included to enhance his points?

7. How would you describe Stevenson's tone, the quality of his writing that reveals his attitude toward his topic and his readers? What specific words, phrases, or sentences contribute to his tone? Does the tone seem appropriate for his purpose and audience?

STUDENT ESSAY

Dennis O'Neil
Katrina Documentary Gives Voice to Survivors

Spike Lee's film *When the Levees° Broke: A Requiem° in Four Acts* cuts straight 　1 to the heart of the Hurricane Katrina tragedy and gives voice to the New Orleans survivors in an unprecedented° way. The epic,° 256-minute documentary provides a multitude° of different perspectives on the disaster and demonstrates the tragic effect that the disaster has had on New Orleans and its citizens.

"It is very important, not just here in the United States but all over the world, 　2 that people hear the stories from these individuals, these witnesses, who saw the horror of what happened in New Orleans," Lee said in a recent interview with HBO. The film is Lee's third collaboration with HBO (after the Oscar-nominated *4 Little Girls* as well as *Jim Brown: All American*), which wanted Lee to craft the "documentary of record" about the tragedy. Three months after Katrina hit, Lee and a small crew made the first of eight trips to New Orleans to shoot raw footage of the disaster and gather subjects for interviews. Ultimately,° close to one hundred subjects appear in

Dennis O'Neil wrote this review of Spike Lee's documentary on Hurricane Katrina for the Louisville Cardinal, *the newspaper of the University of Louisville. The review was published in September 2006.*

Levees: Walls or embankments that hold back water to prevent flooding.   **Requiem:** A solemn chant, song, or other work of art that honors the dead.   **unprecedented:** New; never achieved before.   **epic:** Large in scope.   **a multitude:** Many.   **Ultimately:** Finally; in the end.

the film, all from various walks of life, including academics, military personnel, politicians, celebrities, activists, and residents of New Orleans who were the most affected by the tragedy.

The film is divided into four one-hour acts with acts 1 and 2 encompassing° the   3
period of time between the earliest threats of Katrina to the point where survivors were finally beginning to be evacuated five days after the storm hit. Many of the interview subjects offer strong evidence that the flood of New Orleans was not caused entirely by Katrina but because the city's levee system was not structurally adequate, as it was not strong enough to withstand even a category-three° storm.

What images or voices from the Katrina disaster persist in your memory?

The film offers harrowing° and graphic° images of the disaster while it was in   4
progress, as well as of the aftermath in which the survivors fled their flooded homes for various sanctuaries° around the city. Lee shows the roof on the New Orleans Superdome slowly turning to rust as the storm progresses and how federal aid, which was so quick to assist the tsunami victims in Asia,° didn't arrive until long after the worst had already occurred.

"It was absolutely horrific° conditions," said survivor Fred Johnson to Lee.   5
"It was like being in the middle of a war and all you could do was stand there and feel helpless."

Many of the personal tragedies experienced by the survivors are addressed in the   6
film, such as that of Herbert Freeman Jr., a resident of the Lower Ninth Ward neighborhood of New Orleans, whose mother passed away during the disaster. Freeman was forced to leave her dead body sitting in the Superdome with a note attached to her because she couldn't be airlifted out and Freeman couldn't take her with him. She sat there for days before someone noticed her.

Acts 3 and 4 of the film heavily depict° the aftermath of the tragedy, as the   7
survivors were shepherded° to various areas of the country to restart their lives. Many of them recount° the various hardships of being separated from family members, looking for new homes, fighting with insurance companies, and experiencing the heartache of losing the only home many of them have ever known.

What does "home" mean to you? What do you value in it?

"Thanksgiving was a heart-wrenching situation," said Pastor James Pullings to   8
Lee. "It broke my heart to hear people saying, 'I want to go home, but I have no home to go to.'"

---

encompassing: Covering; consisting of.   **category-three:** A storm characterized by 111- to 130-mph winds and 9- to 12-foot storm surges. Hurricane Katrina made landfall as a category-four storm, with wind speeds up to 140 mph.   **harrowing:** Upsetting. **graphic:** Vivid, often in a disturbing way.   **sanctuaries:** Places of safety.   **tsunami victims in Asia:** A reference to the post-earthquake tidal wave that killed more than 200,000 people in 2004.   **horrific:** Horrifying; terrible.   **depict:** Show or portray.   **shepherded:** Led.   **recount:** Recall; describe.

Many of the film's most poignant° moments involve survivors returning to New   9
Orleans and being confronted by the devastation that has occurred there. In one
scene, the elderly Wilhelmina Blanchard returns to her home and breaks into uncon-
trollable sobs as she sees the horrific state that it is now in. "I had heard of the
devastation," she says through tears, "but I didn't know it was this bad."

"You walk through your old neighborhood," says actor Wendell Pierce, "and you   10
see a house with the number two on the door, and you realize, 'Man, two people died
in that house.' And it's just so deafeningly quiet."

But Lee's ultimate victory with the film is that he doesn't allow the silence to   11
drown out the heart of New Orleans that still beats underneath it. The film's most
moving moment occurs when Terence Blanchard, who composed the film's mournful,
elegiac° score, walks the ghostly silent streets of New Orleans and plays on his
trumpet a soulful jazz lullaby, as if humming a crippled giant to sleep.

"One of the things that I hope this documentary does is remind America that   12
New Orleans is not over with," added Lee. "It's not done."

What does "It's not done" suggest to you?

Questions to Start You Thinking

Meaning

1. Why did Spike Lee make the documentary described in the essay?
2. What content (visual, testimonial, and so on) did Lee include to make his point about the effects of Hurricane Katrina on its survivors and on New Orleans?
3. What is the "ultimate victory" of the film, according to O'Neil?

Writing Strategies

4. What criteria does O'Neil use to judge Lee's documentary? To what extent has the film met these criteria, according to O'Neil?
5. Does O'Neil provide enough evidence to support his judgment? Why or why not?
6. O'Neil makes extensive use of quotations. Do you find the quotations effective or overdone?
7. Using highlighters or marginal notes, identify the essay's introduction, thesis, criteria for evaluation, supporting evidence, and conclusion. How effective is the organization of the essay?

poignant: Touching or moving.   **elegiac:** Sorrowful.

Learning by Writing

THE ASSIGNMENT: WRITING AN EVALUATION

■ For writing activities for evaluating, visit <bedfordstmartins.com/ bedguide> and do a keyword search:

activities

Pick a subject to evaluate — one you have personal experience with and feel competent to evaluate. This might be a movie, a TV program, a piece of music, an artwork, a new product, a government agency, a campus facility or policy, an essay or a reading, or anything else you can think of. Then in a thoughtful essay, analyze your subject and evaluate it. You will need to determine specific criteria for evaluation and make them clear to your readers. In writing your evaluation, you will have a twofold purpose: (1) to set forth your assessment of the quality of your subject and (2) to convince your readers that your judgment is reasonable.

Among the lively student-written evaluations we've seen are these:

A music major evaluated several works by American composer Aaron Copland, finding him trivial and imitative, "without a tenth of the talent or inventiveness that George Gershwin or Duke Ellington had in his little finger."

A student planning a career in business management evaluated a computer firm in which he had worked one summer. His criteria were efficiency, productivity, appeal to new customers, and employee satisfaction.

A student from Brazil, who had seen firsthand the effects of industrial development in the Amazon rain forest, evaluated the efforts of the U.S. government to protect forests and wetlands, comparing them with the efforts of environmentalists in her own country.

GENERATING IDEAS

Find Something to Evaluate.   Try using *brainstorming* or *mapping* to identify as many possible topics as you can think of. Select the ones with most potential — the ones that are most familiar or easiest to find out about. Spend enough time investigating these possibilities that you can comfortably choose one subject for your essay.

Consider Sources of Support.   You'll want to spend time finding material to help you develop a judgment. You may recall a program on television or hunt for an article to read. You might observe a performance or a sports team. An interview or conversation could reveal what others think. Perhaps you'll want to review several examples of your subject: watching several films, listening to several CDs, examining several works of art, or testing several

College production of Romeo and Juliet

Developing a Consensus

Meet with your writing group to discuss the subject you plan to evaluate, and see whether the group can help you arrive at a sound judgment. The others will need to see or hear your detailed report about what you're evaluating. If possible, pass around a product, show a photograph of artwork, play a song on a CD, or read aloud a short literary work or an idea expressed in a reading. Ask your listeners to explain the reasons for their own evaluations. Maybe they'll suggest criteria or evidence that hadn't occurred to you.

FOR GROUP LEARNING

products. You might also browse for information about your subject at several Web sites or attend a campus concert or play.

Establish Your Criteria.   Jot down criteria, standards to apply to your subject based on the features of the subject worth considering. How well, for example, does a popular entertainer score on musicianship, onstage manner, rapport with the audience, selection of material, originality? In evaluating the desirability of Portland as a home for a young careerist, you might ask: Does it provide an ample choice of decent-paying entry-level positions in growth firms? Any criterion you use to evaluate has to fit your subject, your audience, and your purpose. After all, ample entry-level jobs might not matter to an audience of retirees.

■ For more strategies for generating ideas, see Ch. 16.

Try Comparing and Contrasting.   Often you can readily size up the worth of a thing by setting it next to another of its kind. (When you *compare*, you point to similarities; when you *contrast*, you note differences.) To be comparable, of course, your two subjects need to have plenty in common. The quality of a Harley Davidson motorcycle might be judged by contrasting it with a Honda but not with a Hummer.

■ For more on comparing and contrasting, see Ch. 7.

For example, if you are writing a paper for a film-history course, you might compare and contrast the classic German horror movie *The Cabinet of Dr. Caligari* with the classic Hollywood movie *Frankenstein*, concluding that *Caligari* is more artistic. In planning the paper, you might make two columns in which you list the characteristics of each film, point by point:

	CALIGARI	*FRANKENSTEIN*
SETS	Dreamlike and impressionistic	Realistic, but with heavy Gothic atmosphere
	Sets deliberately angular and distorted	Gothic sets
LIGHTING	Deep shadows that throw figures into relief	Torches highlighting monster's face in night scene

By jotting down each point and each bit of evidence side by side, you can outline your comparison and contrast with great efficiency. Once you have listed them, decide on a possible order for the points.

For more on defining, see pp. 356–57.

Try Defining Your Subject.   Another technique for evaluating is to define your subject, indicating its nature so clearly that your readers can easily distinguish it from others of its kind. In defining, you help your readers understand your subject — its structure, its habitat, its functions. In evaluating a classic television show such as *Roseanne* or *The Mary Tyler Moore Show,* you might want to do some *extended* defining, discussing the nature of sitcoms over the years, their techniques, their views of women, their effects on the audience. Unlike a *short definition,* as in a dictionary, an extended definition is intended not simply to explain but to judge: What is the nature of my subject? What qualities make my subject unique, unlike others of its sort?

Develop a Judgment That You Can Explain to Your Audience.   In the end, you will have to come to a decision: Is your subject good, worthwhile, significant, exemplary, preferable — or not? Most writers come to a judgment gradually as they explore their subjects and develop criteria.

Facing the Challenge: Evaluating

The major challenge writers face when writing evaluations is to make clear to their readers the criteria they have used to arrive at their opinion. While you may not be an expert in any field, you should never underestimate your powers of discrimination. When reviewing a movie, for example, you may begin by simply summarizing the story of the film and saying whether you like it or not. However, for readers who are wondering whether to see the movie, you need to go beyond these comments. For example, you might find a movie's special effects, exotic sets, and unpredictable plot effective but wish that the characters had seemed more believable. Based on these criteria, you might come up with the thesis that the movie may not be realistic but is extremely entertaining and well worth seeing.

Once you've chosen a topic, use the following questions to help you clarify and apply standards for evaluating it:

- What features or standards do you plan to use as criteria for evaluating your topic?
- How could you briefly explain each of the criteria for a reader?
- What judgment or evaluation about your topic do these criteria support?

After identifying your criteria, you can examine each in turn. Explaining your criteria will ensure that you move beyond a summary to an opinion or judgment that you can justify to your readers.

To close in on a promising subject, ask yourself a few questions:

DISCOVERY CHECKLIST

—— What criteria do you plan to use in making your evaluation? Are they clear and reasonably easy to apply?

—— What evidence can back up your judgments?

—— Would comparing or contrasting help in evaluating your subject? If so, with what might you compare or contrast your subject?

—— What specific qualities define your subject, setting it apart from all the rest of its class?

PLANNING, DRAFTING, AND DEVELOPING

Start with a Thesis.   Reflect a moment: What is your purpose in this evaluation? What main point do you wish to make? Try writing a paragraph that sums up the purpose of your evaluation, or work on stating a thesis that summarizes your main point.

■ For more on stating a thesis, see pp. 312–19.

| TOPIC + JUDGMENT | campus performance of *Lobby Hero* — liked the seniors featured in it plus the problems the play raised |
| WORKING THESIS | Chosen to showcase the achievements of graduating seniors, the play *Lobby Hero* also brings up ethical problems. |

■ For exercises on choosing effective thesis statements, visit <bedfordstmartins.com/ bedguide> and do a keyword search:

thesis

Consider Your Criteria.   Many writers find that a list of specific criteria gives them confidence and provokes ideas. Consider filling in a chart with three columns — criteria, evidence, judgment — to help focus your thinking.

Develop an Organization.   You may want to begin with a direct statement of your judgment: Based on durability, cost, and comfort, the Classic 7 is an ideal campus backpack. On the other hand, you may want to reserve judgment by opening with a question about your subject: How good a film is *The Departed*? Each approach suggests a different organization:

Thesis or main point	→ Supporting evidence	→ Return to thesis
Opening question	→ Supporting evidence	→ Overall judgment

■ For more on outlining, see pp. 325–33.

In either case, you'll supply plenty of evidence — details, examples, possibly comparisons or contrasts — so that readers find your case compelling. You'll also cluster your evidence around your points or criteria for judgment so that readers know how and why you have reached your judgment. You might try both patterns of organization (or a different one altogether) and see which works better for your subject and purpose.

■ For exercises on supporting a thesis, visit <bedfordstmartins.com/ bedguide> and do a keyword search:

support

FOR PEER RESPONSE

For general questions for a peer editor, see p. 377. For peer response worksheets, visit <bedfordstmartins.com/bedguide> and do a keyword search:

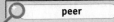
peer

Enlist the advice of a classmate or friend as you determine your criteria for evaluation and your judgment. Ask your peer editor to answer questions like these about your evaluation:

- What is your overall reaction to this essay? Does the writer persuade you to agree with his or her evaluation?

- When you finish the essay, can you tell exactly what the writer thinks of the subject? Where does the writer express this opinion?

- How do you know what criteria the writer is using for evaluation?

- Does the writer give you sufficient evidence for his or her judgment? Put stars wherever more or better evidence is needed.

- What audience does the writer seem to have in mind?

- Would you recommend any changes in the essay's organization?

- If this were your paper, what is the one thing you would be sure to work on before handing it in?

Most writers find that an outline—even a rough list—helps them keep track of points to make. If you intend to compare and contrast your subject with something else, one way to arrange the points is *subject by subject:* discuss subject A, and then discuss subject B. For a longer comparison, a better way to organize is *point by point,* applying each point first to one subject and then to the other. If appropriate and approved by your instructor, you also might plan to include a sketch, photograph, or other illustration of your subject or develop a comparative table summarizing the features of similar items you have compared.

REVISING AND EDITING

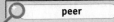 For more on stating a thesis, see pp. 315–18. For more revising and editing strategies, see Ch. 20.

Focus on Your Thesis.   As you begin to revise, make your thesis as precise and clear as possible.

> WORKING THESIS   Chosen to showcase the graduating seniors, the play *Lobby Hero* also brings up ethical problems.
>
> REVISED THESIS   This year's senior showcase play, *Lobby Hero* by Kenneth Lonergan, spotlights outstanding performers and raises timely ethical issues.

Be Fair.   Make your judgments reasonable, not extreme. A reviewer can find fault with a film and still conclude that it is worth seeing. There's nothing wrong, of course, with a fervent judgment ("This is the trashiest excuse for a play I have ever suffered through"), but consider your readers and their

Supporting Judgments

After you have written a draft of your evaluative essay, you will need to consider how well you have linked specific support to your judgments. Scroll through the draft, and highlight each judgment or opinion with color. (Look under "Format" to find "font" choices, including color.) Then go back to the beginning, and this time highlight all facts and evidence with a different color. Are your judgments followed by or related to the evidence to support your claims? Do you need to modify your judgments or revise your support? Do you need to add more support at any points or move sentences around so that your support is more closely linked to your judgments? Connecting your claims with your evidence makes your evaluation persuasive and interesting.

FOR E-WRITERS

likely reactions. Read some reviews in your local newspaper or watch some movie critics on television to see how they balance their judgments. Because readers will have more confidence in your opinions if you seem fair and reasonable, revise your tone and your wording where needed. For example, one writer revised his opening after he realized that he was evaluating the audience rather than the performance.

> The most recent performance by a favorite campus group--Rock Mountain--
> *disappointing concert   Although t*
> was an ~~incredibly revolting~~ experience. ~~The~~ ~~outlandish~~ crowd ignored the DJ who
> *people*
> introduced the group/ and a few ~~nameless members of one social group spent~~
> *ed*
> ~~their time~~ toss~~ing~~ around trash cans in front of the stage/, *the opening number*
>
> *still announced the group's powerful musical presence.*

Use this handy checklist as you think critically about your draft:

REVISION CHECKLIST

___ Is the judgment you pass on your subject unmistakably clear?

___ Have you given your readers evidence to support each point you make?

___ Have you been fair? If you are championing something, have you deliberately skipped over any of its disadvantages or faults? If you are condemning your subject, have you omitted any of its admirable traits?

___ Have you anticipated and answered readers' possible objections?

___ If you compare one thing with another, do you look consistently at the same points in both?

■ For more on comparison and contrast, see Ch. 7 and pp. 366–68.

■ For more editing and proofreading strategies, see pp. 384–87.

After you have revised your evaluation, edit and proofread it. Carefully check grammar, word choice, punctuation, and mechanics — and then correct any problems you find. Make sentences in which you describe the subject of your evaluation as precise and useful as possible. If you have used comparisons or contrasts, make sure these are clear: don't lose your readers in a fog of vague pronouns or confusing references.

Here are some questions to help you start editing and proofreading:

EDITING CHECKLIST

■ For more help turn to the dark-blue-edged pages and find the sections in the Quick Editing Guide noted here.

—— Is the reference of each pronoun clear? Does each pronoun agree with (match) its antecedent?   A6

—— Is it clear what each modifier in a sentence modifies? Have you created any dangling or misplaced modifiers, especially in descriptions of your subject?   B1

—— Have you used parallel structure wherever needed, especially in lists or comparisons?   B2

OTHER ASSIGNMENTS

1. Write an evaluation of a college course you have taken or are now taking. Analyze its strengths and weaknesses. Does the instructor present the material clearly, understandably, and interestingly? Can you confer with the instructor if you need to? Are the assignments pointed and purposeful? Is the textbook helpful, readable, and easy to use? Does this course give you your money's worth?

■ For more on responding to literature, see Ch. 13.

2. Read these two poems on a similar theme critically, and decide which seems to you the better poem. Then, in a brief essay, set forth your evaluation. Some criteria to apply might be the poet's choice of concrete, specific words that appeal to the senses and his awareness of his audience.

Putting in the Seed
ROBERT FROST (1874–1963)

You come to fetch me from my work tonight
When supper's on the table, and we'll see

If I can leave off burying the white
Soft petals fallen from the apple tree
(Soft petals, yes, but not so barren quite,
Mingled with these, smooth bean and wrinkled pea),
And go along with you ere you lose sight
Of what you came for and become like me,
Slave to a springtime passion for the earth.
How Love burns through the Putting in the Seed
On through the watching for that early birth

When, just as the soil tarnishes with weed,
The sturdy seedling with arched body comes
Shouldering its way and shedding the earth crumbs.

Between Our Folding Lips
T. E. BROWN (1830–1897)

Between our folding lips
God slips
An embryon life, and goes;
And this becomes your rose.
We love, God makes: in our sweet mirth
God spies occasion for a birth.
Then is it His, or is it ours?
I know not — He is fond of flowers.

3. Visit a restaurant, a museum, or a tourist attraction, and write an evaluation of it for others who might consider a visit. Or evaluate an unfamiliar magazine, an essay in this textbook, a proposal under consideration
at work, or a source you have read for a college class. Be sure to specify
your criteria for evaluation.

Applying What You Learn: Some Uses of Evaluating

In College Courses.   In writing assignments and on exams, you'll be
asked over and over to evaluate. Evaluation demonstrates to your instructor
your sound understanding and considered opinion of a topic.

- Speech pathology students might be asked to consider the long-standing
controversy that rages in education for the deaf by describing and then
evaluating three currently disputed teaching methods — oral/aural, sign-
ing, and a combination of the two.

- Students of language and linguistics might be asked to evaluate Skin-
ner's behaviorist theory of articulation therapy.

- Students often are asked to evaluate their instructors and courses; outside class, students on some campuses are invited to evaluate their campus facilities or student services.

In the Workplace.   Every executive or professional needs to evaluate people,
projects, goals, and results.

- Political commentators and newspaper editors evaluate the state of the
economy, the actions of the administration or Congress, the decisions
of the Supreme Court, and the merits of proposed legislation.

Career UNIVERSITY Services

return

Evaluating Job Offers

- To evaluate all the factors associated with the position offered and the organization, ask for sufficient time to consider the offer. Sufficient time will depend on your needs and the needs of the organization. The amount of time you need may be different from what the company needs. You may be asked to give your decision sooner than you wish. If, at the end of that time, you have not been able to make a decision, ask for an extension, which may or may not be granted.

- Consider the position, the goals established for the position, the company's track record, what is projected for the company's future, opportunity for promotion, personalities of supervisor and coworkers, management style, and corporate culture.

- Follow up with other organizations that are considering you for employment in which you still have interest. Explain that you have received another offer, but because of your interest in their organization/position, you are following up with them to learn the status of your candidacy.

Web page from George Mason University Career Services

Ratings for video games get more specific

The rating board for the video game industry announced a new age category to fill the gap between "E" for everyone and "T" for teen.

New rating category
E10+ (Everyone 10 and older)
▶ Ages 10 and up
▶ May contain more cartoon, fantasy or mild violence, mild profanity and/or minimally suggestive themes

Existing rating categories

Rating	EC (Early Childhood)	E (Everyone)	T (Teen)	M (Mature)	AO (Adults Only)
Ages	3+	6+	13+	17+	18+
May contain	No material parents would find inappropriate	Minimal cartoon, fantasy or mild violence and/or infrequent use of mild language	Violence, suggestive themes, crude humor, minimal blood and/or infrequent use of strong language	Mature sexual themes, more intense violence and/or strong language	Graphic depictions of sex and/ or violence

SOURCE: Entertainment Software Rating Board

Ratings for video games

- Agencies such as police departments, civil defense units, rescue squads, or the Red Cross evaluate their performance in crisis situations to refine their responses.

- Every job applicant is evaluated by the employer — and every job applicant also evaluates the employer, the workplace, and the job offer.

In Your Community. Written evaluation is common in our daily lives.

- In a posting to an online discussion group, you might explain your evaluation of the topic or of comments of others in the group.

- Friends, peers, or co-workers may ask you to write a letter of recommendation for a job or a commendation for an award. In either case, you'll evaluate relevant characteristics of performance or merit.

- Parents may evaluate the suitability of video games for their children based on industry ratings.

Chapter 12
Supporting a Position with Sources

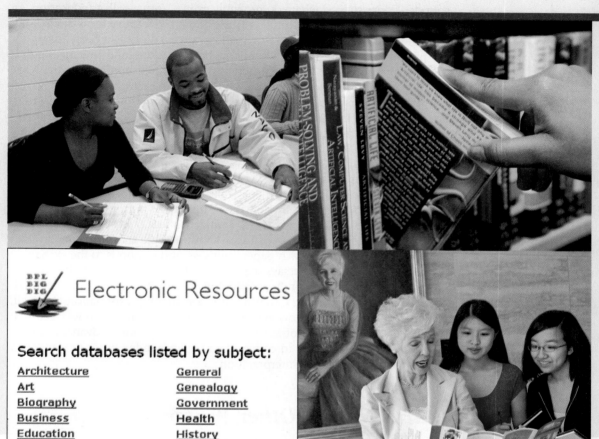

Responding to an Image

These images show activities that might help a student gather evidence from sources to support a position in a college paper. What does each image suggest about possible sources? What do the images suggest about the process of inquiry? Which activities look most intriguing? What other activities might have appeared in images on this page?

Suppose you conducted a survey at your school, asking a random group of students nearing graduation to describe a typical college writing assignment. The odds are good that the typical assignment might boil down to reading a few texts and writing a paper about them. Simple as this description sounds, it does suggest what you probably expect from a college education: an opportunity to absorb and think seriously about provocative ideas. It also suggests the values that lie behind many college expectations — a deep respect for the process of inquiry (the academic method of asking and investigating intriguing questions) and for the products of disciplined inquiry (the analyses, interpretations, and studies that are well regarded in each academic field).

When you first tackle such assignments, you may wonder "How do I figure out what my instructor really wants?" or "How could I possibly do that?" In response, you may turn to peripheral questions such as "How long does my paper have to be?" or "How many sources do I have to use?" instead of facing the central question: "How can I learn the skills I need to use a few sources to develop and support a position in a college paper?" Unlike a presidential debate or a Super Bowl game, a paper that takes a position generally doesn't have two distinct sides or a single winner. Instead of pitting either/or alternatives against each other, the writer of a typical college paper makes a point by joining the ongoing exchange of ideas about a topic that intrigues or challenges others in the field. Each paper builds on and responds to the exchanges of the past — the articles, essays, reports, books, and other texts that convey the perspectives, research findings, and conclusions of others. Although reading such sources may seem daunting, it is a reassuring expectation. After all, you are not expected to know everything yourself but simply to work conscientiously at learning what others know. Your paper, in turn, advances or redirects the exchange in order to convey your well-grounded point of view or to defend your well-reasoned interpretation.

Learning from Other Writers

■ For more on thesis and support, see Chs. 17 and 19.

The selections here illustrate how two different writers draw on evidence from sources to substantiate their points. The notes in the margin of the first reading will help you begin to analyze features such as the thesis, or main idea, and the variety of methods used to introduce and integrate information from sources.

■ For more such writings, visit <bedfordstmartins.com/bedguide> and do a keyword search:

🔍 examples

As You Read These Essays That Support a Position with Sources

As you read these essays, ask yourself the following questions:

1. What thesis, or main idea, expresses the position supported by the essay? How does the writer try to help readers appreciate the importance of this position?

2. In what ways does the writer use information from sources to develop and support a thesis? Do you find this information relevant and persuasive?

3. How does the writer vary the way each source is introduced and the way information is drawn from it?

This excerpt comes from David Callahan's book The Cheating Culture: Why More Americans Are Doing Wrong to Get Ahead *(2004). This selection illustrates the use of MLA style to cite and list sources.*

David Callahan

A Question of Character

Opinion surveys confirm an explosion of material° desires over the past two decades, along with a growing focus on financial success and the increasing linkage in people's minds between meeting these goals and achieving happiness. For example, in 1975, less than 20 percent of Americans surveyed identified a vacation home as being part of the "good life." By the early 1990s, that number had jumped to 35 percent. Less than 15 percent of people put a swimming pool in their dream scenario° in 1975; in 1991, nearly a third of people did. A second car and a second color television became far more important during this period as well, as did travel abroad° and having fashionable clothes.

Financial goals also began pushing aside other aspirations.° The number of Americans who saw the good life as hinging on "a lot of money" and "a job that pays more than average" jumped substantially in the 1980s, rising from a minority of Americans who emphasized these two goals to a majority. As Americans expanded the list of material possessions that they saw as central to the good life, they de-emphasized the importance of other aspects° of life. Even as more people admitted hankering after° swimming pools and vacation homes, they also reported a declining focus on having a happy marriage or an interesting job (Ladd and Bowman 51).

The shifting values and priorities of Americans over the past two decades have been especially evident among young people. Since 1966, the Cooperation Institutional Research Program has tracked the attitudes and demographic° characteristics of college freshman (Astin et al.). Over 700 campuses participate in the surveys every year. In all, more than nine million students have been surveyed. The trends among freshmen perfectly illustrate the rise of the money obsession and the sidelining of less materialistic goals.

In the first years of the survey, during the late 1960s, less than 50 percent of college freshman saw the goal of being well-off financially as either essential or very important, and just over half said the chief benefit of a college education is that it increased their earning potential. The shift toward materialism° among

Margin annotations:

1   **THESIS**
Presenting position

Point 1: goal shifts in general population

2   Supporting evidence, including facts, statistics, and examples to demonstrate a change

Paraphrase (see pp. 218–19)
Source authors and page in parentheses

3   Point 2: goal shifts among young people

Et al. ("and others") used for source with more than three authors

Author's position based on sources cited in next paragraphs

4

---

material: Concerning monetary, as opposed to spiritual, value; concerning physical possessions.   **scenario:** Situation.   **abroad:** Outside of one's country.   **aspirations:** Dreams; goals.   **aspects:** Parts.   **hankering after:** Desiring.   **demographic:** Referring to the characteristics of certain populations.   **materialism:** A concern with physical or material security or possessions rather than intellectual or spiritual pursuits.

Paraphrase
(see pp. 218–19)

Direct quotation
(see pp. 214–15)
Source author and
page numbers cited in
parentheses.

young people began in the mid-1970s, as the idealism° of the 1960s faded
and harsh new economic times arrived. For example, the number of students
who said they went to college to "make more money" climbed ten percentage points in just three years, beginning in 1976. By the mid-1980s, three-
quarters of college students stressed the goal of being well-off financially, a
ratio that held through the 1990s. Today, this goal remains one of two or
three of the highest-rated objectives of college freshman, along with the
status-oriented goal of becoming "an authority in my field" (Astin et al. 46–47).

By 1986, more than a quarter of college freshman reported that they   5
planned to go into business, a career choice that trumped° the closest rival
by nearly three to one. This was also the year in which 40 percent of Yale's
graduating class of 1,300 applied for a job at one investment bank alone,
First Boston. Economics courses were oversubscribed° at Yale and other top
universities as students hurried to qualify themselves to join the gold rush on
Wall Street. The promise of vast riches had an intoxicating° appeal and was
not illusory.° "Never before have so many unskilled twenty-four-year-olds
made so much money in so little time as did in this decade," wrote Yale graduate Michael Lewis, who joined Salomon Brothers.° (This statement, of
course, would be dated by the dot-com era° [Lewis, Liar's 24, 9].)

Short version of title
used because two works
by Michael Lewis are
cited (see para. 7)

As making money moved front and center, young people stopped caring   6
about other things. In the late 1960s, believe it or not, the most important
goal of college freshman was "developing a meaningful philosophy of life,"
cited by over 80 percent of entering students. The centrality of this goal
waned° steadily over the next twenty years, reaching an all-time low of 39
percent in 1987, at the height of the '80s boom. Interest in keeping up with
politics and cleaning up the environment also markedly — and permanently
— declined during the 1980s. The outlook among America's young was epit-
omized° by Alex Keaton, the teenage star of the hit television show Family
Ties. Alex was a briefcase-toting° microyuppie,° played brilliantly by Michael
J. Fox. To the horror of his bohemian° parents, he was all business and
money, brandishing° an inch-thick résumé in one episode. Alex never
doubted that kids like him were the wave of the future.

Author continues
statement-support pattern

Transition from previous
point

He was right. While young people's interest in mainstream business ca-   7
reers dipped sharply after the crash of 1987,° the money obsession morphed°
into a new kind of market populism° by the late 1990s. Making money was

idealism: A concern with high-minded, as opposed to practical, goals.   trumped: Defeated.   oversubscribed: Overenrolled.   intoxicating: Creating enthusiasm; having
an effect like alcohol.   illusory: Imaginary.   Salomon Brothers: An investment bank.
dot-com era: The period, roughly 1997–2001, when many Internet businesses saw sharp
increases in their stock values and received large amounts of investor funds.   waned:
Declined.   epitomized: Clearly illustrated.   briefcase-toting: Briefcase-carrying.
microyuppie: Small, referring to Fox's short stature, young urban professional.   bo-
hemian: Artistic or unconventional.   brandishing: Shaking or waving.   crash of
1987: A record-breaking plunge in the Dow Jones Industrial Average, a measure of stock-
market value.   morphed: Changed.   populism: A concern with the interests of the
average person.

way cool, and you didn't need a suit to do it. Teenagers swapped stock tips and traded over the Internet during lunch breaks. One fifteen-year-old in New Jersey amassed° a nearly million-dollar fortune by masquerading° as multiple people on Yahoo! and hyping° low-priced stocks. The money was rolling in until SEC° investigators arrived at his door (Lewis, "Jonathan" 26). Other teenagers built technology companies in their refinished basements, imagining themselves as the next Steve Jobs.° If Alex Keaton came back to the future° of the late 1990s, he would have staged an IPO° from his bedroom.

For young people, though, the biggest social-health story of the 1990s was the onslaught° of a virulent° new strain of consumerism. The disease begins earlier and earlier with children these days, and it just gets worse. Parents complain endlessly about pressures from their kids to keep up with the Johnnies at the locker next door — with expensive video games, designer-label clothing, digital music players (to play pirated music), home computers, and cell phones. "Over the past ten years, more people have come to think of themselves as having their identities shaped by their consumer goods," commented Alissa Quart, author of Branded, a book about consumerism among teenagers. "But teens and tweens° are more vulnerable° and more open to a warped° relationship that the brands are selling to them. It's an emptied-out relationship where they pour themselves into a brand and see themselves through objects, rather than through people or ideas" (qtd. in Holstein). Quart's book is filled with stories about sixth graders lusting after $500 Kate Spade bags and startling statistics, like how kids spend $600 billion a year of their parents' money and advertisers spend $12 billion a year to influence those buying decisions. She also shows the way in which movies and television programs about teenagers now emphasize an amazingly opulent° lifestyle in places like Beverly Hills.°

A bit of competitive spending might be fine if it weren't so hard to keep up with those who set today's standards of material well-being. As Juliet Schor has documented in The Overspent American, nobody actually compares themselves anymore to the Joneses of yesteryear — that is, the next-door neighbor in a similar income group. We are now likely to compare ourselves with "reference groups" who make much more money than we do. If you're rich, you compare yourself to the superrich. You don't want a "McMansion,"° you want a real mansion — like the one you saw lovingly

8

9

Short title added to identify which work by Lewis

Synthesis and application of ideas (see p. 224)

Point 3: shift toward consumerism

Source quoted in another source, no page needed for one-page article

Summary of information (see p. 220)

---

amassed: Collected; accumulated.   **masquerading:** Playing the role of; acting as. **hyping:** Speaking with excessive enthusiasm about something.   **SEC:** Securities and Exchange Commission, the U.S. government body that investigates misdeeds related to stock trading.   **Steve Jobs:** Cofounder and chief executive officer of Apple Computer. **back to the future:** Reference to the title of the 1985 film in which the main character, played by Michael J. Fox, travels back in time, where he puts his future existence at risk. **IPO:** Initial public offering, a company's first sale of stock on the public market.   **onslaught:** Attack.   **virulent:** Dangerously potent.   **tweens:** Young people *between* childhood and their teenage years.   **vulnerable:** Susceptible to; available to.   **warped:** Distorted.   **opulent:** Luxurious.   **Beverly Hills:** A wealthy part of Los Angeles. **"McMansion":** A large home that, like McDonald's hamburgers, is mass-produced and appeals to many people.

described in a rerun of Lifestyles of the Rich and Famous. If you're upper middle class, you compare yourself to the rich. If you're middle class or lower class, you might compare yourself to both the upper middle class and the rich (Schor). . . .

With pressures like these, it's no surprise that many Americans believe 10 that more money would make them happier. And yet, like a mirage,° people's definition of enough money keeps flitting° farther into the distance. Between 1987 and 1996, a period of only modest income gains for most households, the estimate among Americans as to how much annual income they needed to live in "reasonable comfort" increased by 30 percent, while the amount of money they felt they would need to fulfill all their dreams nearly doubled, from $50,000 to $90,000. According to one survey conducted in the early '90s, 85 percent of American households aspired° to have a lifestyle associated with those in the top fifth of the income ladder. Only 15 percent said they would be satisfied ending up as middle class or just "living a comfortable life." A majority of Americans consistently report that they don't have enough income to live the life they want. Gaps between financial dreams and realities are hardly new in America. Some might even say that these gaps are what America is all about and that they are a good thing, keeping people on their toes and the economy humming. Yet there's a fine line between aspiration and envy, and between a healthy desire to get ahead and a relentless° struggle to keep up. Judging by poll data, America crossed that line quite a while ago (Schor 13; Ladd and Bowman 95).

Conclusion underscoring position

Works Cited

Each source cited in Callahan's essay listed alphabetically by author, with full publication information; first line of entry at left margin; subsequent lines indented ½"

Section and page both supplied for a newspaper article

Author's name listed only once for two works by the same author

Astin, Alexander W., et al. The American Freshman: Thirty-Year Trends. Los Angeles: Higher Education Research Institute, 1997.

Holstein, William. "Marketers Crank It Up for a New Generation." New York Times 26 Jan. 2003: III6.

Ladd, Everett Carll, and Karlyn H. Bowman. Attitudes toward Economic Inequality. Washington: AEI, 1988.

Lewis, Michael. "Jonathan Lebed's Extracurricular Activities." New York Times Magazine 25 Feb. 2001: 26+.

---. Liar's Poker. New York: Penguin, 1989.

Quart, Alissa. Branded: The Buying and Selling of Teenagers. New York: Perseus, 2003.

Schor, Juliet. The Overspent American: Upscaling, Downshifting, and the New Consumer. New York: Basic Books, 1998.

Questions to Start You Thinking

Meaning

1. What position does Callahan take in this essay?

2. What age group particularly concerns Callahan? What has changed about this age group since the mid-1970s?

mirage: A shimmering illusion of water that appears in hot, dry places, like deserts. **flitting:** Moving or shifting.   **aspired:** Hoped.   **relentless:** Never-ending.

3. In paragraph 9, Callahan refers to "competitive spending." What does he mean by this, and what has changed about such spending?

4. How has Callahan arranged the main points in his essay? How do these points develop his thesis (stated in paragraph 1) and lead up to paragraph 10?

Writing Strategies

5. What types of evidence does Callahan use to support his position? How convincing is this evidence to you?

6. Callahan states most source information in his own words rather than quoting sources directly. What seem to be the advantages and disadvantages of these two approaches?

7. How would you describe Callahan's tone, the quality of his writing that reveals his attitude toward his topic and his readers? What specific words, phrases, or sentences contribute to his tone? Does the tone seem appropriate for his purpose and audience?

8. Compare this selection, excerpted from a book, with an article written for a newspaper (see, for example, "Katrina Documentary Gives Voice to Survivors," p. 187). What differences in formatting, style, and presentation do you notice between the two selections?

STUDENT ESSAY

Melissa Lamberth
Overworked!

In the song "Nine to Five," Dolly Parton speaks for the overworked employee whose life is drained away by the clock. The amount of time Americans are working is on the increase, and Americans are growing weary.° Shorter workdays or more opportunities to take time off need to be available in order to provide a safer, happier, and more energetic workplace.

In her book The Overworked American, Schor writes, "The rise of work time was unexpected. For nearly a hundred years, hours had been declining. When this decline abruptly° ended in the late 1940s, it marked the beginning of a new era in work time" (1). Schor explains how this surprising increase has grown during recent years: "Each year, the change is small, amounting to about nine hours, or slightly more than one additional day of work. In any given year, such a small increment° has probably been imperceptible,° but the accumulated increase over two decades is substantial" (2). If Americans are gaining a little over a day of work each year, that is over ten days in a decade! This does not leave much time for family responsibilities or, much less, for leisure time.

Melissa Lamberth wrote this essay for a composition course at Riverside Community College. She used MLA style to cite and list sources. For more on this citation style, see E1–E2 in the Quick Research Guide (the dark-red-edged pages).

1

2

(?) *Do you feel overworked? Why or why not?*

weary: Tired.   **abruptly:** Suddenly.   **increment:** Unit (of growth, in this case).
imperceptible: Not noticeable.

Overworked employees may present a problem not only in the household but also in the workplace and even on the road. In his essay "Four Weeks Vacation," Robinson writes, "The health implications° of sleep-deprived° motorists weaving their way to the office or operating machinery on the job are self-evident" (481). An employee may work a couple of hours of overtime, drive home in traffic for half an hour or an hour, cook or eat dinner with the family, and then clean up after dinner. On top of that, there are errands to run and bills to pay. How much time does that leave the individual to rest? This schedule easily could lead to a "sleep-deprived motorist" or an injured machine operator.   3

The toll that overworked employees take on the family is also evident. In recent years, it has become more and more common for both parents to go to work to support the family. Time is a very important factor in keeping relationships in the household healthy. If both parents are spending a majority of their time working, it may be very difficult to find time to raise the kids and keep a marriage intact. In an article titled "Just What the Worker Needs — Longer Days, No Overtime," Eisenbrey writes, "Women are working many more weeks per year and hours per week, on average, than they did 30 or even 10 years ago. Middle-class married couples with children and a head of household between the ages of 25 and 54 now work an average of 98 weeks a year, compared with 78 weeks in 1969. Overtime for either spouse — but especially the mother — can have serious effects on a family."   4

What do you think of these ideas? Are they practical?

All these added stresses, caused by overworking, are carried straight back to the workplace the next morning. Negative attitudes set in. Employees start to hate work. As a result, morale goes down in the workplace. It is a vicious° cycle that Americans are stuck in. How can this cycle be stopped? Overtime, for one thing, should not be required but only allowed as an option. If employees have too much extra work to do, employers should consider giving the work to someone else. This could mean hiring another employee or dividing the extra work among employees who are not as busy.   5

Employees also need to have more opportunities to take time off. If the employee can't take desired time off due to a heavy workload, which is common in the workplace, employers need to consider hiring temporary employees or going through a temp agency to find employees who will work during the regular employee's time off. This work relief will make for a happier, less stressed employee. In an SFGate.com article titled "You Deserve a Month Off," columnist Mark Morford wrote, "We need more time off. A lot more time. Longer vacations. Extended breaks. Chunks of contiguous° time which you can roll around on the tongue of your id° and feel all swoony° and   6

implications: Consequences.   **sleep-deprived:** Lacking restorative slumber.   **vicious:** Harmful; nasty.   **contiguous:** Uninterrupted.   **id:** The part of the personality concerned with instincts and basic needs.   **swoony:** Given to fainting (in this case, out of happiness).

blissed.° When's the last time you saw an unhappy Aussie°? Exactly." Morford is implying that employees need more time off in order to be happier. He went on to say,
"It prevents burnouts and ameliorates° loathings° and lightens the spirit and lets
the psyche° breathe. . . ."

Some employers may claim that hiring temporary employees so that an   7
employee can have time off would not be cost-effective. However, good employees
are valuable. With that value in mind, hiring someone for a couple of weeks would
be worthwhile so that the regular employee could come back to work rested, re-
freshed, and more productive than ever!

Employers may believe that family- and life-related programs that teach employ-   8
ees how to manage stress and time are the answers to stress in the workplace. That
notion may lead some employees to question "Where are we going to get the time
for such programs?!?" They have their kids' soccer and softball games, meetings with
teachers, dinner to cook, and laundry to do. Employees simply have no time to be
involved in those programs.

An October 11, 2005, press release from an organization named Take Back Your   9
Time announced the sixty-fifth anniversary of the forty-hour workweek (Burger). In
its honor, this group declared October 24th Take Back Your Time Day. In the press release, John de Graaf, Take Back Your Time's national coordinator, stated, "It's 65
years later, productivity is quadruple what it was then, and still most Americans are
working more than 40 hours a week. If 40 hours was enough to support a family
then, it should take even less work time now. We need to start by getting the workweek back down to 40 hours." The organization is fighting for protected 40-hour
workweeks and for higher wages so that Americans don't have to work more than 40
hours to support a family above the poverty line. They are also fighting for salaried
workers who work long hours to be given comp time° for time required of them by
their employers that goes over the 40-hour workweek and for time-and-a-half overtime premiums° to be protected and strengthened.

*If you had more
time, what would you
do with it?*

These goals are positive stepping stones that will lead to a more positive work-   10
place. There should be no need for more than 40 hours of work each week when Americans didn't need to work this much 65 years ago. Technology has radically increased
productivity. Employers need to embrace this and "let their people go!" Let them take
an extra week off! Let them opt out of overtime! Let them get off work a couple of
hours early! In the long run, employees won't be let go, in the literal° sense, because
they will be more productive and punctual.° And that is well worth it.

---

blissed: Happy.   **Aussie:** Australian.   **ameliorates:** Makes better.   **loathings:** Ha-
treds.   **psyche:** Mind.   **comp time:** Compensatory time — time off given for extra
time worked.   **premiums:** Extra payments.   **literal:** Referring to the exact meaning of
a word or expression.   **punctual:** On time.

Works Cited

Burger, Gretchen. "Take Back Your Time." Take Back Your Time. 11 Oct. 2005. 15 Oct.
    2005 <http://www.timeday.org>.

Eisenbrey, Ross. "Just What the Worker Needs--Longer Days, No Overtime."
    Los Angeles Times 14 Feb. 2003. 16 Oct. 2005 <http://www.latimes.com>.

Morford, Mark. "You Deserve a Month Off." SFGate.com 19 Apr. 2002. 12 Oct. 2005
    <http://www.sfgate.com>.

Robinson, Joe. "Four Weeks Vacation." The Bedford Guide for College Writers. 7th ed.
    Ed. X. J. Kennedy, Dorothy M. Kennedy, Sylvia A. Holladay, and Marcia F. Muth.
    Boston: Bedford/St. Martin's, 2005. 479–84.

Schor, Juliet B. The Overworked American: The Unexpected Decline of Leisure. New
    York: Basic, 1992.

Questions to Start You Thinking

Meaning

1. What position does Lamberth support in this essay?

2. According to Lamberth, what difficulties and risks do overworked people face inside and outside of work?

3. What responsibilities do employers have to improve the lives of overworked employees, according to the author?

Writing Strategies

4. What types of evidence does Lamberth use to support her position? How convincing is this evidence to you?

5. Has Lamberth considered alternative views? How does the inclusion (or lack) of these views contribute to or detract from the essay?

6. Exclamation points are used in several places. Do you find this to be an effective or ineffective stylistic choice?

7. Using highlighters or marginal notes, identify the essay's introduction, thesis, major points, supporting evidence for each point, and conclusion. How effective is the organization of this essay?

Learning by Writing

THE ASSIGNMENT: SUPPORTING A POSITION WITH SOURCES

■ For writing activities on supporting a position with sources, visit <bedfordstmartins.com/ bedguide> and do a keyword search:

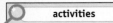
activities

Identify a cluster of readings about a topic that interests you. For example, choose some related readings from one of the thematic groups in *A Writer's Reader*, select several related essays from different thematic groups there, or draw on a group of related readings assigned in your class. If your topic is assigned and you don't begin with any particular interest in it, develop your intellectual curiosity by looking for an angle, an implication, or a vantage point that will engage you or relate in some way to your own experience. Read (or reread) the selections, allowing your curiosity to stimulate your thinking as you consider how each supports, challenges, or deepens your understanding of the topic.

Based on the information in your cluster of readings, develop an enlightening position about the topic that you'd like to share with an audience of college readers. Support this position—your working thesis—using quotations, paraphrases, summaries, and syntheses of the information in the readings as evidence. As you write your paper, be careful to present your information from sources clearly and to credit your sources appropriately.

■ See the contents of *A Writer's Reader* on p. 438.

Papers written in response to this type of assignment encompass great variety:

> One student examined local language usage that combined words from English and Spanish, drawing on essays about language diversity to analyze the patterns and implications of such usage.

> Another writer used a cluster of readings about technology to evaluate the looming privacy issues on a popular Web site for student profiles.

> Yet another, based on personal experience with a blended family and several essays about families, investigated and challenged misconceptions about family units today.

GENERATING IDEAS

Pin Down Your Working Topic and Your Cluster of Readings.   Try to specify what you're going to work on. This task is relatively easy if your instructor has assigned the topic and the required set of readings. If not, figure out what limits your instructor has set and which decisions are yours. Carefully follow any directions about the number or types of sources that you are expected to use. Instead of hunting only for sources that share your initial views about the topic, look for a variety of reliable and relevant sources so that you can broaden, even challenge, your perspective.

■ For more strategies for generating ideas, see Ch. 16.

Consider Your Audience.   You are writing for an audience of college readers intrigued by your topic (unless your instructor specifies some other group). In addition, your instructor probably holds several expectations. One is a broad goal, making sure that you are prepared to succeed when you take on future college writing assignments, including full research papers. For this reason, you'll be expected to quote, paraphrase, and summarize information from sources. Each time you use such material, you'll also need to introduce—or launch—it and credit its source, thus demonstrating essential skills for source-based writing.

■ For advice about finding and evaluating academic sources, turn to B and C in the Quick Research Guide (the dark-red-edged pages).

In addition, your instructor will want to see your own position emerge from the swamp of information that you are reading. Even if you feel that

One Student Thinking through a Topic

General Subject: Men and Women (Ch. 24)

Assigned topic: State and support a position about differences in the behavior of men and women.

What do I know about?   What do I care about?

RECALL PERSONAL EXPERIENCES: Friends at school? Competition for jobs? Pressure on parents to be good role models?

CONSIDER READINGS: Barry? Ehrenreich? Brady? Perrin? Staples? Jensen?

• *Stereotypes of women — emotional and caring*
• *Stereotypes of men — tough and agressive*
• *What about me? I'm a woman in training to be a police officer — and I'm a mother. I'm emotional, caring, aggressive, and tough.*

I bet that men and women are more alike than different. What do the readings say? What evidence do they present?

• **RETURN TO THE READINGS.**
• **TEST AND REFINE YOUR WORKING THESIS.**
• **LOOK FOR EVIDENCE.**

your ideas are like a prehistoric creature, dripping as it struggles out of the swamp onto solid ground, encourage your creature to reach dry land. Jot down your own ideas whenever they pop into mind. Highlight them in color on the page or on the screen. Store them in your writing notebook or in a special file so that you can find them, watch them accumulate, and give them well-deserved prominence in your paper.

■ For more on generating ideas, see Ch. 16.

Take an Academic Approach.   As a writer, you'll find that your experience and imagination remain your own deep well, an endless reservoir from which you can draw ideas whenever you need them. When you write an academic paper, this deep well may help you identify an intriguing topic, raise a compelling question about it, or pursue an unusual slant. For example, you might recall talking with your grandmother about the high cost of her prescriptions and decide to investigate the controversy about importing low-cost prescription medications from other countries.

■ For more on reading critically, see Ch. 2.

Besides drawing on your personal reserves, you'll also be expected to investigate your topic using authoritative sources. These sources — articles,

Facing the Challenge: Finding Your Voice

The major challenge that writers face when using sources to support a position is finding their own voices. You create your voice as a college writer through your choice of language, choice of words, and angle of vision. You probably want to present yourself as a reasonable writer with credible and engaging insights, a thoughtful person a reader will want to hear from. Finding your own voice may be especially difficult because of the complicated process of writing a source-based paper. After all, you need to read carefully to identify information that might strengthen or deepen your discussion. You need to select and capture that information by quoting, paraphrasing, or summarizing. You need to find a place for it in your draft, introduce it, feed it in, and, of course, credit it. By the time you've done all of this, you'll probably feel that your sources have taken over your paper. You may feel that there's no room left for your own voice and, even if there were, it's too soft or shy to jostle past the powerful words of your sources. That, however, is your challenge.

As you develop your voice as a college writer and use it to guide your readers' understanding, you'll restrict your sources to their proper role, acting as supporting evidence. Don't let them get pushy or dominate your writing. Use these questions to help you strengthen your voice:

For more on evidence, see pp. 37–42 and pp. 152–56.

- Can you write out a list or informal passage explaining what you'd like readers to hear from your voice? Where could you add more of this in your draft?

- Have you used your own voice, not quotations or paraphrases from sources, to introduce your topic, state your thesis, and draw your conclusions?

- Have you generally relied on your own voice to open and conclude your paragraphs and to reinforce your main ideas in every passage?

- Have you alternated between your voice and the voices of your sources? Can you strengthen your voice if it gets trampled by a herd of sources?

- Have you used your voice to identify and introduce source material before you present it? Have you used your voice to explain or interpret source material after you include it?

- Have you used your voice to tell readers why your sources are relevant, how they support your points, and what their limits might be?

- Have you carefully created your voice as a college writer, balancing passion and personality with rock-solid reasoning?

Whenever you are uncertain about the answers to these questions, make an electronic copy of your file or print it out. Highlight all of the wording in your own voice in a bright, visible color. Check for the presence and prominence of this highlighting, and then revise the white patches (the material drawn from sources) as needed to strengthen your voice.

Web search

essays, reports, books, Web pages, and other reliable materials — are your second deep well. When one well runs dry for the moment, start pumping the other. As you use your critical reading skills to tap your second reservoir, you join the academic exchange. This exchange is the flow of knowledge from one credible source to the next as writers and researchers raise questions, seek answers, evaluate information, and advance knowledge. As you inquire about your topic, you'll move from what you already know to deeper knowledge and a more complex appreciation of varied perspectives on the topic. Welcome sources that shed light on your inquiry rather than simply agree with a view you already hold.

Skim Your Sources.   When you work with a cluster of readings, you'll need to read them carefully and probably repeatedly. Start out, however, by skimming — quickly reading only enough to find out how the reading is organized and what direction it takes. First, leaf through the reading, glancing at any headings or figure labels. Return to the first paragraph, read it in full, but then read only the first sentence of each subsequent paragraph. At the end, read the final paragraph in full. Then stop to consider what you've already learned about the reading. Do the same with your other selections, classifying or comparing them as you begin to think about what they might contribute to your paper.

Here are a few questions to help you begin the process of juggling your ideas, your sources, and your instructor's expectations:

DISCOVERY CHECKLIST

___ What topic have you been assigned or are you considering? What ideas about it can you generate using brainstorming, freewriting, or another strategy for generating ideas?

___ What cluster of readings will you begin with? What do you already know about these readings? What have you learned about them simply by skimming them?

___ What purpose would you like to achieve in your paper? Who is your primary audience? What will your instructor expect you to accomplish?

___ What clues about how to proceed can you draw from the two sample essays in this chapter or from other readings that your instructor has identified as useful models?

Evaluating Reliable Sources

When you select your own sources, you'll need to evaluate them to be certain that they are reliable choices that your audience will respect. When your sources are identified in your assignment, you'll still need to know their strengths, weaknesses, and limitations so that you introduce and use them effectively. Bring your articles, essays, and other sources to a small-group evaluation session. Using the guidelines in C3 in the Quick Research Guide (the dark-red-edged pages), discuss your common sources or a key source selected by each writer in the group. Look for aspects that you might mention in a paper to bolster a source's credibility with readers (for example, the author's professional affiliation) as well as for limitations that might restrict what the sources can substantiate.

FOR GROUP LEARNING

PLANNING, DRAFTING, AND DEVELOPING

Start with a Working Thesis.   Sometimes you start reading for a source-based paper with a clear position in mind; other times, you begin simply with your initial response to your cluster of sources. Either way, try to state your main idea as a working thesis even if you expect to rewrite it — or even replace it — later on. Once your thesis takes shape in words, you can assess the richness and relevance of your reading based on a clear main idea.

■ For more on stating a thesis, see pp. 312–19.

■ For exercises on choosing effective thesis statements, visit <bedfordstmartins.com/bedguide> and do a keyword search:

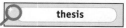

thesis

FIRST RESPONSE TO SOURCES	Joe Robinson, author of "Four Weeks Vacation," and others say that workers need more vacation time, but I can't see my boss agreeing to this.
WORKING THESIS	Although most workers would like longer vacations, many employers do not believe that they would benefit, too.

Read Each Source Thoughtfully.   Before you begin copying quotations from a source, read it through, slowly and carefully, in order to understand what it says. During this reading, don't scribble notes or vigorously highlight. Simply read. After you have figured out what the source says and how it develops its ideas, you are ready to decide how you might use its information to support your own ideas. Read again, this time sifting and selecting as you try to discover what's relevant to your thesis. Think also about the contribution of each source to the academic exchange.

- How does the source use its own sources to support its position?

- Does it review major sources chronologically (by date), thematically (by topic), or by some other method?

- Does it use sources to supply background for its own position? Does it compare its position or research findings with those of other studies?

- What audience does the source address? What was its author's purpose?

- How might you want to use the source as you contribute to the exchange?

Join the Academic Exchange.   When you find a well-researched article that follows academic conventions, it identifies its sources for several reasons. First, it gives honest credit to the work on which it relies — work done by other researchers and writers. They deserve this credit because they have provided useful information that has contributed to the article's credibility and substantiated its points. In addition, the article informs you about its sources so that you, or any other reader, could find them yourself.

The visual on pages 216–17 illustrates how this exchange of ideas and information works and how you, from the moment you begin to use sources in your college writing, join this exchange. The middle of the visual shows the opening of a sample article about a global health problem: obesity. Because this article appears online, it credits its sources by providing a link to each one. A comparable printed article might identify its sources by supplying brief in-text citations (in parentheses in MLA style and APA style), footnotes, numbers keyed to its references, or source identifications in the text itself. To the left of and below the source article are several of its sources. (They, in turn, also supply information about their sources.) The column to the right of the source article illustrates ways that you might capture information from the source.

■ For more on plagiarism, see D1 in the Quick Research Guide (the dark red-edged pages).

■ For an avoiding-plagiarism tutorial, visit <bedfordstmartins.com/rewriting>.

■ For more on critical reading, see Ch. 2.

■ For more on citing and listing sources, see E1 and E2 in the Quick Research Guide (the dark-red-edged pages).

Capture Information and Record Source Details.   Consider how you might eventually want to capture each significant passage or point from a source in your paper — by quoting the exact words of the source, by paraphrasing its ideas in your own words, or by summarizing its essential point. Keeping accurate notes and records as you work with your sources will help you avoid accidental plagiarism (using someone else's words or ideas without giving the credit due). Accurate notes also help to reduce errors or missing information when you add the source material to your draft.

As you capture information, also plan ahead so that you can acknowledge each source following academic conventions. Record the details about the source necessary to identify it in your discussion and to list it with other sources at the end of your paper. Using examples for a paper that relates land use and threats to wildlife, like the tortoise, the next sections illustrate how to capture and credit your sources. Compare the examples with the original passage from the source.

Identify Significant Quotations.   When an author expresses an idea so memorably that you want to reproduce those words exactly, quote them word for word. Direct quotations can add life, color, and authority to your paper. On the other hand, too many quotations can drown your voice and overshadow your point.

ORIGINAL   The tortoise is a creature that has survived virtually unchanged since it first appeared in the geologic record more than 150 million years ago. The species became threatened, however, when ranchers began driving their herds onto Mojave Desert lands for spring grazing, at the very time that the tortoise awakens from hibernation and emerges from its burrows to graze on the greening desert shrubs and grasses. As livestock trampled the burrows and monopolized the scarce desert vegetation, tortoise populations plummeted. (page 152)

Babbitt, Bruce. <u>Cities in the Wilderness: A New Vision of Land Use in America</u>. Washington: Island Press-Shearwater Books, 2005.

TOO MUCH QUOTATION

When "tortoise populations plummeted," a species "that has survived virtually unchanged since it first appeared in the geologic record more than 150 million years ago" (Babbitt 152) had losses that helped to justify setting workable boundaries for the future expansion of Las Vegas.

MEMORABLE QUOTATION

When "tortoise populations plummeted" (Babbitt 152), an unlikely species that has endured for millions of years helped to establish workable boundaries for the future expansion of Las Vegas.

Most writers begin by highlighting or copying too many quotations, often because they are still struggling to master the ideas in the source. The better you understand both the reading and your own thesis, the more effectively you'll choose quotations. After all, a quotation in itself is not necessarily effective evidence, and too many quotations will suggest that your writing is padded or lacks original thought.

HOW TO QUOTE

- Select a quotation that is both notable and pertinent to your thesis.
- Record it accurately, writing out exactly what it says. Include its punctuation and capitalization. Avoid abbreviations that might later be ambiguous.
- Mark both its beginning and ending with quotation marks.
- Note the page or other location (such as an electronic paragraph) where the quotation appears. If the quotation begins on one page but ends on another, mark where the switch occurs so that the credit in your draft will be accurate no matter how much of the quotation you eventually use.
- Double-check the accuracy of each quotation as you record it.

> ▨ For more on quotations, see D3 in the Quick Research Guide (the dark-red-edged pages).

Use an ellipsis mark — three spaced dots (. . .) within a sentence or four dots (. . . .), a period and three spaced dots, concluding a sentence — to show where you leave out any original wording. You may omit wording that doesn't relate to your point, but don't distort the original meaning. For example, if a reviewer calls a movie "a perfect example of poor directing and inept acting," don't quote this comment as "perfect . . . directing and . . . acting."

> ▨ For more on punctuating quotations and using ellipsis marks, see C3 in the Quick Editing Guide (the dark-blue-edged pages).

THE ACADEMIC EXCHANGE

Suppose that you used the center article to support a position. The various ways you might use this source are shown on the right-hand page. In turn, your source drew on other writings, some of which are shown to the left of and below the center article.

Sources Cited in Your Source

Source: U.S. Department of Agriculture

<www.usda.gov>

AREI Chapter 3.5: Global Resources and Productivity

Keith Wiebe

Abstract—*Global food production has grown faster than population in recent decades, due largely to improved seeds and increased use of fertilizer and irrigation. Soil degradation which has slowed yield growth in some areas, depends on farmers' incentives to adopt conservation practices, but does not threaten food security at the global level.*

Introduction

Increased resource use and improvements in technology and efficiency have increased global food production more rapidly than population in recent decades, but 800 million people remain food insecure (fig. 3.5.1). . . . .

Source: World Bank

<web.worldbank.org>

Poverty Analysis: Overview

Trends in poverty over time: Living Standards have improved...

Living standards have risen dramatically over the last decades. The proportion of the developing world's population living in extreme economic poverty -- defined as living on less than $1 per day ($1.08 in 1993 dollars, adjusted to account for differences in purchasing power across countries) -- has fallen from 28 percent in 1990 to 21 percent in 2001.

Substantial improvements in social indicators have accompanied growth in average incomes. Infant mortality rates in low- and middle-income countries have fallen from 86 per 1,000 live births in 1980 to 60 in 2002. Life expectancy in these countries has risen from 60 to 65 between 1980 and 2002. For more health, nutrition and population statistics, see the HNPStats database. . . .

Your Source <www.slate.com>

Please Do Not Feed the Humans

THE GLOBAL EXPLOSION OF FAT.
By William Saletan
Posted Saturday, Sept. 2, 2006, at 8:22 AM ET

In 1894, Congress established Labor Day to honor those who "from rude nature have delved and carved all the grandeur we behold." In the century since, the grandeur of human achievement has multiplied. Over the past four decades, global population has doubled, but food output, driven by increases in productivity, has outpaced it. Poverty, infant mortality, and hunger are receding. For the first time in our planet's history, a species no longer lives at the mercy of scarcity. We have learned to feed ourselves.

We've learned so well, in fact, that we're getting fat. Not just the United States or Europe, but the whole world. Egyptian, Mexican, and South African women are now as fat as Americans. Far more Filipino adults are now overweight than underweight. In China, one in five adults is too heavy, and the rate of overweight in children is 28 times higher than it was two decades ago. In Thailand, Kuwait, and Tunisia, obesity, diabetes, and heart disease are soaring.

Hunger is far from conquered. But since 1990, the global rate of malnutrition has declined an average of 1.7 percent a year. Based on data from the World Health Organization and the U.N. Food and Agriculture Organization, for every two people who are malnourished, three are now overweight or obese. Among women, even in most African countries, overweight has surpassed underweight. The balance of peril is shifting.

Indirect Source: U.S. Department of Labor

<www.dol.gov/opa/aboutdol/laborday.htm>

The History of Labor Day

Labor Day: How it Came About; What it Means

"Labor Day differs in every essential way from the other holidays of the year in any country," said Samuel Gompers, founder and longtime president of the American Federation of Labor. "All other holidays are in a more or less degree connected with conflicts and battles of man's prowess over man, of strife and discord for greed and power, of glories achieved by one nation over another. Labor Day...is devoted to no man, living or dead, to no sect, race, or nation."

Labor Day, the first Monday in September, is a creation of the labor movement and is dedicated to the social and economic achievements of American workers. It constitutes a yearly national tribute to the contributions workers have made to the strength, prosperity, and well-being of our country.

Founder of Labor Day

More than 100 years after the first Labor Day observance, there is still some doubt as to who first proposed the holiday for workers.

Some records show that Peter J. McGuire, general secretary of the Brotherhood of Carpenters and Joiners and a cofounder of the American Federation of Labor, was first in suggesting a day to honor those "who from rude nature have delved and carved all the grandeur we behold."

Information Captured from Your Source

Sample Working Thesis

A clear thesis statement establishes a framework for selecting source material as useful evidence and for explaining its relevance to readers.

> **WORKING THESIS:** In order to counter national and worldwide trends toward obesity, agricultural communities like Grand Junction need to apply their expertise as food producers to the promotion of healthy food products.

Quotation from an Indirect Source

A quotation from an indirect source captures the exact words of an author quoted within the source.

> An 1894 action by Congress created a holiday to recognize workers who "delved and carved" to produce what Americans enjoy (qtd. in Saletan par. 1).

If possible, go to the original source to be sure that the quotation is accurate and that you are using it appropriately. (See the bottom lefthand page.)

> Credit, though disputed, has gone to labor leader Peter McGuire for promoting the recognition of those who "delved and carved all the grandeur we behold" (US Dept. of Labor par. 4).

Quotation from a Source

A quotation captures the author's exact words directly from the source.

> As Saletan observes, "We have learned to feed ourselves" (par. 1), but the success of agricultural enterprise and technology does not guarantee that well-fed people are healthy.

Paraphrase of a Source

A paraphrase restates an author's specific ideas fully and accurately, using your own words and sentences.

> Though the number of hungry people drops nearly 2 percent annually, more people, including African women, are now overfed by a ratio of 3 to 2 and thus have traded the health risks of malnutrition for those of obesity (Saletan par. 3).

Summary of a Source

A summary reduces an author's main point to essentials, using your own words and sentences.

> Given that a worldwide shift in food security has led to an obesity epidemic (Saletan), consumers need lighter, healthier food options, a goal that the Grand Junction agricultural community can actively support.

MLA Works Cited Entry

Author's Name   Title of Article   Title of Magazine   Date

Saletan, William. "Please Do Not Feed the Humans: The Global Explosion of Fat." Slate 2 Sept. 2006.
    28 Sept. 2006 <http://www.slate.com/id/2148756>.

Date of Access   Online Address

Paraphrase Specific Information.   The technique of paraphrasing involves restating an author's ideas in your own language. A paraphrase is generally about the same length as the original. Because it conveys the ideas and emphasis of the original but uses your words and sentences, it helps bring your own voice to the fore. A fresh and creative paraphrase expresses your style without awkwardly jumping between it and your source's style. Be sure to name the source, however, so that your reader knows exactly where you move from one to the other.

Here, again, is the original passage by Bruce Babbitt, followed by a sloppy paraphrase. The paraphrase suffers from a common fault, slipping in too many of the words from the original source. (These borrowed words are underlined in the paraphrase.) Those words need to be expressed in the writer's own language or identified as direct quotations with quotation marks.

ORIGINAL   The tortoise is a creature that has survived virtually unchanged since it first appeared in the geologic record more than 150 million years ago. The species became threatened, however, when ranchers began driving their herds onto Mojave Desert lands for spring grazing, at the very time that the tortoise awakens from hibernation and emerges from its burrows to graze on the greening desert shrubs and grasses. As livestock trampled the burrows and monopolized the scarce desert vegetation, tortoise populations plummeted. (page 152)

Babbitt, Bruce. Cities in the Wilderness: A New Vision of Land Use in America. Washington: Island Press-Shearwater Books, 2005.

SLOPPY PARAPHRASE   Babbitt says that the tortoise is a creature in the Mojave that is virtually unchanged over 150 million years. Over the millennia, the tortoise would awaken from hibernation just in time for spring grazing on the new growth of the region's shrubs and grasses. In recent years the species became threatened. When cattle started to compete for the same food, the livestock trampled the tortoise burrows and monopolized the desert vegetation while the tortoise populations plummeted (152).

To avoid picking up language from the original as you paraphrase, state each sentence afresh instead of just changing a few words in the original. If possible, take a short break, and then check each sentence against the original. Highlight any identical words or sentence patterns, and then rework your paraphrase again. Proper nouns or exact terms for the topic (such as *tortoise*) do not need to be rephrased.

The next example avoids parroting the original by making different word choices while reversing or varying sentence patterns.

> PARAPHRASE   As Babbitt explains, a tenacious survivor in the Mojave is the 150-million-year-old desert tortoise. Over the millennia, the hibernating tortoise would rouse itself each spring just in time to enjoy the new growth of the limited regional plants. In recent years, when cattle began competing for the same territory, the larger animals destroyed tortoise homes, ate tortoise food, and thus eliminated many of the tortoises themselves (152).

A common option is to blend paraphrase with brief quotation, carefully using quotation marks to identify any exact words drawn from the source.

> BLENDED   Babbitt describes a tenacious survivor in the Mojave, the 150-million-year-old desert tortoise. Over the millennia, the hibernating tortoise would rouse itself each spring just in time to munch on the new growth of the sparse regional plants. When cattle started to compete for the same food supply and destroyed the tortoise homes and food, the "tortoise populations plummeted" (152).

In a brief paraphrase, be just as careful to avoid slipping in the author's words or closely shadowing the original sentence structure. If a source says, "President Bush called an emergency meeting of his cabinet to discuss the new crisis," and you write, "The president called his cabinet to hold an emergency meeting to discuss the new crisis," your words are too close to those of the source. One option is to quote the original, though it doesn't seem worth quoting word for word. Or, better, you could write, "Summoning his cabinet to an emergency session, Bush laid out the challenge before them."

HOW TO PARAPHRASE

- Select a passage with detailed information relevant to your thesis.
- Reword the passage, representing it accurately but using your own language.
- Change both its words and its sentence patterns to your own. Replace its words with different expressions. Begin and end sentences differently, simplify long sentences, and reorder information.
- Note the page or other location (such as an electronic paragraph) where the original appears in your source. If the passage runs from one page onto the next, record where the page changes so that your credit will be accurate no matter how much of the paraphrase you use.
- After a break, recheck your paraphrase against the original to be certain that it does not repeat the same words or merely replace a few with synonyms. Revise as needed, placing fresh words in fresh arrangements.

For more on paraphrases, see D4 in the Quick Research Guide (the dark-red-edged pages).

■ For advice on writing a synopsis of a literary work, see pp. 256–58.

Summarize an Overall Point.   Summarizing is a useful way of incorporating the general point of a whole paragraph or section of a work. You briefly state the main sense of the original in your own words and identify the source of the ideas or information. Like a paraphrase, a summary uses your own language and thus increases the prominence of your voice. A summary is generally much shorter than the original; it expresses only the most important ideas — the essence — of the original. The following example summarizes the section of Babbitt's book containing the passage quoted on pages 214–15 and 218.

> SUMMARY   According to Bruce Babbitt, former Secretary of the Interior and governor of Arizona, the isolated federal land in the West traditionally has been open to cattle and sheep ranching. These animals have damaged the arid land by grazing too aggressively, and the ranchers have battled wildlife grazers and predators alike to reduce competition with their stock. Protecting species such as the gray wolf and the desert tortoise has meant limiting grazing, an action supported by the public in order to conserve the character and beauty of the public land.

HOW TO SUMMARIZE

■ For more on summaries, see D5 in the Quick Research Guide (the dark-red-edged pages).

- Select a passage, an article, a chapter, or an entire book whose main idea bears on your thesis.
- Read the selection carefully until you have mastered its overall point.
- Write a sentence or a series of sentences that states its essence in your own words.
- Revise your summary until it is as concise, clear, and accurate as possible. Replace any vague generalizations with precise words.
- Name your source as you begin your summary, or identify it in parentheses.

■ For more on plagiarism, see D1 in the Quick Research Guide (the dark-red-edged pages).

■ For an avoiding plagiarism tutorial, visit <bedfordstmartins.com/rewriting>.

■ For sample source citations and lists, see the readings on pp. 201–08 and the MLA and APA examples in E in the Quick Research Guide (the dark-red-edged pages).

Credit Your Sources Fairly.   As you quote, paraphrase, or summarize, be certain to note which source you are using and exactly where the material appears in the original. Carefully citing and listing your sources will give credit where it's due as it enhances your credibility as a careful writer.

Although academic fields prefer particular formats for their papers, MLA style is widely used in composition, English, and other humanities courses. In MLA style, you credit your source twice. First, briefly note the author's last name (and the page number in the original) in the text as you quote, paraphrase, summarize, or refer to the source. You may wish to mention the author's name (or a short version of the title if the author is not identified) as you introduce the information from the source. If not, note it and the page number of the original in parentheses after you present the

Methods of Capturing Information from Sources	QUOTATION	PARAPHRASE	SUMMARY
FORMAT FOR WORDING	Use exact words from the source, and identify any additions, deletions, or other changes	Use your words and sentence structures, translating the content of the original passage	Use your words and sentence structures, reducing the original passage to its core
COMMON USE	Capture lively and authoritative wording	Capture specific information while conserving its detail	Capture the overall essence of a source or a passage in brief form
ADVANTAGES	Catch a reader's attention; emphasize the authority of the source	Treat specifics fully without shifting from your voice to the source's	Concentrate on a broad but clear point without shifting from your voice to the source's
COMMON PROBLEMS	Quoting too much Quoting inaccurately	Slipping in the original wording Following the original sentence patterns too closely	Losing impact by bogging down in too much detail Drifting into vague generalities
MARKERS	Add quotation marks to show the source's exact words Use ellipses and brackets to mark any changes Identify source in launch statement or text citation and in list of sources	Identify source in launch statement or text citation and in final list of sources	Identify source in launch statement or text citation and in final list of sources

material. Next, fully identify the source in an alphabetical list at the end of your paper.

Let Your Draft Evolve.   No matter how many quotations, paraphrases, and summaries you assemble, chunks of evidence captured from sources do not — on their own — constitute a solid paper. You need to interpret and explain that evidence for your readers, helping them to see exactly why, how, and to what extent it supports your position.

To develop a solid draft, you may want to start with your evidence, using one of these methods to arrange your quotations, paraphrases, and summaries in a logical and compelling order.

■ For exercises on supporting a thesis, visit <bedfordstmartins.com/bedguide> and do a keyword search:

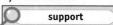

support

- Cut and paste the chunks of evidence, moving them around in a file until they fall into a logical order.
- Print each chunk on a separate page, and arrange the pages on a flat surface like a table, floor, or bed until you reach a workable sequence.
- Label each chunk with a key word, and use the key words to work out an informal outline.

Once your evidence is organized logically, add the commentary needed to connect the chunks for your readers: introduce, conclude, and connect your pieces of evidence with your own explanations and interpretations. (Feel free to ignore any leftovers from your sources unless they cover key points that you still need to integrate.) Let your draft expand as you alternate evidence and interpretation.

For more on planning and drafting, see Chs. 17 and 18.

An alternative is to start with your position or your conclusion, focusing on how you want your paper to present it. You can state your case directly, explaining your thesis and supporting points in your own words, or you can write out directions, telling yourself what to do in each part of a draft (in preparation for actually doing it). Either way, use this working structure to identify where to embed the evidence from your sources. Let your draft grow as you pull in your sources and expand your comments.

DEVELOPMENT CHECKLIST

For sample quotations, paraphrases, and summaries, see D3, D4, and D5 in the Quick Research Guide (the dark-red-edged pages).

—— Have you quoted only notable passages that add support and authority to your discussion?

—— Have you checked your quotations for accuracy and marked where each begins and ends with quotation marks?

—— Have you paraphrased accurately, reflecting both the main points and the supporting details in the original?

—— Does each paraphrase use your own words without repeating or echoing the words or the sentence structure of the original?

—— Have you briefly stated any supporting ideas that you wish to summarize, sticking to the overall point without bogging down in details or examples?

—— Has each summary remained respectful of the ideas and opinions of others, even if you disagree with them?

— Have you identified the source of every quotation, paraphrase, summary, or source reference by noting in parentheses the last name of the writer and the page number (if available) where the passage appears in the source?

— Have you ordered your evidence logically and effectively?

— Have you interpreted and explained your evidence from sources with your own comments?

■ For more on finding your voice, see Facing the Challenge on p. 211.

REVISING AND EDITING

As you read over the draft of your paper, remember what you wanted to accomplish: to develop an enlightening position about your topic and to share this position with a college audience, using sources to support your ideas.

■ For more on reviewing and editing strategies, see Ch. 20.

Strengthen Your Thesis.   As you begin revising, you may decide that your working thesis is ambiguous, poorly worded, hard to support, or simply off the mark. Revise it so that it clearly alerts readers to your main idea.

■ For more on stating a thesis, see pp. 312–19.

WORKING THESIS   Although most workers would like longer vacations, most employers do not believe that they would benefit, too.

REVISED THESIS   Despite assumptions to the contrary, employers who increase vacation time for workers also are likely to increase creativity, productivity, and the bottom line.

Launch Each Source.   Whenever you quote, paraphrase, summarize, or refer to a source, launch it with a suitable introduction. An effective launch sets the scene for your source material, prepares your reader to accept it, and marks the transition from your words and ideas to those of the source.

■ For more about launching sources, see D6 in the Quick Research Guide (the dark-red-edged pages).

As you create a launch statement, often you will first identify the source — by the author's last name or by a short version of the title when the author isn't named — in your introductory sentence or in parentheses. Then try to suggest why you've selected this source and mentioned it at this point, perhaps noting its contribution to your discussion, its credibility, its vantage point, or its relationship to other sources. Vary your launch statements to avoid tedium and to add emphasis. Boost your credibility as a writer by establishing the credibility of your sources.

Here are some typical patterns for launch statements:

As Yung demonstrates, . . .

Although Zeffir maintains . . . , Matson suggests . . .

Many schools educated the young but also unified the community (Hill 22). . . .

In Forward March, Smith's study of the children of military personnel, . . .

Another common recommendation is . . . ("Safety Manual").

Based on years of experience as a travel consultant, Lee explains . . .

■ These examples follow MLA style. See D6 and E1 in the Quick Research Guide (the dark-red-edged pages) for more about how to capture, launch, and cite sources in your text using either MLA or APA style.

When you quote or paraphrase information from a specific page (or other location, such as a paragraph on a Web page), also include that exact location.

The classic definition of . . . (Bagette 18).

Benton distinguishes four typical steps in this process (248–51).

Synthesize Several Sources.   Often you will compare, contrast, or relate two or three sources to deepen your discussion or to illustrate a range of views. When you synthesize, you pull together several sources in the same passage to build a new interpretation or reach a new conclusion. You go beyond the separate contributions of the individual sources to relate the sources to each other and to connect them to your thesis. A synthesis should be easy to follow and use your own wording.

HOW TO SYNTHESIZE

- Summarize (see p. 220) each of the sources you want to synthesize. Boil down each summary to its essence.
- Write a few sentences that state in your own words how the sources are related. For example, are they similar, different, or related? Do they share assumptions and conclusions, or do they represent alternatives, opposites, or opponents? Do they speak to chronology, influence, logical progression, or diversity of opinion?
- Write a few more sentences stating what their relationships mean for your thesis and the position developed in your paper.
- Refine your synthesis statements until they are as clear and illuminating as possible. Embed them as you move from one source summary to the next and as you reach new interpretations or conclusions that go beyond the separate sources.

Use Your Own Voice to Interpret and Connect.   By the time your draft is finished, you may feel that you have found relevant evidence in your sources but that they now dominate your draft. As you reread, you may discover passages that simply string together ideas from sources.

DRAFT

Whole passage repeats "says"

Repeats sentence pattern opening with author

Jumps from one source to the next without transitions

Easterbrook <u>says</u> in "In Search of the Cause of Autism: How about

Television?" that television may injure children who are susceptible to autism.

The Centers for Disease Control and Prevention <u>says</u> that autism trails only mental

retardation among disabilities that affect children's development (par. 3). The Kaiser

Family Foundation study <u>says</u> that parents use television and other electronic entertainment "to help them manage their household and keep their kids

entertained" (Rideout, Hamel, and Kaiser Family Foundation 4).

When your sources overshadow your thesis, your explanations, and your writing style, revise to restore balance. Try strategies such as these to regain control of your draft:

- Add your explanation and interpretation of the source information so that your ideas are clear.
- Add transitions, and state the connections that you assume are obvious.
- Arrange information in a logical sequence, not in the order in which you read it.
- Clarify definitions, justify a topic's importance, and recognize alternative views to help your audience appreciate your position.
- Reword to vary your sentence openings, and avoid repetitive wording.

Your thoughtful revision can help your audience understand what you want to say, why you have included each source, and how you think that it supports your thesis.

REVISION

Two recent studies take very different looks at the development of children in   *Connects two sources*

our society. First, a research study sponsored by the Kaiser Family Foundation

examines how parents use television and other electronic options "to help them   *Adds transitions*

manage their household and keep their kids entertained" (Rideout, Hamel, and

Kaiser Family Foundation 4). Next, based on statistics about how often major

developmental disabilities occur in children, the Centers for Disease Control and

Prevention reports that autism currently trails only mental retardation among

disabilities that affect children's development (par. 3). Journalist and book author   *Identifies author's experience to add credibility*

Gregg Easterbrook pulls together these two views, using the title of his article to raise

his unusual question: "In Search of the Cause of Autism: How about Television?" He

urges study of his speculation that television may injure children who are vulnerable to   *Defines issue and justifies concern*

autism and joins an ongoing debate about what causes autism, a challenging disability

that interferes with children's ability to communicate and interact with other people.

■ For examples of sources cited in the text and listed in MLA or APA style, see E in the Quick Research Guide (the dark-red-edged pages).

List Your Sources as College Readers Expect.   When you use sources in a college paper, you'll be expected to identify them twice: briefly when you draw information from them and fully when you list them at the end of your paper, following a conventional system. The list of sources for the draft and revision in the preceding section would include the following entries.

Centers for Disease Control and Prevention. "How Common Are Autism Spectrum Disorders (ASD)?" <u>Autism</u>. 12 Sept. 2006 <http://www.cdc.gov/ncbddd/autism/ asd_common.htm>.

Easterbrook, Gregg. "In Search of the Cause of Autism: How about Television?" <u>Slate</u> 5 Sept. 2006. 12 Sept. 2006 <http://www.slate.com/id/2149002/>.

Rideout, Victoria, Elizabeth Hamel, and Kaiser Family Foundation. <u>The Media Family: Electronic Media in the Lives of Infants, Toddlers, Preschoolers and Their Parents</u>. Menlo Park, CA: Henry J. Kaiser Family Foundation, May 2006. 12 Sept. 2006 <http://www.kff.org/entmedia/7500.cfm>.

■ To get online help from the Draft Doctor, visit <bedfordstmartins.com/ bedguide>.

Use the Draft Doctor (pp. 228–30) to help you figure out how to improve your draft. Skim down the left column to identify questions you might ask about problems in your draft. When you answer a question with "Yes" or "Maybe," move straight across the row to the Diagnose column next to that question. Use the diagnostic activities to identify gaps or weaknesses, and then move straight across the row to the Treat column on the right. Use the advice that suits your problem as you revise.

FOR E-WRITERS

Checking Your Source Citations

Use your software's search capacity to help you check your source credits. For example, search for all the quotation marks in your paper. As you find each one, make sure that it is one of a pair surrounding every quotation in your paper. Also check that the source and the page (or other location, if available) are identified for each quotation. Use color highlighting to help you spot and refine the details in your list of sources. For instance, if you tend to forget periods or other conventional punctuation after authors' names or titles, go through your list of sources, and highlight those marks in color, adding any that are missing. After all the entries are checked and corrected, restore the passage to the usual black color.

Have several classmates read your draft critically, considering how effectively you have used your sources to support a position. Ask your peer editors to answer questions such as these:

- Can you state the writer's position on the topic?

- Do you have any trouble seeing how the writer's points and the supporting evidence from sources connect? How might the writer make the connections clearer?

- How effectively does the writer capture the information from sources? Would you recommend that any of the quotations, paraphrases, or summaries be presented differently?

- Are any of the source citations unclear? Can you tell where source information came from and where quotations and paraphrases appear in a source?

- Is the writer's voice clear? Do the sources overshadow the writer's voice in any spots?

- If this were your paper, what is the one thing you would be sure to work on before handing it in?

FOR PEER RESPONSE

For general questions for a peer editor, see p. 377. For peer response worksheets, visit <bedfordstmartins.com/bedguide> and do a keyword search:

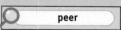

peer

REVISION CHECKLIST

___ Is your thesis, or main idea, clear? Is it distinguished from the points made by your sources?

___ Do you speak in your own voice, interpreting and explaining your sources instead of allowing them to dominate your draft?

___ Have you moved smoothly back and forth between your explanations and your source material?

___ Have you credited every source in the text and in a list at the end of your paper? Have you carefully included each detail expected in the format for crediting sources?

___ Have you been careful to quote, paraphrase, summarize, and credit your sources accurately and ethically? Have you hunted up any missing information, double-checked all quotations, and rechecked the accuracy of anything prepared hastily?

For more on strengthening your voice, see Facing the Challenge on p. 21.

After you have revised your paper, edit and proofread it. Carefully check the grammar, word choice, punctuation, and mechanics — and then correct any problems you find. Be certain to check the punctuation with your quotations, making sure that each quotation mark is correctly placed and that you have used other punctuation, such as commas, correctly. See page 231 for some questions to get you started editing and proofreading.

Draft Doctor: Integrating Source Information Effectively

If you sense a problem, ASK	If you answer *Yes/Maybe*, DIAGNOSE	If you diagnose a problem, TREAT
Too Many Quotations? Have I strung together too many quotations?	• Highlight the words in your draft directly quoted from sources. • Identify any large colored patches where you probably quote too much. • Circle the striking or powerful words, if any, in each clump.	• Reduce your quotations to significant words, presented in a passage or blended with your words. Either way, always set off each quotation with a pair of quotation marks. • Delete the rest, or restate it in your own words. • Clearly identify the source of the quoted or restated material in the style expected.
Too Many Long Quotations? Have I dropped too many long quoted passages into my draft?	• Draw a vertical line in the margin to show the length of each quoted passage. • Check the length and frequency of these lines, looking for any longer than an inch or two. • Read each long quotation critically to master its meaning. Highlight its most significant wording.	• Quote only compelling words; paraphrase, sum up, or delete the rest. • If the significant words are long enough for a block quotation, follow the format for indenting and citing the source in MLA or another style. • Edit each quotation to be sure that you stick to one system at a time: quotation marks for the exact words in a short quotation; indentation without quotation marks for a long quotation.
Too Little Voice? Have I lost my own voice and allowed my sources to take over my draft?	• Highlight the material from sources in one color and your own commentary in another. • Check the color balance in each paragraph. If the source color dominates, consider strengthening your own voice.	• Restore your voice by adding a topic sentence to link each paragraph to your thesis and a concluding sentence to sum up its point. • Add your own transitions (*further, most importantly*) and explanations when you advance from point to point or source to source. • Weave in your ideas until they, not your sources, control your draft.

If you sense a problem, ASK	If you answer *Yes/Maybe*, DIAGNOSE	If you diagnose a problem, TREAT
Weak Launch Statements? Have I tossed source material into my draft without preparing my audience for it?	• Underline each sentence or part of a sentence that introduces source information. • Check each launch statement to see whether it assures a reader that the information is credible, relevant, and logically related to your thesis. (See D6 in the Quick Research Guide.)	• Improve each launch statement by relating the source material to your thesis. • Launch a quotation, paraphrase, or summary by telling readers why they should confidently accept the material. • Note an author's credentials or affiliations significant to readers. • Identify historical or current contributions of a source, or relate it to other sources.
Too Few Source Credits? Have I identified a source only once or twice even though I use its material throughout a passage or paragraph?	• Select a passage that relies heavily on a main source. Use one color to highlight your ideas and different colors to mark material from other sources. • Draw a slash mark at each point in the passage where you make a switch from your ideas to a source (or vice versa) or from source to source. **Draft:** Smith points out X, and Y remains unsolved. [Who says Y is unsolved? Smith? You? Somebody else?]	• At each slash marking a switch between sources, add a launch statement to identify the second source. • At each slash marking a switch to your ideas (or when your color begins), phrase your comment so that it does not sound like more of the source. **Revision:** Although Smith points out X, she discusses but does not solve Y. (Smith says it all.) **Revision:** Although Smith points out X, she does not discuss Y [switch to you] which Wheeler investigates [switch to Wheeler]. • At each slash marking a switch from your ideas (or when your color ends), identify your source again. • When you quote and then continue with material from the same source, identify it again to avoid confusion.

If you sense a problem, ASK	If you answer *Yes/Maybe*, DIAGNOSE	If you diagnose a problem, TREAT
Too Much Repetition? Do I repeat the same words in my launch statements or transitions?	• Identify words (such as *says*) or transitions (such as *also*) that you might overuse. • Search for oft-used words, or highlight them, to see how many times you repeat them.	• Edit your wording for variety and precision. Instead of *says*, try *emphasizes, suggests, reviews, presents,* or *explains*. For *also*, try *in addition, furthermore,* or *similarly.* • Do the same for your own favorite expressions.
Problems with Citation Style? Have I skipped over or confused any details of the formats for crediting sources in my paper? (Make sure you know the style—MLA, APA, or another—expected by your instructor.)	• Go through your draft line by line, marking where you mention and should cite each source in your sentence or in parentheses. • Check that a matching full entry for each source is listed in the correct format in the Works Cited, References, or other bibliography that ends your paper. • Refer to the style examples as you cite and list each source.	• Include the author's name or a short version of the title (if the author is not named) in your sentence or in parentheses. Add the page, line, or other location (if available) for every quotation and paraphrase. Add anything else required. • Make your full entry for each source listed at the end match the pattern expected in the style you are using. Edit the indentation, sequence of details, capitalization, and punctuation.
Any Other Source Problems? After a final look at the sources in my draft, should I revise anything else?	• Read your draft out loud, marking any weak spots in your introduction, use, or citation of sources. • Ask your peer editors how you might improve your use of sources.	• Return to each mark to strengthen your presentation of sources. • Consider the useful suggestions of your peers. • Revise until your draft accomplishes what you want it to do.

EDITING CHECKLIST

—— Do all the verbs agree with their subjects, especially when you   A4
switch from your words to those of a source?

—— Do all the pronouns agree with their antecedents, especially   A6
when you use your words with a quotation from a source?

—— Have you used commas correctly, especially where you   C1
integrate material from sources?

—— Have you punctuated all your quotations correctly?   C3

For more more help, turn to the Quick Editing guide (the dark-blue-edged pages), to the sections noted here.

OTHER ASSIGNMENTS

1. Create a concise Web site that addresses a question of interest to you. Select and read a few reliable sources about that question, and then create several screens or short pages to explain what you have learned. For example, you might want to define or explain aspects of the question, justify the conclusion you have reached, or evaluate alternative answers as well as your own. Identify all of your sources, and supply links when appropriate.

2. Read several sources about the same topic. Instead of using those sources as evidence to support your own position about the topic, analyze how well they function as sources. State your thesis about them, and analyze their strengths and weaknesses using clear criteria. (See, for example, the criteria for evaluating sources in C in the Quick Research Guide, the dark-red-edged pages.)

3. Locate several different accounts of a notable event in newspapers, magazines, published letters or journals, books, blogs, or other sources, depending on the time when the event occurred. State and support a thesis that explains and accounts for the differences among the accounts. Use the accounts as evidence to support your position.

Applying What You Learn: Some Uses of Position Papers Supported by Sources

In College Courses.   In most courses, especially in the humanities and social sciences, you'll be expected to use sources to support a position.

• After reading a short story, poem, or play, students in a literature course might read several critical essays about it and then write essays supporting their own conclusions.

• Students in a sociology course might be asked to read several articles about families and then write a paper reviewing the viewpoints of the articles and supporting a conclusion about them.

- Students in a history course might be asked to read a first-person account, a contemporary secondhand article or report, and a later critical examination of an event or situation in order to develop and support their own thesis about it.

In the Workplace.   Many jobs require reading several reports, technical documents, or other papers and preparing an explanation of the matter, with conclusions that the materials support.

- Newspaper reporters draw on multiple sources to develop a consolidated account of an event or explanation of a situation.

- Organizations such as police departments, fire departments, and social-service agencies assemble multiple accounts and records in order to explain and draw conclusions about something that has happened.

- Employees often must unify reports from different sources in order to make and support a recommendation about how to solve a problem.

Workplace reports

In Your Community.   Partisans, activists, and concerned citizens all gather source materials about issues of concern, consolidating them to persuade others to support and implement their views.

- You might write a letter to the editor, supporting an opinion with information from several respected sources.

- Your civic group might want to raise money for a diabetes clinic, developing a position paper supported by sources to substantiate the need and the possible community benefits.

- Your child's school invites parents to contribute to a grant proposal that includes sources to document a local problem and propose solutions implemented elsewhere.

PART THREE

Special Writing Situations

Introduction

Much of your writing during college will fall into one of the categories covered in Part Two. However, three common situations that you're likely to encounter will call for specialized forms of writing—writing about literature, writing for the workplace, and writing for assessment.

In college English and humanities classes, you'll write papers about literature. You may need to write a personal response, a synopsis, a paraphrase, a review, a comparison and contrast, or—most common in college—a literary analysis. Chapter 13 concentrates on the literary analysis, explaining how to analyze a piece of literature, how to develop a coherent interpretation, and how to present it persuasively. It also provides brief advice on writing a synopsis or a paraphrase of a literary work.

Whether you are working while you attend college or looking forward to a career once you finish, you'll need to use your writing skills in the workplace. As a consumer, a client, or an employee, you may need to write a business letter to straighten out a bill or lodge a complaint. You may need to write memos and e-mail messages as part of your current job. In addition, when you apply for a new position, you may need to write a résumé and letter of application. To simplify such tasks, Chapter 14 offers recommendations and samples for workplace writing.

Finally, as a student you'll face testing situations in which you must demonstrate your knowledge of a subject as well as your proficiency in writing, often constrained by a time limit. Writing essay examinations, short-answer quizzes, impromptu essays, and portfolio entries requires you to use special skills—reading carefully, planning globally, composing quickly, and proofreading independently. Chapter 15 gives valuable tips on how not only to survive but also to thrive in such situations.

Chapter 13

Responding to Literature

As countless readers know, reading fiction gives pleasure and delight. Whether you are reading Stephen King or Stephen Crane, you can be swept up into an imaginative world where you journey to distant lands and meet exotic people. You may also meet characters like yourself and encounter familiar as well as new ways of viewing life. By sharing the experiences of literary characters, you gain insight into your own problems and tolerance of others.

More often than not, a writing assignment in a literature or humanities course will require you first to read closely a literary work (short story, novel, play, or poem) and then to divide it into its elements, explain its meaning, and support your interpretation with evidence from the work. Such analysis is not an end in itself; its purpose is to illuminate the meaning of the work, to help you and others understand it better.

There are certain basic ways of writing about literature, each with its own purpose. We emphasize the *literary analysis*, which requires you to analyze, interpret, and evaluate what you read (pp. 250–56). We also introduce the synopsis, a summary of the events in a narrative, and the paraphrase, an expression of the content of a work in your own words (pp. 256–58). Because literary analysis has its own vocabulary—as do fields as diverse as scuba diving, gourmet cooking, and engineering—we also supply a handy glossary of terms used to discuss the elements of fiction, poetry, and drama (see pp. 248–49).

Literary Analysis

LEARNING FROM OTHER WRITERS

In a composition course, Jonathan Burns was given an assignment to write a literary analysis of "The Lottery," a provocative short story by Shirley Jackson. Read this story yourself to understand its meaning. Then read on to see what Jonathan Burns made of it.

Shirley Jackson
The Lottery

The morning of June 27th was clear and sunny, with the fresh warmth of 1
a full-summer day; the flowers were blossoming profusely and the grass
was richly green. The people of the village began to gather in the square, between the post office and the bank, around ten o'clock; in some towns there
were so many people that the lottery took two days and had to be started on
June 26th, but in this village, where there were only about three hundred
people, the whole lottery took less than two hours, so it could begin at ten
o'clock in the morning and still be through in time to allow the villagers to
get home for noon dinner.

The children assembled first, of course. School was recently over for the 2
summer, and the feeling of liberty sat uneasily on most of them; they
tended to gather together quietly for a while before they broke into boisterous play, and their talk was still of the classroom and the teacher, of books
and reprimands. Bobby Martin had already stuffed his pockets full of stones,
and the other boys soon followed his example, selecting the smoothest and
roundest stones; Bobby and Harry Jones and Dickie Delacroix — the villagers pronounced his name "Dellacroy" — eventually made a great pile of
stones in one corner of the square and guarded it against the raids of the
other boys. The girls stood aside, talking among themselves, looking over
their shoulders at the boys, and the very small children rolled in the dust or
clung to the hands of their older brothers or sisters.

Soon the men began to gather, surveying their own children, speaking 3
of planting and rain, tractors and taxes. They stood together, away from the
pile of stones in the corner, and their jokes were quiet and they smiled
rather than laughed. The women, wearing faded house dresses and sweaters,
came shortly after their menfolk. They greeted one another and exchanged
bits of gossip as they went to join their husbands. Soon the women, standing by their husbands, began to call to their children, and the children came
reluctantly, having to be called four or five times. Bobby Martin ducked
under his mother's grasping hand and ran, laughing, back to the pile of
stones. His father spoke up sharply, and Bobby came quickly and took his
place between his father and his oldest brother.

The lottery was conducted — as were the square dances, the teenage 4
club, the Halloween program — by Mr. Summers, who had time and energy
to devote to civic activities. He was a round-faced, jovial man and he ran the
coal business, and people were sorry for him, because he had no children
and his wife was a scold. When he arrived in the square, carrying the black
wooden box, there was a murmur of conversation among the villagers, and
he waved and called, "Little late today, folks." The postmaster, Mr. Graves,
followed him, carrying a three-legged stool, and the stool was put in the
center of the square and Mr. Summers set the black box down on it. The villagers kept their distance, leaving a space between themselves and the stool,

and when Mr. Summers said, "Some of you fellows want to give me a hand?" there was a hesitation before two men, Mr. Martin and his oldest son, Baxter, came forward to hold the box steady on the stool while Mr. Summers stirred up the papers inside it.

The original paraphernalia for the lottery had been lost long ago, and the black box now resting on the stool had been put into use even before Old Man Warner, the oldest man in town, was born. Mr. Summers spoke frequently to the villagers about making a new box, but no one liked to upset even as much tradition as was represented by the black box. There was a story that the present box had been made with some pieces of the box that had preceded it, the one that had been constructed when the first people settled down to make a village here. Every year, after the lottery, Mr. Summers began talking again about a new box, but every year the subject was allowed to fade off without anything's being done. The black box grew shabbier each year; by now it was no longer completely black but splintered badly along one side to show the original wood color, and in some places faded or stained.

Mr. Martin and his oldest son, Baxter, held the black box securely on the stool until Mr. Summers had stirred the papers thoroughly with his hand. Because so much of the ritual had been forgotten or discarded, Mr. Summers had been successful in having slips of paper substituted for the chips of wood that had been used for generations. Chips of wood, Mr. Summers had argued, had been all very well when the village was tiny, but now that the population was more than three hundred and likely to keep on growing, it was necessary to use something that would fit more easily into the black box. The night before the lottery, Mr. Summers and Mr. Graves made up the slips of paper and put them in the box, and it was then taken to the safe of Mr. Summers's coal company and locked up until Mr. Summers was ready to take it to the square next morning. The rest of the year, the box was put away, sometimes one place, sometimes another; it had spent one year in Mr. Graves's barn and another year underfoot in the post office, and sometimes it was set on a shelf in the Martin grocery and left there.

There was a great deal of fussing to be done before Mr. Summers declared the lottery open. There were the lists to make up — of heads of families, heads of households in each family, members of each household in each family. There was the proper swearing-in of Mr. Summers by the postmaster, as the official of the lottery; at one time, some people remembered, there had been a recital of some sort, performed by the official of the lottery, a perfunctory, tuneless chant that had been rattled off duly each year; some people believed that the official of the lottery used to stand just so when he said or sang it, others believed that he was supposed to walk among the people, but years and years ago this part of the ritual had been allowed to lapse. There had been, also, a ritual salute, which the official of the lottery had had to use in addressing each person who came up to draw from the box, but this also had changed with time, until now it was felt necessary only for the official to speak to each person approaching. Mr. Summers was very good at all this; in his clean white shirt and blue jeans, with one hand resting carelessly on the black box, he seemed very proper and important as he talked interminably to Mr. Graves and the Martins.

Just as Mr. Summers finally left off talking and turned to the assembled   8
villagers, Mrs. Hutchinson came hurriedly along the path to the square, her sweater thrown over her shoulders, and slid into place in the back of the crowd. "Clean forgot what day it was," she said to Mrs. Delacroix, who stood next to her, and they both laughed softly. "Thought my old man was out back stacking wood," Mrs. Hutchinson went on, "and then I looked out the window and the kids was gone, and then I remembered it was the twenty-seventh and came a-running." She dried her hands on her apron, and Mrs. Delacroix said, "You're in time, though. They're still talking away up there."

Mrs. Hutchinson craned her neck to see through the crowd and found   9
her husband and children standing near the front. She tapped Mrs. Delacroix on the arm as a farewell and began to make her way through the crowd. The people separated good-humoredly to let her through; two or three people said, in voices just loud enough to be heard across the crowd, "Here comes your Missus, Hutchinson," and "Bill, she made it after all." Mrs. Hutchinson reached her husband, and Mr. Summers, who had been waiting, said cheerfully, "Thought we were going to have to get on without you, Tessie." Mrs. Hutchinson said, grinning, "Wouldn't have me leave m'dishes in the sink, now, would you, Joe?" and soft laughter ran through the crowd as the people stirred back into position after Mrs. Hutchinson's arrival.

"Well, now," Mr. Summers said soberly, "guess we better get started, get   10
this over with, so's we can go back to work. Anybody ain't here?"

"Dunbar," several people said. "Dunbar, Dunbar."   11

Mr. Summers consulted his list. "Clyde Dunbar," he said. "That's right.   12
He's broke his leg, hasn't he? Who's drawing for him?"

"Me, I guess," a woman said, and Mr. Summers turned to look at her.   13
"Wife draws for her husband," Mr. Summers said. "Don't you have a grown boy to do it for you, Janey?" Although Mr. Summers and everyone else in the village knew the answer perfectly well, it was the business of the official of the lottery to ask such questions formally. Mr. Summers waited with an expression of polite interest while Mrs. Dunbar answered.

"Horace's not but sixteen yet," Mrs. Dunbar said regretfully. "Guess I   14
gotta fill in for the old man this year."

"Right," Mr. Summers said. He made a note on the list he was holding.   15
Then he asked, "Watson boy drawing this year?"

A tall boy in the crowd raised his hand. "Here," he said. "I'm drawing   16
for m'mother and me." He blinked his eyes nervously and ducked his head as several voices in the crowd said things like "Good fellow, Jack," and "Glad to see your mother's got a man to do it."

"Well," Mr. Summers said, "guess that's everyone. Old Man Warner   17
make it?"

"Here," a voice said, and Mr. Summers nodded.   18

A sudden hush fell on the crowd as Mr. Summers cleared his throat and   19
looked at the list. "All ready?" he called. "Now, I'll read the names — heads
of families first — and the men come up and take a paper out of the box.
Keep the paper folded in your hand without looking at it until everyone has
had a turn. Everything clear?"

The people had done it so many times that they only half listened to the   20
directions; most of them were quiet, wetting their lips, not looking around.
Then Mr. Summers raised one hand high and said, "Adams." A man disen-
gaged himself from the crowd and came forward. "Hi, Steve," Mr. Summers
said, and Mr. Adams said, "Hi, Joe." They grinned at one another humor-
lessly and nervously. Then Mr. Adams reached into the black box and took
out a folded paper. He held it firmly by one corner as he turned and went
hastily back to his place in the crowd, where he stood a little apart from his
family, not looking down at his hand.

"Allen," Mr. Summers said. "Anderson. . . . Bentham."   21

"Seems like there's no time at all between lotteries anymore," Mrs.   22
Delacroix said to Mrs. Graves in the back row. "Seems like we got through
with the last one only last week."

"Time sure goes fast," Mrs. Graves said.   23

"Clark. . . . Delacroix."   24

"There goes my old man," Mrs. Delacroix said. She held her breath   25
while her husband went forward.

"Dunbar," Mr. Summers said, and Mrs. Dunbar went steadily to the box   26
while one of the women said, "Go on, Janey," and another said, "There she
goes."

"We're next," Mrs. Graves said. She watched while Mr. Graves came   27
around from the side of the box, greeted Mr. Summers gravely, and selected
a slip of paper from the box. By now, all through the crowd there were men
holding the small folded papers in their large hands, turning them over and
over nervously. Mrs. Dunbar and her two sons stood together, Mrs. Dunbar
holding the slip of paper.

"Harburt. . . . Hutchinson."   28

"Get up there, Bill," Mrs. Hutchinson said, and the people near her   29
laughed.

"Jones."   30

"They do say," Mr. Adams said to Old Man Warner, who stood next to   31
him, "that over in the north village they're talking of giving up the lottery."

Old Man Warner snorted. "Pack of crazy fools," he said. "Listening to   32
the young folks, nothing's good enough for *them*. Next thing you know,
they'll be wanting to go back to living in caves, nobody work anymore, live
that way for a while. Used to be a saying about 'Lottery in June, corn be
heavy soon.' First thing you know, we'd all be eating stewed chickweed and
acorns. There's *always* been a lottery," he added petulantly. "Bad enough to
see young Joe Summers up there joking with everybody."

"Some places have already quit lotteries," Mrs. Adams said.   33

"Nothing but trouble in *that*," Old Man Warner said stoutly. "Pack of   34
young fools."

"Martin." And Bobby Martin watched his father go forward. "Over-   35
dyke. . . . Percy."

"I wish they'd hurry," Mrs. Dunbar said to her older son. "I wish they'd   36
hurry."

"They're almost through," her son said.   37

"You get ready to run tell Dad," Mrs. Dunbar said.   38

Mr. Summers called his own name and then stepped forward precisely   39
and selected a slip from the box. Then he called, "Warner."

"Seventy-seventh year I been in the lottery," Old Man Warner said as he   40
went through the crowd. "Seventy-seventh time."

"Watson." The tall boy came awkwardly through the crowd. Someone   41
said, "Don't be nervous, Jack," and Mr. Summers said, "Take your time, son."

"Zanini."   42

After that, there was a long pause, a breathless pause, until Mr. Sum-   43
mers, holding his slip of paper in the air, said, "All right, fellows." For a
minute, no one moved, and then all the slips of paper were opened. Suddenly, all the women began to speak at once, saying, "Who is it?" "Who's
got it?" "Is it the Dunbars?" "Is it the Watsons?" Then the voices began to
say, "It's Hutchinson. It's Bill." "Bill Hutchinson's got it."

"Go tell your father," Mrs. Dunbar said to her older son.   44

People began to look around to see the Hutchinsons. Bill Hutchinson   45
was standing quiet, staring down at the paper in his hand. Suddenly, Tessie
Hutchinson shouted to Mr. Summers, "You didn't give him time enough to
take any paper he wanted. I saw you. It wasn't fair!"

"Be a good sport, Tessie," Mrs. Delacroix called, and Mrs. Graves said,   46
"All of us took the same chance."

"Shut up, Tessie," Bill Hutchinson said.   47

"Well, everyone," Mr. Summers said, "that was done pretty fast, and   48
now we've got to be hurrying a little more to get done in time." He consulted his next list. "Bill," he said, "you draw for the Hutchinson family. You
got any other households in the Hutchinsons?"

"There's Don and Eva," Mrs. Hutchinson yelled. "Make *them* take their   49
chance!"

"Daughters draw with their husbands' families, Tessie," Mr. Summers   50
said gently. "You know that as well as anyone else."

"It wasn't *fair*," Tessie said.   51

"I guess not, Joe," Bill Hutchinson said regretfully. "My daughter draws   52
with her husband's family, that's only fair. And I've got no other family except the kids."

"Then, as far as drawing for families is concerned, it's you," Mr. Sum-   53
mers said in explanation, "and as far as drawing for households is concerned, that's you, too. Right?"

"Right," Bill Hutchinson said.   54

"How many kids, Bill?" Mr. Summers asked formally.   55

"Three," Bill Hutchinson said. "There's Bill, Jr., and Nancy, and little   56
Dave. And Tessie and me."

"All right, then," Mr. Summers said. "Harry, you got their tickets back?"   57

Mr. Graves nodded and held up the slips of paper. "Put them in the box,   58
then," Mr. Summers directed. "Take Bill's and put it in."

"I think we ought to start over," Mrs. Hutchinson said, as quietly as she   59
could. "I tell you it wasn't *fair*. You didn't give him time enough to choose.
*Every*body saw that."

Mr. Graves had selected the five slips and put them in the box, and he   60
dropped all the papers but those onto the ground, where the breeze caught
them and lifted them off.

"Listen, everybody," Mrs. Hutchinson was saying to the people around   61
her.

"Ready, Bill?" Mr. Summers asked, and Bill Hutchinson, with one quick   62
glance around at his wife and children, nodded.

"Remember," Mr. Summers said, "take the slips and keep them folded   63
until each person has taken one. Harry, you help little Dave." Mr. Graves
took the hand of the little boy, who came willingly with him up to the box.
"Take a paper out of the box, Davy," Mr. Summers said. Davy put his hand
into the box and laughed. "Take just *one* paper," Mr. Summers said. "Harry,
you hold it for him." Mr. Graves took the child's hand and removed the
folded paper from the tight fist and held it while little Dave stood next to
him and looked up at him wonderingly.

"Nancy next," Mr. Summers said. Nancy was twelve, and her school   64
friends breathed heavily as she went forward, switching her skirt, and took a
slip daintily from the box. "Bill, Jr.," Mr. Summers said, and Billy, his face
red and his feet overlarge, nearly knocked the box over as he got a paper out.
"Tessie," Mr. Summers said. She hesitated for a minute, looking around defi-
antly, and then set her lips and went up to the box. She snatched a paper
out and held it behind her.

"Bill," Mr. Summers said, and Bill Hutchinson reached into the box and   65
felt around, bringing his hand out at last with the slip of paper in it.

The crowd was quiet. A girl whispered, "I hope it's not Nancy," and the   66
sound of the whisper reached the edges of the crowd.

"It's not the way it used to be," Old Man Warner said clearly. "People   67
ain't the way they used to be."

"All right," Mr. Summers said. "Open the papers. Harry, you open little   68
Dave's."

Mr. Graves opened the slip of paper and there was a general sigh   69
through the crowd as he held it up and everyone could see that it was blank.
Nancy and Bill, Jr., opened theirs at the same time, and both beamed and
laughed, turning around to the crowd and holding their slips of paper above
their heads.

"Tessie," Mr. Summers said. There was a pause, and then Mr. Summers 70
looked at Bill Hutchinson, and Bill unfolded his paper and showed it. It was
blank.

"It's Tessie," Mr. Summers said, and his voice was hushed. "Show us her 71
paper, Bill."

Bill Hutchinson went over to his wife and forced the slip of paper out of 72
her hand. It had a black spot on it, the black spot Mr. Summers had made
the night before with the heavy pencil in the coal-company office. Bill
Hutchinson held it up, and there was a stir in the crowd.

"All right, folks," Mr. Summers said. "Let's finish quickly."   73

Although the villagers had forgotten the ritual and lost the original 74
black box, they still remembered to use stones. The pile of stones the boys
had made earlier was ready; there were stones on the ground with the blow-
ing scraps of paper that had come out of the box. Mrs. Delacroix selected a
stone so large she had to pick it up with both hands and turned to Mrs.
Dunbar. "Come on," she said. "Hurry up."

Mrs. Dunbar had small stones in both hands, and she said, gasping for 75
breath, "I can't run at all. You'll have to go ahead and I'll catch up with
you."

The children had stones already, and someone gave little Davy Hutchin- 76
son a few pebbles.

Tessie Hutchinson was in the center of a cleared space by now, and she 77
held her hands out desperately as the villagers moved in on her. "It isn't
fair," she said. A stone hit her on the side of the head.

Old Man Warner was saying, "Come on, come on, everyone." Steve 78
Adams was in the front of the crowd of villagers, with Mrs. Graves beside
him.

"It isn't fair, it isn't right," Mrs. Hutchinson screamed, and then they 79
were upon her.

Questions to Start You Thinking

Meaning

1. Where does this story take place? When?

2. How does this lottery differ from what we usually think of as a lottery? Why
   would people conduct a lottery such as this?

3. What does this story mean to you?

Writing Strategies

4. Can you see and hear the people in the story? Do they seem to be real or
   based on fantasy? Who is the most memorable character to you?

5. Are the events believable? Does the ending shock you? Is it believable?

6. Is this story realistic, or is Jackson using these events to represent something
   else?

■ For Burns's synopsis of "The Lottery," see pp. 257–58. For more on writing a summary, see D5 and D6 in the Quick Research Guide (the dark-red-edged pages).

■ For examples of annotated passages, see p. 24 and p. 30.

Read Closely.   As Jonathan Burns read "The Lottery," he was carried along quickly to the startling ending. After the immediate impact of the story wore off, Burns reread it, savoring some of the details he had missed during his first reading. Then he wrote a summary or *synopsis* of "The Lottery" to get a clear fix on the literal events in the story.

But Burns knew that he could not write a good essay without reading the story closely, marking key points in the text. By rereading *at least* three times, he could check his interpretations and be sure that evidence from the story supported his claims. When you analyze a complex work of literature, allow time for several close readings, each for a different reason.

■ For more on literal and critical reading, see Ch. 2.

READING CHECKLIST

Reading to Comprehend

___ What is the literal meaning? Write a few sentences explaining the overall situation — what happens to whom, where, when, why, and how.

___ What are the facts of the situation — the events of the plot, the aspects of the setting, and the major attributes, words, and actions of the characters?

___ What does all the vocabulary mean, especially in titles and in poems? Look up any unfamiliar words or words whose familiar meanings don't seem to fit the context.

Reading to Analyze

___ What are the main parts or elements of the work? Read, read aloud, mark, or make notes on such elements as theme, character, language, style, symbol, or form.

___ What does the literary work mean? What does it imply?

___ What does it suggest about the human condition? How does it expand your understanding? What insights can you apply to your own life?

Reading to Evaluate

___ How do you assess the soundness and plausibility of what the author says?

___ Are the words and tone appropriate for the purpose and audience?

___ Does the author achieve his or her purpose? Is it a worthwhile purpose?

Plan and Organize an Analysis.   Jonathan Burns knew he had to analyze the important elements — such as setting, character, and tone — in "The Lottery" to understand the story well enough to write about it. He immediately thought of the story's undertone of violence but decided that it was so subtle that writing about it would be difficult. Then he considered the especially memorable characters, Mr. Summers and Old Man Warner.

And of course there was Tessie Hutchinson; he could hear her screams as the stones hit her. But he could not think of much to say except the vague statement that they were memorable. All of a sudden, he hit on the surprise ending. How did Jackson manipulate all the details to generate such a shock?

To begin to focus his thinking, he brainstormed for possible essay titles having to do with the ending, some serious, others less so: Death Comes as a Surprise, The Unsuspected Finish, Patience of the Devil. He chose the straightforward title "The Hidden Truth." After reviewing his notes, Burns realized that Jackson uses characterization, symbolism, and ambiguous description to build up to the ending. He listed details from the story under those three headings to make an informal plan for his paper:

For more on brainstorming, see pp. 296–97. For more on seeking motives of characters, see pp. 305–06.

Title: The Hidden Truth
Working Thesis: In "The Lottery" Jackson effectively crafts a shock ending.
1. Characterization that contributes to the shock ending
    –The children of the village
    –The adults of the village
    –Conversations among the villagers
2. Symbols that contribute to the shock ending
    –The stones
    –The black box
3. Ambiguous description that contributes to the shock ending
    –The word "lottery"
    –Comments
        –"clean forgot"
        –"wish they'd hurry"
        –"It isn't fair."
    –Actions
        –Relief
        –Suspense

For more on stating a thesis, see pp. 312–19. For more on organizing ideas and outlining, see pp. 319–33.

Then he drafted the following introduction:

For more on introductions, see pp. 340–42.

Unsuspecting, the reader follows Shirley Jackson's softly flowing tale of a rural community's timeless ritual, the lottery. Awareness of what is at stake--the savage murder of one random member--comes slowly. No sooner does the realization set in than the story is over. It is a shock ending.

What creates the shock that the reader experiences reading "The Lottery"? Shirley Jackson takes great care in producing this effect, using elements such as language, symbolism, and characterization to lure the reader into not anticipating what is to come.

With his synopsis, his plan, his copy of the story, and this beginning of a draft, Burns revised the introduction and wrote the following essay.

STUDENT ESSAY

Jonathan Burns
The Hidden Truth: An Analysis of Shirley Jackson's "The Lottery"

It is as if the first stone thrown strikes the reader as well as Mrs. Hutchinson. And even though there were signs of the stoning to come, somehow the reader is taken by surprise at Tessie's violent death. What factors contribute to the shock ending to "The Lottery"? On closer examination of the story, the reader finds that through all the events leading up to the ending, Shirley Jackson has used unsuspicious characterizations, unobtrusive symbolism, and ambiguous descriptions to achieve so sudden an impact.

By all appearances, the village is a normal place with normal people. Children arrive at the scene first, with school just over for the summer, talking of teachers and books, not of the fact that someone will die today (237). And as the adults show up, their actions are just as stereotypical: the men talk of farming and taxes, while the women gossip (237). The scene conveys no trace of hostility, no sense of dread in anyone: death seems very far away here.

The conversations between the villagers are no more ominous. As the husbands draw slips of paper for their families, the villagers make apparently everyday comments about the seemingly ordinary event of the lottery. Mr. Summers is regarded as a competent and respected figure, despite the fact that his wife is "a scold" (237). Old Man Warner brags about how many lotteries he's seen and rambles on criticizing other towns that have given up the tradition (240–41). The characters' comments show the crowd to be more a closely knit community than a murderous mob.

The symbols of "The Lottery" seem equally ordinary. The stones collected by the boys (237) are unnoticed by the adults and thus seem a trivial detail. The reader thinks of the "great pile" (237) as children's entertainment, like a stack of imaginary coins, rather than an arsenal. Ironically, no stones are ever thrown during the children's play, and no violence is seen in the pile of stones.

Similarly, Jackson describes the box and its history in great detail, but nothing seems unusual about it. It is just another everyday object, stored away in the post office or on a shelf in the grocery (238). Every other day of the year, the box is in plain view but goes virtually unnoticed. The only indication that the box has lethal consequences is that it is painted black (238), yet this is an ambiguous detail, as a black box can also signify mystery or magic, mystical forces that are sometimes thought to exist in any lottery.

In her ambiguous descriptions, Jackson refers regularly to the village's lottery and emphasizes it as a central ritual for the people. The word <u>lottery</u> itself is ironic, as it typically implies a winning of some kind, like a raffle or sweepstakes. It is

The numbers in parentheses are page-number citations following MLA style. For more advice on citing and listing sources, see D6 and E in the Quick Research Guide (the dark-red-edged pages).

paralleled to square dances and to the teenage club, all under the direction of Mr. Summers (237), activities people look forward to. There is no implied difference between the occurrences of this day and the festivities of Halloween: according to Jackson, they are all merely "civic activities" (237). Equally ambiguous are the people's emotions: some of the villagers are casual, such as Mrs. Hutchinson, who arrives late because she "'[c]lean forgot'" what day it is (239), and some are anxious, such as Mrs. Dunbar, who repeats to her son, "'I wish they'd hurry,'" without any sign of the cause of her anxiety (241). With these descriptive details, the reader finds no threat or malice in the villagers, only vague expectation and congeniality.

Even when it becomes clear that the lottery is something no one wants to win,   7
Jackson presents only a vague sense of sadness and mild protest. The crowd is relieved that the youngest of the Hutchinsons, Davy, doesn't draw the fatal slip of paper (242). One girl whispers that she hopes it isn't Nancy (242), and when the Hutchinson children discover they aren't the winners, they beam with joy and proudly display their blank slips (242). Suspense and excitement grow only when the victim is close to being identified. And when Tessie is revealed as the winner of the lottery (243), she merely holds her hands out "desperately" and repeats, "'It isn't fair'" (243).

With a blend of character, symbolism, and description, Jackson paints an overall   8
portrait of a gentle-seeming rural community, apparently no different from any other. The tragic end is sudden only because there is no recognition of violence beforehand, despite the fact that Jackson has provided the reader with plenty of clues in the ample details about the lottery and the people. It is a haunting discovery that the story ends in death, even though such is the truth in the everyday life of all people.

Questions to Start You Thinking

Meaning

1. What is Burns's thesis?
2. What major points does he use to support the interpretation stated in his thesis? What specific elements of the story does he include as evidence?

Writing Strategies

3. How does this essay differ from a synopsis, a summary of the events of the plot? (For a synopsis of "The Lottery," see pp. 257–58.)
4. Does Burns focus on the technique of the short story or on its theme?
5. Is his introduction effective? Compare and contrast it with his first draft (p. 245). What did he change? Which version do you prefer?
6. Why does he explain characterization first, symbolism second, and description last? How effective is this organization? Would discussing these elements in a different order have made much difference?
7. Is his conclusion effective?
8. How does he tie his ideas together as he moves from paragraph to paragraph? How does he keep the focus on ideas and technique instead of plot?

A Glossary of Terms for Literary Analysis

Characters. Characters are imagined people. The author shows you what they are like through their actions, speech, thoughts, attitudes, and background. Sometimes a writer also includes physical characteristics or names or relationships with other people. For example, in "The Lottery," the description of Mr. Summers introduces the lottery official as someone with civic interests who wants to avoid slip-ups (paragraphs 4, 9, and 10).

Figures of Speech. Figures of speech are lively or fresh expressions that vary the expected sequence or sense of words. Some common types of figurative language are the *simile*, a comparison using *like* or *as;* the *metaphor,* an implied comparison; and *personification,* the attribution of human qualities to inanimate or nonhuman creatures or things. In "The Lottery," three boys *guard* their pile of stones "against the *raids*" of others (paragraph 2).

Imagery. Images are words or groups of words that refer to any sense experience: seeing, hearing, smelling, tasting, touching, or feeling. The images in "The Lottery" help readers envision the "richly green" grass (paragraph 1), the smooth and round stones the children gather (paragraph 2), the "hush" that comes over the crowd (paragraph 19), and Mrs. Dunbar "gasping for breath" (paragraph 75).

Irony. Irony results from readers' sense of discrepancy. A simple kind of irony, *sarcasm,* occurs when you say one thing but mean the opposite: "I just love scrubbing the floor." In literature, an *ironic situation* sets up a contrast or incongruity. In "The Lottery," cruel and horrifying actions take place on a sunny June day in an ordinary village. *Ironic dialogue* occurs when a character says one thing, but the audience or reader is aware of another meaning. When Old Man Warner reacts to giving up the lottery as "wanting to go back to living in caves" (paragraph 32), he implies that such a change would return the villages to a more primitive life. His comment is ironic because the reader is aware that this lottery is a primitive ritual. A story has an *ironic point of view* when readers sense a difference between the author and the narrator or the character who perceives the story; Jackson, for instance, clearly does not condone the actions of the villagers.

Plot. Plot is the arrangement of the events of the story—what happens to whom, where, when, and why. If the events follow each other logically and are in keeping with the characters, the plot is *plausible,* or believable. Although the ending of "The Lottery" at first may shock readers, the author uses *foreshadowing,* hints or clues such as the villagers' nervousness about the lottery, to help readers understand future events or twists in the plot.

Most plots place the *protagonist,* or main character, in a *conflict* with the *antagonist,* some other person or group. In "The Lottery," a reader might see Tessie as the protagonist and the villagers as the antagonist. *Conflict* consists of two forces trying to conquer each other or resist being conquered—

not merely vaguely defined turmoil. *External conflicts* occur outside an individual — between two people, a person and a group (Tessie versus the villagers), two groups (lottery supporters and opponents), or even a character and the environment. *Internal conflicts* between two opposing forces or desires occur within an individual (such as fear versus hope as the lottery slips are drawn). The *central conflict* is the primary conflict for the protagonist that propels the action of the story. Events of the plot *complicate* the conflict (Tessie arrives late, Bill draws the slip) and lead to the *climax*, the moment when the outcome is inevitable (Tessie draws the black dot). This outcome is the *resolution*, or conclusion (the villagers stone Tessie). Some stories let events unfold without any apparent plot — action and change occur inside the characters.

Point of View. The point of view, the angle from which a story is told, might be the author's or a character's. The *narrator* is the one who tells the story and perceives the events, perhaps with limited knowledge or a part to play. Three common points of view are those of a *first-person narrator (I)*, the *speaker* who tells the story; a *third-person narrator (he or she)* who participates in the action (often as the protagonist); and a *third-person narrator* who simply observes. The point of view may be *omniscient* (told through several characters' eyes); *limited omniscient* (told through one character's eyes); or *objective* (not told through any character's eyes). In "The Lottery," a third-person objective narrator seemingly looks on and reports what occurs without knowing what the characters think.

Setting. Setting refers to the time and place of events and may include the season, the weather, and the people in the background. The setting often helps establish a literary work's *mood* or *atmosphere*, the emotional climate that a reader senses. For example, the first sentence of "The Lottery" establishes its setting (paragraph 1).

Symbols. Symbols are tangible objects, visible actions, or characters that hint at meanings beyond themselves. In "The Lottery," the black box suggests outdated tradition, resistance to change, evil, cruelty, and more.

Theme. A theme is a work's main idea or insight — the author's observation about life, society, or human nature. Sometimes you can sum up a theme in a sentence ("Human beings cannot live without illusion"); other times, a theme may be implied, hard to discern, or one of several in a work.

To state a theme, go beyond a work's topic or subject by asking yourself, What does the author say about this subject? Details from the story should support your statement of theme, and your theme should account for the details. "The Lottery" treats subjects such as the unexpected, scapegoating, outmoded rituals, and violence; one of its themes might be stated as "People are selfish, always looking out for number one."

LEARNING BY WRITING

The Assignment: Analyzing a Literary Work. For this assignment, you are to be a literary critic—analyzing, interpreting, and evaluating a literary selection for your classmates. Your purpose is to deepen their understanding because you will have devoted time and effort to digging out the meaning and testing it with evidence from the work itself. Even if they too have studied the work carefully, you will try to convince them that your interpretation is valid.

Write an essay interpreting a literary work that intrigues you or expresses a worthwhile meaning. Your instructor may want to approve your selection. After careful analysis of the work, you will become the expert critic, explaining the meaning you discern, supporting your interpretation with evidence from the work, and evaluating the effectiveness of literary elements used by the author and the significance of the theme.

You cannot include everything about the work in your paper, so you should focus on one element (such as character, setting, or theme) or the interrelationship of two or three elements (as Jonathan Burns did when he analyzed characterization, symbolism, and description in his interpretation of "The Lottery"). Although a summary, or *synopsis*, of the plot is a good beginning point, retelling the story is not a satisfactory literary analysis.

These college writers successfully responded to such an assignment:

One showed how the rhythm, rhymes, and images of Adrienne Rich's poem "Aunt Jennifer's Tigers" mesh to convey the poem's theme of tension between a woman's artistic urge and societal constraints.

Another writer who was a musician analyzed the credibility of Sonny as a musician in James Baldwin's "Sonny's Blues"—his attitudes, actions, struggles, relationship with his instrument and with other musicians—and concluded that Sonny is a believable character.

A psychology major concluded that the relationship between Hamlet and Claudius in Shakespeare's *Hamlet* represents in many ways the tension, jealousy, and misunderstanding between stepsons and stepfathers.

Find a Subject. Read several literary works to find two or three you like. You might start with a favorite author or a favorite short story among those read for this course. Next, reread the works that interest you, and select one to concentrate on. Choose the one that strikes you as especially significant—realistic or universal, moving or disturbing, believable or shocking—with a meaning that you wish to share with your classmates.

■ For more on analysis, see pp. 360–63.

Generate Ideas. Analyzing a literary work is the first step in interpreting meaning and evaluating literary quality. As you read the work, identify its elements and analyze them as Jonathan Burns did for "The Lottery." Then focus on *one* significant element or a cluster of related elements. When you write your interpretation, restrict your discussion to that focus.

We provide three checklists to guide you in analyzing different types of literature. Each of these is an aid to understanding, *not* an organizational outline for writing about literature. The first checklist focuses on short stories and novels, but some of its questions can help you analyze setting, character, theme, or your reactions as a reader for almost any kind of literary work.

DISCOVERY CHECKLIST

Analyzing a Short Story or a Novel

—— What is your reaction to the story? Jot it down.

—— Who is the *narrator* — not the author, but the one who tells the story?

—— What is the *point of view?*

—— What is the *setting* (time and place)? What is the *atmosphere* or *mood?*

—— How does the *plot* unfold? Write a synopsis, or summary, of the events in time order, including relationships among those events.

—— What are the *characters* like? Describe their personalities, traits, and motivations based on their actions, speech, habits, and so on. What strategies does the author use to develop the characters? Who is the *protagonist?* The *antagonist?* Do any characters change? Are the changes believable?

—— How would you describe the story's *style,* or use of language? Is it informal, conversational, or formal? Does the story use dialect or foreign words?

—— What are the *external conflicts* and the *internal conflicts?* What is the *central conflict?* Express the conflicts using the word *versus,* such as "dreams versus reality" or "the individual versus society."

—— What is the *climax* of the story? Is there any *resolution?*

—— Are there important *symbols?* What might they mean?

—— What does the *title* of the story mean?

—— What are the *themes* of the story? Are they universal (applicable to all people everywhere at all times)? Write down your interpretation of the main theme. How is this theme related to your own life?

—— What other literary works or experiences from life does the story make you think of? Write them down.

For a glossary of literary terms, see pp. 248–49.

For more on writing a synopsis, see p. 258.

When looking at a poem, consider the elements specific to poetry and those shared with other genres, as the following checklist suggests.

DISCOVERY CHECKLIST

Analyzing a Poem

—— What is your reaction to the poem? Jot it down.

—— Who is the *speaker* — not the author, but the one who narrates?

—— Is there a *setting?* How does it relate to the meaning of the poem? What *mood* or emotional *atmosphere* does it suggest?

___ Can you put the poem into your own words — paraphrase it?

___ What is striking about the poem's language? Is it informal or formal? Does it use irony or figurative language: *imagery, metaphor, personification?* Identify repetition or words that are unusual, used in an unusual way, or *archaic* (no longer commonly used). Consider *connotations,* the suggestions conjured by the words: *house* versus *home,* though both refer to the same place.

___ Is the poem *lyric* (expressing emotion) or *narrative* (telling a story)?

___ How is the poem structured or divided? Does it use *couplets* (two consecutive rhyming lines), *quatrains* (units of four lines), or other units? How do the beginning and end relate to each other and to the poem as a whole?

___ Does the poem use *rhyme* (words that sound alike)? If so, how does the rhyme contribute to the meaning?

___ Does the poem have *rhythm* (regular meter or beat, patterns of accented and unaccented syllables)? How does the rhythm contribute to the meaning?

___ What does the *title* of the poem mean?

___ What is the major *theme* of the poem? How does this underlying idea unify the poem? How is it related to your own life?

___ What other literary works or experiences from life does the poem make you think of? Write them down.

A play is written to be seen and heard, not read. You may analyze what kind it is and how it would appear onstage, as this checklist suggests.

DISCOVERY CHECKLIST

Analyzing a Play

___ What is your reaction to the play? Jot it down.

___ Is the play a serious *tragedy* (which arouses pity and fear in the audience and usually ends unhappily with the death or downfall of the *tragic hero*)? Or is it a *comedy* (which aims to amuse and usually ends happily)?

___ What is the *setting* of the play? What is its *mood?*

___ In brief, what happens? Summarize each act of the play.

___ What are the characters like? Who is the *protagonist?* Who is the *antagonist?* Are there *foil characters* who contrast with the main character and reveal his or her traits? Which characters are in conflict? Which change?

___ Which speeches seem especially significant?

___ What is the plot? Identify the *exposition* or background information needed to understand the story. Determine the main *external* and *internal* conflicts. What is the *central conflict?* What events *complicate* the central conflict? How are these elements of the plot spread throughout the play?

___ What is the *climax* of the play? Is there a *resolution* to the action?

___ What does the *title* mean?

___ Can you identify any *dramatic irony,* words or actions of a character that carry meaning unperceived by the character but evident to the audience?

—— What is the major *theme* of the play? Is it a universal idea? How is it related to your own life?

—— What other literary works or experiences from life does the play make you think of? Write them down.

Consider Your Audience. When you write your analysis, your purpose is to explain the work's deeper meaning. Don't try to impress readers with your brilliance. Instead, regard them as friends in whose company you are discussing something familiar to all, though they may not have studied the work as carefully as you have. This assumption will help you decide how much evidence from the work to include and will reduce summarizing.

Identify Your Support. After you have determined the major element or cluster of elements that you intend to focus on, go through the work again to find all the passages that relate to your main point. Mark them as you find them, or put them on note cards or in a computer file, along with the page references. If you use any quotations, quote exactly.

For more on planning, drafting, and developing, see Chs. 17, 18, and 19.

Develop Your Main Idea or Thesis. Begin by trying to express your point in a thesis statement that identifies the literary work and the author. Suppose you start with a working thesis on the theme of "The Lottery":

For more on stating a thesis, see pp. 312–19.

WORKING THESIS   In "The Lottery," Shirley Jackson reveals the theme.

But this statement is too vague, so you rewrite it to be more precise:

IMPROVED   In "The Lottery" by Shirley Jackson, the theme is tradition.

This thesis is better but still doesn't state the theme clearly or precisely. You try other ways of expressing what Jackson implies about tradition:

IMPROVED   In "The Lottery" by Shirley Jackson, one of the major themes is that outmoded traditions can be harmful.

Adding *one of* shows that this is not the story's only theme, but the rest is vague. What does *outmoded* mean? How are traditions harmful?

MORE PRECISE   In "The Lottery" by Shirley Jackson, one of the major themes is that traditions that have lost their meaning can still move people to act abnormally without thinking.

This thesis is better but may change as you write the analysis. For instance, you might go beyond interpretation of Jackson's ideas by adding *tragic* to convey your evaluation of her observation of the human condition:

EVALUATION   In "The Lottery," Shirley Jackson reveals the tragic theme that
ADDED   traditions that have lost their meaning can still move people to abnormal and thoughtless action.

Or you might say this, alerting readers to your main points:

PREVIEW
ADDED

In "The Lottery," Shirley Jackson effectively uses symbolism and irony to reveal the theme that traditions that have lost their meaning can still move people to abnormal and thoughtless action.

■ For a story that shows character change, see "The Story of an Hour," pp. 259–60.

When planning your essay, focus on analyzing ideas, not retelling events. One way to maintain that focus is to analyze your thesis, dividing it into parts and then developing each part in turn in your essay. The thesis just presented could be divided into (1) use of symbolism to reveal theme and (2) use of irony to reveal theme. Similarly, you might divide a thesis about character change into the character's original traits or attitudes, the events that cause change, and the character's new traits or attitudes.

Introduce Your Essay.   Tie your beginning to your main idea, or thesis. If you are uncertain how to begin, try one of these openings:

- Focus on a character's universality (pointing out that most people might feel as Tessie in "The Lottery" did if their names were drawn).
- Focus on a theme's universality (discussing briefly how traditions seem to be losing their meaning in modern society).

FOR PEER RESPONSE

For general questions for a peer editor, see p. 377. For peer response worksheets, visit <bedfordstmartins.com/ bedguide> and do a keyword search:

🔍 **peer**

Ask one of your classmates to read your draft, considering how effectively you have analyzed the literary work and presented your analysis. Ask your peer editor to answer specific questions such as these:

- What is your first reaction to the literary analysis?
- In what ways does the analysis add to your understanding of the literary work? In what ways does it add to your insights into life?
- Does the introduction make you want to read the rest of the analysis? What changes would you suggest to strengthen the opening?
- Is the main idea clear? Is there sufficient relevant evidence from the work to support that point? Put stars wherever additional evidence is needed. Put a check mark by any irrelevant information.
- Does the writer go beyond plot summary to analyze elements, interpret meaning, and evaluate literary merit? If not, how might the writer revise?
- Is the analysis organized by ideas instead of events? What changes in organization would you suggest?
- Do the transitions guide you smoothly from one point to the next? Do the transitions focus on ideas, not on time or position in the story? Note any places where the writer might add transitions.
- If this were your paper, what is the one thing you would be sure to work on before handing it in?

- Quote a striking line from the work ("and then they were upon her" or " 'Lottery in June, corn be heavy soon' ").

- Start with a statement of what the work is about, with your reaction to the work when you read it, with a parallel personal experience, or with a comment about a technique that the writer uses.

- Ask a "Have you ever?" question to draw readers into your interpretation.

For more on introductions, see pp. 340–42.

Support Your Interpretation. As you develop your analysis, include supporting evidence — descriptions of setting and character, summaries of events, quotations of dialogue, and other specifics. Cite page numbers (for prose) or line numbers (for poetry) where the details can be found in the work. Integrate evidence from the story with your comments and ideas.

For more on citing and listing literary works, see MLA style in E in the Quick Research Guide (the dark-red-edged pages).

Keep the focus on ideas, not events, by using transition markers that refer to character traits and personality change, not to time. Say "Although Mr. Summers was . . ." instead of "At the beginning of the story Mr. Summers was . . . ." Write "Tessie became . . ." instead of "After that Tessie was . . ." State "The villagers in 'The Lottery' changed . . . ," not "On the next page . . . ."

For a list of transitions showing logical connections, see p. 347.

Conclude Your Essay. When you reach the end, don't just stop writing. Use the same techniques you use for introductions — personal experience, comment on technique, quotation — to provide a sense of finality and closing for your readers. Refer to or reaffirm your thesis. Often an effective conclusion ties in directly with the introduction.

For more on conclusions, see pp. 343–44.

Revise and Edit. Consider these questions as you shape your draft:

For more revising and editing strategies, see Ch. 20.

REVISION CHECKLIST

___ Have you clearly identified the literary work and the author near the beginning of the analysis?

___ Is your main idea or thesis clear? Does everything else relate to it?

___ Have you focused on one element or a cluster of related elements in your analysis? Have you organized around these ideas rather than events?

___ Do your transitions focus on ideas, not on plot or time sequence? Do they guide readers easily from one section or sentence to the next?

___ Are your interpretations supported by evidence from the literary work? Do you need to add examples of dialogue, action, or description? Have you selected details relevant to the points of analysis, not interesting sidelights?

___ Have you woven the details from the work smoothly into your text? Have you cited their correct page or line numbers? Have you quoted and cited carefully instead of lifting language without proper attribution?

___ Do you understand all the words and literary terms you use?

___ Have you tried to share your insights into the meaning of the work with your readers, or have you slipped into trying to impress them?

For more editing and proofreading strategies, see pp. 384–87.

After you have revised your literary analysis, check the grammar, word choice, punctuation, and mechanics — and then correct any problems you find. Make sure that you smoothly introduce all of your quotations and references to the work and weave them into your own discussion. Here are some questions to get you started editing and proofreading your paper:

EDITING CHECKLIST

For more help, turn to the dark-blue-edged pages, and find the Quick Editing Guide sections noted here.

____ Have you used the present tense for events in the literary work and for comments about the author's presentation? **A3**

____ Have you used quotation marks correctly whenever you give the exact words of the literary work? **C3**

____ Have you used correct manuscript format for your paper? **D3**

Strategies for Writing about Literature: Synopsis and Paraphrase

LEARNING FROM OTHER WRITERS: SYNOPSIS

In your literature courses you will often be asked to write synopses of short stories and novels and to paraphrase poems. Both skills are valuable because they help you get the chronology straight, pick out the significant events and details, and relate the parts of a work to each other and to the themes of the work.

For more on summarizing and paraphrasing, see Ch. 12 and D in the Quick Research Guide on the dark-red-edged pages.

A *synopsis* is a summary of the plot of a narrative — a short story, a novel, a play, or a narrative poem. It describes the literal meaning, condensing the story to the major events and the most significant details. You do not include your interpretation, but you summarize the work in your own words, taking care not to lift language or sentence structure from the work itself. Like a synopsis, a *paraphrase* conveys the meaning of the original piece of literature and the relationships of its parts in your own words. A paraphrase, however, converts the original poetry to your own prose or the original prose to your own words in a passage about as long as the original.

For "The Lottery," see pp. 237–43.

In preparation for writing his literary analysis of "The Lottery" — to make sure he had the sequence of events clear — Jonathan Burns wrote the following synopsis of the story.

STUDENT EXAMPLE

Jonathan Burns
A Synopsis of "The Lottery"

Around ten o'clock on a sunny June 27, the villagers gathered in the square for   1
a lottery, expecting to be home in time for lunch. The children came first, glad that
school was out for the summer. The boys romped and gathered stones, the girls
talked quietly in small groups, and the little ones hovered near their brothers and
sisters. Then the men came, followed by the women. When parents called, the
children came reluctantly.

Mr. Summers, who always conducted the town lottery, arrived with the black   2
wooden box and set it on the three-legged stool that Mr. Graves had brought out.
The villagers remained at a distance from these men and didn't respond when Mr.
Summers asked for help. Finally, Mr. Martin and his son held the shabby black box as
Mr. Summers mixed the papers in it. Although the townspeople had talked about
replacing the box, they never had, but they had substituted paper slips for the
original wooden chips. To prepare for the drawing, they listed the members of every
household and swore in Mr. Summers. Although they had dropped many aspects of
the original ritual, the official still greeted each person individually.

Tessie Hutchinson rushed into the square, telling her friend Mrs. Delacroix she   3
had almost forgotten what day it was. Then she joined her husband and children.

When Mr. Summers asked if everyone was present, he was told that Clyde Dunbar   4
was absent because of a broken leg but that his wife would draw for the family.
Summers noted that the Watson boy was drawing for his mother and checked to
see if Old Man Warner was present.

The crowd got quiet. Mr. Summers reminded everybody of what they were to   5
do and began to call the names in alphabetical order. People in the group joked
nervously as the names were called. Mrs. Delacroix and Mrs. Graves commented on
how fast time had passed since the last lottery, and Old Man Warner talked about
how important the lottery was to the villagers. When Mr. Summers finished calling
the roll, there was a pause before the heads of households opened their slips.
Everybody wondered who had the special slip of paper, who had won the lottery.
They discovered it was Bill Hutchinson. When Tessie complained that the drawing
hadn't been done fairly, the others told her to "Be a good sport" (241).

Mr. Graves put five slips into the box, one for each member of Bill Hutchinson's   6
family. Tessie kept charging unfairness. The children drew first, then Tessie, then
Bill. The children opened their slips, smiled broadly, and held blank pieces of paper
over their heads. Bill opened his, and it was blank too. Tessie wouldn't open hers;
Bill had to do it for her. Hers had a black spot on it.

Mr. Summers urged the villagers to complete the process quickly. They picked up   7
stones, even little Davy Hutchinson, and started throwing them at Tessie, as she
kept screaming, "It isn't fair, it isn't right" (243). Then they stoned her.

Questions to Start You Thinking

Meaning

1. In what ways does this synopsis help you understand the story better?
2. Why isn't a synopsis as interesting as a short story?
3. Can you tell from this synopsis whether Burns understands Jackson's story beyond the literal level? How can you tell?

Writing Strategies

4. Does Burns retell the story accurately and clearly? Does he get the events in correct time order? How does he show the relationships of the events to each other and to the whole?
5. Does Burns select the details necessary to indicate what happened in "The Lottery"? Why do you think he omits certain details?
6. Are there any details, comments, or events that you would add to his synopsis? Why or why not?
7. How does this synopsis differ from Burns's literary analysis (pp. 246–47)?

LEARNING BY WRITING: SYNOPSIS

The Assignment: Writing a Synopsis of a Story by Kate Chopin.
Whenever you have trouble understanding a story or have a lot of stories to read, writing a synopsis can help you easily review a story's specifics. Keep your synopsis of the plot true to the original, noting accurate details in time order. Condensing a story to a few hundred words forces you to focus on the most important details and the sequence of events, often leading to a statement of theme.

Kate Chopin was a nineteenth-century American writer whose female characters search for their own identity and for freedom from oppression. For practice, write a synopsis of two to three hundred words of Chopin's "The Story of an Hour." Use these questions to help you get started:

DISCOVERY CHECKLIST

____ What are the major events and details of the story?
____ In what time order do events take place?
____ How are the parts of the story related (without adding your interpretations)?
____ Which of the author's words might you want to quote?

Kate Chopin
The Story of an Hour

Knowing that Mrs. Mallard was afflicted with a heart trouble, great care was taken to break to her as gently as possible the news of her husband's death.

It was her sister Josephine who told her, in broken sentences, veiled hints that revealed in half concealing. Her husband's friend Richards was there, too, near her. It was he who had been in the newspaper office when intelligence of the railroad disaster was received, with Brently Mallard's name leading the list of "killed." He had only taken the time to assure himself of its truth by a second telegram, and had hastened to forestall any less careful, less tender friend in bearing the sad message.

She did not hear the story as many women have heard the same, with a paralyzed inability to accept its significance. She wept at once, with sudden, wild abandonment, in her sister's arms. When the storm of grief had spent itself she went away to her room alone. She would have no one follow her.

There stood, facing the open window, a comfortable, roomy armchair. Into this she sank, pressed down by a physical exhaustion that haunted her body and seemed to reach into her soul.

She could see in the open square before her house the tops of trees that were all aquiver with the new spring life. The delicious breath of rain was in the air. In the street below a peddler was crying his wares. The notes of a distant song which someone was singing reached her faintly, and countless sparrows were twittering in the eaves.

There were patches of blue sky showing here and there through the clouds that had met and piled one above the other in the west facing her window.

She sat with her head thrown back upon the cushion of the chair, quite motionless, except when a sob came up into her throat and shook her, as a child who has cried itself to sleep continues to sob in its dreams.

She was young, with a fair, calm face, whose lines bespoke repression and even a certain strength. But now there was a dull stare in her eyes, whose gaze was fixed away off yonder on one of those patches of blue sky. It was not a glance of reflection, but rather indicated a suspension of intelligent thought.

There was something coming to her and she was waiting for it, fearfully. What was it? She did not know; it was too subtle and elusive to name. But she felt it, creeping out of the sky, reaching toward her through the sounds, the scents, the color that filled the air.

Now her bosom rose and fell tumultuously. She was beginning to recognize this thing that was approaching to possess her, and she was striving to beat it back with her will — as powerless as her two white slender hands would have been.

When she abandoned herself a little whispered word escaped her slightly parted lips. She said it over and over under her breath: "Free, free,

free!" The vacant stare and the look of terror that had followed it went from her eyes. They stayed keen and bright. Her pulses beat fast, and the coursing blood warmed and relaxed every inch of her body.

She did not stop to ask if it were not a monstrous joy that held her. A clear and exalted perception enabled her to dismiss the suggestion as trivial. 12

She knew that she would weep again when she saw the kind, tender hands folded in death; the face that had never looked save with love upon her, fixed and gray and dead. But she saw beyond that bitter moment a long procession of years to come that would belong to her absolutely. And she opened and spread her arms out to them in welcome. 13

There would be no one to live for during those coming years; she would live for herself. There would be no powerful will bending her in that blind persistence with which men and women believe they have a right to impose a private will upon a fellow creature. A kind intention or a cruel intention made the act seem no less a crime as she looked upon it in that brief moment of illumination. 14

And yet she had loved him — sometimes. Often she had not. What did it matter! What could love, the unsolved mystery, count for in face of this possession of self-assertion which she suddenly recognized as the strongest impulse of her being. 15

"Free! Body and soul free!" she kept whispering. 16

Josephine was kneeling before the closed door with her lips to the keyhole, imploring for admission. "Louise, open the door! I beg; open the door — you will make yourself ill. What are you doing, Louise? For heaven's sake open the door." 17

"Go away. I am not making myself ill." No; she was drinking in a very elixir of life through that open window. 18

Her fancy was running riot along those days ahead of her. Spring days, and summer days, and all sorts of days that would be her own. She breathed a quick prayer that life might be long. It was only yesterday she had thought with a shudder that life might be long. 19

She arose at length and opened the door to her sister's importunities. There was a feverish triumph in her eyes, and she carried herself unwittingly like a goddess of Victory. She clasped her sister's waist, and together they descended the stairs. Richards stood waiting for them at the bottom. 20

Someone was opening the front door with a latchkey. It was Brently Mallard who entered, a little travel-stained, composedly carrying his gripsack and umbrella. He had been far from the scene of the accident, and did not even know there had been one. He stood amazed at Josephine's piercing cry; at Richards's quick motion to screen him from the view of his wife. 21

But Richards was too late. 22

When the doctors came they said she had died of heart disease — of joy that kills. 23

LEARNING BY WRITING: PARAPHRASE

The Assignment: Writing a Paraphrase of a Poem.   When you study poetry, you can benefit from paraphrasing—expressing the content of a poem in your own words without adding your opinions or interpretations. Writing a paraphrase forces you to divide the poem into logical sections, to figure out what the poet says in each section, and to discern how the parts relate. After paraphrasing a poem, you should find it easier to state its theme—its main idea or insight—in a sentence or two. Use these questions to get started:

For more on paraphrasing, see Ch. 12 and D4 and D6 in the Quick Research Guide (the dark-red-edged pages).

See pp. 196–97 and the Other Assignments section below for poems you might paraphrase.

DISCOVERY CHECKLIST

____ What are the poem's major sections? What does the poet say in each one?

____ How are the sections of the poem related?

____ Are any words unfamiliar or used in a special sense, different from the usual meanings? What do those words mean in the context of the poem?

____ Does the poet use images to create sensory pictures or figurative language to create comparisons? How do these contribute to the meaning?

For more on figures of speech or imagery, see p. 248.

Other Assignments for Writing about Literature

1. Use a poem, a play, or a novel instead of a short story to write the literary analysis assigned in this chapter (p. 250).
2. Write an essay comparing and contrasting a literary element in two or three short stories or poems.
3. Read the poem below by Robert Frost (1874–1963). Write an essay using a paraphrase of the poem as a springboard for your thoughts on a fork in the road of your life—a decision that made a difference for you.

For more on writing a comparison and contrast essay, see Ch. 7.

For another poem by Robert Frost, see pp. 196–97.

The Road Not Taken

Two roads diverged in a yellow wood,
And sorry I could not travel both
And be one traveler, long I stood
And looked down one as far as I could
To where it bent in the undergrowth;

Then took the other, as just as fair,
And having perhaps the better claim,
Because it was grassy and wanted wear;
Though as for that the passing there
Had worn them really about the same,

And both that morning equally lay
In leaves no step had trodden black.
Oh, I kept the first for another day!
Yet knowing how way leads on to way,
I doubted if I should ever come back.

I shall be telling this with a sigh
Somewhere ages and ages hence:
Two roads diverged in a wood, and I —
I took the one less traveled by,
And that has made all the difference.

For more on writing a comparison and contrast essay, see Ch. 7.

4. Read the poem below by Edwin Arlington Robinson (1869–1935). Have you known and envied someone similar to Richard Cory, a person everyone thought had it all? What happened to him or her? What did you discover about your impression of this person? Write a personal response essay to compare and contrast the person you knew with Richard Cory. Be sure to analyze the poem and draw on your own experience.

Richard Cory

Whenever Richard Cory went down town,
We people on the pavement looked at him:
He was a gentleman from sole to crown,
Clean favored, and imperially slim.

And he was always quietly arrayed,
And he was always human when he talked;
But still he fluttered pulses when he said,
"Good-morning," and he glittered when he walked.

And he was rich — yes, richer than a king —
And admirably schooled in every grace:
In fine, we thought that he was everything
To make us wish that we were in his place.

So on we worked, and waited for the light,
And went without the meat, and cursed the bread;
And Richard Cory, one calm summer night,
Went home and put a bullet through his head.

For more about analyzing visuals, see Ch. 22. For more on analysis in general, see pp. 360–63.

5. Write a critical analysis of a song, a movie, or a television program. Be sure to hear or view the work several times to pull out the specific evidence necessary to support your interpretation. If your instructor approves, present your analysis in a podcast, a multimedia format, or a series of Web pages.

Chapter 14
Writing in the Workplace

Most of the world's workplace communication takes place in writing. Although a conversation or voice mail may be forgotten or ignored, a letter, memorandum (memo), or e-mail provides a permanent record of business exchanges, often calling for action.

Personnel managers, the people who do the hiring in large corporations, tend to be keenly interested in applicants who can write clearly, accurately, and effectively. A survey conducted at Cornell University asked executives to rate in importance the qualities they would like employees to possess. Skill in writing was ranked in fourth place, ahead of both managerial and analytical skills, suggesting the practical value of a writing course.

In this chapter, we first outline some general guidelines for workplace writing and then show you four kinds likely to prove useful in your career — letters, memoranda, e-mail, and résumés.

EFFECTIVE WORKPLACE WRITING

Respectful tone

Clear purpose

Concise, clear, well-organized presentation

Reader's point of view

Guidelines for Writing in the Workplace

Good workplace writing succeeds in achieving a clear purpose. When you write to a business, your writing represents you; when you write as part of your job, your writing represents your company as well.

KNOW YOUR PURPOSE

Your purpose, or reason for writing, helps you select and arrange information; it gives you a standard against which to measure your final draft. Most likely, you will want to create a certain response in your readers, informing them about something or motivating them to take a specific action.

DISCOVERY CHECKLIST

____ Do you want to inform — announce something, update others, explain some specialized knowledge, or reply to a request?

____ Do you want to motivate some action — get a question answered, a wrong corrected, a decision made, or a personnel director to hire you?

____ When your readers are finished reading what you've written, what do you want them to think? What do you want them to do?

KEEP YOUR AUDIENCE IN MIND

Consider everything in your workplace writing from your audience's point of view. After all, your purpose is not to express your ideas but to have readers act on them, even if the action is simply to notice your grasp of the situation. If you don't know the person to whom you are writing, make educated guesses based on what you know about the position or company.

Especially when your purpose is to motivate, focus on how "you, the reader" will benefit instead of what "I, the writer" would like.

"I" ATTITUDE   Please send me the form so that I can process your order.

"YOU" ATTITUDE   To make sure that you receive your shipment promptly, please send me the order form.

DISCOVERY CHECKLIST

____ What do your readers already know about the subject? Are they experts in the field? Have they been kept up to date on the situation?

____ What do your readers need to know? What information do they expect you to provide? What information do they need before they can take action?

____ What can you assume about your readers' priorities and expectations? Are they busy executives, deluged with reports and messages? Are they conscientious administrators who will appreciate your attention to detail?

____ What is most likely to motivate your readers to take the action you want?

USE AN APPROPRIATE TONE

Tone is the quality of writing that reveals your attitude toward your topic and your readers. If you show readers that you respect them, their intelligence, and their feelings, they are far more likely to view you and your message favorably. Most workplace writing today ranges from the informal to the slightly formal. Gone are extremely formal phrases such as *enclosed herewith, be advised that,* or *pursuant to the stated request.* At the other extreme, slang, overfriendliness, and a too casual style might cast doubts on your seriousness or credibility. Strive for a relaxed and conversational style, using simple sentences, familiar words, and the active voice.

TOO CASUAL	I hear that thing with the new lackey is a definite go.
TOO FORMAL	This office stands informed that the administration's request for supplementary personnel has been honored.
APPROPRIATE	I understand that a new office assistant has been hired.

In all your business writing, be courteous and considerate. If you are writing to complain, remember that your reader may not be the one who caused the problem — and you are more likely to win your case with courtesy than with sarcasm or insults. When delivering bad news, remember that your reader may interpret a bureaucratic response as cold and unsympathetic. And if you have made a mistake, acknowledge it.

REVISION CHECKLIST

____ Have you avoided slang terms and extremely casual language?

____ Have you avoided unnecessarily formal or sophisticated words?

____ Are your sentences of a manageable length?

____ Have you used the active voice ("I am sending it") rather than the passive voice ("It is being sent")?

____ Does anything you've written sound blaming or accusatory?

____ Do you hear a friendly, considerate, competent person behind your words?

____ Have you asked someone else to read your writing to check for tone?

PRESENT INFORMATION CAREFULLY

In business, time is money: time wasted reading irrelevant, poorly written material is money wasted. To be effective, your business writing should be concise, clear, and well organized.

For advice on document design, see Ch. 21.

Concise writing shows that you respect your readers' time. In most cases, if a letter, memo, or résumé is longer than a page or two, it's too long. You might need to find a better way to present the material, or you might need to cut unneeded information or details.

For sample business documents, see the figures later in this chapter.

Clear writing ensures that the information you convey is accurate, complete, and unambiguous. Put what's most important in a prominent spot (usually at the beginning). Let your readers know exactly what you want them to do — politely, of course. If you have a question, ask it. If you want something, request it.

Well-organized writing helps readers move through it quickly and easily. Write every piece of business correspondence so that it can be skimmed. Make the topic absolutely clear from the beginning, usually the first paragraph of a letter or the subject line of a memo or e-mail message. Use a conventional format that your readers will expect (see Figures 14.1 and 14.3 later in this chapter). Break information into easily processed chunks; order these chunks logically and consistently. Finally, use topic sentences and headings (when appropriate) to label each chunk of information and to give your readers an overview of your document.

■ Clear presentation and organization are also important for PowerPoint slides and Web sites. For examples, see p. 404, p. 407, and p. 411.

REVISION CHECKLIST

■ For more revising and editing strategies, see Ch. 20.

____ Have you kept your letter, memo, or résumé to a page or two?

____ Have you cut all unnecessary or wordy explanations?

____ Have you scrutinized every word to ensure that it can't be misinterpreted? Have you supplied all the background information readers need?

____ Have you emphasized the most important part of your message? Will readers know what you want them to do?

____ Have you followed a consistent, logical order and a conventional format?

____ If appropriate, have you included labels and headings?

Business Letters

■ For advice on job application letters, see pp. 275–76.

To correspond with outside parties, either individual people or other groups, organizations use business letters to request and provide information, motivate action, respond to requests, and sell goods and services. Because letters become part of the permanent record, they can be checked later to determine exactly who said what and when. You should keep a copy of every letter you write, a printout as well as a backup on disk or network.

A good business letter is brief — limited to one page if possible. It supplies whatever information the reader needs, no more. A letter of inquiry might simply request a booklet, a sample, or some promotional material. For a special request, however, you might add why you are writing, what you need, and when you need it. On the other hand, a letter of complaint focuses on your problem — what product is involved, when and where you purchased it, exactly why you are unhappy, and how you'd like the problem solved. Include specifics such as product numbers and dates, and maintain a courteous tone. Because they are so brief, business letters are often judged on details—grammar, punctuation, format, appearance, openings, and closings.

FORMAT FOR BUSINESS LETTERS

The format of business letters (see Figure 14.1) is well established by convention. Remember that the physical appearance of a letter is very important.

For another sample letter, see p. 276.

- Use 8½-by-11-inch bond paper, with matching envelopes. Write on only one side of the page.
- Single-space and use an extra line of space to separate paragraphs and the different elements of the letter. In very short letters, it's acceptable to leave additional space before the inside address.

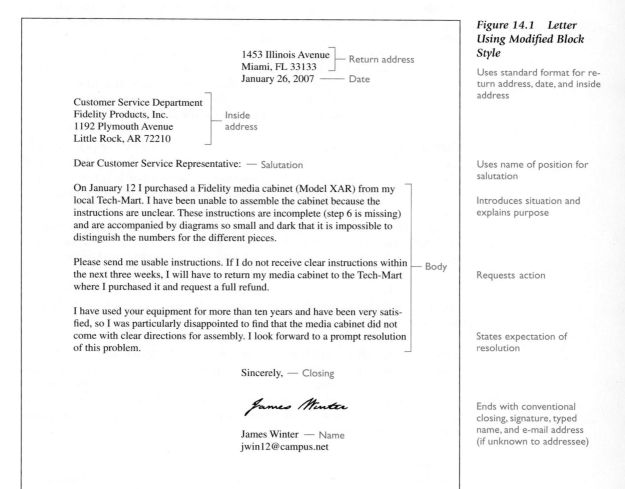

Figure 14.1 Letter Using Modified Block Style

1453 Illinois Avenue — Return address
Miami, FL 33133
January 26, 2007 ——— Date

Customer Service Department
Fidelity Products, Inc.
1192 Plymouth Avenue
Little Rock, AR 72210 — Inside address

Dear Customer Service Representative: — Salutation

On January 12 I purchased a Fidelity media cabinet (Model XAR) from my local Tech-Mart. I have been unable to assemble the cabinet because the instructions are unclear. These instructions are incomplete (step 6 is missing) and are accompanied by diagrams so small and dark that it is impossible to distinguish the numbers for the different pieces.

Please send me usable instructions. If I do not receive clear instructions within the next three weeks, I will have to return my media cabinet to the Tech-Mart where I purchased it and request a full refund.

I have used your equipment for more than ten years and have been very satisfied, so I was particularly disappointed to find that the media cabinet did not come with clear directions for assembly. I look forward to a prompt resolution of this problem.

— Body

Sincerely, — Closing

James Winter

James Winter — Name
jwin12@campus.net

Uses standard format for return address, date, and inside address

Uses name of position for salutation

Introduces situation and explains purpose

Requests action

States expectation of resolution

Ends with conventional closing, signature, typed name, and e-mail address (if unknown to addressee)

- Leave margins of at least one inch on both sides; try to make the top and bottom margins fairly even, although you may have a larger bottom margin if your letter is very short.
- Pay attention to grammar, punctuation, and mechanics. Your readers will.

Return Address. This is your address or the address of the company for which you are writing. Abbreviate only the state using its two-letter postal abbreviation. Omit a return address on preprinted letterhead stationery that already provides this information.

Date. Supply this on the line right after the return address. Spell out the month; follow it by the day, a comma, and the year.

Inside Address. This is the address of the person to whom you are writing. Begin with the person's full name and title (*Mr., Ms., Dr., Professor*); when addressing a woman without a professional title, use *Ms.* unless you know that she prefers *Miss* or *Mrs.* The second line should identify the position the person holds (if any), and the third line should name the organization (if you are writing to one). If you don't know who will read your letter, you may start with the name of the position, department, or organization. Avoid abbreviations in the address except for the state.

Salutation. Skip a line, and then type *Dear* followed by the person's title, last name, and a colon. If you don't know the name of the person who will read your letter, you can use the position that person holds (*Dear Editor*) or the name of the organization (*Dear Angell's Bakery*) in place of a name.

Body. This is your message. Leave one line of space between paragraphs, and begin each paragraph even with the left margin (no indentations). Paragraphs should generally be no longer than seven or eight typed lines.

Closing. Leave one line of space after the last paragraph, and then use a conventional closing followed by a comma: *Sincerely, Sincerely yours, Respectfully yours, Yours truly.*

Typed Name with Position. Leave four lines of space after the closing, and type your name in full, even if you will sign only your first name. Do not include a title before your name. If you are writing on behalf of an organization, you can include your position on the next line. You also may add your e-mail address or telephone number here unless supplied on your stationery or in your message.

Signature. Print the letter, and sign your name in the space above the typed name. Unless you have a personal relationship with the recipient, use both your first and last names. Do not include a title before your name.

Abbreviations at End. Leave at least two lines of extra space between your typed name and any abbreviations used to communicate more information about the letter. Put each abbreviation on a separate line. If you send a copy to someone other than the recipient, use *cc:* followed by the name of the person or organization receiving a copy. If the letter is accompanied by another document in the same envelope, use *Enc.* or *Enclosure.* If the letter has been typed by someone other than the person who wrote and signed it, the writer's initials are given in capital letters, followed by a slash and the initials of the typist in lowercase letters: *VW/dbw.*

Modified and Full Block Style. Two standard formats specify the placement of the elements on the page. To align a letter using *modified block style* (see Figure 14.1), you need to imagine a line running down the center of the page from top to bottom. Place the return address, date, closing, signature, and typed name so that the left side of each aligns with this center line. The *full block style* is generally used only on letterhead stationery with the name and address of the organization. Omit typing the return address, and align all the elements at the left margin.

Envelope Formats. The U.S. Postal Service recommends a format that uses all capital letters, standard abbreviations, and no punctuation; this style makes the information on the envelope easier for the Postal Service to scan and process. However, the conventional envelope format (see Figure 14.2) may be preferred and is always safe to use.

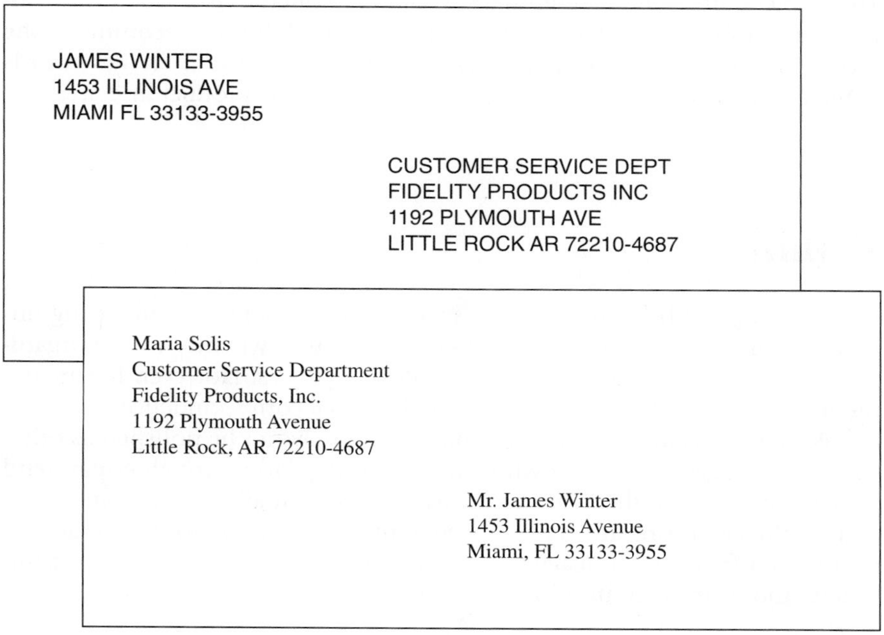

Figure 14.2
Envelope Formats

U.S. Postal Service format

```
JAMES WINTER
1453 ILLINOIS AVE
MIAMI FL 33133-3955


                    CUSTOMER SERVICE DEPT
                    FIDELITY PRODUCTS INC
                    1192 PLYMOUTH AVE
                    LITTLE ROCK AR 72210-4687
```

Conventional format

```
     Maria Solis
     Customer Service Department
     Fidelity Products, Inc.
     1192 Plymouth Avenue
     Little Rock, AR 72210-4687


              Mr. James Winter
              1453 Illinois Avenue
              Miami, FL 33133-3955
```

Memoranda

A *memorandum* (*memo* for short) is a form of communication used within a company to request or exchange information, to make announcements, and to confirm conversations. Memos are frequently used to convey information to large groups — an entire team, department, or organization. Generally, the topic of a memo is quite narrow and should be apparent to the reader at a glance. Memos tend to be written in the first person (*I* or *we*) and can range from the very informal (if written to a peer) to the extremely formal (if written to a high-ranking superior on an important matter). Most are short, but the memo format can be used to convey proposals and reports; long memos freely use headings, subheadings, lists, and other features that are easy to scan. (For a sample, see Figure 14.3.)

FORMAT FOR MEMORANDA

Although every organization has its own format for memos, the heading generally consists of a series of lines with clear labels (followed by colons).

Date:	(date on which memo is sent)
To:	(person or persons to whom it is primarily addressed)
cc:	(names of anyone else who receives a copy)
From:	(name of the writer)
Subject: *or* Re:	(concise, accurate statement of the memo's topic)

The subject line often determines whether a memo is read. (The old-fashioned abbreviation *Re:* for *regarding* is still used, but we recommend the more common *Subject.*) Accurately sum up the topic in a few words ("Agenda for 12/10 meeting," "Sales estimates for new product line").

E-Mail

E-mail is popular because it is easy, speedy, and convenient, combining immediacy with the permanence of letters and memos, whether within organizations or between organizations and outside parties. However, letters and memos are often still preferred for formal, official correspondence.

Because it seems so conversational, e-mail may not be polished as other written messages are. People who correspond regularly through e-mail tend to overlook one another's quirks; however, your e-mail messages are a part of the official record and have no guarantee of privacy. Your confidential chat with a friend or colleague can be intercepted, recorded on other computers, and distributed in print or over a network.

INTERLINK SYSTEMS, INC.

To: All Employees
From: Erica Xiang   *EX*
Subject: Changes in employee benefits
Date: October 26, 2006

Each fall the Human Resources group looks closely at the company's health insurance benefits to make certain that we are providing an excellent level of coverage in a way that makes economic sense. To that end, we have made some changes to our plan, effective January 1, 2007. Let me outline the three major changes.

1. We are pleased to be able to offer employees the opportunity, through a **Flexible Spending Account**, to pay for dependent care and unreimbursed health expenses on a pre-tax basis, a feature that can result in considerable savings. I have attached a summary and will provide more information on this benefit at our staff meeting tomorrow, October 27, at 10:30 A.M. I will be available immediately after the meeting to answer any specific questions.

2. Those of you who have taken advantage of our **vision care benefit** in the past know that it offers significant help in paying for eye exams, eyeglasses, and contact lenses. The current plan will change slightly on January 1. Employees and covered dependents will be eligible to receive up to $50 each year toward the cost of a routine eye exam and up to $100 every two years toward the cost of eyeglasses or contact lenses. If you see a provider within our health insurance network, you will pay only $10 per office visit.

3. We at Interlink Systems feel strongly that our health insurance benefits are excellent, but as you know, the cost of such plans continues to rise every year. In the interest of maintaining excellent coverage for our employees, we will raise our **employee contribution**. Starting January 1, we are asking employees with single coverage to contribute $12.50 more per pay period toward the cost of medical insurance, and employees who cover dependents to contribute $40 more per pay period. Even with this increase, the amount the company asks its employees to contribute towards the premiums (about 8%) is significantly less than the nationwide average of 30%.

Please contact me if you have questions or concerns about the changes that I have outlined in this memo. You can reach me at x462 or at exiang@interlink.net.

Enclosure

Figure 14.3
Memorandum

Uses standard format to identify readers, writer, topic, and date

Explains purpose, noting reader's priorities

Previews clear organization in blocks

Uses friendly tone to note new benefit for employees

Offers assistance

Introduces benefit change with positive background

Presents increased cost carefully, noting coverage quality and high employer contribution

Offers more help and supplies contact information

Notes enclosure

FORMAT FOR E-MAIL

Although e-mail is flexible, its headings are predetermined by your mail system and almost universally follow a memo format: *To:*, *cc:*, *Subject:*, and an automatic *From:* line with your name as sender. Write messages that your audience will find helpful, efficient, and courteous.

- Use a clear subject line to simplify replying and archiving.
- Move promptly to your purpose: state what you need and when.
- Be concise, adding headings and space between sections if needed.
- Follow company practice as you include or delete a trail of message replies.
- Observe company etiquette in copying messages to others.
- Avoid personal statements, humor, or informality that might undermine your professional credibility.

Résumés and Application Letters

The most important business correspondence you write may be the résumé and letter you use to apply for a job. Direct, persuasive, correct prose can help you stand out from the crowd.

RÉSUMÉS

In a résumé, you present yourself as someone who has the qualifications to excel at a job and to be an asset to the organization. Job seekers often have copies of a single résumé on hand, but you may want to customize your résumé for each application if you can easily print attractive copies.

Although a résumé is highly formatted, it also allows a wide variety of decisions about style, organization, and appearance. In this section, we describe a typical résumé, but many formats are acceptable. Unless you have a great deal of relevant work experience, your résumé should be no longer than one page. The standard résumé consists of a heading and labeled sections that detail your experience and qualifications. Within each section, use brief, pointed phrases and clauses rather than complete sentences. Use action verbs (*supervised, ordered, maintained*) and the active voice whenever possible. Highlight labels with underlining, boldface, or a larger type size. Arrange information on the page so that it is pleasing to the eye; use the best paper and clearest printer you can. (For an example, see Figure 14.4.)

■ For more on document design, see Ch. 21.

If you submit electronic applications, you may need to prepare your résumé in several different forms: a text file that you can attach to an e-mail message, an electronically readable version that a company can scan into its database, or a Web version that you can post on your site or a job site (see Figure 14.5). For all these versions, format carefully so that recipients can

Figure 14.4
Conventional Résumé

Anne Cahill
402 Pigeon Hill Road
Windsor, CT 06095
(860) 555-5763
acahill783@yahoo.com

Centers heading with contact information

— Labels sections

Objective	Position as Registered Nurse in pediatric hospital setting
Education	**University of Connecticut**, Storrs, CT. Bachelor of Science, Major in nursing, May 2007. GPA: 3.5; licensed as Registered Nurse by the State of Connecticut in June 2007

Specifies background and experience

Manchester Community Technical College, Manchester, CT. Associate degree in occupational therapy, May 2001. GPA: 3.3.

Work Experience
9/02–present **Certified Occupational Therapy Assistant**, Johnson Memorial Hospital, Stafford Springs, CT
* Assist children with delayed motor development and cerebral palsy to develop skills for the activities of daily life

9/00–9/02 **Nursing Assistant**, Woodlake Healthcare Center, Tolland, CT
* Helped geriatric residents with activities of daily living
* Assisted nursing staff in treating acute care patients

Places current information first

9/98–9/00 **Cashier**, Stop and Shop Supermarket, Vernon, CT
* Trained newly hired cashiers

Clinical Internships **St. Francis Hospital**, Hartford, CT
* Student Nurse, Maternity and Postpartum, spring 2007

Hartford Hospital, Hartford, CT
* Student Nurse, Pediatrics, fall 2006

Visiting Nurse and Community Health, Mansfield, CT
* Student Nurse, Community, spring 2006

Manchester General Hospital, Manchester, CT
* Student Nurse, Medical-Surgical, fall 2005

Computer Skills
* Proficient with Microsoft Office, Database, and Windows applications
* Experienced with Internet research

Adds relevant skills for health-care record keeping

Activities
* Student Union Board of Governors, University of Connecticut, class representative
* Intramural soccer

References Available upon request

Figure 14.5
Résumé for the Web

Uses clear and direct heading

Organizes menu of available information

Creates professional Web design using bullets, color, and white space

Anne Cahill

Objective: **Position as a Registered Nurse in pediatric hospital setting**

- Education

- Experience

- Other Activities

- References

- Contact Me

Profile

New nursing graduate combines proficiency in the latest nursing techniques with significant clinical experience

- Experienced in providing professional, compassionate health-care services to children, others

- Able to work proficiently and productively in hospital settings

- Accustomed to working in a team with a broad range of health professionals and administrators

- Proficient with Microsoft Office, Database, and Windows applications and with Internet research

easily read what you supply. Turn to your campus career center for résumé samples and advice about using alternate formats to your advantage.

Heading.   The heading is generally centered (or otherwise pleasingly aligned) on the page with separate lines for your name; street address, city, state, and zip code; phone number; and e-mail address.

Employment Objective.   This optional section allows personnel officers to see at a glance your priorities and goals. Try to sound confident and eager but not pompous or presumptuous.

Education.   This section is almost always included, often first. Specify each postsecondary school you've attended, your major, your date of graduation (or expected graduation), and your grade point average (if it reflects well on you). You can also add any awards, honors, or relevant course work.

Experience.   In this key section, list each job with the most recent one first. You can include both full-time and part-time jobs. For each, give the name of the organization, your position, your responsibilities, and the dates you held the job. Describe your involvement in any unusual projects or responsibility for any important developments. Highlight details that show relevant work experience and leadership ability. Minimize information unconnected to the job for which you're applying.

Skills.   List any special skills (data processing, technical drawing, multiple languages) that aren't obvious from your education and work experience.

Activities.   You can specify either professional interests and activities (*Member of Birmingham Bricklayers Association*) or personal pursuits (*skiing, hiking, needlepoint*) showing that you are dedicated and well-rounded.

References.   If a job advertisement requests references, provide them. Always contact your references in advance to make sure they are willing to give you a good recommendation. For each person, list the name, his or her organization and position, and the organization's address and phone number. If references have not been requested, you can simply note "Available on request."

APPLICATION LETTERS

When writing a letter applying for a job, you should follow all the guidelines for other business letters. Remember that your immediate objective is to obtain an interview. As you compete against other candidates, your letter and résumé are all the employer has to judge you on. If you're responding to an advertisement, read it critically.

■ For general guidelines for business letters, see pp. 267–69.

- What qualifications are listed? Ideally, you should have all the required qualifications, but if you lack one, try to find something in your background that compensates, some similar experience in a different form.

- What else can you tell about the organization or position from the ad? How does the organization represent itself? If you're unfamiliar with the organization and you can't glean much about it from the ad, check the company's Web site.

- How does the ad describe the ideal candidate? As a team player? A dynamic individual? If you feel that you are the person this organization is looking for, you'll want to portray yourself this way in your letter.

In your letter, you want to spark your readers' interest, convince them that you're a qualified and attractive candidate, and motivate them to interview you. Whenever possible, address your letter to the person responsible for screening applicants and setting up interviews; you may need to call the organization to find out this person's name. In the first paragraph, identify the job, indicate how you heard about it, and summarize your qualifications. In the second paragraph, expand on your qualifications, highlighting key information on your résumé. Supplement it with additional details if necessary to show your readers that you're a better candidate than the other applicants. In the third paragraph, restate your interest in the job, ask for an interview, and let your prospective employer know how to reach you. (For a sample application letter, see Figure 14.6 below.) If you get an interview, follow up with a thank-you note. The note may reemphasize your qualifications and strong interest in the position.

Figure 14.6
Application Letter

Follows standard
letter format

Addresses specific person

Identifies job sought and describes interest

Explains qualifications

Confirms interest and
supplies contact information

Encloses résumé and proof
of certification

402 Pigeon Hill Road
Windsor, CT 06095
July 8, 2007

Sheryl Sullivan
Director of Nursing
Center for Children's Health and Development
St. Francis Hospital and Medical Center
114 Woodland Street
Hartford, CT 06105

Dear Ms. Sullivan:

I am writing to apply for the full-time position as a pediatric nurse at the Center for Children's Health and Development at St. Francis Hospital, which was advertised on the Eastern Connecticut Health Network Web site. I feel that my varied clinical experiences and my desire to work with children ideally suit me for the job. In addition, I am highly motivated to grow and succeed in the field of health care.

For the past five years, I have worked as a certified occupational therapy assistant. In this capacity, I help children with delayed motor function acquire the skills necessary to achieve as high a level of independence as possible. While working as a COTA, I attended nursing school with the ultimate goal of becoming a pediatric nurse. My varied clinical experiences as a student nurse and my previous experience as a nurse's aide in a geriatric center have exposed me to many types of care. I feel that these experiences have helped me to become a well-rounded caregiver; they also, however, have reinforced my belief that my skills and talents are best suited to working with children.

I believe that I would be a strong addition to the medical team at the Children's Center. My clinical experiences have prepared me to deal with a wide range of situations. In addition, I am dedicated to maintaining and enhancing the well-being of children. I am enclosing proof of my recent certification as a Registered Nurse in the state of Connecticut. Please write to me at the address above, e-mail me at acahill783@yahoo.com, or call me at (860) 555-5763. Thank you for your consideration. I look forward to hearing from you.

Sincerely,

Anne Cahill

Anne Cahill

Enclosures

Chapter 15
Writing for Assessment

Most college writing is done for assessment—that is, most of the papers you hand in are eventually evaluated and graded. But some college writing tasks exist *only* as methods of assessment: they are designed not to help you expand your writing skills (or content knowledge) but to allow you to demonstrate that you have mastered them. You often need to do such writing on the spot—a quiz to finish in twenty minutes, a final exam to complete in a few hours, an impromptu essay to dash off in one class period. How do you discover and shape your ideas in a limited time?

In this chapter we provide tips for three types of in-class writing that are commonly used for assessment—the essay exam, the short-answer exam, and the timed writing assignment. We also discuss the writing portfolio, a collection of writing samples that demonstrates your strengths as a writer.

Essay Examinations

In many courses an essay exam is the most important kind of in-class writing. Instructors believe that such writing shows that you haven't just memorized a batch of material but that you have examined it critically and can clearly communicate your thoughts about it to someone else.

For more on critical thinking and college assignments, see pp. 35–36.

PREPARING FOR THE EXAM

Some instructors favor open-book exams, in which you bring your books and perhaps your notes to class for reference. In an open-book exam, ability to memorize and recall is less important than ability to reason and to select what matters. On the other hand—if the exam will be closed book—it's a good idea to fix in your memory vital names, dates, and definitions.

A good way to prepare for any exam, whether the books are closed or open, is to imagine likely questions and then plan answers. If your instructor has supplied sample questions, pattern new ones after them. To study with a textbook, look for the main ideas in relevant chapters. Then ask yourself: What do these ideas have to do with each other? How might they be combined? What conclusions can I draw?

LEARNING FROM ANOTHER WRITER

To look at techniques for answering *any* exam question, let's take one example. A final exam in developmental psychology posed this question:

> What evidence indicates innate factors in perceptual organization? You might find it useful to recall any research that shows how infants perceive depth and forms.

In response, David Ian Cohn sat back in his chair for a few minutes and thought over the reading he'd done for the course. What perception research had used babies for subjects? He jotted down ideas, crossed out a couple of weak ones, and drew lines linking ideas that went together. Then he took a deep breath and wrote this straightforward answer:

For an illustration of linking, see pp. 322–23.

> *Research on infants is probably the best way to demonstrate that some factors in perceptual organization are innate. As the cliff box experiment shows, an infant will avoid what looks like a drop-off, even though its mother calls it and even though it can feel glass covering the drop-off area. The same infant will crawl to the other end of the box, which appears (and is) safe. Apparently, infants do not have to be taught what a cliff looks like.*
>
> *Psychologists have also observed that infants are aware of size constancy. They recognize a difference in size between a 10 cm box at a distance of one meter and a 20 cm box at a distance of two meters. If this phenomenon is not innate, it is at least learned early, for the subjects of the experiment were infants of sixteen to eighteen months.*
>
> *When shown various patterns, infants tend to respond more noticeably to patterns that resemble the human face than to those that appear random. This seemingly innate recognition helps the infant identify people (such as its mother) from less important inanimate objects.*
>
> *Infants also seem to have an innate ability to match sight with sound. When simultaneously shown two television screens, each depicting a different subject, while being played a tape that sometimes matched one screen and sometimes the other, infants looked at whichever screen matched what they heard—not always, but at least twice as often.*

Questions to Start You Thinking

Meaning

1. What is the main idea of Cohn's answer?

2. If you were the psychology instructor, how could you immediately see that Cohn had thoroughly dealt with the question and only with the question?

Writing Strategies

3. In what places is Cohn's answer concrete and specific, not vague and general?

4. Suppose Cohn had tacked on a concluding sentence: "Thus I have conclusively proved that there are innate factors in perceptual organization, by citing much evidence showing that infants definitely can perceive depth and forms." Would that sentence strengthen his answer? Why or why not?

GENERATING IDEAS

When the clock on the wall is ticking away, generating ideas right on the exam sheet will save time. First read over all the questions on the exam carefully. If you don't understand what a question calls for, ask your instructor right away. If you are offered a choice, just cross out questions you are *not* going to answer so you don't waste time on them by mistake. Annotate questions, underline important points, and scribble short definitions. Write reminders that you will notice while you work: TWO PARTS! or GET IN EXAMPLE OF ABORIGINES.

Plan a Concrete Answer.   Few people can dash off an excellent essay exam answer without first taking time to plan. Instructors prefer answers that are concrete and specific rather than those that wander in the clouds of generality. David Cohn's answer to the psychology question cites evidence all the way through — particular experiments in which infants were subjects. Try writing a brief, informal outline like David Cohn's:

> *Thesis: Research on infants is probably the best way to demonstrate that some factors in perceptual organization are innate.*
> *Cliff box — kid fears drop despite glass, mother; knows shallow side safe*
> *Size constancy — learned early if not intrinsic*
> *Shapes — infants respond more/better to face shape than nonformed*
> *Match sound w/ sight — 2 TVs, look twice as much at right one*

■ For David Cohn's complete answer, see p. 278.

Focus on the Question.   Instructors also prefer answers that are organized and coherent rather than rambling. Often a question will contain directive words that help you define your task: *evaluate, compare, discuss, explain, describe, summarize, trace the development of.* You can put yourself on the right track if you incorporate a form of such a word in your first sentence.

■ For more on critical thinking and college assignments, see pp. 34–37.

QUESTION   Define socialism, and give examples of its main varieties.

ANSWER   Socialism is defined as . . .

ANSWER   Socialism is an economic and political concept, difficult to define because it takes many forms. It . . .

PLANNING FOR TYPICAL EXAM QUESTIONS

For examples of many methods of development, see Ch. 19.

Most exam questions fall into types. If you can recognize them, you will
know how to organize and begin to write. Here are examples.

For more on explaining cause and effect, see Ch. 8 and pp. 369–70.

The Cause and Effect Question.   These questions usually mention *causes,
effects,* or both.

> What were the immediate causes of the Dust Bowl in the 1930s?

> Describe the main economic effects of a low prime interest rate.

For more on comparing and contrasting, see Ch. 7 and pp. 366–69.

The Compare or Contrast Question.   This popular type of question asks
you to point out similarities (comparing), discuss differences (contrasting),
or do both. In the process you explain not one subject but two, paralleling
the points you make about each, giving both equal space.

> Compare and contrast *iconic memory* and *eidetic imagery,* defining the terms
> and indicating the ways in which they differ and are related or alike.

After supplying a one-sentence definition of each term, a student proceeded
first to contrast and then to compare, for full credit.

> Iconic memory is a picturelike impression that lasts for only a fraction of a
> second in short-term memory. Eidetic imagery is the ability to take a mental
> photograph, exact in detail, as though its subject were still present. But iconic
> memory soon disappears. Unlike an eidetic image, it does not last long enough
> to enter long-term memory. IM is common; EI is unusual: very few people have
> it. Both iconic memory and eidetic imagery are similar, however: both record
> visual images, and every sighted person of normal intelligence has both abilities
> to some degree.

A question of this kind doesn't always use the words *compare* and *contrast.*
Directions to *show similarities* or *identify likenesses* ask for comparisons, while
those to *distinguish, differentiate,* or *show differences* ask for contrasts, perhaps
to evaluate in what respects one thing is better than the other.

For more on definition, see pp. 356–57.

The Definition Question.   A brief definition may set the stage for answering another question; an extended definition with an illustration or multiple definitions of related terms may stand alone.

> Explain three common approaches to parenting—*permissive, authoritarian-
> restrictive,* and *authoritative.* [Supply a trio of definitions.]

> Define the Stanislavsky method of acting, citing outstanding actors who
> have followed it. [Explain a single method and give examples.]

The Demonstration Question.   This kind of question supplies a statement and asks you to back it up.

> Demonstrate the truth of Freud's contention that laughter may contain elements of aggression.

In other words, you need to explain Freud's claim and then supply evidence to support it. You might refer to crowd scenes you have experienced, analyze a joke or a scene in a film, or use examples from your reading.

The Discussion Question.   A discussion question may tempt the unwary to shoot the breeze.

> Discuss three events that precipitated Lyndon B. Johnson's withdrawal from the 1968 presidential race.

This question looks like an open invitation to ramble about Johnson and the war in Vietnam, but it isn't. Try rewording the question to help you focus your discussion: "Why did President Johnson decide not to seek another term? Analyze the causes and briefly explain each."

Sometimes a discussion question won't announce itself with the word *discuss*, but uses *describe* or *explain* or *explore*.

> Describe the national experience following passage of the Eighteenth Amendment. What did most Americans learn from it?

Provided you know that this amendment banned the sale, manufacture, and transportation of alcoholic drinks and that it was finally repealed, you can discuss its effects — or perhaps the reasons for its repeal.

The Divide or Classify Question.   Sometimes you are asked to slice the subject into sections, sort things into kinds, or break the idea, place, person, or process into its parts.

> For more on division and classification, see pp. 364–66.

> Identify the ways in which each resident of the United States uses, on average, 1,595 gallons of water a day. How and to what degree might a person reduce this amount?

For a start, you would divide up water use into several parts — drinking, cooking, bathing, washing cars, and so on. Then, after that division, you would give tips for water conservation and tell how effective each is.

> What different genres of film did Robert Altman direct? Name at least one outstanding example of each kind.

This classification question asks you to sort films into categories — possibly comedy, war, drama, mystery, western.

The Evaluation Question.   This favorite calls on you to think critically and to present an argument.

> For more on evaluating, see Chs. 9 and 11.

> Evaluate this suggestion, giving reasons for your judgments: cities should stop building highways to the suburbs and instead build public lightrail systems.

Other argument questions might begin "Defend the idea of . . ." or "Show weaknesses in the concept of . . ." or otherwise call on you to take a stand.

For more on process analysis, see pp. 362–64.

The Process Analysis Question.   Often you can spot this kind of question by the word *trace*:

> Trace the stages through which a bill becomes a state law.

> Trace the development of the medieval Italian city-state.

Both questions ask you to tell how something occurs or occurred. In brief, you divide the process into steps and detail each step. The next question calls for the other type of process analysis, the "how-to" variety:

> An employee has been consistently late for work, varying from fifteen minutes to a half hour daily. This employee has been on the job only five months but shows promise of learning skills that your firm needs badly. How would you deal with this situation?

The Response Question.   A question might supply a statement, a comment, or a quotation for close reading, asking you to test the writer's opinion against what you know. Carefully read the statement a few times, and then jot down contrary or supporting evidence.

> Was the following passage written by Gertrude Stein, Kate Chopin, or Tillie Olsen? On what evidence do you base your answer?
>
> > She waited for the material pictures which she thought would gather and blaze before her imagination. She waited in vain. She saw no pictures of solitude, of hope, of longing, or of despair. But the very passions themselves were aroused within her soul, swaying it, lashing it, as the waves daily beat upon her splendid body. She trembled, she was choking, and the tears blinded her.

If you were familiar with the stories of Kate Chopin, who specializes in physical and emotional descriptions of impassioned women, you would point to language (*swaying, lashing*) that marks the passage as hers.

DRAFTING: THE ONLY VERSION

When you have two or more essay questions to answer, block out your time roughly based on the points or minutes your instructor allots to each. Give extra minutes to a complicated question with several parts. Then pace yourself as you write. For example, wrap up question 2 at 10:30 and move on.

As you draft, give yourself room for second thoughts by writing on only one side of the page in your exam booklet and skipping every other line. Should you wish to add material later, you can do so with ease.

Begin with the Easy Questions.   Many students find that it boosts their morale to start with the question they feel best able to answer. Unless your instructor specifies otherwise, why not skip around? Clearly number or label each answer as your instructor does. Then begin in such a way that the instructor will immediately recognize which question you're answering. If the task is "Compare and contrast the depression of the 1930s with the recession of 2001," you might begin in this way:

> *Compared to the paralyzing depression that began in 1929, the recession of 2001 seems like a bad case of measles.*

Try Stating Your Thesis at the Start.   Making your opening sentence a thesis statement — a sentence that immediately makes clear the main point — often makes good sense. Then the rest of your answer can back up that statement. An easy way to get started is to turn the question into a statement and use it to begin an answer.

For more on thesis statements, see pp. 312–19. For David Cohn's thesis and complete answer, see p. 278 and 279.

QUESTION
What reasons for leasing cars and office equipment, instead of purchasing them, can be cited for a two-person partnership?

ANSWER
I can cite at least four reasons for a two-person partnership to lease cars and office equipment. For one thing, under present tax laws, the entire cost of a regular payment under a leasing agreement may be deducted. . . .

Stick to the Question.   You may be tempted to throw into your answer everything you have learned in the course. But to do so defeats the purpose of the examination — to use your knowledge, not to parade it. Answer by selecting and shaping *what matters*. On the other hand, if a question has two parts, answer both.

Name three styles of contemporary architecture and evaluate one of them.

Stay Specific.   Pressed for time, some exam takers think, "I haven't got time to get specific here. I'll just sum this up in general." That's a mistake. Every time you throw in a broad statement ("The Industrial Revolution was beneficial for the peasant"), take time to add specific examples ("In Dusseldorf, as Taine tells us, deaths from starvation among displaced Prussian farmworkers dropped from a peak of almost 10 percent a year").

REVISING: REREADING AND PROOFING

If you have paced yourself, you'll have at least a few minutes left to look over your work. Check that your ideas are clear and hang together. Add sentences wherever new ones are needed. If you recall a key point, add a paragraph on a blank left-hand page. Just draw an arrow to show where it goes.

Naturally, errors occur more often when you write under pressure than when you have time to proofread carefully. On an exam, what you say and how forcefully you say it matter most. Still, no instructor will object to careful corrections. You can add words with carets (∧) or neatly strike them out.

When your paper or blue book is returned, consider these questions as you look it over so that you improve your essay-exam skills:

ESSAY EXAM CHECKLIST

___ Did you answer the whole question, not just part of it?
___ Did you stick to the point, not throw in unrequested information?
___ Did you make your general statements clear by citing evidence or examples?
___ Did you proofread for omissions and lack of clarity?
___ On what questions do you feel you did a good job, whatever your grade?
___ If you had to write this exam over again, how would you now go about it?

Short-Answer Examinations

The *short-answer exam* may call on you to identify names or phrases from your reading, in a sentence or a few words.

Identify the following: Clemenceau, Treaty of Versailles, Maginot line.

Georges Clemenceau — This French premier, nicknamed The Tiger, headed a popular coalition cabinet during World War I and at the Paris Peace Conference demanded stronger penalties against Germany.

For more about writing definitions, see pp. 356–57.

Writing a short identification is much like writing a short definition. Mention the general class to which a thing belongs to make clear its nature.

Treaty of Versailles — pact between Germany and the Allies that . . .
Maginot line — fortifications that . . .

Timed Writings

Many composition instructors give you experience in writing on demand by assigning impromptu in-class essays. Their purpose is to test your writing skills, not your recall. For such writings, your time is limited, the setting is controlled (usually you're at a desk without a dictionary or a spell checker), and you can't choose your subject. Even so, your usual methods of writing, used in a hurry, can still serve you well.

Budget Your Time.   For an in-class essay, if you have forty-five minutes to write, a good rule of thumb is to spend ten minutes preparing, thirty minutes writing, and five minutes rereading and making last-minute changes. Plan quickly to avoid rushing to get your ideas on paper in an essay — the part you will be graded on.

Consider Types of Topics.   Often you can expect the same types of questions for in-class writings as for essay exams. Do what the key words say.

For common types of exam questions, see pp. 279–82.

> What were the *causes* of World War I?
>
> *Compare and contrast* the theories of capitalism and socialism.
>
> *Define* civil rights.

Add your personal twist to a general subject, but note the key words.

> *Analyze* a problem in education that is *difficult to solve.*
>
> *Discuss ways to cope* with stress.

Standardized tests often ask you to respond to a short passage, testing not only your writing ability but also your reading comprehension.

> Thomas Jefferson stated, "If a nation expects to be ignorant and free, in a state of civilization, it expects what never was and never will be." *How* is his comment *relevant* to education today?

Choose Your Topic Wisely.   For on-the-spot writing, the trick is to make the topic your own. If you have a choice, pick the one you know most about, not the one you think will impress your readers. They'll be most impressed by logical argument and solid evidence. If you have to write on a broad subject, bring it down to something you have observed or experienced. Have you witnessed traffic jams, brownouts, or condos ruining beaches? Then write about increased population, using these examples.

Think before You Write.   Despite your limited time, read the instructions or questions carefully, restrict your topic to something you know about, focus on a main idea, and jot down main points for development. If a good hook to open or conclude occurs to you, use it, too.

Thinking Fast

To practice planning quickly for timed writing or tests, brainstorm as a class to explore approaches to sample topics provided in this chapter. Select one class member (or three, in turn) to record ideas on the board. Devote exactly ten minutes of discussion per topic to these key parts of a successful response:

- possible thesis sentences
- possible patterns of organization
- possible kinds and sources of evidence

Expect a wide range of ideas. Spend the last part of class evaluating them.

FOR GROUP LEARNING

Don't Try to Be Perfect. No one expects in-class essays to read as smoothly as reports written over several weeks. You can't polish every sentence or remember the exact word for every spot. And never waste time recopying. Devote your time to the more important parts of writing.

For more on making corrections, see the Quick Editing Guide (the dark-blue-edged pages).

Save Time to Proofread. The last few minutes when you read over your work and correct glaring errors may be the best-spent minutes of all. Cross out errors and make corrections neatly using asterisks (*), arrows, and carets (^). Especially check for the following:

- letters omitted (-*ed* or -*s*), added (develop*e*), or inverted (rec*ie*ve)
- wrong punctuation (a comma instead of a period)
- omitted apostrophes (*dont* instead of *don't*)
- omitted words ("She going" instead of "She *is* going")
- wrong (*except* instead of *accept*) or misspelled words (*mispelled*)

Writing for Portfolio Assessment

The writing portfolio is a popular method of assessment for college classes. It is a printed or electronic collection of pieces of writing that represent the writer's best work. Compiled over time and across projects, a portfolio showcases a writer's talent, hard work, and ability to make thoughtful choices about content and presentation. For a single course, the portfolio is usually due at the end of the term and includes pieces you have written and revised for that course. Most portfolios need some kind of introduction (usually a self-assessment or rationale) addressed to readers, who might be teachers, supervisors, evaluators, parents, or classmates.

Portfolio courses typically emphasize revision and reflection — the ability to identify and discuss your choices, strengths, or learning processes. In such a course, you'll need to save all your drafts and notes, keep track of your choices and changes, and near the end of the term select and submit your best writing.

UNDERSTANDING PORTFOLIO ASSESSMENT

The portfolio is a method of evaluation and teaching that shapes the whole course from beginning to end. For example, your portfolio course will probably emphasize responses to your writing — from your classmates and your instructor — but not necessarily grades on your separate papers. The portfolio method attempts to shift attention to the writing process itself — to discovery, planning, drafting, peer response, revision, editing — allowing time for your skills to develop before the writing "counts" and the portfolio is graded.

The portfolio method is flexible, but you need to read your instructor's syllabus and assignment sheets carefully and listen well in class to determine what kind of portfolio you'll be expected to keep. Below are a few typical types, and more than one might be used in a course.

A Writing Folder.   Students are asked to submit all drafts, notes, outlines, scribbles, doodles, and messy pages — in short, all writing done for the course, whether finished or unfinished. Students may also be asked to revise two or three of their most promising pieces for a "presentation portfolio." The folder is usually not accompanied by a reflective cover letter.

A Learning (or Open) Portfolio.   Students are free to submit a variety of materials that have contributed to their learning. They may even be free to determine the contents, organization, and presentation of the portfolio. A learning portfolio for a composition class might include photos or other nonprint objects collected to demonstrate learning.

A Closed Portfolio.   Students must turn in assignments that are specified by the instructor, or their options for what to include may be limited.

A Midterm Portfolio.   The portfolio is given a trial run at midterm, or the midterm grade is determined by one or two papers that are submitted for evaluation, perhaps accompanied by a brief self-assessment.

A Final or Presentation Portfolio.   The portfolio is evaluated at the end of the course after being revised, edited, and polished for presentation.

A Modified or Combination Portfolio.   The student has some, but not unlimited, choice in what to include. For example, the instructor may ask for three entries that show certain features or parts of the course.

Find out what kind of portfolio your instructor has in mind. Here's one likely scenario. You are required to submit a modified or combination portfolio — one that contains, for example, three revised papers (out of the five or six drafts required). You decide, late in the term, which three to revise and edit. You also may be asked to reflect on what those choices say about you as a writer, to show your learning in the course, or to explain your decisions while writing a paper. Here are some typical questions your instructor, syllabus, or assignment sheets may answer:

- How many papers should you include in the portfolio?
- Do all these papers need to be revised? If so, what level of revision is expected? What criteria will be used to assess them?
- How much of the course grade is determined by the portfolio grade? Are the portfolio entries graded separately, or does the entire portfolio receive one grade?
- May you include papers written for other courses or entries other than texts — such as photos, videos, maps, Web pages, or other visuals?

- Should you preface the portfolio with an introduction or a cover letter? What is expected in this piece: Description? Explanation? Exploration? Application? Reflection? Self-assessment?
- Does each entry need a separate cover sheet? Should descriptions of your processes or choices appear before or after each entry?

TIPS FOR KEEPING A PORTFOLIO

Keep Everything, and Stay Organized.   Don't throw anything away! Keep all your notes, lists, drafts, outlines, clusters, responses from readers, photocopied articles, and references for works cited. If you have your own computer, *back up everything* to a disk. (Better yet, use a jump drive or zip drive, both of which are sturdier than disks.) If you use the computer lab, save your work to a disk, and keep an extra blank disk in your backpack. Use a system to organize everything. For example, invest in a good folder with pockets, and label their contents as you store the drafts, notes, outlines, and peer review forms for each assignment.

Manage Your Time.   The portfolio isn't due until the end of the course (or at midterm), but planning ahead will save you time and frustration. For example, as your instructor returns each assignment with comments, make changes in response while the ideas are fresh. If you don't understand or know how to approach your instructor's comments, ask right away — at the end of class or during office hours that week. Make notes about what you want to do. Then, even if you want to let a paper simmer, you will have both a plan and some fresh insight when you work on it again.

For more help with self-assessment see the For Peer Response questions, the Revision Checklists, and the Draft Doctors throughout *The Bedford Guide*. Also, see "Ask the Draft Doctor" at <bedfordstmartins.com/bedguide>.

Practice Self-Assessment.   For complex activities, it's important to your improvement to step back and evaluate your own performance. Maybe you have great ideas but find it hard to organize them. Maybe you write powerful thesis statements but run out of ideas to support them. Don't wait until the portfolio cover letter is due to begin tracking your learning or assessing your strengths, weaknesses, or preferences.

You can practice self-assessment from the first day of class. For example, after reviewing the syllabus, write one or two paragraphs about how you think you will do in this course. What do you expect to do well on, and why? What may be hard for you, and why? For each paper you share with peers or hand in, write a journal entry about what the paper does well and what it still needs. Keep track, in a log or journal, of your process to plan, research, or draft each paper — where you get stuck and where things click.

For more on keeping a journal, see pp. 306–07.

Choose the Entries Carefully.   If you can select what to include, consider the course emphasis. Of course, you want to select pieces your evaluator will think are "the best," but also consider which show the most promise or potential. Which drafts show creativity, insight, or an unusual approach to the assignment? Which show variety — different purposes, audiences, or voices?

Which show depth—your ability to do thorough research or stay with a topic for several weeks? Also consider the order of the entries—which piece might work best first or last, and how each placement affects the whole.

Write a Strong Reflective Introduction or Cover Letter. Your introduction—usually a self-assessment in the form of a cover letter, a statement, or a description for each of your entries—could be the most important text you write all semester. Besides introducing readers to your collection and portraying you as a writer, it explains your choices in putting the portfolio together and demonstrates that you can evaluate your work and your writing process. For many portfolio-based courses, the reflective introduction or cover letter is the "final exam," testing what you've learned about good writing, readers' needs, and the details of a careful self-presentation.

Ask these questions about writing a reflective introduction or cover letter:

DISCOVERY CHECKLIST

____ Who will read this reflection?

____ What qualities of writing will your reader value?

____ Will the reader suggest changes or evaluate your work?

____ What will the outcome of the reading be? How much can you influence it?

____ What do you want to emphasize about your writing? What are you proud of? What have you learned? What did you have trouble with?

____ How can you present your writing ability in the best light?

If your reader or evaluator is your instructor, look back over responses on your returned papers, and review the course syllabus and assignment sheets. What patterns do you see in your instructor's concerns or directions? What could you tell a friend about this reader's expectations—or pet peeves? Use what you've learned about his or her values as a reader to compose a convincing, well-developed introduction or cover letter.

If your readers or evaluators are unknown, ask your instructor for as much information as possible so you can decide which logical, ethical, or emotional appeals might be most effective. Although you won't know your readers personally, it's safe to assume that they will be trained in portfolio assessment and will share many of your instructor's ideas about good writing. If your college writing program has guidelines, consult them, too.

For more on appeals, see pp. 40–41.

How long should your introduction or cover letter be? Check with your instructor, but regardless of length, develop your ideas or support your claims as in any effective writing. If you are asked to write a letter, follow the format for a business letter: include the date, a salutation, and a closing.

In the reflective introduction, you might try some of the following (but don't try to use all of them):

- Discuss your best entry and why it is your best.
- Detail your revisions — the improvements you want readers to notice.
- Review everything included, touching on the strengths of each.
- Outline your writing and revising process for one or more entries.
- State what the portfolio illustrates about you as a writer, student, researcher, or critical thinker.
- Acknowledge your weaknesses, but show how you've worked to overcome them.
- Acknowledge the influence of your readers on your entries.
- Reflect on what you've learned about writing and reading.
- Lay the groundwork for a positive evaluation of your work.

Polishing the Final Portfolio.   From the first page to the last, your portfolio should be ready for public presentation, a product you can take pride in or show to others. Think about creative ways to give your portfolio a final distinctive feature, such as having it bound at your local copy shop, adding a colorful cover or illustrations, or including a table of contents or a running head. Although a cheerful cover will not make up for weak writing or careless editing, readers will value your extra effort.

PART FOUR

A Writer's Strategies

Introduction

The following seven chapters constitute a manual offering in-depth advice on writing strategies. The word *strategy* may remind you of warfare: in the original Greek sense of the word, it is a way to win a battle. Writing a college paper, you'll probably agree, is a battle of a kind. In this manual you'll find an array of small weapons to use — and perhaps some heavy artillery.

Here are techniques you can learn, methods you can follow, good practices you can observe. The first five chapters offer a wealth of suggestions for approaching each of the stages of the writing process: generating ideas, planning, drafting, developing, and revising and editing. In Part Two, each stage was covered for each assignment, and relevant strategies were mentioned briefly. Here, each stage of the writing process gets a full chapter, and the strategies for each are explained and illustrated more fully. The last two chapters here offer advice on strategies of increasing importance — designing your own documents and understanding visual representations.

No strategy will appeal to every writer, and no writer uses every one for every writing task. Consider this part of the book a reference guide or instruction manual. Turn to it when you need more help, when you're curious, or when you'd like to enlarge your repertoire of writing skills. We can't tell you which of the ideas and techniques covered in these pages will work for you, but we can promise that if you try some of them, you'll be rewarded.

Chapter 16
Strategies for Generating Ideas

For most writers, the hardest part of writing comes first — confronting a blank page. Fortunately, you can prepare for that moment, both for finding ideas and for getting ready to write. All of the tested techniques that follow have worked for some writers — both professionals and students — and some may work for you.

Finding Ideas

When you begin to write, you need to start the ideas flowing. Sometimes ideas appear effortlessly on the paper or screen, perhaps triggered by the opportunities and resources around you — something you read, see, hear, discuss, or think about. (See the top half of the graphic on p. 295.) But at other times you need an arsenal of idea generators, strategies you can use at any point in the writing process — whenever your ideas dry up or you need more examples or evidence. If one strategy doesn't work for a particular writing task, try another. (See the strategies presented in the lower half of the graphic, all detailed in the following pages.)

BUILDING FROM YOUR ASSIGNMENT

Learning to write is learning what questions to ask yourself. Sometimes your assignment triggers this process by raising some questions and answering others. For example, Ben Tran jotted his notes in his book as his instructor and classmates discussed the first assignment for his composition class — recalling a personal experience.

The assignment clarified what audience to address and what purpose to try to accomplish in the paper. It also raised three big questions for Ben:

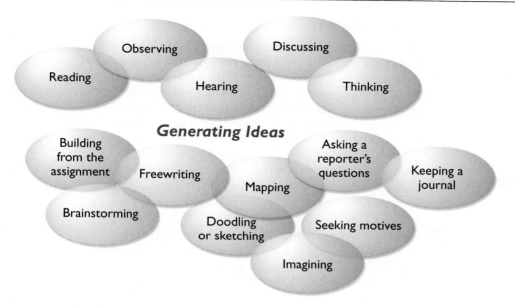

Generating Ideas

Reading · Observing · Discussing · Hearing · Thinking · Building from the assignment · Freewriting · Mapping · Asking a reporter's questions · Keeping a journal · Brainstorming · Doodling or sketching · Seeking motives · Imagining

Which experience should I pick? How did it change me? Why was it so important for me? His classmates asked their instructor other questions about the length, format, and due date for the essay. As class ended, Ben didn't know what he'd write about, but he had figured out the questions to tackle first, using other strategies for generating ideas.

For more detail about this assignment, turn to p. 62 in Ch. 4.

Need to pick one event with consequences

Write about one specific experience that changed how you acted, thought, or felt. Use your experience as a springboard for reflection. Your purpose is not merely to tell an interesting story but to show your readers--your instructor and your classmates--the importance of that experience for you.

What readers? class + prof.

What purpose? 2 parts! Tell the story but do more — reflect & show importance

Sometimes an assignment will assume that you already understand something critical — how to address a particular audience, for example, or what to include in a certain type of writing. When Amalia Blackhawk read her argument assignment, she jotted down several questions about its assumptions to ask her instructor.

Anything OK? Or only newspaper type of issue?

Editor of what?

What's my purpose? Persuading readers to respect my view or to agree?

Select a campus or local issue that matters to you, and write a letter to the editor about it. Be certain to tell readers what the issue is, why it is important, and how you propose to address it. Assume that your letter will appear in a special opinion feature that allows letters longer than the usual word-count limits.

My classmates? The publication's readers?

How long is the usual letter? How long should mine be? Anything else letters like this should do?

Try these steps as you examine an assignment:

1. *Read through the assignment once* simply to discover its overall direction.
2. *Read it again*, this time marking any information that answers questions about your situation as a writer. Does the assignment identify or suggest your audience, your purpose in writing, the type of paper expected, the parts typical of that kind of writing, or the format required?
3. *List the questions that the assignment raises for you.* Figure out exactly what you need to decide — the type of topic to pick, the focus to develop, the issues or aspects to consider, or other guidelines to follow.
4. *Finally, list any questions that the assignment doesn't answer or ask you to answer.* Ask your instructor about these questions during or after class.

■ Activity: Building from Your Assignment

Select an assignment from this book, another textbook, or another class, and make some notes about it. What questions does the assignment answer for you? Which questions or decisions does it direct to you? What other questions might you want to ask your instructor? When you finish your notes, exchange assignments with a classmate, and make notes about that assignment, too. Working with your partner, compare your responses to both assignments.

BRAINSTORMING

A *brainstorm* is a sudden insight or inspiration. As a writing strategy, brainstorming uses free association to stimulate a chain of ideas, often to personalize a topic and break it down into specifics. When you brainstorm, you start with a word or phrase and spend a set period of time simply scribbling a list of ideas as rapidly as possible, writing down whatever comes to mind with no editing or going back.

Brainstorming can be a group activity. In the workplace, it is commonly used to fill a specific need — finding a name for a product, a corporate emblem, a slogan for an advertising campaign. In college, you can try group brainstorming with a few other students or your entire class. Members of the group sit facing one another. They designate one person to record on paper, screen, or chalkboard whatever the others suggest or the best idea in the air at a busy moment. After several minutes of calling out ideas, the group can look over the recorder's list to identify useful results. Online a group might toss out ideas during a chat or post them for all to consider.

On your own, you might brainstorm to define a topic, generate an example while writing, or come up with a title for a finished paper. Angie Ortiz brainstormed after her instructor assigned a paper ("Demonstrate from your own experience how electronic technology is changing our lives"). First, she wrote *electronic technology* at the top of the page and set her alarm for fifteen minutes. Then she began to scribble words and phrases.

Group Brainstorming

Working with a small group of classmates — or the entire class — choose one subject from the list on page 298 that each person knows about. Brainstorm about it individually for ten minutes. Then compare and contrast by exchanging or posting the brainstorming lists of all in the group. Although the group began with the same subject, each writer's treatment will be unique because of differences in experience and perspective. What does this exercise tell you about group brainstorming as a strategy for generating topics?

FOR GROUP LEARNING

Electronic technology
Electronic stuff — iPod, cell phone, laptop, Blackberry. Then there's TV, cable, DVDs. Too much?!
Always on call — at home, in car, at school. Always something playing.
Spend so much time in electronic world — phone calls, IMing, listening to tunes.
Cuts into time really hanging with friends — face-to-face time.
Less aware of my surroundings outside of the electronic world?

When her alarm went off, Ortiz took a break. After returning to her list, she crossed out ideas that did not interest her and circled her final promising question. From her rough list, a focus began to emerge: the capacity of the electronic world to expand information but reduce awareness.

When you want to brainstorm, try this advice:

1. *Start with a key word or phrase* — one that will launch your thoughts in a productive direction. If you need a topic, begin with a general word or phrase (for example, *computer*); if you need an example for a paragraph in progress, use a specific word or phrase (for example, *financial errors computers make*).
2. *Set a time limit.* Ten to fifteen minutes is long enough for strenuous thinking.
3. *Rapidly list brief items.* Stick to words, phrases, or short sentences that you can quickly scan later.
4. *Don't stop.* Don't worry about spelling, repetition, absurdity, or relevance. Don't judge, and don't arrange: just produce. Record whatever comes into your head, as fast as your fingers can type or your pen can fly. If your mind goes blank, keep moving, even if you only repeat what you've just written.

When you finish, circle or check anything that suggests a provocative direction. Scratch out whatever looks useless or dull. Then try some conscious organizing: Are any thoughts related? Can you group them? If so, does the group suggest a topic?

■ **Activity:** Brainstorming

From the following list, choose a subject that interests you, that you know something about, and that you'd like to learn more about — in other words, that you might like to write on. Then brainstorm for ten minutes.

travel	fear	exercise
dieting	dreams	automobiles
family	technology	sports
advertisements	animals	education

Now look over your brainstorming list, and circle any potential topic for a paper. How well did this brainstorming exercise work for you? Can you think of any variations that would make it more useful?

FREEWRITING

To tap your unconscious by *freewriting,* simply write a series of sentences without stopping for fifteen or twenty minutes. The sentences don't have to be grammatical or coherent or stylish; just keep them flowing to unlock an idea's potential.

■ For Ortiz's brain-storming, see pp. 296–97.

Generally, freewriting is most productive if it has an aim — for example, finding a topic, a purpose, or a question you want to answer. Angie Ortiz wrote her topic at the top of a page — and then explored her rough ideas.

> *Electronic devices — do they isolate us? I chat all day on computers and phones, but that's quick communication, not in-depth conversation. I don't really spend much time hanging with friends and getting to know what's going on in their lives. I love listening to my iPod on campus, but maybe I'm not as aware of my surroundings as I could be. I miss seeing things, like the new art gallery that I walk by every day. I didn't even notice the new sculpture park in front! Then, at night, I do assignments on my computer, browse the Web, and watch some cable. I'm in my own little electronic world most of the time. I love technology, but what else am I missing?*

The result, as you can see, wasn't polished prose. Still, in twenty minutes she produced a paragraph to serve as a springboard for her finished essay.

If you want to try freewriting, here's what you do:

1. *Write a sentence or two at the top of your page or computer screen* — the idea you plan to develop by freewriting.
2. *Write steadily without stopping for at least ten minutes.* Express whatever comes to mind, even "My mind is blank," until some new thought floats into view.
3. *Don't censor yourself.* Don't cross out false starts or grammar errors. Don't worry about connecting ideas or finding perfect words.
4. *Feel free to explore.* Your initial sentences can serve as a rough guide, but they shouldn't be a straitjacket. If you find yourself straying from your original idea, a change in direction may be valuable.

Trying Invisible Writing

Invisible writing is a kind of freewriting done on a word processor. After typing your topic at the beginning of a file, darken or turn off your monitor so that you cannot read what's on the screen. Then freewrite. If you feel uneasy, try to relax and concentrate on the ideas. After ten minutes, turn the monitor back on, scroll to the beginning, and read what you have written.

FOR E-WRITERS

5. *Prepare yourself*—if you want to. While you wait for your pencil to start racing, you may want to ask yourself some of these questions:

What interests you about the topic? What aspects do you care most about?

What do you recall about this topic from your own experience? What do you know about it that the next person doesn't?

What have you read about the topic? Observed or heard about it?

How might you feel about this topic if you were someone else (a parent, an instructor, a person from another country)?

6. *Repeat the process, looping back to expand a good idea if you wish.* Poke at the most interesting parts to see if they will further unfold:

What does that mean? If that's true, what then? So what?

What other examples or evidence does this statement call to mind?

What objections might a reader raise? How might you answer them?

■ Activity: Freewriting

Select an idea from your current thinking or from a brainstorming list. Write it at the top of a page or screen. Freewrite about it for fifteen minutes. Share your freewriting with your classmates. If you wish, repeat this process, looping back to explore a provocative idea from your freewriting.

DOODLING OR SKETCHING

If you fill the margins of your notebooks with doodles, harness this artistic energy to generate ideas for writing. Elena Lopez began to sketch her collision with a teammate during a soccer tournament (Figure 16.1). She added stick figures, notes, symbols, and color as she outlined a series of events and their consequences.

Figure 16.1 Doodling or Sketching to Generate Ideas

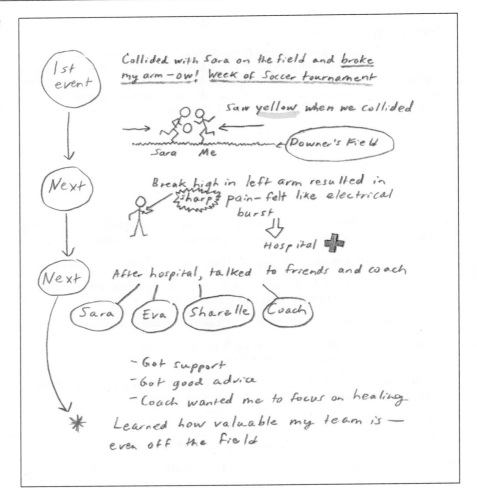

Try this advice as you develop ideas by doodling or sketching:

1. *Give your ideas room to grow.* Open a new file using a drawing program, doodle in pencil on a blank page, or sketch on a series of pages to capture a sequence of events.
2. *Concentrate on your topic, but welcome new ideas.* Begin with a key visual in the center or at the top of a page. Add sketches or doodles as they occur to you; they may embellish, expand, define, or redirect your topic.
3. *Add icons, symbols, colors, figures, labels, notes, or questions.* Freely mix visuals and text, recording ideas without stopping to refine them.
4. *Follow up on your discoveries.* After a break, return to your pages to see how your ideas have evolved. Add notes to make connections, identify sequences, or convert visual concepts into descriptive sentences.

See Ch. 21 for ways to add effective visuals to your writing.

■ **Activity:** Doodling or Sketching

Start with a doodle or sketch that illustrates your topic. Add related events, ideas, or details to develop your topic visually. Share your material with classmates, and then use their observations or questions to help you refine your direction as a writer.

MAPPING

Mapping taps your visual and spatial creativity as you generate ideas. When you use mapping, you position ideas on the page or in a file to show their relationships or relative importance — radiating outward from a key term in the center, dropping down from a key word at the top, sprouting upward from a root idea, branching out from a trunk, flowing across the page or screen in a chronological or causal sequence, or following a circular, spiral, sequential, or other familiar form.

Andrew Choi used mapping to gather ideas for his proposal for revitalizing the campus radio station (Figure 16.2). He noted ideas on colored sticky notes — blue for problems, yellow for solutions, and pink for implementation details. Then he moved the sticky notes around on a blank page, arranging them as he connected ideas.

Here are some suggestions for mapping:

1. *Allow space for your map to develop.* Open a computer file, find some posterboard for arranging sticky notes or cards, or use a large page for notes.
2. *Begin with your topic or a key idea.* Drawing on your imagination, memory, class notes, or reading, place a key word at the center or top of a page or screen.
3. *Add related ideas, examples, issues, or questions.* Quickly and spontaneously place these points above, below, or beside your key word.
4. *Refine the connections.* As your map evolves, use lines, arrows, or loops to connect ideas; box or circle them to focus attention; add colors to relate points or to distinguish source materials from your own ideas.

After a break, continue mapping to probe one part more deeply, refine the structure, add detail, or build an alternate map from a different viewpoint. Because mapping is so versatile, use it also to develop graphics that present ideas in visual form.

See Ch. 21 for ways to add effective visuals to your writing. See also pp. 323–24 on clustering.

■ **Activity:** Mapping

Start with a key word or idea that you know about. Map related ideas, using visual elements to show how they connect. Share your map with classmates, and then use their questions or comments to refine your mapping.

*Figure 16.2 Mapping to
Generate Ideas*

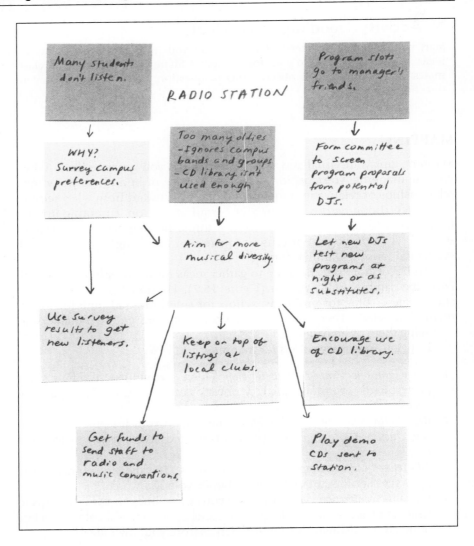

IMAGINING

Your imagination is a valuable resource for exploring possibilities — analyzing an option, evaluating an alternative, or solving a problem. Through imagination, you can discover surprising ideas, original examples, striking expressions, and unexpected relationships.

Suppose that you asked, "What if the average North American life span were more than a century?" No doubt a longer life span would mean that more people would be old. How would that shift affect doctors and nurses, hospitals, and other medical facilities? How might city planners respond to

Group Mapping

Working with a group of three to five classmates, write on a notecard the word or phrase your instructor assigns to the entire class — for example, *campus dining* or *balancing work and college*. Then spend ten or fifteen minutes writing other ideas on new note cards and arranging them around the central card. Move the cards around, and draw connecting lines or arrows if that helps to relate your ideas. Share each group's ideas with the entire class.

FOR GROUP LEARNING

the needs of so many more old people? What would the change mean for shopping centers? For television programming? For leisure activities? For the social security system? For taxes?

Use some of the following strategies to unleash your imagination:

1. *Speculate about changes, alternatives, and options.* What common assumption — something most people take for granted — might you question or deny? What problem or deplorable condition would you like to remedy? What changes in policy, practice, or attitude might avoid problems you foresee for the future? What different paths in life — each with challenges and successes — might you take?
2. *Shift perspective.* Experiment by taking a point of view other than your usual one. How would someone on the opposite side of an issue respond? How would a plant, an animal, or a Martian? Try shifting the debate (to whether people over sixty-five, not teenagers, should be allowed to drink) or the time frame (from present to past or future).
3. *Envision what might be.* Join the many other writers who have imagined a utopia (an ideal state) or an anti-utopia. By envisioning, you can conceive of possible alternatives — a better way of treating illness, electing a president, or finding meaningful order in a chaotic jumble.
4. *Synthesize.* Synthesizing (generating new ideas by combining previously separate ideas) is the opposite of analyzing (breaking ideas down into component parts). Synthesize to make fresh connections, fusing materials — perhaps old or familiar — into something new.

For more about analysis and synthesis, see pp. 34–36.

■ Activity: Imagining

Begin with a problem that cries out for a solution, a condition that requires a remedy, or a situation that calls for change. Ask "What if?" or start with "Suppose that" to trigger your imagination. Speculate about what might be, record your ideas, and share them with your classmates.

ASKING A REPORTER'S QUESTIONS

Journalists, assembling facts to write a news story, ask themselves six simple questions — the five *W*'s and an *H*:

Who?   Where?   Why?
What?   When?   How?

In the *lead,* or opening paragraph, of a good news story, the writer tries to condense the whole story into a sentence or two, answering all six questions.

> A giant homemade fire balloon [*what*] startled residents of Costa Mesa [*where*] last night [*when*] as Ambrose Barker, 79, [*who*] zigzagged across the sky at nearly 300 miles per hour [*how*] in an attempt to set a new altitude record [*why*].

Later in the news story, the reporter will add details, using the six basic questions to generate more about what happened and why.

For your college writing you can use these six helpful questions to generate specific details for your essays. The questions can help you explore the significance of a childhood experience, analyze what happened at some moment in history, or investigate a campus problem. Their purpose is to help you gather ideas. Don't worry if some of them go nowhere or lead to repetitious answers. Later you'll weed out irrelevant points, keeping only those that look promising for your topic.

For a topic that is not based on your personal experience, you may need to do reading or interviewing to answer some of the questions. Take, for example, the topic of the assassination of President John F. Kennedy, and notice how each question can lead to further questions.

- *Who* was John F. Kennedy? What was his background? What kind of person was he? What kind of president? Who was with him when he was killed? Who was nearby? Who do most people believe shot him?

- *What* happened to Kennedy — exactly? What events led up to the assassination? What happened during the assassination? What did the people around him do? What did the media do? What did everyone across the country do? Ask someone who remembers this event what he or she did on hearing about it.

- *Where* was Kennedy assassinated? The city? The street? Where was he going? What was he riding in? Where was he sitting? Where did the shots likely come from? Where did the shots hit him? Where did he die?

- *When* was he assassinated — the day, month, year, time? When did Kennedy decide to go to this city? When — precisely — were the shots fired? When did he die? When was a suspect arrested?

- *Why* was Kennedy assassinated? What are some of the theories of the assassination? What solid evidence is available to explain it? Why has this event caused so much controversy?

- *How* was Kennedy assassinated? What kind of weapon was used? How many shots were fired? Specifically what caused his death? How can we get at the truth of this event?

■ **Activity:** Asking a Reporter's Questions

Choose one of the following topics, or use one of your own:

A memorable event in history or in your life
A concert or other performance that you have attended
An accomplishment on campus
An occurrence in your city
An important speech
A proposal for change
A questionable stand someone has taken

Answer the six reporter's questions about the topic. Then write a sentence or two synthesizing the answers to the six questions. Incorporate that sentence into an introductory paragraph for an essay that you might write later.

SEEKING MOTIVES

In a surprisingly large part of your college writing, you will try to explain the motives behind human behavior. In a history paper, you might consider how George Washington's conduct shaped the presidency. In a psychology report, you might try to explain the behavior of participants in an experiment. In a literature essay, you might analyze the motives of Hester Prynne in *The Scarlet Letter*. Because people, including characters in fiction, are so complex, this task is challenging.

■ For more on writing about literature, see Ch. 13.

If you want to understand any human act, according to philosopher–critic Kenneth Burke, you can break it down into a set of five basic components, a *pentad*, and ask questions about each one. While covering much the same ground as the reporter's questions, Burke's pentad differs in that it can show how the components of a human act affect one another. This line of thought can take you deeper into the motives for human behavior than most reporters' investigations ever go.

Suppose that you are preparing to write a political-science paper on President Lyndon Baines Johnson, known as LBJ. Right after President Kennedy's assassination in 1963, Vice President Johnson was sworn in as president. A year later, in 1964, he was elected to the post by a landslide. By 1968, however, Johnson had decided not to run for a second term. You decide to use Burke's pentad to investigate why he made this decision.

1. *The act:* What was done?

    Announcing the decision to leave office without standing for reelection.

2. *The actor:* Who did it?

    President Johnson.

3. *The agency:* What means did the person use to make it happen?

    A televised address to the nation.

4. *The scene:* Where, when, and under what circumstances did the act happen?

Washington, D.C., March 31, 1968. Protesters against the Vietnam War were gaining numbers and influence. The press was increasingly critical of the escalating war. Senator Eugene McCarthy, an antiwar candidate for president, had made a strong showing against LBJ in the New Hampshire primary election.

5. *The purpose or motive for acting:* What could have made the person do it?

LBJ's motives might have included avoiding a probable defeat, escaping further personal attacks, sparing his family, making it easier for his successor to pull the country out of the war, and easing bitter dissent among Americans.

To carry Burke's method further, you can pair the five components and begin fruitful lines of inquiry by asking questions, as illustrated below, about the pairs:

actor to act	act to scene	scene to agency
actor to scene	act to agency	scene to purpose
actor to purpose	act to purpose	agency to purpose

PAIR   actor to agency

QUESTION   What did LBJ [actor] have to do with his televised address [agency]?

ANSWER   Commanding the attention of a vast audience, LBJ must have felt he was in control — even though his ability to control the situation in Vietnam was slipping.

Not all the paired questions will prove fruitful; some may not even apply. But one or two might reveal valuable connections and start you writing.

■ Activity: Seeking Motives

Choose an action that puzzles you — perhaps something you, a family member, or a friend has done; a decision of a historical or current political figure; or something in a movie, television program, or literary selection. Then apply Burke's pentad to try to determine the motives for the action. If you wish, you can also pair up the components to perceive deeper relationships. When you believe you understand the individual's motivation, write a paragraph explaining the action, and share it with your classmates.

KEEPING A JOURNAL

■ For ideas about keeping a reading journal, see pp. 23–24.

Journal writing richly rewards anyone who engages in it every day or several times a week. You can write anywhere or anytime: all you need is a notebook, a writing implement, and a few minutes to record an entry. To keep a valuable journal, you need only the honesty and willingness to set down what you genuinely think and feel.

Your journal will become a mine studded with priceless nuggets — thoughts and observations, reactions and revelations that are yours for the taking. When you write, you can rifle your well-stocked journal freely—not only for writing topics, but for insights, examples, and other material.

Reflective Journal Writing.   What do you write in your journal? When you make an entry, put less emphasis on recording what happened, as you would in a diary, than on *reflecting* about what you do or see, hear or read, learn or believe. An entry can be a list or an outline, a paragraph or an essay, a poem or a letter you don't intend to send, even a page of doodling. Describe a person or a place, set down a conversation, or record insights into your actions or those of others. Consider your pet peeves, fears, dreams, treasures, convictions or moral dilemmas, or the fate of the world—or the country—if you were in charge. Use your challenges and successes as a writer to nourish and inspire your writing, recording what worked, what didn't, and how you reacted to each.

Responsive Journal Writing.   Sometimes you *respond* to something in particular—to your reading for an assignment, to classroom discussions, to a movie, to a conversation or an observation. This type of journal entry is more focused than the reflective entry. Faced with a long paper to write, you might assign *yourself* a response journal. Then when the time comes to draft your paper, you will have plenty of material to use.

For more on responding to reading, see Ch. 2.

For responsive journal prompts, see the end of each selection in *A Writer's Reader*.

Warm-Up Journal Writing.   To prepare for an assignment, you can group ideas, scribble outlines, sketch beginnings, capture stray thoughts, record relevant material. Of course, what starts as a quick comment on an essay (or a responsive journal entry) may turn into the draft of a paper. In other words, don't let the categories here straitjacket you. A journal can be what you want it to be, and the best journal is the one that's useful to *you*.

■ Activity: Keeping a Journal

Keep a journal for at least a week. Each day record your thoughts, feelings, observations, and reactions. Reflect on what happens, and respond to what you read. Try at least one of the responsive prompts following a selection in *A Writer's Reader*. At the end of the week, bring your journal to class, and read aloud to your classmates the entry you like best.

Keeping an E-Journal

Keeping an e-journal is as simple as creating a file and making entries by date or subject. Record ideas, feelings, images, memories, quotations, and any other writing you wish. You will quickly notice how easy it is to copy and paste inspiring e-mail, quotations from Web pages, or digitized images and sounds into your e-journal. Always identify the source of copied material so that you won't later confuse it with your original writing. As your e-journal grows, you will develop a ready supply of "seeds" and support for writing.

FOR E-WRITERS

Getting Ready

Once you have generated a suitable topic and some ideas related to that topic, you are ready to get down to the job of actually writing.

SETTING UP CIRCUMSTANCES

If you can write only with your shoes off or with a can of soda nearby, set yourself up that way. Some writers need to hear blaring rap music; others need quiet. Create an environment that puts you in the mood for writing.

Devote One Special Place to Writing.   Your place should have good lighting and space to spread out. It may be a desk in your bedroom, the dining room table, or a quiet library cubicle — someplace where no one will bother you and where your mind and body will be ready to settle in for work. Try to make it a place where you can leave your projects and keep handy your pens, paper, computer, dictionary, and reference materials.

Establish a Ritual.   Some writers find that a ritual relaxes them and helps them get started. You might open a soda, straighten your desk, turn music on (or off), and create a new file on the computer.

Relocate.   If you're not getting anywhere with your writing, try moving from the college library to home or from the kitchen to your bedroom. Try an unfamiliar place — a bowling alley, a restaurant, an airport.

Reduce Distractions.   Most of us can't prevent interruptions, but we can reduce them. If you are expecting your boyfriend to call, call him before you start writing. If you have small children, write when they are asleep or at school. Let your voice mail take calls. Block out the noises around you, and concentrate hard on your writing. Let others know you are serious about writing, and allow yourself to give your full attention to it.

Exhaust Your Excuses.   If you, like many writers, are an expert procrastinator, help yourself run out of reasons not to write. Is your room annoyingly jumbled? Straighten it. Sharpen those pencils, throw out that trash, and make that phone call. Then, with your room, your desk, and your mind swept clean, sit down and write.

Write at the Time Best for You.   Some people think best early in the morning, while others favor the small hours when the world is still and their stern self-critic might be asleep, too. Writing at dawn or in the wee hours also reduces distractions from other people.

Write on a Schedule.   Many writers find that it helps to write at a predictable time of day. This method worked marvels for English novelist

Anthony Trollope, who would start at 5:30 A.M., write 2,500 words before 8:30 A.M., and then go to his job at the post office. (He wrote more than sixty books.) Even if you can't set aside the same time every day, it may help to decide, "Today from four to five, I'll sit down and write."

PREPARING YOUR MIND

Sometimes ideas, images, or powerful urges to write will arrive like sudden miracles. When they come, even if you are taking a shower or getting ready to go to a movie, yield to impulse and write. Your words probably will flow with little exertion. Encourage such moments by opening your mind to inspiration.

Talk about Your Writing.   Discuss your ideas with a classmate or friend, encouraging questions, comments, and suggestions. Talk in person, by phone, or through e-mail. Or talk to yourself, using a voice-activated tape recorder, while you sit through traffic jams, walk your dog, or ride your bike.

Lay Out Your Plans.   Tell any nearby listener — student down the hall, spouse, parent, friend — why you want to write this particular paper, what material you'll put into it, how you're going to lay it out. If the other person says, "That sounds good," you'll be encouraged. Even if the reaction is a yawn, you'll have set your own thinking in motion.

Keep a Notebook or Journal Handy.   Always keep some paper in your pocket or backpack or on the night table to write down good ideas that pop into your mind. Imagination may strike in the grocery checkout line, in the doctor's waiting room, or during a lull on the job.

For advice about journals, see pp. 306–07.

Read.   The step from reading to writing is a short one. Even when you're just reading for fun, you start to involve yourself with words. Who knows? You might also hit on something useful for your paper. Or read purposefully: Set out to read and take notes.

Use the following questions to help you get ready to write:

DISCOVERY CHECKLIST

___ Is your environment organized for writing? What changes might help you reduce distractions and procrastination?

___ Have you scheduled enough time to get ready to write? How might you adjust your schedule or your expectations to encourage productivity?

___ Is your assignment clear? What additional questions might you want to ask about what you are expected to do?

___ Have you generated enough ideas that interest you? What other strategies for generating ideas might help you expand, focus, or deepen your ideas?

Chapter 17
Strategies for Stating a Thesis and Planning

S tarting to write often seems a chaotic activity, but you can use the strategies in this chapter to help create order. For most papers, you will first want to consider your purpose and audience and then focus on a central point by discovering, stating, and improving a thesis. To help you sensibly arrange your material, the chapter also includes advice on grouping ideas and on outlining.

Shaping Your Topic for Your Purpose and Your Audience

For critical questions about audience and more about purpose, see p. 311. For more about both, see pp. 14–18.

As you work on your college papers, you may feel as if you're juggling — selecting weighty points and lively details, tossing them into the air, catching each one as it falls, keeping them all moving in sequence. Busy as you are simply juggling, however, your performance almost always draws a crowd —

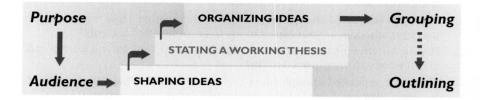

your instructor, your classmates, or other readers. They'll expect you to attend to their concerns as you try to achieve your purpose—probably informing, explaining, or persuading.

Thinking carefully about your audience and purpose can help you plan a
paper more effectively. If you want to show your classmates and instructor
the importance of an event, you'll need to decide how much detail about the
event those readers need. If most of them have gotten speeding tickets, for instance, they'll need less information about that experience than bus riders or
other city commuters might. However, to achieve your purpose, you'll need
to go beyond what happened to why the event mattered to you. No matter
how many tickets your readers have gotten, they won't know exactly how that
experience changed you unless you share that information effectively. In fact,
they may incorrectly assume that you were worrying about being late to class
or paying higher insurance rates when, in fact, you had suddenly realized
how narrowly you had escaped an accident like your cousin's and how that
recognition motivated you to change your driving habits.

Similarly, if you want to persuade county officials to adopt your proposal for changing the way absentee ballots are distributed to college
students, you'll need to support your idea with reasons and evidence—
drawing on the state election laws and legal precedents familiar to these
readers as well as the experiences of student voters. In fact, you may need to
show not only how your proposal would solve existing problems but also
why it would improve the situation more effectively than other proposals.

Although your assignment may help you to define your purpose and audience, you can refine your understanding using questions such as these:

- *What is your general purpose?* What specifically would you like to accomplish in your paper? How would you like your readers to react to your
  paper? Do you want them to smile, think, or agree? To understand,
  learn, accept, respect, care, change, or reply? How might you plan your
  writing to accomplish your aims?

- *Who are your readers?* If they are not clearly identified in your assignment or by your situation, what do you assume about them? What do
  they know or want to know? What opinions do they hold? What do
  they find informative or persuasive? How might you appeal effectively
  to them?

- *How might you narrow and focus your ideas about the topic,* given what you
  know or assume about your purpose and audience? Which slant would
  best accomplish your purpose? What points would appeal most strongly
  to your readers? What details would engage or persuade them?

- *What qualities of good writing have been discussed in your class,* explained
  in your syllabus, or identified in assigned readings? What criteria for
  college writing have emerged from exchanges of drafts with classmates
  or comments from your instructor? How might you shape your writing
  to demonstrate desirable qualities to your readers?

■ **Activity: Considering Purpose and Audience**

Think back to a recent writing task — a college essay, a job application, a report or memo at work, a message to a relative, a letter to a campus office, or some other piece. Write a brief description of your situation as a writer at that time. What was your purpose? Who — exactly — were your readers? How did you account for both as you planned your writing? How might you have made your writing more effective?

Stating and Using a Thesis

Most pieces of effective writing are unified around one main point. That is, all the subpoints and supporting details are relevant to that point. Generally, after you have read an essay, you can sum up the writer's main point in a sentence, even if the author has not stated it explicitly. We call this summary statement a *thesis*.

Often a thesis will be *explicit*, plainly stated, in the piece of writing itself. In "The Myth of the Latin Woman: I Just Met a Girl Named María" from *The Latin Deli* (Athens: University of Georgia Press, 1993), Judith Ortiz Cofer states her thesis in the last sentence of the first paragraph — "You can leave the Island, master the English language, and travel as far as you can, but if you are a Latina, especially one like me who so obviously belongs to Rita Moreno's gene pool, the Island travels with you." This clear statement, strategically placed, helps readers see her main point.

Sometimes a thesis is *implicit*, indirectly suggested rather than directly stated. In "The Niceness Solution," a selection from Bruce Bawer's *Beyond Queer* (New York: Free Press, 1996), Paul Varnell describes an ordinance "banning rude behavior, including rude speech," passed in Raritan, New Jersey. After discussing a 1580 code of conduct, he identifies four objections to such attempts to limit free speech. He concludes with this sentence: "Sensibly, Raritan Police Chief Joseph Sferro said he would not enforce the new ordinance." Although Varnell does not state his main point in one concise sentence, readers know that he opposes the Raritan law and any other attempts to legislate "niceness."

The purpose of most academic and workplace writing is to inform, to explain, or to convince. To achieve any of these purposes, you must make your main point crystal clear. A thesis sentence helps you clarify that idea in your own mind and stay on track as you write. It also helps your readers readily see your point and follow your discussion. Sometimes you may want to imply your thesis, but if you state it explicitly, you ensure that readers cannot miss it.

HOW TO DISCOVER A WORKING THESIS

It's rare for a writer to develop a perfect thesis statement early in the writing process and then to write an effective essay that fits it exactly. What you should aim for is a *working thesis* — a statement that can guide you but that you will ultimately refine. Ideas for a working thesis are probably all around you.

■ Look for specific advice under headings that mention a thesis in Chs. 4–12. Watch for the red labels that identify thesis examples.

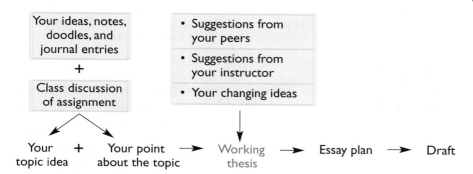

Your topic identifies the area you want to explore. To convert a topic to a thesis, you need to add your own slant, attitude, or point. A useful thesis contains not only the key words that identify your *topic* but also the *point* you want to make or the *attitude* you intend to express.

Topic   +   Slant or Attitude or Point   =   Working Thesis

Suppose you want to identify and write about a specific societal change. After listening to discussion in class and thinking about the topic, you decide to focus on changes in formal courtesy.

TOPIC IDEA   Old-fashioned formal courtesy

Now you experiment, auditioning ideas to make the topic your own.

AUDITION   Old-fashioned formal courtesy is a thing of the past.

FOR GROUP LEARNING

Identifying Theses

Working in a small group, select five essays from Part Two of this book to read carefully (or your instructor may choose the essays for your group). Then, individually, write out the thesis for each essay. Some thesis sentences are stated outright (explicit), but others are indirect (implicit). Compare and contrast the thesis statements that you identified with those your classmates found, and discuss the similarities and differences. How can you account for the differences? Try to agree on a thesis statement for each essay.

Although your audition sentence emphasizes change, it's still a circular statement, repeating rather than advancing a workable point. It doesn't say anything new about old-fashioned formal courtesy; it simply offers a definition of *old-fashioned*. You still need to find and state your own slant — maybe examining why things have changed.

TOPIC IDEA + SLANT	old-fashioned formal courtesy + its decline as gender roles have changed
WORKING THESIS	As the roles of men and women have changed in our society, old-fashioned formal courtesy has declined.

■ For advice about revising a thesis, see pp. 372–73.

Beginning with this working thesis, you could focus on how changing societal attitudes toward gender roles have caused changes in courtesy. Later, when you revise, you may refine your thesis further — perhaps restricting it to courtesy toward the elderly, toward women, or, despite stereotypes, toward men. The chart on page 315 suggests ways to develop a working thesis.

Once you have a working thesis, be sure its point accomplishes the purpose of your assignment. For example, suppose your assignment asks you to compare and contrast two local newspapers' coverage of a Senate election. Ask yourself what the point of that comparison and contrast is. Simply noting a difference won't be enough to satisfy most readers.

NO SPECIFIC POINT	The *Herald*'s coverage of the Senate elections was different from the *Courier*'s.
WORKING THESIS	The *Herald*'s coverage of the Senate elections was more thorough than the *Courier*'s.

■ Activity: Discovering a Thesis

Write a sentence, a working thesis, that unifies each of the following groups of details. Then compare and contrast your theses with those of your classmates. What other information would you need to write a good paper on each topic? How might the thesis statement change as you write the paper?

1. Cigarettes are expensive.
   Cigarettes can cause fires.
   Cigarettes cause unpleasant odors.
   Cigarettes can cause health problems for smokers.
   Secondhand smoke from cigarettes can cause health problems.

2. Clinger College has a highly qualified faculty.
   Clinger College has an excellent curriculum in my field.
   Clinger College has a beautiful campus.
   Clinger College is expensive.
   Clinger College has offered me a scholarship.

3. Crisis centers report that date rape is increasing.
   Most date rape is not reported to the police.
   Often the victim of date rape is not believed.
   Sometimes the victim of date rape is blamed or blames herself.
   The effects of date rape stay with a woman for years.

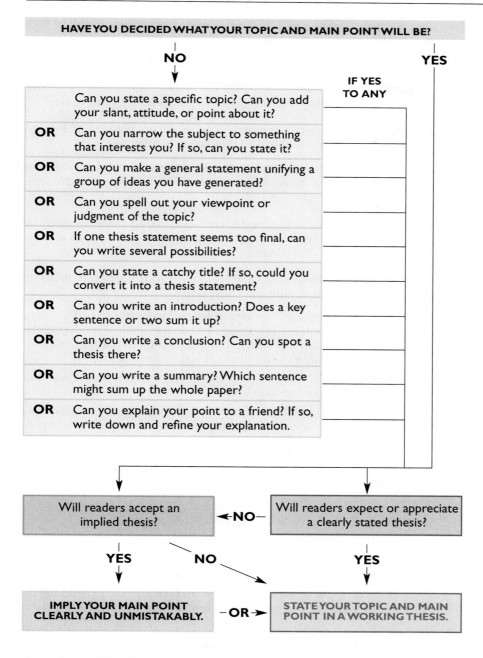

HOW TO STATE A THESIS

Once you have a notion of your topic and main point, these four suggestions may help you state or improve a thesis to guide your planning and
drafting.

- *State the thesis sentence exactly.* Replace vague or general wording with concise, detailed, and down-to-earth language.

  TOO GENERAL   There are a lot of troubles with chemical wastes.

  Are you going to deal with all chemical wastes, throughout all of history, all over the world? Will you list all the troubles they can cause?

  MORE SPECIFIC   Careless dumping of leftover paint is to blame for a recent outbreak of skin rashes in Atlanta.

  If you are writing an argument, you need to take a stand on an issue that is debatable and thus would allow others to take different positions. State yours exactly.

  SPECIFIC STAND   The recent health consequences of carelessly dumped leftover paint require Atlanta officials both to regulate and to educate.

- *State just one central idea in the thesis sentence.* If your paper is to focus on one point, your thesis should state only one main idea.

  TOO MANY IDEAS   Careless dumping of leftover paint has caused a serious problem in Atlanta, and a new kind of biodegradable paint has been developed, and it offers a promising solution to one chemical waste dilemma.

  ONE CENTRAL IDEA   Careless dumping of leftover paint has caused a serious problem in Atlanta.

  OR   A new kind of biodegradable paint offers a promising solution to one chemical waste dilemma.

- *State your thesis positively.* You can usually find evidence to support a positive statement, but you'd have to rule out every possible exception in order to prove a negative one. Negative statements also may sound half-hearted and seem to lead nowhere.

  NEGATIVE   Medical researchers do not know what causes breast cancer.

  POSITIVE   The causes of breast cancer remain a challenge for medical researchers.

  Presenting the topic positively as a "challenge" might lead to a paper about an exciting quest. Besides, to show that researchers are working on the problem would be relatively easy, given an hour of online research.

- *Limit your thesis to a statement that you can demonstrate.* A workable thesis is limited so that you can support it with sufficient convincing evidence. It should stake out just the territory that you can cover thoroughly within the length assigned and the time available, and no more. The shorter the essay, the less development your thesis should promise or require. Likewise, the longer the essay, the more development and complexity your thesis should suggest.

DIFFICULT TO SHOW

For centuries, popular music has announced vital trends in Western society.

DIFFICULT TO SHOW

My favorite piece of music is Beethoven's Fifth Symphony.

The first thesis above could inform a whole encyclopedia of music; the second would require that you explain why that symphony is your favorite, contrasting it with all the other musical compositions you know. The following thesis sounds far more workable for a brief essay.

POSSIBLE TO SHOW

In the past two years, a rise in the number of pre-teenagers has resulted in a comeback for heavy metal on the local concert scene.

Unlike a vague statement or a broad, unrestricted claim, a limited thesis statement narrows and refines your topic, thus restricting your essay to a reasonable scope.

TOO VAGUE

Native American blankets are very beautiful.

TOO BROAD

Native Americans have adapted to many cultural shifts.

POSSIBLE TO SHOW

For some members of the Apache tribe, working in high-rise construction has allowed both economic stability and cultural integrity.

If the suggestions in this chapter have helped you draft a working thesis — even an awkward or a feeble one — you'll find plenty of advice about improving it in the next few pages and more later about revising it. But what if you're freezing up because your thesis simply won't take shape? First, relax. Your thesis will emerge later on — as your thinking matures and you figure out your paper's true direction, as peer readers spot the idea in your paper you're too close to see, as you talk with your instructor and suddenly grasp how to take your paper where you want it to go. In the meantime, plan and write so that you create a rich environment that will encourage your thesis to emerge.

For more on revising a thesis, see pp. 372–73.

■ Activity: Examining Thesis Statements

Discuss each of the following thesis sentences with your classmates. Answer these questions for each:

Is the thesis stated exactly?
Does the thesis state just one idea?
Is the thesis stated positively?
Is the thesis sufficiently limited for a short essay?
How might the thesis be improved?

1. Teenagers should not get married.

2. Cutting classes is like a disease.

3. Students have developed a variety of techniques to conceal inadequate study from their instructors.

■ For exercises on choosing effective thesis statements, visit <bedfordstmartins.com/bedguide> and do a keyword search:

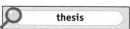
thesis

4. Older people often imitate teenagers.

5. Violence on television can be harmful to children.

6. I don't know how to change the oil in my car.

HOW TO IMPROVE A THESIS

■ To get online help from the Draft Doctor, visit <bedfordstmartins.com/ bedguide>.

Simply knowing what a solid working thesis *should* do may not help you improve your thesis. Whether yours is a first effort or a refined version, turn to the Draft Doctor (pp. 320–21) to help you figure out ways to strengthen your thesis. Skim down the left column to identify questions you might ask about your thesis. When you answer a question with "Yes" or "Maybe," move straight across the row to the Diagnose column next to that question. Use the diagnostic activities to identify gaps or weaknesses, and then move straight across the row again to the Treat column on the right. Use the advice that suits your thesis as you rework it.

HOW TO USE A THESIS TO ORGANIZE

■ For more on using a thesis to develop an outline, see pp. 325–27.

Often a good, clear thesis will suggest an organization for your ideas.

WORKING THESIS	Despite the disadvantages of living in a downtown business district, I wouldn't live anywhere else.
FIRST ¶S	Disadvantages of living in the business district
NEXT ¶S	Advantages of living there
LAST ¶	Affirmation of your fondness for downtown city life

A clear thesis helps to organize you, keeping you on track as you write. Just putting your working thesis into words can stake out your territory. Your thesis can then direct you as you select details and connect sections of the essay. Its purpose is to guide you on a quest, not to limit your ideas.

■ For more on key terms in college assignments, see p. 36 and pp. 280–83.

In addition, your thesis can prepare your readers for the pattern of development or sequence of ideas that you plan to present. As a writer, you look for key words (such as *compare, propose,* or *evaluate*) when you size up an assignment. Such words alert you to what's expected. When you write or revise your thesis, you can use such terms or their equivalents (such as *benefit* or *consequence* instead of *effect*) to preview for readers the likely direction of your paper. Then they, too, will know what to expect.

WORKING THESIS	Expanding the campus program for energy conservation would bring welcome financial and environmental benefits.
FIRST ¶S	Explanation of the campus energy situation and the need for the proposed program expansion
NEXT ¶S	Financial benefits for the college and students
NEXT ¶S	Environmental benefits for the region and beyond
LAST ¶	Concluding assertion of the value of the program

As you write, however, you don't have to cling to a thesis for dear life. If further investigation changes your thinking, you can change your thesis.

WORKING THESIS   Because wolves are a menace to people and farm animals, they ought to be exterminated.

REVISED THESIS   The wolf, a relatively peaceful animal useful in nature's scheme of things, ought to be protected.

You can restate your thesis at any time: as you write, as you revise, as you revise again.

■ Activity: Using a Thesis to Preview Organization

Each of the following thesis statements is from a student paper in a different field of study. Discuss them with your classmates, considering how each one previews the essay to come and how you would expect the essay to be organized into sections.

1. Although the intent of inclusion is to provide the best care for all children by treating both special- and general-education students equally, some people in the field believe that the full inclusion of disabled children in mainstream classrooms may not be in the best interest of either type of student. (From "Is Inclusion the Answer?" by Sarah E. Goers)

2. With ancient Asian roots and contemporary European influences, the Japanese language has continued to change and to reflect cultural change as well. (From "Japanese: Linguistic Diversity" by Stephanie Hawkins)

3. Manifest destiny was an expression by leaders and politicians in the 1840s to clarify continental extension and expansion and in a sense revitalize the mission and national destiny for Americans. (From ethnic studies examination answer by Angela Mendy)

4. By comparing the Aeneid with Troilus and Criseyde, one can easily see the effects of the code of courtly love on literature. (From "The Effect of the Code of Courtly Love: A Comparison of Virgil's Aeneid and Chaucer's Troilus and Criseyde" by Cindy Keeler)

5. The effects of pollutants on the endangered Least Tern entering the Upper Newport Bay should be quantified so that necessary action can be taken to further protect and encourage the species. (From "Contaminant Residues in Least Tern [Sterna antillarum] Eggs Nesting in Upper Newport Bay" by Susanna Olsen)

Organizing Your Ideas

When you organize an essay, you select an order for the parts that makes sense and shows your readers how the ideas are connected. Often your organization will not only help a reader follow your points but also reinforce

Draft Doctor: Building a Stronger Thesis

If you sense a problem, ASK	If you answer Yes/Maybe, DIAGNOSE	If you diagnose a problem, TREAT
Unclear Topic? Could I define or state my topic more clearly?	• Write out your current working thesis. • Circle the words in it that identify your topic. WORKING THESIS:  is essential for World Action volunteers. [What, exactly, does the topic *adaptability* mean?]	• Rework the circled topic. Try to state it more clearly and specify what it means to you. • Define or identify it in terms of your purpose and the likely interests of your audience. REVISED THESIS: An ability to adjust to, even thrive under, challenging circumstances is essential for World Action volunteers.
Unclear Slant? Could I define or state my slant more clearly?	• Write out your current working thesis. • Underline the words that state your slant, attitude, or point about your topic. WORKING THESIS: Volunteering is an invaluable experience. [Why or in what ways is volunteering invaluable?]	• Rework your underlined slant. Jot down possibilities that might sharpen it and express an engaging approach to your topic. • Refine it to address more effectively your purpose as a writer and your audience's interests, concerns, or values. REVISED THESIS: Volunteering builds practical skills while connecting volunteers more fully to their communities.
Broad Thesis? Could I limit my thesis to make sure that I can successfully develop it?	• Write out your current working thesis. • Decide whether it establishes a task that you could accomplish given the time available and the length expected. WORKING THESIS: Rock and roll has evolved dramatically since the 1950s. [Tracing this history in a few pages would be impossible.]	• Restrict your thesis to a slice of the pie, not the whole pie. Focus on one part or element, not several. Break it apart, and pick only a chunk. • Limit its scope by reducing multiple ideas to one point or converting a negative statement to a positive one. REVISED THESIS: The music of the alternative-rock band Wilco continues to evolve as members experiment with vocal moods and instrumentation.

If you sense a problem, ASK	If you answer *Yes/Maybe,* DIAGNOSE	If you diagnose a problem, TREAT
Boring Thesis? Could I make my thesis more interesting for me and for my audience?	• Write out your current working thesis. • Brainstorm about angles or ways to refine it so that you will want to write about it and your audience will want to read about it. WORKING THESIS: Across cultures, weddings include traditions that wish the couple well.	• Reword your thesis until it presents something you'd like to probe, investigate, or show. • Adjust its angle until it expresses the right hold on the topic — seizing the topic from an engaging direction, grasping it securely so it can't slip away, turning it over to reveal the unexpected. REVISED THESIS: From the red clothes and decorations in Chinese weddings to the sugar sprinkled over Iranian brides and grooms, weddings in nearly every culture include traditions aimed at bringing happiness, luck, or fertility to the couple.
Thesis without a Preview? Should I revise my thesis so that it previews the plan for my paper and alerts my audience about what to expect?	• Write out your current working thesis. • List the points about it that you might want to explain and illustrate. • Group your points — first, next, and last — as you might present them to develop your thesis. WORKING THESIS: Raising tuition at Bradley State is counterproductive.	• Rework your thesis to indicate the direction in which your paper goes. • State your preview or prediction clearly in order to prepare readers for the points you raise. REVISED THESIS: Raising tuition at Bradley State is counterproductive because this change would jeopardize both enrollments and income without solving the current financial dilemma.
Any Other Thesis Refinements? After a final look at the refined thesis for my draft, can I improve it further?	• Read your current working thesis out loud to yourself, marking any rough spots. • Ask your peer editors how you might improve the statement and development of your thesis. • Follow any advice about your thesis from your instructor.	• Improve your thesis as needed; for example, smooth out its wording, adjust its slant, reduce its scope, or reverse it. • If your thesis seems entirely misguided or unworkable, toss it out. Make a fresh start. • Consider the useful suggestions of your peers. • Revise until your thesis does what you want it to do.

your emphases by moving from beginning to end or from least to most significant, as the table below illustrates.

GROUPING YOUR IDEAS

While exploring a topic, you will usually find a few ideas that seem to belong together — two facts on New York traffic jams, four actions of New York drivers, three problems with New York streets. But similar ideas seldom appear together in your notes because you did not discover them all at the same time. To identify an effective order for your ideas, you'll need to sort them into groups and arrange them in sequences. Here are five common ways to work:

1. *Rainbow connections.* List all the main points you're going to express. Don't recopy the rest of your material. Use highlighters or colored pencils to mark points that go together with the same color. When you write, follow the color code, and deal with related ideas at the same time.

2. *Linking.* Make a list of major points, and then draw lines (in color if you wish) to link related ideas. Number each linked group to identify a sequence for discussing the ideas. Figure 17.1 illustrates a linked list for an essay on Manhattan driving. The writer has connected related points and supplied each linked group with a heading. Each heading will probably

ORGANIZATION	MOVEMENT	TYPICAL USE	EXAMPLE
Spatial	Left to right, right to left, bottom to top, top to bottom, front to back, outside to inside	• Describing a place, a scene, or an environment • Describing a person's physical appearance	You might describe an ocean vista, moving from the tidepools on the rocky beach to the plastic buoys floating offshore to the sparkling water meeting the sunset sky.
Chronological	What happens first, second, and next, continuing until the end	• Narrating an event • Explaining steps in a procedure • Explaining the development of an idea, a school of thought, or a trend	You might narrate the events that led up to an accident: leaving home late, stopping for an errand, rushing along the highway, racing up to the intersection.
Logical	General to specific, specific to general, least important to most important, cause to effect, problem to solution	• Explaining an idea • Persuading readers to accept a stand, a proposal, or an evaluation	You might analyze the effects of last year's storms by selecting four major consequences, placing the most important one last for emphasis.

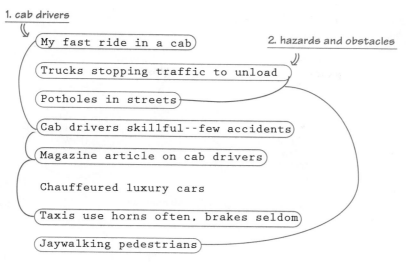

Figure 17.1 The Linking Method for Grouping Ideas

inspire a topic sentence to introduce each major division of the essay. Because one point, chauffeured luxury cars, failed to relate to any other, the writer has a choice: drop the point or develop ideas about it.

3. *Solitaire.* Collect notes and ideas on roomy (5-by-8-inch) file cards. To organize, spread out the cards; arrange and rearrange them, as in a game of solitaire. When each idea seems to lead to the next, gather all the cards into a deck in this order. As you write, deal yourself a card at a time and translate its contents into sentences. This technique is particularly helpful when you write about literature or from research.

4. *Slide show.* If you are familiar with presentation software such as PowerPoint, write your notes and ideas on "slides" (the software equivalent of blank sheets). When you're done, the program gives you the option of viewing your slides one by one or viewing the entire collection. In PowerPoint, choose View and then Slide Sorter. Shuffle and reshuffle your slides into the most promising order.

5. *Clustering.* Like mapping, clustering is a visual method useful for generating as well as grouping ideas. In the middle of a piece of paper, write your topic in a word or a phrase. Then think of the major divisions into which this topic might be organized. For an essay on Manhattan drivers, the major divisions might be the *types* of drivers: (1) taxi drivers, (2) bus drivers, (3) truck drivers, (4) New York drivers of private cars, and (5) out-of-town drivers of private cars. Arrange these divisions around your topic, and circle them too. Draw lines out from the major topic to the subdivisions. You now have a rough plan for an essay. (See Figure 17.2.)

■ For more about mapping, see pp. 301–02.

Figure 17.2 The Cluster-
ing Method for Grouping
Ideas

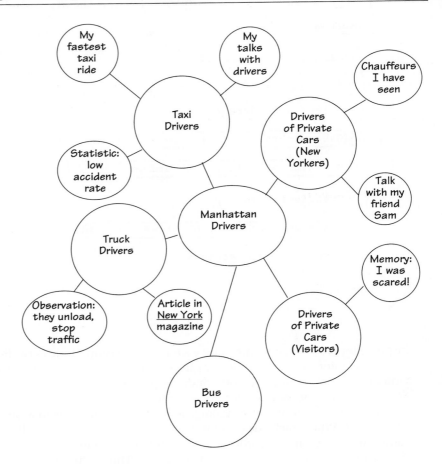

Around each division, make another cluster of details you might in-clude — examples, illustrations, facts, statistics, bits of evidence, opinions. Circle each specific item, and connect it to the appropriate type of driver. When you write your paper, you can expand the details into one paragraph for each type of driver.

This technique lets you know where you have enough specific informa-tion to make your paper clear and interesting — and where you don't. If one subtopic has no small circles around it (such as "bus drivers" in Figure 17.2), you should either think of some specifics to expand it or drop it.

■ Activity: Clustering

Generate clusters for three of the following topics. With your classmates, dis-cuss which one of the three would probably help you write the best paper.

teachers	fast food	civil rights
Internet sites	leisure activities	substance abuse
my favorite restaurants	musicians	technology

OUTLINING

A familiar way to organize is to outline. A written outline, whether brief or detailed, acts as a map that you make before a journey. It shows where to leave from, where to stop along the way, and where to arrive. If you forget where you are going or what you want to say, you can consult your written outline to get back on track. When you turn in your essay, your instructor may request an outline as both a map for readers and a skeletal summary of your material.

How can you arrive at a useful outline? Some writers like to begin with a working thesis. If it's clear, it may suggest how to develop or expand an outline, allowing the plan for the paper to grow naturally from the idea behind it. Others prefer to start with a loose informal outline — perhaps just a list of points to make. If readers find your papers mechanical, such an outline may free up your writing. Still others, especially for research papers or complicated arguments, like to lay out a complex job very carefully in a detailed formal outline. If readers find your writing disorganized and hard to follow, this more detailed plan might be especially useful. In any case, your thesis can be a good guide for planning.

For more on thesis statements, see pp. 312–19.

For more on using outlining for revision, see p. 375.

Thesis-Guided Outlines.   Your working thesis may identify points that you can use to organize your paper. (Of course, if it doesn't, you may want to revise your thesis and then return to your outline or vice versa.) For example, suppose that you are assigned an anthropology paper on the people of Melanesia. You decide to focus on the following idea:

> *Working Thesis: Although the Melanesian pattern of family life may look strange to Westerners, it fosters a degree of independence that rivals our own.*

Emphasizing Ideas

Here are some of the easy computer tools you can use to highlight, categorize, and shape your thinking by distinguishing your points on a screen.

FOR E-WRITERS

Highlighting

Boxing

Showing color

Using **bold**, *italics*, underlining

• Adding bullets

1. Numbering

Changing fonts

Varying print sizes

To use these features, click on their icons on your toolbar, or use your menu. You can also see your experiments with organization by using an option like Track Changes or by creating a table or column of ideas in a separate window to the left of your text.

Laying out ideas in the same order that they follow in the two parts of this thesis statement, you might make a simple outline like this:

1. *Features that appear strange to Westerners*
   - *−A woman supported by her brother, not her husband*
   - *−Trial marriages common*
   - *− Divorce from her children possible for any mother*

2. *Admirable results of system*
   - *−Wives not dependent on husbands for support*
   - *−Divorce between mates uncommon*
   - *−Greater freedom for parents and children*

This informal outline suggests an essay that naturally falls into two parts — features that seem strange and admirable results of the system. When you are creating a thesis-guided outline, look for the key element of your working thesis that can suggest a useful organization, as the table on page 327 illustrates.

Informal Outlines. For in-class writing, brief essays, and familiar topics, a short or informal outline, also called a *scratch outline,* may serve your needs. Jot down a list of points in the order you plan to make them. Use this outline, for your eyes only, to help you get organized, stick to the point, and remember ideas under pressure. The following example outlines a short paper explaining how outdoor enthusiasts can avoid illnesses carried by unsafe drinking water. It simply lists each of the methods for treating potentially unsafe water that the writer plans to explain.

Working Thesis: Campers and hikers need to ensure the safety of the water that they drink from rivers or streams.

Introduction: Treatments for potentially unsafe drinking water

1. *Small commercial filter*
   - *−Remove bacteria and protozoa including salmonella and E. coli*
   - *−Use brands convenient for campers and hikers*

2. *Chemicals*
   - *−Use bleach, chlorine, or iodine*
   - *−Follow general rule: 12 drops per gallon of water*

3. *Boiling*
   - *−Boil for 5 minutes (Red Cross) to 15 minutes (National Safety Council)*
   - *−Store in a clean, covered container*

Conclusion: Using one of three methods of treating water, campers and hikers can enjoy safe water from natural sources.

KEY ELEMENT OF THESIS	EXAMPLES OF KEY ELEMENT	SAMPLE THESIS STATEMENT	QUESTION YOU MIGHT ASK	POSSIBLE ORGANIZATION OF OUTLINE
Plural word	Words such as *benefits, advantages, teenagers,* or *reasons*	A varied personal exercise program has four main *advantages.*	What are the types, kinds, or examples of this word?	List outline headings based on the categories or cases you identify.
Key word identifying an approach or vantage point	Words such as *claim, argument, position, interpretation,* or *point of view*	Wylie's *interpretation* of Van Gogh's last paintings unifies aesthetic and psychological considerations.	What are the parts, aspects, or elements of this approach?	List outline headings based on the components that you identify.
Key word identifying an activity	Words such as *preparing, harming,* or *improving*	*Preparing* a pasta dinner for surprise guests can be an easy process.	How is this activity accomplished, or how does it happen?	Supply a heading for each step, stage, or element that the activity involves.
One part of the sentence subordinate to another	Sentence part beginning with a qualification such as *despite, because, since,* or *although*	*Although* the new wetland preserve will protect only some wildlife, it will bring several long-term benefits to the region.	What does the qualification include, and what does the main statement include?	Use a major heading for the qualification and another for the main statement.
General evaluation that assigns a quality or value to someone or something	Evaluative words such as *typical, unusual, valuable, notable,* or other specific qualities	When other parents meet Sandie Burns on the soccer field sidelines, they may be surprised to see her wheelchair, but they soon discover that she is a *typical* soccer mom.	What examples, illustrations, or clusters of details will show this quality?	Add a heading for each extended example or each group of examples or details you want to use.
Claim or argument advocating a certain decision, action, or solution	Words such as *should, could, might, ought to, need to,* or *must*	In spite of these tough economic times, the student senate *should* strongly recommend extended hours for the library computer lab.	Which reasons and evidence will justify this opinion? Which will counter the opinions of others who disagree with it?	Provide a heading for each major justification or defensive point; add headings for countering reasons.

Outlining

Discuss the formal topic outline on pages 330–31 with some of your class-mates or the entire class, considering the following questions:

- Would this outline be useful in organizing an essay?
- How is the organization logical? Is it easy to follow? What are other possible arrangements for the ideas?
- Is this outline sufficiently detailed for a paper? Can you spot any gaps?
- What possible pitfalls would the writer using this outline need to avoid?

This simple outline could easily fall into a five-paragraph essay or grow to eight paragraphs — introduction, conclusion, and three pairs of paragraphs in between. You probably won't know until you write the paper exactly how many paragraphs you'll need.

An informal outline can be even briefer than the preceding one. To answer an exam question or prepare a very short paper, your outline might be no more than an *outer plan* — three or four phrases jotted in a list:

> *Isolation of region*
> *Tradition of family businesses*
> *Growth of electronic commuting*

The process of making an informal outline can help you figure out how to develop your ideas. Say you plan a "how-to" essay analyzing the process of buying a used car, beginning with this thesis:

> *Working Thesis: Despite traps that await the unwary, preparing yourself before you shop can help you find a good used car.*

The key word in this thesis is *preparing*. When you ask yourself *how* the buyer should prepare before shopping for a used car, you're likely to outline several ideas:

> *—Read car blogs, car magazines, and Consumer Reports.*
> *—Check craigslist, dealer sites, and classified ads.*
> *—Make phone calls to several dealers.*
> *—Talk to friends who have bought used cars.*
> *—Know what to look and listen for when you test-drive.*
> *—Have a mechanic check out any car before you buy it.*

After starting your paper with some horror stories about people who got taken by car sharks, you can discuss, point by point, your bits of advice. Of course, you can always change the sequence, add or drop an idea, or revise your thesis as you go along.

■ **Activity:** Moving from Outline to Thesis

Write a possible thesis statement based on each of the following informal outlines. Be certain that your thesis expresses a possible slant, attitude, or point (even if you don't know enough about the topic to be sure that the position is entirely defensible). Share and compare thesis statements with your classmates. What similarities and differences do you find? How do you account for these?

1. Cell Phones
   Get the financial and service plans of various cell-phone companies.
   Read the cell-phone contracts as well as the promotional offers.
   Look for the time period, flexibility, and cancellation provisions.
   Check the day and evening calling times, total minutes, and other extra charges.
   Find out about the availability and costs for extended calling locations (international, national, and regional calls).

2. Popular Mystery Novels
   Both Tony Hillerman and Margaret Coel write mysteries with Native American characters and settings.
   Hillerman's novels feature members of the Navajo Tribal Police.
   Coel's novels feature a female attorney who is an Arapaho and a Jesuit priest at the reservation mission who grew up in Boston.
   Hillerman's stories take place mostly on the extensive Navajo Reservation in Arizona, New Mexico, and Utah.
   Coel's stories are set mostly on the large Wind River Reservation in Wyoming.
   Hillerman and Coel try to convey tribal culture accurately although their mysteries involve different tribes.
   Both also explore similarities, differences, and conflicts between white and Native American cultures.

3. Downtown Playspace
   The Downtown Playspace project has financial and volunteer support but needs more.
   Statistics indicate the need for a regional facility to expand options for children.
   The Downtown Playspace will be available to visitors of the Children's Museum and to local children in Headstart, preschool, and elementary schools.
   It will combine a state-of-the-art outdoor playground with an indoor technology space.
   Land and a building are available, but both require renovation.

Formal Outlines.   A *formal outline* is an elaborate guide, built with time and care, for a long, complex paper. Because major reports, research papers, and senior theses require so much work, some professors and departments ask a writer to submit a formal outline at an early stage and to include one in the final draft. A formal outline shows how ideas relate one to another — which ones are equal and important (*coordinate*) and which are less important (*subordinate*). It clearly and logically spells out where you are going. If

■ For sample formal outlines, see pp. 330–33.

you outline again after writing a draft, you can use the revised outline to check your logic then as well, perhaps revealing where to revise.

When you make a full formal outline, follow these steps:

- Place your thesis statement at the beginning.
- List the major points that support and develop your thesis, labeling them with roman numerals (I, II, III).
- Break down the major points into divisions with capital letters (A, B, C), subdivide those using arabic numerals (1, 2, 3), and subdivide those using small letters (a, b, c). Continue until your outline is fully developed. If a very complex project requires further subdivision, use arabic numerals and small letters in parentheses.
- Indent each level of division in turn: the deeper the indentation, the more specific the ideas. Align like-numbered or -lettered headings under one another.
- Cast all headings in parallel grammatical form: phrases or sentences, but not both in the same outline.

For more on parallelism, see B2 in the Quick Editing Guide (the dark-blue-edged pages).

For more on analysis and division, see pp. 360–66.

CAUTION: Because an outline divides or analyzes ideas, some readers and instructors disapprove of categories with only one subpoint, reasoning that you can't divide anything into one part. Let's say that your outline on earthquakes lists a 1 without a 2:

> D.   Probable results of an earthquake include structural damage.
>
> > 1. House foundations crack.

Logically, if you are going to discuss the *probable results* of an earthquake, you need to include more than one result:

> D.   Probable results of an earthquake include structural damage.
>
> > 1. House foundations crack.
> >
> > 2. Road surfaces are damaged.
> >
> > 3. Water mains break.

Not only have you now come up with more points, but you have also emphasized the one placed last.

A *formal topic outline* for a long paper might include several levels of ideas, as this outline for Linn Bourgeau's research paper illustrates. Such an outline can help you work out both a persuasive sequence for the parts of a paper and a logical order for any information from sources.

Crucial Choices: Who Will Save the Wetlands If Everyone Is at the Mall?

Working Thesis: Federal regulations need to foster state laws and educational requirements that will help protect the few wetlands that are left, restore as many as possible of those that have been destroyed, and take measures to improve the damage from overdevelopment.

  I.   Illinois wetlands
      A. Loss for nature and humans
          1. More flooding and poorer water quality
          2. Lost ability to prevent floods, clean water, and store water
      B. Need for protection of humankind
 II.   Dramatic floods
      A. Cost in dollars and lives
          1. Thirteen deaths between 1988 and 1998
          2. Cost about $39 million a year
      B. Great Midwestern Flood of 1993
          1. Disregard for wetlands-flood control correlation
          2. Disregard for preventive role of wetlands
III.   Education deficits
      A. Inadequately informed legislators
          1 No "isolated wetland"
          2. Interconnections in natural water systems
          3. Ramifications beyond local area
      B. Uninformed students
          1. High school science courses often electives
          2. College students without knowledge of water systems
 IV.   Changes in laws
      A. Possible transfer of wetlands responsibility from federal government to states
          1. Too much room for interest groups to take over
          2. Need for federal oversight
      B. Perseverance needed (Citizens for Conservation and Deer Point Homes)
      C. New laws for well-researched proposals
          1. Costs of water quality and flooding crises
          2. Misinterpreted or ignored wetlands
          3. Preservation unless no other choice
  V.   Need to save wetlands
      A. New federal definition including all the varieties and watersheds
          1. Concept of interconnectedness, now missing, through re-education
          2. No isolated issue or wetlands
      B. Choices in schools, legislature, and people's daily lives

A topic outline may help you work out a clear sequence of ideas but may not elaborate or connect them. Although you may not be sure how everything will fit together until you write a draft, you may find that a *formal sentence outline* clarifies what you want to say. It also moves you a step closer to drafting topic sentences and paragraphs even though you would still need to add detailed information. Notice how this sentence outline for Linn Bourgeau's research paper expands her ideas.

Crucial Choices: Who Will Save the Wetlands If Everyone Is at the Mall?

Working Thesis: Federal regulations need to foster state laws and educational requirements that will help protect the few wetlands that are left, restore as many as possible of those that have been destroyed, and take measures to improve the damage from overdevelopment.

    I. Over the past 288 years, the people of Illinois have chosen to legislate and drain away 90 percent of the wetlands once abundant across the state.

        A. The degradation of wetlands is a loss for both nature and humans in Illinois.

            1. Destroying wetlands creates more flooding and poorer water quality.

            2. The wetlands have the ability to stave off floods, to clean the water supply, and to add to the aquifers that store water.

        B. The wetlands need to be protected because they protect and serve humankind.

   II. Floods are dramatic and visible consequences of not protecting wetlands.

        A. The cost of flooding can be tallied in dollars spent and in lives lost.

            1. Thirteen people died in floods between 1988 and 1998.

            2. Flooding consistently costs about $39 million a year.

        B. The Great Midwestern Flood of 1993 could have been avoided.

            1. Illinois and other states did not heed the correlation between wetlands and flood control.

            2. Preventing floods is a valuable role of wetlands, whose plants and soil manage excess water.

  III. Education deficits affect both legislators and students.

        A. Legislators are not adequately informed about ecological concepts.

            1. Legislators need to know that an "isolated wetland" simply does not exist.

            2. The law needs to consider interconnections in natural water systems.

            3. People can't escape the ramifications well beyond their local area.

        B. Most students are not informed either.

            1. Science courses often are electives in secondary education.

            2. College students lack knowledge of how water systems work.

IV. Change must begin with laws.

   A. Because federal laws fail to protect wetlands, this task might go to the states.

     1. However, state control leaves too much room for interest groups to take over.

     2. State governments need the guidance of federal oversight.

   B. Perseverance is needed to get politicians to see the value of wetlands, as two cases—Citizens for Conservation and Deer Point Homes—show.

   C. New federal laws should implement well-researched proposals.

     1. Water quality and flooding crises deplete funds and natural resources.

     2. Wetlands have largely been misinterpreted or ignored in the laws.

     3. Wetlands should be preserved unless there is no other choice.

V. Who will save the wetlands if everyone is at the mall?

   A. The federal definition of wetlands should include all the varieties, including watersheds.

     1. The vital concept of interconnectedness, now missing from wetland laws, means a re-education of everyone from legislators to fourth graders.

     2. The value of wetlands is not an isolated issue any more than wetlands are isolated from one another.

   B. The choices made in the schools, the legislature, and people's daily lives will determine the future of water quality and flooding.

■ Activity: Outlining

1. Using one of your groups of ideas from the activities in Chapter 16, construct a formal topic outline that might serve as a guide for an essay.

2. Now turn that topic outline into a formal sentence outline.

3. Discuss both outlines with your classmates and your instructor, bringing up any difficulties you encountered. If you get any better notions for organizing your ideas, change the outline.

4. Write an essay based on your outline.

■ For exercises on organizing support effectively, visit <bedfordstmartins.com/bedguide> and do a keyword search:

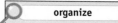

organize

Chapter 18
Strategies for Drafting

Learning to write well involves learning what key questions to ask yourself: How can I begin this draft? What should I do if I get stuck? How can I flesh out the bones of my paper? How can I end effectively? How can I keep my readers with me? In this chapter we offer advice to get you going and keep you going, drafting the first paragraph to the last.

Making a Start Enjoyable

A playful start may get you hard at work before you know it.

- **Time Yourself.**   Set your watch, alarm, or egg timer, and vow to draft a page before the buzzer sounds. Don't stop for anything. If you're writing nonsense, just push on. You can cross out later.
- **Slow to a Crawl.**   If speed quotas don't work, time yourself to write with exaggerated laziness, maybe a sentence every fifteen minutes.
- **Scribble on a Scrap.**   If you dread the blank sheet of paper or screen, try starting on scrap paper, the back of a list, or a small notebook page.
- **Begin Writing the Part You Find Most Appetizing.**   Start in the middle or at the end, wherever the thoughts come easily to mind. As novelist Bill Downey observes, "Writers are allowed to have their dessert first."
- **State Your Purpose.**   Set forth what you want to achieve: To tell a story? To explain something? To win a reader over to your way of thinking?
- **Slip into a Reader's Shoes.**   Put yourself in your reader's place. Start writing what you'd like to find out from the paper.

For more about purpose and audience, see pp. 14–18 and pp. 310–12.

- **Nutshell It.**   Summarize the paper you want to write. Condense your ideas into one small, tight paragraph. Later you can expand each sentence until the meaning is clear and all points are adequately supported.
- **Shrink Your Immediate Job.**   Break the writing task into smaller parts, and do only the first one. Turn out, say, just the first two paragraphs.
- **Seek a Provocative Title.**   Write down a dozen possible titles for your paper. If one sounds strikingly good, don't let it go to waste!
- **Record Yourself.**   Talk a first draft into a tape recorder or your voice mail. Play it back. Then write. Even if it is hard to transcribe your spoken words, this technique may set your mind in motion.
- **Speak Up.**   On your feet, before an imaginary cheering crowd, spontaneously utter a first paragraph. Then — quick! — tape it or write it out.
- **Take Short Breaks.**   Even if you don't feel tired, take a break every half hour or so. Get up, walk around the room, stretch, or get a drink of water. Two or three minutes should be enough to refresh your mind.

Restarting

When you have to write a long or demanding essay that you can't finish in one sitting, you may return to it only to find yourself stalled. You tromp your starter and nothing happens. Your engine seems reluctant to turn over. Try the following suggestions for getting back on the road.

Formatting and Organizing Your Drafts

Use your word processor menu to set the margin widths, line spacing, print size, and other aspects of your paper's format and layout. If your instructor has not specified formatting, customize your files to produce pages with one-inch margins and double spacing, using 12-point type.

Next, whether you store your work on disks or on the hard drive of your own computer, figure out a simple file-naming and folder system to make it easy for you to keep track of your work. Some students prefer file names that identify the course, term, assignment, and draft number, while others note the paper topic or activity with the draft number — Eng101F2007-1-1 or Recall-1. When you revise a draft, duplicate and rename the file — Eng101F2007-1-2 or Recall-2 — instead of simply rewriting the original file. Then all the versions of your paper will be available in case you want to retrieve writing from an early draft or your instructor wants to review the stages of your writing process. Use the menu or the help screen to create a folder for each course; store all your drafts for the class there.

FOR E-WRITERS

■ For more advice on document design, see Ch. 21.

- **Leave Hints for How to Continue.**   If you're ready to quit, jot down any remaining ideas. Tell yourself what you think might come next, or write the first sentence of the next section. When you come back to work, you will face not a blank wall but rich and suggestive graffiti.

- **Pause in Midstream.**   End a writing session by breaking off in midsentence or midparagraph. Just leave a sentence trailing off into space, even if you know what its closing words should be. When you return to your task, you can start writing again immediately.

- **Repeat.**   If the next sentence refuses to appear, simply recopy the last one until that shy creature emerges on the page.

- **Reread.**   When you return to work, spend a few minutes rereading what you have already written or what you have planned.

- **Switch Instruments.**   Do you compose on the computer? Try writing in longhand. Or drop your pen to type. Try writing on note cards or colored paper.

- **Change Activities.**   When words won't come, turn to something quite different. Run, walk your dog, cook a favorite meal, or nap. Or reward yourself — after you reach a certain point in your labors — with a trip to the vending machine, a call to a friend, or a TV show. All the while, your unconscious mind will be working on your writing task.

Paragraphing

For more on developing ideas within paragraphs, see Ch. 19.

An essay is written not in large, indigestible lumps but in *paragraphs* — small units, each more or less self-contained, each contributing some new idea in support of the thesis or main point of the essay. Writers dwell on one idea at a time, stating it, developing it, illustrating it with examples or a few facts — *showing* readers, with plenty of detailed evidence, exactly what they mean.

Paragraphs can be as short as one sentence or as long as a page. Sometimes the length is governed by the audience, the purpose of the writing, or the medium in which it appears. Journalists expect newspaper readers to gobble up facts like popcorn, quickly skimming articles with short one- or two-sentence paragraphs. College writers, in contrast, should assume their readers' willingness to read through well-developed paragraphs.

When readers see a paragraph indentation, they interpret it as a pause, a chance for a deep breath. After that signpost, they expect you to concentrate on a new aspect of your thesis for the rest of that paragraph. The following sections in this chapter give you advice on guiding readers through your writing — using opening paragraphs to draw them in, topic sentences to focus and control body paragraphs within an essay, and concluding paragraphs to wrap up the discussion.

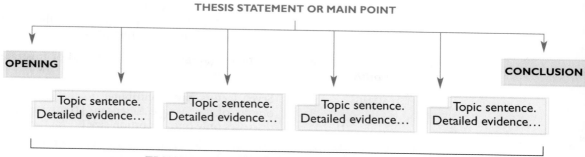

Using Topic Sentences

A *topic sentence* spells out the main idea of a paragraph in the body of an essay. It guides you as you write, and it hooks your readers as they discover what to expect and how to interpret the paragraph. As the topic sentence establishes the focus of the paragraph, it also relates the paragraph to the thesis of the essay, supporting the topic and main point of the essay as a whole. (For this reason, much of the advice on topic sentences for paragraphs also extends to thesis statements for essays.) To convert an idea to a topic sentence, you need to add your own slant, attitude, or point.

For more on thesis statements, see pp. 312–21.

Main Idea   +   Slant or Attitude or Point   =   Topic Sentence

How can you write a good topic sentence? Make it interesting, accurate, and limited. The more pointed and lively your topic sentence, the more it will interest your readers. Even a dull and vague start can be enlivened once you zero in on a specific point.

MAIN IDEA + SLANT	television + everything that's wrong with it
DULL START	There are many things wrong with television.
POINTED TOPIC SENTENCE	Of all the disappointing television programming, what I dislike most is melodramatic news.
¶ PLAN	Illustrate the point with two or three melodramatic news stories.

A topic sentence also should be an accurate guide to the rest of the paragraph so that readers expect just what the paragraph delivers.

INACCURATE GUIDE	All types of household emergencies can catch people off guard. [The paragraph covers steps for emergency preparedness — not the variety of emergencies.]
ACCURATE TOPIC SENTENCE	Although an emergency may not be a common event, emergency preparedness should be routine at every home.

¶ PLAN	Explain how a household can prepare for an emergency with a medical kit, a well-stocked pantry, and a communication plan.

Finally, a topic sentence should be limited so you don't mislead or frustrate readers about what the paragraph covers.

MISLEADING	Seven factors have contributed to the increasing obesity of the average American. [The paragraph discusses only one — portion size.]
LIMITED TOPIC SENTENCE	Portion size is a major factor that contributes to the increasing obesity of average Americans.
¶ PLAN	Define healthy portion sizes, contrasting them with the large portions common in restaurants and packaged foods.

Open with a Topic Sentence.   Usually the topic sentence appears first in the paragraph, followed by sentences that clarify, illustrate, and support what it says. It is typically a statement but can sometimes be a question, alerting the reader to the topic without giving away the punchline. The following example comes from "The Virtues of the Quiet Hero," Senator John McCain's essay about "honor, faith, and service," presented on October 17, 2005, as part of the "This I Believe" series on National Public Radio's *All Things Considered*. Here, as in all the following examples, we have put the topic sentence in *italics*.

> *Years later, I saw an example of honor in the most surprising of places.* As a scared American prisoner of war in Vietnam, I was tied in torture ropes by my tormentors and left alone in an empty room to suffer through the night. Later in the evening, a guard I had never spoken to entered the room and silently loosened the ropes to relieve my suffering. Just before morning, that same guard came back and retightened the ropes before his less humanitarian comrades returned. He never said a word to me. Some months later on a Christmas morning, as I stood alone in the prison courtyard, that same guard walked up to me and stood next to me for a few moments. Then with his sandal, the guard drew a cross in the dirt. We stood wordlessly there for a minute or two, venerating the cross, until the guard rubbed it out and walked away.

This paragraph moves from a general statement to specific examples. The topic sentence clearly states at the outset what the paragraph is about. The second sentence introduces the situation that McCain is recalling. Then the next half-dozen sentences supply two concrete, yet concise, illustrations of his central point.

Place a Topic Sentence near the Beginning.   Sometimes the first sentence of a paragraph acts as a transition, linking what is to come with what has gone before. Then the *second* sentence might be the topic sentence. This pattern is illustrated in the following paragraph from "You Wanna Take This

Online?" by Jeff Chu (*Time*, 8 Aug. 2005). The paragraph before this one recounts thirteen-year-old Taylor Hern's discovery of her name on an online "List of Hos" and ends with her question: "'Who would actually make time in their schedule to do something like that?'"

> Turns out, many of her peers would. *Technology has transformed the lives of teens, including the ways they pick on one another.* If parents and teachers think it's hard to control mean girls and bullying boys in school, they haven't reckoned with cyberspace. Cyberbullying can mean anything from posting pejorative items like the List of Hos to spreading rumors by e-mail to harassing by instant message. It was experienced in the preceding two months by 18 percent of 3,700 middle schoolers surveyed by researchers at Clemson University. Their study is scheduled to be presented at this month's American Psychological Association meeting. The phenomenon peaks at about age thirteen; 21 percent of eighth graders surveyed reported being cyberbullied recently. And incidents of online bullying are like roaches: for every one that's reported, many more go unrecorded. "Our statistics are conservative," says Clemson psychologist Robin Kowalski. "Part of the problem is kids not recognizing that what's happening is a form of bullying."

End with a Topic Sentence.   Occasionally a writer, especially one trying to persuade the reader to agree, piles detail on detail. Then, with a dramatic flourish, the writer *concludes* with the topic sentence, as student Heidi Kessler does.

> A fourteen-year-old writes to an advice columnist in my hometown newspaper that she has "done it" lots of times and sex is "no big deal." At the neighborhood clinic where my aunt works, a hardened sixteen-year-old requests her third abortion. A girl-child I know has two children of her own, but no husband. A college student in my dorm now finds herself sterile from a "social disease" picked up during casual sexual encounters. Multiply these examples by thousands. *It seems clear to me that women, who fought so hard for sexual freedom equal to that of men, have emerged from the battle not as joyous free spirits but as the sexual revolution's walking wounded.*

This paragraph moves from the particular to the general — from four examples about individuals to one large statement about American women at the end. By the time you come to the end of the paragraph, you might be ready to accept the conclusion in the topic sentence.

Imply a Topic Sentence.   It is also possible to find a perfectly unified, well-organized paragraph that has no topic sentence at all, like the following from "New York" (*Esquire,* July 1960) by Gay Talese:

> Each afternoon in New York a rather seedy saxophone player, his cheeks blown out like a spinnaker, stands on the sidewalk playing "Danny Boy" in such a sad, sensitive way that he soon has half the neighborhood peeking out of windows tossing nickels, dimes, and quarters at his feet. Some of the

coins roll under parked cars, but most of them are caught in his out-stretched hand. The saxophone player is a street musician named Joe Gabler; for the past thirty years he has serenaded every block in New York and has sometimes been tossed as much as $100 a day in coins. He is also hit with buckets of water, empty beer cans and eggs, and chased by wild dogs. He is believed to be the last of New York's ancient street musicians.

No one sentence neatly sums up the writer's idea. Like most effective paragraphs that do not state a topic sentence, this one contains something just as good — a *topic idea*. The author doesn't allow his paragraph to wander aimlessly. He knows exactly what he wants to achieve — a description of how Joe Gabler, a famous New York street musician, plies his trade. Because Talese keeps this purpose firmly in mind, the main point — that Gabler meets both reward and abuse — is clear to the reader as well.

■ Activity: Shaping Topic Sentences

Discuss each of the following topic sentences with your peer group, answering these questions:

> Will it catch readers' attention?
> Is it accurate?
> Is it limited?
> How might you develop the idea in the rest of the paragraph?
> Can you improve it?

1. Television commercials stereotype people.
2. Living away from home for the first time is hard.
3. It's good for a child to have a pet.
4. A flea market is a good place to buy jewelry.
5. Pollution should be controlled.
6. Everybody should recycle wastes.

Writing an Opening

Even writers with something to say may find it hard to begin. Often they are so intent on writing a brilliant opening that they freeze, unable to write at all. They forget even the essentials — setting up the topic, sticking to what's relevant, and establishing a thesis. If you feel like a deer paralyzed by headlights when you face your first page, try these ways of tackling the opening:

• Start with your thesis statement, with or without a full opening paragraph. Fill in the rest later.

- Write your thesis statement — the one you planned or one you'd now like to develop — in the middle of a page. Go back to the top of the page, and concisely add the background a reader needs to appreciate where you're going.

- Write a long beginning for your first draft; then cut it down to the most dramatic, exciting, or interesting essentials.

- Simply set down words — any words — on paper, without trying to write an arresting opening. Rewrite later.

- Write the first paragraph last, after you know exactly where your essay goes.

- Move your conclusion to the beginning, and write a new ending.

- Write a summary for yourself and your readers.

Your opening paragraph should intrigue readers — engaging their minds and hearts, exciting their curiosity, drawing them away from their preoccupations into the world set forth in your writing. Use this checklist as you hunt for an effective opening that fits your paper. Then read the sample opening paragraphs that follow.

DISCOVERY CHECKLIST

___ What vital background might readers need?
___ What general situation might help you narrow down to your point?
___ What facts or statistics might make your issue compelling?
___ What powerful anecdote or incident might introduce your point?
___ What striking example or comparison would engage a reader?
___ What question will your thesis — and your essay — answer?
___ What lively quotation would set the scene for your essay?
___ What assertion or claim might be the necessary prelude for your essay?
___ What points should you preview to prepare a reader for what will come?
___ What would compel someone to keep on reading?

Begin with a Story.   Often a simple anecdote can capture your readers' interest and thus serve as a good beginning. Here is how Nicholas Kulish opens his essay "Guy Walks into a Bar" (*New York Times*, 5 Feb. 2006):

> Recently my friend Brandon and I walked along Atlantic Avenue in Brooklyn looking for a place to watch a football game and to quench our thirst for a cold brew. I pushed open the door and we were headed for a pair of empty stools when we both stopped cold. The bar was packed with under-age patrons.

Most of us, after an anecdote, want to read on. What will the writer say next? What has the anecdote to do with the essay as a whole? In this case, Kulish's opening anecdote sets the stage for his objections to parents bringing their babies and toddlers to bars.

Comment on a Topic or Position.   Sometimes a writer expands on a topic, bringing in vital details, as David Morris does to open his article "Rootlessness" (*Utne Reader*, May/June 1990):

> Americans are a rootless people. Each year one in six of us changes residences; one in four changes jobs. We see nothing troubling in these statistics. For most of us, they merely reflect the restless energy that made America great. A nation of immigrants, unsurprisingly, celebrates those willing to pick up stakes and move on: the frontiersman, the cowboy, the entrepreneur, the corporate raider.

After stating his point baldly, Morris supplies statistics to support his contention and briefly explains the phenomenon. This same strategy can be used to present a controversial opinion, then back it up with examples.

Ask a Question.   An essay can begin with a question and answer, as James H. Austin begins "Four Kinds of Chance," in *Chase, Chance, and Creativity: The Lucky Art of Novelty* (New York: Columbia UP, 1978):

> What is chance? Dictionaries define it as something fortuitous that happens unpredictably without discernible human intention. Chance is unintentional and capricious, but we needn't conclude that chance is immune from human intervention. Indeed, chance plays several distinct roles when humans react creatively with one another and with their environment.

Beginning to answer the question in the first paragraph leads readers to expect the rest of the essay to continue the answer.

■ For more on thesis statements, see pp. 312–21.

End with the Thesis Statement.   Opening paragraphs often end by stating the essay's main point. After capturing readers' attention with an anecdote, gripping details, or pertinent examples, you lead readers in exactly the direction your essay goes. In his response to the question "Should Washington stem the tide of both legal and illegal immigration?" ("Symposium," *Insight on the News*, 11 Mar., 2002), Daniel T. Griswold uses this strategy to begin his answer:

> Immigration always has been controversial in the United States. More than two centuries ago, Benjamin Franklin worried that too many German immigrants would swamp America's predominantly British culture. In the mid-1800s, Irish immigrants were scorned as lazy drunks, not to mention Roman Catholics. At the turn of the century a wave of "new immigrants" — Poles, Italians, Russian Jews — were believed to be too different ever to assimilate into American life. *Today the same fears are raised about immigrants from Latin America and Asia, but current critics of immigration are as wrong as their counterparts were in previous eras.*

Writing a Conclusion

The final paragraphs of an essay linger longest in readers' minds, as does E. B. White's conclusion to "Once More to the Lake" (p. 463). In the essay, White describes his return with his young son to a vacation spot he had loved as a child. As the essay ends in an unforgettable image, he recalls how old he really is and realizes the inevitable passing of generations.

> When the others went swimming my son said he was going in, too. He pulled his dripping trunks from the line where they had hung all through the shower and wrung them out. Languidly, and with no thought of going in, I watched him, his hard little body, skinny and bare, saw him wince slightly as he pulled up around his vitals the small, soggy, icy garment. As he buckled the swollen belt, suddenly my groin felt the chill of death.

White's classic ending opens with a sentence that points back to the previous paragraph as it also looks ahead. Then White leads us quickly to his final, chilling insight. And then he stops.

It's easy to say what *not* to do at the end of an essay: don't leave your readers half expecting you to go on. Don't restate everything you've already said. Don't introduce a brand-new topic that leads away from your point. And don't signal that the end is near with an obvious phrase like "As I have said."

"How *do* you write an ending, then?" you might well ask. Use this checklist as you tackle your conclusion. Then read the sample concluding paragraphs that follow.

DISCOVERY CHECKLIST

—— What restatement of your thesis would give readers a satisfying sense of closure?

—— What provocative implications of your thesis might answer "What now?" or "What's the significance of what I've said?"

—— What snappy quotation or statement would wrap up your point?

—— What closing facts or statistics might confirm the merit of your point?

—— What final anecdote, incident, or example might round out your ideas?

—— What question has your essay answered?

—— What assertion or claim might you want to restate?

—— What summary might help a reader pull together what you've said?

—— What would make a reader sorry to finish such a satisfying essay?

End with a Quotation.   An apt quotation can neatly round out an essay, as literary critic Malcolm Cowley shows in *The View from Eighty* (New York: Viking, 1980), his discussion of the pitfalls and compensations of old age.

> "Eighty years old!" the great Catholic poet Paul Claudel wrote in his journal. "No eyes left, no ears, no teeth, no legs, no wind! And when all is said and done, how astonishingly well one does without them!"

State or Restate Your Thesis.   In a sharp criticism of American schools, humorist Russell Baker in "School vs. Education" ends by stating his main point, that schools do not educate.

> Afterward, the former student's destiny fulfilled, his life rich with Oriental carpets, rare porcelain, and full bank accounts, he may one day find himself with the leisure and the inclination to open a book with a curious mind, and start to become educated.

End with a Brief Emphatic Sentence.   For an essay that traces causes or effects, evaluates, or argues, a pointed concluding thought can reinforce your main idea. In "Don't Mess with Mother" (*Newsweek*, 19 Sept. 2005), Anna Quindlen ends her essay about the environmental challenges posed by post-Katrina New Orleans this way:

> New Orleans will be rebuilt, but rebuilt how? In the heedless, grasping fashion in which so much of this country has been built over the past fifty years, which has led to a continuous loop of floods, fires and filth in the air and water? Or could the new New Orleans be the first city of a new era, in which the demands of development and commerce are carefully balanced against the good of the land and, in the long run, the good of its people? We have been crummy stewards of the Earth, with a sense of knee-jerk entitlement that tells us there is always more where this came from.
> There isn't.

Stop When the Story Is Over.   Even a quiet ending can be effective, as long as it signals clearly that the essay is finished. Journalist Martin Gansberg simply stops when the story is over in his true account of the fatal stabbing of a young woman, Kitty Genovese, in full view of residents of a Queens, New York, apartment house. The residents, unwilling to become involved, did nothing to interfere. Here is the last paragraph of his account, "Thirty-eight Who Saw Murder Didn't Call Police" (*New York Times*, 17 Mar. 1964):

> It was 4:25 A.M. when the ambulance arrived to take the body of Miss Genovese. It drove off. "Then," a solemn police detective said, "the people came out."

■ For more exercises on openings and conclusions, visit <bedfordstmartins.com/bedguide> and do a keyword search:

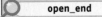 open_end

■ Activity: Opening and Concluding

Openings and conclusions frame an essay, contributing to the unity of the whole. The opening sets up the topic and main idea; the conclusion reaffirms the thesis and rounds off the ideas. Discuss the following with your classmates.

1.   Here are two possible opening paragraphs from a student essay on the importance of teaching children how to swim.

   A. Humans inhabit a world made up of over 70 percent water. In addition to these great bodies of water, we have built millions of swimming pools for sports and leisure activities. At one time or another most people will be faced with either the danger of drowning or the challenge of aquatic recreation. For these reasons, it is essential that we learn to swim. Being a competitive swimmer and a swimming instructor, I fully realize the importance of knowing how to swim.

B. Four-year-old Carl, curious like most children, last spring ventured out onto his pool patio. He fell into the pool and, not knowing how to swim, helplessly sank to the bottom. Minutes later his uncle found the child and brought him to the surface. Because Carl had no pulse, his uncle administered CPR until the paramedics arrived. Eventually the child was revived. During his stay in the hospital, his mother signed him up for beginning swimming classes. Carl was a lucky one. Unlike thousands of other children and adults, he got a second chance.

1. Which introduction is more effective? Why?
2. What would the body of this essay consist of? What kinds of evidence would be included?
3. Write a suitable conclusion for this essay.

2. If you were to read each of the following introductions from professional essays, would you want to read the entire essay? Why?

A. During my ninth hour underground, as I scrambled up a slanting tunnel through the powdered gypsum, Rick Bridges turned to me and said, "You know, this whole area was just discovered Tuesday." (David Roberts, "Caving Comes into Its Golden Age: A New Mexico Marvel," *Smithsonian* Nov. 1988: 52)

B. From the batting average on the back of a George Brett baseball card to the interest rate fluctuations that determine whether the economy grows or stagnates, Americans are fascinated by statistics. (Stephen E. Nordlinger, "By the Numbers," *St. Petersburg Times* 6 Nov. 1988: 11)

C. "What does it look like under there?"

It was always this question back then, always the same pattern of hello and what's your name, what happened to your eye and what's under there. (Natalie Kusz, "Waiting for a Glass Eye," *Road Song* [New York: Farrar, 1990], rpt. in *Harper's* Nov. 1990)

3. How effective are these introductions and conclusions from student essays? Could they be improved? If so, how? If they are satisfactory, explain why. What would be a catchy yet informative title for each essay?

A. Recently a friend down from New York astonished me with stories of several people infected — some with AIDS — by stepping on needles washed up on the New Jersey beaches. This is just one incident of pollution, a devastating problem in our society today. Pollution is increasing in our world because of greed, apathy, and Congress's inability to control this problem. . . .

Wouldn't it be nice to have a pollution-free world without medical wastes floating in the water and washing up on our beaches? Without cars and power plants spewing greenhouse gases? With every corporation abiding by the laws set by Congress? In the future we can have a pollution-free world, but it is going to take the cooperation of everyone, including Congress, to ensure our survival on this Planet Earth.

B. The divorce rate has risen 700 percent in this century and continues to rise. More than one out of every two couples who are married end up divorcing. Over one million children a year are affected by divorce in the family. From these statistics it is clear that one of the greatest problems concerning the family today is divorce and the adverse effects it has on our society. . . .

Divorce causes problems that change people for life. The number of divorces will continue to exceed the 700 percent figure unless married couples learn to communicate, to accept their mates unconditionally, and to sacrificially give of themselves.

4. Choose one of the topics that you generated in Chapter 16, and write at least three different introductions with conclusions. Ask your classmates which is the most effective.

Achieving Coherence

Effective writing proceeds in some sensible order, each sentence following naturally from the one before it. Yet even well-organized prose can be hard to read unless it is *coherent* and effectively integrates its elements. To make your writing coherent, you can use various devices to tie together words in a sentence, sentences in a paragraph, paragraphs in an essay.

Add Transitional Words and Sentences.   You use transitions every day to help your readers and listeners follow your train of thought. For example, you might say to a friend, "Well, *on the one hand,* a second job would help me save money for tuition. *On the other hand,* I'd have less time to study." But some writers rush through, omitting links between thoughts or mistakenly assuming that connections they see will automatically be clear to readers. Often just a word, phrase, or sentence of transition inserted in the right place will transform a disconnected passage into a coherent one.

Many words and phrases specify connections between or within sentences. In the chart on page 347, *transitional markers* are grouped by purpose or the kind of relation or connection they establish.

Occasionally a whole sentence serves as a transition. For example, the first sentence of a new paragraph may hark back to the previous paragraph while simultaneously revealing a new or narrower direction. The following excerpt comes from "Preservation Basics: Why Preserve Film," a page on the Web site of the National Film Preservation Foundation (NFPF) at <http://www.filmpreservation.org/sm_index.html>. The first paragraph introduces the organization's mission; the next two each open with transitional sentences that introduce major challenges to that mission. We have italicized the transitional sentences.

Since Thomas Edison's invention of the kinetoscope in 1893, Americans have traveled the world using motion pictures to tell stories, document traditions, and capture current events. Their work stands as the collective memory of the first century witnessed by the moving image. By saving and sharing these motion pictures, we can illuminate our common heritage with a power and immediacy unique to film.

COMMON TRANSITIONS	
TO MARK TIME	then, soon, first, second, next, recently, the following day, in a little while, meanwhile, after, later, in the past, finally
TO MARK PLACE OR DIRECTION	in the distance, close by, near, far away, above, below, to the right, on the other side, opposite, to the west, next door
TO SUMMARIZE OR RESTATE	in other words, to put it another way, in brief, in simpler terms, on the whole, in fact, in a word, to sum up, in short, in conclusion, to conclude, therefore
TO RELATE CAUSE AND EFFECT OR RESULT	therefore, accordingly, hence, thus, for, so, consequently, as a result, because of, due to, eventually, inevitably
TO ADD OR AMPLIFY OR LIST	and, also, too, besides, as well, moreover, in addition, furthermore, in effect, second, in the second place, again, next
TO COMPARE	similarly, likewise, in like manner, in the same way
TO CONCEDE	whereas, on the other hand, with that in mind, still, and yet, even so, in spite of, despite, at least, of course, no doubt, even though
TO CONTRAST	on the other hand, but, or, however, unlike, nevertheless, on the contrary, conversely, in contrast, instead, counter to
TO INDICATE PURPOSE	to this end, for this purpose, with this aim
TO EXPRESS CONDITION	although, though
TO GIVE EXAMPLES OR SPECIFY	for example, for instance, in this case, in particular, to illustrate
TO QUALIFY	for the most part, by and large, with few exceptions, mainly, in most cases, generally, some, sometimes, typically, frequently, rarely
TO EMPHASIZE	it is true, truly, indeed, of course, to be sure, obviously, without doubt, evidently, clearly, understandably

    Preservationists are working against the clock. Made on perishable plastic, film decays within years if not properly stored.

    Already the losses are high. The Library of Congress has documented that fewer than 20 percent of U.S. feature films from the 1920s survive in complete form in American archives; of the American features produced before 1950, only half still exist. For shorts, documentaries, and independently produced works, we have no way of knowing how much has been lost.

The first paragraph establishes the value of "saving and sharing" the American film legacy. The next two paragraphs use key words related to preservation and its absence (*perishable, decays, losses, lost*) to clarify that what follows builds on what has gone before. Each also opens with a short, dramatic transition to one of the major problems: time and existing loss.

Supply Transition Paragraphs.   Transitions may be even longer than sentences. In a long and complicated essay, moving clearly from one idea to the next will sometimes require a short paragraph of transition.

> So far, the physical and psychological effects of driving nonstop for hundreds of miles seem clear. The next consideration is why drivers do this. What causes people to become addicted to their steering wheels?

Use a transition paragraph only when you sense that your readers might get lost if you don't patiently lead them by the hand. If your essay is short, one question or statement beginning a new paragraph will be enough.

Besides guiding readers through the structure of your essay, a transition paragraph can aid your movement between one branch of argument and your main trunk or between a digression and your main direction. In this excerpt from *The Film Preservation Guide: The Basics for Archives, Libraries, and Museums* (San Francisco: NFPF, 2004; <http://www.filmpreservation.org/preservation/fpg.pdf>), the writer introduces the importance of inspecting a film and then devotes the next paragraph to a digression — referring readers to an inspection sheet in the appendix.

> Inspection is the single most important way to date a film, identify its technical characteristics, and detect damage and decay. Much can be learned by examining your film carefully, from start to finish.
>
> A standardized inspection work sheet (see appendix B) lists things to check and helps organize notes. This type of written report is the foundation for future preservation actions. Collecting the information during inspection will help you make informed decisions and enable you to document any changes in film condition over time.
>
> Signs of decay and damage may vary across the length of the film. . . .

The second paragraph acts as a transition, guiding readers to specialized information in the appendix and drawing readers back to the overall purpose of inspection, assessing the extent of damage to a film. Then the passage continues with the main point: how to learn about a film through an inspection.

Select Repetition.   Another way to clarify the relationship between two sentences, paragraphs, or ideas is to repeat a key word or phrase. Such purposeful repetition almost guarantees that readers will understand how all the parts of a passage fit together. Note the repetition of the word *anger* in the following paragraph (italics ours) from *Of Woman Born* (New York: Norton, 1976) by poet Adrienne Rich. In this complex paragraph, the writer explores her relationship with her mother. The repetition holds all the parts together and makes clear the unity and coherence of the paragraph's ideas.

And I know there must be deep reservoirs of *anger* in her; every mother has known overwhelming, unacceptable *anger* at her children. When I think of the conditions under which my mother became a mother, the impossible expectations, my father's distaste for pregnant women, his hatred of all that he could not control, my *anger* at her dissolves into grief and *anger* for her, and then dissolves back again into *anger* at her: the ancient, unpurged *anger* of the child.

Strengthen Pronouns.   Because they always refer back to nouns or other pronouns, pronouns serve as transitions by making readers refer back as well. Note how certain pronouns (in italics) hold together the following paragraph from "Misunderstood Michelle" by columnist Ellen Goodman in *At Large* (New York: Summit Books, 1981):

> I have two friends who moved in together many years ago. *He* looked upon this step as a trial marriage. *She* looked upon it as, well, moving in together. *He* was sure that in a matter of time, after *they* had built up trust and confidence, *she* would agree that marriage was the next logical step. *She,* on the other hand, was thrilled that here at last was a man *who* would never push *her* back to the altar.

The paragraph contains other transitions, too: time markers like *many years ago, in a matter of time,* and *after; on the other hand,* which indicates a contrast; and repetition of words related to marriage like *trial marriage, marriage,* and *the altar.* All serve the main purpose of transitions — keeping readers on track.

■ **Activity:** Identifying Transitions

Go over one of the papers you have already written for this course, and circle all the transitional devices you can detect. Then share your paper with a classmate. Can the classmate find additional transitions? Does the classmate think you need transitions where you don't have any?

■ For more exercises on transitions, visit <bedfordstmartins.com/bedguide> and do a keyword search:

coherence

Chapter 19
Strategies for Developing

■ For examples of development strategies, visit <bedfordstmartins.com/bedguide> and do a keyword search:

development

How can you spice up your general ideas with the stuff of real life? How can you tug your readers deeper and deeper into your essays until they say, "I see just what you mean"? Well-developed essays have such power because they back up general points with evidence that comes alive for readers. In this chapter we cover nine indispensable methods of development—giving examples, providing details, defining, reasoning inductively and deductively, analyzing a subject, analyzing a process, dividing and classifying, comparing and contrasting, and showing causes and effects. Although you may choose to use only one method within a single paragraph, a strong essay almost always requires a combination of developmental strategies.

Whenever you develop a piece of writing or return to it to revise, you face a challenge: How do you figure out what to do? Sometimes you may suspect that you've wandered into the Writer's Grill, a local hang-out offering a huge buffet lunch. You watch others load their plates, but you still hesitate. Which foods will taste best? Which will be healthy choices? Which will make your meal a relaxing experience? How much will fit on your plate? For you as a writer, the answers to such questions are all individual. They depend on your situation, the clarity of your main idea or thesis, and the state of your draft, as the following checklist suggests.

DISCOVERY CHECKLIST

Purpose

___ Does your assignment recommend or require specific methods of development?

___ Which methods might be most useful to explain, inform, or persuade?

___ What type of development might best achieve your specific purpose?

Audience

___ Which developmental strategies would best clarify your topic for readers?

___ Which would best demonstrate your thesis to your readers?

___ What kinds of evidence will your specific readers prefer? Which strategies might develop this evidence most effectively?

Thesis

___ What development does your thesis promise or imply that you will supply?

___ What sequence of developmental strategies would best support your thesis?

Essay Development

___ Has a reader or peer editor pointed out any ideas in your draft that need fuller or more effective development?

___ Where might your readers have trouble following or understanding without more or better development?

Paragraph Development

___ Should any paragraphs with one or two sentences be developed more fully?

___ Should any long paragraphs with generalizations, repetition, and wordy phrasing be developed differently so that they are richer and deeper?

Giving Examples

An example — the word comes from the Latin *exemplum*, "one thing chosen from among many" — is a typical instance that illustrates a whole type or kind. Giving examples to support a generalization is probably the most often used means of development. This example, from *In Search of Excellence* (New York: Harper and Row, 1982) by Thomas J. Peters and Robert H. Waterman Jr., explains the success of America's top corporations:

> Although he's not a company, our favorite illustration of closeness to the customer is car salesman Joe Girard. He sold more new cars and trucks, each year, for eleven years running, than any other human being. In fact, in a typical year, Joe sold more than twice as many units as whoever was in second place. In explaining his secret of success, Joe said: "I sent out over thirteen thousand cards every month."
>
> Why start with Joe? Because his magic is the magic of IBM and many of the rest of the excellent companies. It is simply service, overpowering service, especially after-sales service. Joe noted, "There's one thing that I do that a lot of salesmen don't, and that's believe the sale really begins *after* the sale — not before. . . . The customer ain't out the door, and my son has made up a thank-you note." Joe would intercede personally, a year later, with the service manager on behalf of his customer. Meanwhile he would keep the communications flowing.

Notice how Peters and Waterman focus on the specific, Joe Girard. They don't write *corporation employees* or even *car salespeople*. Instead, they zero in on one particular man to make the point come alive.

Joe Girard	Level 4: Specific Example
car salespeople	Level 3: Even More Specific Group
corporation employees	Level 2: More Specific Group
America's top corporations	Level 1: General Group or Category

This ladder of abstraction moves from the general — America's top corporations — to a specific person — Joe Girard. The specific example of Joe Girard makes closeness to the customer *concrete* to readers: he is someone readers can relate to. To check the level of specificity in a paragraph or an outline, draw a ladder of abstraction for it. Do the same to restrict a broad subject to a topic manageable in a short essay. If you haven't climbed to the fourth or fifth level, you are probably being too general and need to add specifics.

An example doesn't always have to be a specific individual. Sometimes you can create a picture of something readers have never encountered or give an abstraction a recognizable personality and identity. Using this strategy, Jonathan Kozol makes real the plight of illiterate people in our health-care system in this paragraph from *Prisoners of Silence: Breaking the Bonds of Adult Illiteracy in the United States* (New York: Continuum, 1980):

> Illiterates live, in more than literal ways, an uninsured existence. They cannot understand the written details on a health insurance form. They cannot read waivers that they sign preceding surgical procedures. Several women I have known in Boston have entered a slum hospital with the intention of obtaining a tubal ligation and have emerged a few days later after having been subjected to a hysterectomy. Unaware of their rights, incognizant of jargon, intimidated by the unfamiliar air of fear and atmosphere of ether that so many of us find oppressive in the confines even of the most attractive and expensive medical facilities, they have signed their names to documents they could not read and which nobody, in the hectic situation that prevails so often in those overcrowded hospitals that serve the urban poor, had ever bothered to explain.

Examples aren't trivial doodads you add to a paragraph for decoration; they are what holds your readers' attention and shows them that your writing makes sense. By using examples, you make your ideas more concrete and tangible. To give plenty of examples is one of the writer's chief tasks. When you need more, you can generate them at any point in the writing process. Begin with your own experience, even with a topic about which you know little, or try conversing with others, reading, digging in the library, or browsing on the Web.

For ways to generate ideas, see Ch. 16.

Consider these questions when you use examples in your writing:

DISCOVERY CHECKLIST

___ Are your examples relevant to your main idea or thesis?

___ Are your examples the best ones you can think of? Will readers find them strong and appropriate?

___ Are your examples really specific? Or do they just repeat generalities?

___ From each paragraph, can you draw a ladder of abstraction to at least the fourth level?

■ Activity: Giving Examples

To help you get in the habit of thinking specifically, fill in a ladder of abstraction for five of the following general subjects. Then share your ladders with classmates, and compare and contrast your specifics with theirs.

Examples:

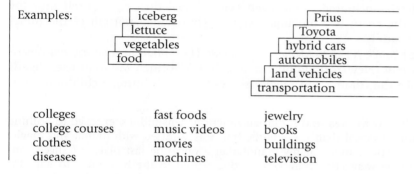

colleges	fast foods	jewelry
college courses	music videos	books
clothes	movies	buildings
diseases	machines	television

Providing Details

A *detail* is any specific, concrete piece of information—a fact, a bit of the historical record, your own observation. Details make scenes and images more realistic and vivid for readers. They also back up generalizations, convincing readers that the writer can make broad assertions with authority.

Mary Harris "Mother" Jones told the story of her life as a labor organizer in *The Autobiography of Mother Jones* (1925; Chicago: Kerr, 1980). She lends conviction to her general statement about a coal miner's lot at the end of the nineteenth century with ample evidence from her own experience and observations.

> Mining at its best is wretched work, and the life and surroundings of the miner are hard and ugly. His work is down in the black depths of the earth. He works alone in a drift. There can be little friendly companionship as there is in the factory; as there is among men who build bridges and houses, working together in groups. The work is dirty. Coal dust grinds itself into the skin, never to be removed. The miner must stoop as he works in the drift. He becomes bent like a gnome.

His work is utterly fatiguing. Muscles and bones ache. His lungs breathe coal dust and the strange, damp air of places that are never filled with sunlight. His house is a poor makeshift and there is little to encourage him to make it attractive. The company owns the ground it stands on, and the miner feels the precariousness of his hold. Around his house is mud and slush. Great mounds of culm [the refuse left after coal is screened], black and sullen, surround him. His children are perpetually grimy from playing on the culm mounds. The wife struggles with dirt, with inadequate water supply, with small wages, with overcrowded shacks.

Although Mother Jones, not a learned writer, relies on short, simple sentences, her writing is clear and powerful because of the specific details she uses. Her opening makes two general statements: (1) "Mining . . . is wretched work," and (2) the miner's "life and surroundings" are "hard and ugly." She supports these generalizations with a barrage of factual evidence and detail, including well-chosen verbs: "Coal dust *grinds* itself into the skin." The result is a moving, convincingly detailed portrait of the miner and his family.

In *Lipstick Jihad: A Memoir of Growing Up Iranian in America and American in Iran* (New York: Public Affairs, 2005), Azadeh Moaveni uses details to evoke the "drama and magic" she experienced during a childhood visit to Iran.

To my five-year-old suburban American sensibilities, exposed to nothing more mystical than the Smurfs, Iran was suffused with drama and magic. After Friday lunch at my grandfather's, once the last plates of sliced cantaloupe were cleared away, everyone retired to the bedrooms to nap. Inevitably there was a willing aunt or cousin on hand to scratch my back as I fell asleep. Unused to the siesta ritual, I woke up after half an hour to find the bed I was sharing with my cousin swathed in a tower of creamy gauze that stretched high up to the ceiling. "Wake up," I nudged him, "we're surrounded!" "It's for the mosquitoes, khareh, ass, go back to sleep." To me it was like a fairy tale, and I peered through the netting to the living room, to the table heaped with plump dates and the dense, aromatic baklava we would nibble on later with tea. The day before I had helped my grandmother, Razi joon, make ash-e gooshvareh, "earring stew"; we made hoops out of the fresh pasta, and dropped them into the vat of simmering herbs and lamb. Here even the ordinary had charm, even the names of stews.

■ For more on transitions, see pp. 346–49.

To guide readers through her details, Moaveni uses transitions — chronological (*After Friday lunch, after half an hour, The day before*), spatial (*through the netting to the living room*), and thematic (*To me it was like a fairy tale*).

Quite different from Moaveni's personal, descriptive details are Guy Garcia's objective facts in "Influencing America" (*Time*, 13 Aug. 2005). Garcia heaps up statistical details to substantiate his claim that Hispanics are "helping to define" mainstream America even though they face "prejudice and enormous social and economic hurdles."

Nearly a quarter of all Latinos live in poverty; the high school drop out rate for Latino youths between the ages of sixteen and nineteen is 21 percent — more than triple that of non-Hispanic whites. Neo-nativists like Pat Buchanan and Samuel Huntington still argue that the "tsunami" of non–English speakers from Latin America will destroy everything that America stands for. Never mind that most Hispanics are religious, family-centric, enterprising, and patriotic. In the *Time* poll, 72 percent said they considered moral issues such as abortion and issues of faith important or very important. This year the government announced that undocumented workers were pouring billions into Social Security and Medicare for benefits that they would never be allowed to claim. Of the 27,000 troops serving in the U.S. armed forces who are not U.S. citizens, a large percentage are from Mexico and the rest of Latin America.

Providing details is one of the simplest yet most effective ways of developing ideas. All it takes on your part is close attention and precise wording to communicate details to readers. If readers were on the scene, what would they see, hear, smell, or feel? Which small details from your reading are most meaningful to you? Would a bit of research turn up just the right fact or statistic? Remember that effective details have a specific purpose: they must help make your images more evocative or your point more convincing. Every detail should support — in some way — your main idea.

■ For more on observing a scene, see Ch. 5.

Here are some questions to consider when you use details:

DISCOVERY CHECKLIST

____ Do all your details support your point of view, main idea, or thesis?

____ Do you have details of sights? Sounds? Tastes? Touch? Smells?

____ Have you included enough details to make your writing clear and interesting?

____ Have you arranged your details in an order that is easy to follow?

■ Activity: Providing Details

To practice using specific details, brainstorm with classmates or alone on one of the following subjects. Include details that appeal to all five senses. Group the details in your list (see pp. 322–24), and write a paragraph or two using your specific details. Begin by stating a main idea that conveys an engaging impression of your subject (not "My grandmother's house was in Topeka, Kansas" but "My grandmother's house was my childhood haven").

■ For more on brainstorming, see pp. 296–98.

■ For more exercises on supporting details, visit <bedfordstmartins.com/bedguide> and do a keyword search:

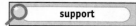

🔍　　　**support**

the things in my room	a memorable event	my job
my grandmother's home	an unusual person	a classroom
a haunted house	my favorite pet	the cafeteria
my old car	a hospital room	an incident

Defining

Define, from the Latin, means "to set bounds to." You define a thing, a word, or a concept by describing it so that it is distinguished from all similar things. If people don't agree on the meaning of a word or an idea, they can't share knowledge about it. Scientists in particular take special care to define their terms precisely. In his article "A Chemist's Definition of pH" from *The Condensed Chemical Dictionary* (New York: Reinhold, 1981), Gessner G. Hawley begins with a brief definition:

> pH is a value taken to represent the acidity or alkalinity of an aqueous solution; it is defined as the logarithm of the reciprocal of the hydrogen-ion concentration of a solution:
>
> $$pH = 1n \ \frac{1}{[H^+]}$$

If you use a word in a special sense or invent a word, you have to explain it or your readers will be lost. In "The Futile Pursuit of Happiness" (*New York Times,* 7 Sept. 2003), Jon Gertner reports on "affective forecasting," an intriguing area of study by economists and psychologists such as Professors Daniel Gilbert of Harvard and Tim Wilson of the University of Virginia. These researchers are exploring what people expect will bring them happiness and how their expectations pan out. Not surprisingly, this new area of study has generated new terms, as the following paragraph explains.

> Gilbert and his collaborator Tim Wilson call the gap between what we predict and what we ultimately experience the *impact bias* — *impact* meaning the errors we make in estimating both the intensity and duration of our emotions and *bias* our tendency to err. The phrase characterizes how we experience the dimming excitement over not just a BMW but also over any object or event that we presume will make us happy. Would a 20 percent raise or winning the lottery result in a contented life? You may predict it will, but almost surely it won't turn out that way. And a new plasma television? You may have high hopes, but the impact bias suggests that it will almost certainly be less cool, and in a shorter time, than you imagine. Worse, Gilbert has noted that these mistakes of expectation can lead directly to mistakes in choosing what we think will give us pleasure. He calls this *miswanting.*

Sometimes you will define an unfamiliar word to save your readers a trip to the dictionary or a familiar but often misunderstood concept to clarify the meaning you intend. For example, what would you mean by *guerilla, liberal,* or *minimum wage*? The more complex or ambiguous an idea, a thing, a movement, a phenomenon, or an organization, the longer the definition you will need to clarify the term for your readers.

Here are some questions to consider when you use definitions:

—— Have you used definitions to help your readers understand the subject matter, not to show off your knowledge?

—— Have you tailored your definition to the needs of your audience?

—— Is your definition specific, clear, and accurate?

—— Would your definition benefit from an example or from details?

■ Activity: Defining

Write an extended definition (a paragraph or so) of one of the following words. Begin with a one-sentence definition of the word. Then, instead of getting most of your definition from a dictionary or textbook, expand and clarify your ideas using some of the strategies in this chapter — examples, details, induction or deduction, analysis (subject, process, causal), division, classification, comparison, contrast. You may also use *negation* (explaining what something is by stating what it is not). Share your definition with your classmates.

education	abuse	exercise	literacy
privacy	jazz	dieting	success
taboo	hip-hop	gossip	fear
prejudice	flu	security	gender

Reasoning Inductively and Deductively

As you develop a typical paragraph in a paper, you are likely to rely on both generalizations and particulars. A *generalization* is a broad statement that establishes the point you want to make, the viewpoint you hold, or the conclusion you have reached. A *particular* is an instance, a detail, or an example — some specific that supplies evidence that a general statement is reasonable. Your particulars support your generalizations; by presenting compelling instances, details, and examples, you back up your broader point. At the same time, your generalizations pull together your particulars, identifying patterns or connections that relate individual cases.

To relate particulars and generalizations, you can use an inductive or deductive process. An *inductive process* begins with the particulars — a convincing number of instances, examples, tests, or experiments. Taken together, these particulars substantiate a larger generalization. In this way a number of long-term studies of weight loss can eventually lead to a consensus about the benefits of walking, eating vegetables, or some other variable. Less formal inductive reasoning is common as people *infer* or conclude that particulars do or do not support a generalization. For example, if your sister ate strawberries three times and got a rash each time, she might infer that she is allergic to strawberries. Induction breaks down when the particulars are too weak or too few to support a generalization: for example, not enough weight-loss studies have

For more on reasoning, see Chs. 3 and 9.

For more on the statement-support pattern, see A3 in the Quick Research Guide (the dark-red-edged pages).

For more on induction and deduction, see Ch. 3.

comparable results or not enough clear instances occur when strawberries—
and nothing else—trigger a reaction.

A *deductive process* begins with a generalization and applies it to another
case. When your sister says no to a piece of strawberry pie, she does so because,
based on her assumptions, she *deduces* that it, too, will trigger a rash. Deduction breaks down when the initial generalization is flawed or when a particular
case doesn't fit the generalization. For instance, suppose that each time your
sister ate strawberries she drizzled them with lemon juice, the real culprit. Or
suppose that the various weight-loss studies defined low-fat food so differently
that no one could determine how their findings might be related.

Once you have reached your conclusions as a writer—either by using
particulars to support generalizations or by applying reliable generalizations
to other particulars—you still need to decide how to present your reasoning
to your readers. Do you want your readers to follow your own process, perhaps examining numerous cases before reaching a conclusion about them?
Or do you want them to learn what you've concluded first and then review
the evidence? Because academic audiences tend to expect conclusions first,
many writers begin essays with thesis statements and paragraphs with topic
sentences. On the other hand, if your readers are likely to reject an unexpected thesis initially, you may need to show them the evidence first and
then lead them gently but purposefully to your point.

In "The Good Heart" (*Newsweek*, 3 Oct. 2005), Anne Underwood opens
with a paragraph organized inductively: she describes a particular situation
that has helped substantiate the broad, even surprising, generalization with
which she concludes the paragraph.

> You can call it the Northridge Effect, after the powerful earthquake that
> struck near Los Angeles at 4:30 on a January morning in 1994. Within an
> hour, and for the rest of the day, medics responding to people crushed or
> trapped inside buildings faced a second wave of deaths from heart attacks
> among people who had survived the tremor unscathed. In the months that
> followed, researchers at two universities examined coroners' records from
> Los Angeles County and found an astonishing jump in cardiovascular
> deaths, from 15.6 on an average day to 51 on the day of the quake itself.
> Most of these people turned out to have a history of coronary disease or risk
> factors such as high blood pressure. But those who died were not involved
> in rescue efforts or trying to dig themselves out of the rubble. Why did they
> die? In the understated language of the *New England Journal of Medicine*,
> "emotional stress may precipitate cardiac events in people who are predis-
> posed to such events." To put it simply, they were scared to death.

Underwood goes on to review the impact on heart attack patients of various factors such as anxiety, depression, and childhood trauma. Then, in the following
passage, she first states and supports a generalization about the effects of common stresses in adult life, citing the results of an inductive study. In the second
paragraph, she deductively applies the generalization to a particular case.

> And if stress in childhood can lead to heart disease, what about current
> stressors—longer work hours, threats of layoffs, collapsing pension funds?

A study last year in the *Lancet* examined more than 11,000 heart-attack sufferers from 52 countries and found that in the year before their heart attacks, patients had been under significantly more strains — from work, family, financial troubles, depression, and other causes — than some 13,000 healthy control subjects. "Each of these factors individually was associated with increased risk," says Dr. Salim Yusuf, professor of medicine at Canada's McMaster University and senior investigator on the study. "Together, they accounted for 30 percent of overall heart-attack risk." But people respond differently to high-pressure work situations. The key to whether it produces a coronary seems to be whether you have a sense of control over life, or live at the mercy of circumstances and superiors.

That was the experience of John O'Connell, a Rockford, Illinois, laboratory manager who suffered his first heart attack in 1996, at the age of 56. In the two years before, his mother and two of his children had suffered serious illnesses, and his job had been changed in a reorganization. "My life seemed completely out of control," he says. "I had no idea where I would end up." He ended up on a gurney with a clot blocking his left anterior descending artery — the classic "widowmaker." Two months later he had triple bypass surgery. A second heart attack when he was 58 left his cardiologist shaking his head. There's nothing more we can do for you, doctors told him.

Use these questions to help you present your reasoning clearly and persuasively:

DISCOVERY CHECKLIST

___ Do your generalizations follow logically from your particulars? Can you substantiate what and how much you claim?

___ Are your particulars typical, numerous, and relevant enough to support your generalizations? Are your particulars substantial enough to warrant the conclusion you have drawn?

___ Are both your generalizations and your particulars presented clearly? Have you identified your assumptions for your readers?

___ How do you expect your reasoning patterns to affect your readers? What are your reasons for opening with generalizations or reserving them until the end of a paragraph or passage?

___ Is your reasoning in an explanatory paper clear and logical? Is your reasoning in an argumentative paper rigorous enough to withstand the scrutiny of readers? Have you avoided generalizing too broadly or illogically connecting generalizations and particulars?

■ Activity: Reasoning Inductively and Deductively

Look through a recent magazine for an article that explores a health, an environmental, or an economic issue. Read the article, looking for paragraphs organized inductively and deductively. Why do you think the writer chose one pattern or the other in the various sections of the article? How well do those patterns work from a reader's point of view?

Analyzing a Subject

When you *analyze* a subject, you divide it into its parts and then examine one part at a time. If you have taken any chemistry, you probably analyzed water: you separated it into hydrogen and oxygen, its two elements. You've heard many a commentator or blogger analyze the news, telling us what made up an event—who participated, where it occurred, what happened. Analyzing a news event may produce results less certain and clear-cut than analyzing a chemical compound, but the principle is similar—to take something apart for the purpose of understanding it better.

For more on division and classification, see pp. 364–66. For more on process analysis, see pp. 362–64. For more on cause and effect, see pp. 369–70.

Analysis helps readers grasp something complex: they can more readily take in the subject in a series of bites than in one gulp. For this reason, college textbooks do a lot of analyzing: an economics book divides a labor union into its component parts, an anatomy text divides the hand into its bones, muscles, and ligaments. In your college papers, you might analyze and explain to readers anything from a contemporary subculture (What social groups make up the homeless population of Los Angeles?) to an ecosystem (What animals, plants, and minerals coexist in a rain forest?). Analysis is so useful that you can apply it in many situations: breaking down the components of a subject to classify them, separating the stages in a process to see how it works, or identifying the possible results of an event to project consequences.

In *Cultural Anthropology: A Perspective on the Human Condition* (St. Paul: West, 1987), Emily A. Schultz and Robert H. Lavenda briefly but effectively demonstrate by analysis how a metaphor like "the Lord is my shepherd" makes a difficult concept ("the Lord") easy to understand.

> The first part of a metaphor, the metaphorical subject, indicates the domain of experience that needs to be clarified (e.g., "the Lord"). The second part of a metaphor, the metaphorical predicate, suggests a domain of experience which is familiar (e.g., sheep-herding) and which may help us understand what "the Lord" is all about.

In much the same way, Lillian Tsu, a government major at Cornell University, uses analysis in her essay "A Woman in the White House" to identify major difficulties faced by female politicians in the United States.

Although traditionally paternalistic societies like the Philippines and Pakistan and socially conservative states like Great Britain have elected female leaders, particular characteristics of the United States' own electoral system have complicated efforts to elect a female president. Despite social modernization and the progress of the women's movement, the voters of the United States have lagged far behind those of other nations in their willingness to trust in the leadership of a female executive. While the women's movement succeeded in changing Americans' attitudes as to what roles are socially acceptable for women, female candidates have faced a more difficult task in U.S. elections than their male counterparts have. Three factors have been responsible for this situation--political socialization, lack of experience, and open discrimination.

Next, Tsu treats these three factors in turn, beginning each section with a transition that emphasizes the difficulties faced: "One obstacle," "A second obstacle," "A third obstacle." The opening list and the transitions direct readers through a complicated essay, moving from the explanation of the three factors to the final section on implications.

When you plan an analysis, you might label slices in a pielike circle or arrange subdivisions in a list running from smallest to largest or from least to most important. Make sure that your analysis has a purpose—that it will demonstrate something about your subject or tell your readers something they didn't know before. For example, to show the ethnic composition of New York City, you might divide the city geographically into neighborhoods—Harlem, Spanish Harlem, Yorkville, Chinatown, Little Italy. To explain New York's social classes, however, you might start with homeless people and work up to the wealthy elite. The way you slice your subject into pieces will depend in part on the point you want to make about it—and the point you end up making will depend in part on how you've sliced it up. As you develop your ideas, you may also find that you have a stronger point to make—that New York City's social hierarchy is oppressive and unstable, for example.

How can you help your readers follow your analysis? Some writers begin by identifying the subdivisions into which they are going to slice their subject ("The federal government has three branches"). If you name or label each part you mention, define the terms you use, and clarify with examples, you will also help distinguish each part from the others. Finally, using transitions, leading readers from one part to the next, helps make your essay readable.

For more on transitions, see pp. 346–49.

Here are some questions to consider when you use analysis:

DISCOVERY CHECKLIST

____ Exactly what will you try to achieve in your analysis?
____ How does your analysis support your main idea or thesis?
____ How will you break your subject into parts?
____ How can you make each part clear to your readers?
____ What definitions, details, and examples would help clarify each part?
____ What transitions would clarify your movement from part to part?

■ Activity: Analyzing a Subject

Analyze one of the following subjects by making a list of its basic parts or elements. Then use your list as the basis for a paragraph or short essay explaining each part. Be sure to identify the purpose or point of your analysis. Compare your analysis with those of others in your class who chose the same subject.

a college	a choir, orchestra, or other musical group
a news source	a computer or other technological device
a reality TV show	a basketball, baseball, hockey, or other team
effective teaching	a family
a healthy lifestyle	leadership, heroism, or service

Analyzing a Process

Analyzing a process means telling step by step how something is, was, or could be done. You can analyze an action or a phenomenon — how a skyscraper is built, how a revolution begins, how sunspots form, how to make chili. This strategy can also explain large, long-ago events that a writer couldn't possibly have witnessed or complex technical processes that a writer couldn't personally duplicate. Here, for instance, is a paragraph from "The Case for Cloning" (*Time* 9 Feb. 1998) in which Madeleine Nash describes the process of cloning cells. Her *informative* process analysis sets forth how something happens.

> Cloning individual human cells . . . is another matter. Biologists are already talking about harnessing for medical purposes the technique that produced the sheep called Dolly. They might, for example, obtain healthy cells from a patient with leukemia or a burn victim and then transfer the nucleus of each cell into an unfertilized egg from which the nucleus has been removed. Coddled in culture dishes, these embryonic clones — each genetically identical to the patient from which the nuclei came — would begin to divide. The cells would not have to grow into a fetus, however. The addition of powerful growth factors could ensure that the clones develop only into specialized cells and tissue. For the leukemia patient, for example, the cloned cells could provide an infusion of fresh bone marrow, and for the burn victim, grafts of brand-new skin. Unlike cells from an unrelated donor, these cloned cells would incur no danger of rejection; patients would be spared the need to take powerful drugs to suppress the immune system.

In contrast, the *directive* or "how-to" process analysis tells readers how to do something (how to box, invest for retirement, clean a painting) or how to make something (how to draw a map, blaze a trail, set up a computer). Especially on Web sites, directions may consist of simple step-by-step lists designed for browsers who want quick advice. In essays and articles, however, the basics may be supplemented with advice, encouragement, or relevant experience. In the following example from "How to Catch More Trout" (*Outdoor Life* May 2006), Joe Brooks identifies the critical stages in the process in his first paragraph:

> Every move you make in trout fishing counts for or against you. The way you approach a pool, how you retrieve, how you strike, how you play the fish, how you land him — all are important factors. If you plan your tactics according to the demands of each situation, you'll catch a lot more trout over a season.

Then Brooks introduces the first stage:

> The first thing you should do is stand by the pool and study it awhile before you fish. Locate the trout that are rising consistently. Choose one (the lowest in the pool, preferably), and work on him. If you rush right in and start casting, you'll probably put down several fish that you haven't seen. And you can scare still more fish by false-casting all over the place. A dozen fish you might have caught with a more careful approach may see the line and go down before you even drop the fly on the surface.

He continues with stages and advice until he reaches the last step:

> The safest way to land a fish is to beach it. If no low bank is handy, you can fight a fish until he is tired and then pull his head against a bank or an up-jutting rock and pick him up. Hold him gently. The tighter your grip, the more likely he is to spurt from your fingers, break your leader tippet, and escape. Even if you intend to put him back, you want to feel that he is really yours — a trout you have cast and caught and released because you planned it that way.

Throughout the article, Brooks skillfully addresses his audience — readers of *Outdoor Life*, people who probably already know how to fish, hunt, and enjoy outdoor recreation. As his title indicates, Brooks isn't explaining how to catch trout but how to catch *more* trout. For this reason, he skips topics for beginners (such as how to cast) and instead urges readers to plan and implement more sophisticated tactics to increase their catch.

Process analysis can also be turned to humorous ends, as illustrated in this paragraph from "How to Heal a Broken Heart (in One Day)" by student Lindsey Schendel.

> To begin your first day of mourning, you will wake up at 11 a.m., thus banishing any feelings of fatigue. Forget eating a healthy breakfast; toast two waffles, and plaster them with chocolate syrup instead of maple. Then make sure you have a room of serenity so you may cry in peace. It is important that you go through the necessary phases of denial and depression. Call up a friend or family member while you are still in your serious, somber mood. Explain to that person the hardships you are facing and how you don't know if you can go on. Immediately afterwards, turn on any empowering music, get up, and dance.

Like more serious process directions, this paragraph includes steps or stages (sleeping late, eating breakfast, crying and calling, and getting up and dancing). They are arranged in chronological order with transitions marking the movement from one to the other (*To begin, then, while, immediately afterwards*).

■ For more on transitions, see pp. 346–49.

Process analyses are wonderful ways to show your readers the inside workings of events or systems, but they can be difficult to follow. Be sure to divide the process into logical steps or stages and to put the steps in a sensible chronological order. Add details or examples wherever your description might be ambiguous or abstract; use transitions to mark the end of one step and the beginning of the next.

Here are some questions to consider when you use process analysis:

DISCOVERY CHECKLIST

___ Do you thoroughly understand the process you are analyzing?

___ Do you have a good reason to analyze a process at this point in your writing? How does your analysis support your main idea or thesis?

___ Have you broken the process into logical and useful steps? Have you adjusted your explanation of the steps for your audience?

___ Is the order in which you present these steps the best one possible?

___ Have you used transitions to guide readers from one step to the next?

■ **Activity: Analyzing a Process**

Analyze one of the following processes or procedures as the basis of a paragraph or short essay. Then share your process analysis with classmates. Can they follow your analysis easily? Do they spot anything you left out?

registering for college classes   falling in love
studying for a test   buying a used car
having the flu (or another illness)   moving

Dividing and Classifying

■ For more on analyzing a subject, see pp. 360–61.

To divide is to break something down, identifying or analyzing its components. It's far easier to take in a subject, especially a complex one, a piece at a time. The thing divided may be as concrete as a medical center (which a writer might divide into specialty units) or as abstract as a person's knowledge of art (which the writer might divide into knowledge of sculpture, painting, drawing, and other forms). To classify is to make sense of a complicated and potentially bewildering array of things — works of literature, this year's movies — by sorting them into categories (*types* or *classes*) that you can deal with one at a time. Literature is customarily arranged by genre — novels, stories, poems, plays. Movies might be sorted by audience (movies for children, teenagers, or mature audiences).

Dividing and classifying are like two sides of the same coin. In theory, any broad subject can be *divided* into components, which can then be *classified* into categories. In practice, it's often difficult to tell where division stops and classification begins.

In the following paragraph from his college textbook *Wildlife Management* (San Francisco: Freeman, 1978), Robert H. Giles Jr. uses division to simplify an especially large, abstract subject: the management of forest wildlife in America. To explain which environmentalists assume which duties and responsibilities, Giles divides forest wildlife management into six levels or areas of concern, arranged roughly from large to small, all neatly explained in fewer than two hundred words.

There are six scales of forest wildlife management: (1) national, (2) regional, (3) state or industrial, (4) county or parish, (5) intra-state region, management unit, or watershed, and (6) forest. Each is different. At the national and regional levels, management includes decisions on timber harvest quotas, grazing policy in forested lands, official stance on forest taxation bills, cutting policy relative to threatened and endangered species, management coordination of migratory species, and research fund allocation. At the state or industrial level, decision types include land acquisition, sale, or trade; season setting; and permit systems and fees. At the county level, plans are made, seasons set, and special fees levied. At the intra-state level, decisions include what seasons to recommend, what stances to take on bills not affecting local conditions, the sequence in which to attempt land acquisition, and the placement of facilities. At the forest level, decisions may include some of those of the larger management unit but typically are those of maintenance schedules, planting stock, cutting rotations, personnel employment and supervision, road closures, equipment use, practices to be attempted or used, and boundaries to be marked.

In a textbook lesson on how babies develop, Kurt W. Fischer and Arlyne Lazerson, writing in *Human Development* (New York: Freeman, 1984), describe a research project that classified individual babies into three types according to temperament.

The researchers also found that certain of these temperamental qualities tended to occur together. These clusters of characteristics generally fell into three types — the easy baby, the difficult baby, and the baby who was slow to warm up. The *easy infant* has regular patterns of eating and sleeping, readily approaches new objects and people, adapts easily to changes in the environment, generally reacts with low or moderate intensity, and typically is in a cheerful mood. The *difficult infant* usually shows irregular patterns of eating and sleeping, withdraws from new objects or people, adapts slowly to changes, reacts with great intensity, and is frequently cranky. The *slow-to-warm-up infant* typically has a low activity level, tends to withdraw when presented with an unfamiliar object, reacts with a low level of intensity, and adapts slowly to changes in the environment. Fortunately for parents, most healthy infants — 40 percent or more — have an easy temperament. Only about 10 percent have a difficult temperament, and about 15 percent are slow to warm up. The remaining 35 percent do not easily fit one of the three types but show some other pattern.

When you divide and classify, your point is to make order out of a complex or overwhelming jumble.

- Make sure the components and categories you identify are sensible, given your purpose, and follow the same principle of classification or analysis for all categories. For example, if you're trying to discuss campus relations, it makes sense to divide the school population into *instructors*, *students*, and *support staff*; it would make less sense to divide it into *people from the South*, *people from the other states*, and *people from overseas*.

- Try to group apples with apples, not with oranges, so that all the components or categories are roughly equivalent. For example, if you're classifying television shows and you've come up with *reality shows*, *dramas*, *talk shows*, *children's shows*, *news*, and *cartoons*, then you've got a problem: the last category is probably part of *children's shows*.

- Check that your final system is simple and easy for your readers to understand. Most people can handle only about seven things at once. If you've got more than five or six components or categories, perhaps you need to combine or eliminate some.

Consider these questions when you use division or classification:

DISCOVERY CHECKLIST

___ How does your division or classification support your main idea or thesis?

___ Do you use the most logical principle to divide or classify for your purpose?

___ Do you stick to one principle throughout?

___ Have you identified components or categories that are comparable?

___ Have you arranged your components or categories in the best order?

___ Have you given specific examples for each component or category?

___ Have you made a complex subject more accessible to your readers?

■ Activity: Dividing and Classifying

For more on brainstorming, see pp. 296–98.

To practice dividing and classifying, choose one or two of the following subjects. Brainstorm for five minutes on each, trying to come up with as many components as you can. With your classmates, create one large list by combining items from all who chose each subject. Working together, take the largest list and try to classify the items on it into logical categories. Feel free to add or change components or categories if you've overlooked something.

students	customers	sports	families
teachers	Web sites	vacations	drivers

Comparing and Contrasting

For advice on writing a comparison and contrast essay, see Ch. 7.

Often you can develop ideas by setting a pair of subjects side by side, comparing and contrasting them. When you compare, you point out similarities; when you contrast, you discuss differences. In daily life, we compare and contrast to decide which menu item to choose, which car (or other product) to buy, which college course to sign up for. A comparison and contrast can lead to a final evaluation and a decision about which thing is better, but it doesn't have to.

Working together, these twin strategies use one subject to clarify another. The dual method works well for a pair similar in nature — two cities, two films, two economic theories. Because this method shows that you have observed and understood both subjects, college instructors will often ask you to compare and contrast on exams ("Discuss the chief similarities and differences between nineteenth-century French and English colonial policies in West Africa").

You can use two basic methods of organization for comparison and contrast — the opposing pattern and the alternating pattern. Using the *opposing pattern*, you discuss all the characteristics or subdivisions of the first subject in the first half of the paragraph or essay and then discuss all the characteristics of the other subject. Using the *alternating pattern*, you move back and forth between the two subjects. This pattern places the specifics close together for immediate comparison and contrast. Whichever pattern you choose, be sure to cover the same subpoints for each subject and to follow the same order in each part, as illustrated for a comparison and contrast of two brothers.

For more on these organizing patterns, see pp. 114–17.

OPPOSING PATTERN, SUBJECT BY SUBJECT	ALTERNATING PATTERN, POINT BY POINT
Subject A: Jim	Point 1: Appearance
Point 1: Appearance	Subject A: Jim
Point 2: Personality	Subject B: Jack
Point 3: Interests	Point 2: Personality
Subject B: Jack	Subject A: Jim
Point 1: Appearance	Subject B: Jack
Point 2: Personality	Point 3: Interests
Point 3: Interests	Subject A: Jim
	Subject B: Jack

When you compare and contrast, think carefully about why you are doing so. Compare Jack and Jim to do more than point out lanky or curly hair. Instead, use their differences to highlight their powerful bond as brothers or their similarities to support a generalization about a family strength.

The following selection opens Chapter One of *Rousseau's Dog* by David Edmonds and John Eidinow (New York: HarperCollins, 2006). The book tells the story of the bitterness that grew between David Hume and Jean-Jacques Rousseau, two eighteenth-century philosophers with very different views and styles.

On the evening of January 10, 1766, the weather in the English Channel was foul — stormy, wet, and cold. That night, after being held in harbor by unfavorable winds, a packet boat beat its way, rolling and plunging, from Calais to Dover. Among the passengers were two men who had met for the first time some three weeks earlier in Paris, a British diplomat and a Swiss refugee. The refugee was accompanied by his beloved dog, Sultan, small and brown with a curly tail. The diplomat stayed below, tormented by sea-sickness. The refugee remained on deck all night; the frozen sailors marveled at his hardiness.

If the ship had foundered, she would have carried to the bottom of the Channel two of the most influential thinkers of the eighteenth century.

The diplomat was David Hume. His contributions to philosophy on induction, causation, necessity, personal identity, morality, and theism are of such enduring importance that his name belongs in the league of the most elite philosophers, the league that would also include Plato, Aristotle, Descartes, Kant, and Wittgenstein. A contemporary and friend of Adam Smith's, he paved the way to modern economics; he also modernized historiography.

The refugee was Jean-Jacques Rousseau. His intellectual range and achievements were equally staggering. He made epochal contributions to political theory, literature, and education. His autobiography, *The Confessions,* was a stunningly original work, one that has spawned countless successors but still sets the standard for a narrative of self-revelation and artistic development. *Émile,* his educational tract, transformed the debate about the upbringing of children and was instrumental in altering our perceptions of childhood. *On the Social Contract,* his most significant political publication, has been cited as an inspiration for generations of revolutionaries. More fundamentally, Rousseau altered the way we view ourselves, our emotions, and our relationship to society and to the natural world.

■ For a sample paper and outline using the alternating pattern, see pp. 108–10 and pp. 115–17.

In the first paragraph of this selection, the authors use a short form of the alternating pattern to introduce the two men — moving briefly from diplomat to refugee, diplomat to refugee. The next paragraph asserts their significance, providing a transition to the third and fourth paragraphs, which use the opposing pattern to introduce the contributions, stature, and legacy of the two. As the first chapter continues comparing and contrasting, the difference between the temperaments of the two men — and the potential for deep conflict — grows increasingly clear to readers.

■ For another example using the opposing pattern, see p. 105.

Consider these questions when you use comparison and contrast:

DISCOVERY CHECKLIST

___ Is your reason for comparing and contrasting unmistakably clear? Does it support or develop your main idea or thesis?

___ Have you chosen to write about the *major* similarities and differences?

___ Have you compared or contrasted like things? Have you discussed the same categories or features for each item?

___ Have you selected points of comparison and supporting details that will intrigue, enlighten, and persuade your audience?

___ Have you used the best possible arrangement, given your subject and the point you're trying to make?

___ If you are making a judgment, have you treated both subjects fairly?

___ Have you avoided moving mechanically from "On the one hand" to "On the other hand"?

■ **Activity:** Comparing and Contrasting

Write a paragraph or two in which you compare and contrast the subjects in one of the following pairs:

baseball and football (or two other sports)
living in an apartment (or dorm) and living in a house
two cities or towns you are familiar with
two musicians
communicating by phone and e-mail
watching a sports event on television and in person

Identifying Causes and Effects

From the time we are children, we ask why. Why can't I go out and play? Why is the sky blue? Why did my goldfish die? Seeking causes and effects continues into adulthood, so it's natural that explaining causal relationships is a common method of development. To use this method successfully, you must think about the subject critically, gather evidence, draw judicious conclusions, and clarify relationships.

■ For advice on writing a cause and effect essay, see Ch. 8.

In the following paragraph from "What Pop Lyrics Say to Us" (*New York Times,* 24 Feb. 1985), Robert Palmer speculates on the causes that led young people to turn to rock music for inspiration as well as the effects of their expectations on the musicians of the time.

> By the late '60s, the peace and civil rights movement were beginning to splinter. The assassinations of the Kennedys and Martin Luther King had robbed a generation of its heroes, the Vietnam War was escalating despite the protests, and at home, violence was on the rise. Young people turned to rock, expecting it to ask the right questions and come up with answers, hoping that the music's most visionary artists could somehow make sense of things. But rock's most influential artists — Bob Dylan, the Beatles, the Rolling Stones — were finding that serving as the conscience of a generation exacted a heavy toll. Mr. Dylan, for one, felt the pressures becoming unbearable, and wrote about his predicament in songs like "All Along the Watchtower."

Instead of focusing on causes *or* effects, often writers trace a *chain* of cause and effect relationships, as Charles C. Mann and Mark L. Plummer do in "The Butterfly Problem" *(Atlantic Monthly* Jan. 1992).

> More generally, the web of species around us helps generate soil, regulate freshwater supplies, dispose of waste, and maintain the quality of the atmosphere. Pillaging nature to the point where it cannot perform these functions is dangerously foolish. Simple self-protection is thus a second motive for preserving biodiversity. When DDT was sprayed in Borneo, the biologists Paul and Anne Ehrlich relate in their book *Extinction* (1981), it killed all the houseflies. The gecko lizards that preyed on the flies ate their pesticide-filled corpses and died. House cats consumed the dying lizards; they died

too. Rats descended on the villages, bringing bubonic plague. Incredibly, the housefly in this case was part of an intricate system that controlled human disease. To make up for its absence, the government was forced to parachute cats into the area.

Consider these questions when you identify causes and effects:

For more on faulty thinking and logical fallacies, see pp. 46–47 and pp. 162–63.

DISCOVERY CHECKLIST

____ Is your use of cause and effect clearly tied to your main idea or thesis?

____ Have you identified actual causes? Have you supplied persuasive evidence to support them?

____ Have you identified actual effects, or are they conjecture? If conjecture, are they logical possibilities? Can you find persuasive evidence to support them?

____ Have you judiciously drawn conclusions about causes and effects? Have you avoided faulty thinking and logical fallacies?

____ Have you presented your points clearly and logically so that your readers can follow them easily?

____ Have you considered other causes or effects, immediate or long-term, that readers might find relevant?

■ Activity: Identifying Causes and Effects

1. Identify some of the *causes* of *five* of the following. Then discuss possible causes with your classmates.

failing an exam	stage fright	losing a job
an automobile accident	losing/winning a game	losing weight
poor health	stress	going to college
good health	getting a job	getting a scholarship

2. Identify some of the *effects* of *five* of the following. Then discuss possible effects with your classmates.

an insult	dieting	divorce
a compliment	speeding	traveling to another country
learning to read	winning the lottery	drinking while driving

3. Identify some of the *causes and effects* of *one* of the following. You may need to do a little research to identify the chain of causes and effects for the event. How might you use what you have discovered as part of an essay? Discuss your findings with your classmates.

the online shopping boom	the bird flu
the Vietnam War	recycling
the attacks of September 11, 2001	a gay-marriage court case
the discovery of atomic energy	the uses of solar energy
a major U.S. Supreme	global climate change
Court decision	racial tension

Chapter 20
Strategies for Revising and Editing

Good writing is rewriting. When Ernest Hemingway was asked what made him rewrite the last page of the novel *A Farewell to Arms* thirty-nine times, he replied, "Getting the words right." His comment reflects the care that serious writers take in revising their work. In this chapter we provide strategies for revising and editing—ways to rethink muddy ideas and emphasize important ones, to rephrase obscure passages and restructure

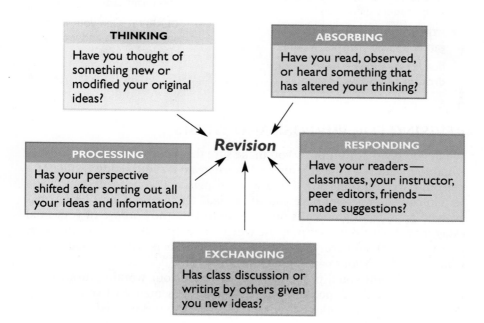

THINKING
Have you thought of something new or modified your original ideas?

ABSORBING
Have you read, observed, or heard something that has altered your thinking?

PROCESSING
Has your perspective shifted after sorting out all your ideas and information?

Revision

RESPONDING
Have your readers—classmates, your instructor, peer editors, friends—made suggestions?

EXCHANGING
Has class discussion or writing by others given you new ideas?

garbled sentences. Our advice applies not only to rewriting whole essays but also to rewriting sentences and paragraphs. In addition, we give you tips for editing and proofreading grammar, spelling, punctuation, and mechanics.

Re-viewing and Revising

Revision means "seeing again" — discovering again, conceiving again, shaping again. As an integral aspect of the total writing process, it may occur at any and all stages of the process, and most writers do a lot of it. *Macro revising* is making large, global, or fundamental changes that affect the overall direction or impact of writing — its purpose, organization, or audience. Its companion is *micro revising*, paying attention to the details of language. It involves sentences, words, punctuation, and grammar — including ways to create emphasis and eliminate wordiness.

MACRO REVISING	MICRO REVISING
• **PURPOSE:** Have you refined what you want to accomplish?	• **EMPHASIS:** Can you position your ideas more effectively?
• **THESIS:** Could you state your main point more accurately?	• **CONCISENESS:** Can you spot extra words that you might cut?
• **AUDIENCE:** Should you address your readers differently?	• **CLARITY:** Can you make any sentences and words clearer?
• **STRUCTURE:** Should you reorganize any part of your writing?	
• **SUPPORT:** Do you need to add, drop, or rework your support?	

REVISING FOR PURPOSE AND THESIS

When you revise for purpose, you make sure that your writing accomplishes what you want it to do. If your goal is to create an interesting profile of a person, have you done so? If you want to persuade your readers to take a certain course of action, have you succeeded? Of course, if your project has evolved or your assignment is now clearer to you, the purpose of your final essay may differ from your purpose when you began. To revise for purpose, try to step back and see your writing as other readers will. Concentrate on what's actually in your paper, not what you assume is there.

At this point you'll probably want to revise your working thesis statement (if you've developed one) or create a thesis sentence (if you haven't). First scrutinize your working thesis. Reconsider how it is worded:

■ For more on stating and improving a working thesis, see pp. 312–18.

- Is it stated exactly in concise yet detailed language?
- Is it focused on only one main idea?
- Is it stated positively rather than negatively?
- Is it limited to a demonstrable statement?

Then consider how accurately your thesis now represents your main idea and your draft as a whole:

- Does each part of your essay directly relate to your thesis?
- Does each part of your essay develop and support your thesis?
- Does your essay deliver everything your thesis promises?

If you find unrelated or contradictory passages, you have several options: revise the thesis, revise the essay, or revise both.

You may find that your ideas have deepened, your topic has become more complex, or your essay has developed along new lines during the process of writing. If so, you may want to refine or expand your thesis statement so that it accurately represents this evolution.

WORKING THESIS	The *Herald*'s coverage of the Senate elections was more thorough than the *Courier*'s.
REVISED THESIS	The *Herald*'s coverage of the Senate elections was less timely but more thorough and more impartial than the *Courier*'s.
WORKING THESIS	As the roles of men and women have changed in our society, old-fashioned formal courtesy has declined.
REVISED THESIS	As the roles of men and women have changed in our society, old-fashioned formal courtesy has declined not only toward women but also toward men.

Here are helpful questions about revising for purpose and thesis:

REVISION CHECKLIST

—— Do you know exactly what you want your essay to accomplish? Can you put it in one sentence: "In this paper I want to . . ."?

—— Is your thesis stated outright in the essay? If not, have you provided clues so that your readers will know precisely what it is?

—— Does every part of the essay work to achieve the same goal?

—— Have you tried to do too much? Does your coverage of your topic seem too thin? If so, how might you reduce the scope of your thesis and essay?

—— Does your essay say all that needs to be said? Is everything — ideas, connections, supporting evidence — on paper, not just in your head?

—— In writing the essay, have you changed your mind, rethought your assumptions, made a discovery? Does anything now need to be recast?

—— Do you have enough evidence? Is every point developed fully enough to be clear? To be convincing?

■ To see one student's revising and editing process, visit <bedfordstmartins.com/bedguide> and do a keyword search:

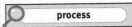

REVISING FOR AUDIENCE

An essay is successful only if it succeeds with its particular audience, and what works with one audience can fall flat with another. Visualize one of your readers poring over the essay, sentence by sentence, reacting to what you have written. What expressions do you see on that reader's face? Where does he or she have trouble understanding? Where have you hit the mark? Your organization, your selection of details, your word choice, and your tone all affect your readers, so pay special attention to these aspects.

Here are some helpful questions about revising for your audience:

REVISION CHECKLIST

___ Who will read this essay?

___ Does the essay tell your readers what they want to know rather than what they probably know already?

___ Are there any places where readers might fall asleep? If so, can you shorten, delete, or liven up such passages?

___ Does the opening of the essay mislead your readers by promising something that the essay never delivers?

___ Do you unfold each idea in enough detail to make it both clear and interesting? Would readers appreciate more detailed evidence?

___ Have you anticipated questions your audience might ask?

___ Where might readers raise serious objections? How might you anticipate their objections and answer them?

___ Have you used any specialized or technical language that your readers might not understand? If so, have you worked in brief definitions?

___ What is your attitude toward your audience? Are you chummy, angry, superior, apologetic, condescending, preachy? Should you revise to improve your attitude? Ask your peers for an opinion.

___ Will your readers think you have told them something worth knowing?

REVISING FOR STRUCTURE AND SUPPORT

When you revise for structure and support, you make sure that the order of your ideas, your selection of supporting material, and its arrangement are as effective as possible. You may have all the ingredients of a successful essay — but they may be a confusing mess.

■ For more on paragraphs, topic sentences, and transitions, see Ch. 18.

In a well-structured essay, each paragraph, sentence, and phrase serves a clear function. Are your opening and closing paragraphs relevant, concise, and interesting? Is everything in each paragraph on the same topic? Are all ideas adequately developed? Are the paragraphs arranged in the best possible order? Finally, review each place where you lead readers from one idea to the next to be certain that the transition is clear and painless.

An outline can be useful for discovering what you've succeeded in getting on paper. Start by finding the topic sentence of each paragraph in your draft (or creating one, if necessary) and listing them in order. Label the sentences I., II., A., B., and so on to indicate the logical relationships of ideas in your essay. Do the same with the supporting details under each topic sentence, labeling them also with letters and numbers and indenting appropriately. Now look at the outline. Does it make sense on its own, without the essay to explain it? Would a different order or arrangement be more effective? Do any sections look thin and need more evidence? Are the connections between parts in your head but not on paper? Maybe too many ideas are jammed into too few paragraphs. Maybe you don't include as many specific details and examples as you need — or maybe you need stronger ones. Work on the outline until you get it into strong shape, and then rewrite the essay to follow it.

For more on using outlining for planning, see pp. 325–33.

Try these helpful questions about revising for structure and support:

REVISION CHECKLIST

—— Does your introduction set up the whole essay? Does it both grab readers' attention and hint at what is to follow?

—— Does the essay fulfill all that you promise in your opening?

—— Would any later passage make a better beginning?

—— Is your thesis clear early in the essay? If explicit, is it positioned prominently?

—— Do the paragraph breaks seem logical?

—— Is the main idea of each paragraph clear? Have you used a topic sentence in every paragraph?

—— Is the main idea of each paragraph fully developed? Where might you need more details or better evidence to be convincing?

—— Within each paragraph, is each detail or piece of evidence relevant to the topic sentence? If you find a stray bit, should you omit it or move it to another paragraph?

—— Are all the ideas directly relevant to the main point of the essay?

—— Would any paragraphs make more sense in a different order?

—— Does everything follow clearly? Does one point smoothly lead to the next? Would transitions help make the connections clearer?

—— Does the conclusion follow from what has gone before, or does it seem arbitrarily tacked on?

■ Activity: Tackling Macro Revision

Even if you don't know exactly what needs to be changed in a draft, this activity will help you get started making productive changes. Select a draft that would benefit from revision. Then, based on your sense of the draft's greatest need, choose one of the revision checklists, and use it to guide a first revision. Let the draft sit for a few hours or a day or so. Then consider what else you'd like to improve, and select one of the remaining checklists to work with.

FOR E-WRITERS

Exchanging Drafts

E-mail can be an efficient way for writers and readers to exchange drafts. You can either copy and paste a document into the e-mail message or attach a document. Copying the draft into the message may remove some formatting, such as italics or bold but usually works well and avoids spreading computer viruses. If you want to preserve the formatting and believe your reader has compatible software, you may attach the document instead. If you use the Save As option, probably under the File menu, you can create a duplicate version of your file in another format such as Rich Text Format (rtf) which can be opened in any word-processing software.

WORKING WITH A PEER EDITOR

Of course, there's no substitute for having someone else go over your writing. Many college assignments ask you to write for an audience of classmates, but even if your essay is written for a different group (the town council or readers of *Newsweek*, for example), having a classmate read your essay is a worthwhile revision strategy. To gain all you can as a writer from a peer review, you need to play an active part in the discussion of your work:

- Ask your reader questions. (If this prospect seems difficult, write a "Dear Editor" letter or memo ahead of time, and bring it to your meeting.)
- Be open to new ideas — for focus, organization, or details.
- Use what's helpful, but trust yourself as the writer.

To be a helpful, supportive peer editor, try to offer honest, intelligent feedback, not judgment.

- Look at the big picture: purpose, focus, clarity, coherence, organization, support.
- When you spot strengths or weaknesses, be specific: note examples.
- Answer the writer's questions, and also use the questions supplied throughout this book to concentrate on essentials, not details.

See specific checklists in the "Revising and Editing" sections in Chs. 4 to 12.

As a writer, you can ask your peer editor to begin with your specific questions or use applicable questions from the general checklist on page 377.

Revising for Emphasis, Conciseness, and Clarity

After you've revised for the large issues in your draft — purpose, thesis, audience, structure, and support — you're ready to turn your attention to micro revising. Now is the time to look at your language, to emphasize what matters most, and to communicate it concisely and clearly.

Questions for a Peer Editor

FIRST QUESTIONS FOR A PEER EDITOR

What is your first reaction to this paper?

What is this writer trying to tell you?

What are this paper's greatest strengths?

Does it have any major weaknesses?

What one change would most improve the paper?

QUESTIONS ON MEANING

Do you understand everything? Is the draft missing any information that you need to know?

Does this paper tell you anything you didn't know before?

Is the writer trying to cover too much territory? Too little?

Does any point need to be more fully explained or illustrated?

When you come to the end, has the paper delivered what it promised?

Could this paper use a down-to-the-ground revision?

QUESTIONS ON ORGANIZATION

Has the writer begun in a way that grabs your interest and quickly draws you into the paper's main idea? Or can you find a better beginning at some later point?

Does the paper have one main idea, or does it juggle more than one?

Would the main idea stand out better if anything were removed or added?

Might the ideas in the paper be more effectively arranged? Do any ideas belong together that now seem too far apart?

Can you follow the ideas easily? Are transitions needed? If so, where?

Does the writer keep to one point of view — one angle of seeing?

Does the ending seem deliberate, as if the writer meant to conclude, not just run out of gas? How might the writer strengthen the conclusion?

QUESTIONS ON WRITING STRATEGIES

Do you feel that this paper addresses you personally?

Do you dislike or object to any statement the writer makes or any wording the writer uses? Is the problem word choice, tone, or inadequate support to convince you? Should the writer keep or change this part?

Does the draft contain anything that distracts you or seems unnecessary?

Do you get bored at any point? How might the writer keep you reading?

Is the language of this paper too lofty and abstract? If so, where does the writer need to come down to earth and get specific?

Do you understand all the words used? Do any specialized words need clearer definitions?

■ For online peer response worksheets, visit <bedfordstmartins.com/bedguide> and do a keyword search:

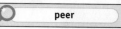

peer

FOR E-WRITERS

Tracking Comments and Exchanges

A simple way to work with a peer editor's help is to start by saving your file with a new title. Add a "+" and your peer's initials to the file name to keep track of different drafts. When you and your peer exchange texts, you may each want to use all capitals for your comments in each other's drafts. The capitalized comments will be easy to distinguish from the original.

Some word processors also offer editing systems, such as Track Changes in the Tools menu. This resource allows peer editors to highlight possible changes in your draft using underlining, color differences, and strikeouts. You can easily see suggestions, even from several readers.

STRESSING WHAT COUNTS

An ineffective writer treats all ideas as equals. An effective writer decides what matters most and shines a bright light on it. You can't emphasize merely by <u>underlining</u>, putting things in "quotation marks," or throwing them into <u>CAPITALS</u>. Such devices grow monotonous, stressing nothing at all. Instead, emphasize things that count using the most emphatic positions in an essay, a paragraph, or a sentence — the beginning and the end.

Stating It First.   In an essay, you might start with what matters most. For an economics paper on import quotas (such as the number of foreign cars allowed into a country), student Donna Waite summed up her conclusion.

> Although an import quota has many effects, both for the nation imposing the quota and for the nation whose industries must suffer from it, I believe that the most important effect is generally felt at home. A native industry gains a chance to thrive in a marketplace of lessened competition.

A paper that takes a stand or makes a proposal might open with the writer's position.

> Our state's antiquated system of justices of the peace is inefficient.

> The United States should orbit a human observer around Mars.

In a single sentence, as in an essay, you can stress things at the start. Consider the following unemphatic sentence:

> When Congress debates the Hall-Hayes Act removing existing protections for endangered species, as now seems likely to occur on May 12, it will be a considerable misfortune if this bill should pass, since the extinction of many rare birds and animals would certainly result.

The debate and its probable timing consume the start of the sentence. Here's a better use of this emphatic position:

> The extinction of many rare birds and animals would certainly follow passage of the Hall-Hayes Act.

Now the writer stresses what he most fears — the dire consequences of the act. (A later sentence might add the date and his opinion about passage.)

Stating It Last.   To place an idea last can throw weight on it. Emphatic order, proceeding from least important to most, is dramatic: it builds up and up. In a paper on import quotas, however, a dramatic buildup might look contrived. Still, in an essay on how city parks lure visitors to the city, the thesis sentence — summing up the point of the essay — might stand at the very end: "For the urban core, improved parks could bring about a new era of prosperity." Giving the evidence first and leading up to the thesis at the end is particularly effective in editorials and informal persuasive essays.

A sentence that uses climactic order, suspending its point until the end, is a *periodic* sentence. Notice how novelist Julian Green builds to his point of emphasis.

> Amid chaos of illusions into which we are cast headlong, there is one thing that stands out as true, and that is — love.

CUTTING AND WHITTLING

Like pea pickers who throw out dirt and pebbles, good writers remove needless words that clog their prose. One of the chief joys of revising is to watch 200 paunchy words shrink to a svelte 150. To see how saving words helps, let's first look at some wordiness. In what she imagined to be a gracious style, a New York socialite once sent this dinner invitation to Hu Shi, the Chinese ambassador:

> O learned sage and distinguished representative of the numerous Chinese nation, pray deign to honor my humble abode with your noble presence at a pouring of libations, to be followed by a modest evening repast, on the forthcoming Friday, June Eighteenth, in this Year of the Pig, at the approximate hour of eight o'clock, Eastern Standard Time. Kindly be assured furthermore, O most illustrious sire, that a favorable reply at your earliest convenience will be received most humbly and gratefully by the undersigned unworthy suppliant.

In reply, the witty diplomat sent this telegram:

> CAN DO. HU SHI.

Hu Shi's reply disputes a common assumption — that the more words an idea takes, the more impressive it will seem. Most good contemporary writers know that the more succinctly they can state an idea, the clearer and more forceful it will be.

■ For more on transitions, see pp. 346–49.

Cut the Fanfare.   Why bother to announce that you're going to say something? Cut the fanfare. We aren't, by the way, attacking the usefulness of transitions that lead readers along.

WORDY	As far as getting ready for winter is concerned, I put antifreeze in my car.
REVISED	To get ready for winter, I put antifreeze in my car.
WORDY	The point should be made that . . . Let me make it perfectly clear that . . . In this paper I intend to . . . In conclusion I would like to say that . . .

Use Strong Verbs.   Forms of the verb *be* (*am, is, are, was, were*) followed by a noun or an adjective can make a statement wordy, as can *There is* or *There are*. Such weak verbs can almost always be replaced by active verbs.

WORDY	The Akron game was a disappointment to the fans.
REVISED	The Akron game disappointed the fans.
WORDY	There are many people who dislike flying.
REVISED	Many people dislike flying.

Use Relative Pronouns with Caution.   When a clause begins with a relative pronoun (*who, which, that*), you often can whittle it to a phrase.

WORDY	Venus, which is the second planet of the solar system, is called the evening star.
REVISED	Venus, the second planet of the solar system, is called the evening star.

Cut Out Deadwood.   The more you revise, the more shortcuts you'll discover. Phrases such as *on the subject of, in regard to, in terms of,* and *as far as . . . is concerned* often simply fill space. Try reading the sentences below without the words in *italics*.

Howell spoke for the sophomores, and Janet *also spoke* for the seniors.

He is *something of* a clown but *sort of the* lovable *type*.

As a major in *the field of* economics, I plan to concentrate on *the area of* international banking.

The decision as to whether *or not* to go is up to you.

Cut Descriptors.   Adjectives and adverbs are often dispensable. Contrast these two versions:

WORDY	Johnson's extremely significant research led to highly important major discoveries.
REVISED	Johnson's research led to major discoveries.

Be Short, Not Long.   While a long word may convey a shade of meaning that a shorter synonym doesn't, in general favor short words over long ones. Instead of *the remainder*, write *the rest*; instead of *activate*, *start* or *begin*; instead of *adequate* or *sufficient*, *enough*. Look for the right word—one that wraps an idea in a smaller package.

> WORDY   Andy has a left fist that has a lot of power in it.
>
> REVISED   Andy has a potent left.

By the way, it pays to read. From reading, you absorb words like *potent* and set them to work for you.

KEEPING IT CLEAR

Recall what you want to achieve—clear communication with your readers using specific, unambiguous words arranged in logical order. Aim for direct, forceful expression.

> WORDY   He is more or less a pretty outstanding person in regard to good looks.
>
> REVISED   He is strikingly handsome.

Try to read your draft as a brand-new reader would. Be sure to return, after a break, to passages that you have struggled to write; heal any battle scars by focusing on clarity.

> UNCLEAR   Thus, after a lot of thought, it should be approved by the board even though the federal funding for all the cow-tagging may not be approved yet because it has wide support from local cattle ranchers.
>
> CLEAR   In anticipation of federal funding, the Livestock Board should approve the cow-tagging proposal widely supported by local cattle ranchers.

Here is a list of questions to use in slimming and clarifying your writing:

MICRO REVISION CHECKLIST

—— Have you positioned what counts at the beginning or the end?

—— Are you direct, straightforward, and clear?

—— Do you announce an idea before you utter it? If so, consider chopping out the announcement.

—— Can you substitute an active verb wherever you use a form of the verb *be* (*is, was, were*)?

—— Can you recast any sentence that begins *There is* or *There are*?

—— Can you reduce to a phrase any clause beginning with *which, who,* or *that*?

—— Have you added deadwood or too many adjectives and adverbs?

—— Do you see any long words where short words would do?

—— Have you kept your writing clear?

■ **Activity:** Tackling Micro Revision

Think back over the revisions you've already made to your draft and the advice you've received from peer editors or other readers. Is your paper more likely to seem bland (because it lacks emphasis), wordy (because it needs a good trimming), or foggy (because it needs to be more clear, direct, and logical)? Pick one issue as your focus for the moment, and concentrate on adding emphasis, cutting extra words, or expressing ideas clearly.

For his composition class, Daniel Matthews was assigned a paper using a few sources. He was to write about an "urban legend," a widely accepted and emotionally appealing—but untrue—tale about events. The following selection from his paper, "The Truth about 'Taps,'" introduces his topic and briefly explains both the legend and the true story about it. The first draft illustrates macro revisions (highlighted in the margin) and micro revisions (marked in the text). Following the draft is the clear and concise final version.

FIRST DRAFT

Avoid "you" in case readers have not shared this experience.

Anyone who has ever
~~As you know, whenever you have~~ attended the funeral services for a fallen

veteran of the United States of America, ~~you have~~ *has* stood fast as a lone bugler filled the

air with the mournful ~~and sullenly appropriate~~ last tribute to a defender of the ~~United~~

~~States of America.~~ ~~As most of us know,~~ *T* he name of the bugle call is "Taps," and the *nation*

legend *has* *ed* *has*
~~story~~ behind its origin ~~is one that is~~ gain~~ing a~~ popularity ~~of its own~~ as it ~~is more and~~

~~more frequently being~~ circulated in this time of war on terror. Although ~~it is~~

Rework paragraph to summarize legend when first mentioned.

~~clear that~~ this tale ~~of the origin~~ of a beautiful ode to a fallen warrior is heartfelt ~~and~~

As such, i
~~full of purposeful intent,~~ it is an "urban legend." ~~It~~ fails to provide due justice to the

INSERT:
According to this story, Union Captain Robert Ellicombe discovered that a Confederate casualty was, in fact, his son, a music student in the South. The father found "Taps" in his son's pocket, and the tune was first played at a military burial as his son was laid to rest (Coulter).

memories of the men responsible for the true origin of "Taps."

true
General Daniel Butterfield is the originator of the bugle call "Taps," ~~formerly~~

~~known as "Lights Out."~~ Butterfield served ~~as a general~~ in the Union army during the

Civil War and was awarded the Medal of Honor for actions during that time. One of

his most endearing claims to fame is the bugle call "Taps," which he composed at

Harrison's Landing in 1862 (Warner 167). ~~The bugle call~~ "Taps" originates from another call named "Lights Out"; this call was used by the Army to signal the end of the day.

Butterfield, wanting a new and original call unique to his command, summoned

bugler Oliver Willcox Norton to his tent one night. and rather than compose an altogether

new tune, he instead modified the notes to the call "Lights Out" (US Military District of

Shortly thereafter
Washington). Then this call could be heard being used up and down the Union lines as

the other commanders who had heard the call liked it and adapted it for their own use.

and itself   *"Tattoo," a*
This call, the modified version of "Lights Out" is also in a way a derivative of the British

bugle call "Tattoo" which is very similar in both sound and purpose to "Lights Out,"

(Villanueva). notes this as well in his paper "24 Notes That Tap Deep Emotion."

Group all the discussion of the versions in one place.

Divide long sentence to keep it clear.

Strengthen paragraph conclusion by sticking to its focus.

REVISED DRAFT

Anyone who has ever attended the funeral services for a fallen veteran of the

United States of America has stood fast as a lone bugler filled the air with a mournful

last tribute to a defender of the nation. The name of the bugle call is "Taps," and

the legend behind its origin has gained popularity as it has circulated in this time of

war on terror. According to this story, Union Captain Robert Ellicombe discovered

that a Confederate casualty was, in fact, his son, a music student in the South. The

father found "Taps" in his son's pocket, and the tune was first played at a military

burial as his son was laid to rest (Coulter). Although this tale of a beautiful ode to a

fallen warrior is heartfelt, it is an "urban legend." As such, it fails to provide due

justice to the memories of the men responsible for the true origin of "Taps."

General Daniel Butterfield is the true originator of the bugle call "Taps."

Butterfield served in the Union army during the Civil War and was awarded the Medal

of Honor for actions during that time. One of his most endearing claims to fame is

the bugle call "Taps," which he composed at Harrison's Landing in 1862 (Warner

167). "Taps" originates from another call named "Lights Out," used by the army to signal the end of the day and itself a derivative of "Tattoo," a British bugle call similar in both sound and purpose (Villanueva). Butterfield, wanting a new and original call unique to his command, summoned bugler Oliver Willcox Norton to his tent one night. Rather than compose an altogether new tune, he instead modified the notes to the call "Lights Out" (US Military District of Washington). Shortly thereafter this call could be heard up and down the Union lines as other commanders heard the call and adapted it for their own use.

Editing and Proofreading

Editing means correcting and refining grammar, punctuation, and mechanics. Proofreading means taking a final look at your paper to check correctness and to catch spelling or word-processing errors. Don't edit and proofread too soon. In your early drafting, don't fret over the correct spelling of an unfamiliar word; it may be revised out in a later version. If the word stays in, you'll

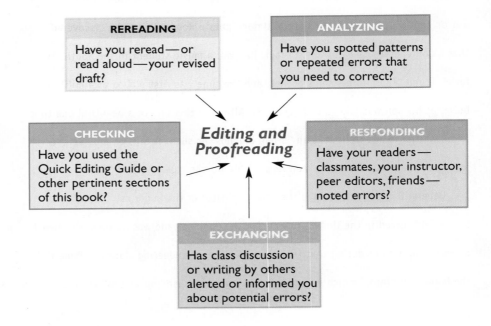

REREADING
Have you reread—or read aloud—your revised draft?

ANALYZING
Have you spotted patterns or repeated errors that you need to correct?

CHECKING
Have you used the Quick Editing Guide or other pertinent sections of this book?

Editing and Proofreading

RESPONDING
Have your readers—classmates, your instructor, peer editors, friends—noted errors?

EXCHANGING
Has class discussion or writing by others alerted or informed you about potential errors?

have time to check it later. After you have revised, however, you are ready to refine and correct. In college, good editing and proofreading can make the difference between a C and an A. On the job, it may help you get a promotion. Readers, teachers, and bosses like careful writers who take time to edit and proofread.

EDITING

As you edit, whenever you doubt whether a word or construction is correct, consult a good reference handbook. Learn the grammar conventions you don't understand so you can spot and eliminate problems in your own writing. Practice until you easily recognize major errors such as fragments and comma splices. Ask for assistance from a peer editor or a tutor in the writing center if your campus has one.

EDITING	PROOFREADING
• **GRAMMAR:** Are your sentences and their parts correct?	• **SPELLING:** Have you spell-checked and reread attentively?
• **SENTENCES:** Are your sentences clear and effective?	• **INCORRECT WORDS:** Have you mistakenly picked any wrong words?
• **WORD CHOICE:** Are your words correct and well selected?	• **MISSING WORDS:** Have you left out any words?
• **PUNCTUATION:** Do you need to add, correct, or drop any marks?	• **MINOR ERRORS:** Can you see any small mistakes?
• **MECHANICS:** Do you need to correct capitals, italics, or other matters?	• **MINOR DETAILS:** Do you need to correct any details?
• **FORMAT:** Do you need to adjust margins, spacing, or headings?	

Use the "Quick Editing Guide" at the end of this book to get you started (look for the pages with dark blue edges). It briefly reviews grammar, style, punctuation, and mechanics problems typically found in college writing and supplies definitions, examples, and a checklist to help you tackle each one. Here is an editing checklist for the problems explained there, along with the section letter and number:

■ For more help, turn to the dark-blue-edged pages, and find the Quick Editing Guide sections noted there.

■ For help documenting any sources in your paper, turn to the dark-red-edged pages, and find D6 and E1–E2 in the Quick Research Guide there.

EDITING CHECKLIST

Common and Serious Problems in College Writing

Grammar Problems

___ Have you avoided writing sentence fragments?	**A1**
___ Have you avoided writing comma splices or fused sentences?	**A2**
___ Have you used the correct form for all verbs in the past tense?	**A3**
___ Do all verbs agree with their subjects?	**A4**
___ Have you used the correct case for all pronouns?	**A5**
___ Do all pronouns agree with their antecedents?	**A6**
___ Have you used adjectives and adverbs correctly?	**A7**

Sentence Problems

___ Does each modifier clearly modify the appropriate sentence element?	**B1**
___ Have you used parallel structure where necessary?	**B2**

Punctuation Problems

___ Have you used commas correctly?	**C1**
___ Have you used apostrophes correctly?	**C2**
___ Have you punctuated quotations correctly?	**C3**

Mechanics and Format Problems

___ Have you used capital letters correctly?	**D1**
___ Have you spelled all words correctly?	**D2**
___ Have you used correct manuscript form?	**D3**

PROOFREADING

All writers make mistakes as they put ideas on paper. Because the mind works faster than the pencil (or the word processor), when you are distracted by someone talking or your cell phone ringing, you may omit a word or put in the wrong punctuation. A moment's break in concentration can lead to errors. Making such mistakes isn't bad — you simply need to take the

FOR E-WRITERS

Understanding Checkers and Their Limits

Spell checkers are handy tools, but they aren't foolproof. They can't tell you that you've used *their* when you meant *there*, *affect* when you meant *effect*, or *won* when you meant *own*. Grammar checkers also can alert you to many types of sentence problems, but you have to reason through the suggestions carefully. A checker may question long sentences and unusual constructions that are perfectly correct. As the writer, you, not the software, should always have the final word. (See also p. A-1.)

Proofreading in Pairs

Select a passage, from this textbook or elsewhere, that is about one hundred words long. Type up the passage, intentionally adding ten errors in grammar, spelling, punctuation, or capitalization. Swap passages with a classmate; proofread, then check each other's work against the originals. Share your proofreading strategies.

FOR GROUP LEARNING

time to find and correct them. Proofreading does take patience but is a skill you can develop. For instance, when you simply glance at the spelling of *environment*, you may miss the second *n*. When you read normally, you usually see only the shells of words — the first and last letters. You fix your eyes on the print only three or four times per line or less. When you proofread, try to create a situation that will help you concentrate on detail.

- Let a paper sit several days, overnight, or at least a few hours before proofreading so that you allow time to gain perspective.

- Budget enough time to proofread thoroughly. For a long essay or complex research paper with a list of sources, schedule several sessions.

- Ask someone else to read your paper and tell you if it is free of errors. But take pride in your own work. *Don't* let someone else do it for you.

- Use a dictionary or a spell checker whenever you can.

- Keep a list of your habitual errors, especially those your instructor has already pointed out. Double-check for these errors (such as leaving off *-s* or *-ed* endings or putting in unnecessary commas).

To proofread effectively, you should try to look at the letters in each word and the punctuation marks between words without sliding over these symbols. Use the following questions to help you slow down and concentrate:

PROOFREADING CHECKLIST

— Have you read what you have written very slowly, looking at every word and letter? Have you tried to see what you have actually written, not what you think is there?

— Have you read your paper aloud? Have you used speaking to slow yourself down so you can see and hear mistakes?

— Have you read the essay backward so that you look at each word instead of getting caught up in the flow of ideas?

— Have you read your essay several times, focusing each time on a specific area of difficulty? (For example, read once for spelling, once for punctuation, and once for a problem that recurs in your writing.)

■ Activity: Editing and Proofreading

■ For editing exercises, visit Exercise Central at <bedfordstmartins.com/ bedguide>.

Read the following passage carefully. Assume that the organization of the paragraph is satisfactory, but find and correct fifteen errors in sentence structure, grammar, spelling, punctuation, and capitalization. After you have corrected the passage, discuss with your classmates the changes you have made and your reasons for making those changes.

Robert Frost, one of the most poplar American poets. He was born in San Francisco in 1874, and died in Boston in 1963. His family moved to new England when his father died in 1885. There he completed highschool and attended colledge but never graduate. Poverty and problems filled his life. He worked in a woll mill, on a newspaper, and at varous odd jobs. Because of ill health he settled on a farm and began to teach school to support his wife and children. Throughout his life he dedicated himself to writing poetry, by 1915 he was in demand for public readings and speaking engagements. He was awarded the Pulitzer Prize for poetry four times—in 1924, 1931, 1937, and 1943. The popularity of his poetry rests in his use of common themes and images. everyone can relate to his universal poems, such as "Birches" and "Stopping by Woods on a Snowy Evening." Students read his poetry in school from seventh grade through graduate school, so almost everyone recognize lines from his best-loved poems. America is proud of it's son, the homespun poet Robert Frost.

Chapter 21

Strategies for Designing Your Document

Whether the document you prepare is an essay, a research paper, or a business letter, creating an effective design for it helps you achieve your purpose and meet the expectations of your audience. Through your own reading, you may have noticed that you respond differently to documents depending upon their appearance. For example, look quickly at Figure 21.1. Which of the two newspapers there seems more appealing to you?

If you prefer *USA Today*, you're like many Americans — you like the look of a colorful, casual newspaper and may even consider it easier to read. But if someone asked which of the two newspapers seems more credible or trustworthy, many would say the *Wall Street Journal*. Its closely typed text, narrow columns, and limited use of color create a look more "respectable" than that of the open, friendly *USA Today* with its abundant pictures, more colorful design, and playful tone. As you can see, the same features that make the *Wall Street Journal* seem more credible than *USA Today* may also make it less inviting to read. Like other newspapers, however, the *Wall Street Journal* freely uses headlines, short paragraphs, column dividers, white space, page numbers, and other visual markers that help the reader grasp the structure of the text at a glance and decide where to plunge in. Without such visual markers, the pages of the *Wall Street Journal* would provide the reader few pathways into its content.

Occasionally, college students are assigned a composition that looks and reads like a newspaper. But most of the papers you will write are not as visually complex as the *Wall Street Journal* or *USA Today*. Instead of calling for multiple columns, headlines, and graphics, your teacher will most likely expect to see double spacing, one-inch margins, numbered pages, and indented block quotations — visual markers typical of college compositions. Figure 21.2 shows two pages — the first page and the list of sources — of a typical college composition that follows the guidelines of the Modern Language Association (MLA).

For more on manuscript format, turn to D3 in the Quick Editing Guide (the dark-blue-edged pages).

389

Figure 21.1
Front Pages of USA Today *and the* Wall Street Journal *(with common features labeled)*

Figure 21.2
The First Page and Works
Cited Page of a Student
Research Paper in MLA
Format

1″

½″
Goers 1

Sarah E. Goers   Writer's name

Professor Day   Instructor's name

English 101   Course

29 January 2007   Date

½″ or
5 spaces   Is Inclusion the Answer?

→Inclusion is one of the most passionately debated

issues in public education today. Full inclusion, defined as

placing all students with disabilities in general education

classes, has three main components: the integration of

→ special education students into the mainstream

1″   classroom, educational planning and programming, and   1″

the clarification of responsibility for appropriate

instruction (Heinich 292). Although the intent is to

provide the best car...

special and general...

people in the field b...

disabled children in...

in the best interest...

children will not be...

program unless the6...

their needs; if place...

not met due to low...

lack of necessary re...

these reasons, the...

inclusion or separat...

1″

Writer's last name and
page number in running
head

Title, centered

Double-spacing
throughout

Citation with author's
name and page number
in parentheses

List of works cited on a
separate page

1″

Centered
heading

½″
Goers 8

Works Cited

Block, Martin E. "Did We Jump on the Wrong Bandwagon?

Problems with Inclusion." Palestra 15.3 (1999) 4-10.

10 Dec. 2006 <http://www.palestra.com/Inclusion.html>.

Gaskins, Jacob. "Teaching Writing to Students with

Learning Disabilities: The Landmark Method."

Teaching English in the Two-Year College 22.2

(1995): 71-76.

Heinich, Robert, ed. Educating All Handicapped Children.

Englewood Cliffs: Educational Technology

Publications, 1979.

Hewett, Beth. "Helping Students with Learning

Disabilities: Collaboration between Writing Centers

and Special Services." Writing Lab 25.3 (2000):

1-4.

Jacobson, Linda. "Disabled Kids Moving into Regular

Classrooms." Atlanta Journal 5 May 1994: C1.

Maushard, Mary. "Special Schools Fall Victim to 'Inclusion.'"

Sun [Baltimore] 13 June 1993: B1. NewsBank.

½″ Boston Public Lib. 21 Dec. 2006 <http://

www.newsbank.com>.

Radebaugh, Barbara. "NEA vs. AFT." Education 201-002

Lecture. William Rainey Harper Coll., Palatine, IL.

21 Jan. 1999.

Rios, Denise A. "Special Students Joining Regular

Classrooms." Orange County Register 9 June 1994:

A24. NewsBank. Boston Public Lib. 11 Dec. 2006.

<http://www.newsbank.com>.

List alphabetized by
author's last name

First line of entry at left
margin

Subsequent lines
indented ½″ or
5 spaces

Understanding Four Basic Principles of Document Design

■ For more advice on designing documents, visit <bedfordstmartins.com/ bedguide> and do a key-word search:

🔍 designing

Four key principles of document design will help you to produce effective documents in and out of the classroom. Use these questions based on the principles to help you design college papers or other documents:

DISCOVERY CHECKLIST

___ Who are your readers? What are their key concerns? How might your document design acknowledge their concerns?

___ What form or genre do readers expect? What features do they see as typical of that form? What visual evidence would they expect or accept as appropriate?

___ What problems or constraints will your readers face? How can your document design help to address these constraints?

___ What is the purpose of your document? How can its design help achieve this purpose? How can it enhance your credibility as a writer?

PRINCIPLE 1: KNOW YOUR AUDIENCE

Whether you are writing an essay for class or preparing a different type of document, identifying your audience is a good first step toward creating an effective design. For most papers for a composition course, your primary reader is your teacher and your secondary readers include your peers. For some assignments, you might include other readers as well.

■ For more on purpose and audience, see pp. 14–18 and pp. 310–12.

Suppose you've written a paper explaining the benefits of a longer school year to a real-world audience. An audience of parents would have different concerns than an audience of community leaders or of school officials or teachers. Teachers, for example, would need to be assured that their paychecks would keep pace with the longer work year. The school board would need to be convinced that the increased costs for salaries, building operations, and transportation would pay off in higher student achievement. And other civic leaders might want to know the effects on community safety, traffic congestion, and seasonal employment rates.

In deciding how to design your document, you might consider ways to acknowledge, even highlight, the concerns of your particular audience, perhaps using headings, white space, and variations in type style. You might also consider whether your audience is likely to read every word of your argument or to skim it for key points. Perhaps tables, graphs, or diagrams would make information more accessible. Thinking about such issues means you'll have a better chance of reaching your audience.

PRINCIPLE 2: SATISFY YOUR AUDIENCE'S EXPECTATIONS

When you think about a newspaper, a particular type of publication comes to mind because the newspaper is a familiar *genre*, or form. As Figure 21.1 shows, almost all newspapers share a set of defined features: a masthead, headlines, pictures with captions, graphics, and articles arranged in columns of text. Even if details of the form vary, newspapers are still recognized as newspapers. Similarly, *Utne Reader* and *Parenting* both belong to the genre of the magazine: both feature articles arranged in columns, notable quotations set in larger type, and photographs. Despite significantly different content, magazines share a common genre identification, as Figure 21.3 illustrates.

For samples of work-place genres, see Ch. 14.

Like the newspaper and the magazine, the college paper can be thought of as a genre. Readers, including your teacher and your peers, have expectations about what topics are appropriate for such documents, how they should be written, and how they should look. Readers also have expectations about visual evidence such as graphs, tables, photographs, or other illustrations, depending on the field and the assignment. Check your syllabus to see if a specific document design is required.

For advice about a general format for papers, see D3 in the Quick Editing Guide (the dark-blue-edged pages).

Usually your readers expect your paper to be word processed, double-spaced with numbered pages. Some teachers want a cover page with your name, the title of your paper, your course number and section, the date, and perhaps other information. Others prefer that you follow the MLA paper format, simply supplying a four-line identifier and a centered title on the first page (see Figure 21.2). Some will ask you to include your last

Creating a Template

Unless your teacher encourages unusual or creative formatting, don't experiment too much with the appearance of a college paper. In fact, you can easily apply expected features to your papers by creating a template for papers with the same specifications. First, format your paper the way you want it to look. Then, create a document template that you can use any time you begin a new paper:

FOR E-WRITERS

1. Create a duplicate copy of your formatted file.
2. Delete all of the text in the document.
3. Use the Save As feature to save the file as a document template.
4. Give the template a name, such as "English paper" or "Paper form."
5. When you create a new file, choose this template from the options in your template folder. (Use the Help box for more on templates.)

Figure 21.3
Common Features in Magazine Design: Page Spread from Utne Reader, *November–December 2006 (top) and* Parenting, *June/July 2003 (bottom)*

Photograph

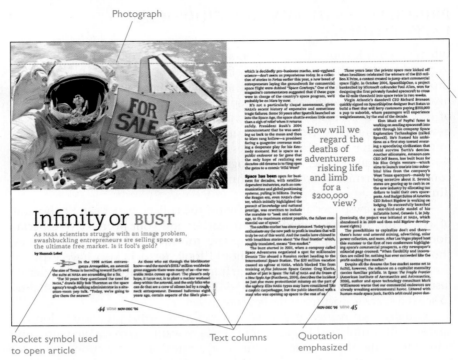

Image and text unit and framed by dotted line

Rocket symbol used to open article

Text columns

Quotation emphasized

Text column

Photograph

Quotation emphasized

Text and image united and framed by border

Arrow symbol used to catch reader's eye

name or a shortened title with the page number at the top or bottom of each page.

Although you should follow any specific guidelines that your instructor supplies, some genre features might be flexible. For example, you might use larger, boldface type for your paper title or use underlining or boldface to set off any headings. Perhaps you might want to separate your page numbers from the rest of the text with a horizontal line or insert a little extra white space between paragraphs. Such features could help to make your standard paper distinctive and easier for your teacher to read.

PRINCIPLE 3: CONSIDER YOUR AUDIENCE'S CONSTRAINTS

Your teacher probably expects you to print your paper in a crisp, black, 12-point type, double-spaced, on one side of a white sheet of paper with one-inch margins. You also may be asked to reprint a paper if your toner cartridge is nearly empty. Before accusing your teacher of being overly picky, remember that he or she may read and grade compositions in batches of a hundred or more. Papers that are printed clearly in a standard format are easier on the eyes than those with faint print or unusual formats. In addition, your teacher needs enough margin space for comments. If you try to save paper by using a smaller point size, narrower margins, or single spacing, the paper may be more difficult to read and to grade.

When you address readers besides your teacher, they too will have some constraints. Some may read your document on a computer screen if it arrives as an e-mail attachment. Others may skim a text's main points during the morning commute or sort through a stack of résumés before lunch. Just as you want to write an effective paper that addresses your readers' information needs, you also want to design a usable, readable paper — one that readers can readily absorb regardless of constraints.

PRINCIPLE 4: REMEMBER YOUR PURPOSE

Like most writers, you have in mind a particular reason for writing. As you take into account your readers' concerns, their expectations, and the conditions under which they read, your challenge is to write convincingly for them. When you do so, you also increase your credibility as a writer. Although good document design is no substitute for a clear and orderly essay, it can help you achieve your purpose and enhance the message you are trying to convey, as the rest of this chapter will explain.

For more on purpose and audience, see pp. 14–18 and pp. 310–12.

Creating an Effective Design for Your Document

When you design a document, you direct a reader's attention using tools such as type options, lists, white space, headings, repetition, color, and visuals. Although you may not be accustomed to thinking about design issues, you already make design choices whenever you type something in your word processor. The following guidelines can help you design effective documents that achieve your purpose and appeal to your audience.

USING A PROMINENT ELEMENT

Artists and designers aim to attract readers' attention by making important elements prominent. Consider Figure 21.4, for example, which shows two of six panels of a student-designed brochure. The image of the mannequin on the brochure's cover immediately draws the eye, but the pattern of light guides readers to the central question: "Is your life out of control?" Other words on the left panel (such as "broken," "stuck," "lost," and "depressed") serve as a suggestive backdrop, but there is no mistaking the main message.

For more on white space, see pp. 402–04; for more on headings, see pp. 405–09; and for more on color, see p. 410.

Providing a prominent element helps your readers focus on what you think is most important. As you begin work on any visual document ask, "What is the main message I want to get across?" Once you have decided on that message, think of ways to give it prominence. For example, if you are designing a brochure, flyer, poster, or postcard, you might want to surround one large headline by a significant amount of space, as the designer of the brochure did in the left panel. Note also in the right panel how the headings — all questions, parallel in form — appear in color, separated by white space so that readers clearly see the breaks between topics. The inside panels of the brochure respond to the questions posed in the headings, pointing readers toward helpful resources.

For more on parallel structure, see B2 in the Quick Editing Guide (the dark-blue-edged pages).

For more on understanding visuals, see Ch. 22.

You can get ideas about how to present prominent elements by looking at visual documents designed by others. Learning to spot these elements — and figure out how they are given prominence — can also help you analyze and interpret visual documents.

CHOOSING FONTS

Typography refers to the appearance of typeset letters on a page. When you add boldface type, use all capital letters, or change type size, you make a typographic choice. Such choices can make your document clear and attractive, but an inappropriate or excessive option can clutter your work.

Current word-processing software allows changing typefaces, commonly called *fonts*, to increase readability, achieve special effects, add emphasis, or set a particular tone. Although most college papers use a conventional font

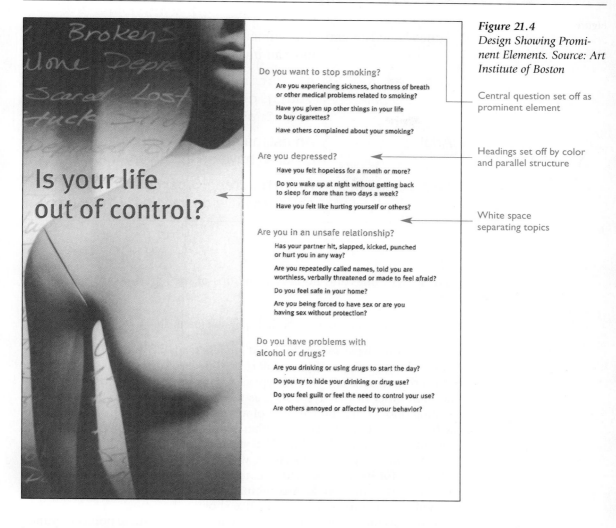

Figure 21.4
Design Showing Prominent Elements. Source: Art Institute of Boston

Central question set off as prominent element

Headings set off by color and parallel structure

White space separating topics

in a 12-point size, sometimes you may need to use larger type for signs, posters, and visuals (such as PowerPoint slides) for oral presentations. Test such materials for readability by printing samples in various type sizes and standing back from them at the distance of your intended audience.

For examples of PowerPoint slides, see p. 404.

Figure 21.5 shows the same sentence written in four different 12-point fonts: Times New Roman, Courier New, Arial, and Comic Sans MS. Although the examples are all written in the standard 12-point size, the typefaces occupy different amounts of horizontal space on the page.

Serif or Sans Serif Fonts.   Times New Roman and Courier New are called *serif* fonts. A serif font has small tails, or serifs, at the ends of the letters. Arial and Comic Sans MS are *sans serif* — without serifs — and thus have

Figure 21.5
Space Occupied by
Different Typefaces

Times New Roman	An estimated 40 percent of young children have an imaginary friend.
Courier New	An estimated 40 percent of young children have an imaginary friend.
Arial	An estimated 40 percent of young children have an imaginary friend.
Comic Sans MS	An estimated 40 percent of young children have an imaginary friend.

solid, straight lines and no tails at the tips of the letters, as these examples show:

Times New Roman (serif)   K k P p   Arial (sans serif)   K k P p

Sans serif fonts have a clean look but are less readable than serif fonts, especially in long passages. If you look over your local newspaper, you may see both serif and sans serif fonts. Typically, sans serif fonts are used for headlines and other display type, such as advertisements and "pull quotes" (interesting quotations "pulled out" of an article and printed in larger type to catch the reader's eye). On the other hand, most newspapers choose serif fonts for their article (or "body") text. In fact, Times New Roman, the default font on many word processors, was developed for the *Times* newspaper in London for its own use. Other common serif fonts include Palatino and New Century Schoolbook. A combination of fonts can provide maximum readability and emphasis, as Figure 21.6 shows.

If you decide to combine two different fonts, keep these points in mind:

- Serif and sans serif fonts can be combined in the same document, though document designers recommend using only one of each.

- For further emphasis, you may vary the type size or type style, such as italics or bold, for each font.

Novelty Fonts.   For most college and professional writing, novelty fonts — those that are unusual or decorative — are inappropriate. **Comic Sans MS** is a novelty font, as are *Brush Script* and **Tempus Sans**. While these casual, playful typefaces may suit some writing situations, novelty fonts can set the wrong tone for your paper, especially if your subject is technical or serious.

For example, if you are writing a paper about civil liberties, Comic Sans MS might suggest that readers don't need to take your arguments seriously

Watching TV with a Critical Eye

By second grade, kids have figured out, often from personal experience, that the toys they see in commercials don't always measure up in real life. Children this age are old enough to get into more sophisticated discussions about fact and opinion.

Figure 21.6
Sans Serif Heading Used with Serif Body Font.
Source: Kiplinger's, February 2000

or that you lack respect for a serious subject. Figure 21.7 shows two versions of the same text — one set in Times New Roman, which is appropriate for an academic setting, and the other set in Comic Sans MS, which generally is not. In academic or other serious writing, stick with standard fonts that are familiar to readers and that set a professional tone.

For more on typefaces in visuals, see pp. 426–27.

Italics.   When you *italicize* words, you call the reader's attention to them.

- Use italics for book, film, magazine, or electronic database titles.
  My favorite novel is *Wuthering Heights.*
- Use italics for foreign words.
  My Finnish grandmother called me *Kultani* ("my golden one").

Times New Roman	Comic Sans MS
Does Heightened Surveillance Make Us More or Less Secure?	**Does Heightened Surveillance Make Us More or Less Secure?**
Since the terrorist attacks of September 11, 2001, a wide-ranging debate has ensued over whether face-recognition systems and other surveillance tools should be used to identify potential terrorists. While proponents see these tools as an essential defense when loosely organized terrorist "cells" might strike at any time, opponents say these systems are flawed at best and jeopardize the civil liberties of all citizens.	Since the terrorist attacks of September 11, 2001, a wide-ranging debate has ensued over whether face-recognition systems and other surveillance tools should be used to identify potential terrorists. While proponents see these tools as an essential defense when loosely organized terrorist "cells" might strike at any time, opponents say these systems are flawed at best and jeopardize the civil liberties of all citizens.

Figure 21.7   *Identical Text Set in Two Fonts. Sources: See Figure 21.9*

FOR E-WRITERS

Changing Your Type Style

Your word-processing program is likely to supply several ways of changing type style. When you look at the screen, your toolbar probably includes boxes that identify the font you are using (such as Times New Roman) and the point size of the characters (such as 12). Nearby you may spot other small boxes or icons that, with a click, shift what you type to bold, italics, or underlined text—all necessary in academic papers if only for the various styles of documenting sources. You can also use your mouse to highlight sections of text and then click on these icons to change the text style for that passage. Clicking on the Format menu and then on Font generally supplies a menu of design options, such as shadows or small capitals.

- Use italics for your first use of a technical or scientific term, and provide a definition for the reader. After that, use regular type without emphasis.

  AIDS patients monitor their levels of *helper T-cells* because these cells detect antigens in the body and activate other cells to fight the antigens. Because HIV destroys helper T-cells, this information indicates the status of a patient's immune system.

Italicized words appear lighter in weight than nonitalicized words. This lightness, coupled with the slant of the letters, makes italics unsuitable for sustained reading. Use italics for emphasis, not for large blocks of text.

▨ For examples of bold-face type in résumés, see p. 273.

Boldface.   Boldface type is suitable for emphasis only. Too much produces the "raisin bread" effect, a random scattering of dark spots across a light page, illustrated in Figure 21.8. Because this scattering encourages the reader to "hear" the words as emphasized, it creates a choppy, unnatural rhythm.

Many teachers expect you to choose emphatic words, not to rely on boldface type for emphasis in academic papers. In other documents, use boldface selectively, highlighting only words that you want the reader to see or "hear" with emphasis added. In general, reserve boldface type primarily for headings, key points in a list of factors, or similar uses.

Longevity.   People are living longer today, so Social Security funds need to stretch to accommodate these longer lives.

Inflation.   Dollars paid into the system in 1980 are worth less today, and interest on the fund has not kept pace with the need for the dollars.

Figure 21.8
The Raisin-Bread Effect Produced by Too Much Boldface

Treating Carpal Tunnel Syndrome

Physicians **generally** suggest one of **three** methods of treating patients with carpal tunnel syndrome. **First,** reducing the amount of repeated **wrist** movement **can** allow the median nerve to heal. **This** can be accomplished by changing habits or **positions** or by using a wrist **splint.** . . .

PREPARING LISTS

The organization or placement of material on a page — its layout — can make information more accessible for readers. For example, lists are easier to read when they are displayed rather than integrated.

INTEGRATED LIST   Movies are rated by the film-rating board of the Classification and Rating Administration (CARA) based on several criteria, including these: overall theme, use of language, presence of violence, presence of nudity and sexual content, and combined use of these elements in the context of an individual film.

DISPLAYED LIST   Movies are rated by the film-rating board of the Classification and Rating Administration (CARA) based on several criteria, including these:
- overall theme
- use of language
- presence of violence
- presence of nudity and sexual content
- combined use of these elements in the context of an individual film

Bulleted List.   One type of displayed list uses a mark called a *bullet* to set off a bit of information. The most common bullet is the small round one often available in a word processor's bulleted list function (•). Bulleted lists are common in business and other documents but not necessarily in academic papers.

Use a bulleted list to enumerate steps, reasons, or items, especially when the order isn't significant, as in this example:

Controversy surrounding the 2000 presidential election climaxed in Florida, where several balloting issues converged.

- A controversial Palm Beach County ballot was blamed for several thousand votes possibly cast in error for a third-party candidate, Pat Buchanan.

Creating Lists

Your toolbar may show small icons or boxes for developing bulleted or numbered lists. If so, one click on an icon adds a number or bullet to your text, while a second click removes it from a passage. When you type a return at the end of one listed item, the next bullet or number appears. Your Insert menu probably includes a Symbol option. Click here for alternative symbols — for example, square bullets or different sizes of round bullets. Generally, a click on the selected item (perhaps with an Insert command) adds it to your text. For academic papers, use such devices conservatively, always following any specific directions from your instructor or from the style guide preferred by the field. In APA style, for instance, simply type out a list within a sentence, placing letters inside pairs of parentheses: (a), (b), and (c).

FOR E-WRITERS

- A Florida law triggered a statewide ballot recount when the votes for the two main candidates were separated by less than 1 percent.

- Outstanding absentee ballots had to be counted to determine which candidate had received the most votes.

■ For examples of the use of bullets in résumés, see p. 273.

Bullets — perhaps combined with headings, white space, and boldface type — can highlight skills or titles in a résumé, making it easier for readers to spot a job applicant's relevant experience. Web résumés, like other Web pages, divide information to fit the screen. They may use design devices to emphasize links and categories, such as education and experience.

Numbered List.   Another type of displayed list, the numbered list, can emphasize important sequences, especially in activity plans, how-to advice, instructional writing, or other process descriptions. Here is a simplified sequence of activities for making an article of clothing:

1. Select your pattern and fabric.
2. Lay out the pattern and pin it to the fabric, paying careful attention to the arrows and grain lines.
3. Cut out the fabric pieces following the outline of the pattern.
4. Sew the garment together using the pattern's step-by-step instructions.

USING WHITE SPACE STRATEGICALLY

■ For examples of the use of white space in print and Web résumés, see p. 273 and p. 274. For more about white space in visuals, see pp. 424–25.

White space is just that: space within a document that is free of text. Blank space gives the eye a rest and can frame important information, increasing emphasis as you guide the reader through your document.

College Papers.   When you write college papers, you use white space to assist your readers. For example, one-inch margins and double-spacing provide some respite for the reader's eyes. Adding extra white space to indent the first line of your paragraphs helps the reader immediately differentiate one paragraph from the next. In addition, indenting an extended "block" quotation sets it off as a special kind of text.

■ For sample pages from an academic paper, see p. 391. For advice on the format for a college paper, see D3 in the Quick Editing Guide (the dark-blue-edged pages).

As you can see in Figure 21.9, white space is crucial to the appearance of your papers. Were this example single-spaced, its closely spaced lines would be much too cramped, interfering with readers' ability to keep their place in the text and possibly intimidating them. When text elements are close together and look fairly uniform, readers may feel as if they are trying to merge onto a congested freeway. Some may give up if they don't see openings where they can easily jump in and begin to navigate the text.

However, if you separate sections of your paper by hitting the enter key an extra time or two — especially if your paper is double-spaced — you will trap too much white space between sections. This extra space may create a gap that prevents the reader's eye from making natural connections within the text and seeing your paper as a cohesive unit.

Does Heightened Surveillance ← Centered title with
Make Us More or Less Secure?   space on both sides

Indented → Since the terrorist attacks of September 11, 2001, a wide-
paragraph   ranging debate has ensued over whether face-recognition systems and
other surveillance tools should be used to identify potential terrorists.
While proponents see these tools as an essential defense when loosely
organized terrorist "cells" might strike at any time, opponents say
these systems are flawed at best and jeopardize the civil liberties of
all citizens.

Barry Steinhardt, director of the Technology and Liberty Program
of the American Civil Liberties Union, sees a clear threat to personal
freedom:

Extended   Many people still do not grasp that Big Brother surveillance
quotation   is no longer the stuff of books and movies.... Given
indented as   the capabilities of today's technology, the only thing
a block   protecting us from a full-fledged surveillance society are
the legal and political institutions we have inherited as
Americans. Unfortunately, the September 11 attacks
have led some to embrace the fallacy that weakening
the Constitution will strengthen America. ("'Big Brother'")

However, others argue that technology can make us safer-- and,
in fact, already has. Video monitoring systems using closed-circuit
televisions have been in use for years in such places as the United
Kingdom, where officials say that crime has declined significantly as a
result ("Law, Order, and Terrorism").

Figure 21.9
Text Using White Space.
Sources: "'Big Brother'
Is No Longer a Fiction,
ACLU Warns in New
Report," American Civil
Liberties Union, *15 Jan.*
2003. 23 June 2003
<www.aclu.org>. *"Law,*
Order, and Terrorism:
Other Nations' Remedies,"
Dahlia Lithwick,
Slate.com, *5 Oct. 2001.*
23 June 2003
<www.slate.com>.

Readable double-
spaced lines

Text framed
by margins

Visuals.   Effective use of space is important in visuals — such as trans-
parencies or PowerPoint slides — for presentations. Providing ample space
and limiting the text on each slide helps readers absorb your major points.
For example, the slide in Figure 21.10 contains too much text, making it hard
to read and potentially distracting for the audience. In contrast, Figure 21.11
contains less text and more open space, making each point easier to read. It
also uses bullets effectively to highlight the main points. These points are
meant only to summarize major issues and themes, not to detail all of
them; you can flesh out your main points during your talk. Though the
slides have been reduced to fit in this book, the original type sizes were large

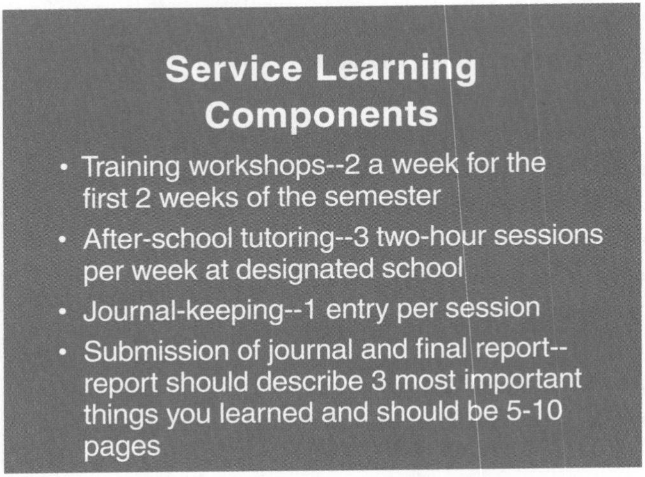

Figure 21.10
PowerPoint Slide with Too
Much Text and Too Little
Space

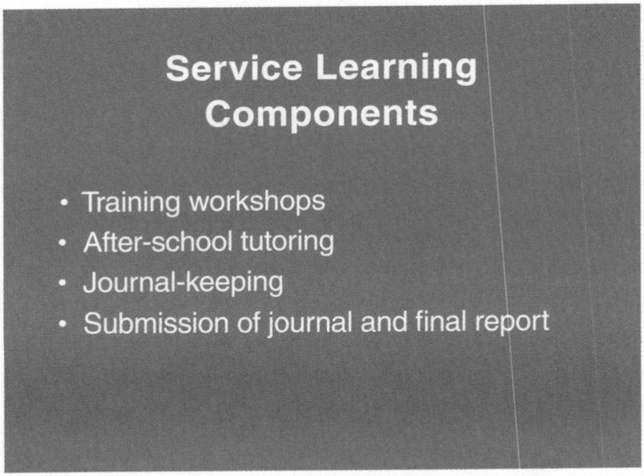

Service Learning Components

- Training workshops--2 a week for the first 2 weeks of the semester
- After-school tutoring--3 two-hour sessions per week at designated school
- Journal-keeping--1 entry per session
- Submission of journal and final report-- report should describe 3 most important things you learned and should be 5-10 pages

Figure 21.11
PowerPoint Slide with
Brief Text and Effective
Use of Space

Service Learning Components

- Training workshops
- After-school tutoring
- Journal-keeping
- Submission of journal and final report

enough to be viewed by the presenter's classmates: 44 points for the heading and 32 points for the body.

Finally, as you can see, the "white space" without text in these slides is actually blue. Some public-speaking experts believe that black type on a white background can be too stark for a slide; instead, they recommend a dark blue background with yellow or white type. However, others believe that black on white is fine and may in fact be what the audience is accustomed to. Presentation software like PowerPoint makes it easy for you to experiment with these options.

Does Heightened Surveillance ◄———— Centered title with
Make Us More or Less Secure?   space on both sides

Indented ———► Since the terrorist attacks of September 11, 2001, a wide-
paragraph
ranging debate has ensued over whether face-recognition systems and
other surveillance tools should be used to identify potential terrorists.
While proponents see these tools as an essential defense when loosely
organized terrorist "cells" might strike at any time, opponents say
these systems are flawed at best and jeopardize the civil liberties of
all citizens.

Barry Steinhardt, director of the Technology and Liberty Program
of the American Civil Liberties Union, sees a clear threat to personal
freedom:

Many people still do not grasp that Big Brother surveillance
is no longer the stuff of books and movies.... Given
the capabilities of today's technology, the only thing
protecting us from a full-fledged surveillance society are
Extended   the legal and political institutions we have inherited as
quotation
indented as   Americans. Unfortunately, the September 11 attacks
a block   have led some to embrace the fallacy that weakening
the Constitution will strengthen America. ("'Big Brother'")

However, others argue that technology can make us safer -- and,
in fact, already has. Video monitoring systems using closed-circuit
televisions have been in use for years in such places as the United
Kingdom, where officials say that crime has declined significantly as a
result ("Law, Order, and Terrorism").

Figure 21.9
Text Using White Space.
Sources: "'Big Brother'
Is No Longer a Fiction,
ACLU Warns in New
Report," American Civil
Liberties Union, *15 Jan.
2003. 23 June 2003*
<www.aclu.org>. *"Law,
Order, and Terrorism:
Other Nations' Remedies,"
Dahlia Lithwick,
Slate.com, 5 Oct. 2001.
23 June 2003*
<www.slate.com>.

Readable double-
spaced lines

Text framed
by margins

Visuals.   Effective use of space is important in visuals — such as trans-
parencies or PowerPoint slides — for presentations. Providing ample space
and limiting the text on each slide helps readers absorb your major points.
For example, the slide in Figure 21.10 contains too much text, making it hard
to read and potentially distracting for the audience. In contrast, Figure 21.11
contains less text and more open space, making each point easier to read. It
also uses bullets effectively to highlight the main points. These points are
meant only to summarize major issues and themes, not to detail all of
them; you can flesh out your main points during your talk. Though the
slides have been reduced to fit in this book, the original type sizes were large

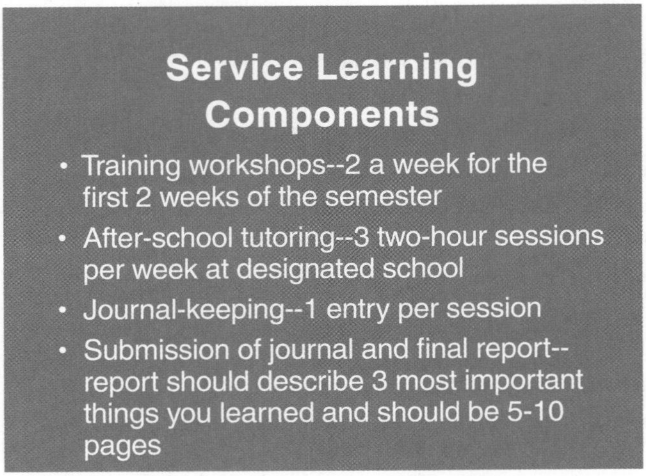

Figure 21.10
PowerPoint Slide with Too
Much Text and Too Little
Space

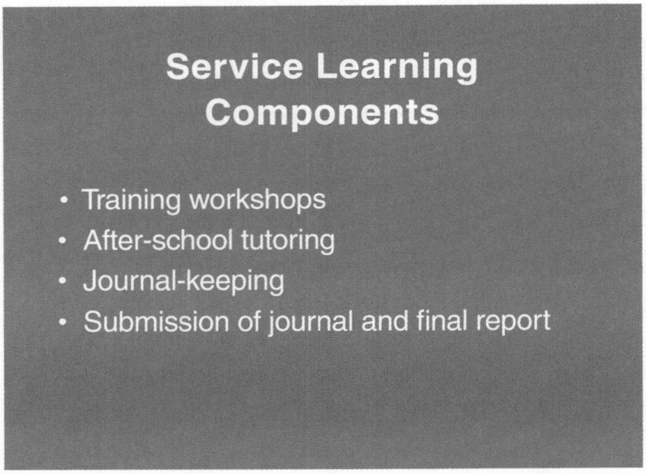

Figure 21.11
PowerPoint Slide with
Brief Text and Effective
Use of Space

enough to be viewed by the presenter's classmates: 44 points for the heading and 32 points for the body.

Finally, as you can see, the "white space" without text in these slides is actually blue. Some public-speaking experts believe that black type on a white background can be too stark for a slide; instead, they recommend a dark blue background with yellow or white type. However, others believe that black on white is fine and may in fact be what the audience is accustomed to. Presentation software like PowerPoint makes it easy for you to experiment with these options.

USING HEADINGS AND ALIGNMENT

Readers look for cues about what's most important and about how components are related to one another. Effective document design provides just such cues through features like headings and subheadings. Clear headings help your readers navigate by showing a document's hierarchy of ideas. Appropriately aligned headings guide the reader's eye.

Heading Levels.   The relative size and prominence of the section headings indicate how a document is structured and which sections are most important. Headings also name the sections so that readers know where they are and where they are going. Though headings are often unnecessary in short essays, they can focus the attention of readers while providing a useful pathway through complex documents such as research papers, lab reports, business proposals, and Web-based documents.

Use typographical elements to distinguish clearly between levels of headings and subheadings within your document. Once you decide what a major section (or *level-one*) heading should look like — boldfaced and italicized, for example — be consistent with comparable headings. Treat minor headings consistently as well. In this book, you'll notice that all of the major headings within a chapter are set like this:

Level-One Heading   [17-point, boldfaced, italicized, in color]

Level-two and level-three headings are set like this:

LEVEL-TWO HEADING   [12-point, capitalized, boldfaced]

Level-Three Heading   [10-point, boldfaced]

Each of these styles is used consistently in order to give readers visual cues to both content and organization. The headings differ from each other and from the main text in size, style, and color. Differentiating headings in such ways makes your text easier to read and easier to use whether your reader is scrutinizing every word or scanning only key points.

If your instructor asks you to follow the guidelines of a particular style, you may have less flexibility in formatting headings. For example, the American Psychological Association (APA) illustrates five levels of headings, all in the same regular font style and size as the body text but varying capitalization, placement (centered or left), and underlining to distinguish the levels. MLA, however, does not recommend headings or discuss their design.

Heading Consistency.   The headings in your document should be brief, clear, and informative. The four most common styles of headings are *-ing*

■ For more on MLA and APA style, see E1–E2 in the Quick Research Guide (the dark-red-edged pages). For even more MLA help, consult the *MLA Handbook for Writers of Research Papers,* or go to <www.mla.org/style>. For even more APA help, consult the *Publication Manual of the American Psychological Association* or <www.apastyle.org>.

■ For more on parallel structure, see B2 in the Quick Editing Guide (the dark-blue-edged pages).

(gerund) phrases, noun phrases, questions, and imperative sentences. Effective writers use consistent parallel phrasing, whatever the style they choose. In other words, if you write a level-one heading as an *-ing* phrase, make sure that all of the level-one headings that follow are also *-ing* phrases.

Here are some examples of each style of heading:

-ING PHRASES
Using the College Catalog
Choosing Courses
Declaring a Major

NOUN PHRASES
The Benefits of Electronic Commerce
The Challenges of Electronic Commerce
The Characteristics of the Online Shopper

QUESTIONS
What Is Hepatitis C?
Who Is at Risk?
How Is Hepatitis C Treated?

IMPERATIVE SENTENCES
Initiate Your IRA Rollover
Learn Your Distribution Options
Select New Investments

■ For more information on Web design, visit the Web Style Guide at <www.webstyleguide.com>.

In general, Web pages — especially home pages and site guides — tend to have more headings than other types of documents because they are designed to help readers find information quickly, within a small viewing frame. If you are designing a Web page, consider what different users might want to find on your site. Then clearly connect your headings and content to users' needs.

The Web page shown in Figure 21.12 organizes links under three major categories — Connecting, Organizing, and Sponsoring. All three are identified by *-ing* words that suggest action in progress. Under these broad headings are links to other content on the site, most identified by nouns and noun phrases (such as Member Benefits or Summer Institutes). However, two links that urge action by the viewer — Join and Update — both begin with verbs. Such headings use parallel structure to identify and group topics and also to accomplish a purpose, here to encourage participation in service learning.

Heading Alignment.   Besides being consistently styled and phrased, headings should also be consistently placed, or aligned, along the same vertical line. Figure 21.13 illustrates confusing alignment, mixing left-aligned, right-aligned, and fully justified text running out to both the left and right margins. Because your title is generally centered, you might be tempted to center all of your headings, but doing so may introduce nonfunctional white space that detracts from the design of your paper. Instead, rely on the graphic designer's principle of alignment: each element should be aligned with at least one other item, rather than having an alignment all its own.

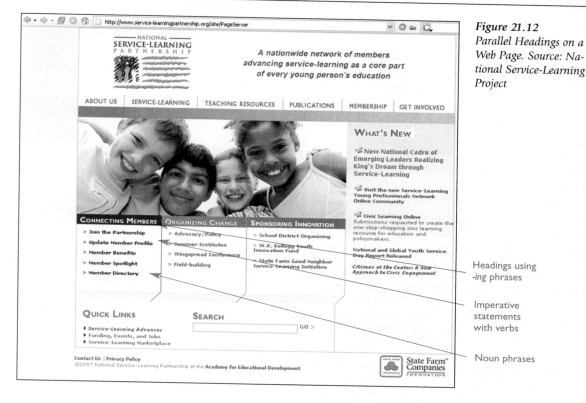

Figure 21.12
Parallel Headings on a Web Page. Source: National Service-Learning Project

Headings using -ing phrases

Imperative statements with verbs

Noun phrases

The Progressive Party Platform of 1912

Centered title

The Rule of the People

The National Progressive party, committed to the principles of government by a self-controlled democracy expressing its will through representatives of the people, pledges itself to secure such alterations in the fundamental law of the several States and the United States as shall insure the representative character of the government.

In particular, the party declares for direct primaries for the nomination of State and National officers; for nationwide preferential primaries for candidates for presidency; for the direct election of the United States Senators by the people; and we urge on the States the policy of the short ballot, with responsibility to the people secured by the initiative, referendum and recall.

Left-aligned text

Amendment of Constitution

The Progressive party, believing that a free people should have the power from time to time to amend their fundamental law so as to adapt it progressively to the changing needs of the people, pledges itself to provide a more easy and expeditious method of amending the Federal Constitution. . . .

Equal Suffrage

The Progressive party, believing that no people can justly claim to be a true democracy which denies political rights on account of sex, pledges itself to the task of securing equal suffrage to men and women alike.

Fully justified text, aligned at left and right

Right-aligned text

Figure 21.13
Centered Title over Text with Varying Alignments. Source: "The Progressive Party Platform of 1912." From National Party Platforms 1840–1964. *Kirk H. Porter and Donald Bruce Johnson, comps. U of Illinois P., 1966, 175–78.*

But centering *is* an alignment, you might protest. Indeed, centering all of your headings and subheadings should create a uniform alignment throughout your paper. Except in cases of coincidence, however, each centered heading will be a different length and thus, to the reader's eye, will have a different alignment, as you can see in Figure 21.14.

In contrast, in Figure 21.15 the headings are positioned at the left margin (or "flush left," as designers call it) to create a strong line down the left

Figure 21.14
Centered Headings
(no strong alignment).
Source: See Figure 21.13

> ### The Progressive Party Platform of 1912
>
> #### The Rule of the People
> The National Progressive party, committed to the principles of government by a self-controlled democracy expressing its will through representatives of the people, pledges itself to secure such alterations in the fundamental law of the several States and the United States as shall insure the representative character of the government.
>
> In particular, the party declares for direct primaries for the nomination of State and National officers; for nationwide preferential primaries for candidates for presidency; for the direct election of the United States Senators by the people; and we urge on the States the policy of the short ballot, with responsibility to the people secured by the initiative, referendum and recall.
>
> #### Amendment of Constitution
> The Progressive party, believing that a free people should have the power from time to time to amend their fundamental law so as to adapt it progressively to the changing needs of the people, pledges itself to provide a more easy and expeditious method of amending the Federal Constitution. . . .
>
> #### Equal Suffrage
> The Progressive party, believing that no people can justly claim to be a true democracy which denies political rights on account of sex, pledges itself to the task of securing equal suffrage to men and women alike.

Figure 21.15
Left-aligned Title, Head-
ings, and Text (strong
alignment). Source:
See Figure 21.13

> ### The Progressive Party Platform of 1912
>
> #### The Rule of the People
> The National Progressive party, committed to the principles of government by a self-controlled democracy expressing its will through representatives of the people, pledges itself to secure such alterations in the fundamental law of the several States and the United States as shall insure the representative character of the government.
>
> In particular, the party declares for direct primaries for the nomination of State and National officers; for nationwide preferential primaries for candidates for presidency; for the direct election of the United States Senators by the people; and we urge on the States the policy of the short ballot, with responsibility to the people secured by the initiative, referendum and recall.
>
> #### Amendment of Constitution
> The Progressive party, believing that a free people should have the power from time to time to amend their fundamental law so as to adapt it progressively to the changing needs of the people, pledges itself to provide a more easy and expeditious method of amending the Federal Constitution. . . .
>
> #### Equal Suffrage
> The Progressive party, believing that no people can justly claim to be a true democracy which denies political rights on account of sex, pledges itself to the task of securing equal suffrage to men and women alike.

side of the page. This line helps keep the reader's eye moving downward and forward through the paper. The indented paragraphs also line up with each other, creating another strong alignment on the page. The text itself lines up along the left margin. The Web page in Figure 21.12 also groups and aligns the headings.

Much of the time you will use both left-aligned text and left-aligned headings in your document. Right-aligned text is rare in a college paper, except for special elements such as running headers and footers (discussed below). Some people like the tidy look of fully justified text, even on both sides, but you should use it with caution. The computer justifies text by adding extra white space between words and by hyphenating words that don't fit on a line; both techniques make text harder to read. Many teachers prefer left alignment only and no automatic hyphenation, as the MLA and APA guidelines advise.

USING REPETITION PURPOSEFULLY

Though common in poetry and in technical writing, too much verbal repetition may be frowned upon in academic writing. *Visual* repetition, however, can assist a reader. If you were driving along a freeway and the familiar navigation signs — the green and white rectangles — suddenly changed to purple triangles, you might wonder whether you had strayed into a different country. Similarly, if the font or alignment suddenly changes in a paper, the reader immediately asks: What is this new navigational cue? What am I expected to do now?

To avoid disorienting readers, repeat one or two fonts throughout your paper to sustain a clean, uncluttered look. Consistent headings and subheadings also serve as a kind of road map to guide the readers' progress. Another simple design strategy is the use of running, or repeated, headers and footers. A *running header* is a line of information that appears consistently at the top of each page of your document, while a *running footer* appears consistently at the bottom of pages. Check the top of this page and the few after or before it to figure out the pattern for this book's running headers. As part of the header or the footer, writers sometimes include information such as the document title, its file name, or a distinctive graphic. Once you create a header or footer, your word processor can automatically insert it on each page with the page number, if you've selected that option, or with the date. Figure 21.16 illustrates the type of header required in MLA style.

Fallon 2

Claremont's third message is that activism is needed to combat this

terrorism and hatred, and he provides clear models for activism. . . .

Figure 21.16
Sample Header (running header) in MLA Style, from Geoffrey Fallon's "Hatred within an Illustrated Medium: Those Uncanny X-Men"

FOR E-WRITERS

Adding Running Heads

Most word-processing programs can add running heads to your papers, automatically supplying your last name and the page number (or other information) at the top of each page. Check the View or Format menu for a Header or Footer option. In the Header box, use the tab key or your mouse to move to the header location you desire — generally the far right side for an academic paper. Type the header information — such as your last name (in MLA style), a key word from your title (in APA style), or your own identifier for a draft — and then click on the Page Number option or icon. Each page will be correctly numbered in sequence even if you delete or add passages.

USING COLOR EFFECTIVELY

Until recently, college papers typically have not included much color. However, word-processing software and other programs now make it possible to include color graphics, photographs, and other images in papers. Make sure that color serves a purpose — for instance, to highlight key information — instead of being used merely as decoration. For example, a good use of color would be to distinguish the slices in a pie chart (see p. 414).

If you are creating documents beyond college papers, you may have even more opportunities to use color. For example, on a Web page you can use color to highlight headings and key information, as in Figure 21.17, or to emphasize a theme such as the patriotic nature of service learning, as in Figure 21.12. On any given page, avoid using too many colors because they can overload readers and defeat the purpose of helping them find important information. Also, choose your colors carefully. For example, although yellow is an attention-getting color, as school buses and traffic signs illustrate, words written in yellow on a white background are hard to read.

Using Visuals to Reinforce Your Content

Some of your documents may benefit from the addition of graphs, diagrams, maps, photographs, or other materials that add visual interest, convey information, and reinforce your text. You might prepare these yourself or incorporate such materials from other sources, giving credit and requesting permission, if needed (see p. 415). In either case, visual materials should suit your purpose and your audience, not be used as decoration. Check your software for tools for creating graphics like pie charts, bar charts, and tables. If you are unfamiliar with these functions, ask for advice at the computer lab.

ADDING VISUALS

When could your document benefit from visuals? To answer this question, think about the ways in which visual material can support your point.

- To discuss a conflict in a certain geographical area, supply a map.
- To illustrate an autobiographical essay, scan an image of yourself as a baby or at some important moment in your life.
- To clarify the stages or steps in a process, a procedure, or a set of directions, include a diagram.
- To present statistical information, add graphs, charts, or tables.

Process Diagrams and Illustrations.   A paper explaining a process such as wastewater treatment in King County, Washington, might include a diagram, as in Figure 21.18. On the other hand, Figure 21.19 shows another way to illustrate a process. Notice how the drawings and descriptions work together to provide an overview of the tasks at an archaeological site.

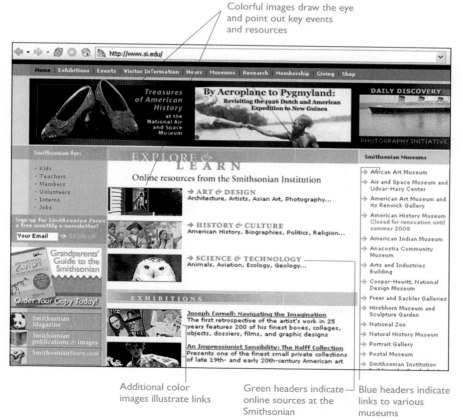

Figure 21.17
Use of Color on a Web Page. Source: The Smithsonian Institution

Figure 21.18
A Diagram Showing the
Process of Wastewater
Treatment in King County,
Washington. Source: King
County, Washington,
Department of Natural
Resources Wastewater
Treatment Division

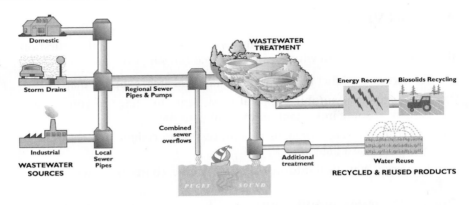

Figure 21.19
Illustration of Work at an
Archaeological Dig.
Source: *Dorling Kindersley,*
Children's Illustrated
Encyclopedia

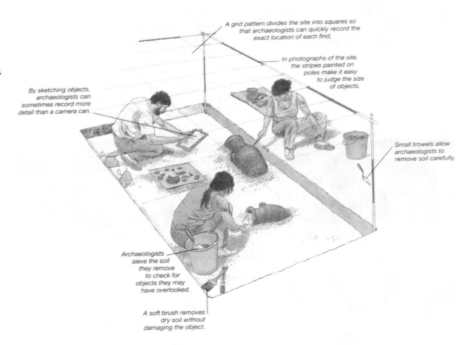

For more advice on
preparing graphs and
charts, visit
<bedfordstmartins.com/
bedguide> and do a key-
word search:

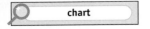

Comparative Graphs and Charts.   Graphics in college papers, magazines, Web sites, and other publications also consolidate information —
both numerical and verbal — in visual form. As the following examples
show, the various types of graphics convey information through visual elements such as size, shape, direction, and color.

• To illustrate a trend, a relationship, a comparison, or a contrast — the
number of children who use the Internet or the ratio of men to women

Adding Visuals to Your Text

How can you add visuals to your paper? In a few cases — such as using material from a print source with a deadline only hours away — your simplest method may be the old-fashioned one: add an extra page break in your text where you want to place the material, print the final version of your file, and then use the numbered blank page to photocopy or present the material in your paper. Much of the time, however, you can create your own material right in your text file. To prepare a table, use the Insert or the Table menu. Simply add page breaks before and after it if you wish to present it on its own page, as some instructors and academic style manuals prefer.

Other options for adding boxes, graphs, pie charts, bar charts, or art may be available through the Insert menu, a Drawing or Clip Art option, or related spreadsheet or presentation software. Use a scanner to integrate printed material, or try an image editor to scan photographs or add digital photos. Turn to your computer lab for help in using or accessing sophisticated software applications or equipment more advanced than your own. For a complex project, get help well ahead of your deadline, and allow plenty of time to learn new techniques for integrating visuals. Be sure to request permission to use images when needed, and acknowledge visual sources as carefully as textual sources.

FOR E-WRITERS

at your college — create a graph in a spreadsheet. For example, Figure 21.20 compares trends in album sales for two years.

• To illustrate percentages or shares of a whole, add a pie chart, such as those in Figure 21.21. These charts indicate how much of the complete (100%) market for albums (total and current month) is controlled by various distributors.

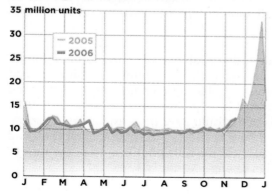

Weekly Album Sales

Figure 21.20
A Graph Comparing Album Sales in 2005 and 2006 (Months— January to January). Source: Billboard, *week ending November 29, 2006*

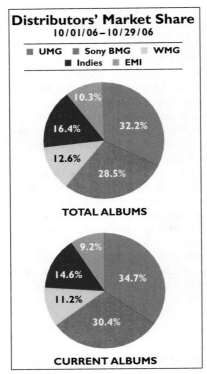

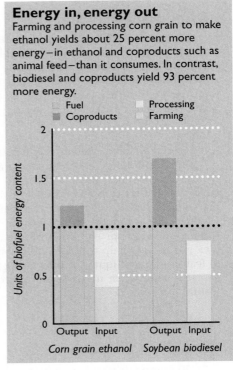

Figure 21.21   Pie Charts Showing Album Distributors' Market Share. Source: Billboard, *week ending October 29, 2006*

Figure 21.22   A Bar Chart Presenting Numerical Comparisons. Source: Technology Review, *September/October 2006; Jason Hill, University of Minnesota,* Proceedings of the National Academy of Sciences.

- To compare various values or amounts, provide a bar chart like the one in Figure 21.22. This chart illustrates an advantage of soybean-based biodiesel over corn-based ethanol by contrasting the energy required to produce each alternative fuel.

Comparative Tables.   Consider using a table to organize textual information for easier reading. Typically, tables have columns (running up and down) and rows (running across). Tables are common in academic and workplace writing but are also used in popular magazines, as Figure 21.23 shows. The information in this table could have been explained in a paragraph, but a block of text would have been less accessible for readers — and far less visually interesting. Notice how the little photographs of the various objects described bring the design to life.

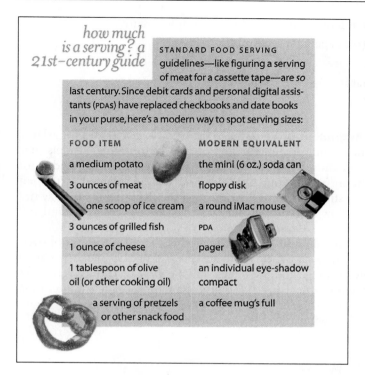

Figure 21.23
A Table Organiz-
ing Textual Data.
Source: Health,
May 2002, page
35

CREDITING SOURCES

If you include visual materials from another source, printed or electronic, credit that source in your essay. Be sure to ask permission, if required, to use an image so that you don't risk violating the copyright. If you download an image from the Web, check the site for its guidelines for the use of images. Follow these guidelines, asking permission if necessary and giving credit to the owner of the copyright. If you are uncertain about whether you can use an image from a source, check with your teacher.

■ For more on the MLA and APA documentation styles, see E1–E2 in the Quick Research Guide (the dark-red-edged pages).

ARRANGING VISUALS AND TEXT IN YOUR DOCUMENT

Using visuals can create problems in *layout*, the arrangement of text and graphics on a page. Here are some guidelines for ensuring that your layout is effective and appropriate for your purpose and audience.

Integration of Visuals and Text.   Because you are including the visual to support an idea in your text, your reader will make better sense of the graph, chart, diagram, or photograph if you provide a context for it. In an introductory sentence, you should give your reader this information:

- The number or letter of the visual (for example, Figure 6)
- Its location (on page 9, in section 3)
- Its content
- The point that it helps you to make

Also supply a label with your visual to identify its topic and number.

Placement and Alignment of Visuals.   Placing a visual close to the related discussion will make your document easy for readers to follow. Readers may get distracted if they must flip from the body of the text to an appendix, for example. In addition, when your headings and text are aligned at the left margin to sustain a strong forward flow through the document, you may not want to disrupt the flow by centering your visuals. Let your eye be the judge.

Balance between Visuals and Text.   The visuals should support, not overshadow, the content of your paper. Try to strike a balance between the size of any single graphic or image and the related chunks of text. Though a reader's eye should be drawn to the visual, try to give it an appropriate — rather than excessive — share of the page layout.

Consider the following questions as you design your document:

DOCUMENT DESIGN CHECKLIST

____ Does your document design meet your readers' expectations and acknowledge their constraints?

____ Does your document design help to achieve your purpose? Does it help emphasize your key points and clear organization?

____ Have you used appropriate fonts, or typefaces, in your document? Do you use boldface and italic type sparingly for emphasis? Have you used bulleted or numbered lists when appropriate to call out information?

____ Do you use white space strategically, calling attention to or linking portions of text rather than creating gaps between textual elements?

____ Do your headings, subheadings, and alignment provide readers with clear and purposeful navigational cues?

____ Have you used repeated elements, such as running headers or footers, that increase visual coherence?

____ Do your diagrams, photographs, or other illustrations clarify your content? Do your graphs, charts, or tables present numerical or textual information "at a glance"?

____ Have you used color effectively to highlight, distinguish, or organize information?

____ Does your layout integrate the visuals using appropriate placement, size, and alignment?

____ Have you secured any permission needed to use copyrighted material? Have you credited the source of each visual?

■ Activities and Assignments

1. Experiment with the fonts available on your computer. Using a paragraph or two from a recent paper, go through the font list to see how your sentences look in various fonts. Test different sizes as well as the bold and italic versions. How readable is each font?

2. Look at a bulletin board, literature rack, magazine shelf, or other location that displays different examples of printed material. Identify different uses of fonts to establish a mood or convey a message. Select one example that you find particularly effective, and briefly explain how the font helps to convey the desired mood or message to the audience. If possible, include a copy of the example with your paper.

3. Using your favorite search engine (Google or Yahoo!, for example), locate an online example of a research paper or report. (The keywords "research paper" or "research report" should return several examples.) Or find a technical or government report online or in the library. Read the abstract or introduction to get an idea of the author's topic. Then quickly skim the report in order to answer the following questions:

   a. What is the purpose of the report?

   b. Who is the intended audience? How can you tell?

   c. In what ways does the writer use document design to address readers' needs and constraints?

   d. How does the writer use document design to help make his or her point?

   e. What design revisions would you recommend to the writer? How might these changes improve the audience's reading experience?

   Write a brief essay presenting your findings.

4. FOR GROUP WORK: Assemble several different documents that you are reading or might read — perhaps a textbook, a newspaper, a magazine, an online article, a brochure, a catalog, or a campus publication. Examine each document carefully, considering which aspects of the design seem effective or ineffective in achieving the writer's purpose and meeting the reader's needs. Then, bring your documents and notes to class. In groups of three to five students, share your findings.

5. FOR GROUP WORK: In a small group, examine several different documents — one supplied by each group member or one or two of the sets prepared for activity 4. For each document, consider what other design choices might have made the visual presentation more effective. When you've finished your analysis, share your findings with the class.

Chapter 22
Strategies for Understanding Visual Representations

On a street-corner billboard, a man is biting into a jelly doughnut while driving, a look of horror on his face. He's horrified because a big blob of purple jelly (captured in midair) is about to land in the middle of his white dress shirt. The only other picture on the billboard is a detergent manufacturer's logo.

Other billboards on this corner advertise such diverse commodities as fast food, cell-phone services, and the radiology department at a local hospital. Thousands of drivers pause at this intersection to wait out a red light — a captive audience for aggressive and compelling visual representations. It's a good location for the detergent ad: drivers who pass the billboard, especially those who are eating in their cars, will relate to the problem of food spills on nice clothes. Obviously, the company that sponsored the ad hopes these people will remember its brand — the one that can tackle even the worst stains on the whitest shirts — the next time they buy laundry detergent.

The specific images on these billboards change with time, but images are a constant and persistent presence in our lives. The sign atop a taxi invites us to try the new ride at a local tourist attraction. A celebrity sporting a milk moustache smiles from the side of a city bus, accompanied by the familiar question, "Got milk?" The lettering on a pickup truck urges us to call for a free landscaping estimate. On television, video, and the Web, advertising images surround us, trying to shape our opinions about everything from personal hygiene products to snack foods to political candidates.

Advertisements are not the only visual representations that affect us. Cartoons, photographs, drawings, paintings, logos, graphics, and other two-dimensional media originate from a variety of sources with a variety of purposes — and all work to evoke responses. The critical skills you develop for analyzing these still images also apply to other types of visual representations, including television commercials, films, and stage productions. We can't help but notice visual images, and whether we respond with a smile or a frown, one thing is certain: visuals help to structure our views of reality.

Using Strategies for Visual Analysis

Begin a visual analysis by conducting a *close reading* of the image. Like a literal and critical reading of a written text, a close reading of an image involves careful, in-depth examination of the advertisement, photograph, cartoon, artwork, or other visual representation. Your close reading should focus on the following three levels of questions:

- **What is the big picture?** What is the source of the image? What is its purpose? What audience does it address? What prominent element in the image stands out? What focal point draws the eye?

- **What characteristics of the image can you observe?** What story does the image tell? What people or animals appear in the image? What are the major elements of the image? How are they arranged?

- **How can you interpret what the image suggests?** What feeling or mood does it create? What is its cultural meaning? What are the roles of any signs, symbols, or language that it includes? What is the image about?

The rest of the chapter explains these three levels of visual analysis in more detail. You may discover that your classmates respond differently to some images than you do. Your personal cultural background and your experiences may influence how you interpret the meaning of an image. If you plan

■ For a model visual analysis and visual-analysis activity, visit <bedfordstmartins.com/bedguide> and do a keyword search:

visual

■ For more on literal and critical reading of texts, see Ch. 2. For a checklist for analyzing images, see pp. 433–34.

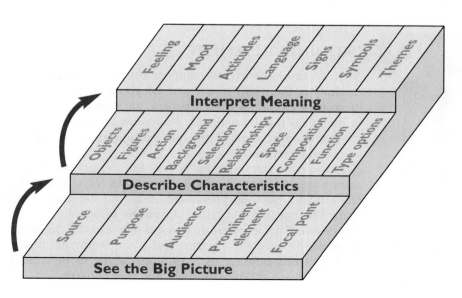

to write about the image you analyze, take notes or use your journal to record your observations and interpretations. Be sure to include a copy of the image, if one is available, when you solicit peer review of your essay or submit it to your teacher.

Level One: Seeing the Big Picture

Begin your close reading of an image by discovering what you can about its source and overall composition. If you include the image in a paper, you will need to cite the source and its "author" or artist, just as you would if you were including text from a reading, an article, or a literary work.

■ For more on crediting sources of visuals, see p. 415.

PURPOSE AND AUDIENCE

■ For more on purpose and audience, see pp. 14–18 and pp. 310–12.

Identifying the purpose and intended audience for an image is sometimes complicated. For example, an image may appear in its original context or in a different situation, used seriously, humorously, or allusively. Use these questions to help you explore the purpose of and audience for the image:

DISCOVERY CHECKLIST

Figure 22.1
Public-Service Advertisement with One Prominent Element. Source: Act Against Violence.org/Ad Council

____ What is the context for the image? For example, if it is an advertisement, when and where did it run? If it is a photograph, painting, or other work of art, who is the artist? Where has it been published or exhibited?

____ What is the purpose of the image?

____ What audience does the image aim to attract?

PROMINENT ELEMENT

Next, examine the overall composition of the image. Look carefully at the whole image and ask yourself, "Is there one prominent element — object, person, background, writing — in the image that immediately attracts my attention?" Examine that element in detail to figure out how and why it draws you into the image.

Answering that question is easy for a visual that showcases a single object or person, as in Figure 22.1. There, the child is the obvious prominent element. Her dark eyes, framed by her dark hair, draw the viewer to her alert, intent expression. That expression suggests her capacity to learn from all she observes. The text above and below her image reinforces this message as it cautions adults to be careful what they teach children through their own conduct.

Identifying the prominent element can be more complicated for a visual with several characters. For example, consider which form draws your eye in Figure 22.2. Many people would first notice the dark-haired Caucasian girl. Her prominence in the picture can be explained in part by her position at the left side of the photograph, framed by the white porch railing. People who read from left to right and top to bottom — including most Americans and Europeans — also typically read photographs in the same way, which means that the viewer's eye is likely to be drawn into the photograph at the upper left corner. For this reason, artists and photographers often position key elements — those they want viewers to see right away — somewhere in the upper left quadrant of the image. (See Figure 22.3.)

FOCAL POINT

There is another reason the reader's eye might be drawn first to the girl on the left: notice that all of the other children are turned slightly toward her, straining to see the pages of the magazine she is holding. Not only is she positioned so as to provide a focal point for the viewer, but she is also the focal point of action within the photograph.

Now, take a look at the child on the right side of the picture. You may have noticed her first. Or, once you did notice her, you may have been surprised that she didn't attract your attention right away. After all, she provides some contrast within the photograph because she sits apart from the other girls, seems to be a little younger, and does not appear to be included in their little group. What's more, she's not wearing any clothes. Still, most people won't notice her first because of the path the eye typically travels within a photograph. Because of the left-to-right and top-to-bottom reading pattern that Americans and Europeans take for granted, most of us view photographs in a Z pattern, as depicted in Figure 22.4. Even though most viewers would notice the child on the far right last, they would still pause to look at her. Thus, the bottom right corner of an image is a second very important position that a skilled photographer can use to retain the viewers' attention. When you look at the "big picture" in this way, you can see the overall composition of the image, identify its prominent element, and determine its focal point.

Level Two: Observing the Characteristics of an Image

As you concentrate on the literal reading of a written text, you become aware of the information it presents, you comprehend what it means, and you are able to apply it in relation to other situations. Similarly, your close reading of an image includes observing its *denotative* or literal characteristics. At this stage, you focus on exactly what the image depicts — observing it objectively — rather than probing what it means or signifies.

For more about reading on a literal level, see pp. 25–29. For a checklist for analyzing images, see pp. 433–34.

Figure 22.2 (top)
Photograph of Four Children,
Kodak Picture of the Day,
October 22, 2000

Figure 22.3 (above left)
Photograph Divided into
Quarters

Figure 22.4 (above right)
Z Pattern Often Used to Read
Images

Figure 22.5 (right)
Close-Up Detail of Photograph

CAST OF CHARACTERS

Objects.   Examine the condition, colors, sizes, functions, and positions of the objects included in the image. In Figure 22.2, for example, only one object is depicted in the image: a large magazine. Everything else in the image is either a figure or part of the background.

Figures.   Look closely at any figures (men, women, children, animals) in the image. Consider their facial expressions, poses, hairstyles and colors, ages, sexes, ethnicity, possible education, suggested occupations, apparent relationships to each other, and so on.

Figure 22.2 shows four girls, three about eight or nine years old and the fourth a few years younger. Three of the girls are Caucasian, and one is African American. The dark-haired Caucasian girl is wearing a colorful bathing suit as is the African American girl. Between them sits a light-haired Caucasian girl, wearing shorts and a short-sleeved blue and white flowered T-shirt. All three appear to be dressed appropriately for the weather. The three girls pore over the magazine held by the dark-haired Caucasian girl. Judging from their facial expressions, they are totally engrossed in the magazine, as well as a little puzzled. The girls seem to be looking at a picture; the magazine is turned sideways with the spine at the bottom.

The fourth child, the youngest in the photograph, sits slightly apart from the others. Her light hair appears damp — possibly from swimming, we might conclude, because two of the other girls are attired in swimsuits. We can see that her skin is tanned and that she has several small bruises on her legs, probably acquired during play. Her right leg is crossed over her left, causing her body to turn slightly away from the other girls. Her face is turned toward them, however, and she seems to be trying to see what they are looking at. Her hands are raised, her eyes are bright, and she's smiling at whatever she is able to see of the magazine.

STORY OF THE IMAGE

Action.   The action shown in an image suggests its "plot" or story, the events surrounding the moment captured in the image. In Figure 22.2, four children are seated on the steps of a house looking at a magazine on a summer day. Because no adults appear in the picture and the children look puzzled, we might assume that they are looking at something they don't understand, possibly something adults might frown on. On the other hand, they are not being secretive, so this impression may not be accurate.

Background.   The background in an image shows where and when the action takes place. In Figure 22.2, the children are seated on the wooden steps of a blue house. We might conclude that the steps are part of a back porch rather than a front porch because the porch is relatively small and the steps begin immediately: there is no deck and consequently nowhere to sit except on the steps themselves. The top step is painted blue, and the railing is painted white to match the white metal door and window frames. In a few places the paint is chipped or worn away. But these signs of disrepair simply seem to indicate that the house is lived in and comfortable; they are not severe enough to suggest that the occupants are poor. In the windows next to the steps and on the door, we can see the reflections of trees. The children's clothes identify the season as summer.

DESIGN AND ARRANGEMENT

Selection of Elements.   When you look at the design of an image, you might reflect on both the elements within the image and their organization.

- What are the major colors and shapes?
- How are they arranged?
- Does the image appear balanced? Are light and dark areas arranged symmetrically?
- Does the image appear organized or chaotic?
- Is one area of the picture darker (heavier) or brighter (lighter) than other areas?
- What does the design make you think of—does it evoke a particular emotion, historical period, or memory?

In Figure 22.2, the most prominent shape is the white porch railing that frames the children and draws the viewer's eye in toward the action. The image appears balanced, in that the white door provides the backdrop for the youngest child, while the blue siding and white porch railing frame the other girls. Therefore, the image is split down the center, both by the separation of the figures and by the shapes that make up the background. The brightly colored summer clothing worn by the girls on the left side also accentuates the youngest child's monochromatic nakedness.

Relationship of Elements.   Visual elements may be related to one another or to written material that appears with them. As you notice such relationships, consider what they tell you. In Figure 22.2, for instance, the three older girls are grouped together around the magazine, and the youngest child is clearly not part of their group. She is separated physically from the others by a bit of space and by the vertical line formed by the doorframe, which splits the background in two. Moreover, her body is turned slightly away from them, and she is not clothed. However, her gaze, like the other girls', is on the magazine that they are scrutinizing; this element of the picture connects all of the children.

■ For more information on white space in document design, see pp. 402–04.

Use of Space.   An image may be surrounded by a lot of "white space"— empty space without text or graphics — or it may be "busy," filled with visual and written elements. White space is effective when it provides relief from an otherwise busy layout or when it directs the reader's eye to key elements of the image. The image in Figure 22.2 does not include any empty space; its shapes and colors guide the viewer's eye.

Figure 22.6
Volkswagen Advertise-
ment, about 1959

In contrast, look at the image in Figure 22.6. It specifically uses white space to call attention to the Volkswagen's small size. When this advertisement was produced back in 1959, many American cars were large and heavy. The VW, a German import, provided consumers with an alternative type of vehicle, and the advertising emphasized this contrast.

ARTISTIC CHOICES

Whether an image is a photograph, a drawing, or another form of representation, the person who composes it considers its artistic effect, its function, and its connection to related text.

Composition Decisions.   Aesthetic or artistic choices may vary with the preferences of the designer and the characteristics of the medium. For example, if an image is a photograph, the photographer might use a close-up, medium, or wide-angle shot to compose it—and also determine the angle of the shot, the lighting, and the use of color.

The picture of the four children in Figure 22.2 (p. 422) is a medium shot and has been taken at the children's eye level. If the photograph were a close-up, only one aspect of the image would be visible. Notice in Figure 22.5 how the meaning of the picture changes when we view the girls' faces as a close-up. We have no way of telling where the picture was taken or what the girls are doing; moreover, by moving in closer, this view completely cuts out the youngest child. The girls' attentiveness is still apparent, but we can't quite tell what its object is.

In contrast, in the Volkswagen ad (Figure 22.6), the white space creates the effect of a long shot taken from below with a telephoto lens. We see the car as it might appear if we were looking down at it through the wrong end of a pair of binoculars. This vantage point shrinks the car so that an already small vehicle looks even smaller.

For more about the ways visuals support content, see pp. 410–14.

Function Decisions.   When using an image to illustrate a point, either alone or in connection with text, a writer must make sure that the illustration serves the overall purpose of the document. In other words, form should follow function. For example, the 1959 Oldsmobile ad, Figure 22.7, shows people who seem to be having a good time; in fact, one scene is set near the shore. These illustrations suggest that those who purchase the cars will enjoy life, a notion that undoubtedly suits the advertiser's goals.

For a sample pie chart, see Figure 21.21, p. 414. For sample photographs, turn to the images opening Chs. 4 to 12 and 23 to 27.

Writers have many choices available to them for illustrations—not only photographs and drawings but also charts, graphs, and tables. Certain types of visuals are especially suited to certain functions. For example, a pie chart is perhaps the best way to convey parts of a whole visually. A photograph effectively captures the drama and intensity of the moment—a child's rescue, a family's grief, or an earthquake's toll. When you look at newspapers, magazines, and other publications, consider how the visuals function and why the writer might have chosen to include them.

For more on typefaces, see pp. 396–400.

Typeface Options.   Many images, especially advertisements, combine image and text, using the typeface to set a particular mood and convey a particular impression. For example, Times New Roman is a common typeface, easy to read and somewhat conservative, whereas **Comic Sans MS** is considered informal—almost playful—and looks handwritten. Any printed element included in an image may be trendy or conservative, large or small, in rela-

Figure 22.7
Oldsmobile Advertisement,
1959

tion to the image as a whole. Further, it may be meant to inform, evoke emotion, or decorate the page.

    Look back at Figure 22.6 (p. 425), the 1959 Volkswagen ad. The words "Think small" are printed in a sans serif typeface—spare and unadorned, just like the VW itself. The ad also includes a significant amount of text across the bottom of the page. While this text is difficult to read in the

▦ For a definition and example of sans serif type, see pp. 397–98.

Figure 22.8   *Stairway.*
Source: Design for Communica-
tion: Conceptual Graphic Design
Basics

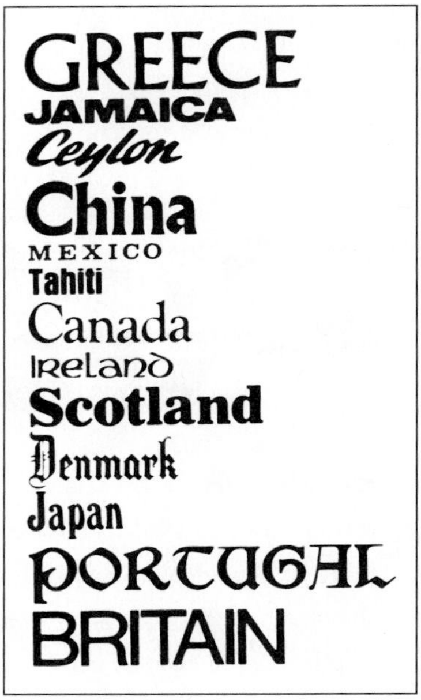

Figure 22.9   *Type as Cultural Cliché.*
Source: Publication Design

reproduction in this book, it humorously points out the benefits of driving a small imported vehicle instead of one of the many large, roomy cars common at the time.

In contrast to the VW ad campaign, the 1959 Oldsmobile marketing strategy promoted a big vehicle, not a small one, as Figure 22.7 illustrates. Here the cars are shown in medium to close-up view to call attention to their length. Happy human figures positioned in and beside the cars emphasize their size, and the cars are painted in bright colors, unlike the VW's service-able black. The type in the ad, like the other visual elements, reflects and pro-motes the Oldsmobile's size. The primary text in the center of the page is large enough to be read in the reproduction here. It introduces the brand name by opening the first sentence with the Oldsmobile '59 logo and praises the cars' expansive size, space, power, and other features. Near the bottom of each car image, however, are a few lines of "fine print" that are difficult to read in the reproduction — brief notes about other features of the car.

Other images besides advertisements use type to set a mood or convey feelings and ideas. Figure 22.8 is a design student's response to an assign-ment that called for using letters to create an image. The student used a simple typeface and a stairlike arrangement to help viewers "experience" the word *stairway*. Figure 22.9 illustrates how certain typefaces have become asso-ciated with particular countries — even to the point of becoming clichés. In fact, designers of travel posters, travel brochures, and other such publications often draw on predictable typographical choices like these to suggest a feel-ing or mood — for example, boldness, tradition, adventure, history.

Just as type can establish a mood or tone, the absence of any written language in an image can also affect how we view that image. Recall Figure 22.2 (p. 422), the photograph of the children sitting on the porch looking at a magazine. Because we can't see the magazine's title, we are left to wonder — perhaps with amusement — about what has so engrossed the children. If the title of the magazine — *Sports Illustrated, Wired, People* — were revealed to us, the photograph might seem less intriguing. By leaving us to speculate about the identity of the magazine, the photographer may keep us looking longer and harder at the image.

Level Three: Interpreting the Meaning of an Image

When you read a written text on an analytical level, you engage actively with the text. You analyze its parts from different angles, synthesize the material by combining it with related information, and finally evaluate or judge its significance. When you interpret an image, you do much the same, actively questioning and examining what the image *connotes* or suggests, speculating about what it signifies.

For more on reading analytically, see pp. 25–29. For a checklist for analyzing images, see pp. 433–34.

Because interpretation is more personal than observation, this process can reveal deep-seated individual and cultural values. In fact, interpreting an image is sometimes emotional or difficult because it may require you to examine beliefs that you are unaware of holding. You may even become impatient with visual analysis, perhaps feeling that too much is being read into the image. Like learning to read critically, however, learning to interpret images is a valuable skill. When you see an image that attracts you, chances are good that you like it because it upholds strong cultural beliefs. Through close reading of images, you can examine how image makers are able to perpetuate such cultural values and speculate about why — perhaps analyzing an artist's political motivations or an advertiser's economic motivations. When you interpret an image, you go beyond literal observation to examine what the image suggests and what it may mean.

GENERAL FEELING OR MOOD

To begin interpreting an image, consider what feeling or mood it creates and how it does so. If you are a woman, you probably recall huddling, around age eight or nine, with a couple of "best friends" as the girls do in Figure 22.2. As a result, the interaction in this photograph may seem very familiar and may evoke fond memories. If you are a man, this photograph may call up somewhat different memories. Although eight-year-old boys also cluster in small groups, their motivations may differ from those behind little girls' huddles. Moreover, anyone who was ignored or excluded at a young age

Figure 22.10
Photograph Conveying a Mood. Source: Jonathan Nourok, PhotoEdit

may feel a rush of sympathy for the youngest child; her separation from the older children may dredge up age-old hurt feelings.

For many viewers, the image may also suggest a mood associated with summer: sitting on the back porch after a trip to the swimming pool, spending a carefree day with friends. This "summer" mood is a particular cultural association related to the summers of childhood. By the time we reach college, summer no longer has the same feeling. Work, summer school, separations, and family responsibilities—maybe even for children like those in the picture—obliterate the freedoms of childhood summer vacations. However, another image might capture or represent a different version of this feeling or mood. As Figure 22.10 illustrates, an adult version of the "summer mood" might use similar colors and bright light to evoke a similar feeling. In this image, the cluster of childhood friends has been replaced by a solitary, reflective person, tapping the beauty of a summer scene through the creative experience of painting.

SOCIOLOGICAL, POLITICAL, ECONOMIC, OR CULTURAL ATTITUDES

On the surface, the Volkswagen ad in Figure 22.6 (p. 425) is simply an attempt to sell a car. But its message might be interpreted to mean "scale down"—lead a less consumer-oriented lifestyle. If Volkswagen had distributed this ad in the 1970s, it would have been unremarkable—faced with the first energy crisis that adversely affected American gasoline prices, many advertisers used ecological consciousness to sell cars. In 1959, however, energy conservation was not really a concern. Contrasted with other automobile ads of its time, the Volkswagen ad seems somewhat eccentric, making the novel suggestion that larger cars are excessively extravagant.

Figure 22.11
Photograph Using a Missing Element to Convey a Message. Source: Public Service Announcement, Americans for National Parks

Whereas the Volkswagen ad suggests that "small" refers both to size and affordability, the Oldsmobile ad in Figure 22.7 (p. 427) depicts a large vehicle and implies a large price tag. By emphasizing the Vista-Panoramic view and increased luggage space and by portraying the car near a seashore, the ad leads viewers to think about going on vacation. It thus implies luxury and exclusivity—not everyone can afford this car or the activities it suggests.

Sometimes what is missing from an image is as important as what is included. For instance, Figure 22.11 deliberately contrasts presence and absence, projecting a possible future scene—without the bear—to bring home its message about the need to protect and preserve our national parks and their residents. What's missing also may be more subtle, especially for viewers who wear the blinders of their own times, circumstances, or expecta-

Here today...

tions. For example, viewers of today might readily notice the absence of people of color in the 1959 Oldsmobile ad, An interesting study might investigate what types of magazines originally carried this ad, whether their readers recognized what was missing, and whether (and if so, how) Oldsmobiles were also advertised in publications aimed at Asian, African, or Spanish-speaking Americans.

LANGUAGE

Just as you would examine figures, colors, and shapes when you observe the literal characteristics of an image, so you need to examine its words, phrases, and sentences when you interpret what it suggests. Does its language provide information, generate an emotional response, or do both? Do its words repeat a sound or concept, signal a comparison (such as a "new, improved" product), carry sexual overtones, issue a challenge, or offer a definition or philosophy of life? The words in the center of the Oldsmobile ad in Figure 22.7, for instance, are calculated to associate the car with a leisurely, affluent lifestyle. On the other hand, VW's "Think small" ad in Figure 22.6 turns compactness into a goal, a quality to be desired in a car and, by extension, in life.

Frequently advertisements employ wordplay — lighthearted or serious — to get their messages across. Consider, for example, the public-service advertisement in Figure 22.12, which was created by a graphic-design student. This ad features a play on the word *tolerance*, which is scrambled on the chalkboard so that the letters in the center read *learn*. The chalkboard, a typical feature of the classroom, suggests that tolerance is a basic lesson to be learned. Also, the definition of tolerance at the bottom of the ad is much like other definitions students might look up in a dictionary. (It reads, "The capacity for, or practice of, recognizing or respecting the behavior, beliefs, opinions, practices, or rights of others, whether agreeing with them or not.")

Wordplay can also challenge viewers' preconceptions about a visual image. The billboard in Figure 22.13 shows a romantic — indeed, seductive — scene. The sophisticated couple gaze deeply into each other's eyes as the man kisses the woman's hand. However, the verbal exchange undermines that intimate scene and viewers' expectations about what happens next. Instead of a similar compliment in response to "Your scent is intoxicating," the billboard makes plain its antismoking position with the reply: "Yours is carcinogenic." In just seven words, the billboard counters the suave, romantic image of smoking with the reality of smelly, cancer-causing tobacco smoke.

Figure 22.12
Public-Service Advertisement Showing Wordplay.
Source: Design for Communication: Conceptual Graphic Design Basics

Figure 22.13
Billboard Showing Wordplay.
Source: Photograph by Bill
Aron, PhotoEdit

SIGNS AND SYMBOLS

Signs and symbols, such as product logos, are images or words that communicate key messages. In the Oldsmobile ad in Figure 22.7 (p. 427), the product logo doubles as the phrase that introduces the description of the 1959 model. Sometimes a product logo alone may be enough, as in the Hershey chocolate company's holiday ads that include little more than a single Hershey's Kiss. The shape of the Kiss serves as a logo or symbol for the company.

If you look back at the second magazine spread in Figure 21.3 (see p. 394), you'll see a prominent cultural symbol — the U.S. flag. The flag is held by a little boy who is sitting on a man's shoulders, presumably his father's. In this spread, the flag is associated not only with the Fourth of July, the article's subject, but also with a family's values. Even without the headings and quotations, the symbolism comes across clearly.

Figure 22.14 also combines a widely recognizable symbol — the bars and locked door of a jail cell — with the image of a child. This child, however, is not riding securely on dad's shoulders while celebrating a patriotic holiday. Instead, the child is confined in what looks like a bedroom scattered with toys. This public-service announcement turns around the usual message of the cell-door symbol, applying it not only to the potential offender but also to that person's family. The surprising image of the young child behind bars suggests the complex and potentially long-lasting effects of a prison sentence on families and relatives.

Figure 22.14
Public-Service Advertisement Using Symbolism.
Source: Project Safe Neighborhoods/Ad Council

THEMES

The theme of an image is not the same as its plot. When you identify the plot, you identify the story that is told by the image. When you identify the theme, on the other hand, you explain what the image is about. An ad for a diamond ring may tell the story of a man surprising his wife with a ring on their twenty-fifth wedding anniversary, but the advertisement's theme could be sex, romance, commitment, or some other concept. Similarly, the theme of a soft-drink ad might be competition, community, compassion, or individualism. A painting of the ocean might be about cheerfulness, fear, or loneliness.

Through a close reading, you can unearth clues and details to support your interpretation of the theme and convince others of its merit. For example, when you first glance at the image in Figure 22.15, it appears to illustrate a recipe for a tasty margarita. As you read the list of ingredients, you find that they suggest a tale of too many drinks and a drunk-driving accident after running a red light. Instead of promoting an alcoholic beverage or promising relaxing fun, this public-service announcement challenges the assumption that risky behavior won't carry consequences. Its text counters its suggestive image and reminds viewers of its theme—that well-being comes not from alcohol-fueled confidence but from responsible choices.

Ask the following questions as you analyze an image, such as a chapter opener in this book or an example in this chapter, or as you prepare to present your analysis in an essay:

Figure 22.15
Poster Conveying a Theme. Source: U.S. Department of Transportation/Ad Council

VISUAL ANALYSIS CH\ECKLIST

Seeing the Big Picture

What is the source of the image? What is its purpose and audience?

What prominent element in the image immediately attracts your attention? How and why does it draw you into the image?

____ What is the focal point of the image? How does the image direct your attention to this point? What path does your eye follow as you observe the image?

Observing the Characteristics of an Image

____ What objects are included in the image?

____ What figures (people or animals) appear in the image?

____ What action takes place in the image? What is its "plot" or story?

____ What is in the background of the image? Where does the action of the image take place? What kind of place is it?

____ What elements contribute to the design of the image? What colors and shapes does the image include? How are they arranged or balanced? What feeling, memory, or association does the design evoke?

____ How are the pictorial elements related to one another? How are they related to any written material? What do these relationships tell you as a viewer?

____ How does the image use space? Does it include a lot of white space, or does it seem cluttered and busy?

____ What composition decisions has the designer or artist made? What type of shot, shot angle, lighting, or color is used?

____ What is the function of the image? How does form support function?

____ What typefaces are used? What impressions do they convey?

Interpreting the Meaning of an Image

____ What general feeling do you get from looking at the image? What mood does it create? How does it create this mood?

___ What sociological, political, economic, or cultural attitudes are reflected in the image?

___ What language is included in the image? How does the language function?

___ What signs and symbols can you identify? What role do these play?

___ What theme or themes can you identify in the image?

■ Activities and Assignments

1. Find a print ad that evokes a strong emotional response. Study the ad closely, observing its characteristics and interpreting its meaning. Write an essay in which you explain the techniques by which the ad evokes your emotional response. Include a copy of the ad with your essay, and consult others to determine whether they have the same response to the ad.

For a sample analysis of a Volkswagen ad, see "Wham! Bam! Buy a VW, Ma'am!" (p. 184).

2. Volkswagen continues to produce thought-provoking advertisements like the one shown in Figure 22.6 on page 425. Video clips of some of the company's recent television ads can be found on its Web site at <www.vw.com/vwlife/commercial.html>. View one or two of these advertisements, considering such features as their stories or "plots"; the choice of figures, settings, and images; the angles from which subjects are filmed; and any text messages included. Based on your analysis of the ads, decide what message you think that the company wants to communicate about its cars. In an essay, describe this message and the audience that Volkswagen seems to be aiming for, and discuss how the artistic choices in the ads might appeal to this audience.

3. Compile a design notebook. Over several weeks, collect ten or twelve images that appeal to you. You may wish to choose examples of a particular genre, or your teacher may assign a genre or theme. For example, you might select advertisements, portraits, or photographs of campus landmarks. You might choose landscape paintings by different artists or snack food advertisements from magazines aimed at different audiences. On the other hand, your collection might revolve around a theme, such as friendship, competition, community, or romance. As you collect these images, "read" each one closely, and write short responses explaining your reactions to the images. At the end of the collection period, choose two or three images. Write an essay in which you compare or contrast them, analyzing how they illustrate the same genre, convey a theme, or appeal to different audiences.

4. Visit a music store, and find a CD cover whose design interests you. Make notes about design choices such as its prominent element and focal point, the use of color and imagery, and the use of typography. Based on the design, try to predict what kind of music is on the CD. If the store has CD-listening stations, try to listen to a track or two. Did the music match your expectations based on the CD design? If you were the CD designer, would you have made any different artistic choices? Write a brief essay discussing your observations, and attach a copy of the CD cover, if possible. (You might be able to print it out from the Web.) As an alternative assignment, listen to some music that's new to you, and design a CD cover for it, applying the elements described in this chapter. Describe in a brief paper the

visual elements you would include on your CD cover. If you wish, sketch your design for the cover, using colored pencils or markers or pasting in images or type from print sources, such as magazines or newspapers.

5. **FOR GROUP WORK:**   Select some type of image (for example, an advertisement; a visual from a magazine or image database; a CD, DVD, or video-cassette cover) and, on your own, make notes on its "literal" characteristics. (For guidance, see "Observing the Characteristics of an Image," pp. 421–29.) Then, bring your image and notes to class. In small groups of three to five students, share your images and discuss your literal readings.

6. **FOR GROUP WORK:**   In a small group, pick one or two of the images that the group members analyzed for activity 5. Ask each group member, in turn, to suggest possible interpretations of the images. (For guidance, see "Interpreting the Meaning of an Image," pp. 429–33.) What different interpretations do group members suggest? How do you account for their differences? Share your findings with the rest of the class.

A
Writer's
Reader

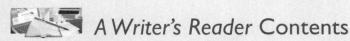

Introduction:
Reading to Write

A *Writer's Reader* is a collection of thirty-two carefully selected professional essays. We hope, first of all, that you will read these pieces simply for the sake of reading — enjoying and responding to the ideas presented. Good writers read widely, and in doing so, they increase their knowledge of the craft of writing. Second, we hope that you will actively study these essays as solid examples of the situations and strategies explored in *A Writer's Guide*. The authors represented in this reader, experts from varied fields, have faced the same problems and choices you do when you write. You can learn from studying their decisions, structures, and techniques. Finally, we hope that you will find the content of the essays intriguing — and that the essays, along with the questions posed after each one, will give you ideas to write about.

Each chapter in *A Writer's Reader* concentrates on a familiar broad theme — families, men and women, popular culture, electronic technology, and education. In some essays the writers focus on the inner world and write personal experience and opinion papers. In others the authors turn their attention to the outer world and write informational and persuasive essays. Within each chapter, the last two selections are a pair of essays on the same subject. We've provided these pairs so that you can see how different writers use different strategies to address similar issues.

Each chapter in the reader begins with an image, a visual activity, and a Web search activity, all intended to stimulate your thinking and writing. Each reading selection is preceded by biographical information about the author, placing him or her — and the piece itself — into a cultural and informational context. Next a reading note, As You Read, suggests a way to consider the selection. Following each reading are five Questions to Start You Thinking that consistently cover the same ground: meaning, writing strategies, critical thinking, vocabulary, and connections with one or more of the other selections in *A Writer's Reader*. Each paired essay is also followed by a question that asks you about a link between the essays. After these questions come a couple of journal prompts designed to get your writing juices flowing. Finally, two possible assignments make specific suggestions for writing. The first assignment is directed toward your inner world, asking you to draw generally on your personal experience and your understanding of the essay. The second is outer directed, asking you to look outside yourself and write an evaluative or argumentative paper, one that may require further reading or research.

For more on journal writing, see pp. 306–07.

439

Chapter 23
Families

Responding to an Image

Carefully examine this family photograph, making thorough notes about the clothing, positions, facial expressions, posture, race, gender, and other attributes of the people. Also, make notes about the surroundings. What might these attributes and surroundings indicate about the occasion? What kind of family does this photograph portray? Does this family portrait remind you of any others you've seen?

Search the Library of Congress online archive called American Memory <http://memory.loc.gov/ammem/> by entering a subject related to your family's history, such as a state or city where your ancestors or family have lived, an industry a relative has worked in, or a historical event or natural disaster that affected your family in some way. Locate and study a specific photograph or document on this subject. Imagine that your family has a direct connection to the photo or document you have found. Write an imaginary narrative about one or more members of your family based on your finding.

■ For reading activities linked to this chapter, visit <bedfordstmartins.com/bedguide> and do a keyword search:

reading

Christy De'on Miller
Give Me Five More Minutes

Christy De'on Miller *was born in 1955 and grew up in Texas and New Mexico. After serving in the military and working secretarial jobs, she earned a BA in English from Texas Tech University in 2003. Four months after she graduated, her son, Lance Corporal Aaron C. Austin, was killed in Iraq during his second tour of duty as a marine. Miller is currently working with journalist Steve Ramos on a book about Aaron. The following selection, published on* Salon.com *in 2006, is Miller's moving account of learning the news that her son was killed. A longer version of the essay first appeared in* Operation Homecoming: Iraq, Afghanistan, and the Home Front, in the Words of U.S. Troops and Their Families *(2006), a compilation of writings that soldiers and their loved ones submitted to a project funded by the National Endowment for the Arts.*

AS YOU READ: *Identify the objects Miller uses to help her recall her son.*

■ For more about Christy De'on Miller, visit <bedfordstmartins.com/bedguide> and do a keyword search:

author

On April 26, 2004, I woke up around 4:00 in the morning and turned on 1 the television in my bedroom. At least 12 marines had been injured, and by 6:00 A.M., reporters were saying that one had died. I typed Aaron a letter, as I'd been doing daily for several weeks, trying to sound positive. Outside of mentioning that we had one marine down, I avoided the hard news of the day.

It was around 4:00 or 5:00 P.M. when the two marines drove up to my 2 house. The noncommissioned officer began to approach me. It seemed to take an eternity for him to cross my lawn — I think I must have walked some, gone to meet him halfway.

He began, "Ma'am, are you Christy Miller? Can we go inside? We need 3 to talk to you." His wasn't an easy job.

"No, we've got to do this outside." Mine, still the harder. 4

The other marine, the officer, said, "Ma'am, your son was killed in ac- 5 tion today in Al Anbar Province."

I said, "My son was killed in the firefight that's on the television right 6 now. He was killed in Fallujah. There's been one marine killed today."

There, in that moment, the tiniest and longest length of time, there 7
must've been a mechanical failure, an embodiment of someone's (it couldn't
have been mine) heart and brain colliding.

"Mine," I finished. Yes, the marine was mine.   8

My son, Lance Corporal Aaron C. Austin, United States Marine Corps 9
machine gunner, team leader Echo Company, Second Battalion, First Marine
Regiment, First Marine Division was killed in action on April 26, 2004, in
Fallujah, Iraq. He was born on July 1, 1982, at 8:53 P.M. central daylight savings time in Amherst, Texas. Circumcised and sent home on the Fourth of
July, he was my breast-fed, blanket-sucking baby boy, a little Linus° look-
alike. He threw his blanket away when he was ten. God, how I wish for that
blanket now. It surely would carry some scent.

Aaron's company commander, Captain Zembiec, wrote me right after it 10
happened. He wrote,

> Your son was killed in action today. He was conducting a security patrol
> with his company this morning, in enemy territory. His company had
> halted in two buildings, strongpointing them and looking for insurgents. A
> large number of enemy personnel attacked Aaron and his platoon at
> around 1100. Despite intense enemy machine gun and rocket propelled
> grenade fire, your son fought like a lion. He remained in his fighting posi-
> tion until all his wounded comrades could be evacuated from the rooftop
> they were defending. . . . We held a memorial service this afternoon in
> honor of your son. With the exception of the marines on security, every
> man in the company attended the service. Aaron was respected and admired
> by every marine in his company. His death brought tears to my eyes, tears
> that fell in front of my marines. I am unashamed of that fact.

From the men who first told me the news, who had stood outside my 11
home, compassionate marines in dress blues, to those who entered my living room and placed before me the one remaining box of my son's life, and
then, on bent knee, took out a smaller box from within the larger, and
handed over to me Aaron's watch, the one removed from his body at the
time of death — it is to these men that I owe so much.

I began to wear Aaron's watch, which was still on Baghdad time. His 12
watch became my watch. His alarm would go off at 3:28:24. Then again at
3:33:20. Aaron always said, "Give me five more minutes, Mom." This early
alarm, its hidden meaning, meant only for him, for duty on a rooftop possibly,
is 5:30 P.M. (the evening before) my time.

When the battery goes dead on a digital watch — it's gone. Blank. Not 13
even a zero. Aaron's watch stopped somewhere between late afternoon on
the twenty-eighth of November and noon on the thirtieth. Since then, I've
experienced the first Mother's Day without my son, his twenty-second birthday, and the homecoming of his unit. More of the "firsts" will soon be behind me. I don't know if the seconds, thirds, and fourths get any better.

At times I believe I can learn to live a life without my son. After all, I 14
must. There are other mothers who have lost their boys — car accidents, war,

---

Linus: Character who carries a security blanket in the *Peanuts* comic strip .

illness—who can shop for dinner at the local grocer's without the macaroni-and-cheese boxes suddenly causing them grief. But the memory of him is planted in everything around me. Inside of me. So much of him has been lost, is fading, breaking down. His blanket, his watch, his uniform.

The military uses commercial washers to clean personal items before 15 they are handed over to the families. Understandable, but it leaves a synthetic laundry smell. Aaron's scent is gone. These are the realizations, the moments I've most dreaded. And they come out of nowhere.

I went through several rounds of "looking for him." Articles, pictures, 16 his voice, things like that. He used to chew on the caps of pens, his dog tags, everything, so I saved a few things I found like that. You're not ever preparing for this day, so everything had pretty much been washed, given away, or thrown out when Aaron deployed.° I did find his voice on a couple of tapes, including when he was in the third grade, and he was studying for a spelling test, spelling dinosaur words over and over. Then his voice for a few minutes back in '98, I think, and then, after his first trip to Iraq when a news station interviewed him. Each and every new little discovery is uplifting for a while, it lends hope, and then you remember why you're doing it.

Then one day, I was in a closet, and I looked down and saw a pair of 17 Aaron's house shoes, lizard-striped ones. The shoes brought a smile and tears and when I grabbed them up, and noticed a kind of grimy stain in the bottom, I sniffed, over and over. I cried, of course, but I was still so happy. It was the smell of his feet. No one ever expects that kind of smell to be a gift, but to me, that day, it was. Still, every once in a while, I go and get them out of his room. Now they sit by his bed, close to our two pairs of boots: jungle boots I wore in Panama and his pair, from Iraq.

The days have become different. Sorrow is a tile in the mosaic° and 18 flashes of grief still come. But I believe that time does heal. I think it teaches. The moments pass. I can't say how. It's not of my doing. Sometimes I question. Why has God taken the only child that remained? Left me with no hope for a grandchild? I'm certain there can be no more. No more children.

And yet I have no particular animosity° for my son's killer. He's a name- 19 less and faceless combatant to me. Should I ever have the opportunity to meet him, I hope that I'd forgive him. To me, the buck° stops with the Father. His power stings at times. But He's listened to me; perhaps He's even cried with me. And yes, I do know what I'm talking about here. It's a belief, man. Aaron's words. You either believe in God or you don't. Yes, I'd forgive. I do forgive. There is absolutely nothing I'd do to keep myself from spending eternity with God and Aaron.

The words *forever* and *eternity* mean something to me now. Before, I 20 wouldn't concentrate on their true definition, on their essence. I thought they were for later. Now, I have an aching need to know that forever and

---

deployed: Traveled with other military personnel to the site of battle.   **mosaic:** A pattern created through the arrangement of small tiles.   **animosity:** Ill-will, hostility. **the buck:** A reference to the saying, "The buck stops here," meaning that responsibility for a problem or situation ultimately rests at this point.

eternity started long before my time — way before Aaron, before the marines came to my home that day.

Questions to Start You Thinking

1. CONSIDERING MEANING: Where in the essay does Miller refer to its title? What is her point in doing so? What other meaning might the essay's title have for Miller?

2. IDENTIFYING WRITING STRATEGIES: Miller uses recall to open her essay with a powerful anecdote (paragraphs 1–8). Why do you think she chose this strategy? How do you respond to this opening, and how effective do you find it?

3. READING CRITICALLY: How would you describe Miller's tone in her essay? How does she avoid bitterness in writing about the circumstances of her son's death?

4. EXPANDING VOCABULARY: In paragraphs 2, 19, and 20, Miller uses the word *eternity*. What does she mean by *eternity*? What subtle differences can you detect in her three uses of the word?

5. MAKING CONNECTIONS: Both Miller and E. B. White in "Once More to the Lake" (pp. 463–68) write about their relationships with their sons, as well as the need to hold on to memories. What similarities can you find in the ideas presented by these two writers? In the tone of their writing? What are some differences? (Consider, in particular, the final paragraph of each essay.)

Journal Prompts

1. Miller seems almost obsessed with recapturing her son's scent. Why do you think smells have the power to call up vivid memories? Write about a time or two when you responded nostalgically to a smell.

2. Respond to the saying, "Children should not die before their parents do." Why do you think it is considered more difficult for a parent to lose a child than for a child to lose a parent?

Suggestions for Writing

1. Recall a time when you lost someone for whom you cared a great deal — perhaps due to death, a breakup, a move, a family change, or some other circumstance. Write an essay in which you describe how you responded to this loss. Like Miller, you might use examples and description to bring your recollections to life. As you draft, consider how your tone could help you convey your feelings through the words you choose.

2. The war in which Miller's son died has sparked considerable controversy. Write an essay exploring your responses to the war in Iraq. If they have changed over time, then detail those changes. Why do you think ending the conflict in Iraq has proved more difficult than originally anticipated? To prepare for this essay, you may want to do some brief research to help you recall the sequence of events leading up to or following the invasion of Iraq.

Amy Tan
Mother Tongue

Amy Tan *was born in 1952 in Oakland, California, a few years after her parents immigrated to the United States from China. After receiving a BA in English and linguistics and an MA in linguistics from San Jose State University, Tan worked as a specialist in language development before becoming a freelance business writer in 1981. Tan's first short story (1985) became the basis for her first novel,* The Joy Luck Club *(1990), which was a phenomenal best-seller and was made into a movie. Tan's second novel,* The Kitchen God's Wife *(1991), was equally popular. She has also written children's books,* The Moon Lady *(1992) and* The Chinese Siamese Cat *(1994). With her next novels,* The Hundred Secret Senses *(1995) and* The Bonesetter's Daughter *(2001), Tan returned to themes of family relationships, loyalty, and ways of reconciling the past with the present. Most recently she published* The Opposite of Fate *(2003), a book of autobiographical essays, and* Saving Fish from Drowning *(2005), a novel. "Mother Tongue" first appeared in* Threepenny Review *in 1990; in this essay, Tan explores the effect of her mother's "broken" English — the language Tan grew up with — on her life and writing.*

■ For more about Amy Tan, visit <bedfordstmartins.com/bedguide> and do a key-word search:

🔍 **author**

AS YOU READ: *Identify the difficulties Tan says exist for a child growing up in a family that speaks nonstandard English.*

I am not a scholar of English or literature. I cannot give you much more than personal opinions on the English language and its variations in this country or others.

I am a writer. And by that definition, I am someone who has always loved language. I am fascinated by language in daily life. I spend a great deal of my time thinking about the power of language — the way it can evoke an emotion, a visual image, a complex idea, or a simple truth. Language is the tool of my trade. And I use them all — all the Englishes I grew up with.

Recently, I was made keenly aware of the different Englishes I do use. I was giving a talk to a large group of people, the same talk I had already given to half a dozen other groups. The nature of the talk was about my writing, my life, and my book, *The Joy Luck Club*. The talk was going along well enough, until I remembered one major difference that made the whole talk sound wrong. My mother was in the room. And it was perhaps the first time she had heard me give a lengthy speech, using the kind of English I have never used with her. I was saying things like, "The intersection of memory upon imagination" and "There is an aspect of my fiction that relates to thus-and-thus" — a speech filled with carefully wrought° grammatical phrases, burdened, it suddenly seemed to me, with nominalized° forms,

wrought: Crafted.   **nominalized:** Made into a noun from a verb.

past perfect tenses, conditional phrases, all the forms of Standard English that I had learned in school and through books, the forms of English I did not use at home with my mother.

Just last week, I was walking down the street with my mother, and I again found myself conscious of the English I was using, and the English I do use with her. We were talking about the price of new and used furniture and I heard myself saying this: "Not waste money that way." My husband was with us as well, and he didn't notice any switch in my English. And then I realized why. It's because over the twenty years we've been together I've often used that same kind of English with him, and sometimes he even uses it with me. It has become our language of intimacy, a different sort of English that relates to family talk, the language I grew up with.

So you'll have some idea of what this family talk I heard sounds like, I'll quote what my mother said during a recent conversation which I video-taped and then transcribed.° During this conversation, my mother was talking about a political gangster in Shanghai who had the same last name as her family's, Du, and how the gangster in his early years wanted to be adopted by her family, which was rich by comparison. Later, the gangster became more powerful, far richer than my mother's family, and one day showed up at my mother's wedding to pay his respects. Here's what she said in part:

"Du Yusong having business like fruit stand. Like off the street kind. He is like Du Zong—but not Tsung-ming Island people. The local people call putong, the river east side, he belong to that side local people. That man want to ask Du Zong father take him in like become own family. Du Zong father wasn't look down on him, but didn't take seriously, until that man big like become a mafia. Now important person, very hard to inviting him. Chinese way, came only to show respect, don't stay for dinner. Respect for making big celebration, he shows up. Mean gives lots of respect. Chinese custom. Chinese social life that way. If too important won't have to stay too long. He come to my wedding. I didn't see, I heard it. I gone to boy's side, they have YMCA dinner. Chinese age I was nineteen."

You should know that my mother's expressive command of English belies° how much she actually understands. She reads the *Forbes* report, listens to *Wall Street Week*, converses daily with her stockbroker, reads all of Shirley MacLaine's books with ease—all kinds of things I can't begin to understand. Yet some of my friends tell me they understand fifty percent of what my mother says. Some say they understand eighty to ninety percent. Some say they understand none of it, as if she were speaking pure Chinese. But to me, my mother's English is perfectly clear, perfectly natural. It's my mother tongue. Her language, as I hear it, is vivid, direct, full of observation and imagery. That was the language that helped shape the way I saw things, expressed things, made sense of the world.

transcribed: Made a written copy of what was said.   belies: Shows to be false.

Lately, I've been giving more thought to the kind of English my mother 8
speaks. Like others, I have described it to people as "broken" or "fractured"
English. But I wince when I say that. It has always bothered me that I can
think of no way to describe it other than "broken," as if it were damaged
and needed to be fixed, as if it lacked a certain wholeness and soundness.
I've heard other terms used, "limited English," for example. But they seem
just as bad, as if everything is limited, including people's perceptions of the
limited English speaker.

I know this for a fact, because when I was growing up, my mother's 9
"limited" English limited *my* perception of her. I was ashamed of her English. I believed that her English reflected the quality of what she had to say.
That is, because she expressed them imperfectly her thoughts were imperfect. And I had plenty of empirical evidence to support me: the fact that
people in department stores, at banks, and at restaurants did not take her
seriously, did not give her good service, pretended not to understand her, or
even acted as if they did not hear her.

My mother has long realized the limitations of her English as well. 10
When I was fifteen, she used to have me call people on the phone to pretend I was she. In this guise, I was forced to ask for information or even to
complain and yell at people who had been rude to her. One time it was a
call to her stockbroker in New York. She had cashed out her small portfolio
and it just so happened we were going to go to New York the next week, our
very first trip outside California. I had to get on the phone and say in an
adolescent voice that was not very convincing, "This is Mrs. Tan."

And my mother was standing in the back whispering loudly, "Why he 11
don't send me check, already two weeks late. So mad he lie to me, losing me
money."

And then I said in perfect English, "Yes, I'm getting rather concerned. 12
You had agreed to send the check two weeks ago, but it hasn't arrived."

Then she began to talk more loudly. "What he want, I come to New 13
York tell him front of his boss, you cheating me?" And I was trying to
calm her down, make her be quiet, while telling the stockbroker, "I can't
tolerate any more excuses. If I don't receive the check immediately, I am
going to have to speak to your manager when I'm in New York next week."
And sure enough, the following week there we were in front of this astonished stockbroker, and I was sitting there red-faced and quiet, and my
mother, the real Mrs. Tan, was shouting at his boss in her impeccable broken English.

We used a similar routine just five days ago, for a situation that was far 14
less humorous. My mother had gone to the hospital for an appointment, to
find out about a benign brain tumor a CAT scan had revealed a month ago.
She said she had spoken very good English, her best English, no mistakes.
Still, she said, the hospital did not apologize when they said they had lost
the CAT scan and she had come for nothing. She said they did not seem to
have any sympathy when she told them she was anxious to know the exact
diagnosis, since her husband and son had both died of brain tumors. She

said they would not give her any more information until the next time and she would have to make another appointment for that. So she said she would not leave until the doctor called her daughter. She wouldn't budge. And when the doctor finally called her daughter, me, who spoke in perfect English — lo and behold — we had assurances the CAT scan would be found, promises that a conference call on Monday would be held, and apologies for any suffering my mother had gone through for a most regrettable mistake.

I think my mother's English almost had an effect on limiting my possibilities in life as well. Sociologists and linguists probably will tell you that a person's developing language skills are more influenced by peers. But I think that the language spoken in the family, especially in immigrant families which are more insular, plays a large role in shaping the language of the child. And I believe that it affected my results on achievement tests, IQ tests, and the SAT. While my English skills were never judged as poor, compared to math, English could not be considered my strong suit. In grade school I did moderately well, getting perhaps B's, sometimes B-pluses, in English and scoring perhaps in the sixtieth or seventieth percentile on achievement tests. But those scores were not good enough to override the opinion that my true abilities lay in math and science, because in those areas I achieved A's and scored in the ninetieth percentile or higher. 15

This was understandable. Math is precise; there is only one correct answer. Whereas, for me at least, the answers on English tests were always a judgment call, a matter of opinion and personal experience. Those tests were constructed around items like fill-in-the-blank sentence completion, such as, "Even though Tom was _____ , Mary thought he was _____ ." And the correct answer always seemed to be the most bland combinations of thoughts, for example, "Even though Tom was shy, Mary thought he was charming," with the grammatical structure "even though" limiting the correct answer to some sort of semantic° opposites, so you wouldn't get answers like, "Even though Tom was foolish, Mary thought he was ridiculous." Well, according to my mother, there were very few limitations as to what Tom could have been and what Mary might have thought of him. So I never did well on tests like that. 16

The same was true with word analogies, pairs of words in which you were supposed to find some sort of logical, semantic relationship — for example, "*Sunset* is to *nightfall* as _____ is to _____ ." And here you would be presented with a list of four possible pairs, one of which showed the same kind of relationship: *red* is to *stoplight*, *bus* is to *arrival*, *chills* is to *fever*, *yawn* is to *boring*. Well, I could never think that way. I knew what the tests were asking, but I could not block out of my mind the images already created by the first pair, "*sunset* is to *nightfall*" — and I would see a burst of colors against a darkening sky, the moon rising, the lowering of a curtain of stars. And all the other pairs of words — *red, bus, stoplight, boring* — just threw up a 17

semantic: Relating to the meaning of language.

mass of confusing images, making it impossible for me to sort out something as logical as saying: "A sunset precedes nightfall" is the same as "a chill precedes a fever." The only way I would have gotten that answer right would have been to imagine an associative situation, for example, my being disobedient and staying out past sunset, catching a chill at night, which turns into feverish pneumonia as punishment, which indeed did happen to me.

I have been thinking about all this lately, about my mother's English, 18 about achievement tests. Because lately I've been asked, as a writer, why there are not more Asian Americans enrolled in creative writing programs. Why do so many Chinese students go into engineering? Well, these are broad sociological questions I can't begin to answer. But I have noticed in surveys—in fact, just last week—that Asian students, as a whole, always do significantly better on math achievement tests than in English. And this makes me think that there are other Asian American students whose English spoken in the home might also be described as "broken" or "limited." And perhaps they also have teachers who are steering them away from writing and into math and science, which is what happened to me.

Fortunately, I happen to be rebellious in nature and enjoy the challenge 19 of disproving assumptions made about me. I became an English major my first year in college, after being enrolled as pre-med. I started writing nonfiction as a freelancer the week after I was told by my former boss that writing was my worst skill and I should hone my talents toward account management.

But it wasn't until 1985 that I finally began to write fiction. And at first I 20 wrote using what I thought to be wittily crafted sentences, sentences that would finally prove I had mastery over the English language. Here's an example from the first draft of a story that later made its way into *The Joy Luck Club,* but without this line: "That was my mental quandary in its nascent° state." A terrible line, which I can barely pronounce.

Fortunately, for reasons I won't get into today, I later decided I should 21 envision a reader for the stories I would write. And the reader I decided upon was my mother, because these were stories about mothers. So with this reader in mind—and in fact she did read my early drafts—I began to write stories using all the Englishes I grew up with: the English I spoke to my mother, which for lack of a better term might be described as "simple"; the English she used with me, which for lack of a better term might be described as "broken"; my translation of her Chinese, which could certainly be described as "watered down"; and what I imagined to be her translation of her Chinese if she could speak in perfect English, her internal language, and for that I sought to preserve the essence, but neither an English nor a Chinese structure. I wanted to capture what language ability tests can never reveal: her intent, her passion, her imagery, the rhythms of her speech, and the nature of her thoughts.

nascent: Beginning; only partly formed.

Apart from what any critic had to say about my writing, I knew I had 22
succeeded where it counted when my mother finished reading my book and
gave me her verdict: "So easy to read."

Questions to Start You Thinking

1. CONSIDERING MEANING: What are the Englishes that Tan grew up with?
   What other Englishes has she used in her life? What does each English have
   that gives it an advantage over the other Englishes in certain situations?

2. IDENTIFYING WRITING STRATEGIES: What examples does Tan use to analyze
   the various Englishes she uses? How has Tan been able to synthesize her
   Englishes successfully into her present style of writing fiction?

3. READING CRITICALLY: Although Tan explains that she writes using "all the
   Englishes" she has known throughout her life (paragraph 21), she doesn't
   do that in this essay. What are the differences between the English Tan uses
   in this essay and the kinds she says she uses in her fiction? How does the
   language she uses here fit the purpose of her essay?

4. EXPANDING VOCABULARY: In paragraph 9, Tan writes that she had "plenty of
   empirical evidence" that her mother's "limited" English meant that her
   mother's thoughts were "imperfect" as well. Define *empirical*. What does
   Tan's use of this word tell us about her present attitude toward the way she
   judged her mother when she was growing up?

5. MAKING CONNECTIONS: Tan and Richard Rodriguez ("Public and Private
   Language," pp. 571–76) recount learning English as they grew up in homes
   where English was a second language. What similarities do you find in
   their experiences and the obstacles they faced? How did learning English
   affect their self-images? How did it influence their relationships with their
   families?

Journal Prompts

1. Describe one of the Englishes you use to communicate. When do you use it,
   and when do you avoid using it?

2. In what ways are you a "translator," if not of language, then of current
   events and fashions, for your parents or other members of your family?

Suggestions for Writing

1. In a personal essay explain an important event in your family's history,
   using your family's various Englishes or other languages.

2. Take note of and, if possible, transcribe one conversation you have had with
   a parent or other family member, one with a teacher, and one with a close
   friend. Write an essay comparing and contrasting the "languages" of the
   three conversations. How do the languages differ? How do you account for
   these differences? What do you think would happen if someone used
   "teacher language" to talk to a friend or used "friend language" in a class
   discussion or paper?

Anna Quindlen
Evan's Two Moms

Anna Quindlen *was born in 1953 in Philadelphia. After graduating from Barnard College in 1974, she worked briefly as a reporter for the* New York Post *before moving to the* New York Times. *There she wrote the "About New York" column and then two syndicated columns: "Life in the 30s," which drew on her experiences with her family and neighborhood, and until 1994, when she left the* Times, *"Public and Private," which explored political issues. She is currently a contributing editor and columnist for* Newsweek. *Quindlen won the Pulitzer Prize for Commentary in 1992, and many of her columns have been collected in the books* Living Out Loud *(1986),* Thinking Out Loud *(1993), and* Loud and Clear *(2005). Quindlen also has written five novels — Object Lessons (1991), One True Thing (1994), Black and Blue (1998), Blessings (2002), and Rise and Shine (2007) — as well as the advice books A Short Guide to a Happy Life (2000) and Being Perfect (2005). In "Evan's Two Moms," written in 1992, Quindlen emphatically argues that gay marriage should be legalized.*

■ For more about Anna Quindlen, visit <bedfordstmartins.com/bedguide> and do a keyword search:

author

AS YOU READ: *Identify the main points Quindlen uses to support her position.*

Evan has two moms. This is no big thing. Evan has always had two 1
moms — in his school file, on his emergency forms, with his friends. "Ooooh, Evan, you're lucky," they sometimes say. "You have two moms." It sounds like a sitcom, but until last week it was emotional truth without legal bulwark.° That was when a judge in New York approved the adoption of a six-year-old boy by his biological mother's lesbian partner. Evan. Evan's mom. Evan's other mom. A kid, a psychologist, a pediatrician. A family.

The matter of Evan's two moms is one in a series of events over the last 2
year that lead to certain conclusions. A Minnesota appeals court granted guardianship of a woman left a quadriplegic in a car accident to her lesbian lover, the culmination of a seven-year battle in which the injured woman's parents did everything possible to negate the partnership between the two. A lawyer in Georgia had her job offer withdrawn after the state attorney general found out that she and her lesbian lover were planning a marriage ceremony; she's brought suit. The computer company Lotus announced that the gay partners of employees would be eligible for the same benefits as spouses.

Add to these public events the private struggles, the couples who go 3
from lawyer to lawyer to approximate legal protections their straight counterparts take for granted, the AIDS survivors who find themselves shut out of their partners' dying days by biological family members and shut out of

---

bulwark: Strong support.

their apartments by leases with a single name on the dotted line, and one solution is obvious.

Gay marriage is a radical notion for straight people and a conservative 4 notion for gay ones. After years of being sledgehammered by society, some gay men and lesbian women are deeply suspicious of participating in an institution that seems to have "straight world" written all over it.

But the rads of twenty years ago, straight and gay alike, have other 5 things on their minds today. Family is one, and the linchpin of family has commonly been a loving commitment between two adults. When same-sex couples set out to make that commitment, they discover that they are at a disadvantage: No joint tax returns. No health insurance coverage for an uninsured partner. No survivor's benefits from Social Security. None of the automatic rights, privileges, and responsibilities society attaches to a marriage contract. In Madison, Wisconsin, a couple who applied at the Y with their kids for a family membership were turned down because both were women. It's one of those small things that can make you feel small.

Some took marriage statutes that refer to "two persons" at their word 6 and applied for a license. The results were court decisions that quoted the Bible and embraced circular argument: marriage is by definition the union of a man and a woman because that is how we've defined it.

No religion should be forced to marry anyone in violation of its tenets,° 7 although ironically it is now only in religious ceremonies that gay people can marry, performed by clergy who find the blessing of two who love each other no sin. But there is no secular° reason that we should take a patchwork approach of corporate, governmental, and legal steps to guarantee what can be done simply, economically, conclusively, and inclusively with the words "I do."

"Fran and I chose to get married for the same reasons that any two 8 people do," said the lawyer who was fired in Georgia. "We fell in love; we wanted to spend our lives together." Pretty simple.

Consider the case of *Loving v. Virginia,* aptly named. At the time, sixteen 9 states had laws that barred interracial marriage, relying on natural law, that amorphous° grab bag for justifying prejudice. Sounding a little like God throwing Adam and Eve out of paradise, the trial judge suspended the one-year sentence of Richard Loving, who was white, and his wife, Mildred, who was black, provided they got out of the State of Virginia.

In 1967 the Supreme Court found such laws to be unconstitutional. 10 Only twenty-five years ago and it was a crime for a black woman to marry a white man. Perhaps twenty-five years from now we will find it just as incredible that two people of the same sex were not entitled to legally commit themselves to each other. Love and commitment are rare enough; it seems absurd to thwart them in any guise.

---

tenets: Principles.   **secular:** Relating to nonreligious matters.   **amorphous:** Having no specific shape.

Questions to Start You Thinking

1. CONSIDERING MEANING: According to Quindlen, what is unjust about not allowing gay men and lesbians to marry *legally*?

2. IDENTIFYING WRITING STRATEGIES: Quindlen ends her essay with a comparison of gay marriage and interracial marriage (paragraphs 9 and 10). How does she use this comparison to support her argument? Do you think it is a valid comparison? Why or why not?

3. READING CRITICALLY: What kinds of appeals does Quindlen use in her essay? How are they appropriate or inappropriate for addressing her opponents' arguments? (See pp. 40–41 for an explanation of kinds of appeals.)

4. EXPANDING VOCABULARY: Define *marriage* as Quindlen would define it. How does her definition of the term differ from the one in the dictionary?

5. MAKING CONNECTIONS: What privileges of the majority culture are gay families and immigrant families (Tan, "Mother Tongue," pp. 445–50) sometimes denied?

Journal Prompts

1. In your opinion, is the dictionary definition of *marriage* inadequate? If so, how do you think it should be revised? If you think the dictionary definition is fine, defend it against attack.

2. Imagine that you have the power to design and create the perfect parents. What would they be like? What criteria would they have to meet to live up to your vision of ideal parents?

Suggestions for Writing

1. Describe the most unconventional family you know. How is this family different from other families? How is it the same?

2. In your opinion, would two parents of the same gender help or hurt a child's development? Write an essay comparing and contrasting the possible benefits and disadvantages of this type of family. Use specific examples — hypothetical or gathered from your own observation or reading — to illustrate your argument.

Anjula Razdan
What's Love Got to Do with It?

Anjula Razdan *was a senior editor of the* Utne Reader, *where she wrote on topics ranging from international politics to pop culture. The daughter of Indian immigrants whose marriage was arranged, Razdan grew up in Illinois and currently works as a freelance writer and editor in Washington, D.C. In this selection, which appeared in the* Utne Reader *in 2003, Razdan asks her readers to consider whether arranging marriages might more effectively create lasting relationships*

■ For more about Anjula Razdan, visit <bedfordstmartins.com/ bedguide> and do a keyword search:

author

than choosing mates based on romantic attraction. To explore this question, she draws on her own experiences and observations as well as the testimony of experts.

AS YOU READ: *Look for Razdan's account of both the benefits and the drawbacks of arranged marriages.*

One of the greatest pleasures of my teen years was sitting down with a bag of cinnamon Red Hots and a new LaVyrle Spencer romance, immersing myself in another tale of star-crossed lovers drawn together by the heart's mysterious alchemy.° My mother didn't get it. "Why are you reading that?" she would ask, her voice tinged with both amusement and horror. Everything in her background told her that romance was a waste of time.

Born and raised in Illinois by parents who emigrated from India thirty-five years ago, I am the product of an arranged marriage, and yet I grew up under the spell of Western romantic love — first comes love, *then* comes marriage — which both puzzled and dismayed my parents. Their relationship was set up over tea and samosas° by their grandfathers, and they were already engaged when they went on their first date, a chaperoned trip to the movies. My mom and dad still barely knew each other on their wedding day — and they certainly hadn't fallen in love. Yet both were confident that their shared values, beliefs, and family background would form a strong bond that, over time, would develop into love.

"But, what could they possibly know of *real love*?" I would ask myself petulantly° after each standoff with my parents over whether or not I could date in high school (I couldn't) and whether I would allow them to arrange my marriage (I wouldn't). The very idea of an arranged marriage offended my ideas of both love and liberty — to me, the act of choosing whom to love represented the very essence of freedom. To take away that choice seemed like an attack not just on my autonomy as a person, but on democracy itself.

And, yet, even in the supposedly liberated West, the notion of choosing your mate is a relatively recent one. Until the nineteenth century, writes historian E. J. Graff in *What Is Marriage For? The Strange Social History of Our Most Intimate Institution* (Boston: Beacon Press, 1999), arranged marriages were quite common in Europe as a way of forging alliances, ensuring inheritances, and stitching together the social, political, and religious needs of a community. Love had nothing to do with it.

Fast forward a couple hundred years to twenty-first-century America, and you see a modern, progressive society where people are free to choose their mates, for the most part, based on love instead of social or economic gain. But for many people, a quiet voice from within wonders: Are we really better off? Who hasn't at some point in their life — at the end of an ill-fated

---

alchemy: A medieval predecessor of chemistry that aimed to turn base metals into gold.   **samosas:** Small, fried Indian pastries filled with seasoned vegetables or meat.
petulantly: Irritably.

relationship or midway through dinner with the third "date-from-hell" this
month — longed for a matchmaker to find the right partner? No hassles. No
effort. No personal ads or blind dates.

The point of the Western romantic ideal is to live "happily ever after,"   6
yet nearly half of all marriages in this country end in divorce, and the number of never-married adults grows each year. Boundless choice notwith-
standing, what does it mean when the marital success rate is the statistical
equivalent of a coin toss?

"People don't really know how to choose a long-term partner," offers   7
Dr. Alvin Cooper, the director of the San Jose Marital Services and Sexuality
Centre and a staff psychologist at Stanford University. "The major reasons
that people find and get involved with somebody else are proximity and
physical attraction. And both of these factors are terrible predictors of long-
term happiness in a relationship."

At the moment we pick a mate, Cooper says, we are often blinded by   8
passion and therefore virtually incapable of making a sound decision.

Psychology Today editor Robert Epstein agrees. "[It's] like getting drunk   9
and marrying someone in Las Vegas," he quips. A former director of the
Cambridge Center for Behavioral Studies, Epstein holds a decidedly unro-
mantic view of courtship and love. Indeed, he argues it is our myths of "love
at first sight" and "a knight in a shining Porsche" that get so many of us into
trouble. When the heat of passion wears off — and it always does, he says —
you can be left with virtually nothing "except lawyer's bills."

Epstein points out that many arranged marriages result in an enduring   10
love because they promote compatibility and rational deliberation ahead of
passionate impulse. Epstein himself is undertaking a bold step to prove his
theory that love can be learned. He wrote an editorial in *Psychology Today* last
year seeking women to participate in the experiment with him. He proposed
to choose one of the "applicants," and together they would attempt to fall in
love — consciously and deliberately. After receiving more than 1,000 responses, none of which seemed right, Epstein yielded just a little to impulse,
asking Gabriela, an intriguing Venezuelan woman he met on a plane, to join
him in the project. After an understandable bout of cold feet, she eventually
agreed.

In a "love contract" the two signed on Valentine's Day this year to seal   11
the deal, Epstein stipulates that he and Gabriela must undergo intensive
counseling to learn how to communicate effectively and participate in a variety of exercises designed to foster mutual love. To help oversee and guide
the project, Epstein has even formed an advisory board made up of high-
profile relationship experts, most notably Dr. John Gray, who wrote the
best-selling *Men Are from Mars, Women Are from Venus*. If the experiment
pans out, the two will have learned to love each other within a year's time.

It may strike some as anathema° to be so premeditated about the   12
process of falling in love, but to hear Epstein tell it, most unions fail exactly

anathema: An abomination; blasphemy.

because they aren't intentional enough; they're based on a roll of the dice and a determination to stake everything on love. What this means, Epstein says, is that most people lack basic relationship skills, and, as a result, most relationships lack emotional and psychological intimacy.

A divorced father of four, Epstein himself married for passion — "just 13 like I was told to do by the fairy tales and by the movies" — but eventually came to regret it. "I had the experience that so many people have now," he says, "which is basically looking at your partner and going, 'Who are you?'" Although Epstein acknowledges the non-Western tradition of arranged marriage is a complex, somewhat flawed institution, he thinks we can "distill key elements of [it] to help us learn how to create a new, more stable institution in the West."

Judging from the phenomenon of reality-TV shows like *Married by* 14 *America* and *Meet My Folks* and the recent increase in the number of professional matchmakers, the idea of arranging marriages (even if in nontraditional ways) seems to be taking hold in this country — perhaps nowhere more powerfully than in cyberspace. Online dating services attracted some twenty million people last year (roughly one-fifth of all singles — and growing), who used sites like Match.com and Yahoo Personals to hook up with potentially compatible partners. Web sites' search engines play the role of patriarchal grandfathers, searching for good matches based on any number of criteria that you select.

Cooper, the Stanford psychologist and author of *Sex and the Internet: A* 15 *Guidebook for Clinicians* (Brunner-Routledge, 2002) — and an expert in the field of online sexuality — says that because online interaction tends to downplay proximity, physical attraction, and face-to-face interaction, people are more likely to take risks and disclose significant things about themselves. The result is that they attain a higher level of psychological and emotional intimacy than if they dated right away or hopped in the sack. Indeed, online dating represents a return to what University of Chicago Humanities Professor Amy Kass calls the "distanced nearness" of old-style courtship, an intimate and protected (cyber)space that encourages self-revelation while maintaining personal boundaries.

And whether looking for a fellow scientist, someone else who's HIV- 16 positive, or a B-movie film buff, an online dater has a much higher likelihood of finding "the one" due to the computer's capacity to sort through thousands of potential mates. "That's what computers are all about — efficiency and sorting," says Cooper, who believes that online dating has the potential to lower the nation's 50 percent divorce rate. There is no magic or "chemistry" involved in love, Cooper insists. "It's specific, operationalizable factors."

Love's mystery solved by "operationalizable factors"! Why does that 17 sound a little less than inspiring? Sure, for many people the Internet can efficiently facilitate love and help to nudge fate along. But, for the diehard romantic who trusts in surprise, coincidence, and fate, the cyber-solution to love lacks heart. "To the romantic," observes English writer Blake Morrison in *The Guardian*, "every marriage is an arranged marriage — arranged by fate, that is, which gives us no choice."

More than a century ago, Emily Dickinson mocked those who would 18
dissect birds to find the mechanics of song:

> *Split the Lark — and you'll find the Music*
> *Bulb after Bulb, in Silver rolled —*
> *Scantily dealt to the Summer Morning*
> *Saved for your Ear when Lutes be old.*

> *Loose the Flood — you shall find it patent —*
> *Gush after Gush, reserved for you —*
> *Scarlet Experiment! Skeptic Thomas!*
> *Now, do you doubt that your Bird was true?*

In other words, writes Deborah Blum in her book, *Sex on the Brain* (Pen- 19
guin, 1997), "kill the bird and [you] silence the melody." For some, nurturing the ideal of romantic love may be more important than the goal of love itself. Making a more conscious choice in mating may help partners handle the complex personal ties and obligations of marriage; but romantic love, infused as it is with myth and projection and doomed passion, is a way to live *outside* of life's obligations, outside of time itself — if only for a brief, bright moment. Choosing love by rational means might not be worth it for those souls who'd rather roll the dice and risk the possibility of ending up with nothing but tragic nobility and the bittersweet tang of regret.

In the end, who really wants to examine love too closely? I'd rather curl 20
up with a LaVyrle Spencer novel or dream up the French movie version of my life than live in a world where the mechanics of love — and its giddy, mysterious buzz — are laid bare. After all, to actually unravel love's mystery is, perhaps, to miss the point of it all.

Questions to Start You Thinking

1. CONSIDERING MEANING: According to the experts whom Razdan quotes, why is cyberspace an ideal venue for facilitating relationships?

2. IDENTIFYING WRITING STRATEGIES: How does Razdan use cause and effect to explain the high divorce rate in the United States?

3. READING CRITICALLY: What type of evidence does Razdan use to explore whether arranged marriages are more successful than relationships based on romantic attraction? Do you think the evidence is relevant, credible, and sufficient? Why, or why not? What other type of evidence might she have used?

4. EXPANDING VOCABULARY: In commenting on her parents' arranged marriage, Razdan asks in paragraph 3, "But, what could they possibly know of *real love*?" How do you define *real love*? Do you think that Razdan would agree with your definition?

5. **MAKING CONNECTIONS:** The statement that "nearly half of all marriages in this country end in divorce" (paragraph 6) applies to Noel Perrin's marriage ("A Part-Time Marriage," pp. 494–96). Given his experiences, how do you think he would respond to Razdan's essay? Would he be in favor of arranged marriages?

Journal Prompts

1. Write a brief personal ad for a mate, using the writing style associated with personals. Keep in mind that the words you choose and the way you organize your ad reveal something about your personality.

2. One of the experts whom Razdan quotes mentions the myth of "love at first sight" (paragraph 9). Write about a time when you fell in love at first sight or present your opinion on whether such a thing exists.

Suggestions for Writing

1. Write an essay that uses your personal experiences and observations to develop a specific idea presented in Razdan's essay. For example, you might recall your own "date-from-hell" (paragraph 5), a friend's experience with an online dating service, or a matchmaker friend's success rate. Based on your experiences and observations, you might write about current dating practices or about "relationship skills" needed for a successful marriage.

2. Drawing examples from this reading and your own observations, write an essay arguing for or against arranged marriages. You might also do some research to find additional support for your argument.

Danzy Senna
The Color of Love

■ For more about Danzy Senna, visit <bedfordstmartins.com/ bedguide> and do a key-word search:

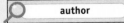
author

Danzy Senna, *born in 1970 in Boston, earned her BA at Stanford University and her MFA from the University of California, Irvine. Senna's essays and short stories have been widely anthologized, and her journalistic writing has appeared in such publications as the* Nation, *the* Utne Reader, *and* Newsweek. *Her best-selling novel* Caucasia *(1988) won several awards, and in 2002 she received a prestigious Whiting Award, given each year to ten writers of exceptional ability and promise. Her most recent book is the psychological thriller* Symptomatic *(2004). Senna recently moved from Massachusetts to Los Angeles and is currently working on a screenplay and on a nonfiction book about her father's life. In "The Color of Love," Senna, the daughter of a white mother and a black father, explores the complexities — racial and otherwise — of her relationship with her grandmother. The essay originally appeared in* O: The Oprah Magazine *in 2000.*

AS YOU READ: *Consider how her grandmother displays both love for Senna and prejudice toward her. How does Senna respond?*

We had this much in common: We were both women, and we were 1
both writers. But we were as different as two people can be and still
exist in the same family. She was ancient — as white and dusty as chalk —
and spent her days seated in a velvet armchair, passing judgments on the
world below. She still believed in noble bloodlines; my blood had been
mixed at conception. I believed there was no such thing as nobility or class
or lineage, only systems designed to keep some people up in the big house
and others outside, in the cold.

She was my grandmother. She was Irish but from that country's Protes- 2
tant elite, which meant she seemed more British than anything. She was an
actress, a writer of plays and novels, and still unmarried in her thirties when
she came to America to visit. One night while in Boston, she went to a dinner party, where she was seated next to a young lawyer with blood as blue as
the ocean. Her pearl earring fell in his oyster soup — or so the story goes —
and they fell in love. My grandmother married that lawyer and left her native Ireland for New England.

How she came to have black grandchildren is a story of opposites. It 3
was 1968 in Boston when her daughter — my mother — a small, blonde
Wasp° poet, married my father, a tall and handsome black intellectual, in
an act that was as rebellious as it was hopeful. The products of that unlikely
union — my older sister, my younger brother, and I — grew up in urban
chaos, in a home filled with artists and political activists. The old lady across
the river in Cambridge seemed to me an endangered species. Her walls were
covered with portraits of my ancestors, the pale and dead men who had
conquered Africa and built Boston long before my time. When I visited,
their eyes followed me from room to room with what I imagined to be an
expression of scorn. Among the portraits sat my grandmother, a bird who
had flown in to remind us all that there had indeed been a time when lineage and caste° meant something. To me, young and dark and full of energy,
she was the missing link between the living and the dead.

But her blood flowed through me, whether I liked it or not. I grew up to 4
be a writer, just like her. And as I struggled to tell my own stories — about
race and class and post–civil rights America — I wondered who my grandmother had been before, in Dublin, when she was friend and confidante to
literary giants such as William Butler Yeats and Samuel Beckett. Once, while
snooping in her bedroom, I discovered her novels, the ones that had been
published in Ireland when she was my age. I stared at her photograph on
the jacket and wondered about the young woman who wore a mischievous
smile. Had she ever worried about becoming so powerful that no man would
want her? Did she now feel that she had sacrificed her career and wild Irish-
woman dreams to become a wife and mother and proper Bostonian?

I longed to know her — to love her. But the differences between us were 5
real and alive, and they threatened to squelch our fragile connection. She

Wasp: An acronym (for White Anglo-Saxon Protestant) referring to a member of the
prevailing American social class.   **caste:** Class or social group.

was an alcoholic. In the evening, after a few glasses of gin, she could turn vicious. Though she held antiquated racist views, my grandmother would still have preferred to see my mother married and was saddened when my parents split in the seventies. She believed that a woman without a man was pitiable. The first question she always asked me when she saw me: "Do you have a man?" The second question: "What is he?" That was her way of finding out his race and background. She looked visibly pleased if he was a Wasp, neutral if he was Jewish, and disappointed if he was black.

My mother ignored her hurtful comments but felt them just the same. 6
She spent her visits to my grandmother's house slamming dishes in the kitchen, hissing her anger just out of hearing range, then raving, on the drive home, about what awful thing her mother had said this time. Like my mother, I knew the rule: I was not to disrespect elders. She was old and gray and would soon be gone. But I had inherited my grandmother's short temper. When I got angry, even as a child, I felt as if blood were rushing around in my head, red waves battering the shore. Words spilled from my mouth — cutting, vicious words that I regretted.

One autumn day in Cambridge, at my grandmother's place, I lost my 7
temper. I was home from college for the holidays, staying in her guest room. I woke from a nap to the sound of her enraged voice shouting at what I could only imagine was the television.

"Idiot! You damn fool!" she bellowed. "You stupid, stupid woman!" It 8
has to be *Jeopardy!*, I thought. She must be yelling at those tiny contestants on the screen. She knows the answers to those questions better than they do. But when the shouting went on for a beat too long, I went to the top of the stairs and looked down into the living room. She was speaking to a real person: her cleaning lady, a Greek woman named Mary, who was on her hands and knees, nervously gathering the shards of a broken vase. My grandmother stood over her, hands on hips, cursing.

"You fool," my grandmother repeated. "How in bloody hell could you 9
have done something so stupid?"

"Grandma." I didn't shout her name but said it loudly enough that she, 10
though hard of hearing, glanced up.

"Oh, darling!" she piped, suddenly cheerful. "Would you like a cup of 11
tea? You must be dreadfully tired."

Mary was on her feet again. She smiled nervously at me, then rushed 12
into the kitchen with the pieces of the broken vase.

I told myself to be a good girl, to be polite. But something snapped. I 13
marched down the stairs, and even she noticed something on my face that made her sit in her velvet chair.

"Don't you ever talk to her that way," I shouted. "Where do you think 14
you are? Slavery was abolished long ago."

I stood over her, tall and long-limbed, daring her to speak. My grand- 15
mother shook her head. "It's about race, isn't it?"

"Race?" I said, baffled. "Mary's white. This is about respect — treating 16
other human beings with respect."

She wasn't hearing me. All she saw was color. "The tragedy about you," 17
she said soberly, "is that you are mixed." I felt those waves in my head:
"Your tragedy is that you're old and ignorant," I spat. "You don't know the
first thing about me."

She cried into her hands. She seemed diminished, a little old woman. 18
She looked up only to say, "You are a cruel girl."

I left her apartment trembling yet feeling exhilarated by what I had 19
done. But my elation soon turned to shame. I had taken on an old lady. And
for what? Her intolerance was, at her age, deeply entrenched. My rebuttals
couldn't change her.

Yet that fight marked the beginning of our relationship. I've since de- 20
cided that when you cease to express anger toward those who have hurt you,
you are essentially giving up on them. They are dead to you. But when you
express anger, it is a sign that they still matter, that they are worth the fight.

After that argument, my grandmother and I began a conversation. She 21
seemed to see me clearly for the first time, or perhaps she, a "cruel girl" herself, had simply met her match. And I no longer felt she was a relic. She was
a living, breathing human being who deserved to be spoken to as an equal.

I began visiting her more. I would drive to Cambridge and sit with 22
her, eating mixed nuts and sipping ginger ale, regaling° her with tales of my
latest love drama or writing project. In her presence, I was proudly black and
young and political, and she was who she was: subtly racist, terribly elitist,
and awfully funny. She still said things that angered me: She bemoaned my
mother's marriage to my father, she said that I should marry not for love but
for money, and she told me that I needn't identify as black, since I didn't
look it. I snapped back at her. But she, with senility creeping in, didn't seem
to hear me; each time I came, she said the same things.

Last summer I went into hiding to work on my second novel at a writ- 23
ers' retreat in New Hampshire. The place was a kind of paradise for creative
souls, a hideaway where every writer had his or her own cabin in the woods
with no phone or television — no distractions to speak of. But I was miser-
able. I could not write. Even the flies outside my window seemed to whisper,
"Go out and play. Forget the novel. Leave it till tomorrow."

I woke one morning at four, the light outside my window still blue. I 24
felt panic and sadness, though I didn't know why. I got up, dressed, and
went outside for a walk through the forest. But the panic persisted, and I
began to cry. I assumed that my writer's block had seized me suddenly.

That night I ate dinner in the main house and received a call on the pay 25
phone from my mother. She told me my grandmother had fallen and broken her leg. But that wasn't all; she had subsequently suffered a heart attack.
Her other organs were failing. I had to hurry if I wanted to say good-bye.

I drove to Boston that night, not believing that we could be losing her. 26
She would make it. I was certain. Sure, she was ninety-two, frail, unable to
walk steadily. But she was lucid,° and her tongue was as sharp as ever.

---

regaling: Entertaining.   **lucid:** Mentally sound.

Somehow I had imagined her as indestructible, made immortal by power and cruelty and wit.

The woman I found in the hospital bed was barely recognizable. My 27 grandmother had always been fussy about her appearance. She never showed her face without makeup. Even in the day, when it was just she and the cleaning lady, she dressed as if she were ready for a cocktail party. At night she usually had cocktail parties; doddering° old men hovered around her, sipping Scotch and bantering about theater and politics.

My grandmother's face had swollen to twice its normal size, and tubes 28 came out of her nose. She had struggled so hard to pull them out that the nurses had tied her wrists to the bed rails. Her hair was gray and thin. Her body was withered and bruised, barely covered by the green hospital gown.

Her hazel eyes were all that was still recognizable, but the expression in 29 them was different from any I had ever seen on her — terror. She was terrified to die. She tried to rise when she saw me, and her eyes pleaded with me to help her, to save her, to get her out of this mess. I stood over her, and I felt only one thing: overwhelming love. Not a trace of anger. That dark gray rage I'd felt toward her was gone as I stroked her forehead and told her she would be okay, even knowing she would not.

For two days, my mother, her sisters, and I stood beside my grand- 30 mother, singing Irish ballads and reading passages to her from the works of her favorite novelist, James Joyce. For the first time, she could not talk. At one point, she gestured wildly for pen and paper. I brought her the pen and the paper and held them up for her, but she was too weak for even that. What came out was only a faint, incomprehensible line.

In death we are each reduced to our essence: the spirit we are when we 31 are born. The trappings we hold on to our whole lives — our race, our money, our sex, our age, our politics — become irrelevant. My grandmother became a child in that hospital bed, a spirit about to embark on an unknown journey, terrified and alone, no matter how many of us were crowded around her. In the final hours, even her skin seemed to lose its wrinkles and take on a waxy glow. Then, finally, the machines around us went silent as she left us behind to squabble in the purgatory of the flesh.

Questions to Start You Thinking

1. CONSIDERING MEANING: What are the similarities and differences between Senna and her grandmother? How do the differences result in conflict?

2. IDENTIFYING WRITING STRATEGIES: Identify some ways Senna makes her grandmother come alive for readers. Where is her description vivid enough for you to see her as Senna does? Which details are particularly effective? Why?

3. READING CRITICALLY: How would you describe the tone of the essay? Support your opinion with specific passages.

doddering: Feeble.

4. **EXPANDING VOCABULARY:** In describing her grandmother, Senna explains, "I had imagined her as indestructible, made immortal by power and cruelty and wit" (paragraph 26). In your own words, define *immortal*. How can "power and cruelty and wit" make someone immortal?

5. **MAKING CONNECTIONS:** In "Evan's Two Moms" (pp. 451–52), Anna Quindlen makes a comparison between gay marriage and interracial marriage. How is Senna's situation both similar to and different from that of a child of same-sex parents? What advice might Senna give about the prejudice that such a child might encounter?

Journal Prompts

1. Recall a time when you or someone you know was verbally abused. How did you respond?

2. At the end of her life, Senna's grandmother "gestured wildly for pen and paper" (paragraph 30), but she was unable to write. If she had been able to write a sentence or two, what might she have written to Senna?

Suggestions for Writing

1. Senna notes that "when you cease to express anger toward those who have hurt you, you are essentially giving up on them" (paragraph 20). Write an essay about a time when expressing anger had a positive effect on a relationship. Be sure to recall the events leading up to the confrontation as well as the resolution to the problem.

2. Senna suggests that her grandmother's prejudice is a result of age and ignorance. What other factors might contribute to an individual's prejudices? Write an essay presenting your views about how prejudice develops and what can be done to prevent it.

E. B. White
Once More to the Lake

E. B. (Elwyn Brooks) White *(1899–1985) was born in Mount Vernon, New York. After serving in the army, he graduated from Cornell University and moved to Seattle to work as a reporter. His career led him back to the East Coast, where he joined the staff of the recently established* New Yorker *magazine in 1927. For half a century, his satires, poems, and essays helped define that magazine's distinctive style of elegant wit and social comment. He moved to Maine in 1933, and his widely read books for children,* Stuart Little *(1945),* Charlotte's Web *(1952), and* The Trumpet of the Swan *(1970), draw on his familiarity with the country to celebrate life's blend of sadness, happiness, love, and loss. In the following essay, first published in* Harper's *magazine in 1941, White reflects on the experience of returning with his son to a favorite scene from his own childhood. In the paired selection*

■ For more about
E. B. White, visit
<bedfordstmartins.com/
bedguide> and do a key-
word search:

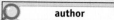
author

that follows (pp. 470–72), Nancy Gibbs offers a different view of summer vacations, proposing that parents relax summer rules and schedules so their children can enjoy memorable experiences like the one that White describes.

As YOU READ: *Notice what, according to White, changes a person's perspective from childhood to adulthood.*

August 1941

One summer, along about 1904, my father rented a camp on a lake in Maine and took us all there for the month of August. We all got ring-worm from some kittens and had to rub Pond's Extract on our arms and legs night and morning, and my father rolled over in a canoe with all his clothes on; but outside of that the vacation was a success and from then on none of us ever thought there was any place in the world like that lake in Maine. We returned summer after summer—always on August 1 for one month. I have since become a salt-water man, but sometimes in summer there are days when the restlessness of the tides and the fearful cold of the sea water and the incessant wind that blows across the afternoon and into the evening make me wish for the placidity of a lake in the woods. A few weeks ago this feeling got so strong I bought myself a couple of bass hooks and a spinner and returned to the lake where we used to go, for a week's fishing and to revisit old haunts. 1

I took along my son, who had never had any fresh water up his nose and who had seen lily pads only from train windows. On the journey over to the lake I began to wonder what it would be like. I wondered how time would have marred this unique, this holy spot—the coves and streams, the hills that the sun set behind, the camps and the paths behind the camps. I was sure that the tarred road would have found it out, and I wondered in what other ways it would be desolated. It is strange how much you can remember about places like that once you allow your mind to return into the grooves that lead back. You remember one thing, and that suddenly reminds you of another thing. I guess I remembered clearest of all the early mornings, when the lake was cool and motionless, remembered how the bedroom smelled of the lumber it was made of and of the wet woods whose scent entered through the screen. The partitions in the camp were thin and did not extend clear to the top of the rooms, and as I was always the first up I would dress softly so as not to wake the others, and sneak out into the sweet outdoors and start out in the canoe, keeping close along the shore in the long shadows of the pines. I remembered being very careful never to rub my paddle against the gunwale° for fear of disturbing the stillness of the cathedral. 2

The lake had never been what you would call a wild lake. There were cottages sprinkled around the shores, and it was in farming country al- 3

---

gunwale: Upper edge of the side of a boat.

though the shores of the lake were quite heavily wooded. Some of the cottages were owned by nearby farmers, and you would live at the shore and eat your meals at the farmhouse. That's what our family did. But although it wasn't wild, it was a fairly large and undisturbed lake and there were places in it that, to a child at least, seemed infinitely remote and primeval.

I was right about the tar: it led to within half a mile of the shore. But 4 when I got back there, with my boy, and we settled into a camp near a farmhouse and into the kind of summertime I had known, I could tell that it was going to be pretty much the same as it had been before—I knew it, lying in bed the first morning smelling the bedroom and hearing the boy sneak quietly out and go off along the shore in a boat. I began to sustain the illusion that he was I, and therefore, by simple transposition, that I was my father. This sensation persisted, kept cropping up all the time we were there. It was not an entirely new feeling, but in this setting it grew much stronger. I seemed to be living a dual existence. I would be in the middle of some simple act, I would be picking up a bait box or laying down a table fork, or I would be saying something and suddenly it would be not I but my father who was saying the words or making the gesture. It gave me a creepy sensation.

We went fishing the first morning. I felt the same damp moss covering 5 the worms in the bait can, and saw the dragonfly alight on the tip of my rod as it hovered a few inches from the surface of the water. It was the arrival of this fly that convinced me beyond any doubt that everything was as it always had been, that the years were a mirage, and that there had been no years. The small waves were the same, chucking the rowboat under the chin as we fished at anchor, and the boat was the same boat, the same color green and the ribs broken in the same places, and under the floorboards the same fresh water leavings and debris—the dead hellgrammite, the wisps of moss, the rusty discarded fishhook, the dried blood from yesterday's catch. We stared silently at the tips of our rods, at the dragonflies that came and went. I lowered the tip of mine into the water, tentatively, pensively dislodging the fly, which darted two feet away, poised, darted two feet back, and came to rest again a little farther up the rod. There had been no years between the ducking of this dragonfly and the other one—the one that was part of memory. I looked at the boy, who was silently watching his fly, and it was my hands that held his rod, my eyes watching. I felt dizzy and didn't know which rod I was at the end of.

We caught two bass, hauling them in briskly as though they were mack- 6 erel, pulling them over the side of the boat in a businesslike manner without any landing net, and stunning them with a blow on the back of the head. When we got back for a swim before lunch, the lake was exactly where we had left it, the same number of inches from the dock, and there was only the merest suggestion of a breeze. This seemed an utterly enchanted sea, this lake you could leave to its own devices for a few hours and come back to, and find that it had not stirred, this constant and trustworthy body of water. In the shallows, the dark, water-soaked sticks and twigs, smooth and old, were undulating in clusters on the bottom against the clean ribbed sand,

and the track of the mussel was plain. A school of minnows swam by, each minnow with its small individual shadow, doubling the attendance, so clear and sharp in the sunlight. Some of the other campers were in swimming, along the shore, one of them with a cake of soap, and the water felt thin and clear and unsubstantial. Over the years there had been this person with the cake of soap, this cultist, and here he was. There had been no years.

Up to the farmhouse to dinner through the teeming dusty field, the 7 road under our sneakers was only a two-track road. The middle track was missing, the one with the marks of the hooves and the splotches of dried, flaky manure. There had always been three tracks to choose from in choosing which track to walk in; now the choice was narrowed down to two. For a moment I missed terribly the middle alternative. But the way led past the tennis court, and something about the way it lay there in the sun reassured me; the tape had loosened along the backline, the alleys were green with plantains° and other weeds, and the net (installed in June and removed in September) sagged in the dry noon, and the whole place steamed with midday heat and hunger and emptiness. There was a choice of pie for dessert, and one was blueberry and one was apple, and the waitresses were the same country girls, there having been no passage of time, only the illusion of it as in a dropped curtain — the waitresses were still fifteen; their hair had been washed, that was the only difference — they had been to the movies and seen the pretty girls with the clean hair.

Summertime, oh, summertime, pattern of life indelible° with fade- 8 proof lake, the wood unshatterable, the pasture with the sweetfern and the juniper forever and ever, summer without end; this was the background, and the life along the shore was the design, the cottages with their innocent and tranquil design, their tiny docks with the flagpole and the American flag floating against the white clouds in the blue sky, the little paths over the roots of the trees leading from camp to camp and the paths leading back to the outhouses and the can of lime for sprinkling, and at the souvenir counters at the store the miniature birchbark canoes and the postcards that showed things looking a little better than they looked. This was the American family at play, escaping the city heat, wondering whether the newcomers in the camp at the head of the cove were "common" or "nice," wondering whether it was true that the people who drove up for Sunday dinner at the farmhouse were turned away because there wasn't enough chicken.

It seemed to me, as I kept remembering all this, that those times and 9 those summers had been infinitely precious and worth saving. There had been jollity and peace and goodness. The arriving (at the beginning of August) had been so big a business in itself, at the railway station the farm wagon drawn up, the first smell of the pine-laden air, the first glimpse of the smiling farmer, and the great importance of the trunks and your father's enormous authority in such matters, and the feel of the wagon under you for the long ten-mile haul, and at the top of the last long hill catching the

---

plantains: Common wild plants.   **indelible:** Unable to be removed.

first view of the lake after eleven months of not seeing this cherished body
of water. The shouts and cries of the other campers when they saw you, and
the trunks to be unpacked, to give up their rich burden. (Arriving was less
exciting nowadays, when you sneaked up in your car and parked it under a
tree near the camp and took out the bags and in five minutes it was all over,
no fuss, no loud wonderful fuss about trunks.)

Peace and goodness and jollity. The only thing that was wrong now,   10
really, was the sound of the place, an unfamiliar nervous sound of the
outboard motors. This was the note that jarred, the one thing that would
sometimes break the illusion and set the years moving. In those other
summertimes all motors were inboard; and when they were at a little distance, the noise they made was a sedative, an ingredient of summer sleep.
They were one-cylinder and two-cylinder engines, and some were make-and-
break and some were jump-spark, but they all made a sleepy sound across
the lake. The one-lungers throbbed and fluttered, and the twin-cylinder ones
purred and purred, and that was a quiet sound, too. But now the campers
all had outboards. In the daytime, in the hot mornings, these motors made
a petulant, irritable sound; at night in the still evening when the afterglow
lit the water, they whined about one's ears like mosquitoes. My boy loved
our rented outboard, and his great desire was to achieve single-handed mastery over it, and authority, and he soon learned the trick of choking it a little
(but not too much), and the adjustment of the needle valve. Watching him I
would remember the things you could do with the old one-cylinder engine
with the heavy flywheel,° how you could have it eating out of your hand if
you got really close to it spiritually. Motorboats in those days didn't have
clutches, and you would make a landing by shutting off the motor at the
proper time and coasting in with a dead rudder. But there was a way of reversing them, if you learned the trick, by cutting the switch and putting it on
again exactly on the final dying revolution of the flywheel, so that it would
kick back against compression and begin reversing. Approaching a dock in a
strong following breeze, it was difficult to slow up sufficiently by the ordinary coasting method, and if a boy felt he had complete mastery over his
motor, he was tempted to keep it running beyond its time and then reverse
it a few feet from the dock. It took a cool nerve, because if you threw the
switch a twentieth of a second too soon you would catch the flywheel when
it still had speed enough to go up past center, and the boat would leap
ahead, charging bull-fashion at the dock.

We had a good week at the camp. The bass were biting well and the   11
sun shone endlessly, day after day. We would be tired at night and lie down
in the accumulated heat of the little bedrooms after the long hot day and
the breeze would stir almost imperceptibly outside and the smell of the
swamp drift in through the rusty screens. Sleep would come easily and in
the morning the red squirrel would be on the roof, tapping out his gay routine. I kept remembering everything, lying in bed in the mornings — the

flywheel: A heavy wheel revolving on a shaft to regulate machinery.

small steamboat that had a long rounded stern like the lip of a Ubangi,° and how quietly she ran on the moonlight sails, when the older boys played their mandolins° and the girls sang and we ate doughnuts dipped in sugar, and how sweet the music was on the water in the shining night, and what it had felt like to think about girls then. After breakfast we would go up to the store and the things were in the same place — the minnows in a bottle, the plugs and spinners disarranged and pawed over by the youngsters from the boys' camp, the Fig Newtons and the Beeman's gum. Outside, the road was tarred and cars stood in front of the store. Inside, all was just as it had always been, except there was more Coca-Cola and not so much Moxie and root beer and birch beer and sarsaparilla. We would walk out with the bottle of pop apiece and sometimes the pop would backfire up our noses and hurt. We explored the streams, quietly, where the turtles slid off the sunny logs and dug their way into the soft bottom; and we lay on the town wharf and fed worms to the tame bass. Everywhere we went I had trouble making out which was I, the one walking at my side, the one walking in my pants.

One afternoon while we were at that lake a thunderstorm came up. It 12 was the revival of an old melodrama that I had seen long ago with childish awe. The second-act climax of the drama of the electrical disturbance over a lake in America had not changed in any important respect. This was the big scene. The whole thing was so familiar, the first feeling of oppression and heat and a general air around camp of not wanting to go very far away. In midafternoon (it was all the same) a curious darkening of the sky, and a lull in everything that had made life tick; and then the way the boats suddenly swung the other way at their moorings with the coming of a breeze out of the new quarter, and the premonitory° rumble. Then the kettle drum, then the snare, then the bass drum and cymbals, then crackling light against the dark, and the gods grinning and licking their chops in the hills. Afterward the calm, the rain steadily rustling in the calm lake, the return of light and hope and spirits, and the campers running out in joy and relief to go swimming in the rain, their bright cries perpetuating the deathless joke about how they were getting simply drenched, and the children screaming with delight at the new sensation of bathing in the rain, and the joke about getting drenched linking the generations in a strong indestructible chain. And the comedian who waded in carrying an umbrella.

When the others went swimming my son said he was going in, too. He 13 pulled his dripping trunks from the line where they had hung all through the shower and wrung them out. Languidly, and with no thought of going in, I watched him, his hard little body, skinny and bare, saw him wince slightly as he pulled up around his vitals the small, soggy, icy garment. As he buckled the swollen belt, suddenly my groin felt the chill of death.

Ubangi: People who live near the Ubangi River in the Central African Republic and Zaire. The women traditionally pierce and stretch their lips around flat wooden disks. **mandolins:** Small stringed instruments often used in ballads and folk music. **premonitory:** Warning.

Questions to Start You Thinking

1. CONSIDERING MEANING: How have the lake and the surrounding community, as White depicts them, changed since he was a boy?

2. IDENTIFYING WRITING STRATEGIES: Notice the details White uses to describe life at the lake. How many different sensory experiences do his images evoke? Identify and then analyze at least four memorable images from the essay, explaining what makes each memorable.

3. READING CRITICALLY: White compares the past with the present to show that "there had been no years" since his childhood at the lake (paragraph 5). How does this comparison shape the tone of White's essay? How does the tone change at the end? What is the effect of this sudden change?

4. EXPANDING VOCABULARY: Define *primeval* (paragraph 3), *transposition* (paragraph 4), *hellgrammite* (paragraph 5), *undulating, cultist* (paragraph 6), and *petulant* (paragraph 10). What is White's purpose in using adult words rather than a child's words to look back on his childhood experience?

5. MAKING CONNECTIONS: Both White and Danzy Senna ("The Color of Love," pp. 458–62) write about a relationship with a close family member. While they both use narration to reveal the intricacies of these relationships, Senna adds dialogue to her narration. As a reader, are you affected more by one approach than the other? Which approach do you find more successful? Or do you find each effective in its own way?

Link to the Paired Essay

While White and Nancy Gibbs ("Free the Children," pp. 470–72) both address childhood summers, their essays have very different purposes. How would you define each writer's purpose? How do the strategies they use in developing their essays differ? Are they similar in any ways?

Journal Prompts

1. Describe a place that has special meaning for you. Why is it special?

2. Use White's description of a thunderstorm (paragraph 12) as a model to describe a natural event that you have witnessed.

Suggestions for Writing

1. Think of a place you knew as a child and then visited again as an adult. Write an essay explaining how the place had changed and not changed. Use observation and recall to make the place as memorable for your readers as it was for you.

2. How do you think nostalgia—the desire to return to an important and pleasant time in the past—influences the way we remember our own experiences? Use examples from White's essay and from your experience to illustrate your explanation.

Nancy Gibbs
Free the Children

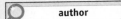 For more about
Nancy Gibbs, visit
<bedfordstmartins.com/
bedguide> and do a key-
word search:

author

Nancy Gibbs *was born in New York, received a BA in history from Yale University, and then studied politics and philosophy at Oxford University. Gibbs joined* Time *magazine in 1985 as a reporter for the International section and is currently editor-at-large. She has written over one hundred cover stories on topics including the September 11 terrorist attacks, the war in Iraq, Hurricane Katrina, and stem-cell research. Gibbs is also a visiting professor of journalism at Princeton University, where she teaches a seminar about the divided political culture of the United States. She lives near New York City with her husband and two daughters. In "Free the Children," which first appeared in* Time *in 2003, Gibbs voices her concern over modern parents' tendency to overprotect their children. Both she and E. B. White ("Once More to the Lake," pp. 464–68) idealize summer as a time for exploration, a time for kids simply to enjoy their freedom with, as Gibbs puts it, "no one keeping score."*

AS YOU READ: *Note some of the specific things Gibbs suggests allowing children to do when they are out of school for the summer. How do you respond to her suggestions?*

My daughters are upstairs shrieking. And thumping. Nothing sounds 1 broken, so I am leaving them alone to savor the outlaw feeling of playing hooky from the afternoon session of camp. They know absences don't count against them on some Permanent Record somewhere.

I long for them to have a whole summer that doesn't matter. When they 2 can read for fun, even books that don't appear on the officially sanctioned summer reading list. When even the outfielders get to play first base sometimes because the game doesn't count. When they can ruin their brand-new sneakers because they found a great new creek. When a rule can be bent, if only to test its strength, and they can play all they want, without playing for keeps.

I want summer not to count because what happens as a result counts 3 for so much. Maybe we adults idealize our own red-rover° days, the hot afternoons spent playing games that required no coaches, eating foods that involved no nutrition, getting dirty in whole new ways and rarely glancing in the direction of a screen of any kind. Ask friends about the people and places that shaped them, and summer springs up quickly when they tell their story: their first kiss, first beer, first job that changed everything. The best summer moments were stretchy enough to carry us all through the year, which is why it's worth listening to all the warnings from social scientists about our Hurried Children who for the rest of the year wear their schedules like clothes that are too tight.

red-rover: An outdoor children's game.

The experts have long charted the growing stress and disappearing 4 downtime of modern children; now they say the trend extends across class and region. The combination of double shifts, shrinking vacations, fear of boredom, and competitive instincts conspires to clog our kids' summer just as much as the rest of the year. Even camp isn't likely to be about s'mores and spud° anymore: there is math camp and weight camp and leadership camp, as though summer were about perfecting ourselves, when in fact the opposite may be true.

That's because summer should be a season of grace — not of excuses but 5 of exceptions, ice cream an hour before dinner just because it's so hot out, bedtimes missed in honor of meteor showers, weekdays and weekends that melt together because nothing feels like work. It's not just about relaxing; it's about rehearsing. All our efforts to guard and guide our children may just get in the way of the one thing they need most from us: to be deeply loved yet left alone so they can try a new skill, new slang, new style, new flip-flops. So they can trip a few times, make mistakes, cross them out, try again, with no one keeping score.

This may require some reeducation, a kind of summer school of play 6 that teaches kids not to expect to be entertained every moment, to adjust to days measured out not in periods of practices but in large clumps of opportunity called Morning and Afternoon. Go build a fort. Use every single art supply in the house to make something big. Be bored and see where it takes you, because the imagination's dusty wilderness is worth crossing if you want to sculpt your soul.

Giving children some summer privacy and freedom takes nerve, and not 7 just because this is also precious time to be together as a family. Last summer, the Amber Alert° summer, who could take their eyes off their kids in the front yard? When my seven-year-old was half an hour late coming home one afternoon and the lifeguards and counselors starting asking me what she looked like, what she was wearing, I couldn't get enough air in my lungs to tell them, the fear was so strangling.

But when we finally found her, happily engrossed near Dead Man's 8 Cave catching frogs with a friend, I had to take a deep breath and remember that maybe I had neglected to teach her to call home if she was going to be late, because I had never needed to. She is shuttled from school to playdate to soccer to chess, and only in the summer does she control her own time and whereabouts at all. Do I punish her for savoring liberty the first time she ever tasted it? So we had a long talk while sitting under a tree before I grounded her for a day.

We are bombarded with reasons to stay inside: we're afraid of mosquitoes 9 because of West Nile° and grass because of pesticides and sun because of cancer and sunscreen because of vitamin-D deficiency. Ours is the generation that knows too much, including what other kids are doing in the summer to get a

spud: Another children's game.   **Amber Alert:** A missing-child bulletin issued by law enforcement agencies.   **West Nile:** A virus spread by infected mosquitoes.

head start in the marathon that ends with a fat envelope from a top school. So apart from the challenge of trusting our kids, there is the challenge of trusting ourselves, steering by the stars of instinct and memory rather than parent peer pressure or all those guidebooks on how to raise a Successful Child.

I send my girls out to play in the hope that by summer's end I will see 10 the gifts that freedom brings. Kids seem four inches taller in September than in June, whether they've grown any or not. And the measuring stick is marked off in bruises healed and flags captured, friends lost and found, goals achieved without anyone's help. I hope for the discipline not to discipline them too much because that's how I will learn how strong they have become.

Questions to Start You Thinking

1. **CONSIDERING MEANING:** According to Gibbs, what are some of the benefits of allowing children unsupervised free time during the summer?

2. **IDENTIFYING WRITING STRATEGIES:** In paragraphs 7 and 8, Gibbs uses recall to share a specific experience involving one of her daughters. What is her point in including this anecdote? What does it contribute to the essay as a whole?

3. **READING CRITICALLY:** In paragraph 3, Gibbs refers to "all the warnings from social scientists about our Hurried Children," and in the next paragraph she mentions "experts" who have "charted the growing stress and disappearing downtime of modern children." Is this evidence sufficient to establish that a problem exists? Why or why not? What do these brief references suggest about Gibbs's intended audience?

4. **EXPANDING VOCABULARY:** Reread paragraph 5, in which Gibbs writes that summer is "not just about relaxing; it's about rehearsing." What does she mean by *rehearsing* in this context, and why is the word important to her point?

5. **MAKING CONNECTIONS:** In "They've Got to Be Carefully Taught" (pp. 564–66), Susan Brady Konig argues that our educational system forces ideas on children rather than allowing them to develop more naturally, as Gibbs feels they should. How do you think that freedom and structure affect the development of children?

Link to the Paired Essay

In "Once More to the Lake" (pp. 464–68), E. B. White writes about a summer vacation that he and his son spend at a rustic fishing camp. How might Gibbs respond to White's vacation with his son? Does White allow his son the "summer privacy and freedom" that Gibbs advocates (paragraph 7)? What might White think of the world of children today?

Journal Prompts

1. Do you agree with Gibbs that children today experience significant stress and a lack of downtime? Why or why not?

2. How closely supervised was your free time when you were a child? If you have children, how closely do you supervise their free time? Do you think that Gibbs diminishes the benefits of parental supervision? Why or why not?

Suggestions for Writing

1. In a personal essay, write about a special experience you had as a child during a summer break. In what ways does your experience support or counter Gibbs's point about the importance of allowing children unsupervised free time?

2. Write an essay, addressed to parents of children under the age of twelve, proposing what you see as the ideal way to treat their children's summer break. What sorts of activities should be available to them? What should parents participate in, and when should they leave their children alone? Develop your ideas as specifically as possible.

Chapter 24
Men and Women

Responding to an Image

Examine this photograph, including the setting and the body language of the man and woman. What similarities and differences do you note? What emotions are apparent? If you were to add dialogue to this picture, what might the man and woman be saying or thinking? Based on your analysis, what general point does the photograph make about relationships? (You also might want to compare and contrast this image with the one on p. 529.)

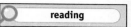
Robert Jensen
The High Cost of Manliness

Robert Jensen *was born in 1958 and grew up in Fargo, North Dakota. After earning a BA in social studies and secondary education from Moorhead State University and graduate degrees in journalism from American University and the University of Minnesota, Jensen started his career as a newspaper journalist. He is now a professor of journalism at the University of Texas at Austin, where he teaches courses on media law, ethics, and politics and also regularly contributes to a variety of publications. His scholarly books include* Pornography: The Production and Consumption of Inequality *(1998),* Writing Dissent: Taking Radical Ideas from the Margins to the Mainstream *(2001),* Citizens of the Empire: The Struggle to Claim Our Humanity *(2004), and* The Heart of Whiteness: Confronting Race, Racism, and White Privilege *(2005). An outspoken critic of current U.S. foreign policy, Jensen gained widespread attention over his series of controversial opinion pieces in the* Houston Chronicle *soon after the September 11 terrorist attacks. In the following essay, which first appeared on Alternet.org in September 2006, Jensen calls for abandoning the prevailing definition of masculinity, arguing that it is "toxic" to both men and women.*

AS YOU READ: *Identify what Jensen sees as the dominant conception of masculinity in contemporary culture. What does he think of this conception?*

It's hard to be a man; hard to live up to the demands that come with the dominant conception of masculinity, of the tough guy. 1

So, guys, I have an idea—maybe it's time we stop trying. Maybe this masculinity thing is a bad deal, not just for women but for us. 2

We need to get rid of the whole idea of masculinity. It's time to abandon the claim that there are certain psychological or social traits that inherently come with being biologically male. If we can get past that, we have a chance to create a better world for men and women. 3

The dominant conception of masculinity in U.S. culture is easily summarized: men are assumed to be naturally competitive and aggressive, and being a real man is therefore marked by the struggle for control, conquest, and domination. A man looks at the world, sees what he wants, and takes it. Men who don't measure up are wimps, sissies, fags, girls. The worst insult one man can 4 hurl at another—whether it's boys on the playground or CEOs in the board-room—is the accusation that a man is like a woman. Although the culture acknowledges that men can in some situations have traits traditionally associated with women (caring, compassion, tenderness), in the end it is men's strength-expressed-as-toughness that defines us and must trump any femalelike softness. Those aspects of masculinity must prevail for a man to be a "real man."

That's not to suggest, of course, that every man adopts that view of masculinity. But it is endorsed in key institutions and activities—most notably in business, the military, and athletics—and is reinforced through the mass media. It is particularly expressed in the way men—straight and gay alike—talk about sexuality and act sexually. And our culture's male heroes reflect those characteristics: they most often are men who take charge rather than seek consensus, seize power rather than look for ways to share it, and are willing to be violent to achieve their goals. 5

That view of masculinity is dangerous for women. It leads men to seek to control "their" women and define their own pleasure in that control, which leads to epidemic levels of rape and battery. But this view of masculinity is toxic for men as well. 6

If masculinity is defined as conquest, it means that men will always struggle with each other for dominance. In a system premised on hierarchy° and power, there can be only one king of the hill. Every other man must in some way be subordinated to the king, and the king has to always be nervous about who is coming up that hill to get him. A friend who once worked on Wall Street—one of the preeminent° sites of masculine competition—described coming to work as like walking into a knife fight when all the good spots along the wall were taken. Masculinity like this is life lived as endless competition and threat. 7

No one man created this system, and perhaps none of us, if given a choice, would choose it. But we live our lives in that system, and it deforms men, narrowing our emotional range and depth. It keeps us from the rich connections with others—not just with women and children, but other men—that make life meaningful but require vulnerability. 8

This doesn't mean that the negative consequences of this toxic masculinity are equally dangerous for men and women. As feminists have long pointed out, there's a big difference between women dealing with the possibility of being raped, beaten, and killed by the men in their lives and men not being able to cry. But we can see that the short-term material gains that men get are not adequate compensation for what we men give up in the long haul—which is to surrender part of our humanity to the project of dominance. 9

Of course there are obvious physical differences between men and women—average body size, hormones, reproductive organs. There may be other differences rooted in our biology that we don't yet understand. Yet it's also true that men and women are more similar than we are different, and that given the pernicious° effects of centuries of patriarchy° and its re- 10

hierarchy: A grouping based on relative rank.   preeminent: Most important.   pernicious: Destructive.   patriarchy: Social organization in which the father is supreme; male control of most of the power in a society.

lentless devaluing of things female, we should be skeptical of the perceived differences.

What we know is simple: in any human population, there is wide indi- 11 vidual variation. While there's no doubt that a large part of our behavior is rooted in our DNA, there's also no doubt that our genetic endowment is highly influenced by culture. Beyond that, it's difficult to say much with any certainty. It's true that only women can bear children and breast-feed. That fact likely has some bearing on aspects of men's and women's personalities. But we don't know much about what the effect is, and given the limits of our tools to understand human behavior, it's possible we may never know much.

At the moment, the culture seems obsessed with gender differences, in the 12 context of a recurring intellectual fad (called "evolutionary psychology" this time around, and "sociobiology" in a previous incarnation) that wants to ex- plain all complex behaviors as simple evolutionary adaptations — if a pattern of human behavior exists, it must be because it's adaptive in some ways. In the long run, that's true by definition. But in the short term it's hardly a convinc- ing argument to say, "Look at how men and women behave so differently; it must be because men and women are fundamentally different" when a politi- cal system has been creating differences between men and women.

From there, the argument that we need to scrap masculinity is fairly 13 simple. To illustrate it, remember back to right after 9/11. A number of com- mentators argued that criticisms of masculinity should be rethought. Can- not we now see — recognizing that male firefighters raced into burning buildings, risking and sometimes sacrificing their lives to save others — that masculinity can encompass a kind of strength that is rooted in caring and sacrifice? Of course men often exhibit such strength, just as do women. So, the obvious question arises: What makes these distinctly masculine charac- teristics? Are they not simply human characteristics?

We identify masculine tendencies toward competition, domination, and 14 violence because we see patterns of differential behavior; men are more prone to such behavior in our culture. We can go on to observe and analyze the ways in which men are socialized to behave in those ways, toward the goal of chang- ing those destructive behaviors. That analysis is different than saying that ad- mirable human qualities present in both men and women are somehow pri- marily the domain of one gender. To assign them to a gender is misguided and demeaning to the gender that is then assumed not to possess them to the same degree. Once we start saying "strength and courage are masculine traits," it leads to the conclusion that woman are not as strong or courageous.

Of course, if we are going to jettison° masculinity, we have to scrap fem- 15 ininity along with it. We have to stop trying to define what men and women are going to be in the world based on extrapolations° from physical sex differences. That doesn't mean we ignore those differences when they mat- ter, but we have to stop assuming they matter everywhere.

jettison: Throw out.   **extrapolations:** Predictions.

I don't think the planet can long survive if the current conception of 16
masculinity endures. We face political and ecological challenges that can't
be met with this old model of what it means to be a man. At the more intimate level, the stakes are just as high. For those of us who are biologically
male, we have a simple choice: we men can settle for being men, or we can
strive to be human beings.

Questions to Start You Thinking

1. CONSIDERING MEANING: What does Jensen see as the negative consequences
   of the commonly held idea of masculinity?

2. IDENTIFYING WRITING STRATEGIES: Where in the essay does Jensen use comparison and contrast in writing about men and women? What is his point
   in doing so?

3. READING CRITICALLY: In paragraph 5, Jensen admits that not all men conceive
   of masculinity in terms of competition and aggression. Do you think he goes
   on to provide enough evidence to support his claim that this view of masculinity is dominant in U.S. culture? Why or why not?

4. EXPANDING VOCABULARY: In paragraph 12, Jensen refers to the current obsession with gender differences in the United States as a "recurring intellectual
   fad." What does he mean by this phrase, and what does it contribute to his
   argument?

5. MAKING CONNECTIONS: In "Guys Just Want to Have Fun" (pp. 482–84),
   Barbara Ehrenreich also writes about views of men and women in con-
   temporary U.S. culture. In what ways do her observations correspond with
   Jensen's? In what ways do they differ?

Journal Prompts

1. Do you agree, as Jensen puts it, that the "worst insult one man can hurl at
   another . . . is the accusation that a man is like a woman" (paragraph 4)?
   What do you think about insults that liken a woman to a man?

2. In the essay's final paragraph, Jensen writes that he doesn't think "the
   planet can long survive if the current conception of masculinity endures."
   How do you respond to this statement?

Suggestions for Writing

1. Jensen writes in paragraph 13 about the idea of strength. In an essay, discuss how you define *human strength*, considering the physical, the intellectual, and the emotional.

2. Jensen acknowledges that gender differences are in some part determined
   by biological factors. However, he is more concerned about the influence of
   social conditioning. Write an essay analyzing how a particular social force
   does or does not contribute to stereotypes of masculinity and femininity.
   For example, you might consider the influence of some aspect of popular
   culture, education, sports, or children's toys. Use examples from your experience as well as other evidence to support your point.

Brent Staples
Black Men and Public Space

Brent Staples *was born in 1951 in Chester, Pennsylvania, and earned a PhD in psychology from the University of Chicago. He wrote for the* Chicago Sun-Times *and* Down Beat *magazine before joining the* New York Times *in 1985, where he moved from metropolitan news to the* New York Times Book Review. *Since 1990, Staples has been a member of the* Times *editorial board, writing regular columns on politics and culture. His work also has appeared in such magazines as* New York Woman, Ms., *and* Harper's, *and he is the author of the memoir* Parallel Time: Growing Up in Black and White *(1994). In the following essay, published in a slightly different version in* Ms. *magazine in September 1986, Staples considers how his presence affects other pedestrians at night.*

AS YOU READ: *Identify why other pedestrians respond to Staples with anxiety.*

■ For more about Brent Staples, visit <bedfordstmartins.com/bedguide> and do a keyword search:

author

My first victim was a woman — white, well dressed, probably in her late twenties. I came upon her late one evening on a deserted street in Hyde Park, a relatively affluent neighborhood in an otherwise mean, impoverished section of Chicago. As I swung onto the avenue behind her, there seemed to be a discreet, uninflammatory distance between us. Not so. She cast back a worried glance. To her, the youngish black man — a broad six feet two inches with a beard and billowing hair, both hands shoved into the pockets of a bulky military jacket — seemed menacingly close. After a few more quick glimpses, she picked up her pace and was soon running in earnest. Within seconds, she disappeared into a cross street.

That was more than a decade ago. I was twenty-one years old, a graduate student newly arrived at the University of Chicago. It was in the echo of that terrified woman's footfalls that I first began to know the unwieldy inheritance I'd come into — the ability to alter public space in ugly ways. It was clear that she thought herself the quarry of a mugger, a rapist, or worse. Suffering a bout of insomnia, however, I was stalking sleep, not defenseless wayfarers. As a softy who is scarcely able to take a knife to a raw chicken — let alone hold one to a person's throat — I was surprised, embarrassed, and dismayed all at once. Her flight made me feel like an accomplice in tyranny. It also made it clear that I was indistinguishable from the muggers who occasionally seeped into the area from the surrounding ghetto. The first encounter, and those that followed, signified that a vast, unnerving gulf lay between nighttime pedestrians — particularly women — and me. And I soon gathered that being perceived as dangerous is a hazard in itself. I only needed to turn a corner into a dicey situation, or crowd some frightened, armed person in a foyer somewhere, or make an errant move after being pulled over by a policeman. Where fear and weapons meet — and they often do in urban America — there is always the possibility of death.

In that first year, my first away from my hometown, I was to become 3
thoroughly familiar with the language of fear. At dark, shadowy intersections,
I could cross in front of a car stopped at a traffic light and elicit the *thunk,
thunk, thunk, thunk* of the driver — black, white, male, or female — hammering down the door locks. On less traveled streets after dark, I grew accustomed to but never comfortable with people crossing to the other side of the street rather than pass me. Then there were the standard unpleasantries with policemen, doormen, bouncers, cabdrivers, and others whose business it is to screen out troublesome individuals *before* there is any nastiness.

I moved to New York nearly two years ago and I have remained an avid 4
night walker. In central Manhattan, the near-constant crowd cover minimizes tense one-on-one street encounters. Elsewhere — in SoHo, for example, where sidewalks are narrow and tightly spaced buildings shut out the sky — things can get very taut indeed.

After dark, on the warrenlike° streets of Brooklyn where I live, I often see 5
women who fear the worst from me. They seem to have set their faces on neutral, and with their purse straps strung across their chests bandolier-style, they forge ahead as though bracing themselves against being tackled. I understand, of course, that the danger they perceive is not a hallucination. Women are particularly vulnerable to street violence, and young black males are drastically overrepresented among the perpetrators of that violence. Yet these truths are no solace against the kind of alienation that comes of being ever the suspect, a fearsome entity with whom pedestrians avoid making eye contact.

It is not altogether clear to me how I reached the ripe old age of twenty- 6
two without being conscious of the lethality nighttime pedestrians attributed to me. Perhaps it was because in Chester, Pennsylvania, the small, angry industrial town where I came of age in the 1960s, I was scarcely noticeable against a backdrop of gang warfare, street knifings, and murders. I grew up one of the good boys, had perhaps a half-dozen fistfights. In retrospect, my shyness of combat has clear sources.

As a boy, I saw countless tough guys locked away; I have since buried 7
several, too. They were babies, really — a teenage cousin, a brother of twenty-two, a childhood friend in his mid-twenties — all gone down in episodes of bravado played out in the streets. I came to doubt the virtues of intimidation early on. I chose, perhaps unconsciously, to remain a shadow — timid, but a survivor.

The fearsomeness mistakenly attributed to me in public places often has 8
a perilous flavor. The most frightening of these confusions occurred in the late 1970s and early 1980s, when I worked as a journalist in Chicago. One day, rushing into the office of a magazine I was writing for with a deadline story in hand, I was mistaken for a burglar. The office manager called security and, with an ad hoc° posse, pursued me through the labyrinthine halls, nearly to my editor's door. I had no way of proving who I was. I could only move briskly toward the company of someone who knew me.

warrenlike: Like a maze.   **ad hoc:** Spur of the moment.

Another time I was on assignment for a local paper and killing time be- 9
fore an interview. I entered a jewelry store on the city's affluent Near North
Side. The proprietor excused herself and returned with an enormous red
Doberman pinscher straining at the end of a leash. She stood, the dog extended toward me, silent to my questions, her eyes bulging nearly out of her
head. I took a cursory look around, nodded, and bade her good night.

Relatively speaking, however, I never fared as badly as another black 10
male journalist. He went to nearby Waukegan, Illinois, a couple of summers
ago to work on a story about a murderer who was born there. Mistaking the
reporter for the killer, police officers hauled him from his car at gunpoint
and but for his press credentials would probably have tried to book him.
Such episodes are not uncommon. Black men trade tales like this all the time.

Over the years, I learned to smother the rage I felt at so often being taken 11
for a criminal. Not to do so would surely have led to madness. I now take
precautions to make myself less threatening. I move about with care, particularly late in the evening. I give a wide berth° to nervous people on subway
platforms during the wee hours, particularly when I have exchanged business
clothes for jeans. If I happen to be entering a building behind some people
who appear skittish, I may walk by, letting them clear the lobby before I return, so as not to seem to be following them. I have been calm and extremely
congenial on those rare occasions when I've been pulled over by the police.

And on late-evening constitutionals I employ what has proved to be an 12
excellent tension-reducing measure: I whistle melodies from Beethoven and
Vivaldi and the more popular classical composers. Even steely New Yorkers
hunching toward nighttime destinations seem to relax, and occasionally
they even join in the tune. Virtually everybody seems to sense that a mugger
wouldn't be warbling bright, sunny selections from Vivaldi's *Four Seasons*. It
is my equivalent of the cowbell that hikers wear when they know they are in
bear country.

Questions to Start You Thinking

1. **CONSIDERING MEANING:** What misconceptions do people have about
   Staples because he is a young black man? What does he feel causes such
   misconceptions?

2. **IDENTIFYING WRITING STRATEGIES:** At the end of the essay, how does Staples
   use comparison to explain his behavior?

3. **READING CRITICALLY:** What kinds of appeals — emotional, logical, ethical —
   does Staples use? Are his appeals appropriate for the purpose of his essay?
   Why or why not? (For an explanation of kinds of appeals, see pp. 40–41.)

4. **EXPANDING VOCABULARY:** Define *affluent, uninflammatory* (paragraph 1), *unwieldy, quarry, errant* (paragraph 2), *bandolier, solace* (paragraph 5), *lethality*
   (paragraph 6), and *bravado* (paragraph 7). Why do you think Staples uses
   such formal language in this essay?

berth: Space.

5. **MAKING CONNECTIONS:** In "The Color of Love" (pp. 458–62), Danzy Senna writes about being the daughter of a black father and a white mother and, in particular, about her relationship with her prejudiced white grandmother. How might Senna and Staples respond to one another's experiences?

Journal Prompts

1. Are stereotypes ever useful? Why or why not?
2. Have you or someone you know ever been wrongfully stereotyped or pre-judged? How did you react?

Suggestions for Writing

1. Staples describes his feelings about being the object of racial fear. Have you or someone you know ever been the object of such a fear or of other mis-conceptions based on prejudice or stereotyping? Write a short personal essay discussing the causes and effects of the experience. What preconcep-tions were you or your acquaintance the victim of? How did you or your ac-quaintance respond?
2. What do you think causes the stereotype of African American men that Staples is addressing? Write an essay that analyzes this stereotype, drawing on several outside sources to support your analysis.

Barbara Ehrenreich
Guys Just Want to Have Fun

■ For more about Barbara Ehrenreich, visit <bedfordstmartins.com/bedguide> and do a key-word search:

author

Barbara Ehrenreich, *born in 1941, holds a BA from Reed College and a PhD from Rockefeller University. A writer and social activist, her critiques of such issues as health-care policy and workplace rights have appeared in publications including* Ms., Mother Jones, Nation, New Republic, *and* Time, *and she currently writes a regular column for the* Progressive. *She is also the author of several books, includ-ing* Fear of Falling: The Inner Life of the Middle Class *(1988),* Snarling Citi-zen: Essays *(1995),* Blood Rites: Origins and History of the Passion of War *(1997),* Bait and Switch: The (Futile) Pursuit of the American Dream *(2006), and* Dancing in the Streets: A History of Collective Joy *(2007). To write the best-selling* Nickel and Dimed: On (Not) Getting by in America *(2001), in which she explores the harsh realities of surviving on a wage of six to seven dollars an hour, Ehrenreich spent two years waiting tables, cleaning houses, and performing other low-wage jobs. In "Guys Just Want to Have Fun," from* Time *magazine in 2006, Ehrenreich examines evolving gender roles in education and the workplace. Al-though women are now more likely than men to earn a college degree, she argues that a shift in corporate culture is continuing to favor men in the business world.*

AS YOU READ: *Identify what you see as Ehrenreich's underlying purpose in writing this essay. What point does she want to impress on readers?*

When I was in college, I followed a simple strategy: go where the boys   1
are. Sure, that led me into many settings where inebriants° flowed,
but my reasoning was strictly practical. Men ruled the world, as anyone
could see, so the trick was to do as they did. No girlie major like art history
or French lit for me. I started in chemistry and then proceeded up the gender gradient to physics, finally achieving in Classical Mechanics the exalted
status of only girl in the class.

But that was an era when the cool kids smoked Gauloises° and argued   2
about Kierkegaard° and Trotsky.° Today, as two recent reports have revealed,
it's the girls who achieve and the boys who coast along on gut courses congenial to hangovers. Boys are less likely to go to college in the first place
(only 45 percent of college students under twenty-five are male) and are less
likely to graduate as well. If I tried to follow my original strategy now, I
would probably end up with an MA in *Madden*, the football video game,
and a postgraduate stay in rehab.

The trend has occasioned some predictions of a coming matriarchy in   3
which high-achieving women will rule over a nation of slacker guys. We've
all seen the movie, an endless loop culminating most recently in *You, Me
and Dupree*.° That little girls' T-shirt slogan — GIRLS RULE, BOYS DROOL — is
beginning to look less like a slur and more like an empirical° observation.

But it may be that the boys still know what they're doing. Among other   4
things that have changed since the '60s is the corporate culture, which once
valued literacy, numeracy, high GPAs and the ability to construct a simple
sentence. No doubt there are still workplaces where such achievements are
valued, but when I set out as an undercover journalist seeking a white-collar
corporate job for my book *Bait and Switch*, I was shocked to find the emphasis entirely on such elusive qualities as "personality," "attitude," and "lika-
bility." Play down the smarts, the career coaches and self-help books advised, cull° the experience and exude a "positive attitude."

In a June article on corporate personality testing, the *Washington Post* re-   5
ported on a woman who passed the skills test for a customer-care job but
wasn't hired because she failed the personality test. Those tests, including
the ubiquitous Myers-Briggs test, have no scientific credibility or predictive
value, as Annie Murphy Paul showed in her 2004 book, *Cult of Personality*.
You can have one Myers-Briggs personality on Tuesday and another when
you retake the test on Thursday. Their chief function, as far as I could tell
when I took them, was to weed out the introverts. When asked whether
you'd rather be the life of the party or curl up with a book, the correct answer is always "Party!"

---

inebriants: Substances that make one drunk.   **Gauloises:** A brand of French cigarettes.   **Kierkegaard:** Søren Kierkegaard (1813–1855), a nineteenth-century Danish
philosopher.   **Trotsky:** Leon Trotsky (1879–1940), leader of the Communist revolution
in Russia.   ***You, Me and Dupree:*** A 2006 comic film about a lazy, immature male character.   **empirical:** Based on evidence.   **cull:** Remove inferior parts from.

So the best preparation for that all-important personality test may well   6
be a college career spent playing poker and doing tequila shots. An Atlanta
woman I interviewed, a skilled Web-site writer, was fired without explanation after a few weeks at a job. "I tried to fit in," she told me. "I went to
lunch with the guys, but all they talked about was sports, which I know
nothing about, and they all seemed to know each other from college." Poor
thing, she had probably wasted her college years in the library.

The business world isn't totally hostile to higher education—an MBA   7
still counts for something. But as G. J. Meyer wrote in his classic 1995 book,
Executive Blues: Down and Out in Corporate America, a higher degree in something other than business or law—or, worse, a stint of college teaching—
can impart a deadly "academic stench" to one's résumé. And what are we to
make of the growing corporate defiance of elementary grammar? At a job
fair I attended, AT&T Wireless solicited sales reps with the question, if it was
a question, "Are you ready to put your skills to work. Like the way you're a
quick study. How you're good at finding solutions." Take that, you irritating,
irrelevant English 101 professors!

Maybe we need a return to gender-segregated higher education, with   8
the academic equivalent of Pinocchio's Pleasure Island for boys, where they
can hone their "people skills" at keg parties. But we will need those high-
achieving girls more than ever. Someone, after all, is going to have to figure
out how to make an economy run by superannuated° slacker boys competitive again in a world filled with Chinese and Indian brainiacs. I'd still major
in physics if I were doing it again, just because there ought to be at least a
few Americans, of whatever gender, who know something beyond the technology of beer bongs.

Questions to Start You Thinking

1. CONSIDERING MEANING: According to Ehrenreich, what are the general differences between today's male and female college students? In general, what
   character traits does Ehrenreich think are most valued in today's business
   world, and which gender is more likely to hold these qualities?

2. IDENTIFYING WRITING STRATEGIES: Where in the essay does Ehrenreich discuss causes and effects? How does this strategy contribute to her purpose?

3. READING CRITICALLY: What point is Ehrenreich making in her final paragraph? How convincing do you find her argument here?

4. EXPANDING VOCABULARY: In paragraph 3, what does Ehrenreich mean by "a
   coming matriarchy"? Discuss whether she is using the term *matriarchy* literally or in a special sense here

5. MAKING CONNECTIONS: In "Why Not a Dollar?" (pp. 488–93), Evelyn F.
   Murphy writes about the increasing wage gap between men and women in
   the U.S. workforce. How might Ehrenreich explain that gap?

superannuated: Advancing in age.

Journal Prompts

1. Does your experience bear out what Ehrenreich says about the differences between male and female college students? If so, how do you explain these differences? If not, how would you describe the work habits of male and female students?

2. What do you think are the most important qualities employers should seek in potential employees? To what extent are these qualities shared equally by women and men?

Suggestions for Writing

1. Analyze the employee characteristics and work ethic valued by your current or recent employer. Then write an essay that agrees with, disagrees with, or qualifies Ehrenreich's position, using that recent experience to support your view.

2. In the final paragraph of this selection, Ehrenreich refers to "gender-segregated higher education." Do some research about current views on this topic. Then write an essay either summarizing the arguments on both sides or taking a stand of your own on the topic.

Dave Barry

From Now On, Let Women Kill Their Own Spiders

Dave Barry *was born in 1947 in Armonk, New York. According to his own biographical statement, he has been "steadily growing older ever since without ever actually reaching maturity." He attended Haverford College and started his career in* journalism at the Daily Local News *in West Chester, Pennsylvania. As a syndicated writer for the* Miami Herald *from 1983 to 2005, Barry's humorous columns appeared in hundreds of newspapers, and he won the Pulitzer Prize for Commentary in 1988. Barry is the author of numerous books, which include* Babies and Other Hazards of Sex *(1984),* Dave Barry's Complete Guide to Guys *(1995),* Dave Barry Is from Mars and Venus *(1997),* Boogers Are My Beat *(2003), and his recent* Dave Barry's Money Secrets *(2006) and* The Shepherd, the Angel, and Walter the Christmas Miracle Dog *(2006). The article "From Now On, Let Women Kill Their Own Spiders" first appeared in the* Miami Herald. *In this piece, Barry pokes fun at miscommunication between men and women. Identifying with both, he laughs at how the sexes inevitably bewilder and infuriate each other.*

AS YOU READ: *Try to discover what Barry is really criticizing.*

From time to time I receive letters from a certain group of individuals that I will describe, for want of a better term, as "women." I have such a letter here, from a Susie Walker of North Augusta, S.C., who asks the following

For more about Dave Barry, visit <bedfordstmartins.com/bedguide> and do a keyword search:

author

question: "Why do men open a drawer and say, 'Where is the spatula?' instead of, you know, looking for it?"

This question expresses a commonly held (by women) negative stereotype 2
about guys of the male gender, which is that they cannot find things around
the house, especially things in the kitchen. Many women believe that if you
want to hide something from a man, all you have to do is put it in plain sight
in the refrigerator, and he will never, ever find it, as evidenced by the fact that a
man can open a refrigerator containing 463 pounds of assorted meats, poultry,
cold cuts, condiments, vegetables, frozen dinners, snack foods, desserts, etc.,
and ask, with no irony whatsoever, "Do we have anything to eat?"

Now I could respond to this stereotype in a snide° manner by making 3
generalizations about women. I could ask, for example, how come your average woman prepares for virtually every upcoming event in her life, including dental appointments, by buying new shoes, even if she already owns as
many pairs as the entire Riverdance troupe. I could point out that, if there
were no women, there would be no such thing as Leonardo DiCaprio. I
could ask why a woman would walk up to a perfectly innocent man who is
minding his own business watching basketball and demand to know if a
certain pair of pants makes her butt look too big, and then, no matter what
he answers, get mad at him. I could ask why, according to the best scientific
estimates, 93 percent of the nation's severely limited bathroom-storage
space is taken up by decades-old, mostly empty tubes labeled "moisturizer."
I could point out that, to judge from the covers of countless women's magazines, the two topics most interesting to women are (1) Why men are all
disgusting pigs, and (2) How to attract men.

Yes, I could raise these issues in response to the question asked by Susie 4
Walker of North Augusta, S.C., regarding the man who was asking where the
spatula was. I could even ask WHY this particular man might be looking for the
spatula. Could it be that he needs a spatula to kill a spider, because, while he
was innocently watching basketball and minding his own business, a member
of another major gender — a gender that refuses to personally kill spiders but
wants them all dead — DEMANDED that he kill the spider, which nine times
out of ten turns out to be a male spider that was minding its own business? Do
you realize how many men arrive in hospital emergency rooms every year,
sometimes still gripping their spatulas, suffering from painful spider-inflicted
injuries? I don't have the exact statistics right here, but I bet they are chilling.

As I say, I could raise these issues and resort to the kind of negativity in- 5
dulged in by Susie Walker of North Augusta, S.C. But I choose not to. I
choose, instead, to address her question seriously, in hopes that, by improving the communication between the genders, all human beings — both men
and women, together — will come to a better understanding of how dense°
women can be sometimes.

I say this because there is an excellent reason why a man would open 6
the spatula drawer and, without looking for the spatula, ask where the spat-

snide: Sarcastic, especially in a nasty manner.   dense: Slow-witted.

ula is: the man does not have TIME to look for the spatula. Why? Because he is busy thinking. Men are almost always thinking. When you look at a man who appears to be merely scratching himself, rest assured that inside his head, his brain is humming like a high-powered computer, processing millions of pieces of information and producing important insights such as, "This feels good!"

We should be grateful that men think so much, because over the years 7 they have thought up countless inventions that have made life better for all people, everywhere. The shot clock in basketball is one example. Another one is underwear-eating bacteria. I found out about this thanks to the many alert readers who sent me an article from *New Scientist* magazine stating that Russian scientists — and you KNOW these are guy scientists — are trying to solve the problem of waste disposal aboard spacecraft, by "designing a cocktail of bacteria to digest astronauts' cotton and paper underpants." Is that great, or what? I am picturing a utopian future wherein, when a man's briefs get dirty, they will simply dissolve from his body, thereby freeing him from the chore of dealing with his soiled underwear via the labor-intensive, time-consuming method he now uses, namely, dropping them on the floor.

I'm not saying that guys have solved all the world's problems. I'm just 8 saying that there ARE solutions out there, and if, instead of harping endlessly about spatulas, we allow guys to use their mental talents to look for these solutions, in time, they will find them. Unless they are in the refrigerator.

Questions to Start You Thinking

1. CONSIDERING MEANING: What is Barry satirizing in his essay?

2. IDENTIFYING WRITING STRATEGIES: Barry's essay is filled with rhetorical questions. Locate some of these, and consider how he answers them. What evidence does he provide to support his answers? How does this evidence affect his tone? How does it affect meaning?

3. READING CRITICALLY: What generalizations about women does Barry make in paragraph 3? How do these serve to support his main point?

4. EXPANDING VOCABULARY: Define *utopian* (paragraph 7). According to Barry, how would underwear-eating bacteria contribute to a utopian future?

5. MAKING CONNECTIONS: Both Barry and Judy Brady ("I Want a Wife," pp. 497–99) use satire, humorously attacking human mistakes and shortcomings in their essays. Compare and contrast their use of satire.

Journal Prompts

1. Put your imagination to work to suggest other inventions — besides underwear-eating bacteria — that would benefit man- (or woman-) kind. Follow Barry's model and have fun.

2. Discuss a conversation you've heard that involved man or woman bashing. What was the tone of the conversation? How serious were the participants? What are the effects of such remarks?

Suggestions for Writing

1. Stereotypes can be useful in literature and film, but in real life they may be damaging. Write an essay in which you examine real-life stereotypes, recalling behavior you have observed and experienced.

2. Using Barry's essay as a model, write an essay satirizing an issue you find unfair, irritating, or just amusing.

Evelyn F. Murphy
Why Not a Dollar?

■ For more about Evelyn F. Murphy, visit <bedfordstmartins.com/ bedguide> and do a keyword search:

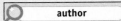

author

Evelyn F. Murphy *was born in Panama in 1940, where her father was stationed during World War II. She and her family moved from one army base to the next throughout her childhood. She received a bachelor's degree and a PhD from Duke University and a master's degree from Columbia University. Using her education in mathematics and economics initially as an economist, she began her public career in the late 1970s as secretary of environmental affairs for Massachusetts and later served as the state's secretary of economic affairs. In 1986, she was elected lieutenant governor of Massachusetts, becoming the first woman in the state's history to hold constitutional office. She is now president of The WAGE Project, Inc., a nonprofit group that aims to end wage discrimination against working women. The following selection is a chapter from Murphy's* Getting Even: Why Women Don't Get Paid Like Men — and What to Do about It *(2005), cowritten with E. J. Graff. Murphy uses sources to show that women's earnings aren't catching up to men's; in fact, she argues, the gender wage gap is actually widening.*

AS YOU READ: *Pay attention to Murphy's use of statistics. To what extent does she rely on statistics to make her point?*

Sometimes I ask people, "What should women be earning today com- 1 pared with men?" I don't ask what women *are* earning, which hardly anyone can answer with certainty, but what women *should* be earning. Most people shrug and say they have no idea, or guess that it should be about eighty cents to a man's dollar.

No one says "One dollar." That is the correct answer. There should be 2 no gender wage gap at all.

Is that an exaggeration? Statisticians point out that women do not yet 3 have quite as many years' experience in the workforce as men have. It's true that for the generation that began working in the 1960s, fewer women than men have a steady forty or fifty years of on-the-job experience. So maybe there should be a gap of a few pennies — at most! — to reflect that slight disadvantage. But not 23 cents' worth. Social scientists hedge° their conclusions about what causes that broad gap with disclaimers. They acknowledge

hedge: Make excuses for.

that biases exist in their measurements. They admit that they cannot say for sure that differences between women and men in what's called "merit"—education, experience, and other personal capital—add up to 23 cents. But despite the absence of rock-hard proof, this explanation has been accepted. Instead of demanding an immediate end to the wage gap, most Americans believe that it's closing slowly, at an evolutionary pace, moving women penny by penny toward equality.

But that's just not so. If the explanations heard forty years ago were 4 correct—if the reason for the wage gap was indeed that there was a "merit gap" and that in 1965 women had inferior qualifications, little experience, and less career commitment—that gap would have disappeared by now. The wage gap should have closed more than a decade ago. Instead, for several years during the 1990s, it actually widened.[1] It should have disappeared at every rung, from entry level to executive suite. Women have closed the education, career time, and commitment gap. So why hasn't the wage gap closed as well?

Some commentators answer this question by pulling out little slivers of 5 data—comparing, say, male and female engineering graduates' starting salaries in a particular year—to announce that women are already even. Their claim is that young women and young men (in that job category, at least, for that year) made just about the same amount when they got their first jobs. Therefore, the claim goes, the gender wage gap is over: the very newest generation of adults has gotten even.

But that's just plain wrong. The only way to reach such a conclusion is 6 to cherry-pick the most equal job category during its most equal year (ignoring the vast majority of working women, who are far from equal)—and then to ignore how those young women fare as the years go by. Otherwise, here's what you find: women start out behind, and the longer they work, the further behind they fall. One former bank clerk (now an administrator) told me that when she and her husband entered the job market in the 1970s, doing the same work, they "started off at the same range of pay and he just completely left me behind. His salary just kept going up and up every year, and mine just went up incrementally."

That experience has continued for every generation since. We have heard 7 in recent years that young women have caught up within high school and college, matching or surpassing young men as valedictorians, school newspaper editors, and the like. But that's no longer true once women and men start competing not for grades and accolades but for dollars. No matter how *nearly* equal some are at that first job, the wage gap between men and women in their age group keeps widening throughout their lives.

Take those new graduates just entering the job market, the data sliver 8 sometimes held up as proof of emerging equality. For a brief shining moment in 1991, young women and young men in their first postcollege jobs did get much closer to even: the women earned $20,556 while the men earned $22,479, just (just!), a 9 percent difference. That sounds terrific: 9 percent, when only thirty years before it had been 41 percent. Had that apparent trend continued, women and men might be even by now. But it did not—not for that generation of women, who rapidly fell farther behind, and not for their little sisters, for whom even the *entering* wage gap widened. The young women and men who entered the job market in 2003 were actually *farther* apart than their counterparts in 1991.[2] When these women started working, they earned 16 percent less than young men college grads. So much for the optimistic belief that the gender wage gap is steadily declining with each successive generation of workers.

Why have so many of us held that belief? Because most people thought 9 that the wage gap was narrowing over the last forty years because women were catching up on "merit." A close analysis of the data proves that it's not so. The largest drop in the wage gap—a hefty 8 cents during the 1980s— came not because women were catching up, but because men's real wages were declining, as manufacturing left the United States. Women caught up at men's expense. That's much of the story in the post–World War II American economy: in bad economic times, men's wages flatten, even decline; women catch up only by comparison, not because they're actually gaining more equal treatment on the job. Look at that unpleasant *increase* in the starting wage gap between female and male college graduates in 1991 and 2003. American women's hard work, increasing skills, and improving qualifications do *not* put us on an inevitable course toward equal pay.

If You Graduated in 1991, Your Raises
Have Not Kept Pace with Men's

Let's illustrate that more fully by looking at what's happened to a single gen- 10 eration of women and men—a generation whose mothers worked, whose entire lives had been spent under the assumption that they could and would be equal on the job.

What happened to your wages if you graduated from college and en- 11 tered the job market in 1991? Over the decade, *their raises did not keep pace with men's.* At the beginning of the decade, they were making 91 cents to a man's dollar. By the end of the decade, these very same women were making only 89 cents to a man's dollar. These women fell behind. They lost money. Their wage gap widened.

Let me repeat that: their wage gap expanded during the nation's biggest 12 economic expansion since the 1950s. It expanded for the generation of women and men *most equally prepared* for the job market in history. The wage gap widened. In 2003, the twenty-five-to-thirty-four-year-old women who had graduated from college were making, on average, $47,364—and the men who had graduated alongside them were making, on average, $53,271. Women's real wages had grown by 130 percent—while men's real wages had grown by 137 percent.

Remember, these are no longer baby boomers, the ones who were just 13 breaking open the doors to women's employment, fighting male chauvinist attitudes and general social resistance, and who may have aimed too low, considering that often their mothers didn't work. These young adults grew up with mothers who were just as educated, qualified, employed, and employable as their fathers. These young men and women didn't simply grow up believing that women *could* work, if given the chance; they actually knew women who were bus drivers and doctors, heavy-metal guitarists and helicopter pilots, corporate managers and professional tennis players, state senators and Supreme Court justices. These aren't the trailblazers. These are the trail followers.

Remember, too, that most of these college-educated women could not af- 14 ford to drop out of work for a couple of years to be stay-at-home moms. These women took their maternity leave (and some husbands even took paternity leave) to have a child — and then had to go right back to full-time work. Those families needed both paychecks — the wife's *and* the husband's — just to keep up their standard of living.[3]

These full-time, year-round working women hadn't even hit their thirty- 15 fifth birthdays, and they were already behind by $6,000 a year — when they had started only $2,000 a year behind. That's a lot of tamales, diapers, or movies. Add that up for a few years, and that's a Ford F150 SuperCrew instead of a Chevy Cavalier. That's a renovated kitchen, a year's college tuition, a time-share in Florida, a significant retirement fund contribution.

Young women with only a high school diploma fell even further behind 16 during these years. When between the ages of eighteen to twenty-four these women entered the job market in 1991, working year-round and full-time, they were earning an average of $13,558 — while men with their age, education, and experience earned $16,559. That was a nasty 18 percent gap.[4] By 2003, these women earned 22 cents less for every dollar their male counterparts took home. Having started out earning $3,000 a year less than their male peers, these women were now earning $7,000 a year less — an enormous bite out of a low-wage paycheck.

Women who graduated from professional schools and started their 17 working careers in 1991 fared a little better than these other working women. When between the ages of twenty-five and thirty-four these women entered the job market, working year-round and full-time, they were earning an average of $43,429 — while men with their age, credentials, and experience earned $61,038. That was a nasty 29 percent gap for a group of people with the same qualifications. By the year 2003, female JDs, MBAs, and MDs between the ages of thirty-five and forty-four were making an average of $97,756 each year while men their age, with the same credentials, made $113,805, outearning them by only — *only!* — 14 percent.

Except for that small number of high-earning women with professional 18 degrees, this recent generation of women starting their working careers followed that same old trend: the longer they worked, the more they fell behind.

Women Fall Farther Behind Men over a Lifetime

The wage gap is an expanding bullet in a woman's finances, tearing away at 19 her checkbook more and more each year. Perhaps that's why, for so many women, the creeping suspicion that things are unfair transforms into a smoldering sense of outrage somewhere between the ages of thirty-five and forty-five. Having expected that by working hard they would earn the appropriate rewards, they look around in some shock — and reluctantly realize that the men they graduated with or were hired alongside are farther along in their finances and careers. They come to the distressing conclusion that either they've utterly bungled their careers — or they've been cheated out of their rightful earnings.

Heidi Hartmann, president of the Institute for Women's Policy Research, 20 who's been tracking the shifts in men's and women's wages for decades, says that when times are good, men advance more than women do. Nobody knows why. But understanding why is important. For that brief moment between 1993 and 2000, women should have gotten even. These were the most promising set of circumstances since the mid-1960s, which saw the Equal Pay Act passed in 1963; Title VII of the Civil Rights Acts, which banned gender discrimination at work, passed in 1964; and an Executive Order banning discrimination by federal employees and federal contractors, issued in 1965. That's when we as a nation started paying attention to the idea that women deserve equal pay.

In the 1990s, more than a generation later, women were as qualified as 21 men in just about every particular. This was the decade in which the economy's transformation from brawn to brains, from a manufacturing to a service- and information-based economy, seemed complete. And that's where women are just as well equipped as men: in human relations, in verbal and numeric skills (if you look at the SATs or GREs), in solving problems and creating ideas. America's commitment to reaching wage equality for women — and all that meant for women and men becoming socially equal as well — had failed.

If women's earnings could not catch up to men's in a time of nearly un- 22 real prosperity, at a time when women's qualifications had caught up, what was holding them back?

The answer is simple: discrimination.   23

Notes

1. Policy analysts pinned the explanation of why the gender wage gap widened in the mid-1990s on "welfare reform." Their theory: since almost all — 90 percent — of welfare recipients were women, when these low-skilled, untrained mothers lost their welfare support and were forced to join the full-time workforce in low-paying jobs, their wages dragged the average of women's overall wages down. That explanation sounds plausible. But it's wrong. Women's average wages dropped between 1993 and 1996 — *before* Congress passed the welfare reform law in 1996. A number of states experimented with reforming welfare before national legislation took effect. In these states, some welfare recipients did trickle into minimum-wage work before national welfare reform passed — but not enough of them to drag down the overall average of women's wages. Even in August 1996, when welfare reform passed, welfare recipients still had more time before they had to seek work. Not until 1997, 1998, and 1999 did large numbers of former welfare recipients start working in low-paying jobs. And in those years, contrary to welfare reform theories, average women's wages *increased* — and the wage gap narrowed.
2. Table P-32, "Educational Attainment — Full-Time, Year-Round Workers 18 Years Old and Over, by Mean Earnings, Age, and Sex: 1991 to 2003," U.S. Census Bureau, *Historical Income Tables — People*, Washington, D.C., 2005.
3. Lawrence Michel, Jared Berstein, John Schmitt, *State of Working America 1998–99*, Economic Policy Institute, Washington, D.C., Chapter 1: Family Income.

4. "Educational Attainment—People 25 Years Old and Over by Median Income and Sex: 1991 to 2001," in U.S. Census Bureau, *Historical Income Tables—People,* Washington, D.C.

Questions to Start You Thinking

1. CONSIDERING MEANING: Why, according to Murphy, should the wage gap between women and men have disappeared for people who entered the workforce since the early 1990s? Why does she think it has not?

2. IDENTIFYING WRITING STRATEGIES: Consider Murphy's use of italics throughout the essay. What is the effect of the italicized words and phrases? What do they contribute to Murphy's tone?

3. READING CRITICALLY: How convincing do you find Murphy's explanation for the wage gap between women and men? Can you think of other possible reasons why women, on average, earn less than men?

4. EXPANDING VOCABULARY: In paragraph 13, Murphy refers to "male chauvinist attitudes." What does the term *chauvinist* mean in this context, and what is its origin? Why do you think it is less commonly used today than in the 1960s and 1970s?

5. MAKING CONNECTIONS: Tamara Draut's "What's a Diploma Worth, Anyway?" (pp. 561–63) focuses on declining wages for both males and females entering the workforce since 2000. How do the statistics Draut offers affect your view of Murphy's argument?

Journal Prompts

1. How do you respond to Murphy's argument? Are you surprised to learn of the wage gap between women and men? What do you think of Murphy's comment in paragraph 1 that many people she questioned believed a woman should earn "about eighty cents to a man's dollar"?

2. In paragraph 13, Murphy refers to "young adults [who] grew up with mothers who were just as educated, qualified, employed, and employable as their fathers . . . [who] actually knew women who were bus drivers and doctors, heavy-metal guitarists and helicopter pilots, corporate managers and professional tennis players, state senators and Supreme Court justices." Do you feel women have achieved equality with men? Why or why not?

Suggestions for Writing

1. In the selection's final paragraph, Murphy claims that what has kept the gender wage gap from closing is discrimination. How would you define *discrimination*? In what ways might different groups be discriminated against? As you plan your essay, consider examples from your own experience, the experience of friends, and your reading.

2. Write an essay about another controversial workplace issue. For example, you might explore one of these questions: Should employers be allowed to monitor employees' electronic communications? Is drug testing in the workplace an invasion of privacy? Why are women underrepresented in certain careers? Support your conclusions with evidence from sources, as Murphy does.

Noel Perrin

A Part-Time Marriage

■ For more about
Noel Perrin, visit
<bedfordstmartins.com/
bedguide> and do a key-
word search:

author

Noel Perrin *(1927–2004) was born in New York City. He earned degrees at Williams College, Duke University, and Cambridge University and for over forty years taught English and environmental studies at Dartmouth College. For all his academic credentials, much of his fame as a writer comes from three volumes of essays on part-time farming — Second Person Rural (1980), Third Person Rural (1983), and Last Person Rural (1991). After his death in 2004, some of his finest essays from these books were collected in Best Person Rural (2006). Perrin's A Child's Delight (1997) is a collection of essays celebrating some of his favorite but underappreciated children's books. In the following essay, first published in the New York Times Magazine on September 9, 1984, Perrin satirizes the postdivorce behavior of many middle-class couples and proposes a somewhat unusual remedy for the problems that plague modern marriages. In the paired selection that follows (pp. 497–99), Judy Brady also satirizes marital roles, but with a very different purpose.*

AS YOU READ: *Identify the problems with marriage that Perrin addresses.*

When my wife told me she wanted a divorce, I responded like any nor- 1
mal college professor. I hurried to the college library. I wanted to get hold of some books on divorce and find out what was happening to me.

Over the next week (my wife meanwhile having left), I read or skimmed 2
about twenty. Nineteen of them were no help at all. They offered advice on financial settlements. They told me my wife and I should have been in counseling. A bit late for *that* advice.

What I sought was insight. I especially wanted to understand what was 3
wrong with me that my wife had left, and not even for someone else, but just to be rid of *me*. College professors think they can learn that sort of thing from books.

As it turned out, I could. Or at least I got a start. The twentieth book was 4
a collection of essays by various sociologists, and one of the pieces took my breath away. It was like reading my own horoscope.

The two authors had studied a large group of divorced people much like 5
my wife and me. That is, they focused on middle-class Americans of the straight-arrow persuasion. Serious types, believers in marriage for life. Likely to be parents — and, on the whole, good parents. Likely to have pillar-of-the-community potential. But, nevertheless, all divorced.

Naturally there were many different reasons why all these people had 6
divorced, and many different ways they behaved after the divorce. But there was a dominant pattern, and I instantly recognized myself in it. Recognized my wife, too. Reading the essay told me not only what was wrong with me, but also with her. It was the same flaw in both of us. It even gave me a hint as to what my postdivorce behavior was likely to be, and how I might find happiness in the future.

494

This is the story the essay told me. Or, rather, this is the story the essay   7
hinted at, and that I have since pieced together with much observation, a
number of embarrassingly personal questions put to divorced friends, and
to some extent from my own life.

Somewhere in some suburb or small city, a middle-class couple separate.   8
They are probably between thirty and forty years old. They own a house and
have children. The conscious or official reason for their separation is quite
different from what it would have been in their parents' generation. Then, it
would have been a man leaving his wife for another, and usually younger,
woman. Now it's a woman leaving her husband in order to find herself.

When they separate, the wife normally stays in the house they occupied   9
as a married couple. Neither wants to uproot the children. The husband
moves to an apartment, which is nearly always going to be closer to his
place of employment than his house was. The ex-wife will almost certainly
never see that apartment. The husband, however, sees his former house all
the time. Not only is he coming by to pick up the children for visits; if he
and his ex-wife are on reasonably good terms, he is apt to visit them right
there, while she makes use of the time to do errands or to see a friend.

Back when these two were married, they had an informal labor division.   10
She did inside work, he did outside. Naturally there were exceptions: she
gardened, and he did his share of the dishes, maybe even baked bread. But
mostly he mowed the lawn and fixed the lawn mower; she put up any new
curtains, often enough ones she had made herself.

One Saturday, six months or a year after they separated, he comes to see   11
the kids. He plans also to mow the lawn. Before she leaves, she says, "That
damn overhead garage door you got is off the track again. Do you think
you'd have time to fix it?" Apartment life makes him restless. He jumps at
the chance.

She, just as honorable and straight-arrow as he, has no idea of asking   12
for this as a favor. She invites him to stay for an early dinner. She may put
it indirectly — "Michael and Sally want their daddy to have supper with
them" — but he is clear that the invitation also proceeds from her.

Provided neither of them has met a really attractive other person yet,   13
they now move into a routine. He comes regularly to do the outside chores,
and always stays for dinner. If the children are young enough, he may read
to them before bedtime. She may wash his shirts.

One such evening, they both happen to be stirred not only by physical   14
desire but by loneliness. "Oh, you might as well come upstairs," she says
with a certain self-contempt. He needs no second invitation; they are upstairs
in a flash. It is a delightful end to the evening. More delightful than anything
they remember from their marriage, or at least from the later part of it.

That, too, now becomes part of the pattern. He never stays the full   15
night, because, good parents that they are, they don't want the children to
get any false hopes up — as they would, seeing their father at breakfast.

Such a relationship may go on for several years, may even be inter-   16
rupted by a romance on one side or the other and then resume. It may even

grow to the point where she's mending as well as washing his shirts, and he is advising her on her tax returns and fixing her car.

What they have achieved postdivorce is what their marriage should have   17
been like in the first place. Part-time. Seven days a week of marriage was too much. One afternoon and two evenings is just right.

Although our society is even now witnessing de facto part-time arrange-   18
ments, such as the couple who work in different cities and meet only on weekends, we have no theory of part-time marriage, at least no theory that has reached the general public. The romantic notion still dominates that if you love someone, you obviously want to be with them all the time.

To me it's clear we need such a theory. There are certainly people who   19
thrive on seven-day-a-week marriages. They have a high level of intimacy and they may be better, warmer people than the rest of us. But there are millions and millions of us with medium or low levels of intimacy. We find full-time family memberships a strain. If we could enter marriage with more realistic expectations of what closeness means for us, I suspect the divorce rate might permanently turn downward. It's too bad there isn't a sort of glucose tolerance test for intimacy.

As for me personally, I still do want to get married again. About four   20
days a week.

Questions to Start You Thinking

1. CONSIDERING MEANING: How did Perrin's divorce affect him?

2. IDENTIFYING WRITING STRATEGIES: How does Perrin use cause and effect to support the solution he proposes?

3. READING CRITICALLY: What is Perrin's purpose in writing this essay? Do you think he is serious about his proposal for a part-time marriage? What evidence in his essay leads you to your conclusion?

4. EXPANDING VOCABULARY: Notice Perrin's use of the words *straight-arrow*, *pillar-of-the-community* (paragraph 5), *dominant* (paragraph 6), *self-contempt* (paragraph 14), *de facto* (paragraph 18), and *glucose tolerance test* (paragraph 19). How does Perrin's vocabulary fit or challenge your expectations of how a college professor writes? Find other examples to support your answer.

5. MAKING CONNECTIONS: How might Perrin respond to Dave Barry's more comic view of relations between men and women in "From Now On, Let Women Kill Their Own Spiders" (pp. 485–87)? What do these two essays suggest about the roles taken on by wives and husbands? Do they reflect the kinds of roles you are familiar with?

■ For useful links to Web sources on topics including *families*, visit <bedfordstmartins.com/ toplinks>.

Link to the Paired Essay

How might Perrin react to Judy Brady's point of view in "I Want a Wife" (pp. 497–99)? By reading Brady's essay, might Perrin have a better understanding of why his wife left him to "find herself"? Would he appreciate Brady's satire?

Journal Prompts

1. Would you prefer a full- or part-time marriage? Why?

2. Sketch out a theory or a plan for part-time marriage. What elements or rules would be needed to make it successful?

Suggestions for Writing

1. Write an essay explaining how divorce has affected you or those around you.

2. Take a stand on the solution Perrin proposes. In a short essay, agree or disagree with the idea of part-time marriage. Is it a constructive response to problems of marital incompatibility? Why or why not?

Judy Brady
I Want a Wife

Judy Brady *was born in 1937 in San Francisco, where she now makes her home. A graduate of the University of Iowa, Brady has contributed to various publications and has traveled to Cuba to study class relationships and education. She edited the book* 1 in 3: Women with Cancer Confront an Epidemic *(1991), drawing on her own struggle with the disease, and she continues to write and speak about cancer and its possible environmental causes. In the following piece, which has been reprinted frequently since its appearance in* Ms. *magazine in December 1971, Brady considers the role of the American housewife. While she has said that she is "not a 'writer,'" this essay shows Brady to be a satirist adept at taking a stand and provoking attention.*

AS YOU READ: *Ask yourself why Brady says she wants a wife rather than a husband.*

For more about Judy Brady, visit <bedfordstmartins.com/bedguide> and do a keyword search:

    🔍 author

I belong to that classification of people known as wives. I am A Wife. And, 1 not altogether incidentally, I am a mother.

Not too long ago a male friend of mine appeared on the scene fresh 2 from a recent divorce. He had one child, who is, of course, with his ex-wife. He is looking for another wife. As I thought about him while I was ironing one evening, it suddenly occurred to me that I, too, would like to have a wife. Why do I want a wife?

I would like to go back to school so that I can become economically 3 independent, support myself, and, if need be, support those dependent upon me. I want a wife who will work and send me to school. And while I am going to school I want a wife to take care of my children. I want a wife to keep track of the children's doctor and dentist appointments. And to keep track of mine, too. I want a wife to make sure my children eat properly and are kept clean. I want a wife who will wash the children's clothes and keep them mended. I want a wife who is a good nurturant° attendant to my children, who arranges for their schooling, makes sure that they have an adequate social life with their peers, takes them to the park, the zoo, etc. I want a wife who takes care of the children when they are sick, a wife who arranges to be around when the children need special care, because, of course, I cannot miss classes at school. My wife must arrange to lose time at work and not lose the job. It may mean a small cut in my wife's income from time to time, but I guess I can tolerate that. Needless to say, my wife will arrange and pay for the care of the children while my wife is working.

I want a wife who will take care of *my* physical needs. I want a wife who   4 will keep my house clean. A wife who will pick up after my children, a wife who will pick up after me. I want a wife who will keep my clothes clean, ironed, mended, replaced when need be, and who will see to it that my personal things are kept in their proper place so that I can find what I need the minute I need it. I want a wife who cooks the meals, a wife who is a *good* cook. I want a wife who will plan the menus, do the necessary grocery shopping, prepare the meals, serve them pleasantly, and then do the cleaning up while I do my studying. I want a wife who will care for me when I am sick and sympathize with my pain and loss of time from school. I want a wife to go along when our family takes a vacation so that someone can continue to care for me and my children when I need a rest and change of scene.

I want a wife who will not bother me with rambling complaints about   5 a wife's duties. But I want a wife who will listen to me when I feel the need to explain a rather difficult point I have come across in my course of studies.

I want a wife who will take care of the details of my social life. When   6 my wife and I are invited out by my friends, I want a wife who will take care of the babysitting arrangements. When I meet people at school that I like and want to entertain, I want a wife who will have the house clean, will prepare a special meal, serve it to me and my friends, and not interrupt when I talk about things that interest me and my friends. I want a wife who will have arranged that the children are fed and ready for bed before my guests arrive so that the children do not bother us. I want a wife who takes care of the needs of my guests so that they feel comfortable, who makes sure that they have an ashtray, that they are passed the hors d'oeuvres, that they are offered a second helping of the food, that their wine glasses are replenished when necessary, that their coffee is served to them as they like it. And I want a wife who knows that sometimes I need a night out by myself.

I want a wife who is sensitive to my sexual needs, a wife who makes   7 love passionately and eagerly when I feel like it, a wife who makes sure that I am satisfied. And, of course, I want a wife who will not demand sexual

nurturant: Kind, loving, nourishing.

attention when I am not in the mood for it. I want a wife who assumes the complete responsibility for birth control, because I do not want more children. I want a wife who will remain sexually faithful to me so that I do not have to clutter up my intellectual life with jealousies. And I want a wife who understands that *my* sexual needs may entail more than strict adherence to monogamy. I must, after all, be able to relate to people as fully as possible.

If, by chance, I find another person more suitable as a wife than the wife   8 I already have, I want the liberty to replace my present wife with another one. Naturally, I will expect a fresh, new life; my wife will take the children and be solely responsible for them so that I am left free.

When I am through with school and have a job, I want my wife to quit   9 working and remain at home so that my wife can more fully and completely take care of a wife's duties.

My God, who *wouldn't* want a wife?   10

Questions to Start You Thinking

1. CONSIDERING MEANING: How does Brady define the traditional role of the wife? Does she think that a wife should perform all of the duties she outlines? How can you tell?

2. IDENTIFYING WRITING STRATEGIES: How does Brady use observation to support her stand? What other approaches does she use?

3. READING CRITICALLY: What is the tone of this essay? How does Brady establish it? Considering that she was writing for a predominantly female — and feminist — audience, do you think Brady's tone is appropriate?

4. EXPANDING VOCABULARY: Why does Brady use such simple language in this essay? What is the effect of her use of such phrases as *of course* (paragraph 2), *Needless to say* (paragraph 3), and *Naturally* (paragraph 8)?

5. MAKING CONNECTIONS: In "Why Not a Dollar?" (pp. 488–92), Evelyn F. Murphy writes about the wage gap between women and men in the workplace. How might the traditional role assigned to women that Brady describes contribute to women on average getting paid less than men?

Link to the Paired Essay

Does Noel Perrin's presentation of himself as a husband in "A Part-Time Marriage" (pp. 494–96) strike you as similar to or different from the kind of husband suggested by Brady in "I Want a Wife"? Point to specific passages in Perrin's essay to support your answer. Given Brady's purpose in her essay, what do you think she might have to say to Perrin about his proposed "solution" to the problems of modern marriages?

Journal Prompts

1. Exert your wishful thinking — describe your ideal mate.

2. Begin with a stereotype of a husband, wife, boyfriend, girlfriend, father, or mother, and write a satirical description of that stereotype.

Suggestions for Writing

1. In a short personal essay, explain what you want or expect in a wife, husband, or life partner. Do your hopes and expectations differ from social and cultural norms? If so, in what way(s)? How has your parents' relationship shaped your attitudes and ideals?

2. How has the role of a wife changed since this essay was written? Write an essay comparing and contrasting the post-2000 wife with the kind of wife Judy Brady claims she wants.

Chapter 25
Popular Culture

Responding to an Image

Read this comic strip frame by frame, and summarize its basic story. What is the significance of its title? Overall, what is the comic strip's purpose? How does it combine text and visual images to comment on our ability to counter the effects of advertising? Why do you think the writer/artist chose to convey her message through a comic strip?

■ For reading activities linked to this chapter, visit <bedfordstmartins.com/bedguide> and do a keyword search:

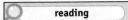
reading

Web Search

Visit adflip <www.adflip.com/>, a site that archives both classic and modern print advertisements. Click on "Current Ads," and choose one that interests you. Then search one of the site's classic-ad collections, looking for a similar product from a different decade. Compare and contrast the two ads. How do their visual and written components differ? What techniques or appeals do the advertisers use to sell the products? What does each ad reveal about the culture of its decade or about its intended audience? Write an essay using specific details from the ads to support your thesis or main idea about the pair.

Tara Parker-Pope
Custom-Made

■ For more about Tara Parker-Pope, visit <bedfordstmartins.com/bedguide> and do a keyword search:

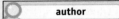
author

Tara Parker-Pope *is the author of the weekly Health Journal column for the* Wall Street Journal, *where she enjoys "taking this really technical, complicated stuff and distilling it down into something that people can understand and use to make decisions about their health." After graduating from the University of Texas with an MA in sociology, she went on to work as a political and government reporter for the* Houston Chronicle *and the* Austin-American Statesman. *She joined the* Wall Street Journal *in 1993, where she wrote about consumer products, marketing, and advertising before starting the Health Journal column in 2000. She is the author of* Cigarettes: Anatomy of an Industry from Seed to Smoke *(2001) and* The Hormone Decision *(2007). "Custom-Made" was first published in the* Wall Street Journal Europe *in 1996. Using numerous examples, Parker-Pope illustrates how global brands such as Domino's, McDonald's, and Heinz adapt their products and marketing tactics to appeal to local tastes.*

AS YOU READ: *Notice the many different countries Parker-Pope writes about. What do you learn about the tastes and lifestyles of people in these different countries?*

Pity the poor Domino's Pizza Inc. delivery man. 1

In Britain, customers don't like the idea of him knocking on their 2 doors — they think it's rude. In Japan, houses aren't numbered sequentially — finding an address means searching among rows of houses numbered willy-nilly.° And in Kuwait, pizza is more likely to be delivered to a waiting limousine than to someone's front door.

"We honestly believe we have the best pizza-delivery system in the 3 world," says Gary McCausland, managing director of Domino's international division. "But delivering pizza isn't the same all over the world."

And neither is making cars, selling soap, or packaging toilet paper. Inter- 4 national marketers have found that just because a product plays in Peoria, that doesn't mean it will be a hit in Helsinki.

willy-nilly: Without a particular order.

502

To satisfy local tastes, products ranging from Heinz ketchup to Cheetos 5
chips are tweaked, reformulated, and reflavored. Fast-food companies such
as McDonald's Corporation, popular for the "sameness" they offer all over
the world, have discovered that to succeed, they also need to offer some
local appeal — selling beer in Germany and adding British Cadbury chocolate sticks to their ice-cream cones in England.

The result is a delicate balancing act for international marketers: How 6
does a company exploit the economies of scale° that can be gained by
global marketing while at the same time making its products appeal to local
tastes?

The answer: be flexible, even when it means changing a tried-and-true 7
recipe, even when consumer preferences, like Häagen-Dazs green tea ice
cream, sound awful to the Western palate.

"It's a dilemma we all live with every day," says Nick Harding, H. J. 8
Heinz Company's managing director for northern Europe. Heinz varies the
recipe of its famous ketchup in different markets, selling a less-sweet version
in Belgium and Holland, for instance, because consumers there use ketchup
as a pasta sauce (and mayonnaise on french fries). "We're looking for the
economies from globalizing our ideas, but we want to maintain the differences necessary for local markets," says Mr. Harding.

For those who don't heed such advice, the costs are high. U.S. auto 9
makers, for instance, have done poorly in Japan, at least in part because they
failed to adapt. Until recently, most didn't bother even to put steering
wheels on the right, as is the standard in Japan. While some American makers are beginning to conform, European companies such as Volkswagen AG,
Daimler-Benz AG, and Bayerische Motoren Werke AG did it much sooner,
and have done far better in the Japanese market as a result.

For Domino's, the balancing act has meant maintaining the same basic 10
pizza-delivery system worldwide — and then teaming up with local franchisers
to tailor the system to each country's needs. In Japan, detailed wall maps,
three times larger than those used in its stores elsewhere, help delivery
people find the proper address despite the odd street-numbering system.

In Iceland, where much of the population doesn't have phone service, 11
Domino's has teamed with a Reykjavik drive-in movie theater to gain access
to consumers. Customers craving a reindeer-sausage pizza (a popular flavor
there) flash their turn signal, and a theater employee brings them a cellular
phone to order a pizza, which is then delivered to the car.

Local Domino's managers have developed new pizza flavors, including 12
mayo jaga (mayonnaise and potato) in Tokyo and pickled ginger in India.
The company, which now has 1,160 stores in 46 countries, is currently trying to develop a nonbeef pepperoni topping for its stores in India.

When Pillsbury Company, a unit of Britain's Grand Metropolitan PLC, 13
wanted to begin marketing its Green Giant brand vegetables outside the United
States, it decided to start with canned sweet corn, a basic product unlikely to

---

economies of scale: A decrease in the average per unit cost of production that occurs
with an increase in the number of units produced.

require any flavor changes across international markets. But to Pillsbury's surprise, the product still was subject to local influences. Instead of being eaten as a hot side dish, the French add it to salad and eat it cold. In Britain, corn is used as a sandwich and pizza topping. In Japan, school children gobble down canned corn as an after-school treat. And in Korea, the sweet corn is sprinkled over ice cream. . . .

The drive for localization has been taken to extremes in some cases: 14 Cheetos, the bright orange and cheesy-tasting chip brand of PepsiCo Inc.'s Frito-Lay unit, are cheeseless in China. The reason? Chinese consumers generally don't like cheese, in part because many of them are lactose intolerant. So Cheetos tested such flavors as Peking duck, fried egg, and even dog to tempt the palates of Chinese.

Ultimately, says Tom Kuthy, vice president of marketing for PepsiCo 15 Foods International's Asia-Pacific operations, the company picked a butter flavor, called American cream, and an Asianized barbecue flavor called Japanese steak. Last year, Frito rolled out its third flavor, seafood.

In addition to changing the taste, the company also packaged Cheetos 16 in a 15-gram size priced at one yuan, about 12 cents, so that even kids with little spending money can afford them.

The bottom line: these efforts to adapt to the local market have paid off. 17 Mr. Kuthy estimates that close to 300 million packages of Cheetos have been sold since they were introduced two years ago in Guangzhou. Cheetos are now available in Shanghai and Beijing as well.

Frito isn't through trying to adapt. Now the company is introducing a 18 33-gram pack for two yuan. Mr. Kuthy also is considering more flavors, but dog won't be one of them. "Yes, we tested the concept, but it was never made into a product," he says. "Its performance was mediocre."

Other PepsiCo units have followed with their own flavor variations. In 19 Thailand, Pizza Hut has a tom yam-flavored pizza based on the spices of the traditional Thai soup. In Singapore, you can get a KFC Zinger chicken burger that is hot and spicy with Asia's ubiquitous chili. The Singaporean pizza at Pizza Hut comes with ground beef, green peppers, and chili. Elsewhere in Asia, pizzas come in flavors such as Mongolian, with pork, chili, and garlic; salmon, with a creamy lobster sauce; and Satay, with grilled chicken and beef.

Coming up with the right flavor combinations for international con- 20 sumers isn't easy. Part of the challenge is building relationships with customers in far-flung markets. For years, the founders of Ben & Jerry's Homemade Inc. had relied on friends, co-workers, and their own taste buds to concoct such unusual ice-cream flavors as Chunky Monkey and Cherry Garcia.

But introducing their ice cream abroad, by definition, meant losing that 21 close connection with their customers that made them successful. "For Ben and me, since we've grown up in the United States, our customers were people like us, and the flavors we made appealed to us," says cofounder Jerry Greenfield, scooping ice cream at a media event in the Royal Albert Hall in London. "I don't think we have the same seat-of-the-pants feel for places like England. It's a different culture."

As a result, one of the company's most popular flavors in the United 22
States, Chocolate Chip Cookie Dough, flopped in Britain. The nostalgia
quotient of the ice cream, vanilla-flavored with chunks of raw cookie dough,
was simply lost on the Brits, who historically haven't eaten chocolate-chip
cookies. "People didn't grow up in this country sneaking raw cookie-dough
batter from Mom," says Mr. Greenfield.

The solution? Hold a contest to concoct a quintessential British ice cream. 23
After reviewing hundreds of entries, including Choc Ness Monster and Cream
Victoria, the company in July introduced Cool Britannia, a combination of
vanilla ice cream, strawberries, and chocolate-covered Scottish shortbread.
(The company plans to sell Cool Britannia in the United States eventually.)

And in a stab at building a quirky relationship with Brits, the duo opted 24
for a publicity stunt when Britain's beef crisis° meant farmers were left with
herds of cattle that couldn't be sold at market. Ben & Jerry's creative solution: use the cows to advertise. The company's logo was draped across the
backs of grazing cattle, and the stunt made the front page of major London
newspapers.

The company has just begun selling ice cream in France but isn't sure 25
whether the company will try contests for a French flavor in that market.
One reason: it's unclear whether Ben & Jerry's wry humor, amusing to the
Brits, will be understood by the laconic° French. "We're going to try to get
more in touch, more comfortable with the feel of the French market first,"
says Mr. Greenfield.

But for every success story, there have been a slew of global marketing 26
mistakes. In Japan, consumer-products marketer Procter & Gamble Company
made several stumbles when it first entered the market in the early 1970s.

The company thought its thicker, more-absorbent Pampers diapers in 27
big packs like those favored in America would be big sellers in Japan. But
Japanese women change their babies twice as often as Americans and prefer
thin diapers. Moreover, they often have tiny apartments and no room to
store huge diaper packs.

The company adapted by making thinner diapers packaged in smaller bags. 28
Because the company shifted gears quickly, Procter & Gamble is now one of the
largest and most successful consumer-goods companies in Japan, with more
than $1 billion in annual sales and market leadership in several categories.

Questions to Start You Thinking

1. **CONSIDERING MEANING:** Why is it important that U.S. companies learn to
   adapt their product lines for different international markets?

2. **IDENTIFYING WRITING STRATEGIES:** Which examples do you find particularly
   effective in illustrating Parker-Pope's point about product adaptation? Why
   do you suppose she included so many examples? What is their effect?

---

beef crisis: A reference to mad cow disease, which infected many British cattle and pre-
vented their consumption as meat.   **laconic:** Marked by using few words.

3. **READING CRITICALLY:** Throughout the essay, Parker-Pope includes quotations from executives of U.S. companies. Is this strategy effective for the point she is trying to make? Why or why not?

4. **EXPANDING VOCABULARY:** Consider Parker-Pope's title for the essay. In what sense does "Custom-Made" have a double meaning?

5. **MAKING CONNECTIONS:** In "Latino Style Is Cool. Oh, All Right: It's Hot" (below), Ruth La Ferla examines how young Hispanics have adopted fashions that reflect their heritage. How might U.S. product manufacturers adapt themselves to this Latino market? Have you noticed any examples of companies doing so in their advertising, for example?

Journal Prompts

1. Which of the product adaptations that Parker-Pope writes about sound appealing to you? Which sound like something you wouldn't want to try? What do you suppose contributes to your response?

2. Think of a snack you enjoy eating. Then be creative and come up with ways you might adapt its flavor for alternative versions that could broaden its share of the market.

Suggestions for Writing

1. Choose a type of consumer product that inspires intense competition among different companies — soft drinks, for example, or running shoes or toothpaste or cellular phone service. Then analyze some print and television ads for different brands of the product, considering how they appeal to you or might appeal to others. In an essay, compare and contrast each brand's advertising, and make some conjectures about the target audience in each case.

For more advice on evaluating, see Ch. 11.

2. Pick a type of product (jeans, shoes, fast food, cars), and list at least three criteria that you think are essential for it. For example, for jeans, you might select good fit, stylishness, and a price below fifty dollars. Then evaluate two or three different examples of this product based on how well they meet your criteria. What suggestions might you make to the manufacturers to improve their products?

Ruth La Ferla
Latino Style Is Cool. Oh, All Right: It's Hot

For more about Ruth La Ferla, visit <bedfordstmartins.com/bedguide> and do a keyword search:

author

Ruth La Ferla was born in 1936, in Munich, Germany, and moved to Chicago, Illinois, with her family in 1939. She earned a bachelor's degree from Knox College and a master's degree in German literature from the University of Illinois. From 1985 to 1991, she wrote for the New York Times Sunday Magazine *and then went on to work for* Elle. *In 2000, she returned to the* New York Times *as a fashion writer, publishing articles in the Thursday Styles pages and in the Sunday Lifestyle section. She has also worked as a fashion editor for* Women's Wear Daily *and* Avenue. *"Latino Style Is Cool. Oh, All Right: It's Hot" first appeared in the* New York Times *on April 15, 2001, around the time that Jennifer Lopez introduced her new clothing line, JLo. La Ferla wanted to explore the rise of Latino stars in the media and how their visibility might affect the fashion industry. During her investigation, she discovered Latino culture's proud expression of heritage through fashion.*

AS YOU READ: *Identify the primary characteristics of the Latino style that La Ferla describes.*

On a recent Friday afternoon, Lisa Forero, her dark, shoulder-length 1 hair parted in the center, stalked the corridors of La Guardia High School of Performing Arts in Manhattan, perched on four-inch platform boots. Ms. Forero, a drama major, played up her curves in a form-fitting gray spandex dress and wore outsize gold hoops on her ears. Her fingertips were airbrushed in tints of pink and cream.

Did she fret that her image — that of a saucy bombshell — bordered on 2 self-parody? Not a bit. Dressing up as a familiar stereotype is Ms. Forero's pointedly aggressive way of claiming her Latino heritage, she says. Ms. Forero, seventeen, acknowledged that she had not always been so bold. "Two or three years ago, I didn't usually wear gold," she said, "and I usually wouldn't get my nails done. But as I've gotten older, I've needed to identify more with my cultural background."

Her sandy-haired classmate Kenneth Lamadrid, seventeen, is just as 3 brash. "Because of the way I look and because my parents called me Ken, a lot of people don't know that I'm Cuban," he said. But Mr. Lamadrid takes pains to set them straight. That afternoon, he was wearing a souvenir from a recent family reunion, a snug T-shirt emblazoned with the names of all of his relatives who have emigrated to the United States from Cuba. "I'm wearing my family history," he said. "You have to be proud of who you are."

Ms. Forero and Mr. Lamadrid are members of a population that, accord- 4 ing to the 2000 census, seems on the verge of becoming America's largest minority group. Wildly heterogeneous,° its members come from more than twenty countries and represent a mixture of races, backgrounds, and even religions. What Latinos share, as Ms. Forero well knows, is a common language — Spanish — and rapidly expanding cultural clout.°

"Hispanic is hip," she observed dryly. "Right now, it's the thing to be." 5 Indeed, in the last couple of years Latinos have been surprised and flattered to find themselves courted as voters, consumers, workers, and entertainers. And now many are bemused to discover that, like hip-hop–influenced African Americans before them, they are admired as avatars° of urban chic.

heterogeneous: From diverse sources.   **clout:** Power.   **avatars:** Perfect representations of.

"There is an emerging Latino style, and I think it appeals to more than 6 just Latinos," said Clara Rodriguez, a professor of sociology at Fordham University in Manhattan and the author of *Latin Looks: Images of Latinas and Latinos in the U.S. Media* (Westview Press, 1997). Dr. Rodriguez made a point of distinguishing between pervasive archetypes — the smoldering vamp, the brilliantined° Lothario° — and the fashion personas adopted by young urban Hispanics, which allude to those types without aping them. These Latin Gen X-ers are rediscovering their roots and flaunting them, she said, while communicating solidarity by the way they dress.

Rodrigo Salazar, the editor of *Urban Latino*, a general-interest magazine for 7 young Hispanics, expressed a similar view. "As we stake our claim in the culture, we are starting to take control of our own images," Mr. Salazar said. Young, trend-conscious Latinos do that in part, he said, by experimenting with fashion and cultivating a street-smart style that is more overtly sensual than hip-hop and is at the same time heavily steeped in Hispanic iconography.°

Flounces, ruffles, and ear hoops are among the generic, ostentatiously° 8 Hispanic symbols being tossed into a pan-Latino° blender these days. Even crosses are part of the mix, not as a symbol of faith but as a hip accessory. Mr. Salazar conceded that such items lend themselves to ethnic stereotyping but argued that perhaps that is all the more reason to flaunt them. For many young Hispanics, he said, they are a visual shorthand that signals their identity.

Latino style also incorporates the provocative cropped T-shirts, low- 9 slung chinos, stacked heels, and chains that are the fashion insignia of cholos, members of Latin street gangs. And it incorporates components of a style adopted by young Puerto Rican New Yorkers in the late 1970s: fitted shirts in phantasmagorical° patterns, hip-riding denims, cropped halters, blouses tied at the midriff, navel-baring T-shirts, and platform shoes. Similar regalia survives as the style uniform of pop icons like Ricky Martin and Jennifer Lopez.

But the look is also indebted to the traditional garb favored by an earlier 10 generation of Latino immigrants. On some days, for example, Mr. Lamadrid, the drama student, wears a guayabera, a loose multipocket shirt like the ones his Cuban grandfather used to wear. Nowadays, the shirts, worn by many young Hispanics as a badge of their heritage, have been appropriated by non-Hispanics as well.

"We take our lead from the things we've seen our parents wear and the 11 things we've seen in movies," Mr. Salazar said, "but our style is evolving as our influence is growing. We're seeing ourselves in the street, and we're following the cues of our friends and celebrities who are Latino."

Mr. Salazar was describing a cultural pastiche° that has become increas- 12 ingly identifiable — and some maintain, consummately marketable. Its po-

---

brilliantined: Hair slicked back with a shiny pomade.   **Lothario:** A man known for seducing women.   **iconography:** Symbolism.   **ostentatiously:** Marked by showiness.   **pan-Latino:** Across Latino culture.   **phantasmagorical:** Fantastic, as related to what is not real.   **pastiche:** Mixture.

tential mass appeal is surely not lost on Ms. Lopez, the singer and actress, who is negotiating with Andy Hilfiger, Tommy's younger brother, to market her own brand of Latina glam in a fashion line.

At the same time, Latina chic is being packaged for mass consumption by 13 some leading apparel makers. In the last several months, Ralph Lauren, Nike, Tommy Hilfiger, and the Gap have played to the current fascination with Latina exoticism in advertisements featuring variations on the full-lipped, south-of-the-border sexpot. Ralph Lauren's campaign showcases the Spanish film star Penélope Cruz in a snug top and a swirling skirt, performing what looks like flamenco. Both Guess and Sergio Valente display ads in which halter tops and rump-clutching denims encase Brazilian brunettes. And Vertigo, a midprice sportswear company, is showing its scarlet trouser suit on a raven-haired vamp, a ringer — it can't be coincidence — for a young Bianca Jagger.

"Our industry has become enamored with the dark, mysterious confidence 14 that these women portray," said Steven Miska, the president of Sergio Valente.

Magazine editors, too, find the Latin look compelling. The March issue 15 of Italian *Vogue*, the fashionista's bible, has a feature in which young Latino-Americans model the season's key looks.

Is the industry trying to market Latinness as a commodity? "Definitely," 16 said Sam Shahid, the president and creative director of Shahid, a New York advertising agency with fashion clients. Mr. Shahid employed Hispanic models for the latest Abercrombie & Fitch catalog. "No one moves as freely," he said, then added: "Selling a Latin look doesn't mean it has to be a Carmen Miranda,° cha-cha type thing. 'Latin' can simply be a sultry sex appeal."

Should Mr. Hilfiger and Ms. Lopez reach an agreement, industry insiders speculate that the collection will draw heavily on Ms. Lopez's Puerto Rican heritage. "Her flash look, the stacked heels, the low-rise jeans — these things are already being emulated by people well outside the Hispanic community," said Tom Julian, a trend analyst for Fallon Worldwide, a Minneapolis branding company.

Deliberately packaging an urban Hispanic look for mass consumption 18 makes sense to Mr. Julian. "Ethnicity is good in today's marketplace," he said. "All of a sudden you are talking about hair, makeup, clothing, and accessories that are part of a lifestyle that is distinctive, that has a point of view." Noting that so-called urban apparel — the streetwise casual wear favored by young blacks and Hispanics — is a $5 billion-a-year business, he ventured that a Latino subgenre could generate at least half that amount.

Some Hispanics bristle at the reduction of their identity to a handful of 19 styling cues, which might then be peddled as Latin chic. They are uneasy about being lumped by outsiders into an undifferentiated cultural mass. "I think the world would often like to describe us as a bunch of hot tamales," said Betty Cortina, the editorial director of *Latina*, a lifestyle magazine for

---

Carmen Miranda: Brazilian singer, actress, and star of 1940s American movie musicals, noted for her outrageous costumes (including headdresses made from fruit) and thick, comic accent.

young women. "That happens to be the way many Latinas see themselves," she conceded, "but if our cultural identity is all wrapped up in a sexy sense of style, then we have a lot of work to do."

Others maintain that a degree of cultural stereotyping is inevitable and 20 may not be all bad. "It's important for people to understand that within the Latin community there is range," said Elisa Jimenez, a New York fashion designer and performance artist of part-Mexican descent. At the same time, an attraction to certain cultural stereotypes can be positive, she asserted, if "it inspires us to be happier, more expressive — any or all of those things that we want to be more of."

Latino-influenced apparel and grooming are seductive to many non- 21 Latins intent on borrowing elements of a culture that they perceive as more authentic, spontaneous, and alluring than their own. "Latin equals sexy," said Kim Hastreiter, the editor of *Paper*, a magazine that features a generous sampling of Latino artists, models, fashion, film and pop stars in its April issue. "It's heat and a certain aliveness."

Ms. Hastreiter might have been describing Cindy Green, a New York 22 performance artist and the graphic design director of the DKNY fashion house. Ms. Green flaunts acrylic-tipped nails airbrushed in hot pink and silver, a hyperfeminine look copied from the young Latina women she sees on her way to work. "I'm completely obsessed with my nails," she said, adding that she is just as much taken with the tight ponytails, dark lip liner, and extreme makeup worn by many young Hispanic women. "I come from Ohio," she said, "and all this is very exotic to me."

Danielle Levitt, a New York City fashion photographer, is equally besot- 23 ted. "I can't explain my attraction to things that are Latin," she said. "I think it's the glamour." Ms. Levitt likes to pile on Latina-style gold bangles and heart-shaped pendants. At her throat she wears an elaborate gold nameplate, similar to those worn on the air by the stars of *Sex and the City*, a show that is arguably influenced by Latina style.

Ms. Jimenez had never designed clothes that were identifiably Latin 24 until Kbond, a vanguard Los Angeles clothing store, asked her recently for a look that was patently Hispanic. She responded by lopping the sleeves off a series of ruffled men's tuxedo shirts — "tricking them out," as she put it, into "sexy little halters" for women.

At the moment she is selling a line of sportswear steeped in Latin kitsch 25 — "La Vida Loca" T-shirts, for example, printed with the characteristically Mexican images of a rose, a pair of dice, and a skull. "It's time to get our heritage out there," Ms. Jimenez declared with mingled defiance and mirth. She envisions her designs teamed with uptight little handbags and immaculate white jeans.

Who's going to wear them?   26

"Are you kidding?" she said. "They're going to be the height of Upper 27 East Side° chic."

Upper East Side: An upper-class neighborhood in New York City.

Questions to Start You Thinking

1. CONSIDERING MEANING: What are some of the reasons La Ferla gives for young Latino women and men adopting exotic styles associated with traditional Hispanic culture?

2. IDENTIFYING WRITING STRATEGIES: How does La Ferla use cause and effect in this essay? Why is this strategy particularly appropriate to her purpose?

3. READING CRITICALLY: Skim through the essay again, paying particular attention to the quotations La Ferla includes — from teenage Latinos and Latinas, a sociology professor, fashion editors and designers, and advertising and marketing experts. Why do you think she chose to interview this wide variety of people? What is the effect of the many quotations?

4. EXPANDING VOCABULARY: Define *allude, aping, flaunting,* and *solidarity* (paragraph 6). How do these words help readers understand the sources of contemporary Latino style?

5. MAKING CONNECTIONS: In "They've Got to Be Carefully Taught" (pp. 564–66), Susan Brady Konig writes somewhat critically about her daughter's preschool teacher requiring the young students in her class to identify with their cultural background and heritage. In contrast, the teenagers quoted in the beginning of La Ferla's essay enthusiastically present theirs. To what extent might aggressively asserting one's heritage be a positive thing? To what extent might it be a negative thing?

Journal Prompts

1. What do you identify as your cultural or ethnic heritage? How does this identification contribute to your personal style? (Keep in mind that your personal style may be a reaction against your family heritage.)

2. How fashion conscious are you? Do you follow the latest trends, intentionally buck them, or just ignore them altogether? Why do you feel about fashion as you do?

Suggestions for Writing

1. Take some time to observe the different fashion choices (clothing, hairstyles, accessories, and so forth) that characterize various groups in your community. You might, for example, choose to observe people on your campus, at a shopping mall or supermarket, or, if you live in a city, simply on the street. Make notes on your observations, and then write an essay in which you classify the various styles you observed.

2. In paragraph 4, La Ferla refers to the fact that 2000 census data suggest that Hispanic residents are "on the verge of becoming America's largest minority group." Do some research about the causes of this boom in the Hispanic population and the kinds of responses it has generated among both non-Hispanics and Hispanics. Then write an essay explaining these causes and effects.

Stephen King
Why We Crave Horror Movies

■ For more about Stephen King, visit <bedfordstmartins.com/bedguide> and do a keyword search:

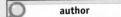

Stephen King was born in 1947 in Portland, Maine, and attended the University of Maine at Orono. He now lives in Bangor, Maine, where he writes his best-selling horror novels, many of which have been made into popular movies. The prolific King is also the author of screenplays, teleplays, short fiction, essays, e-books, and (under the pseudonym Richard Bachman) novels. His well-known horror novels include Carrie *(1974),* Firestarter *(1980),* Pet Sematary *(1983),* Misery *(1987),* The Green Mile *(1996),* Wizard and Glass *(1997), and* Hearts in Atlantis *(1999). His most recent books include* On Writing: A Memoir of the Craft *(2000), the novels* Cell *(2006) and* Lisey's Story *(2006), and the final installments of his epic fantasy series* The Dark Tower, *which he is currently adapting into a comic-book series for Marvel. Since 2003, King has also written a regular column on pop culture for* Entertainment Weekly. *In the following essay, first published in* Playboy *in December 1981, King draws on his extensive experience with horror to explain the human craving to be frightened.*

AS YOU READ: *Identify the needs that King says horror movies fulfill for viewers.*

I think that we're all mentally ill; those of us outside the asylums only hide it a little better — and maybe not all that much better, after all. We've all known people who talk to themselves, people who sometimes squinch their faces into horrible grimaces when they believe no one is watching, people who have some hysterical fear — of snakes, the dark, the tight place, the long drop . . . and, of course, those final worms and grubs that are waiting so patiently underground. 1

When we pay our four or five bucks and seat ourselves at tenth-row center in a theater showing a horror movie, we are daring the nightmare. 2

Why? Some of the reasons are simple and obvious. To show that we can, that we are not afraid, that we can ride this roller coaster. Which is not to say that a really good horror movie may not surprise a scream out of us at some point, the way we may scream when the roller coaster twists through a complete 360 or plows through a lake at the bottom of the drop. And horror movies, like roller coasters, have always been the special province° of the young; by the time one turns forty or fifty, one's appetite for double twists or 360-degree loops may be considerably depleted. 3

We also go to reestablish our feelings of essential normality; the horror movie is innately conservative, even reactionary. Freda Jackson as the horrible melting woman in *Die, Monster, Die!* confirms for us that no matter how far we may be removed from the beauty of a Robert Redford or a Diana Ross, we are still light-years from true ugliness. 4

province: Area.

And we go to have fun.   5

Ah, but this is where the ground starts to slope away, isn't it? Because   6
this is a very peculiar sort of fun indeed. The fun comes from seeing others
menaced — sometimes killed. One critic suggested that if pro football has
become the voyeur's° version of combat, then the horror film has become
the modern version of the public lynching.

It is true that the mythic, "fairy-tale" horror film intends to take away   7
the shades of gray. . . . It urges us to put away our more civilized and adult
penchant° for analysis and to become children again, seeing things in pure
blacks and whites. It may be that horror movies provide psychic relief on
this level because this invitation to lapse into simplicity, irrationality, and
even outright madness is extended so rarely. We are told we may allow our
emotions a free rein . . . or no rein at all.

If we are all insane, then sanity becomes a matter of degree. If your in-   8
sanity leads you to carve up women like Jack the Ripper or the Cleveland
Torso Murderer, we clap you away in the funny farm (but neither of those
two amateur-night surgeons was ever caught, heh-heh-heh); if, on the other
hand, your insanity leads you only to talk to yourself when you're under
stress or to pick your nose on your morning bus, then you are left alone to
go about your business . . . though it is doubtful that you will ever be invited to the best parties.

The potential lyncher is in almost all of us (excluding saints, past and   9
present; but then, most saints have been crazy in their own ways), and every
now and then, he has to be let loose to scream and roll around in the grass.
Our emotions and our fears form their own body, and we recognize that
it demands its own exercise to maintain proper muscle tone. Certain of
these emotional muscles are accepted — even exalted — in civilized society;
they are, of course, the emotions that tend to maintain the status quo° of
civilization itself. Love, friendship, loyalty, kindness — these are all the emotions that we applaud, emotions that have been immortalized in the couplets of Hallmark cards and in the verses (I don't dare call it poetry) of
Leonard Nimoy.

When we exhibit these emotions, society showers us with positive rein- 10
forcement; we learn this even before we get out of diapers. When, as children, we hug our rotten little puke of a sister and give her a kiss, all the
aunts and uncles smile and twit and cry, "Isn't he the sweetest little thing?"
Such coveted treats as chocolate-covered graham crackers often follow. But if
we deliberately slam the rotten little puke of a sister's fingers in the door,
sanctions follow — angry remonstrance° from parents, aunts, and uncles; instead of a chocolate-covered graham cracker, a spanking.

But anticivilization emotions don't go away, and they demand periodic 11
exercise. We have such "sick" jokes as "What's the difference between a

---

voyeur: One who takes inordinate pleasure in the act of watching.   **penchant:** Strong
inclination.   **status quo:** Existing state of affairs.   **remonstrance:** Objection.

truckload of bowling balls and a truckload of dead babies?" (You can't unload the truckload of bowling balls with a pitchfork . . . a joke, by the way, that I heard originally from a ten-year-old.) Such a joke may surprise a laugh or a grin out of us even as we recoil, a possibility that confirms the thesis: if we share a brotherhood of man, then we also share an insanity of man. None of which is intended as a defense of either the sick joke or insanity but merely as an explanation of [how] the best horror films, like the best fairy tales, manage to be reactionary, anarchistic, and revolutionary all at the same time.

The mythic horror movie, like the sick joke, has a dirty job to do. It deliberately appeals to all that is worst in us. It is morbidity unchained, our most base instincts let free, our nastiest fantasies realized . . . and it all happens, fittingly enough, in the dark. For those reasons, good liberals often shy away from horror films. For myself, I like to see the most aggressive of them — *Dawn of the Dead*, for instance — as lifting a trapdoor in the civilized forebrain and throwing a basket of raw meat to the hungry alligators swimming around in that subterranean river beneath. 12

Why bother? Because it keeps them from getting out, man, it keeps them down there and me up here. It was Lennon and McCartney who said that all you need is love, and I would agree with that. 13

As long as you keep the gators fed. 14

Questions to Start You Thinking

1. CONSIDERING MEANING: What does King mean when he says that "we're all mentally ill" (paragraph 1)? Is this a serious statement? Why or why not?

2. IDENTIFYING WRITING STRATEGIES: How does King use analysis, breaking a complex topic into parts, to support his argument?

3. READING CRITICALLY: Why do you think King uses the inclusive pronoun *we* so frequently throughout his essay? What effect does the use of this pronoun have on your response to his argument?

4. EXPANDING VOCABULARY: Define *innately* (paragraph 4). What does King mean when he says horror movies are "innately conservative"? Does he contradict himself when he says they are also "reactionary, anarchistic, and revolutionary" (paragraph 11)? Why or why not?

5. MAKING CONNECTIONS: How do King's reasons for our craving for horror movies relate to James Poniewozik's reasons for the popularity of reality television ("Why Reality TV Is Good for Us," pp. 520–24)? In what ways do the two writers agree or disagree about viewers' needs and about the capacity of movies or television to address those needs?

Journal Prompts

1. What is your response to "sick" jokes? Why?

2. Recall a movie that exercised your "anticivilization emotions" (paragraph 11). Describe your state of mind before, during, and after the movie.

Suggestions for Writing

1. What genre of movie do you prefer to watch, and why? What cravings does this type of movie satisfy?

2. Do you agree that "the horror film has become the modern version of the public lynching" (paragraph 6)? Write an argument in which you defend or refute this suggestion, citing examples from King's essay and from your own moviegoing experience to support your position.

Michael Abernethy
Male Bashing on TV

Michael Abernethy *was born in Bristol, Tennessee, in 1960. He holds a BA from Baylor University and an MA from the University of North Texas. He currently teaches communication studies and writing at Indiana State University, and he is also a film and television critic for PopMatters.com. Before becoming a full-time writer and educator, Abernethy worked in hotel and restaurant management. "Male Bashing on TV," first published on PopMatters.com in 2003, takes on an issue that some may find trivial. To Abernethy, however, the increasingly negative portrayal of men on sitcoms and commercials is no laughing matter.*

AS YOU READ: *Why, according to Abernethy, is male bashing on television a serious problem?*

■ For more about
Michael Abernethy, visit
<bedfordstmartins.com/
bedguide> and do a key-
word search:

author

Warning for our male readers: the following article contains big words 1
and complex sentences. It might be a good idea to have a woman nearby to explain it to you.

It's been a hard day. Your assistant at work is out with the flu and there 2
is another deadline fast approaching. Your wife is at a business conference, so you have to pick up your son at daycare, make dinner, clean the kitchen, do a load of laundry, and get Junior to bed before you can settle down on the sofa with those reports you still need to go over.

Perhaps a little comedy will make the work more bearable, you think, 3
so you turn on CBS's Monday night comedies: *King of Queens, Yes, Dear, Everybody Loves Raymond,* and *Still Standing.* Over the next two hours, you see four male lead characters who are nothing like you. These men are selfish and lazy, inconsiderate husbands and poor parents.

And the commercials in between aren't any better. Among them: A feminine hygiene ad: two women are traveling down a lovely country road, 4
laughing and having a great time. But wait. One of them needs to check the freshness of her minipad, and, apparently, the next rest area is six states away. A woman's voice-over interjects, "It's obvious that the interstate system was designed by men."

A digital camera ad: a young husband walks through a grocery store, try- 5
ing to match photos in his hand with items on the shelves. Cut to his wife
in the kitchen, snapping digital pictures of all the items in the pantry so that
hubby won't screw up the shopping.

A family game ad: a dorky guy and beautiful woman are playing Trivial 6
Pursuit. He asks her, "How much does the average man's brain weigh?" Her
answer: "Not much."

A wine ad: a group of women are sitting around the patio of a beach 7
house, drinking a blush wine. Their boyfriends approach, but are denied re-
freshment until they have "earned" it by building a sand statue of David.

Welcome to the new comic image of men on TV: incompetence at its 8
worst. Where television used to feature wise and wonderful fathers and husbands, today's comedies and ads often feature bumbling husbands and
inept, uninvolved fathers. On *Still Standing*, Bill (Mark Addy) embarrasses
his wife Judy (Jamie Gertz) so badly in front of her reading group that she
is dropped from the group. On *Everybody Loves Raymond*, Raymond (Ray
Romano) must choose between bathing the twin boys or helping his daughter with her homework. He begrudgingly agrees to assist his daughter, for
whom he is no help whatsoever.

CBS is not the only guilty party. ABC's *My Wife and Kids* and *According to* 9
Jim, Fox's *The Bernie Mac Show*, *The Simpsons*, *Malcolm in the Middle*, and (the
recently cancelled) *Titus* and the WB's *Reba* also feature women who are better organized and possess better relational skills than their male counterparts. While most television dramas tend to avoid gender stereotypes, as
these undermine "realism," comic portrayals of men have become increasingly negative. The trend is so noticeable that it has been criticized by men's
rights groups and some television critics.

It has also been studied by academicians Dr. Katherine Young and Paul 10
Nathanson in their book, *Spreading Misandry°: The Teaching of Contempt for
Men in Popular Culture*. Young and Nathanson argue that in addition to
being portrayed as generally unintelligent, men are ridiculed, rejected, and
physically abused in the media. Such behavior, they suggest, "would never
be acceptable if directed at women." Evidence of this pattern is found in a
2001 survey of one thousand adults conducted by the Advertising Standards
Association in Great Britain, which found two-thirds of respondents thought
that women featured in advertisements were "intelligent, assertive, and caring," while the men were "pathetic and silly." The number of respondents
who thought men were depicted as "intelligent" was a paltry° 14 percent.
(While these figures apply to the United Kingdom, comparable advertisements air in the United States.)

Some feminists might argue that, for decades, women on TV looked 11
mindless, and that turnabout is fair play. True, many women characters

misandry: Hatred of men.   **paltry:** Trivial; small.

through the years have had little more to do than look after their families. From the prim housewife whose only means of control over her children was, "Wait till your father gets home!" to the dutiful housewife whose husband declares "My wife: I think I'll keep her," women in the '50s and '60s were often subservient. (This generalization leaves out the unusual someone like Donna Reed, who produced her own show, on which she was not subservient.)

Then, during the "sexual revolution," TV began to feature independent 12 women who could take care of themselves (Mary and Rhoda on *The Mary Tyler Moore Show, Julia,* Alice and Flo on *Alice,* Louise and Florence on *The Jeffersons*). So now, thirty years later, you'd think that maybe we'd have come to some parity.° Not even.

Granted, men still dominate television, from the newsroom to prime- 13 time. And men do plenty on their own to perpetuate the image of the immature male, from Comedy Central's *The Man Show* to the hordes of drunken college boys who show up every year on MTV's Spring Break. What's the problem with a few jokes about how dumb men can be? C'mon, can't we take a few jokes?

If only it was just a few. The jokes have become standard fare. Looking 14 at a handful of sitcoms makes the situation seem relatively insignificant, but when those sitcoms are combined with dozens of negative ads which repeat frequently, then a poor image of men is created in the minds of viewers.

According to *Gender Issues in Advertising Language,* television portrayals 15 that help create or reinforce negative stereotypes can lead to problems with self-image, self-concept, and personal aspirations. Young men learn that they are expected to screw up, that women will have the brains to their brawn, and that childcare is over their heads. And it isn't just men who suffer from this constant parade of dumb men on TV. Children Now reports a new study that found that two-thirds of children they surveyed describe men on TV as angry and only one-third report ever seeing a man on television performing domestic chores, such as cooking or cleaning. There are far too few positive role models for young boys on television.

Moreover, stereotypical male-bashing portrayals undermine the core 16 belief of the feminist movement: equality. Just think. What if the butt of all the jokes took on another identity? Consider the following fictional exchanges:

"It is so hard to get decent employees."
"That's because you keep hiring blacks."

"I just don't understand this project at all."
"Well, a woman explained it to you, so what did you expect?"

parity: Equality.

"I can't believe he is going out again tonight."

"Oh please, all Hispanics care about is sex."

All of these statements are offensive, and would rightfully be objected to by advocates of fair representation in the media. However, put the word "man" or "men" in place of "blacks," "woman," and "Hispanics" in the above sentences and they're deemed humorous. Are men who ask to be treated civilly overly sensitive or are we as justified in our objections as members of NOW,° the NAACP,° GLAAD,° and other groups which protest demeaning television portrayals, whether those portrayals are on sitcoms, dramas, advertisements, or moronic TV like *The Man Show*?

Most of the shows I'm talking about are popular. Maybe that means that 17 I am being too sensitive. Yet, many U.S. viewers didn't have a problem with *Amos and Andy* or *I Dream of Jeannie*, both famous for their offensive stereotypes. These shows enjoyed good ratings, but neither concept is likely to be revived anytime soon, as "society" has realized their inappropriateness.

All this is not to say buffoonery — male or female — isn't a comic staple. 18 Barney on *The Andy Griffith Show*, Ted on *The Mary Tyler Moore Show*, and Kramer on *Seinfeld* were all vital characters, but the shows also featured intelligent males. And these clowns were amusing because they were eccentric personalities, not because they were men. The same could be said of many female characters on TV, like *Alice*'s Flo, *Friends*' Phoebe, or Karen on *Will & Grace*. Good comedy stems from creative writing and imaginative characterizations, not from degrading stereotypes.

Fortunately, some people are working to change the way television 19 portrays men. J. C. Penney recently ran an ad for a One Day sale, with a father at the breakfast table, with his infant crying and throwing things. The father asks the child when his mother will be home. Lana Whited of the *Roanoke Times*, syndicated columnist Dirk Lammers, and the National Men's Resource Center were just a few who objected to this image of an apparently incompetent and uncaring father, one who would let his child cry without making any attempt to calm him. Penney's got the message; their recent holiday ad featured a father, mother, and son all happily shopping together.

Few men I know want a return to the "good ole days." Those generaliza- 20 tions were as unrealistic as the idea that all men are big slobbering goofballs. Hope lies beyond such simplistic oppositions, in shows like *The Cosby Show* or *Mad about You*, which placed their protagonists on level playing fields. Paul Reiser and Cosby did, on occasion, do moronic things, but so did Helen Hunt and Phylicia Rashad. People — because they are people, not just gendered people — are prone to fall on their faces occasionally.

Undoubtedly, there are men out there who are clones of Ward Cleaver, 21 just as there are men who resemble Al Bundy. But the majority is some-

NOW: National Organization for Women.   **NAACP:** National Association for the Advancement of Colored People.   **GLAAD:** Gay and Lesbian Alliance Against Defamation.

where in between. We're trying to deal the best we can with the kids, the spouse, the job, the bills, the household chores, and the countless crises that pop up unexpectedly. After all that, when we do get the chance to sit down and relax, it would be nice to turn on the TV and not see ourselves reflected as idiots.

Questions to Start You Thinking

1. **CONSIDERING MEANING:** In Abernethy's opinion, what generates the best kind of comedy?

2. **IDENTIFYING WRITING STRATEGIES:** What strategies does Abernethy use to help readers understand the complexity and extent of male bashing on television?

3. **READING CRITICALLY:** Abernethy states that jokes about men's incompetence have become "standard fare" on television (paragraph 14). Does he provide sufficient relevant evidence to support this statement? Which of his examples are particularly striking?

4. **EXPANDING VOCABULARY:** In paragraph 10, Abernethy cites a study in which only 14 percent of respondents thought that men on television were depicted as "intelligent." How do you define *intelligent*? What kind of intelligence do you think Abernethy would like to see male sitcom characters display?

5. **MAKING CONNECTIONS:** In paragraph 18, Abernethy declares, "Good comedy stems from creative writing and imaginative characterizations, not from degrading stereotypes." How might Dave Barry ("From Now On, Let Women Kill Their Own Spiders," pp. 485–87) respond to this statement?

Journal Prompts

1. As Abernethy points out in paragraph 11, "Some feminists might argue that, for decades, women on TV looked mindless, and that turnabout is fair play." Do you agree or disagree with this attitude? Why?

2. How do you define *good comedy*? In your opinion, does stereotyping add to or detract from humor?

Suggestions for Writing

1. Is Abernethy overreacting? Using additional examples from television shows or commercials that you have seen, write an essay responding to his point of view.

2. Select a magazine geared to women and one geared to men, and then thumb through the advertisements. How are males portrayed in each magazine's ads? Does the treatment differ between the two magazines? In what ways does it support or refute Abernethy's point? Present your analysis in a comparison-and-contrast essay.

James Poniewozik

Why Reality TV Is Good for Us*

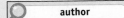 For more about
James Poniewozik, visit
<bedfordstmartins.com/
bedguide> and do a key-
word search:

author

James Poniewozik, *a native of Monroe, Michigan, is a graduate of the Univer-sity of Michigan and New York University. Since 1999 he has been the media and television critic for* Time *magazine, writing on subjects ranging from the television series* The Sopranos *to the effects of September 11 on popular culture. Before join-ing the staff of* Time, *Poniewozik served as the media critic and Media section edi-tor for* Salon.com. *He also has written for such publications as* Fortune, Rolling Stone, New York, *the* New York Times Book Review, *and* Talk *and regularly contributes to NPR's* On the Media *and* All Things Considered. *With a viewpoint markedly different from that of Terry Golway ("A Nation of Idol-Worshipers," pp. 525–27), Poniewozik extols the virtues of the often criticized but hugely popular genre of reality television in the following selection from a 2003 issue of* Time.

AS YOU READ: *Determine why Poniewozik suggests that reality-television characters set a good example for viewers.*

For eight single professional women gathered in Dallas, it is holy 1 Wednesday — the night each week that they gather in one of their homes for the Traveling *Bachelorette* Party. Munching snacks and passing a bottle of wine, they cheer, cry, and cackle as their spiritual leader, Trista Rehn, braves heartache, indecision, and the occasional recitation of bad po-etry to choose from among her twenty-five swains.° Yet something is unset-tling Leah Hudson's stomach, and it's not just the wine. "I hate that we've been sucked into the Hoover vac of reality TV," says Hudson, thirty. "Do we not have anything better to do than to live vicariously through a bunch of fifteen-minute-fame seekers?"

There you have the essence of reality TV's success: it is the one mass- 2 entertainment category that thrives because of its audience's contempt for it. It makes us feel tawdry, dirty, cheap — if it didn't, we probably wouldn't bother tuning in. And in this, for once, the audience and critics agree. Just listen to the raves for America's hottest TV genre.

"The country is gripped by misanthropy!"° — New York *Observer* 3

"Ridiculous and pernicious!° *Many kinds of cruelty are passed off as enter-* 4 *tainment!"* — Washington *Post*

"So-called reality television just may be killing the medium!" — San Fran- 5 cisco *Chronicle*

O.K., we added the exclamation points, but you get the idea. Yes, view- 6 ers are tuning in to *Joe Millionaire, The Bachelorette,* and *American Idol* by the tens of millions. Yet, to paraphrase Winston Churchill,° never have so many watched so much TV with so little good to say about it.

* Reported by *Time's* Amy Lennard Goehner, Jeanne McDowell, and Adam Pitluk.

swains: Admirers.   **misanthropy:** Hatred of humanity.   **pernicious:** Cruel.   **Win-ston Churchill:** British prime minister during World War II.

Well, that ends here. It may ruin reality producers' marketing plans for a   7
TV critic to say it, but reality TV is, in fact, the best thing to happen to television in several years. It has given the networks water-cooler buzz again; it
has reminded viewers jaded by sitcoms and dramas why TV can be exciting;
and at its best, it is teaching TV a new way to tell involving human stories.

A few concessions up front. First, yes, we all know that there's little real-   8
ity in reality TV: those "intimate" dates, for instance, are staged in front of
banks of cameras and sweltering floodlights. But it's the only phrase we've
got, and I'm sticking with it. Second, I don't pretend to defend the indefen-
sible: *Are You Hot? The Search for America's Sexiest People* isn't getting any
help from me. And finally, I realize that comparing even a well-made reality
show with, say, *The Simpsons* is not merely comparing apples with oranges;
it's comparing onions with washing machines — no reality show can match
the intelligence and layers of well-constructed fiction.

On a sheer ratings level, the latest wave of reality hits has worked a sea   9
change for the networks. And it has put them back on the pop-cultural map,
after losing the buzz war to cable for years. Reality shows don't just reach
tens of millions of viewers but leave them feeling part of a communal experience — what network TV does best, but sitcoms and dramas haven't done
since *Seinfeld* and *Twin Peaks*. (When was the last time *CSI* made you call
your best friend or holler back at your TV?) "Reality has proven that network
television is still relevant," says Mike Fleiss, creator of the *Bachelor* franchise.

This has sitcom and drama writers praying for the reality bust. "The   10
networks only have so much time and resources," says Amy Sherman-
Palladino, creator of *Gilmore Girls*. "Rather than solely focusing on convincing the Olsen twins to allow themselves to be eaten by bears in prime time,
I wish they would focus on coming up with something that would really
last." TV does seem to be in overkill mode, as the networks have signed up
dozens of dating shows, talent searches, and other voyeurfests. And like an
overheated NASDAQ, the reality market is bound to correct. But unlike earlier TV reality booms, this one is supported by a large, young audience that
grew up on MTV's *The Real World* and considers reality as legitimate as dramas and sitcoms — and that, for now, prefers it.

And why not? It would be easier to bemoan reality shows' crowding out   11
sitcoms and dramas if the latter weren't in such a rut. But the new network
shows of fall 2002 were a creatively timid mass of remakes, bland family
comedies, and derivative° cop dramas. Network executives dubbed them
"comfort" — i.e., familiar and boring — TV. Whereas reality TV — call it "dis-
comfort TV" — lives to rattle viewers' cages. It provokes. It offends. But at
least it's trying to do something besides help you get to sleep. Some upcoming reality concepts are idealistic, like FX's *American Candidate*, which aims
to field a "people's candidate" for president in 2004. Others are lowbrow,
like ABC's *The Will* (relatives battle for an inheritance), Fox's *Married by
America* (viewers vote to help pair up a bride and groom), and NBC's *Around
the World in 80 Dates* (American bachelor seeks mates around the world;

---

derivative: Unoriginal.

after all, how better to improve America's image then to send a stud to other countries to defile their women?). But all of them make you sit up and pay attention. "I like to make a show where people say, 'You can't put that on TV,'" says Fleiss. "Then I put it on TV."

By and large, reality shows aren't supplanting° creative successes like *24* or *Scrubs;* they're filling in for duds like *Presidio Med* and *MDs.* As NBC reality chief Jeff Gaspin says, "There is a little survival-of-the-fittest thing this ends up creating." When sitcoms started cloning goofy suburban dads and quirky, pretty yuppies, we got *The Osbournes.* And now reality TV is becoming our source for involved stories about personal relationships. This used to be the stuff of dramas like the canceled *Once and Again,* until programmers began concentrating on series like *CSI* and *Law & Order,* which have characters as detailed and individuated as checkers pieces. By the time *Survivor* ends, you know its players better than you know *Law & Order'*s Detective Briscoe after eleven years. Likewise, the WB's *High School Reunion,* which brings together classmates after ten years, is really asking whether you're doomed to live out your high school role — "the jock," "the nerd," or whatnot — for life. Last fall two scripted shows, *That Was Then* and *Do Over,* asked the same questions but with cardboard characters and silly premises involving time travel. They got canceled. *High School Reunion* got a second season.

In Britain, where reality has ruled Britannia's (air)waves for years, TV writers are starting to learn from reality's success. The sitcom *The Office* uses reality-TV techniques (jerky, handheld camera work, "confessional" interviews) to explore the petty politics of white-collar workers. Now airing on BBC America, it's the best comedy to debut here this season, because its characters are the kind of hard-to-pigeonhole folks you find in life — or on reality TV. On *Survivor* and *The Amazing Race,* the gay men don't drop Judy Garland references in every scene. MTV's *Making the Band 2* — a kind of hip-hop *American Idol* — gave center stage to inner-city kids who would be portrayed as perps or victims on a cop drama.

But aesthetics° aside, the case against reality TV is mainly moral — and there's a point to it. It's hard to defend the deception of *Joe Millionaire* — which set up twenty women to court construction worker Evan Marriott by telling them he was a multimillionaire — as hilarious as its fool's-gold chase can be. Even the show's Potemkin° Croesus° contends that producers hid the show's premise from him until the last minute. "The day before I left for France, I signed confidentiality papers which said what the show was about," Marriott tells *Time.* "At that point, could I really back out?" Others are concerned about the message of meanness. "There's a premium on the lowest common denominator of human relationships," James Steyer, author

12

13

14

supplanting: Replacing.   **aesthetics:** Artistic beauty and taste.   **Potemkin:** Something that appears impressive on the surface but is shabby underneath, referring to Grigori Aleksandrovich Potemkin's construction of fake villages for Catherine the Great's tours of the Ukraine and the Crimea.   **Croesus:** A very wealthy man, referring to a king of Lydia who was renowned for his riches.

of *The Other Parent: The Inside Story of the Media's Effect on Our Children.* "It's often women degrading themselves. I don't want my nine-year-old thinking that's the way girls should behave."

So *The Bachelorette* is not morally instructive for grade-schoolers. But 15 wallowing in the weaknesses and failings of humanity is a trademark of satire — people accused Jonathan Swift and Mark Twain of being misanthropes too — and much reality TV is really satire boiled down to one extreme gesture. A great reality-TV concept takes some commonplace piety of polite society and gives it a wedgie. Companies value team spirit; *Survivor* says the team will screw you in the end. The cult of self-esteem says everybody is talented; *American Idol's* Simon Cowell says to sit down and shut your pie hole. Romance and feminism says a man's money shouldn't matter; *Joe Millionaire* wagers $50 million that they're wrong.

The social criticisms of reality TV rest on two assumptions: that millions 16 of other people are being taken in by reality TV's deceptions (which the critic himself — or herself — is able to see through) or are being led astray by its unsavory messages (to which the critic is immune). When a reality show depicts bad behavior, it's immoral, misanthropic, sexist, or sick. When *The Sopranos* does the same thing, it's nuanced storytelling. We assume that viewers can empathize with Tony Soprano without wanting to be him; we assume they can maintain critical distance and perceive ironies between his words and the truth. Why? Because we assume that people who like *The Sopranos* are smarter, more mature — better — than people who like *The Bachelorette.*

And aren't they? Isn't there something simply wrong with people who 17 enjoy entertainment that depends on ordinary people getting their heart broken, being told they can't sing, or getting played for fools? That's the question behind the protests of CBS's plans to make a real-life version of *The Beverly Hillbillies* with a poor rural family. Says Dee Davis, president of the Center for Rural Strategies, "If somebody had proposed, 'Let's go into the barrio° in L.A. and find a family of immigrants and put them in a mansion, and won't it be funny when they interview maids?' then people could see that's a step too far." It's hard to either defend or attack a show that doesn't exist yet, but it's also true that the original sitcom was far harder on Mr. Drysdale than the Clampetts. And on *The Osbournes,* Ozzy — another Beverly Hills fish out of water — was "humiliated" into becoming the most beloved dad in America.

Indeed, for all the talk about "humiliation TV," what's striking about 18 most reality shows is how good humored and resilient most of the participants are: the *American Idol* rejectees stubbornly convinced of their own talent, the *Fear Factor* players walking away from vats of insects like Olympic champions. What finally bothers their detractors is, perhaps, not that these people are humiliated but that they are not. Embarrassment, these shows demonstrate, is survivable, even ignorable, and ignoring embarrassment is a skill we all could use. It is what you risk — like injury in a sport — in order

barrio: Spanish-speaking neighborhood in the United States.

to triumph. "What people are really responding to on these shows is people pursuing their dreams," says *American Candidate* producer R. J. Cutler. A reality show with all humiliation and no triumph would be boring.

And at their best, the shows offer something else entirely. One of the 19 most arresting moments this TV season came on *American Idol*, when a single mom and professional boxer from Detroit flunked her audition. The show went with her backstage, with her adorable young son, as she told her life story. Her husband, a corrections officer, was murdered a few years before. She had taken up boxing—her ring name is "Lady Tiger"—because you can't raise a kid on waitress money. Her monologue went from defiance ("You'll see my album. Lady Tiger don't stop") to despair ("You ain't going nowhere in Detroit. Nowhere") to dignified resolve for her son's sake ("We're never going to quit, are we, angel?"). It was a haunting slice of life, more authentic than any *ER* subplot.

Was Lady Tiger setting a bad example for her son on national TV? 20 Or setting a good example by dreaming, persevering and being proud? *American Idol* didn't say. It didn't nudge us to laugh at her or prod us to cry for her. In about two minutes, it just told a quintessentially° American story of ambition and desperation and shrinking options, and it left the judgment to us. That's unsettling. That's heartbreaking. And the reality is, that's great TV.

Questions to Start You Thinking

1. CONSIDERING MEANING: According to Poniewozik, what are the main reasons that "reality TV is . . . the best thing to happen to television in several years" (paragraph 7)?

2. IDENTIFYING WRITING STRATEGIES: What criteria does Poniewozik use to evaluate reality television? In his opinion, how do traditional sitcoms and dramas fare when judged according to the same criteria?

3. READING CRITICALLY: Where does Poniewozik address arguments against reality television? Does he present sufficient evidence to support his evaluation in the face of these opposing viewpoints?

4. EXPANDING VOCABULARY: Define *individuated* (paragraph 12). What does Poniewozik mean when he finds today's fictional television characters "as detailed and individuated as checkers pieces"? Does the comparison work?

5. MAKING CONNECTIONS: How do reality shows like *The Bachelor* or *Beauty and the Geek* relate to or differ from the institution of arranged marriage that Anjula Razdan analyzes ("What's Love Got to Do with It?" pp. 453–57)?

Link to the Paired Essay

Compare and contrast Poniewozik's essay with Terry Golway's "A Nation of Idol-Worshipers" (pp. 525–27) in terms of each writer's purpose, intended audience, use of evidence, and tone. Which argument do you find more convincing, and why?

■ For useful links to Web sources on topics including *popular culture*, visit <bedfordstmartins.com/toplinks>.

quintessentially: Most representative; classic.

Journal Prompts

1. Are you offended by reality television or entertained? Explain why.

2. Would you like to participate in a reality television show? Why, or why not? Which program would you like to be on, if any?

Suggestions for Writing

1. Imagine that you have the opportunity to create a reality television show. Write an essay in which you pitch the show to a television producer. Describe your show's premise, purpose, intended audience, and participants' characteristics. Include a paragraph that convinces the producer that your show, sure to be a blockbuster, is a must-have for the next television season.

2. Do additional research on the factors that have led to the success or failure of a specific reality television show. Based on what you learn from your research and from this reading, develop criteria for evaluating reality television programs. Using your criteria, write an essay that reviews, either negatively or positively, a reality television show.

Terry Golway

A Nation of Idol-Worshipers

Terry Golway, *born in 1955, is a freelance writer based in New Jersey, where he is currently curator of the John Kean Center for American History at Kean University. A veteran journalist, Golway is also the author or coauthor of several books on Irish and Irish American history, including* Irish Rebel: John Devoy and America's Fight for Ireland's Freedom *(1998),* For the Cause of Liberty: A Thousand Years of Ireland's Heroes *(2000), and* The Irish in America *(1997), a companion volume to the PBS television series* Long Journey Home: The Irish in America. *In one of his most recent books,* So Others Might Live: A History of New York's Bravest *(2003), Golway — whose father, father-in-law, godfather, and uncles were all firefighters — traces the history of the New York City Fire Department from its beginnings as a volunteer force in the 1700s to its tragic losses on September 11, 2001. In "A Nation of Idol-Worshipers," first published in* America *on July 31, 2006, Golway laments America's obsession with the cult of celebrity, which is fueled in large part by shows like* American Idol.

AS YOU READ: *Think about why Golway might have written this essay. What effect do you suppose he hoped it would have on his readers?*

■ For more about Terry Golway, visit <bedfordstmartins.com/ bedguide> and do a keyword search:

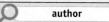
author

The columnist Russell Baker once wrote a piece about the discovery he made one evening after he retired to his basement and, with nothing else to do, turned on the television set. All sorts of new and alien life forms invaded the basement. There was, he would write, a country living in his cellar — a country with which he was not particularly acquainted.

That's how I felt several months ago when I found myself in the pres- 2
ence of actual grown-ups, who were parsing° the results of a television show
called *American Idol*. In addition to being unaware that so-called talent
shows had been a staple of broadcasting since Guglielmo Marconi° figured
out wireless communications, these grown-ups admitted that their children
were hooked on the show. One grown-up announced that his teenage
daughter, who likes to sing in the shower, has decided that one day she will
be an "American Idol."

When I suggested that there were other avenues to "idolhood," like 3
medicine, social work, engineering, or teaching, my friend laughed. Apparently he thought I was kidding. I wasn't. Was I being a killjoy? Yes. Snob-
bish? Perhaps. But kidding? Not a chance.

The startling popularity of *American Idol* and its knockoffs provides fur- 4
ther proof that America is, in the words of writer Neil Postman, amusing itself to death. As never before, young people are being taught to believe that
genuine American idols sing and dance and look beautiful in front of a television camera, that pop culture is the only culture that matters, and that
achievement that doesn't bring the dubious° reward of fame is hardly worth
the effort.

One of the new *Idol* knockoffs is called *America's Got Talent*. The title 5
suggests that television executives were stunned to learn about this surfeit°
of American talent, but given their line of work, their surprise is understandable. As talented as America may be, however, the country doesn't have
enough engineers, mathematicians, scientists, and systems analysts. The culture no longer recognizes this kind of work as worthy of aspiration.

That's absurd, and most of us know that. Surely the people who put on 6
these awful shows know they're selling dubious goods. After all, many of
them are products of America's finest universities. (That thought alone
ought to tell us something about our society.) They are familiar, presumably,
with the work of genuine American idols — people who have actually contributed to society rather than merely distracted it.

For the men and women who are the "brains" behind shows like *Ameri-* 7
can Idol and its imitators, all of this is an exercise in postmodern irony.° But
for the kids who watch, and even for some of the grown-ups, it is completely serious. And that's the frightening part.

At the risk of sounding like a middle-aged crank, I remember when chil- 8
dren aspired to be astronauts, rocket scientists, cancer-conquering doctors,
firefighters, clergy and religious and, yes, even political leaders. Not every aspiring president made it to the Oval Office. And not every would-be fire-
fighter passed the physical. But at least those dreams were born of a society
that valued service and citizenship. Today's "Idol-worshipers" are the products of a society that values extreme narcissism and shallow fame.

Parsing: Analyzing.   **Guglielmo Marconi:** Inventor of the radio.   **dubious:** Doubtful.   **surfeit:** Overabundance.   **irony:** Referring to something that is deliberately
contrary to what one would expect, often in an amusing way.

That's not to say that serious people cannot spend a few frivolous moments watching a silly show just for fun. I've spent more than a few hours this summer following the exploits of the golfer Phil Mickelson. This curious pastime could be regarded as an even more serious sign of American decline than the popularity of *American Idol*. But then again, at least Phil Mickelson is not hostage to the whims of a snooty British judge. 9

I realize that actors and singers have long been regarded as secular° gods — this did not start with *American Idol*. The cult of celebrity and fame has been around for generations. Kids in the 1960s worshiped the Beatles, so I am told. Bobby-soxers° fainted at the sight of the young Frank Sinatra. Young men fell in love with the likes of Elizabeth Taylor and Betty Grable. Movie fan magazines have been chronicling the lives of the famous since the Roaring Twenties. 10

Still, it seems clear to me that today's Americans devote more time, money, and energy in pursuit of trivial pop culture than ever before. Entire television channels are devoted to one of my favorite oxymorons,° "entertainment news." A word from a single talk-show host can and does inspire millions of people to buy a book that most of them probably will never read. Serious magazines struggle to find new readers, but magazines devoted to the lives of movie stars make their owners rich, if not famous. 11

And, of course, there is this business of what makes an "American Idol." In the aftermath of 9/11, we swore that we were changed people, that we would forever honor the sacrifices of society's true heroes. We claimed that we understood how we had let trivia consume our lives. 12

For a while our idols were people who gave of themselves, who put their own lives at risk for the sake of others. Fame and glamour were put in their rightful place. Eternal values reasserted themselves. We saw the difference between reality and fantasy. 13

Today, less than five years after that life-altering outrage, we debate the merits of singers who wish to be seen as an American idol. We encourage our children to worship these idols, to go forth and do likewise. 14

We really haven't learned much, have we? 15

Questions to Start You Thinking

1. CONSIDERING MEANING: What does Golway see as the negative effects of the American obsession with a "cult of celebrity and fame" (paragraph 10)? What does he think society should value more highly than celebrity?

2. IDENTIFYING WRITING STRATEGIES: Where in the essay does Golway suggest that the issue he is writing about is not completely one-sided? Why do you suppose he does so? How does he then go about picking up the thread of his own argument?

---

secular: Not pertaining to religion.   **Bobby-soxers:** Teenage girls in the 1940s. **oxymorons:** Contradictions in terms.

3. READING CRITICALLY: Golway presents little hard evidence to back up his claims about the "cult of celebrity and fame"; for example, he might have cited the ratings for *American Idol* or compared the readership of celebrity-centered magazines with more serious publications. What does the fact that he didn't do so suggest to you about his intended audience and his thoughts about the "cult of celebrity" more generally?

4. EXPANDING VOCABULARY: In paragraph 8, Golway refers to the United States as "a society that values extreme narcissism." Define *narcissism*. To what extent do you feel that shows such as *American Idol* celebrate this concept?

5. MAKING CONNECTIONS: How might Golway's views relate to Barbara Ehrenreich's point in "Guys Just Want to Have Fun" (pp. 482–84) that employers increasingly value personality over education and demonstrated competence when hiring and promoting employees? What do both writers' observations suggest about contemporary society?

Link to the Paired Essay

James Poniewozik ("Why Reality TV Is Good for Us," pp. 520–24) offers a much more positive take on *American Idol* than does Golway. What do the two writers see differently about the program? To what extent might the fact that Poniewozik is a television critic, someone who watches a considerable amount of television, as opposed to Golway, who seems not to watch much television at all, contribute to their differing opinions?

Journal Prompts

1. What is your attitude toward shows like *American Idol*? Are you a big fan, an occasional viewer, or an active avoider of such television fare? Explain why.

2. How do you account for the popularity of *American Idol* and other programs that are essentially talent contests, whether for amateurs or for celebrities competing in an activity for which they are not known, such as *Dancing with the Stars*?

Suggestions for Writing

1. As this essay illustrates, reality television shows can provide a glimpse into our society, mirroring our values, desires, and way of life. What Golway sees in shows like *American Idol* is a self-absorbed society obsessed with shallow fame. To what extent do you agree or disagree with Golway's view? Write an essay in which you analyze one or more of these shows, explaining what *you* think they reveal about American society.

2. Do some research about the most highly rated programs on television, in both primetime and daytime, on the networks and on cable. Be sure to consider as well what programs appeal to various age groups. Then write an essay in which you explore what seems to appeal to the majority of Americans and why.

Chapter 26
E-Technology

Responding to an Image

At first glance, how would you describe the overall feeling conveyed by this image? What is significant about the directions in which the man and woman are facing and about what they are doing? How does the background contribute to the mood of the picture? What point does the image seem to be making about the impact of communication technology? Translate that point into a caption for the illustration or into a thesis for an essay. (You also might want to compare and contrast this image with the one on p. 474.)

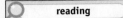For reading activities linked to this chapter, visit <bedfordstmartins.com/bedguide> and do a keyword search:

🔍 **reading**

Web Search

Think of a topic of great personal interest to you—a hobby, a political or social issue, a subject of study, something you know a lot about. Then look for varied Web sites devoted to this topic, especially message boards, chat rooms, blogs, and other interactive sites where individuals come together to share their thoughts on and experiences with the topic. As you browse through such sites, think about the kinds of communities the Web creates. How do people relate to one another online? What do they learn from one another, and where do they fail to connect? Ultimately, do you think of the Internet as a unifying force—bringing together people who would not normally come into contact? Or do you view the Internet as an isolating force—allowing people to remain anonymous and to avoid direct human contact?

Harvard Magazine

Creating Community, Online and Off

Harvard Magazine was founded in 1898 by alumni of Harvard University. Published bimonthly, it covers campus news as well as current social and political issues. Although affiliated with Harvard University, the magazine is independently edited to maintain an objective viewpoint. According to its Web site, the magazine's mission is "keeping alumni of Harvard University connected to the university and to each other." The following article, from the January–February 2004 issue of the magazine, discusses the popularity of blogging, examining its benefits and drawbacks as well as its capacity for building community among students and faculty at a campus.

AS YOU READ: *Think about the various bloggers the essay quotes. How are they similar, and how are they different?*

The weeks leading up to Thanksgiving were especially busy for Harvard 1 bloggers.

Robert John Bennett '68, who's writing a novel online, posted chapters 2 4 through 12 of part V ("Harvard—The Fourth Year") on his blog—short for Weblog, or online journal. Another blogger, Cynthia Rockwell, a sociology department staff member and freelance movie reviewer, debated the value of scholarly film criticism: "Does this kind of criticism illuminate, or does it bleach raw? I don't know. Do artists need critics? I don't know." Harvard Law School (HLS) librarian Vernica Downey used her blog to remind readers about National Children's Book Week ("The theme this year is 'Free to Read'"). And in his blog, Nathan Paxton cheered that month's landmark state-court decision lifting the ban on same-sex marriages. "This is great," the PhD candidate in government wrote. "The issue of the place of gays in our society is going to be the hot-button culture-wars issue of 2004."

Meanwhile, one particularly prolific commentator, known online only 3
as The Redhead, waxed wistful about single life. "How is it that some people
find their soulmates (if there is such a thing) at sixteen?" she mused one
bleak November afternoon. "Where are all the beautiful souls in this city
(they're too young, or they're married, or they're smokers, or they're in love
with someone else)? There's no justice in the universe."

Welcome to Weblogs at Harvard Law, an experimental community where 4
more than 350 students, faculty and staff members, and alumni have signed
up to publicly express their thoughts about everything from social issues to
software, from literature to love. Based at the Berkman Center for Internet
and Society, the initiative is free and available to anyone with a Harvard.edu
e-mail address. And except for a few private blogs limited to specific classes,
all Harvard-hosted blogs can be read by anybody on the Web.

Harvard's blogging project stems from a November 2002 conference, 5
sponsored by the Berkman Center, to examine the university's "digital identity." Provost Steven E. Hyman challenged those present to use the Internet
to unify their famously decentralized° institution, building bridges among
isolated departments and schools. "The question became how we could set
up the different parts of Harvard to talk to each other better," says center director John Palfrey '94, JD '01. Participants also hoped to create exciting new
online communities and fresh ways to use technology in teaching.

With their grassroots appeal, blogs seemed like a good first step. Shortly 6
after the conference, the center recruited a new fellow, blogging pioneer
Dave Winer, to spearhead the online community. Winer's own tech-talk
journal, DaveNet, was among the Internet's first blogs; founded in 1994, it
predated the term identifying it by several years. "I found this way of telling
stories that didn't have a filter, and it worked," says Winer, who went on to
found UserLand Software Inc. of Los Altos, California, which makes Web-
publishing products, and to launch an even better-known blog, Scripting
News. After arriving at Harvard in early 2003, Winer quickly adapted his
blogging software, Manila, for the university's Weblog community and
launched the program in March.

Blogs are public online journals, written in reverse chronological order, 7
with the most recent entries at the top. Unlike most graphic-rich Web sites,
they consist primarily of unadorned text and links to other sites, although
serious bloggers also upload photographs, audio, and video. Blogs usually
present a single author's voice, but increasingly groups and organizations
are using the format as well: the law school's LLM class of '04, the library at
Harvard's Rowland Institute, and the Berkman Center itself, among others,
maintain Weblogs.

All are part of a fast-growing worldwide community dubbed the "blogo- 8
sphere." About five million blogs now exist, according to Perseus Development Corporation; the Braintree, Massachusetts–based market-research firm
expects that number to double before 2005.

---

decentralized: Lacking a central point of focus.

What draws people to blogging? First, of course, they have something to 9
say. "I blog to talk, to let it out, to experiment with words, to Be Heard," The
Redhead writes. "I miss standing onstage in plays I believed in; I miss projecting my voice across a thousand seats. I'm loud for a reason. I have a lot
to say, and a strong set of lungs, and passion. And maybe out there, someone's got a question I can help answer."

In addition, blogging is refreshingly simple, requiring virtually no tech- 10
nical design know-how, or special software. Harvard users simply go to the
project's Web site (http://blogs.law.harvard.edu), where they can create a
blog in two or three minutes by following the instructions. From there, they
can post text, links, and photographs as easily as they send e-mail messages.

Blogging is also a cheap — or, in the Berkman Center's case, free — form 11
of publishing using existing space on university computers. And from a
user's perspective, it's wonderfully liberated from editorial interference. "You
know that old saying that freedom of the press belongs to whoever has the
press?" Winer asks. "Now *everybody* has the press."

As Harvard's diverse blogger population illustrates, "everybody" isn't the 12
stereotypical bored, barely literate teenager. Today lawyers, librarians, and
researchers use online journals for networking and sharing information; en-
trepreneurs use them for marketing and customer service; college professors
and students use them to extend in-class discussion. They're increasingly
popular among journalists, too. Several correspondents (and at least one
Iraqi citizen) maintained high-profile blogs at the height of last year's war in
Iraq, and Harvard's Nieman Foundation for Journalism devoted a chunk of
the fall 2003 issue of its quarterly magazine to examining the role of blogs
in newsrooms. Politicians are adopting blogs as well. By late 2003, nearly
every presidential candidate had one, though most real blogging was being
done by campaign staff members.

At Harvard, as elsewhere, blog styles are as different as the people behind 13
them. Many are online diaries, often featuring an online persona or alter ego.
The Redhead — who by mid November hadn't missed a single day of blogging
since the project's launch — writes about anything on her mind: her job, a
class, a party, a conversation, an observation. "I let myself have fun, but I try to
make sure there's a point," she says. Sometimes she prepares a single long
entry first thing in the morning or late at night; sometimes she writes several
and posts quick-hit entries — one or two sentences on a single topic, written as
rapidly as an e-mail message — throughout her day. (Fortunately, The Redhead, a.k.a. Wendy Koslow, is program coordinator for the Berkman Center,
where occasional on-the-job blogging is not only permitted, but encouraged.)

Many Harvard bloggers specialize. Vernica Downey, the HLS librarian, 14
writes primarily about research, rare books, and children's literature. Her
blog, titled "Thinking While Typing," draws a small but loyal audience of
regular readers. "I'm very popular among German librarians, for some reason," says Downey, who writes primarily outside work. HLS fellow Christopher Lydon, a former public-radio talk-show host, uses his site to explore

the social and cultural effects of blogging. He posts extensive text and audio interviews with leading bloggers, including some of those managing the on-line presidential campaigns.

Some educators use blogs as teaching tools. John Palfrey, a lecturer at   15 both HLS and the Extension School, posts syllabi, reading materials, and lectures on class blogs; he encourages, but doesn't require, students to use them. He views the technology as a way to extend the classroom experience, and to provide a new forum for people who might be too shy to speak up in person. "This helps us explore how people express themselves," says Palfrey, who also maintains an HLS blog on legal issues.

One Harvard staff member blogs to support a blossoming stage career.   16 Erin Judge, an assistant to two HLS professors by day, does stand-up comedy in Boston-area clubs at night. Her blog, "On Being (un)Funny," prompts some people to see her shows, she says. Its real strength, though, is as a testing ground for new material. "When I go onstage, I have five to seven minutes. There's no room to try out something you're taking a risk on — certainly not at first," she says. "So I find it very valuable to have this forum. I try to write something of length three times a week." Then she collects feedback from regular readers — friends, fellow comics, other bloggers, her mother in Texas — and revises her routines before performing them.

Like other communities, Harvard's Weblog project relies on rules. Users   17 can't run businesses or political campaigns using the university's technology, and they can't imply that Harvard endorses anything they write. At the same time, the project's coordinators — who believe the experiment will work only if bloggers know they can publish freely — never censor content. That is a critical factor for participants, who tend to become passionate about free speech. "I feel like I can say whatever I want," Judge says. "If anybody else I know had a blog at the place where they work, they wouldn't feel comfortable posting certain things."

Asked how coordinators would handle, for instance, a blog containing   18 hate speech, Palfrey says that hasn't been a problem — yet. "The community is self-policed, and that works remarkably well."

Until late October, the university hadn't interfered, either. But then col-   19 lege junior Derek Slater posted internal memos from Diebold Election Systems, an electronic voting-machine manufacturer, on his blog. The documents, which described possible security flaws in the company's equipment, had already been widely circulated online. After Slater posted them, Diebold complained to Harvard, arguing that Slater — and Harvard, as host — had violated U.S. copyright law. Initially, Harvard told Slater to "cease and desist" and warned him that, in keeping with school policy, he would be banned from University computer systems for a year if it happened again. Slater, backed by the Berkman Center, argued that posting the memos fell within the copyright law's "fair use" provision. In November, Harvard's general counsel agreed, saying the university no longer considered the matter a violation. Diebold later dropped the complaint.

Despite blogging's popularity, it has some drawbacks. The biggest prob- 20
lem: many blogs are downright boring. The worst offenders take the most
mundane material imaginable and share it with the world. One typical example, from a Harvard-hosted blog: "After approximately twenty years of
use, my GE toaster oven broke last night. Today I went to Target to buy a
new one. . . . They had a very nice Black & Decker toaster oven for $29.99
and I purchased it. My mother purchased a toaster oven for less about a year
ago. However, hers does not work. But she won't admit it."

Another pitfall: abandonment. Perseus, the market-research company, 21
says two-thirds of all blogs languish° unattended (which researchers define
as having no posts for two months), while one-quarter are "one-day wonders," created and then forgotten. Not surprisingly, the Harvard project's directory is littered with apparently abandoned blogs. In one case, an incom-
ing freshman kept a detailed diary of his first few days on campus this past
fall, even creating Dickens-style headings for his chapters ("In Which I Do
Something Entirely Unexpected"). By the following week, though, he'd apparently lost interest; he never blogged again.

Because the Web is a public medium, bloggers occasionally attract un- 22
wanted attention. Koslow's high-spirited site briefly attracted a male fan
whose constant e-mail messages made her uncomfortable. "I e-mailed him
and said, 'Please don't contact me anymore,'" says Koslow, who doesn't
know whether the man was part of the Harvard community. "The second
time I did that, it worked." The experience made her more cautious about
posting personal information: she took her work e-mail address off the blog
and now uses nicknames or initials when referring to friends and colleagues.

Despite the growing pains, most bloggers remain true believers in their 23
medium's value and promise. Downey, for instance, feels guilty if she gets so
busy she goes several days without blogging. When that happens, she says,
she posts a message letting readers know "I'm still here; this Weblog hasn't
been abandoned." Once she decided to take a break from blogging, perhaps
permanently—but she missed it so much she found herself back online
within a week.

Coordinators can't yet say whether Harvard's blog project is, in fact, 24
building intellectual bridges on campus. "It's way too early to declare victory," Palfrey says. But it *is* building community. Some participants have become fast friends off-line, gathering for weekly meetings at the law school.
In October, many attended the HLS-sponsored BloggerCon, a conference
that attracted 150 participants from as far away as Japan. Meanwhile, Palfrey
says, Stanford Law School expects to offer Weblogs to all its students, beginning this fall.

Online, many Harvardians faithfully stop by fellow participants' blogs to 25
read and comment on each other's posting. "I feel like my blog has a little
neighborhood," says Koslow. Dave Winer, project coordinator and medium

languish: Lie idle.

pioneer, skims maybe a dozen blogs daily. "Every one of them is a teacher of mine," he says, "and they teach me something new every day."

Questions to Start You Thinking

1. CONSIDERING MEANING: What are some of the reasons that blogging has become so popular? What are some of the drawbacks to blogging?

2. IDENTIFYING WRITING STRATEGIES: This essay is clearly organized into specific sections. What is the focus of each section, and where does each begin and end? How are the transitions between the sections signaled?

3. READING CRITICALLY: Who seems to be the intended audience for this essay? What do you think is the writer's intended purpose? How well do you think this purpose is achieved?

4. EXPANDING VOCABULARY: Paragraph 6 refers to the "grassroots appeal" of blogs. What is the meaning of this phrase, and how does it relate to the point of the essay?

5. MAKING CONNECTIONS: In "How Computers Change the Way We Think" (pp. 552–58), Sherry Turkle argues that blogging and other online technologies have affected the way we view privacy. Do the people interviewed for this essay seem to have concerns about privacy issues? Should they?

Journal Prompts

1. What kinds of communication do you participate in online? What do you see as the positive and negative aspects of electronic communication?

2. If you were to start your own blog, what would you write about? Your daily life? A hobby? An issue you feel passionate about? Explain why you would choose this topic. If you already have a blog, what do you write about? What have you gained from the experience?

Suggestions for Writing

1. In the conclusion of the essay, the author makes the point that Harvard's blog project is "building community." Write an essay about a community that you are a part of—your family, a church or other religious organization, a school, a sports team, a club, or some other group. Discuss how this group could (or already does) use the Internet to foster a greater sense of community.

2. Spend some time reading a variety of blogs, either at the Harvard Web site (see paragraph 10) or elsewhere on the Internet. You might start at *Technorati* <http://technorati.com>, where you can see a list of the most popular blogs and do a keyword search of blog postings. Make notes about the kinds of things bloggers write about. Then write an essay classifying the different kinds of blogs you encountered. Be sure to use plenty of examples as support.

David Gelernter
Computers Cannot Teach Children Basic Skills

■ For more about
David Gelernter, visit
<bedfordstmartins.com/
bedguide> and do a key-
word search:

🔍　　author

David Gelernter *was born in 1955. Although his undergraduate degree from Yale University is in classical Hebrew literature, he went on to receive a PhD in computer science from the State University of New York at Stony Brook. Gelernter has been a professor of computer science at Yale since 1983, and his writings and theories on technology have been highly influential. He is also a painter and an art critic, and he serves on the National Council for the Arts. In 1993, he lost part of his right hand and the sight in one eye after opening a mail bomb sent by Theodore Kaczynski, the "Unabomber" terrorist opposed to the advancement of technology, who targeted prominent professors and business executives. Gelernter chronicled his recovery in the memoir* Drawing Life: Surviving the Unabomber *(1997). His other books include* Mirror Worlds *(1991),* The Muse in the Machine: Computerizing the Poetry of Human Thought *(1994),* 1939: The Lost World of the Fair *(1995), and* Machine Beauty *(1998). He has written for such publications as* Commentary, *the* New York Times, *the* Wall Street Journal, *the* Washington Post, *the* National Review, *and* Time. *In "Computers Cannot Teach Children Basic Skills," first published in* New Republic *in 1994, Gelernter challenges the widely held view that computers are always a "godsend" in the classroom.*

AS YOU READ: *Identify the solution Gelernter proposes for making effective use of computers in the classroom.*

Over the last decade an estimated $2 billion has been spent on more than 1
2 million computers for America's classrooms. That's not surprising. We constantly hear from Washington that the schools are in trouble and that computers are a godsend. Within the education establishment, in poor as well as rich schools, the machines are awaited with nearly religious awe. An inner-city principal bragged to a teacher friend of mine recently that his school "has a computer in every classroom . . . despite being in a bad neighborhood!"

Computers Teach Some Things Well

Computers should be in the schools. They have the potential to accomplish 2
great things. With the right software, they could help make science tangible or teach neglected topics like art and music. They could help students form a concrete idea of society by displaying on-screen a version of the city in which they live — a picture that tracks real life moment by moment.

In practice, however, computers make our worst educational nightmares 3
come true. While we bemoan the decline of literacy, computers discount words in favor of pictures and pictures in favor of video. While we fret about the decreasing cogency° of public debate, computers dismiss linear argu-

---

cogency: Logic, persuasiveness.

ment and promote fast, shallow romps across the information landscape. While we worry about basic skills, we allow into the classroom software that will do a student's arithmetic or correct his spelling.

Computers Lower Reading Skills

Take multimedia. The idea of multimedia is to combine text, sound, and pictures in a single package that you browse on-screen. You don't just *read* Shakespeare; you watch actors performing, listen to songs, view Elizabethan buildings. What's wrong with that? By offering children candy-coated books, multimedia is guaranteed to sour them on unsweetened reading. It makes the printed page look even more boring than it used to look. Sure, books will be available in the classroom, too — but they'll have all the appeal of a dusty piano to a teen who has a Walkman handy. 4

So what if the little nippers don't read? If they're watching Olivier° instead, what do they lose? The text, the written word along with all of its attendant pleasures. Besides, a book is more portable than a computer, has a higher-resolution display, can be written on and dog-eared, and is comparatively dirt cheap. 5

Hypermedia, multimedia's comrade in the struggle for a brave new classroom,° is just as troubling. It's a way of presenting documents on-screen without imposing a linear start-to-finish order. Disembodied paragraphs are linked by theme; after reading one about the First World War, for example, you might be able to choose another about the technology of battleships, or the life of Woodrow Wilson, or hemlines in the '20s. This is another cute idea that is good in minor ways and terrible in major ones. Teaching children to understand the orderly unfolding of a plot or a logical argument is a crucial part of education. Authors don't merely agglomerate° paragraphs; they work hard to make the narrative read a certain way, prove a particular point. To turn a book or a document into hypertext is to invite readers to ignore exactly what counts — the story. 6

The real problem, again, is the accentuation° of already bad habits. Dynamiting documents into disjointed paragraphs is one more expression of the sorry fact that sustained argument is not our style. If you're a newspaper or magazine editor and your readership is dwindling, what's the solution? Shorter pieces. If you're a politician and you want to get elected, what do you need? Tasty sound bites. Logical presentation be damned. 7

Another software species, "allow me" programs, is not much better. These programs correct spelling and, by applying canned grammatical and stylistic rules, fix prose. In terms of promoting basic skills, though, they have all the virtues of a pocket calculator. 8

Olivier: Lawrence Olivier, a British actor noted for his Shakespearean performances. **brave new classroom:** Reference to the Aldous Huxley novel *Brave New World,* in which technology makes life happy but empty.   **agglomerate:** Jumble together.   **accentuation:** Making more intense.

In Kentucky, as the *Wall Street Journal* reported, students in grades K–3   9
are mixed together regardless of age in a relaxed environment. It works
great, the *Journal* says. Yes, scores on computation tests have dropped 10 percent at one school, but not to worry: "Drilling addition and subtraction in
an age of calculators is a waste of time," the principal reassures us. Meanwhile, a Japanese educator informs University of Wisconsin mathematician
Richard Akey that in his country, "calculators are not used in elementary or
junior high school because the primary emphasis is on helping students develop their mental abilities." No wonder Japanese kids blow the pants off
American kids in math. Do we really think "drilling addition and subtraction in an age of calculators is a waste of time"? If we do, then "drilling
reading in an age of multimedia is a waste of time" can't be far behind.

Prose-correcting programs are also a little ghoulish, like asking a com-   10
puter for tips on improving your personality. On the other hand, I ran this
viewpoint through a spell checker, so how can I ban the use of such programs in schools? Because to misspell is human; to have no idea of correct
spelling is to be semiliterate.

Conditions on the Use of Computers

There's no denying that computers have the potential to perform inspiring   11
feats in the classroom. If we are ever to see that potential realized, however,
we ought to agree on three conditions. First, there should be a completely
new crop of children's software. Most of today's offerings show no imagination. There are hundreds of similar reading and geography and arithmetic
programs, but almost nothing on electricity or physics or architecture. Also,
they abuse the technical capacities of new media to glitz up old forms instead of creating new ones. Why not build a time-travel program that gives
kids a feel for how history is structured by zooming you backward? A spectrum program that lets users twirl a frequency knob to see what happens?

Second, computers should be used only during recess or relaxation peri-   12
ods. Treat them as fillips,° not as surrogate teachers. When I was in school
in the '60s, we all loved educational films. When we saw a movie in class,
everybody won: teachers didn't have to teach, and pupils didn't have to
learn. I suspect that classroom computers are popular today for the same
reasons.

Most important, educators should learn what parents and most teachers   13
already know: you cannot teach a child anything unless you look him in the
face. We should not forget what computers are. Like books — better in some
ways, worse in others — they are devices that help children mobilize their
own resources and learn for themselves. The computer's potential to do
good is modestly greater than a book's in some areas. Its potential to do
harm is vastly greater, across the board.

---

fillips: Things that are added for excitement but are not essential.

Questions to Start You Thinking

1. CONSIDERING MEANING: What are the primary shortcomings Gelernter believes computers have as educational tools?

2. IDENTIFYING WRITING STRATEGIES: Where in the essay does Gelernter present his solution as to how computers should be used in the classroom? Do you find this placement effective? Why or why not?

3. READING CRITICALLY: In several places in the essay, Gelernter compares computers with books. Review what he has to say about computers and books. Do you think he makes an effective argument here? Why or why not?

4. EXPANDING VOCABULARY: Define *bemoan, literacy, fret, linear,* and *romps* (paragraph 3). Then, in your own words, summarize Gelernter's point in paragraph 3. What does his word choice suggest about his intended audience?

5. MAKING CONNECTIONS: What might Gelernter have to say about the kind of education Annie Dillard describes in the selection from her autobiography on pages 577–79? Could she have learned the same thing by simply using a computer? Why or why not?

Journal Prompts

1. What kind of learning have you done on computers? How effective do you find such learning?

2. In the essay's final paragraph, Gelernter writes that "you cannot teach a child anything unless you look him in the face." What does he mean? Do you agree?

Suggestions for Writing

1. To what extent do you agree or disagree with Gelernter's position? Write an essay in which you take a stand about the value of computers in the classroom. Focus, in particular, on the basic skills of reading, writing, and mathematics, but feel free to consider other areas in which computers may or may not be effective teaching tools.

2. Gelernter wrote this essay in 1994. Do some research on how computers have come to be used in classrooms since then. For example, what kinds of software have been developed for educational purposes? How much time does the average student spend using a computer in the classroom? Are computers being used to teach basic skills? Write an essay in which you use your findings to support your position about how Gelernter would feel about the use of computers in education today.

Steven Levy
From *The Perfect Thing*

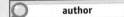 For more about
Steven Levy, visit
<bedfordstmartins.com/
bedguide> and do a key-
word search:

author

Steven Levy, *senior editor of* Newsweek *and author of the magazine's "The Tech-nologist" column, is one of America's most acclaimed technology writers. Born in 1951, Levy grew up in Philadelphia and earned his undergraduate degree from Temple University. He then received an MA in literature from Pennsylvania State University. He began his journalism career covering everything from sports to rock music to wedding announcements before joining* Newsweek *in 1995. Levy's work also has appeared in such publications as the* New Yorker, *the* New York Times Magazine, Harper's, *and* Premiere, *and he is a regular contributor to* Wired *magazine. Levy's six books include* Hackers: Heroes of the Computer Revolution *(1984), which brought the word* hacker *into people's daily vocabulary and was named by* PC Magazine *as the best sci-tech book written in the last twenty years, and* Crypto: How the Code Rebels Beat the Government — Saving Privacy in the Digital Age *(2001), winner of the grand eBook prize at the 2001 Frankfurt Book festival. The following selection is from his latest book,* The Perfect Thing: How the iPod Shuffles Commerce, Culture, and Coolness *(2006). In this excerpt, Levy questions the social impact of the groundbreaking device: "Has the iPod destroyed the social fabric? Has it transmogrified us into a zombie culture?"*

AS YOU READ: *Think about how Levy describes iPod users. How does he characterize them?*

In February 2005, the writer Andrew Sullivan visited New York City and 1 became severely discombobulated. The energizing, cacophonous° racket he had associated with New York had fallen silent. Even more disconcert-ing,° the city's formerly boisterous° population had apparently been mind-jacked by some alien force. Staring at the suddenly quiescent street life, he fingered the culprit. It was the Gizmo That Stole Gotham:

> There were little white wires hanging down from their ears, or tucked into pockets, purses, or jackets. The eyes were a little vacant. Each was in his or her own musical world, walking to their soundtrack, stars in their own music video, almost oblivious to the world around them. These are the iPod people. Even without the white wires you can tell who they are. They walk down the street in their own MP3 cocoon, bumping into others, deaf to small social cues, shutting out anyone not in their bubble.

Even Sullivan's own status as an iPod owner — "I joined the cult a few 2 years ago; the sect of the little white box worshipers," he confessed — did not mitigate his sorrow at what had been lost. "Walk through any airport in the United States these days and you will see person after person gliding through the social ether as if on autopilot," he wrote. "Get on a subway and

---

cacophonous: Noisy.   **disconcerting:** Disturbing.   **boisterous:** Noisily enthusiastic.

you're surrounded by a bunch of Stepford° commuters staring into mid-space as if anaesthetized by technology. Don't ask, don't tell, don't overhear, don't observe. Just tune in and tune out."

Has the iPod destroyed the social fabric? Has it transmogrified us into a   3
zombie culture? Has love of our own tunes lured us into aural narcissism,°
locking us in a cycle of self-love, from our hand-picked music library
straight to our brains, via earbuds? It's something an unplugged observer
might well ask. In certain places — the gym, the subway, the airplane, the
schoolyard — it may seem that the immediate environment, and the people
in it, gets less attention than the increasingly inevitable iPod.

Outsiders are getting frustrated at the party they haven't been invited to.   4
To those who depend on making cold connections, it's beyond frustration.
Pity the poor beggars and street musicians who must now compete with the
personal concerts buzzing in the heads of potential donors. For politicians
seeking to press voter flesh, it's a nightmare. "This is a whole new hazard in
campaigning!" Gifford Miller, striving to be New York City's mayor in 2005,
told *New York* magazine, "We have to come up with something to jam the
iPods!" (Miller, of course, lost the primary.)

And it's not just mendicants,° pols,° and social critics who worry about   5
the effect; even some enthusiastic iPod owners are concerned about the impact on the social dynamic. Wayne Coyne, the singer and guitarist for the
Flaming Lips, for instance, loves the access to his music that the iPod gives
him but admits, "There's an insulation that happens. I can see space is at a
premium in a community like Manhattan, but in a way it's saying, 'I'm with
you people, but I don't want to deal with you.' I don't really like that sometimes — I like the idea of 'Let's deal with each other, why not?'"

Coyne's lament is typical of this form of social criticism. But it's mis-   6
guided. Think of your experiences in the subway and gym before the iPod became standard issue and supposedly made everyone into an extra from *The
Village of the Damned*. Did people in those pre-'pod environments spontaneously break out into chatter, exchange intimacies, and otherwise "deal with
each other"? No. They avoided eye contact and counted the minutes until the
torturous boredom of those social hells might end. Now people happily listen
to their favorite music, marvel at how their personal soundscapes enliven their
surroundings, and appreciate the cozy (albeit virtual) protective covering that
their iPods provide them. Amazingly, *that* seems to make observers crazy.

Questions to Start You Thinking

1. CONSIDERING MEANING: According to Levy, what concerns do critics have
   about the popularity of iPods?
2. IDENTIFYING WRITING STRATEGIES: In paragraphs 1 and 2, Levy quotes Andrew Sullivan quite extensively. What is the effect of these quotations?

Stepford: Robotic, zombielike. The word originates from *The Stepford Wives,* a 1972
novel in which the men of the fictional town of Stepford replace their wives with robots.
narcissism: Self-love.   **mendicants:** Beggars.   **pols:** Politicians.

3. **READING CRITICALLY:** Levy devotes most of this selection to laying out various criticisms of iPods. Where does he begin to counter these concerns? Do you find his defense of iPods sufficient to counteract these criticisms?

4. **EXPANDING VOCABULARY:** Define *discombobulated* (paragraph 1) and *transmogrified* (paragraph 3). Why might Levy have chosen to use these words rather than simpler synonyms?

5. **MAKING CONNECTIONS:** The *Harvard Magazine* essay "Creating Community, Online and Off" (pp. 530–35) discusses how modern technology can bring people together. Levy, on the other hand, reminds readers how it can push people apart. What do you think is the main effect of personal technologies — portable music players, cell phones, laptop computers, and so on? What examples support your opinion?

Journal Prompts

1. What is your opinion of iPods? How do you respond to the criticisms that Levy mentions?

2. If you could create a "personal soundtrack," what would it consist of? What kind of music would you use to characterize your daily life?

Suggestions for Writing

1. Consider another electronic device that some people criticize and others embrace — cell phones, for example, or video games or even television. Write an essay in which you evaluate both the pros and the cons of your subject.

2. One issue related to the use of iPods and other such devices is that of copyright infringement when music is downloaded without specific permission. Do some research about the arguments on both sides of this issue, and then write an essay in which you take a stand for or against greater enforcement of copyright protection.

Merrill Markoe
Who Am I?

 For more about Merrill Markoe, visit <bedfordstmartins.com/bedguide> and do a keyword search:

author

Merrill Markoe *was born in New York City in 1951. After earning an MFA from the University of California at Berkeley and spending a year as an art instructor, she left teaching to try her hand at comedy writing. Markoe says that "nobody was more surprised" than she when her first script landed her a job as a writer for the television program* Laugh In 2. *She went on to become the Emmy-winning cocreator and original head writer of* Late Night with David Letterman. *After leaving the show in 1988, Markoe worked as a television news correspondent and freelance writer for such shows as* Newhart, Moonlighting, *and* Sex and the City. *Markoe now spends much of her time writing books, including the humorous essay collections* What the Dogs Have Taught Me and Other Amazing Things I've Learned *(1992),* How to Be Hap-Hap-Happy Like Me *(1994), and* Merrill Markoe's

Guide to Love *(1997). She also has published two novels,* It's My F —— ing
Birthday *(2002) and* Walking in Circles Before Lying Down *(2006), and has
written for such publications as* Rolling Stone, Time, New York Woman, *the* New
York Times, *and the* Los Angeles Times. *In this essay, first published in* ON *Magazine in March 2001, Markoe offers a humorous take on online personality quizzes.*

AS YOU READ: *Note the different results of each personality quiz that Markoe takes.
Do the quizzes help her answer the question in the essay's title?*

Having spent a fair amount of time and money in therapy, debating my   1
every move with a licensed and supposedly caring professional, I was
under the impression that I had a pretty good idea of what I was all about.
At least until I started taking personality quizzes on the Internet. As any
reader of cheesy women's magazines will tell you, this quiz-taking business
can be both time-consuming and pointless in terms of gaining meaningful
advice. But it can also be as utterly seductive as the horoscope pages. For
about a minute and a half, the quiz glistens like a beacon of knowledge before you, offering answers to all the important questions in life. Five minutes later, awash in self-loathing, you can't even remember what it said or
why you ever buy that magazine.

As it turns out, the Internet is so full of this kind of self-improvement   2
quiz that it could be argued that the only thing that separates the Net from
an average issue of *Cosmopolitan* is that *Cosmo* offers only one quiz at a time.
And the Internet seems to have fewer ads for panty liners.

I came to know of this one day when, quite by accident, I encountered a   3
quiz at a handy site called QuizBox.com that promised to tell me how "attractive" I was. I guess I needed a little reassurance (with emphasis on the word
little — if the quiz couldn't see me, how reassuring could it be?). I willingly
submitted to seemingly irrelevant questions like "Which city would you like
to visit?" (I chose Paris over Tokyo or Beijing because, in the montage° in my
imagination, I thought I looked more attractive in Paris.) I also selected a peck
over a big kiss as my first-date kissing style because a rash of unappealing recent first dates was still fresh in my mind, and this quiz didn't specify whether
the guy I was allegedly going on this first date with had any sex appeal.

After my scores were tallied, the quiz passed judgment. It said, in no un-   4
certain terms, that I needed to improve my personality. I also needed to be
more optimistic and smile more. I could be attractive if I would try, it
sighed, but clearly it didn't think I was trying hard enough.

So there I was, alone in my house and suddenly a lot less attractive than   5
I had been a few minutes earlier. I wasn't going to take this lying down. To
recoup my losses, like a woman feverishly playing the slot machines, I continued to take more quizzes.

Instantly I was able to wrest myself from the jaws of low self-esteem via   6
the "What kind of personality do you have?" quiz. This time, when asked to
answer the question "If you could wish for anything what would it be?" I

montage: A series of images.

chose "Become a beauty queen." (After all, my health was already pretty good, my eyes are already pretty nice, and being clever was apparently getting me nowhere.) Much to my delight, the quiz was favorably impressed. "People with your kind of character are few and far between," it informed me. "Everybody likes to be around people with your personality."

Feeling a bit more confident, I was also getting genuinely curious about the possibility of learning something new about myself this way. So I went on taking quizzes. Which is how I came to find out that every single thing I did defined my personality.   7

There was an egg test that revealed that because I eat fried eggs white-part first, instead of yolk first, I am "logical, smart, and inventive . . . though sometimes too cold and selfish." That I only eat egg whites, period, didn't seem to factor in one way or another.   8

Next, by picking toilet stall No. 2 out of a drawing of three empty stalls ("The Toilet Test"), I learned I was "an efficient person" yet also "a romantic person" who can be "too hasty making decisions in love." I guess it serves me right for being so cavalier° about my toilet-stall selections.   9

On "The Eating Test," I made the mistake of picking eggs and toast over cereal for breakfast, while also admitting to sometimes skipping lunch entirely because of worry about my weight. Now I had inadvertently shown myself to be "jealous of people who are smarter and better looking" than I am. A harsh evaluation, I felt, for someone "with my kind of character."   10

So I left QuizBox.com's petty judgments behind and typed "personality quiz" into the Yahoo! search engine. This led me to "The Ultimate Personality Test." Three cups of coffee later (and still in my pajamas at one in the afternoon), I was saddened to learn that I was a "secret agent" who "professionally, likes to work in a cubicle and eat lunch at the desk."   11

But my mood improved considerably once I clicked on the next test I could find, and my choice of an abstract pattern from an assortment of designs offered me a complete reevaluation. Now, thank heavens, I was "dynamic, active, extroverted" and "willing to accept certain risks and to make a strong commitment in exchange for interesting and varied work."   12

So which was it? Was I a cubicle worker or a risk taker? Hoping to get off this emotional roller coaster, I wandered over to TheSpark.com, where yet another personality test branded me "an accountant. Reserved. Meticulous. Dependable." And this despite the fact that on the very same page "The Sexy Test" said I was 75 percent sexier than their average quiz taker! Because this puzzling new image of "sexy accountant" didn't provide me with anything except an idea for a horrible new sitcom, I took a deep, cleansing breath and dived into the elaborate "How Others See You" quiz, where I emerged "extroverted, agreeable but neurotic and not very conscientious." I found this confusing because a quiz at a women's financial site insisted that I was "thorough, meticulous, and calm" only a few minutes later.   13

By the end of a long day, I also learned that my taste in room decor is "middle class" ("What Class Are You?"), despite the fact that my "plant per-   14

cavalier: Arrogant; disdainful.

sonality" is "woodland natural." My "workout personality" is "40% inspirational, 30% spontaneous, and 30% analytical (sailing, training for a triathlon, and softball recommended)." And my religious beliefs are Unitarian Universalist, neopagan, or Malayan Buddhist.

Although the Ayurvedic Foundation's site tells me I have a Pitta constitution, meaning I am "hot, sharp, liquid, and oily," an insurance company's longevity quiz says that I will live to be ninety-five.   15

So there it is: I am extroverted and reserved, passive and active, risk taking and afraid of change. I am also calm, neurotic, and meticulous, dependable and not very conscientious. So what if my workout program of alternating the gym with yoga does not fit my personality? Who cares if I should belong to a religion I have never heard of? All things considered, I have to say that it feels great to really get to know myself at last.   16

Questions to Start You Thinking

1. **CONSIDERING MEANING:** How do you interpret Markoe's final sentence in this selection?

2. **IDENTIFYING WRITING STRATEGIES:** In paragraph 4, Markoe writes about the first quiz as if it were an actual person criticizing her. How does she do this? What is the effect?

3. **READING CRITICALLY:** What is Markoe's purpose in writing this essay? How do you think she wants readers to respond? Do all the quizzes she quotes from seem to be real? Why or why not?

4. **EXPANDING VOCABULARY:** Define the adjectives Markoe uses to describe herself in the first two sentences of paragraph 16. How do these words contribute to the point she is making in the essay as a whole?

5. **MAKING CONNECTIONS:** In "What's Love Got to Do with It?" (pp. 453–57), Anjula Razdan discusses online dating services, which often use personality questionnaires to match up potential mates. Razdan quotes several experts on Internet dating, including one who says, "That's what computers are all about—efficiency and sorting" (paragraph 16). How might Markoe respond to this statement? How do you think she might feel about online dating services?

Journal Prompts

1. Find a personality quiz, either online or in a popular magazine, and answer the questions as honestly as you can. To what extent do the quiz results match the personality you see yourself as having?

2. Do you ever feel that you or others you know spend too much time online? Explain why you think Internet surfing can become addictive.

Suggestions for Writing

1. Spend an hour or so taking as many different online personality quizzes as you can. Then, like Markoe, write an essay in which you use examples to share your results with readers. Your tone will depend on how seriously you take those results.

2. Markoe makes the point in paragraph 1 that quiz taking can be "as utterly seductive as the horoscope pages." Write an essay in which you analyze what lies behind the appeal of quizzes, horoscopes, and other tools that claim to reveal people's personalities. What is it that people are looking for when they seek out these guides?

Alex Koppelman
MySpace or OurSpace?

■ For more about Alex Koppelman, visit <bedfordstmartins.com/ bedguide> and do a keyword search:

 author

Alex Koppelman *was born in 1982 in Baltimore, Maryland. He graduated from the University of Pennsylvania in 2005 and is currently a staff writer for* Salon.com, *where he covers news and politics. Before joining* Salon, *he helped found the online magazine* Dragonfire, *serving as the Arts and Entertainment editor and media critic, and he also has written for the* Huffington Post *blog. In addition to writing for* Salon, *he is currently a contributing editor for SMITH Magazine, a new interactive magazine that aims to publish "the best in personal media . . . blogs, memoirs, diaries, viral videos, social networking, the mash-up between the professional and the amateur." In this article, first published on Salon.com in June 2006, Koppelman reports on privacy concerns raised by cases in which students have been suspended from school or arrested based on their postings to social-networking sites. In the paired essay that follows, Sherry Turkle also takes a close look at how social-networking sites — among other computer technologies — are affecting the ways people think and behave.*

AS YOU READ: *Consider how school authorities and law-enforcement agents have responded to teenagers' postings on MySpace. What are the primary concerns of people on both sides of the issue — those who support such monitoring and those who criticize it?*

In October, seventeen-year-old Dimitri Arethas posted a doctored photo 1 on his MySpace page depicting his public high school's black vice principal as RoboCop. Arethas said he found the photo, which had a racial slur scrawled on it, on another student's Web site, and that he posted it to his own MySpace page thinking it was funny. Arethas, of Charlotte, North Carolina, claims he didn't mean the post to be racist and says that most of his fellow students thought the post was funny too.

But one anonymous student didn't, and brought it to the attention of 2 school administrators. As a result, Arethas says principal Joel Ritchie, who did not respond to a request for comment, suspended Arethas for ten days.

Arethas, who says he apologized and removed the photo when he was 3 initially confronted, was incensed° by the suspension, and contacted his local paper, the *Charlotte Observer,* and the American Civil Liberties Union.

incensed: Angered.

With the help of ACLU lawyers, Arethas was able to convince the school to end the suspension. He returned after two days.

"Maybe what I did was wrong, morally," Arethas said in a recent e-mail, 4 "but I had every right to express myself. I just chose to do it as a picture, instead of rambling down the hallways yelling, 'Man! This school sucks.'"

Arethas isn't the only student to be disciplined for what he posted to his 5 MySpace profile. The past few years have seen an explosion in the number of schools taking to the Web to find out what students are saying and doing. And punishment has followed, from a Pennsylvania school that suspended one student for creating a parody MySpace profile of his principal to a California school that suspended twenty students simply for viewing one student's MySpace profile, which contained threats against another student. And some public school systems, like Illinois's Community High School District 128, are even taking steps to monitor everything their students say on sites like MySpace. According to the *Chicago Tribune*, under new guidelines, students who participate in extracurricular activities will need to sign a pledge in which they agree that the school can discipline them if it finds evidence that they have posted any "illegal or inappropriate" material online. Even some police are beginning to patrol MySpace, seeing the site as an effective tool for catching teenage criminals.

All of this new scrutiny poses a vital question for MySpace, which claims 6 76 million users and is now the largest of all the Web's social-networking sites: What will happen to the site if and when users no longer feel safe expressing themselves there? And in an age where teenagers are accustomed to living their lives online, what will happen when they learn that what they thought was private is, in fact, public, and not without consequence?

"I never thought [this] would happen," Arethas says of his suspension. 7 "I figured only my friends would see my profile page."

Most large online social-networking services have undergone similar 8 challenges as they've grown, with users feeling safe in the widely held though mistaken perception that what they posted was private, or at least that it would only be seen by a select group of people. Other sites have also, like MySpace, dealt with users who have preyed on other more gullible° ones, as with the recent high-profile arrests of men who used MySpace to lure young girls. But few sites have grown as large, and as quickly, as MySpace, which was acquired in July 2005 by Rupert Murdoch's News Corporation for $580 million. And few have specialized so effectively in encouraging kids to get comfortable and open up.

As with all forms of electronic media, people still have a hard time 9 wrapping their minds around the fact that little online is truly private. A sampling of MySpace's offerings reveals the evidence: posts explore almost every aspect of users' personal lives, from typical teenage angst about acne and unrequited° crushes to more incriminating fare — sexually suggestive images and photos of drinking and drug use — as well as professions of love, anger, and every emotion in between.

gullible: Easily fooled.   **unrequited:** Not returned.

"MySpace has encouraged its users to be aware that what they post on   10
their MySpace profile is available for the public to see," says MySpace
spokesman Matthew Grossman, adding that "part of why MySpace has been
so successful is because people can share their feelings." While Grossman
stresses that MySpace does not spy on its users, or share their information,
the site will work with law enforcement "if they [law enforcement] go
through the proper legal channels," such as a subpoena or warrant. The
site's privacy statement makes that caveat° explicit. But many users haven't
heeded those warnings. They do so now at their peril, because more and
more, they are being watched.

"We patrol the Internet like we patrol the streets," Officer James McNamee,   11
a member of the Barrington, Illinois, police department's Special Crimes
Unit, says. "We'll go in on a MySpace or a Xanga, we'll pick out our area,
and we'll just start surfing it, checking it, seeing what's going on."

McNamee says the fact that police have only recently realized what a   12
powerful tool social-networking sites can be for investigative purposes may
be what makes MySpace users feel the site is their own private realm.

"We're still playing catch-up," McNamee says. "I wouldn't say we're   13
super far behind, but we're learning as we go and I think that's the reason
some [teens] feel like, 'Oh, this is an invasion of our privacy.' Well, no, it's
not, it's just that we were behind on learning that we should have been paying attention to this, and now we're paying attention."

McNamee says they've found pictures of graffiti, with the artists stand-   14
ing next to it, "smiling, all happy about their activity," they've found evidence of drug dealing — "where they could hook up, who was dealing drugs
. . . photos of their money . . . photos of their drugs" — they've even found a
"We Hate Barrington Police Department" blog. ("We don't care," McNamee
says of the blog. "It's kind of funny to us; we'll let them vent that way.")

The question of what public-school students have the right to say, and   15
where they have the right to say it, remains murky, with little in the way of
definitive jurisprudence to guide schools and courts. Indeed, just about the
only thing experts on the topic seem to agree on is that no one really knows
what the law is.

"There have been some court decisions, and in all honesty they've been a   16
little bit confused," says Mark Goodman, the executive director of the Student Press Law Center. "And it really isn't just Internet-based speech, but actually any kind of expression by students outside of school. There really have
been relatively few cases going to court on this issue, so it's understandable
[to a certain extent] why there would be some confusion surrounding it."

Goodman, for his part, believes that the law is on the students' side.   17

In a public school, I believe the law's pretty clear that the school does not
have the authority to punish students for expression they engage in outside
of school. There are really important fundamental reasons for that. At the
very least, it's a major usurpation° of parental authority. Outside of school,

caveat: Warning.   usurpation: Wrongful taking away.

parents have the authority to discipline their children. . . . I think the problem is a lot of people simply presume that the Internet in effect becomes school expression, and I simply don't believe it does. I think there are legally important distinctions, and very good policy reasons why the school shouldn't have that authority.

Marc Rotenberg, who teaches information privacy law at the Georgetown University Law Center and is the executive director of the Electronic Privacy Information Center, believes the issue is not so clear-cut. 18

"The key point is whatever is publicly accessible," Rotenberg says. "If a student writes an article in the town paper that defames one of the teachers, the fact that it didn't happen in a school publication really is irrelevant. The school will still act on that information if it's public and available to the community. . . . The courts have not, particularly in the last few years, been sympathetic to student privacy claims, and I don't think there's any reason to think it would be otherwise when the conduct is posted to publicly available Web sites. . . . The critical point here is that yes, I think students should have the freedom to express their views, and I don't think there should be any type of prior restraint on publication, whether it's in print or online media. But that doesn't mean what you say may not have some repercussions." 19

There are no such questions about whether the police have a right to patrol MySpace. 20

"If it is a public forum that is accessible to others, then presumably the police are welcome to participate, as they would be welcome to enter a shopping mall or something like that," Rotenberg says. 21

Kurt Opsahl, a staff lawyer with the Electronic Frontier Foundation, a nonprofit organization whose mission is to defend Internet free speech, agrees. 22

"You have of course a constitutional right not to incriminate yourself, but you have to exercise that right by not incriminating yourself," Opsahl says. "If you post a photo of yourself engaged in apparently illegal activity with text confirming what you're doing, that can be used against you. Anything you say can and will be used against you, as they say in the Miranda warnings." 23

But according to James McNamee, MySpace's younger users, or at least the ones he sees in his virtual patrols, haven't yet caught on to that. 24

"Some people criticize MySpace, and there's no reason to criticize it," he says. "It's a social-networking Internet site that's doing a great function, in my view. The problem is young people aren't sure how to handle it yet. They're not understanding that it's the World Wide Web, they don't get that concept. They think only their friends are looking at it." 25

Eight MySpace users in Wilkes-Barre, Pennsylvania, learned the hard way that the people visiting their MySpace profiles were not just friends. Wilkes-Barre police, stumped by a rash of graffiti in the downtown area, turned to MySpace to seek suspects. 26

"The police dug very deep to find me," says one of those arrested in the case, who asked to remain anonymous because of ongoing legal proceedings, and who would communicate only through MySpace. "I didn't have my name, 27 phone number, or any info on me online. I've never used my real name, I've never had my own Internet connection (always another person's name), and I never had my address or name at all posted or registered online."

That user, who denies any involvement in the graffiti, says he was aware 28 of the public nature of the site — "I always think that people are looking," he says — but that some of his friends were not, and that he thinks the police overstepped their bounds.

"I feel that police shouldn't lie and disguise their identity to gain friend- 29 ship with people they can't see, or ever meet without [informants]."

Dimitri Arethas also feels his rights were violated. "A home page is basi- 30 cally as private as it gets," he told the *Observer* at the time of his suspension.

When asked recently if he still felt that way, his answer was much the 31 same.

"Private like exclusive to only your friends? No, not that kind of pri- 32 vate," he said. "[But] someone has to personally seek out your name and find you in order to view your MySpace, which is what stirs me up. That's where I got some sense of privacy. I could have never imagined someone printing out my profile page and then turning it in."

Mark Goodman worries about the lessons students like Arethas will 33 learn as more face consequences for what they post to sites like MySpace.

> What I would hate to see happen, and I think it has happened in some communities at least, is students deciding they can't publish unpopular or controversial viewpoints on their MySpace page or an independent Web site because they're afraid school officials will punish them for it. That, I think, is very disturbing, and those are the young people who, as adults, are going to believe the government should be regulating what the public says. It has very troubling implications for their appreciation of the First Amendment in the world outside of school.

Arethas says that he has become more cautious about what he posts. 34 "Gotta play the political game now," he says. He took his MySpace profile down for a week after the incident, but decided to put it back up — without the offending photo — when he realized, he says, that he "could pretty much get away with it," and that he "had won the case" by being reinstated to school. He still believes the school was wrong to suspend him.

Goodman thinks, though, that few students would act as Arethas did. He 35 points to a study on high school students' attitudes toward the First Amendment, conducted by researchers at the University of Connecticut. Released early last year, the study found that 49 percent of students thought that newspapers should need government approval for their stories, 75 percent didn't realize flag burning was legal, and more than a third thought the First Amendment went too far. Half believed the government could censor the Internet.

"I think the point of it, ultimately, is how can we expect anything differ- 36 ent [than the survey results]," Goodman says. "A direct result of these actions is young people's dismissiveness of the fundamental values of free expression that we as a nation supposedly hold dear."

The MySpace user arrested in the Wilkes-Barre case agrees.   37

I think that MySpace is the epitome° of free speech, and censorship, all rolled in one. And I think that America with[out] free speech is not free at all. Just think about the people that have been censored. Go to another country, like Denmark and there is no censorship at all, and the kids growing up there don't look at it as dirty, just as life. When we make things illegal, or "dirty to look at" we create the feeling that it's bad.

Questions to Start You Thinking

1. CONSIDERING MEANING: Why are some people concerned about school and other authorities policing teenagers' Web postings? How can this issue be seen as involving freedom of speech?

2. IDENTIFYING WRITING STRATEGIES: Consider Koppelman's use of quotations in this selection. How do the quotations help him to develop his point? Why do you think he chose to quote his sources so extensively?

3. READING CRITICALLY: Does Koppelman present a balanced view of his topic? Or does he seem to lean toward one side of the issue — either in favor of or opposed to the policing of students' Web postings? Explain what you see as his purpose in writing the selection.

4. EXPANDING VOCABULARY: Define *murky, definitive,* and *jurisprudence* (paragraph 15). What point is Koppelman making in this paragraph?

5. MAKING CONNECTIONS: The essay from *Harvard Magazine,* "Creating Community, Online and Off" (pp. 530–35), mentions that the Harvard blogs are not censored. Do you feel that schools should have the right to censor content on blog sites that they provide to students? Why or why not?

Link to the Paired Essay

In the essay that follows ("How Computers Change the Way We Think," pp. 552–58), Sherry Turkle writes that "in a democracy, privacy is a right, not merely a privilege" (paragraph 11). Of the people whom Koppelman quotes in his essay, which do you think would agree with Turkle's statement? Which would disagree? Explain your reasoning, as well as where you stand on the issue.

Journal Prompts

1. Write about the kinds of personal information you share online. How safe do you feel providing this information? Did Koppelman's essay change the way you feel about your online privacy?

2. What is your response to Dimitri Arethas's case? Explain why you think his suspension was fair or unfair. Would your response be different if the photograph had not contained a racial slur?

epitome: Most perfect example.

Suggestions for Writing

1. Why do you think young people are so eager to create pages on sites such as MySpace, to share photographs and information about their personal lives with anyone who happens upon the page? Write an essay in which you explain some reasons for the phenomenal popularity of MySpace and other sites like it.

2. Write an essay in which you take a stand on students' freedom of speech. For example, should schools be able to discipline students for what they post to Web sites? Should administrators have a say in what students can publish in school newspapers or in letters to community newspapers? What about messages written on students' clothing? Support your position by citing examples from Koppelman's essay as well as from additional research.

Sherry Turkle
How Computers Change the Way We Think

■ For more about Sherry Turkle, visit <bedfordstmartins.com/bedguide> and do a keyword search:

author

Sherry Turkle *was born in 1948 in New York City. A graduate of Radcliffe College, the University of Chicago, and Harvard University, she is a clinical psychologist and a professor of sociology at the Massachusetts Institute of Technology. She also founded and directs the MIT Initiative on Technology and Self, a research center devoted to "the social and psychological dimensions of technological change." Turkle's teaching and writing, which focus on people's relationship with technology, have earned her the nickname* cybershrink. *Her books include* Psychoanalytic Politics: Jacques Lacan and Freud's French Revolution *(1978, revised 1992);* The Second Self: Computers and the Human Spirit *(1984, revised 2005); and* Life on the Screen: Identity in the Age of the Internet *(1995). She is currently writing a book on how technology — rapidly evolving to become more humanlike — is changing what it means to be human. In the following essay, first published in* the Chronicle of Higher Education *in 2004, Turkle explores how technologies such as online chat, PowerPoint, word processors, and simulation games are radically affecting our "habits of mind."*

AS YOU READ: *Identify the areas in which Turkle sees computers changing the way people think. Does she present her opinions on whether these changes are good or bad?*

The tools we use to think change the ways in which we think. The invention of written language brought about a radical shift in how we process, organize, store, and transmit representations of the world. Although writing remains our primary information technology, today when we think about the impact of technology on our habits of mind, we think primarily of the computer.

My first encounters with how computers change the way we think came soon after I joined the faculty at the Massachusetts Institute of Technology in the late 1970s, at the end of the era of the slide rule and the beginning of the era of the personal computer. At a lunch for new faculty members, several senior professors in engineering complained that the transition from slide rules to calculators had affected their students' ability to deal with issues of scale. When students used slide rules, they had to insert decimal points themselves. The professors insisted that that required students to maintain a mental sense of scale, whereas those who relied on calculators made frequent errors in orders of magnitude. Additionally, the students with calculators had lost their ability to do "back of the envelope" calculations, and with that, an intuitive feel for the material.

That same semester, I taught a course in the history of psychology. There, 3 I experienced the impact of computational objects on students' ideas about their emotional lives. My class had read Freud's essay on slips of the tongue, with its famous first example: the chairman of a parliamentary session opens a meeting by declaring it closed. The students discussed how Freud interpreted such errors as revealing a person's mixed emotions. A computer-science major disagreed with Freud's approach. The mind, she argued, is a computer. And in a computational dictionary—like we have in the human mind— "closed" and "open" are designated by the same symbol, separated by a sign for opposition. "Closed" equals "minus open." To substitute "closed" for "open" does not require the notion of ambivalence or conflict.

"When the chairman made that substitution," she declared, "a bit was 4 dropped; a minus sign was lost. There was a power surge. No problem."

The young woman turned a Freudian slip into an information-processing 5 error. An explanation in terms of meaning had become an explanation in terms of mechanism.

Such encounters turned me to the study of both the instrumental and 6 the subjective sides of the nascent° computer culture. As an ethnographer and psychologist, I began to study not only what the computer was doing *for* us, but what it was doing *to* us, including how it was changing the way we see ourselves, our sense of human identity.

In the 1980s, I surveyed the psychological effects of computational ob- 7 jects in everyday life—largely the unintended side effects of people's tendency to project thoughts and feelings onto their machines. In the twenty years since, computational objects have become more explicitly designed to have emotional and cognitive effects. And those "effects by design" will become even stronger in the decade to come. Machines are being designed to serve explicitly as companions, pets, and tutors. And they are introduced in school settings for the youngest children.

Today, starting in elementary school, students use e-mail, word process- 8 ing, computer simulations, virtual communities, and PowerPoint software. In the process, they are absorbing more than the content of what appears on their screens. They are learning new ways to think about what it means to know and understand.

What follows is a short and certainly not comprehensive list of areas 9 where I see information technology encouraging changes in thinking. There

nascent: Just being born.

can be no simple way of cataloging whether any particular change is good or bad. That is contested terrain. At every step we have to ask, as educators and citizens, whether current technology is leading us in directions that serve our human purposes. Such questions are not technical; they are social, moral, and political. For me, addressing that subjective side of computation is one of the more significant challenges for the next decade of information technology in higher education. Technology does not determine change, but it encourages us to take certain directions. If we make those directions clear, we can more easily exert human choice.

Thinking about Privacy

Today's college students are habituated to a world of online blogging, in- 10
stant messaging, and Web browsing that leaves electronic traces. Yet they have had little experience with the right to privacy. Unlike past generations of Americans, who grew up with the notion that the privacy of their mail was sacrosanct,° our children are accustomed to electronic surveillance as part of their daily lives.

I have colleagues who feel that the increased incursions on privacy have 11
put the topic more in the news, and that this is a positive change. But middle-school and high-school students tend to be willing to provide personal information online with no safeguards, and college students seem uninterested in violations of privacy and in increased governmental and commercial surveillance. Professors find that students do not understand that in a democracy, privacy is a right, not merely a privilege. In ten years, ideas about the relationship of privacy and government will require even more active pedagogy.° (One might also hope that increased education about the kinds of silent surveillance that technology makes possible may inspire more active political engagement with the issue.)

Avatars° or a Self?

Chat rooms, role-playing games, and other technological venues offer us 12
many different contexts for presenting ourselves online. Those possibilities are particularly important for adolescents because they offer what Erik Erikson described as a moratorium, a time out or safe space for the personal experimentation that is so crucial for adolescent development. Our dangerous world — with crime, terrorism, drugs, and AIDS — offers little in the way of safe spaces. Online worlds can provide valuable spaces for identity play.

But some people who gain fluency in expressing multiple aspects of self 13
may find it harder to develop authentic selves. Some children who write narratives for their screen avatars may grow up with too little experience of how to share their real feelings with other people. For those who are lonely yet afraid of intimacy, information technology has made it possible to have the illusion of companionship without the demands of friendship.

sacrosanct: Most sacred or holy.   **pedagogy:** Teaching.   **avatars:** Graphic representations of people in a virtual reality environment such as the Internet.

From Powerful Ideas to PowerPoint

In the 1970s and early 1980s, some educators wanted to make programming 14
part of the regular curriculum for K–12 education. They argued that because
information technology carries ideas, it might as well carry the most powerful ideas that computer science has to offer. It is ironic that in most elementary schools today, the ideas being carried by information technology are not
ideas from computer science like procedural thinking, but more likely to be
those embedded in productivity tools like PowerPoint presentation software.

PowerPoint does more than provide a way of transmitting content. It 15
carries its own way of thinking, its own aesthetic° — which not surprisingly
shows up in the aesthetic of college freshmen. In that aesthetic, presentation
becomes its own powerful idea.

To be sure, the software cannot be blamed for lower intellectual stan- 16
dards. Misuse of the former is as much a symptom as a cause of the latter.
Indeed, the culture in which our children are raised is increasingly a culture
of presentation, a corporate culture in which appearance is often more important than reality. In contemporary political discourse, the bar has also
been lowered. Use of rhetorical devices at the expense of cogent° argument
regularly goes without notice. But it is precisely because standards of intellectual rigor outside the educational sphere have fallen that educators must
attend to how we use, and when we introduce, software that has been designed to simplify the organization and processing of information.

In *The Cognitive Style of PowerPoint* (Graphics Press, 2003), Edward R. 17
Tufte suggests that PowerPoint equates bulleting with clear thinking. It does
not teach students to begin a discussion or construct a narrative. It encourages presentation, not conversation. Of course, in the hands of a master
teacher, a PowerPoint presentation with few words and powerful images can
serve as the jumping-off point for a brilliant lecture. But in the hands of
elementary-school students, often introduced to PowerPoint in the third
grade, and often infatuated with its swooshing sounds, animated icons, and
flashing text, a slide show is more likely to close down debate than open it up.

Developed to serve the needs of the corporate boardroom, the software 18
is designed to convey absolute authority. Teachers used to tell students that
clear exposition depended on clear outlining, but presentation software has
fetishized° the outline at the expense of the content.

Narrative, the exposition of content, takes time. PowerPoint, like so 19
much in the computer culture, speeds up the pace.

Word Processing versus Thinking

The catalog for the Vermont Country Store advertises a manual typewriter, 20
which the advertising copy says "moves at a pace that allows time to compose
your thoughts." As many of us know, it is possible to manipulate text on

---

aesthetic: Conception of beauty.   **cogent:** Logical.   **fetishized:** Turned into an object of irrational devotion.

a computer screen and see how it looks faster than we can think about what the words mean.

Word processing has its own complex psychology. From a pedagogical 21 point of view, it can make dedicated students into better writers because it allows them to revise text, rearrange paragraphs, and experiment with the tone and shape of an essay. Few professional writers would part with their computers; some claim that they simply cannot think without their hands on the keyboard. Yet the ability to quickly fill the page, to see it before you can think it, can make bad writers even worse.

A seventh grader once told me that the typewriter she found in her 22 mother's attic is "cool because you have to type each letter by itself. You have to know what you are doing in advance or it comes out a mess." The idea of thinking ahead has become exotic.

Taking Things at Interface Value

We expect software to be easy to use, and we assume that we don't have to 23 know how a computer works. In the early 1980s, most computer users who spoke of transparency meant that, as with any other machine, you could "open the hood" and poke around. But only a few years later, Macintosh users began to use the term when they talked about seeing their documents and programs represented by attractive and easy-to-interpret icons. They were referring to an ability to make things work without needing to go below the screen surface. Paradoxically, it was the screen's opacity that permitted that kind of transparency. Today, when people say that something is transparent, they mean that they can see how to make it work, not that they know how it works. In other words, transparency means epistemic opacity.

The people who built or bought the first generation of personal com- 24 puters understood them down to the bits and bytes. The next generation of operating systems were more complex, but they still invited that old-time reductive understanding. Contemporary information technology encourages different habits of mind. Today's college students are already used to taking things at (inter)face value; their successors in 2014 will be even less accustomed to probing below the surface.

Simulation and Its Discontents

Some thinkers argue that the new opacity is empowering, enabling anyone 25 to use the most sophisticated technological tools and to experiment with simulation in complex and creative ways. But it is also true that our tools carry the message that they are beyond our understanding. It is possible that in daily life, epistemic opacity can lead to passivity.

I first became aware of that possibility in the early 1990s, when the first 26 generation of complex simulation games were introduced and immediately became popular for home as well as school use. SimLife teaches the principles of evolution by getting children involved in the development of complex ecosystems; in that sense it is an extraordinary learning tool. During one session in which I played SimLife with Tim, a thirteen-year-old, the screen before us flashed a message: "Your orgot is being eaten up." "What's an orgot?" I asked. Tim didn't know. "I just ignore that," he said confidently. "You don't need to know that kind of stuff to play."

For me, that story serves as a cautionary tale. Computer simulations en- 27 able their users to think about complex phenomena as dynamic, evolving systems. But they also accustom us to manipulating systems whose core assumptions we may not understand and that may not be true.

We live in a culture of simulation. Our games, our economic and politi- 28 cal systems, and the ways architects design buildings, chemists envisage molecules, and surgeons perform operations all use simulation technology. In ten years the degree to which simulations are embedded in every area of life will have increased exponentially. We need to develop a new form of media literacy: readership skills for the culture of simulation.

We come to written text with habits of readership based on centuries of 29 civilization. At the very least, we have learned to begin with the journalist's traditional questions: who, what, when, where, why, and how. Who wrote these words, what is their message, why were they written, and how are they situated in time and place, politically and socially? A central project for higher education during the next ten years should be creating programs in information-technology literacy, with the goal of teaching students to interrogate simulations in much the same spirit, challenging their built-in assumptions.

Despite the ever-increasing complexity of software, most computer envi- 30 ronments put users in worlds based on constrained choices. In other words, immersion in programmed worlds puts us in reassuring environments where the rules are clear. For example, when you play a video game, you often go through a series of frightening situations that you escape by mastering the rules — you experience life as a reassuring dichotomy° of scary and safe. Children grow up in a culture of video games, action films, fantasy epics, and computer programs that all rely on that familiar scenario of almost losing but then regaining total mastery: there is danger. It is mastered. A still-more-powerful monster appears. It is subdued. Scary. Safe.

Yet in the real world, we have never had a greater need to work our way 31 out of binary° assumptions. In the decade ahead, we need to rebuild the culture around information technology. In that new sociotechnical culture, assumptions about the nature of mastery would be less absolute. The new culture would make it easier, not more difficult, to consider life in shades of gray, to see moral dilemmas in terms other than a battle between Good and Evil. For never has our world been more complex, hybridized, and global. Never have we so needed to have many contradictory thoughts and feelings at the same time. Our tools must help us accomplish that, not fight against us.

Information technology is identity technology. Embedding it in a cul- 32 ture that supports democracy, freedom of expression, tolerance, diversity,

dichotomy: Division into two opposite groups.   **binary:** Marked by two parts.

and complexity of opinion is one of the next decade's greatest challenges. We cannot afford to fail.

When I first began studying the computer culture, a small breed of   33 highly trained technologists thought of themselves as "computer people." That is no longer the case. If we take the computer as a carrier of a way of knowing, a way of seeing the world and our place in it, we are all computer people now.

Questions to Start You Thinking

1. CONSIDERING MEANING: In your own words, explain the six major ways in which Turkle says that computers are changing the way people think. Why does she think it is important that we pay attention to these changes?

2. IDENTIFYING WRITING STRATEGIES: Why do you think Turkle presents the six areas of change in the order that she does? Does there seem to be a logic behind this order?

3. READING CRITICALLY: How clearly does Turkle establish causes and effects in this selection? Do you find her arguments convincing? Why or why not?

4. EXPANDING VOCABULARY: Reread paragraph 23, in which Turkle writes about the fact that most computer users have little understanding of how computers work. Define *transparency*, *epistemic*, and *opacity*, and explain what Turkle means at the end of this paragraph when she says that "transparency means epistemic opacity."

5. MAKING CONNECTIONS: How might Turkle respond to David Gelernter's arguments in "Computers Cannot Teach Children Basic Skills" (pp. 536–38)? How might Gelernter respond to Turkle? Explain whether the two are basically in agreement or disagreement.

Link to the Paired Essay

In paragraph 32, Turkle writes, "Information technology is identity technology. Embedding it in a culture that supports democracy, freedom of expression, tolerance, diversity, and complexity of opinion is one of the next decade's greatest challenges." In "MySpace or OurSpace?" (pp. 546–51), Alex Koppelman deals with a similar theme. Nevertheless, these essays differ in many ways. Compare and contrast the two writers' purposes, audiences, and writing styles, pointing to specific passages in each essay to support your opinion.

Journal Prompts

1. Choose one of the changes Turkle writes about here, and explore your own thoughts about it. Do you essentially agree with Turkle? Why or why not?

2. To what extent do you rely on computers in your daily life? How would your life be different without computers?

Suggestions for Writing

1. What are some possible negative effects of people's reliance on computers? Drawing on your own observations, write an essay in which you explore a cause-and-effect relationship between computer use and some particular human behavior or ways of thinking.

2. In paragraph 31, Turkle writes, "Never has our world been more complex, hybridized, and global. Never have we so needed to have many contradictory thoughts and feelings at the same time." What would you point to as some of the important challenges the world faces over, say, the next fifty years? Write an essay in which you identify several challenges and discuss the extent to which computer technology might contribute to solving them or to making them worse. Consult outside sources to support your position.

For more on supporting a position with sources, see Ch. 12. For more on finding and documenting sources, see the Quick Research Guide (the dark-red-edged pages).

Chapter 27
Education

Responding to an Image

At first glance, this cartoon may appear to be about nothing more than a school basketball game. However, a closer look reveals a deeper message. Why does the scene include two scoreboards? How does the composition of the image guide a viewer's eye to them? What does the cartoon suggest about the role of sports in today's schools, the relationship between sports and academics, or the standards for evaluating athletes and other students? Could the cartoon also be making a comment about standardized testing? Write a brief editorial that might accompany this cartoon.

The educational system is facing many challenges, two of which are highlighted in this cartoon — the role of sports in education and standardized testing. Conduct your own investigation into these and other challenges by visiting Education Week on the Web <www.edweek.org/context/topics/> or the National Education Association home page <www.nea.org/>. Which of the issues highlighted on these Web sites do you consider the most important and deserving of immediate attention? Why? Use the Internet to find at least one other reliable source of information on this topic. Be able to explain how you found your source and which criteria you used to evaluate its reliability and usefulness.

■ For Web reading activities linked to this chapter, visit <bedfordstmartins.com/ bedguide> and do a key-word search:

🔍 reading

Tamara Draut
What's a Diploma Worth, Anyway?

Tamara Draut *holds an MPA from Columbia University and a BSJ from Ohio University. As the director of the Economic Opportunity Program at Demos, a policy-research organization in New York City, Draut is currently studying the challenges faced by low- and middle-income households struggling to pay off debt and work their way into the middle class. She is the coauthor of several Demos reports, including "Millions to the Middle: Three Strategies to Grow the Middle Class," "Retiring in the Red: The Growth of Debt among Older Americans," and "Borrowing to Make Ends Meet: The Growth of Credit Card Debt in the '90s." She recently published the book* Strapped: Why America's 20- and 30-Somethings Can't Get Ahead *(2006). Draut's research has been cited in many newspapers and magazines, and she has appeared as a commentator on television news shows. "What's a Diploma Worth, Anyway?" first appeared on the Web site TomPaine.com on September 5, 2006, and it was later reposted on Alternet.org. In this piece, Draut offers a dismal answer to the question that she poses in the essay's title. In today's economy, she claims, a bachelor's degree doesn't mean what it used to.*

AS YOU READ: *Identify Draut's three main concerns regarding the economic situation of college graduates today.*

■ For more about Tamara Draut, visit <bedfordstmartins.com/ bedguide> and do a key-word search:

🔍 author

Go to college. Work hard. Save money. For the baby-boom generation, 1 this mantra was considered the tried-and-true recipe for getting ahead in America. If you're a parent of a twenty-something today, chances are you gave this advice to your own kids as they emerged from teen-hood into adulthood.

And indeed, a generation ago, most people found that if they followed 2 these three rules, they'd earn a spot under the security blanket of America's middle class. But as one famous boomer said so eloquently, "the times, they are a-changin'."

The recently released *2006 Economic Report of the President* reported that 3 earnings for workers with college degrees declined between 2000 and 2004 — yet another thread of evidence in a growing mound that for those just starting out, the golden rules are no longer so golden.

Getting a bachelor's degree is the required ticket for entry into the 4 middle class today, but the security once implied in that status is gone. In addition to the exigencies° now felt by middle-class Americans of all ages — rising health-care costs, soaring home prices, and flat or falling incomes — today's new generation of college grads bear an added vulnerability of massive debt.

"Middle class" for a college-educated twenty- or thirty-something today 5 means carrying five-figure student-loan debt. Two-thirds of college graduates borrow money to help pay for school, putting them $20,000 in the red on average. At current interest rates for federal student loans of 6.8 percent, that amounts to a $230 monthly payment for the next ten years. And for those trying to buy more security with an advanced degree — just try getting ahead without one — leaves today's aspiring professionals with a combined student loan debt of $46,900 on average.

So, what about hard work? Surely young workers who put their nose to 6 the grindstone can earn enough to pay off those debts and earn their way to economic security. They are certainly trying. According to one study, Generation X — those now twenty-five to forty years old, work nearly three hours more per week than did young baby boomers in 1977. But those extra work hours aren't adding up to enough additional earnings to counter the effect of student-loan debts. Compared to 1980, the median earnings for a young worker aged twenty-five to thirty-four with a bachelor's degree or higher were only 6.6 percent higher in 2004. During the same time period, student-loan debt has more than doubled.

Even if student-loan debt hadn't risen, young workers would still find 7 getting ahead to be harder today than it was for the previous generation. Remember that the bulk of today's under-thirty-four crowd entered the labor force during the 1990s — the culmination of America's post-industrial transition. By the beginning of the 1990s, the rules of the game had been totally rewritten. Wall Street investors pushed short-term profits over long-term stability. Global competition created new pressures for companies to cut costs. The new economy had found its sea legs. Gen Xers became the first group of young adults faced with building their lives in this volatile° new economy.

A generation ago, the labor market was like an escalator: productivity 8 went up and so did wages. So young workers back then experienced a steady and swift progression in earnings. Today's labor market is like an automated airport walkway: the economy grows faster, but wages remain flat.

Now, the hardest nut for Americans of all ages: savings. Over the last 9 twenty years, our nation's personal saving rate has plummeted from about 8

---

exigencies: Urgent demands.   **volatile:** Characterized by unexpected change.

percent through the 1980s and early 1990s to zero (actually negative) today. These figures are just for run-of-mill savings. How are young people doing with other types of saving, like retirement? Forty percent of people under age thirty-five had a retirement account in 2004, with $11,000 in holdings on average.

The living standards of America's college graduates, particularly those 10 under thirty-five, are declining. Of course, lesser-educated Americans experienced this painful reality much sooner, and much more dramatically. But now that all three main pillars of American success — education, hard work, and savings — show signs of serious weakness, we're running out of options. Young people are enrolling in college in record numbers, working longer hours, and doing their best to save for retirement. Yet, in all likelihood, this will be the first generation to not surpass their parents' standard of living.

America's declining economic future didn't just happen. Like global 11 warming, we've arrived at this point because for too long our leaders refused to acknowledge the problem, or made policy decisions that helped get us here. Recognizing this is now our only option.

Questions to Start You Thinking

1. CONSIDERING MEANING: According to Draut, why are today's college graduates less well-off than previous generations?

2. IDENTIFYING WRITING STRATEGIES: How does Draut's opening paragraph forecast the organization of her essay? What are the essay's three main parts? Where does each begin, and how does Draut signal the beginning of each section? Do you find her organization effective?

3. READING CRITICALLY: In paragraph 10, Draut writes that the "living standards of America's college graduates, particularly those under thirty-five, are declining." Has she presented enough evidence to convince you of this? Why or why not?

4. EXPANDING VOCABULARY: In paragraph 1, Draut refers to the "baby-boom generation." What is this generation, and how did it get its name?

5. MAKING CONNECTIONS: In "The Right to Fail" (pp. 567–70), first published in 1970, William Zinsser offers a different take on the relative value of a college education. How do his views differ from Draut's, and what might account for these differences? What do you suppose Draut would think of Zinsser's argument?

Journal Prompts

1. What are your reasons for being in college? How do your criteria for evaluating the value of your education resemble or differ from Draut's?

2. Where do you see yourself after you finish your college degree? Describe what you hope your life will be like five to ten years from now.

Suggestions for Writing

1. Write an essay of your own titled "What's a Diploma Worth, Anyway?" Drawing on your own experience, explain what a college diploma means to you.

2. Do some research about the baby-boom generation and Generation X. Drawing on outside sources as well as interviews with people you know, write an essay in which you compare and contrast the two generations in terms of their general values, goals, economic and social situations, and any other characteristics that interest you.

Susan Brady Konig
They've Got to Be Carefully Taught

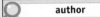

For more about Susan Brady Konig, visit \<bedfordstmartins.com/bedguide> and do a keyword search:

author

Susan Brady Konig *was born in 1951 in Paris, France, and grew up in New York City, where she now lives with her husband and four children. After graduating from Georgetown University, Konig worked at the* Washington Post *as an assistant to the Style section's fashion editor. She later became an editor for* Seventeen *magazine and a regular columnist for the* New York Post. *Konig currently writes about everything from pop culture to parenting to politics for* National Review Online *and* Catholic Digest, *and her writing also has appeared in such publications as* Ladies' Home Journal, Travel & Leisure, Us, *and* Parade. *Her first book,* Why Animals Sleep So Close to the Road (and Other Lies I Tell My Children), *was published in 2005. In "They've Got to Be Carefully Taught," an event at her daughter's preschool prompts Konig to question the emphasis that many schools place on teaching cultural diversity. The essay originally appeared in the* National Review *in 1997.*

AS YOU READ: *Note how the preschoolers respond to the cultural diversity activities that Konig describes.*

At my daughter's preschool it's time for all the children to learn that they are different from one another. Even though these kids are at that remarkable age when they are thoroughly color blind, their teachers are spending a month emphasizing race, color, and background. The little tots are being taught in no uncertain terms that their hair is different, their skin is different, and their parents come from different places. It's Cultural Diversity Month.

I hadn't really given much thought to the ethnic and national backgrounds of Sarah's classmates. I can guarantee that Sarah, being two and a half, gave the subject absolutely no thought. Her teachers, however, had apparently given it quite a lot of thought. They sent a letter asking each parent to contribute to the cultural-awareness effort by "providing any information and/or material regarding your family's cultural background. For example:

favorite recipe or song." All well and good, unless your culture isn't diverse enough.

The next day I take Sarah to school and her teacher, Miss Laura, anxious 3 to get this Cultural Diversity show on the road, begins the interrogation.

"Where are you and your husband from?" she cheerily demands.   4

"We're Americans," I reply — less, I must confess, out of patriotism than 5 from sheer lack of coffee. It was barely 9:00 A.M.

"Yes, of course, but where are you from?" I'm beginning to feel like a 6 nightclub patron being badgered by a no-talent stand-up comic.

"We're native New Yorkers."   7

"But where are your people from?"   8

"Well," I dive in with a sigh, "my family is originally Irish on both sides. 9 My husband's father was from Czechoslovakia and his mother is from the Bronx, but her grandparents were from the Ukraine."

"Can you cook Irish?"   10

"I could bring in potatoes and beer for the whole class."   11

Miss Laura doesn't get it.   12

"Look," I say, "we're Americans. Our kids are Americans. We tell them 13 about American history and George Washington and apple pie and all that stuff. If you want me to do something American, I can do that."

She is decidedly unexcited.   14

A few days later, she tells me that she was trying to explain to Sarah that 15 her dad is from Ireland.

"Wrong," I say, "but go on."   16

"He's not from Ireland?"   17

"No," I sigh. "He's from Queens. I'm from Ireland. I mean I'm Irish — 18 that is, my great-grandparents were. Don't get me wrong, I'm proud of my heritage — but that's entirely beside the point. I told you we tell Sarah she's American."

"Well, anyway," she smiles, "Sarah thinks her Daddy's from *Iceland!* Isn't 19 that cute?"

Later in the month, Miss Laura admits that her class is not quite getting 20 the whole skin-color thing. "I tried to show them how we all have different skin," she chuckled. Apparently, little Henry is the only one who successfully grasped the concept. He now runs around the classroom announcing to anyone who'll listen, "I'm white!" Miss Laura asked the children what color her own skin was. (She is a light-skinned Hispanic, which would make her skin color . . . what? Caramel? Mochaccino?) The kids opted for purple or orange. "They looked at me like I was crazy!" Miss Laura said. I just smile.

The culmination of Cultural Diversity Month, the day when the parents 21 come into class and join their children in a glorious celebration of multicultural disparity,° has arrived. As I arrive I see a large collage on the wall depicting the earth, with all the children's names placed next to the country they are from. Next to my daughter's name it says "Ireland." I politely remind

disparity: Difference.

Miss Laura that Sarah is, in fact, from America and suggest that, by insisting otherwise, she is confusing my daughter. She reluctantly changes Sarah's affiliation to USA. It will be the only one of its kind on the wall.

The mom from Brazil brings in a bunch of great music, and the whole   22
class is doing the samba and running around in a conga line. It's very cute. Then I get up to teach the children an indigenous folk tune from the culture of Sarah's people, passed down through the generations from her grandparents to her parents and now to Sarah — a song called "Take Me Out to the Ballgame." First I explain to the kids that Sarah was born right here in New York — and that's in what country, Sarah? Sarah looks at me and says, "France." I look at Miss Laura, who just shrugs.

I stand there in my baseball cap and sing my song. The teacher tries to   23
rush me off. I say, "Don't you want them to learn it?" They took long enough learning to samba! I am granted permission to sing it one more time. The kids join in on the "root, root, root" and the "1, 2, 3 strikes you're out," but they can see their teacher isn't enthusiastic.

So now these sweet, innocent babies who thought they were all the   24
same are becoming culturally aware. Two little girls are touching each other's hair and saying, "Your hair is blonde, just like mine." Off to one side a little dark-haired girl stands alone, excluded. She looks confused as to what to do next. She knows she's not blonde. Sure, all children notice these things eventually, but, thanks to the concerted efforts of their teachers, these two- and three-year-olds are talking about things that separate rather than connect.

And Sarah only knows what she has been taught: Little Henry is white,   25
her daddy's from Iceland, and New York's in France.

Questions to Start You Thinking

1. CONSIDERING MEANING: What does Konig suggest are the consequences of introducing ideas of race, color, and national background to young children?

2. IDENTIFYING WRITING STRATEGIES: How does Konig go about drawing Miss Laura as a character? What impression does she create of her?

3. READING CRITICALLY: This essay originally appeared in the *National Review,* a politically conservative magazine of news and commentary. How do you think the majority of the magazine's readers would have responded to the essay?

4. EXPANDING VOCABULARY: Define *indigenous.* In paragraph 22, Konig writes about teaching the children "an indigenous folk tune," which turns out to be "Take Me Out to the Ballgame." In what sense is her use of the word *indigenous* ironic?

5. MAKING CONNECTIONS: Amy Tan ("Mother Tongue," pp. 445–50) and Richard Rodriguez ("Public and Private Language," pp. 571–76) also write about issues of ethnicity and education. How might Konig react to their observations? How might students be introduced to matters of cultural difference without contributing to a sense of separateness?

Journal Prompts

1. How was the subject of cultural diversity treated in your early education? How did you respond?

2. Konig writes in the first paragraph that young children are "color blind." Later in the essay, she says that "all children notice [differences in race and so forth] eventually" (paragraph 24). What are your earliest memories of recognizing racial and ethnic differences?

Suggestions for Writing

1. Write an essay recalling a classroom experience that you feel had more negative results than positive ones for you and your classmates. Like Konig, be sure to bring the classroom experience to life with specific details.

2. Konig makes a point of referring to her family as "Americans." Is there a difference in being "American" and in being "Hispanic American" or "Asian American" or "African American" or "Native American"? Write an essay in which you explore your own responses to such labels. Why might some ethnic Americans prefer simply to be called "Americans"? Conversely, why might some prefer the more specific term that indicates their heritage? What do you see as positive and negative consequences of such labeling?

William Zinsser
The Right to Fail

William Zinsser *was born in New York City in 1922. After receiving his BA from Princeton University in 1944, he worked as a feature writer for the* New York Herald Tribune *and later became the newspaper's drama and film critic. Zinsser has written numerous books and contributed articles to magazines including* Life, *the* New Yorker, *and the* Atlantic. *Although he has covered subjects ranging from American landmarks to jazz, he is probably best known for his classic guides to writing:* On Writing Well *(1976),* Writing with a Word Processor *(1983),* Inventing the Truth *(1987),* Writing to Learn *(1988), and* Writing about Your Life *(2004). Zinsser has taught humor and nonfiction writing at Yale University, and he currently teaches at the New School University and the Columbia University Graduate School of Journalism in New York City. In "The Right to Fail," an excerpt from* The Lunacy Boom *(1970), Zinsser makes the case that failure is an important aspect of human experience.*

AS YOU READ: *Identify the benefits of failure that Zinsser presents.*

■ For more about William Zinsser, visit <bedfordstmartins.com/ bedguide> and do a keyword search:

🔍 author

I like "dropout" as an addition to the American language because it's brief and it's clear. What I don't like is that we use it almost entirely as a dirty word.

We only apply it to people under twenty-one. Yet an adult who spends 2
his days and nights watching mindless TV programs is more of a dropout
than an eighteen-year-old who quits college, with its frequently mindless
courses, to become, say, a VISTA volunteer. For the young, dropping out is
often a way of dropping in.

To hold this opinion, however, is little short of treason in America. A boy 3
or girl who leaves college is branded a failure — and the right to fail is one of
the few freedoms that this country does not grant its citizens. The American
dream is a dream of "getting ahead," painted in strokes of gold wherever we
look. Our advertisements and TV commercials are a hymn to material success, our magazine articles a toast to people who made it to the top. Smoke
the right cigarette or drive the right car — so the ads imply — and girls will be
swooning into your deodorized arms or caressing your expensive lapels. Happiness goes to the man who has the sweet smell of achievement. He is our
national idol, and everybody else is our national fink.°

I want to put in a word for the fink, especially the teen-age fink, because 4
if we give him time to get through his finkdom — if we release him from the
pressure of attaining certain goals by a certain age — he has a good chance of
becoming our national idol, a Jefferson° or a Thoreau,° a Buckminster
Fuller° or an Adlai Stevenson,° a man with a mind of his own. We need
mavericks° and dissenters and dreamers far more than we need junior vice
presidents, but we paralyze them by insisting that every step be a step up to
the next rung of the ladder. Yet in the fluid years of youth, the only way for
boys and girls to find their proper road is often to take a hundred side trips,
poking out in different directions, faltering, drawing back, and starting again.

"But what if we fail?" they ask, whispering the dreadful word across the 5
Generation Gap to their parents, who are back home at the Establishment,
nursing their "middle-class values" and cultivating their "goal-oriented society." The parents whisper back: "Don't!"

What they should say is "Don't be afraid to fail!" Failure isn't fatal. 6
Countless people have had a bout with it and come out stronger as a result.
Many have even come out famous. History is strewn with eminent dropouts,
"loners" who followed their own trail, not worrying about its odd twists and
turns because they had faith in their own sense of direction. To read their bi-
ographies is always exhilarating, not only because they beat the system, but
because their system was better than the one that they beat.

Luckily, such rebels still turn up often enough to prove that individual- 7
ism, though badly threatened, is not extinct. Much has been written, for in-

---

fink: Tattletale or other contemptible person.   **Jefferson:** Thomas Jefferson
(1743–1826), the third president of the United States and the main author of the Decla-
ration of Independence.   **Thoreau:** Henry David Thoreau (1817–1862), an American
writer and naturalist.   **Buckminster Fuller:** American inventor, architect, and engineer
(1895–1983) who dropped out of Harvard to work on solving global resource and environmental problems.   **Adlai Stevenson:** American politician (1900–1965) who was
greatly admired for championing liberal causes but badly lost two presidential elections.
mavericks: Nonconformists.

stance, about the fitful scholastic career of Thomas P. F. Hoving, New York's former Parks Commissioner and now director of the Metropolitan Museum of Art. Hoving was a dropout's dropout, entering and leaving schools as if they were motels, often at the request of the management. Still, he must have learned something during those unorthodox years, for he dropped in again at the top of his profession.

His case reminds me of another boyhood—that of Holden Caulfield in   8
J. D. Salinger's *The Catcher in the Rye*, the most popular literary hero of the postwar period. There is nothing accidental about the grip that this dropout continues to hold on the affections of an entire American generation. Nobody else, real or invented, has made such an engaging shambles of our "goal-oriented society," so gratified our secret belief that the "phonies" are in power and the good guys up the creek. Whether Holden has also reached the top of his chosen field today is one of those speculations that delight fanciers of good fiction. I speculate that he has. Holden Caulfield, incidentally, is now thirty-six.

I'm not urging everyone to go out and fail just for the sheer therapy   9
of it, or to quit college just to coddle° some vague discontent. Obviously it's better to succeed than to flop, and in general a long education is more helpful than a short one. (Thanks to my own education, for example, I can tell George Eliot from T. S. Eliot. I can handle the pluperfect tense in French, and I know that Caesar beat the Helvetii because he had enough frumentum.°) I only mean that failure isn't bad in itself, or success automatically good.

Fred Zinnemann, who has directed some of Hollywood's most honored   10
movies, was asked by a reporter, when *A Man for All Seasons* won every prize, about his previous film *Behold a Pale Horse*, which was a box-office disaster. "I don't feel any obligation to be successful," Zinnemann replied. "Success can be dangerous—you feel you know it all. I've learned a great deal from my failures." A similar point was made by Richard Brooks about his ambitious money loser, *Lord Jim*. Recalling the three years of his life that went into it, talking almost with elation about the troubles that befell his unit in Cambodia, Brooks told me that he learned more about his craft from this considerable failure than from his many earlier hits.

It's a point, of course, that applies throughout the arts. Writers, play-   11
wrights, painters, and composers work in the expectation of periodic defeat, but they wouldn't keep going back into the arena if they thought it was the end of the world. It isn't the end of the world. For an artist—and perhaps for anybody—it is the only way to grow.

Today's younger generation seems to know that this is true, seems will-   12
ing to take the risks in life that artists take in art. "Society," needlessly to say, still has the upper hand—it sets the goals and condemns as a failure everybody who won't play. But the dropouts and the hippies are not as afraid of failure as their parents and grandparents. This could mean, as their elders

---

coddle: Indulge; satisfy.   **frumentum:** Latin word for corn or grain.

might say, that they are just plumb lazy, secure in the comforts of an affluent state. It could also mean, however, that they just don't buy the old standards of success and are rapidly writing new ones.

Recently it was announced, for instance, that more than two hundred   13
thousand Americans have inquired about service in VISTA (the domestic
Peace Corps) and that, according to a Gallup survey, "more than three million American college students would serve VISTA in some capacity if given
the opportunity." This is hardly the road to riches or to an executive suite.
Yet I have met many of these young volunteers, and they are not pining
for traditional success. On the contrary, they appear more fulfilled than the
average vice president with a swimming pool.

Who is to say, then, if there is any right path to the top, or even to say   14
what the top consists of? Obviously the colleges don't have more than a partial answer — otherwise the young would not be so disaffected with an education that they consider vapid.° Obviously business does not have the
answer — otherwise the young would not be so scornful of its call to be an
organization man.

The fact is, nobody has the answer, and the dawning awareness of this   15
fact seems to me one of the best things happening in America today. Success
and failure are again becoming individual visions, as they were when the
country was younger, not rigid categories. Maybe we are learning again to
cherish this right of every person to succeed on his own terms and to fail as
often as necessary along the way.

Questions to Start You Thinking

1. CONSIDERING MEANING: What does Zinsser mean when he says that "dropping out is often a way of dropping in" (paragraph 2)? Why is this especially true for young adults?

2. IDENTIFYING WRITING STRATEGIES: Identify some of the concrete examples
   that Zinsser uses to illustrate his points. Are his examples extensive and varied enough to be convincing? Why or why not?

3. READING CRITICALLY: Zinsser is savvy enough to admit that his position is
   "little short of treason in America" (paragraph 3). Where else does he acknowledge that his advice might seem outlandish? How does he counter
   the opposition?

4. EXPANDING VOCABULARY: In paragraph 3, Zinsser writes, "Our advertisements and TV commercials are a hymn to material success." Define *hymn*.
   What does the word suggest about the American attitude toward material
   success? How does Zinsser feel about the American dream?

5. MAKING CONNECTIONS: If Carl T. Rowan ("Unforgettable Miss Bessie,"
   pp. 580–83) were to write a journal response to Zinsser's essay, what do you
   think he would write? How, suggests Rowan, is school success important in
   ways perhaps not considered by Zinsser?

vapid: Dull.

Journal Prompts

1. What is your definition of the "American dream" (paragraph 3)?
2. Who would you like to share Zinsser's essay with in order to open up that person's mind about failure? Why?

Suggestions for Writing

1. In paragraph 10, Zinsser offers the following quote from a movie director: "Success can be dangerous — you feel you know it all. I've learned a great deal from my failures." Write an essay in which you recall a personal experience that illustrates this statement.
2. Originally written in 1970, Zinsser's essay includes some examples that may not be familiar to you. Write an essay that supports and updates Zinsser's position by drawing on more current examples from history, literature, sports, current events, or popular culture. Imagine a specific audience for your essay (perhaps a sibling, a friend, or a high school class), and be sure that your examples will have an impact on those readers.

Richard Rodriguez
Public and Private Language

Richard Rodriguez, *the son of Spanish-speaking Mexican American parents, was born in 1944 and grew up in San Francisco, where he currently lives. He earned a BA at Stanford University and received graduate degrees in English from Columbia University and the University of California at Berkeley. A full-time writer and lecturer, Rodriguez is an editor at Pacific News Service and has served as a contributing editor for* Harper's Magazine, U.S. News & World Report, *and the Sunday "Opinion" section of the* Los Angeles Times. *His work has appeared in numerous publications including the* New York Times, *the* Wall Street Journal, *the* American Scholar, Time, Mother Jones, *and the* New Republic, *and he is a regular contributor to PBS's* News Hour with Jim Lehrer. *His books, which often draw on autobiography to explore race and ethnicity in American society, include* Hunger of Memory *(1982), from which the following selection is drawn,* Days of Obligation: An Argument with My Mexican Father *(1992), and* Brown: The Last Discovery of America *(2002). In "Public and Private Language," he recounts the origin of his complex views of bilingual education.*

AS YOU READ: *Discover the ways in which learning English changed Rodriguez's life and his relationship with his family.*

For more about Richard Rodriguez, visit <bedfordstmartins.com/bedguide> and do a keyword search:

> author

S upporters of bilingual education today imply that students like me miss   1
a great deal by not being taught in their family's language. What they seem not to recognize is that, as a socially disadvantaged child, I considered

Spanish to be a private language. What I needed to learn in school was that I had the right—and the obligation—to speak the public language of *los gringos.*° The odd truth is that my first-grade classmates could have become bilingual, in the conventional sense of that word, more easily than I. Had they been taught (as upper-middle-class children are often taught early) a second language like Spanish or French, they could have regarded it simply as that: another public language. In my case such bilingualism could not have been so quickly achieved. What I did not believe was that I could speak a single public language.

Without question, it would have pleased me to hear my teachers address me in Spanish when I entered the classroom. I would have felt much less afraid. I would have trusted them and responded with ease. But I would have delayed—for how long postponed?—having to learn the language of public society. I would have evaded—and for how long could I have afforded to delay?—learning the great lesson of school, that I had a public identity. 2

Fortunately, my teachers were unsentimental about their responsibility. What they understood was that I needed to speak a public language. So their voices would search me out, asking me questions. Each time I'd hear them, I'd look up in surprise to see a nun's face frowning at me. I'd mumble, not really meaning to answer. The nun would persist, "Richard, stand up. Don't look at the floor. Speak up. Speak to the entire class, not just to me!" but I couldn't believe that the English language was mine to use. (In part, I did not want to believe it.) I continued to mumble. I resisted the teacher's demands. (Did I somehow suspect that once I learned public language my pleasing family life would be changed?) Silent, waiting for the bell to sound, I remained dazed, diffident,° afraid. 3

Because I wrongly imagined that English was intrinsically° a public language and Spanish an intrinsically private one, I easily noticed the difference between classroom language and the language of home. At school, words were directed to a general audience of listeners. ("Boys and girls. . . .") Words were meaningfully ordered. And the point was not self-expression alone but to make oneself understood by many others. The teacher quizzed: "Boys and girls, why do we use that word in this sentence? Could we think of a better word to use there? Would the sentence change its meaning if the words were differently arranged? And wasn't there a better way of saying much the same thing?" (I couldn't say. I wouldn't try to say.) 4

Three months. Five. Half a year passed. Unsmiling, ever watchful, my teachers noted my silence. They began to connect my behavior with the difficult progress my older sister and brother were making. Until one Saturday morning three nuns arrived at the house to talk to our parents. Stiffly, they sat on the blue living room sofa. From the doorway of another room, spying 5

---

los gringos: Spanish for "foreigner," often used as a derogatory term for English-speaking Americans.   **diffident:** Shy.   **intrinsically:** Essentially; inherently.

the visitors, I noted the incongruity° — the clash of two worlds, the faces and voices of school intruding upon the familiar setting of home. I over-heard one voice gently wondering, "Do your children speak only Spanish at home, Mrs. Rodriguez?" While another voice added, "That Richard especially seems so timid and shy."

That Rich-heard!   6

With great tact the visitors continued, "Is it possible for you and your 7 husband to encourage your children to practice their English when they are home?" Of course, my parents complied. What would they not do for their children's well-being? And how could they have questioned the Church's authority which those women represented? In an instant, they agreed to give up the language (the sounds) that had revealed and accentuated our family's closeness. The moment after the visitors left, the change was observed. *"Ahora,*° speak to us *en inglés,"*° my father and mother united to tell us.

At first, it seemed a kind of game. After dinner each night, the family 8 gathered to practice "our" English. (It was still then *inglés,* a language foreign to us, so we felt drawn as strangers to it.) Laughing, we would try to define words we could not pronounce. We played with strange English sounds, often overanglicizing our pronunciations. And we filled the smiling gaps of our sentences with familiar Spanish sounds. But that was cheating, somebody shouted. Everyone laughed. In school, meanwhile, like my brother and sister, I was required to attend a daily tutoring session. I needed a full year of special attention. I also needed my teachers to keep my attention from straying in class by calling out, *Rich-heard* — their English voices slowly prying loose my ties to my other name, its three notes, *Ri-car-do.* Most of all I needed to hear my mother and father speak to me in a moment of seriousness in broken — suddenly heartbreaking — English. The scene was inevitable: one Saturday morning I entered the kitchen where my parents were talking in Spanish. I did not realize that they were talking in Spanish however until, at the moment they saw me, I heard their voices change to speak English. Those *gringo* sounds they uttered startled me. Pushed me away. In that moment of trivial misunderstanding and profound insight, I felt my throat twisted by unsounded grief. I turned quickly and left the room. But I had no place to escape to with Spanish. (The spell was broken.) My brother and sisters were speaking English in another part of the house.

Again and again in the days following, increasingly angry, I was obliged 9 to hear my mother and father: "Speak to us *en inglés.*" (*Speak.*) Only then did I determine to learn classroom English. Weeks after, it happened: one day in school I had my hand raised to volunteer an answer. I spoke out in a loud voice. And I did not think it remarkable when the entire class understood. That day, I moved very far from the disadvantaged child I had been only days earlier. The belief, that calming assurance that I belonged in public, had at last taken hold.

incongruity: Lack of harmony or appropriateness.   *Ahora:* Spanish for "now."
en inglés: Spanish for "in English."

Shortly after, I stopped hearing the high and loud sounds of *los gringos*. 10
A more and more confident speaker of English, I didn't trouble to listen to
how strangers sounded, speaking to me. And there simply were too many
English-speaking people in my day for me to hear American accents anymore. Conversations quickened. Listening to persons whose voices sounded
eccentrically pitched, I usually noted their sounds for an initial few seconds
before I concentrated on *what* they were saying. Conversations became
content-full. Transparent. Hearing someone's *tone* of voice — angry or questioning or sarcastic or happy or sad — I didn't distinguish it from the words
it expressed. Sound and word were thus tightly wedded. At the end of a day,
I was often bemused, always relieved, to realize how "silent," though
crowded with words, my day in public had been. (This public silence measured and quickened the change in my life.)

At last, seven years old, I came to believe what had been technically true 11
since my birth: I was an American citizen.

But the special feeling of closeness at home was diminished by then. 12
Gone was the desperate, urgent, intense feeling of being at home; rare was
the experience of feeling myself individualized by family intimates. We remained a loving family, but one greatly changed. No longer so close; no
longer bound tight by the pleasing and troubling knowledge of our public
separateness. Neither my older brother nor sister rushed home after school
anymore. Nor did I. When I arrived home there would often be neighborhood kids in the house. Or the house would be empty of sounds.

Following the dramatic Americanization of their children, even my par- 13
ents grew more publicly confident. Especially my mother. She learned the
names of all the people on our block. And she decided we needed to have a
telephone installed in the house. My father continued to use the word *gringo*.
But it was no longer charged with the old bitterness or distrust. (Stripped of
any emotional content, the word simply became a name for those Americans not of Hispanic descent.) Hearing him, sometimes, I wasn't sure if he
was pronouncing the Spanish word *gringo* or saying gringo in English.

Matching the silence I started hearing in public was a new quiet at 14
home. The family's quiet was partly due to the fact that, as we children
learned more and more English, we shared fewer and fewer words with our
parents. Sentences needed to be spoken slowly when a child addressed his
mother or father. (Often the parent wouldn't understand.) The child would
need to repeat himself. (Still the parent misunderstood.) The young voice,
frustrated, would end up saying, "Never mind" — the subject was closed.
Dinners would be noisy with the clinking of knives and forks against dishes.
My mother would smile softly between her remarks; my father at the other
end of the table would chew and chew at his food, while he stared over the
heads of his children.

My *mother*! My *father*! After English became my primary language, I no 15
longer knew what words to use in addressing my parents. The old Spanish
words (those tender accents of sound) I had used earlier — *mamá* and *papá* —
I couldn't use anymore. They would have been all-too-painful reminders of

how much had changed in my life. On the other hand, the words I heard neighborhood kids call *their* parents seemed equally unsatisfactory. *Mother* and *Father; Ma, Papa, Pa, Dad, Pop* (how I hated the all-American sound of that last word especially) — all these terms I felt were unsuitable, not really terms of address for *my* parents. As a result, I never used them at home. Whenever I'd speak to my parents, I would try to get their attention with eye contact alone. In public conversations, I'd refer to "my parents" or "my mother and father."

My mother and father, for their part, responded differently, as their chil- 16 dren spoke to them less and less. My mother grew restless, seemed troubled and anxious at the scarcity of words exchanged in the house. It was she who would question me about my day when I came home from school. She smiled at the small talk. She pried at the edges of my sentences to get me to say something more. (What?) She'd join conversations she overheard, but her intrusions often stopped her children's talking. By contrast, my father seemed reconciled to the new quiet. Though his English improved some-what, he retired into silence. At dinner he spoke very little. One night his children and even his wife helplessly giggled at his garbled English pronun-ciation of the Catholic Grace before Meals. Thereafter he made his wife recite the prayer at the start of each meal, even on formal occasions, when there were guests in the house. Hers became the public voice of the family. On official business, it was she, not my father, one would usually hear on the phone or in stores, talking to strangers. His children grew so accustomed to his silence that, years later, they would speak routinely of his shyness. (My mother would often try to explain: both his parents died when he was eight. He was raised by an uncle who treated him like little more than a menial servant. He was never encouraged to speak. He grew up alone. A man of few words.) But my father was not shy, I realized, when I'd watch him speaking Spanish with relatives. Using Spanish, he was quickly effusive.° Es-pecially when talking with other men, his voice would spark, flicker, flare alive with sounds. In Spanish, he expressed ideas and feelings he rarely re-vealed in English. With firm Spanish sounds, he conveyed confidence and authority English would never allow him.

The silence at home, however, was finally more than a literal silence. 17 Fewer words passed between parent and child, but more profound was the silence that resulted from my inattention to sounds. At about the time I no longer bothered to listen with care to the sounds of English in public, I grew careless about listening to the sounds family members made when they spoke. Most of the time I heard someone speaking at home and didn't dis-tinguish his sounds from the words people uttered in public. I didn't even pay much attention to my parents' accented and ungrammatical speech. At least not at home. Only when I was with them in public would I grow alert to their accents. Though, even then, their sounds caused me less and less concern. For I was increasingly confident of my own public identity.

effusive: Talkative; unreserved.

Today I hear bilingual educators say that children lose a degree of "indi- 18
viduality" by becoming assimilated into public society. (Bilingual schooling
was popularized in the seventies, that decade when middle-class ethnics
began to resist the process of assimilation — the American melting pot.) But
the bilingualists simplistically scorn the value and necessity of assimilation.
They do not seem to realize that there are *two* ways a person is individualized. So they do not realize that while one suffers a diminished sense of *private* individuality by becoming assimilated into public society, such assimilation makes possible the achievement of *public* individuality.

Questions to Start You Thinking

1. CONSIDERING MEANING: What created the new "silence" in the Rodriguez
   household? Explain why.
2. IDENTIFYING WRITING STRATEGIES: How does Rodriguez use comparison and
   contrast to convey his experience learning English?
3. READING CRITICALLY: How does Rodriguez use dialogue to make the experience he recalls more vivid for his readers? Is this strategy effective in helping
   him achieve his purpose? Why or why not?
4. EXPANDING VOCABULARY: Rodriguez uses the terms *private* and *public*. What
   do these words mean when used as adjectives to describe "language" and
   "identity"?
5. MAKING CONNECTIONS: Both Rodriguez and Amy Tan ("Mother Tongue,"
   pp. 445–50) are from homes in which English was spoken as a second language. Compare and contrast how each writer's mastery of English affected
   his or her mother.

Journal Prompts

1. Recall a time when your public identity was at odds with your private self.
2. Has an accomplishment that you are proud of ever had a negative effect on
   another aspect of your life or on other people around you?

Suggestions for Writing

1. If you speak a second language, write an essay recalling your experience
   learning it. What were some of your struggles? Can you relate to Rodriguez's
   experience? How do you use that language today? If you do not know a second language, write an essay in which you analyze the possible benefits of
   learning one. What language would you like to learn? Why?
2. According to Rodriguez, "Supporters of bilingual education today imply
   that students like me miss a great deal by not being taught in their family's
   language" (paragraph 1). Rodriguez counters this assumption by showing
   how his immersion in English allowed him to develop a public identity that
   ultimately led to his success. At the same time, however, his English-only
   immersion hurt his family life. Write an essay in which you take a stand on
   the complex topic of bilingual education, using further reading and research
   to support your position about how it does or does not benefit students.

Annie Dillard
From *An American Childhood*

Annie Dillard, *born in 1945 in Pittsburgh, Pennsylvania, is an acclaimed poet and essayist known for her nature and spiritual writing. After graduating from Hollins College in Virginia, Dillard settled in the Blue Ridge Mountains to write her first volume of poetry,* Tickets for a Prayer Wheel *(1974). Her second book, a collection of essays titled* Pilgrim at Tinker Creek *(1974), won a Pulitzer Prize. Since then, Dillard has published numerous books including* Holy the Firm *(1978), a prose poem;* Living by Fiction *(1982), a book of literary criticism;* Teaching a Stone to Talk *(1982), a collection of essays;* An American Childhood *(1987), a memoir; and* The Writing Life *(1989), a volume of short meditations on the writing process. Her most recent books include* For the Time Being *(1999) and* The Maytrees: A Novel *(2007). Dillard is currently professor emeritus at Wesleyan University. In this selection from* An American Childhood, *Dillard vividly describes how viewing an amoeba through a microscope leads to a sudden epiphany that would guide her throughout her education.*

AS YOU READ: *Think about what Dillard was like as a child. What words would you use to describe her?*

■ For more about Annie Dillard, visit <bedfordstmartins.com/bedguide> and do a keyword search:

author

After I read *The Field Book of Ponds and Streams* several times, I longed for 1 a microscope. Everybody needed a microscope. Detectives used microscopes, both for the FBI and at Scotland Yard. Although usually I had to save my tiny allowance for things I wanted, that year for Christmas my parents gave me a microscope kit.

In a dark basement corner, on a white enamel table, I set up the micro- 2 scope kit. I supplied a chair, a lamp, a batch of jars, a candle, and a pile of library books. The microscope kit supplied a blunt black three-speed microscope, a booklet, a scalpel, a dropper, an ingenious device for cutting thin segments of fragile tissue, a pile of clean slides and cover slips, and a dandy array of corked test tubes.

One of the test tubes contained "hay infusion." Hay infusion was a wee 3 brown chip of grass blade. You added water to it, and after a week it became a jungle in a drop, full of one-celled animals. This did not work for me. All I saw in the microscope after a week was a wet chip of dried grass, much enlarged.

Another test tube contained "diatomaceous earth." This was, I believed, 4 an actual pinch of the white cliffs of Dover.° On my palm it was an airy, friable chalk. The booklet said it was composed of the siliceous bodies of diatoms — one-celled creatures that lived in, as it were, small glass jewelry boxes with fitted lids. Diatoms, I read, come in a variety of transparent geometrical shapes. Broken and dead and dug out of geological deposits, they made chalk, and a fine abrasive used in silver polish and toothpaste. What I

---

white cliffs of Dover: A famous British geological landmark.

saw in the microscope must have been the fine abrasive — grit enlarged. It was years before I saw a recognizable, whole diatom. The kit's diatomaceous earth was a bust.

All that winter I played with the microscope. I prepared slides from things 5 at hand, as the books suggested. I looked at the transparent membrane inside an onion's skin and saw the cell. I looked at a section of cork and saw the cells, and at scrapings from the inside of my cheek, ditto. I looked at my blood and saw not much; I looked at my urine and saw a long iridescent crystal, for the drop had dried.

All this was very well, but I wanted to see the wildlife I had read about. I 6 wanted especially to see the famous amoeba, who had eluded me. He was supposed to live in the hay infusion, but I hadn't found him there. He lived outside in warm ponds and streams, too, but I lived in Pittsburgh, and it had been a cold winter.

Finally late that spring I saw an amoeba. The week before, I had gath- 7 ered puddle water from Frick Park; it had been festering in a jar in the basement. This June night after dinner I figured I had waited long enough. In the basement at my microscope table I spread a scummy drop of Frick Park puddle water on a slide, peeked in, and lo, there was the famous amoeba. He was as blobby and grainy as his picture; I would have known him anywhere.

Before I had watched him at all, I ran upstairs. My parents were still at 8 the table, drinking coffee. They, too, could see the famous amoeba. I told them, bursting, that he was all set up, that they should hurry before his water dried. It was the chance of a lifetime.

Father had stretched out his long legs and was tilting back in his chair. 9 Mother sat with her knees crossed, in blue slacks, smoking a Chesterfield. The dessert dishes were still on the table. My sisters were nowhere in evidence. It was a warm evening; the big dining-room windows gave onto blooming rhododendrons.

Mother regarded me warmly. She gave me to understand that she was 10 glad I had found what I had been looking for, but that she and Father were happy to sit with their coffee, and would not be coming down.

She did not say, but I understood at once, that they had their pursuits 11 (coffee?) and I had mine. She did not say, but I began to understand then, that you do what you do out of your private passion for the thing itself.

I had essentially been handed my own life. In subsequent years my par- 12 ents would praise my drawings and poems, and supply me with books, art supplies, and sports equipment, and listen to my troubles and enthusiasms, and supervise my hours, and discuss and inform, but they would not get involved with my detective work, nor hear about my reading, nor inquire about my homework or term papers or exams, nor visit the salamanders I caught, nor listen to me play the piano, nor attend my field hockey games, nor fuss over my insect collection with me, or my poetry collection or stamp collection or rock collection. My days and nights were my own to plan and fill.

When I left the dining room that evening and started down the dark 13
basement stairs, I had a life. I sat down to my wonderful amoeba, and there
he was, rolling his grains more slowly now, extending an arc of his edge for
a foot and drawing himself along by that foot, and absorbing it again and
rolling on. I gave him some more pond water.

I had hit pay dirt. For all I knew, there were paramecia, too, in that 14
pond water, or daphniae, or stentors, or any of the many other creatures I
had read about and never seen: volvox, the spherical algal colony; euglena
with its one red eye; the elusive, glassy diatom; hydra, rotifers, water bears,
worms. Anything was possible. The sky was the limit.

Questions to Start You Thinking

1. CONSIDERING MEANING: Why was Dillard's discovery of the amoeba so important to her childhood development? How did her parents respond to
   her excitement? What did this experience help her to learn?

2. IDENTIFYING WRITING STRATEGIES: Where in the essay does Dillard use specific descriptive details to help readers see what she sees? How effective do
   you find her use of such details?

3. READING CRITICALLY: How does Dillard go about communicating to readers
   her excitement over discovering the amoeba? What sort of picture does she
   paint of herself as a girl, and how do you think she expects readers to respond?

4. EXPANDING VOCABULARY: Define *friable* and *siliceous* (paragraph 4). Why do
   you suppose Dillard chose to use this sophisticated vocabulary in this paragraph? Also consider the scientific vocabulary she uses in her final paragraph. Do you think she expects readers to be familiar with these terms?

5. MAKING CONNECTIONS: In "Public and Private Language" (pp. 571–76),
   Richard Rodriguez also writes about discovering a life independent of his parents. What do he and Dillard have in common, and how are they different?

Link to the Paired Essay

In "Unforgettable Miss Bessie" (pp. 580–83), Carl T. Rowan also writes of
struggling to achieve educational goals. Despite their many differences, what
attitudes do Dillard and Rowan share?

Journal Prompts

1. What activities did you enjoy pursuing by yourself as a child? Recall a specific
   time when you pursued one of these activities on your own and reflect on
   what you learned from the experience.

2. Think about something, like Dillard's microscope, that you wanted very
   badly when you were young. If you finally received it as a gift or were able
   to buy it for yourself, what was your response? Did it meet your expectations, or did it disappoint you in any way? How long did it continue to occupy you? If you didn't receive it, write about how the disappointment affected you.

■ For more about
Carl T. Rowan, visit
<bedfordstmartins.com/
bedguide> and do a key-
word search:

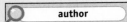
author

Suggestions for Writing

1. Recall a time when you struggled to accomplish something important to you, as Dillard struggled to see the amoeba. Write an essay in which you relate your struggle, your triumph (or failure), and the effects of the experience. Be sure that readers understand why the goal meant so much to you.

2. In paragraph 12, Dillard writes, "I had essentially been handed my own life. . . . My days and nights were my own to plan and fill." Through her story of discovering the amoeba on her own, Dillard makes the implicit point that children should be allowed the freedom to explore and learn and grow without their parents watching over their every move. Write an essay that supports Dillard's position by drawing on examples from your own experience and from the essays in this book.

Carl T. Rowan
Unforgettable Miss Bessie

Journalist and political figure **Carl T. Rowan** *(1925–2000) was born in Ravenscroft, Tennessee. After graduating from Oberlin College, he received a master's degree in journalism from the University of Minnesota. Rowan then wrote for the Minneapolis Tribune before becoming deputy secretary of state under President John F. Kennedy. He later served as a delegate to the United Nations and as U.S. ambassador to Finland. Rowan eventually returned to journalism, writing a syndicated column for the* Chicago Sun-Times *until 1998. In 1987, he founded Project Excellence, a scholarship program for African American high school students. His several books include* Just Between Us Blacks *(1974),* Breaking Barriers: A Memoir *(1991), and* The Coming Race War in America: A Wake-Up Call *(1996). In the following essay, published in* Reader's Digest *in 1985, Rowan tells the story of a teacher who had a lasting impact on his life and on his view of himself.*

AS YOU READ: *Note how Miss Bessie affected the author as a young man.*

She was only about five feet tall and probably never weighed more than 110 pounds, but Miss Bessie was a towering presence in the classroom. She was the only woman tough enough to make me read *Beowulf*° and think for a few foolish days that I liked it. From 1938 to 1942, when I attended Bernard High School in McMinnville, Tennessee, she taught me English, history, civics — and a lot more than I realized.

I shall never forget the day she scolded me into reading *Beowulf.*   2

"But Miss Bessie," I complained, "I ain't much interested in it."   3

Her large brown eyes became daggerish slits. "Boy," she said, "how dare   4
you say 'ain't' to me! I've taught you better than that."

"Miss Bessie," I pleaded, "I'm trying to make first-string end on the foot-   5
ball team, and if I go around saying 'it isn't' and 'they aren't,' the guys are
gonna laugh me off the squad."

Beowulf: A long story in poetic form, written in the eighth century in Old English.

"Boy," she responded, "you'll play football because you have guts. But   6
do you know what *really* takes guts? Refusing to lower your standards to
those of the crowd. It takes guts to say you've got to live and be somebody
fifty years after all the football games are over."

I started saying "it isn't" and "they aren't," and I still made first-string   7
end — and class valedictorian — without losing my buddies' respect.

During her remarkable 44-year-career, Mrs. Bessie Taylor Gwynn   8
taught hundreds of economically deprived black youngsters — including
my mother, my brother, my sisters, and me. I remember her now with
gratitude and affection — especially in this era when Americans are so
wrought-up° about a "rising tide of mediocrity"° in public education and
the problems of finding competent, caring teachers. Miss Bessie was an
example of an informed, dedicated teacher, a blessing to children, and an
asset to the nation.

Born in 1895, in poverty, she grew up in Athens, Alabama, where there   9
was no public school for blacks. She attended Trinity School, a private institution for blacks run by the American Missionary Association, and in 1911
graduated from the Normal School (a "super" high school) at Fisk University in Nashville. Mrs. Gwynn, the essence of pride and privacy, never talked
about her years in Athens; only in the months before her death did she reveal that she had never attended Fisk University itself because she could not
afford the four-year course.

At Normal School she learned a lot about Shakespeare, but most of all   10
about the profound importance of education — especially, for a people
trying to move up from slavery. "What you put in your head, boy," she
once said, "can never be pulled out by the Ku Klux Klan,° the Congress,
or anybody."

Miss Bessie's bearing of dignity told anyone who met her that she was   11
"educated" in the best sense of the word. There was never a discipline problem in her classes. We didn't dare mess with a woman who knew about the
Battle of Hastings, the Magna Carta, and the Bill of Rights — and who could
also play the piano.

This frail-looking woman could make sense of Shakespeare, Milton,   12
Voltaire, and bring to life Booker T. Washington and W. E. B. DuBois. Believing that it was important to know who the officials were that spent taxpay-
ers' money and made public policy, she made us memorize the names of
everyone on the Supreme Court and in the President's Cabinet. It could be
embarrassing to be unprepared when Miss Bessie said, "Get up and tell the
class who Frances Perkins° is and what you think about her."

---

wrought-up: Worked up; upset.   **"rising tide of mediocrity":** A reference, from a 1983
report from the National Commission on Excellence in Education, to sinking standards
said to be threatening the U.S. educational system.   **Ku Klux Klan:** The collective name
of several organizations that have persecuted African Americans and other groups since
the 1860s.   **Frances Perkins:** Secretary of labor under U.S. President Franklin D. Roosevelt and the first woman to hold a cabinet post.

Miss Bessie knew that my family, like so many others during the Depres- 13
sion,° couldn't afford to subscribe to a newspaper. She knew we didn't even
own a radio. Still, she prodded me to "look out for your future and find
some way to keep up with what's going on in the world." So I became a delivery boy for the Chattanooga *Times*. I rarely made a dollar a week, but I got
to read a newspaper every day.

Miss Bessie noticed things that had nothing to do with schoolwork, but 14
were vital to a youngster's development. Once a few classmates made fun of
my frayed, hand-me-down overcoat, calling me "Strings." As I was leaving
school, Miss Bessie patted me on the back of that old overcoat and said,
"Carl, never fret about what you *don't* have. Just make the most of what you
do have — a brain."

Among the things that I did not have was electricity in the little frame 15
house that my father had built for $400 with his World War I bonus. But be-
cause of her inspiration, I spent many hours squinting beside a kerosene
lamp reading Shakespeare and Thoreau, Samuel Pepys and William Cullen
Bryant.

No one in my family had ever graduated from high school, so there was 16
no tradition of commitment to learning for me to lean on. Like millions of
youngsters in today's ghettos and barrios, I needed the push and stimulation
of a teacher who truly cared. Miss Bessie gave plenty of both, as she im-
mersed me in a wonderful world of similes, metaphors, and even ono-
matopoeia. She led me to believe that I could write sonnets as well as
Shakespeare, or iambic-pentameter verse to put Alexander Pope to shame.

In those days the McMinnville school system was rigidly "Jim Crow,"° 17
and poor black children had to struggle to put anything in their heads. Our
high school was only slightly larger than the once-typical little red school-
house, and its library was outrageously inadequate — so small, I like to say,
that if two students were in it and one wanted to turn a page, the other one
had to step outside.

Negroes, as we were called then, were not allowed in the town library, 18
except to mop floors or dust tables. But through one of those secret Old
South arrangements between whites of conscience and blacks of stature,
Miss Bessie kept getting books smuggled out of the white library. That is
how she introduced me to the Brontës, Byron, Coleridge, Keats, and Ten-
nyson. "If you don't read, you can't write, and if you can't write, you might
as well stop dreaming," Miss Bessie once told me.

So I read whatever Miss Bessie told me to, and tried to remember the 19
things she insisted that I store away. Forty-five years later, I can still recite her
"truths to live by," such as Henry Wadsworth Longfellow's lines from "The
Ladder of St. Augustine":

Depression: Severe economic downturn lasting from the stock market crash of 1929
until the start of World War II.   **"Jim Crow":** Segregation of African Americans under
discriminatory laws and customs.

The heights by great men reached and kept
Were not attained by sudden flight.
But they, while their companions slept,
Were toiling upward in the night.

Years later, her inspiration, prodding, anger, cajoling, and almost os- 20
motic° infusion of learning finally led to that lovely day when Miss Bessie
dropped me a note saying, "I'm so proud to read your column in the
Nashville *Tennessean.*"

Miss Bessie was a spry 80 when I went back to McMinnville and visited 21
her in a senior citizens' apartment building. Pointing out proudly that her
building was racially integrated, she reached for two glasses and a pint of
bourbon. I was momentarily shocked, because it would have been scan-
dalous in the 1930s and '40s for word to get out that a teacher drank, and
nobody had ever raised a rumor that Miss Bessie did.

I felt a new sense of equality as she lifted her glass to mine. Then she re- 22
vealed a softness and compassion that I had never known as a student.

"I've never forgotten that examination day," she said, "when Buster Mar- 23
tin held up seven fingers, obviously asking you for help with question number seven, 'Name a common carrier.'° I can still picture you looking at your
exam paper and humming a few bars of 'Chattanooga Choo Choo.' I was so
tickled, I couldn't punish either of you."

Miss Bessie was telling me, with bourbon-laced grace, that I never 24
fooled her for a moment.

When Miss Bessie died in 1980, at age 85, hundreds of her former stu- 25
dents mourned. They knew the measure of a great teacher: love and motivation. Her wisdom and influence had rippled out across generations.

Some of her students who might normally have been doomed to 26
poverty went on to become doctors, dentists, and college professors. Many,
guided by Miss Bessie's example, became public-school teachers.

"The memory of Miss Bessie and how she conducted her classroom did 27
more for me than anything I learned in college," recalls Gladys Wood of
Knoxville, Tennessee, a highly respected English teacher who spent 43 years
in the state's school system. "So many times, when I faced a difficult classroom problem, I asked myself, *How would Miss Bessie deal with this?* And I'd
remember that she would handle it with laughter and love."

No child can get all the necessary support at home, and millions of 28
poor children get *no* support at all. This is what makes a wise, educated,
warm-hearted teacher like Miss Bessie so vital to the minds, hearts, and
souls of this country's children.

---

osmotic: Like the transfer of substances through a cell membrane (osmosis).   **common
carrier:** A public transportation system, such as a railway or airline.

Questions to Start You Thinking

1. CONSIDERING MEANING: Why did Rowan look up to Miss Bessie? How did she influence him?

2. IDENTIFYING WRITING STRATEGIES: How does Rowan use both recall and cause and effect to illustrate the power of a caring teacher? Which details and bits of dialogue seem especially engaging? How does he organize them in a logical sequence?

3. READING CRITICALLY: What is Rowan's purpose in this essay? How does his selection of details and dialogue work toward achieving this purpose?

4. EXPANDING VOCABULARY: Define *dignity*. How does Rowan apply this word to Miss Bessie, and how could it also apply to him?

5. MAKING CONNECTIONS: In "Public and Private Language" (pp. 571–76), Richard Rodriguez refers to the "private language" of his Spanish-speaking home as opposed to the "public language" of school. In what way might the type of speech criticized by Miss Bessie in paragraph 4 be considered a form of "private language"? What larger point is she making about such language, and how might Rodriguez respond?

Link to the Paired Essay

Taken together, Rowan's essay and Annie Dillard's excerpt from *An American Childhood* (pp. 577–79) suggest that a person's motivation to become educated can come from both internal and external sources. To what extent, and in what ways, were Rowan and Dillard internally and externally motivated?

Journal Prompts

1. Write about an accomplishment that you are proud of.

2. Rowan describes delivering the newspaper so that he would be able to read it. Write about a time when you made an extra effort to better yourself.

Suggestions for Writing

1. Write about a time when a teacher, a work supervisor, or some other influential person took a special interest in helping you to succeed. Recall how this person influenced you and how he or she changed your life. Include plenty of detail to bring that person to life.

2. Rowan writes that Miss Bessie contributed to the success of "students who might normally have been doomed to poverty." Write an essay in which you argue that education is the key to success. Use the readings in this text and your own experiences and observations to support your point.

Appendix
Quick Research Guide

When you begin college, you may feel awkward, uncertain about what to say and how to speak up. As you gain experience, you will join the intellectual exchange around you by reading, thinking, and writing with sources. For many college papers, you will be expected to turn to sources such as articles, books, and Web sites for the evidence needed to support your thesis and develop your ideas about it. This expectation reflects the academic view that knowledge advances through exchange: each writer reads and responds to the writing of others, building on earlier discussion while expanding the conversation.

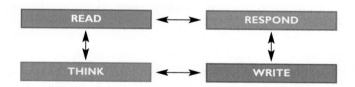

This Quick Research Guide is designed to help you succeed in several common research situations. Conducting any research requires time to explore, to think, and to respond. However, efficient and purposeful research can produce greater success in less time than random searching or optimistic browsing.

Perhaps you are writing a paper based primarily on your own experience or observation, but you want to add a dash of supporting evidence from a source or two, using a simple research process. Maybe you want a warm-up to build your confidence before you tackle an extensive research project. Possibly you need good advice fast: you've procrastinated, you're overwhelmed by conflicting demands on your time, or you're uncertain about how to succeed as a college researcher.

For more on writing processes, see Ch. 1, any chapter (4–12) in Part Two, or Chs. 16–20.

To help you in such cases, this Quick Research Guide concentrates on five key steps: defining your quest, searching for recommended sources, evaluating those you find, adding evidence from them to your paper, and citing them correctly.

TURNING TO SOURCES FOR SUPPORTING EVIDENCE

DEFINE → SEARCH → EVALUATE → ADD → CITE

A   *Defining Your Quest*

Especially when your research goals are limited to finding pertinent evidence from only a few sources, you're more likely to be successful if you try to define the hunt in advance by considering questions such as these.

PURPOSE CHECKLIST

For more about stating and using a thesis, see pp. 312–19.

___ What is the thesis that you want to support, the point that you want to demonstrate, or the question you want to answer?
___ Does the assignment require or suggest any specific research focus — certain types of supporting evidence, sources, or presentations of material?
___ Which of your ideas do you want to support with good evidence?
___ Which of your ideas might you want to check, clarify, or change based on your research?
___ Which ideas or opinions of others do you want to verify or counter?
___ Do you want to analyze material yourself (for example, comparing different articles or Web sites) or to find someone else's analysis?

For more about types of evidence, see pp. 40–41.

___ What kinds of evidence do you want to use — facts, statistics, or expert testimony? Do you also want to add your own firsthand observation of the situation or scene?

A1   Consider the criteria of writers and readers.

Although supporting evidence can come from many sources — your experience, observation, imagination, or interaction with others — college instructors often expect you to turn to the writings of others. In those books, articles, and reports, you can find pertinent examples, illustrations, details, and expert testimony — in short, reliable information that will show that your claims and statements are sound. That evidence should satisfy you as a writer and also meet the criteria of your college readers — your instructors and possibly your classmates.

TWO VIEWS OF SUPPORTING EVIDENCE

COLLEGE WRITER	COLLEGE READER
• Does it answer my question and support my thesis?	• Is it relevant to the purpose and assignment?
• Does it seem accurate?	• Is it reliable, given academic standards?
• Is it recent enough?	• Is it current, given the standards of the field?
• Does it add enough depth?	• Is it of sufficient quantity, variety, and strength?
• Is it balanced enough?	• Is it typical, fair, and complex?
• Will it persuade my audience?	• Does the writer make a credible case?

For evidence checklists, see p. 40 and p. A-6.

A2 Decide what supporting evidence you need.

When you need to add muscle to your college papers, the right resources can supply the facts, statistics, and expert testimony to back up your point. Sometimes you won't need comprehensive information about the topic, but you will want to hunt — quickly and efficiently — for exactly what you do need. Suppose, for example, that you are proposing solutions to your community's employment problem. Because you already have ideas based on your firsthand observations and the experiences of people you know, your research goals are limited. First, you want to add accurate facts and figures that will show why you believe a compelling problem exists. Next, you want to visit the Web sites of local educational institutions and possibly locate someone to interview about existing career development programs.

WORKING THESIS

Many residents of Aurora need more — and more innovative — postsecondary educational opportunities to improve their job skills and career alternatives.

Types of Evidence	DEFINITION	EXAMPLE	SOURCE
FACTS	Statements that can be verified objectively	When employment opportunities drop, college enrollments tend to go up because people are motivated to increase their skills.	Colorado Commission on Higher Education, "Governor's Task Force to Strengthen and Improve the Community College System: Final Report, April 5, 2004," page 16, at <www.state.co.us/cche>
STATISTICS	Facts stated in numbers	According to the U.S. Census Bureau, 85% of Aurora residents over age 25 have graduated from high school, 4.6% more than the national average. However, only 24.6% of this group have graduated from college, only 0.2% better than the 24.4% national average.	"Profile of Selected Social Characteristics: 2000" for Aurora, Colorado, and for United States, *U.S. Census Bureau Fact* at <http://factfinder.census.gov/home/saff/main.html?_lang=en>
EXPERT TESTIMONY	Information from a knowledgeable person who has studied or gained experience about the topic	According to information supplied by a representative of the Center for Workforce Development, students who join the Essential Skills certificate program gain computer and customer relations skills, earn college credits, and participate in an internship.	Center for Workforce Development Web page, <http://www.ccaurora.edu/industry/workforce_development.html>, and Essential Skills for the Workplace Certificates, <http://www.ccaurora.edu/programs/certificates/2006_2007/Essential%20Skills%20Cert%2006-07.pdf>
FIRSTHAND OBSERVATION	Your own unbiased, accurate eyewitness account	At the campus Web site and during my visit to the Community College of Aurora to interview a workforce specialist, I observed publicity for programs in computer systems, paramedic training, criminal justice, law enforcement, and early childhood education.	Your notes, your collection of campus materials, and your Web printouts

For more about these types of evidence, see pp. 40–41.

A3   Decide where you need supporting evidence.

Sometimes you will know exactly what your paper needs. In fact, as you plan or draft, you may tuck in notes to yourself—find this, look that up, add some numbers here. Other times, you may sense that your paper isn't as strong as you want it to be, but you may not know exactly what to add or where to add it. One way to determine where you need supporting evidence is to examine your draft, sentence by sentence.

- What does each sentence claim or promise to a reader?
- Where do you provide supporting evidence to demonstrate the claim or fulfill the promise?

The answers to these questions — your statements and your supporting evidence — often fall into a common alternating pattern:

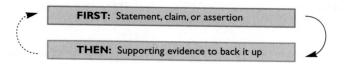

FIRST: Statement, claim, or assertion

THEN: Supporting evidence to back it up

When you spot a string of assertions without much support, you have found a place where you might need more evidence. Select your evidence carefully so that it substantiates the exact statement, claim, or assertion that precedes it. Likewise, if you spot a string of examples, details, facts, quotations, or other evidence, introduce or conclude it with an interpretive statement that explains the point the evidence supports. Make sure your general statement connects and pulls together all of the particular evidence.

■ For more about arguments based on claims of substantiation, evaluation, or policy, see pp. 152–54.

When Carrie Williamson introduced the topic of her cause-and-effect paper, "Rain Forest Destruction," she made a general statement and then supported it by quoting facts from a source. Then she repeated this statement-support pattern, backing up her next statement in turn. By using this pattern from the very beginning, Carrie reassured her readers that she was a trustworthy writer who would try to supply convincing evidence throughout the rest of her paper.

■ For more on inductive and deductive reasoning, see pp. 42–43.

■ For the source entries from Carrie Williamson's MLA list of works cited, see pp. A-22–A-24.

The tropical rain forests are among the most biologically diverse communities in the world. According to Rainforestweb.org, "More than 50 percent of the Earth's species live in tropical rainforests," and the "typical four-square-mile patch of tropical rainforest contains up to 1,500 species of flowering plants, 750 tree species, 125 mammal species, 400 bird species, 100 reptile species, 60 amphibian species, and 150 butterfly species" ("Rainforest Data"). These amazing communities that depend on each part being intact in order to function properly and successfully are being destroyed at an alarming rate. Each year "an area larger than Italy" (Soltani) is destroyed. Many rain forest conservationists debate what the leading cause of deforestation is. Regardless of which one is the major cause, the fact remains that both logging and slash-and-burn farming are destroying more and more acres of rain forests each year.

⊐— Statement

Supporting evidence: Statistics about species

⊢ Statement

⊐ Supporting evidence: Facts about destruction

Statement identifying cause-and-effect debate

Statement previewing points to come

Besides checking for the statement-support pattern, consider your paper's overall purpose, organization, and line of reasoning. The table on page A-6 shows some of the many ways this common statement-support pattern can be used to clarify and substantiate your ideas.

FIRST: STATEMENT, CLAIM, OR ASSERTION	THEN: POSSIBLE SUPPORTING EVIDENCE
Introduces a topic	Facts or statistics to justify the importance or significance of the topic
Describes a situation	Factual examples or illustrations to convey the reality or urgency of the situation
Introduces an event	Accurate firsthand observations to describe an event that you have witnessed
Presents a problem	Expert testimony or firsthand observation to establish the necessity or urgency of a solution
Explains an issue	Facts and details to clarify or justify the significance of the issue
States your point	Facts, statistics, or examples to support your viewpoint or position
Interprets and prepares readers for evidence that follows	Facts, examples, observations, or research findings to define and develop your case
Concludes with your recommendation or evaluation	Facts, examples, or expert testimony to persuade readers to accept your conclusion

Use the following checklist to help you decide whether — and where — you might need supporting evidence from sources.

EVIDENCE CHECKLIST

___ What does your thesis promise that you'll deliver? What additional evidence would ensure that you effectively demonstrate your thesis?

___ Are your statements, claims, and assertions backed up with supporting evidence? If not, what evidence might you add?

___ What evidence would most effectively persuade your readers?

___ What criteria for useful evidence are most important to your readers? What evidence would best meet these criteria?

___ Which parts of your paper sound weak or incomplete to you?

___ What facts or statistics would clarify your topic?

___ What examples or illustrations would make the background or the current circumstances clearer and more compelling for readers?

___ What does a reliable expert say about the situation your topic involves?

___ What firsthand observation would add authenticity?

___ Where have peer editors or your instructor suggested adding more evidence or stronger evidence?

B *Searching for Recommended Sources*

Even researchers who need specific evidence from only a source or two may turn first to the nearly limitless Internet. However, random Web sites are likely to require you to do extra work—checking all the information presented as fact, looking for biases or financial motives, and searching for what's not stated rather than simply accepting what is. Such caution is required because anyone—expert or not—can build a Web site, write a blog, post a message in a public forum, or circulate an e-mail message. Repetition does not ensure the accuracy, reliability, or integrity of online information because the Internet as a whole has no quality controls.

On the other hand, when your college library buys books, subscribes to scholarly journals, and acquires reference materials, whether print or electronic, these publications are expected to follow accepted editorial practices. Well-regarded publishers and professional groups turn to peer reviewers—experts in the field—to assess articles or books before they are selected for publication. Their readers, in turn, count on these traditional quality controls to bring them material that meets academic or professional standards. When you need to conduct an efficient search, quick and focused, try to begin with reliable sources, already screened and recommended by professionals.

B1 Seek advice about reliable sources.

Although popular search engines can turn up sources on nearly any topic, you always need to ask whether those sources meet your criteria and your readers'. After all, your challenge is not simply to find any sources but to find solid sources with reliable evidence for a college paper. Very often your instructors will guide your search by specifying their requirements or general expectations. In addition, the following short-cuts can help you find solid sources fast—ideally already screened, selected, and organized for you.

RESOURCE CHECKLIST

____ Has your instructor suggested to the class where you might begin? Have you talked with your instructor after class, during office hours, or by e-mail to ask for specific advice about resources for your topic? Have you checked the assignment sheet, syllabus, handouts, or class Web site?

____ Have your classmates recommended useful academic databases, disciplinary Web sites, or similar resources?

____ Does the department offering the course have a Web site with lists of resources available at the library or links to sites well regarded in that field?

____ Does your textbook Web site provide links to additional resources?

___ Which library databases does the librarian at the reference desk recommend for your course level and your topic?

___ Which databases or links on your library's Web site lead to government (federal, state, or local) resources or articles in journals and newspapers?

___ Which resources are available on library terminals, in the new periodicals room, or in the reference area of your college library?

B2   Select reliable sources that meet your readers' criteria.

If you planned to investigate common Internet hoaxes for a paper about online practices, you might deliberately turn to sources that are, by definition, unreliable. However, in most cases, you want to turn right away to reliable sources. The charts on pages A-10–A-11 explain how to recognize different types of sources, gauge their currency, and select those appropriate for a given topic or assignment.

Each type of source analyzed in these charts might be credible and useful for a paper. For certain assignments, you might be expected to use sources as varied as reports from journalists, advice from practitioners in the field, accounts of historical eyewitnesses, or opposing opinions on civic policy. However, college instructors often expect you to turn not to popular sources but to scholarly ones — also identified as peer-reviewed or refereed sources — with characteristics such as these:

- in-depth investigation or interpretation of an academic topic or research problem
- discussion of previous studies, which are cited in the text and listed at the end for easy reference by readers
- use of research methods accepted in a discipline or several fields
- publication by a reputable company or sponsoring organization
- acceptance for publication based on reviews by experts (peer reviewers) who assess the quality of the study
- preparation for publication supervised by academic or expert editors or by authors and professional staff

Your instructors may be more confident of the quality controls of established publications, appearing in print or in simultaneous print and online versions, than of the procedures of newer or unfamiliar electronic sources. Your campus librarian can help you limit your searches to peer-reviewed journals or check the scholarly reputation of sources that you find.

C   *Evaluating Possible Sources*

You may dream that your research will instantly turn up the perfect source. Like the perfect wave, the perfect snowy slope, or the perfect day, such a source is likely to be hard to come by. After all, by what standards will you judge perfection? And what are the odds that you will find such perfection ever, much less during your limited research schedule? Instead of looking for perfect sources, most college researchers evaluate sources on the basis of their own practical needs, the standards of their readers, and the shared concern of writers and readers for reliable, appropriate evidence.

■ For exercises on evaluating Web sources in particular, visit <bedfordstmartins.com/bedguide> and do a keyword search:

🔍   **evaluate**

C1   Evaluate sources as a practical researcher.

Your situation as a writer may determine how long or how widely you can search for what you need or how deeply you can delve into the sources you find. For example, if you are worried about finishing your paper on time or about juggling several assignments at once, you will need to search efficiently, evaluating sources first in terms of your own practical criteria.

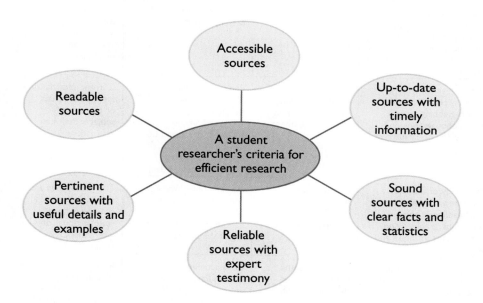

- Accessible sources
- Readable sources
- Up-to-date sources with timely information
- A student researcher's criteria for efficient research
- Pertinent sources with useful details and examples
- Sound sources with clear facts and statistics
- Reliable sources with expert testimony

C2   Evaluate sources as your readers would.

You will want to consider what your readers expect of the sources you select and the way that you use them. If you are uncertain about college requirements, start with recommended sources that are easily accessible, readable, and

Understanding Print Sources and Their Applications	LIKELY APPEARANCE	TYPICAL PUBLICATION TIME FRAME	EXAMPLES	BEST FOR
SCHOLARLY BOOK	In-depth discussion, often hardbound with a plain cover, that presents research findings, references, and few, if any, illustrations to an academic audience	Months or years, probably following months or years for research and writing	*Improving Classroom Testing, The Information Society: A Skeptical View, The Psychology of Aggression, Theodore Roosevelt and His Times*	In-depth analysis and research into established academic topics
POPULAR NONFICTION BOOK	Trendy or topical hardbound or paperback publication, often with an eye-catching cover, that conveys information, advice, or instructions to general readers	Months or years, possibly following months or years for writing	*The World Is Flat, The Year of Magical Thinking, General Ike, A Short History of Nearly Everything*	Overview of current trends or issues, informative advice, personal experience, or life story
SCHOLARLY JOURNAL	Quarterly or monthly text-heavy publication, often sponsored by a scholarly group, with prominent table of contents listing long articles directed to specialists	Months (or longer), probably following months or years of research and writing	*American Economic Review, Journal of the American Medical Association (JAMA), PMLA (Publications of the Modern Language Association), Science and Technology Review*	In-depth, up-to-date research on discipline-specific topics
NEWS MAGAZINE	Weekly or monthly publication with color cover, photographs, and short articles (sometimes collaborative) on news stories, current events, and societal trends	Days or weeks, following current or long-term investigation	*Time, Newsweek, U.S. News & World Report*	The latest news on topics of regional, national, or international significance
POPULAR MAGAZINE	Colorful weekly, biweekly, or monthly publication with attention-grabbing cover, sidebars, photographs, and articles on its special interest	Days, weeks, or months, following immediate or long-term development	Range from *Atlantic Monthly, National Geographic, Psychology Today,* and *Smithsonian* to *People, Redbook,* and *US* (serious topics and in-depth stories to hobbies or celebrities)	Current information on popular issues or trends and subjects that interest readers
NEWSPAPER	Daily, weekly, or monthly publication with oversized pages, headlines, columns, photographs, graphics, and stories on current news and timely issues	Days or weeks, following current or long-term investigation	*New York Times, Washington Post, Wall Street Journal, Chronicle of Higher Education,* your local or regional newspaper	The latest news and opinions on topics of local, regional, state, national, or international significance
PAMPHLET OR BOOKLET	Brief paperbound publications, appearing irregularly, individually, or in a series, often sponsored by a scholarly, civic, business, government, or other group or agency	Days or months, following development of material	*GE Annual Report, The Unicorn Tapestries, Children of John and Sophia Walz, Medical History of Washington County with Some Personal Recollections*	In-depth coverage of specific topics, viewpoints, advice, or recollections of groups or individuals
REFERENCE WORK	Book or multivolume encyclopedia, handbook, dictionary, directory, almanac, atlas, fact book, or other informative guide, usually in the library's reference area	Months or years, probably following months or years for research and writing	*Encyclopedia of the Harlem Renaissance, Biographical Dictionary of Hispanic Americans, Oxford Dictionary of Literary Quotations, Facts on File, Atlas of World Cultures*	Concise background explanations, definitions, facts, statistics, biographies, and other specifics

Understanding Electronic Sources and Their Applications	LIKELY APPEARANCE	TYPICAL PUBLICATION TIME FRAME	EXAMPLES	BEST FOR
ONLINE REFERENCE SITE	Prominent search box, search options for fields or topics, links to specialized gateways or resources	Immediate, daily, or regular updates	*Infomine* at <http://infomine.ucr.edu>, *Internet Public Library* at <www.ipl.org>, *Librarians' Internet Index* at <www.lii.org>, *WWW Virtual Library* at <http://vlib.org>, *or Ask* at <www.ask.com>	Quick access to prescreened resources and links for researchers
GATEWAY SITE FOR A TOPIC OR FIELD	Prominent focus on discipline or topic with search or category options	Regular or irregular updates, depending on sponsor or Webmaster	*The American Civil-War Homepage* at <http://sunsite.utk.edu/civil-war>, *William Faulkner on the Web* at <www.mcsr.olemiss.edu/~egjbp/faulkner/faulkner.html>	Quick access to prescreened resources and links on specific subjects
ONLINE DOCUMENT COLLECTION	List of available documents, groups of documents, or search options such as author or title	Regular or irregular updates, depending on materials or Webmaster	*Bartleby* at <http://bartleby.com>, *Project Gutenberg* at <http://gutenberg.org>, *American Memory* at <http://memory.loc.gov>	Easy access to large collections of texts and visuals
PROFESSIONAL WEB SITE	Conspicuous promotion of sponsor such as scholarly or field group, nonprofit agency, corporation, or foundation (.org, .net, or .com)	Regular or irregular updates, depending on sponsor	American Educational Research Association at <www.aera.net>, Better Business Bureau at <http://bbb.org>, MetLife Foundation, search at <www.metlife.com>	Resources or specialized materials related to sponsor's interests
ACADEMIC WEB SITE	Attractive presentation of institution (.edu) and its academic and other units	Regular or irregular updates, depending on academic or other unit maintaining page	College Web sites such as your campus site, library home page, or department or course page	Disciplinary and cross-disciplinary resources from campus units
GOVERNMENT WEB SITE	Prominent focus on federal, state, local, or other agencies (.gov), often with links and a search box	Regular or irregular updates, depending on government agency	Government gateways at <www.usa.gov>, agencies such as the Census Bureau at <http://factfinder.census.gov> or Environmental Protection Agency at <www.epa.gov>	Topic-specific statistics, reports, information about legislation and policies, consumer publications
ONLINE NEWSPAPER OR NEWS SERVICE	Banner headline of news organization with breaking news, section options, and archives	Immediate updates as events occur along with archives of past coverage	Online *New York Times, Washington Post, Wall Street Journal,* or local newspapers	The latest national or international news and views
INTEREST-GROUP OR PERSONAL WEB SITE	Logo or banner for partisan or special-interest group, discussion group, or individual pages or blogs (Web logs)	Regular or irregular updates, depending on individual or group	Democracy for America at <www.democracyforamerica.com>, Young Republicans at <www.yrnf.org>, ArtsJournal at <www.artsjournal.com>	Wide range of views, resources, opinions, and counterarguments which require evaluation of bias

up-to-date — and chock full of the reliable facts, statistics, research findings, case studies, observations, examples, illustrations, and expert testimony that will persuade your readers.

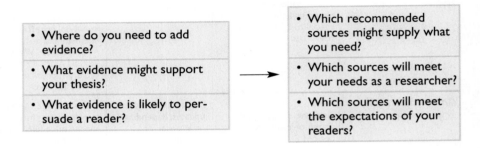

• Where do you need to add evidence?
• What evidence might support your thesis?
• What evidence is likely to persuade a reader?

• Which recommended sources might supply what you need?
• Which sources will meet your needs as a researcher?
• Which sources will meet the expectations of your readers?

C3   Evaluate sources for reliable and appropriate evidence.

When you use evidence from sources to support your points, both you and your readers are likely to hold two simple expectations:

- that your sources are reliable so you can trust their information
- that the information you select from them is appropriate for your paper

After all, how could an unreliable source successfully support your ideas? And what could unsuitable or mismatched information contribute to your paper? The difficult task, of course, is learning how to judge what is reliable and appropriate. The following checklist suggests how you can use the time-tested journalist's questions — who, what, when, where, why, and how — to evaluate each print or electronic source that you consider using.

EVALUATION CHECKLIST

Who?

___ Who is the author of the source? What are the author's credentials and experience?

___ Who is the intended audience of the source?

___ Who publishes the source or sponsors the site? Is this publisher well regarded? Is the source aimed at an academic or a general audience?

___ Who has reviewed the source before publication? Only the author? Expert peer reviewers? An editorial staff?

What?

___ What is the purpose of the publication or Web site? Is it trying to sell, inform, report, or shape opinion?

—— What bias or point of view might affect the reliability of the source?

—— What evidence does the source present? Does the source seem trustworthy and logical? Does it identify its sources or supply active links?

When?

—— When was the source published or created?

—— When was it revised to stay up-to-date?

Where?

—— Where did you find the source?

—— Where is the source recommended? Has your library prescreened it?

Why?

—— Why would you use this source rather than others?

—— Why is its information relevant to your research question?

How?

—— How does the source reflect its author, publisher or sponsor, and audience? How might you need to qualify its use in your paper?

—— How would this source support your thesis and provide persuasive evidence?

D *Capturing, Launching, and Citing Evidence Added from Sources*

Sometimes researchers concentrate so hard on hunting for reliable sources that they forget what comes next. The value of every source remains potential until you successfully capture its facts, statistics, expert testimony, examples, or other information in a form that you can incorporate into your paper. In addition, you need to launch — or introduce — the information in order to identify its source or its contribution to your paper. Finally, you must accurately cite, or credit, both in the text of your paper and in a final list of sources, each source whose words or ideas you use. (Follow the advice of the Modern Language Association, supplied here, or whatever other system your instructor requires.)

■ For exercises on supporting a thesis statement, visit <bedfordstmartins.com/ bedguide> and do a keyword search:

    support

■ For examples in both MLA and APA style, see E1–E2.

```
CAPTURE  →  LAUNCH  →  CITE
```

D1 Avoid plagiarism.

Be sure to allow enough time to add information from sources skillfully and correctly. Find out exactly how your instructor expects you to credit sources. Even if you do not intend to plagiarize — to use another writer's words or

■ For exercises on incorporating source material and avoiding plagiarism, visit <bedfordstmartins.com/ bedguide> and do a keyword search:

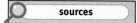
    sources

ideas without appropriately crediting them — a paper full of sloppy or careless short cuts can look just like a paper deliberately copied from unacknowledged sources. Instead, borrow carefully and honestly, fully acknowledging your debt to writers from whom you borrow anything.

Identify the source of information, an idea, a summary, a paraphrase, or a quotation right away, as soon as you write it in your notes. Carry that acknowledgment into your first draft and all that follow. You generally do not need to identify a source if you use what is called "common knowledge" — quotations, expressions, or information widely known and widely accepted. If you are uncertain about whether you need to cite a source, ask your instructor, or simply provide the citation.

The following chart reviews accepted methods of adding source material and identifies good research practices. These practices will help prevent common errors that may call into question your integrity or your attentiveness as a research writer.

■ For more on critical reading, see Ch. 2.
For more on evaluating evidence, see pp. 39–40.
For more on logical fallacies, see pp. 162–63.

D2 Read your source critically.

Before you pop any outside material into your paper, read critically to evaluate the reliability and suitability of the source. If you cannot understand a complicated source that requires specialized background, don't use it in your paper. If its ideas, facts, claims, or viewpoint seem unusual, incorporate only what

Accepted Methods of Adding and Crediting Source Material	OBJECTIVES OF METHOD	GOOD PRACTICES TO AVOID ERRORS
QUOTATION	Select and identify the exact words of a source in order to capture its vitality, authority, or incisiveness for your paper.	• Repeat the exact words of the source or properly indicate changes. • Use both opening and closing quotation marks. • Provide the page number or other location of the quotation in the source. • Supply complete identification of the source.
PARAPHRASE	Restate the detailed ideas of a source in your own words and sentences, with credit to the original source, in order to capture the content of a passage.	• Read carefully so that you can paraphrase accurately without distorting the source. • Use your own words and sentences to avoid following the pattern, sequence, or wording of the original. • Rephrase or add quotation marks to identify words from the source that slip into or add to your paraphrase.

Accepted Methods of Adding and Crediting Source Material	OBJECTIVES OF METHOD	GOOD PRACTICES TO AVOID ERRORS
PARAPHRASE (CONTINUED)		• Provide the page number or other location of the original passage in the source. • Clearly distinguish between the paraphrase and your own ideas to avoid confusing switches. • Supply complete identification of the source.
SUMMARY	Very briefly express the main point or key ideas of a source or passage in your own words, with credit to the original source, in order to capture its essential ideas or conclusion.	• Read carefully so that you can summarize accurately without distorting the source. • Rephrase or add quotation marks to identify words from the source that slip into your summary. • Give specific credit to the source for ideas that you include in your discussion. • Clearly distinguish between the summary and your own ideas to avoid confusing switches. • Supply complete identification of the source.
IN-TEXT CITATION	Credit each quotation, paraphrase, summary, or other reference to a source in short form by giving the author's last name in the text of the paper or with the page number in parentheses (MLA style).	• Supply consistent citations without forgetting or carelessly omitting sources. • Spell names of authors and titles correctly. • Provide accurate page references.
CONCLUDING LIST OF WORKS CITED	Credit each source cited in the text with a corresponding full entry in an alphabetical list at the end of the paper.	• Match each source citation in the text with an entry in the final list. • Provide consistent entries without forgetting or carelessly omitting sources. • Supply every detail expected in an entry, even if you must return to the library or go online to complete your source notes. • Follow the exact sequence, capitalization, punctuation, indentation pattern, and other details required by MLA or another style. • Check that each entry in your final list appears in alphabetical order.

you can substantiate in other unrelated sources. On the other hand, if its evidence seems accurate, logical, and relevant, consider exactly how you might want to add it to your paper — by quoting, paraphrasing, or summarizing.

For advice about how to quote, see pp. 214–15; for more examples see E1.

For more on punctuating quotations and using ellipsis marks, see C3 in the Quick Editing Guide (the dark-blue-edged pages).

D3   Quote accurately.

When you are taking notes from a source, record as many quotations as you want if that process helps you master the material. When you add quotations to your paper, however, be selective. Limit your direct quotations to compelling selections; after all, a quotation in itself is not necessarily effective evidence, and too many quotations will suggest that your writing is padded or lacks original thought. Be certain that you quote exactly, and credit your source using the format expected. Use the following questions to check the accuracy of your quotation.

QUOTATION CHECKLIST

____ Have you quoted only a notable passage that adds support and authority to your discussion?

____ Have you checked your quotation to be sure that it repeats your source word for word?

____ Have you marked the beginning and the ending of the quotation with quotation marks?

____ Have you used ellipses (. . .) to mark any spot where you have left out words in the original?

____ Have you identified the source of the quotation in a launch statement (see p. A-18) or in parentheses?

____ Have you specified in parentheses the page number where the quotation appears in the source?

D4   Paraphrase carefully.

For advice about how to paraphrase, see pp. 218–19.

While a quotation presents an idea in the exact and memorable words of a source, a paraphrase does the reverse. A paraphrase presents a passage from a source in your own words and sentences. It may include the same level of detail that the original does, but it should not slip into the wording of the original (unless you identify those snippets with quotation marks). Be sure to credit the original source when you paraphrase, just as you do when you quote. Use the following questions to help you keep your paraphrase fresh.

PARAPHRASE CHECKLIST

____ Have you read the passage critically to be sure that you fully understand it?

____ Have you paraphrased accurately, reflecting both the main points and the supporting details in the original?

— Does your paraphrase use your own words without repeating or echoing the words or the sentence structure of the original?

— Does your paraphrase stick to the ideas of the original without tucking in your own thoughts?

— Have you reread and revised your paraphrase so that it reads smoothly and clearly?

— Have you identified the source of the paraphrase in a launch statement (see p. A-18) or in parentheses?

— Have you specified in parentheses the page number where the passage appears in the source?

D5   Summarize fairly.

Unlike a quotation or a paraphrase, a summary reduces the ideas of a source to their essence. Even though a summary uses your own words, you still must clearly identify the source. Your summary may boil a book, a chapter, an article, or a section down to a few sentences that accurately and clearly sum up the sense of the original. Use the following questions to help you assess the success of your summary.

For advice about how to summarize, see p. 220.

SUMMARY CHECKLIST

— Have you fairly stated the author's thesis, or main point, in your own words in a sentence or two?

— Have you briefly stated any supporting ideas that you wish to summarize?

— Have you stuck to the overall point without getting bogged down in details or examples?

— Has your summary remained respectful of the ideas and opinions of others, even if you disagree with them?

— Have you reread and revised your summary so that it reads smoothly and clearly?

— Have you identified the source of the summary in a launch statement (see D6) or in parentheses?

— Have you specified in parentheses the page number where any specific passage appears in the source?

D6   Launch and cite each quotation, paraphrase, and summary.

Instead of dropping ideas from sources into your paper as if they had just arrived by flying saucer, weave them in so that they effectively support the point you want to make. As you integrate each idea from a source, take three steps.

1. Capture. Begin with the supporting evidence you have captured from your source in a quotation, paraphrase, or summary. Refine this material so that it will fit smoothly into your paper. Reduce your quotation to its most memorable words, freshen the wording of your paraphrase, or increase the precision of your summary. Position the evidence where it is needed to support your statements, claims, or assertions.

2. Launch. Launch, or introduce, the material captured from each source. Avoid tossing stand-alone quotations into your paper or stacking up a series of paraphrases and summaries. Instead, lead smoothly into your source information. As you write a launch statement, try to draw on the authority of the source, mention the author's credentials, or connect the material to other sources or your points. Let readers know why you have selected this evidence and what you think it contributes to your paper.

■ For more on launch statements, see pp. 223–24.

Dalton, long an advocate of "green" construction, recommends a five-year plan to . . . (18).

As a specialist in elder law, attorney Tamara Diaz suggests . . . .

■ For more on punctuating quotations, see C3 in the Quick Editing Guide (the dark-blue-edged pages).

Like Westin, regional director Neil urges that ". . ." (308). Brown, however, takes an innovative approach to local conservation practices and recommends . . . (108).

Another policy analyst, arguing from principles expressed in the Bill of Rights, maintains . . . (Frank 96).

While Congress pits secure borders against individual liberties, immigration analyst Smith proposes a third possibility that might . . . (42).

■ For examples showing how to cite and list sources in your paper, see section E.

3. **Cite.** Identify each source briefly yet accurately.

- Name the author in parentheses (unless already named in your launch statement).
- In APA style, add the date of the source.
- Add the page number to locate the original passage.
- If a source has no author, begin the citation with the first words of the title.
- Add a full entry for each source to a list at the end of your paper.

E *Citing and Listing Sources in MLA or APA Style*

■ For exercises on citing and listing sources in MLA style, visit <bedfordstmartins.com/ bedguide> and do a keyword search:

🔍 cite

MLA style is the format for crediting sources that is recommended by the Modern Language Association and often required in English classes. APA style is the format recommended by the American Psychological Association, often used in the social sciences, business, and some composition classes. These two styles are widely used in college papers, but your specialized courses may require other academic styles, depending on the field. Because instructors expect you to credit sources carefully, follow any direc-

tions or examples supplied, or refer to the style manual required. Although academic styles all credit sources, they have many detailed differences. Stick to the one expected.

In both the MLA and APA styles, your sources need to be identified twice in your paper: first, briefly, at the very moment you draw upon the source material and later, in full, at the end of your paper. The short reference includes the name of the author of the source (or a short form of the title if the source does not name an author), so it's easy for a reader to connect that short entry in your text with the related full entry in the final alphabetical list.

E1   Cite sources in your text.

MLA STYLE

Right in the text, at the moment you add a quotation, a paraphrase, or a summary, you need to identify the source. Your citation generally follows a simple pattern: name the author, and note the page in the original where the material is located.

(Last Name of Author ##)   (Talia 35)   (Smitt and Gilbert 152–53)

Place this citation immediately after a direct quotation or paraphrase.

> When "The Lottery" begins, the reader thinks of the "great pile of stones" (Jackson 191) as children's entertainment.

When the author is named in your launch statement, the citation can be even simpler.

> According to Hunt, the city faced "deficits and drought" (54) for ten more years.

For quotations from poems, plays, or novels, supply line, act and scene, or chapter numbers rather than page numbers.

> The speaker in Robinson's poem describes Richard Cory as "richer than a king" (line 9), an attractive man who "fluttered pulses when he said, / 'Good-morning'" (7–8).

If you use only one source in your paper, identify it at the beginning of your essay. Then just give page or line numbers in parentheses after each quotation or paraphrase.

Use the following checklist to improve your source citations.

CITATION CHECKLIST

____ Have you placed your citation right after your quotation, paraphrase, or summary?

____ Have you enclosed your citation with a pair of parenthesis marks?

____ Have you provided the last name of the author either in your launch statement or in your citation?

____ Have you used the title for a work without an identified author?

___ Have you added the exact page, as numbered in the source, or another location number (such as a Web paragraph, poetry line, novel chapter, or play act and scene) to identify where the source material appears?

APA STYLE

After the author's last name, add the date. Use p. (for "page") or pp. (for "pages") before the page numbers.

(Last Name of Author, Date, p. ##)   (Talia, 2007, p. 35)
(Smith & Gilbert, 2004, pp. 152–153)

E2   List sources at the end.

At the end of your paper, add a list of your sources. For each source mentioned in the text, supply a corresponding full entry. Use this checklist to improve the accuracy of your entries.

WORKS CITED CHECKLIST

___ Have you figured out what type of source you have used? Have you followed the sample pattern for that type as exactly as possible?

___ Have you used quotation marks and underlining (MLA) or italics (APA) correctly for titles?

___ Have you used correct punctuation — periods, commas, colons, parentheses — in your entry?

___ Have you checked the accuracy of the numbers in your entry—pages, volume, and dates?

___ Have you accurately recorded the name of the author, title, publisher, and so on?

___ Have you correctly typed the address of an electronic source (or supplied a simpler address for the source's search page)?

___ Have you correctly arranged your entries in alphabetical order?

___ Have you checked your final list against your text citations so that every source appears in both places?

___ Have you double-spaced your list just like your paper, without any extra space between entries?

___ Have you begun the first line of each entry in your list at the left margin? Have you indented each additional line as you would indent a paragraph? (To do this automatically, use your software's "hanging" indentation option, possibly in the Format-Paragraph-Indentation-Special menu.)

The secret to figuring out what to include in a Works Cited entry generally comes down to this question about your source: What is it? Once you identify the type of source you have used, you can find a general pattern for it in this book or in your style guide. Then, using this pattern, you can examine the title page or other parts of your source to find the details needed to complete the pattern.

MLA STYLE

Call your list of sources Works Cited. Use the following examples as patterns for your entries. For each type of source, supply the same information in the same order using the same punctuation or other features.

BOOK

TEXT CITATION

(Rosenzweig 7)

WORKS CITED ENTRY

Author's name   Period   Title of book, underlined

Rosenzweig, Michael L. Win-Win Ecology: How the Earth's Species Can Survive in the

Midst of Human Enterprise. New York: Oxford UP, 2003.

Period / City of publication   Publisher (shortened name)   Year of publication   Period

■ If you need to find formats for other types of sources, consult the current *MLA Handbook for Writers of Research Papers*, often available in the library, or check your research manual or research guide for more information.

ESSAY, STORY, OR POEM FROM A BOOK

TEXT CITATION

(Brady 498)

WORKS CITED ENTRY

Author of selection   Title of selection, in quotation marks   Title of book or anthology, underlined

Brady, Judy. "I Want a Wife." The Bedford Guide for College Writers. 8th ed.

Ed. X. J. Kennedy, Dorothy M. Kennedy, and Marcia F. Muth. —— Authors or editors of book

Boston: Bedford/St. Martin's, 2008. 497-99.

City of publication   Publisher of book   Year of publication   Page numbers of the selection

■ See the title page of this book and the reading on page 497 to find the details needed for this entry.

POPULAR MAGAZINE ARTICLE

The author's name and the title generally appear at the beginning of an article. Typically, the magazine name, the date, and page numbers appear at the bottom of pages. Arrange the date in this order: 4 Oct. 2007.

■ See the *Utne Reader* and *Parenting* samples on p. 394.

TEXT CITATION

(Lobel 45)

WORKS CITED ENTRY

Author's name Title of article, Title of magazine,
                in quotation marks underlined

Lobel, Hannah. "Infinity or Bust." <u>Utne Reader</u> Nov-Dec. 2006: 44-46.

Date of publication Page numbers of the article

If the author is not identified, simply begin with the title of the article.

"How We Celebrate July 4th." <u>Parenting</u> June-July 2003: 22-23.

SCHOLARLY JOURNAL ARTICLE

If each issue of a journal begins with page 1, add the issue number after the volume: 98.5.

TEXT CITATION

(Baller 30)

WORKS CITED ENTRY

Author's name Title of journal article in quotation marks

Baller, William. "Farm Families and the American Revolution." <u>Journal of Family History</u>

31 (2006): 28-44. Title of journal,
                    underlined

Volume Year Page numbers
number Colon of the article

ARTICLE FROM A LIBRARY DATABASE

For databases like *InfoTrac*, the full publication information for the print source often appears at the top of the online entry. A printout of the article usually will record this information as well as your date of access and any URL provided. Note that the first page number of the print source can be followed by a hyphen if the full page range is not known.

TEXT CITATION

■ See p. A-5 for the text reference from Carrie Williamson's paper.

The page number is not included because it is not available in the online version.

(Soltani)

WORKS CITED ENTRY

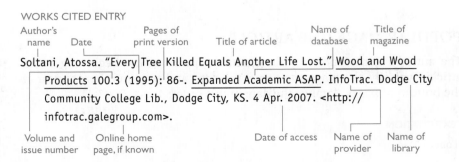

Author's   Pages of   Name of   Title of
name   Date   print version   Title of article   database   magazine

Soltani, Atossa. "Every Tree Killed Equals Another Life Lost." <u>Wood and Wood</u>
     Products 100.3 (1995): 86-. Expanded Academic ASAP. InfoTrac. Dodge City
     Community College Lib., Dodge City, KS. 4 Apr. 2007. <http://
     infotrac.galegroup.com>.

Volume and   Online home   Date of access   Name of   Name of
issue number   page, if known   provider   library

PAGE FROM A WEB SITE

The page title and site title often appear at the top of a given page. The date when a site was posted or last updated often appears at the bottom, as does the name of the sponsor. (However, sponsor information may appear as a link.) A print-out of the page will record this information as well as the date of access and URL. Note that the URL appears in the address bar of the Internet browser.

TEXT CITATION

The site is identified by title because it does not name an author. The page number is not included because it is not available for the Web page.

According to Rainforestweb.org, . . .

See p. A-5 for the text reference from Carrie Williamson's paper.

WORKS CITED ENTRY

No author identified   Title of page, in quotation marks   Name of sponsor   Title of site underlined

"Rainforest Data and Research." Rainforestweb.org: World Rainforest Information Portal. 2001. Rainforest Action Network. 5 Apr. 2007 <http://www.rainforestweb.org/Rainforest_Information/Rainforest_Data_and_Research/>.

Date posted or updated

Date of visit

Online address of site or its search page, divided only following a slash

APA STYLE

Call your list of sources References. Use the following examples as patterns for your entries. For each type of source, supply the same information in the same order using the same punctuation or other features.

If you need to find formats for other types of sources, consult the current *Publication Manual of the American Psychological Association,* often available in the library, or check your research manual or research guide for more information.

BOOK

TEXT CITATION

(Rosenzweig, 2003, p. 7)

REFERENCES ENTRY

Rosenzweig, M. L. (2003). *Win-win ecology: How the earth's species can survive in the midst of human enterprise.* Oxford, England: Oxford University Press.

WORK OR SECTION IN A BOOK

TEXT CITATION

(Brady, 1971/2008, p. 497)

Turn to the title page of this book and the reading selection on p. 497 to find the details needed for this entry.

REFERENCES ENTRY

Brady, J. (2008). I want a wife. In X. J. Kennedy, D. M. Kennedy, & M. F. Muth (Eds.), *The Bedford guide for college writers* (8th ed., pp. 497-499). Boston: Bedford/ St. Martin's. (Original work published 1971)

POPULAR MAGAZINE ARTICLE

Add any volume number (in italics) and a comma after the magazine title.

TEXT CITATION

("How We Celebrate," 2003, p. 22)

See the *Parenting* sample on p. 394.

REFERENCES ENTRY

How we celebrate July 4th. (2003, June/July). *Parenting*, 22–23.

SCHOLARLY JOURNAL ARTICLE

TEXT CITATION

(Niemi & Herrnson, 2003, p. 318)

REFERENCES ENTRY

Nieme, R. G., & Herrnson, P. S. (2003). Beyond the butterfly: The complexity of U.S. ballots. *Perspectives on Politics, 1*, 317-326.

ARTICLE FROM A LIBRARY DATABASE

IN-TEXT CITATION

See p. A-5 for the text reference from Carrie Williamson's paper.

Neither a page nor a paragraph number is available for the online article.

(Soltani, 1995)

REFERENCES ENTRY

Soltani, A. (1995). Every tree killed equals another life lost. *Wood and Wood Products, 100*(3), 86-87. Retrieved from Expanded Academic ASAP database.

PAGE FROM A WEB SITE

TEXT CITATION

The site is identified by title because it does not identify an author.

According to *Rainforestweb.org* ("Rainforest Data," 2001), . . .

REFERENCES ENTRY

Add your access date if the site may change.

Rainforest data and research. (2001). *Rainforestweb.org: World rainforest information portal*. Retrieved April 7, 2007, from http://www.rainforestweb.org/ Rainforest_Information/Rainforest_Data_and_Research/

Appendix
Quick Editing Guide

Editing and proofreading are needed at the end of the writing process be-cause writers — *all* writers — find it difficult to write error-free sentences the very first time they try. Sometimes as a writer you pay more attention to

Editing with a Computer

Computers can help you edit in several ways. Grammar checkers will catch some errors, but not others. For this reason, you always need to consider the grammar checker's suggestions carefully before accepting them.

FOR E-WRITERS

- A grammar checker cannot always correctly identify the subject or verb in a sentence; it may question whether a sentence is complete or whether its subject and verb agree, even when the sentence is correct.

- Grammar checkers are likely to miss certain problems such as misplaced modifiers, faulty parallelism, possessives without apostrophes, or incor-rectly positioned commas.

- Most grammar checkers do a good job of spotting problems with adjec-tives and adverbs, such as confusing *good* and *well*.

You can also use your word processor to search for your own typical problems. Begin by keeping track of your mistakes so that you can develop an "error hit list." Then try to figure out how to use your software's Find and Re-place capacity (probably in the Edit menu) to check quickly for some of these problems. For instance, you might search for all instances of *each* (always sin-gular) or *few* (always plural) to see if all the verbs agree.

The computer can also help you read your draft more closely. For ex-ample, you can automatically isolate each sentence so that you are less likely to skip over sentence errors. First make a copy of your draft. Then select Re-place in your software's Edit menu. Ask the software to find every period in the file and replace it with a period and two returns. This change will create a version with each sentence separated by several spaces so that you can easily check every one for fragments, comma splices, or other problems.

what you want to say than to how you say it. Sometimes you inaccurately remember spelling or grammar or punctuation. At other times you are distracted or simply make keyboarding errors. Once you are satisfied that you have expressed your ideas, you should make sure that each sentence and word is concise, clear, and correct.

■ For advice on writing more concisely, see pp. 379–81.

This Quick Editing Guide provides an overview of grammar, style, punctuation, and mechanics problems typical of college writing. Certain common errors in Standard Written English are like red flags to careful readers: they signal that the writer is either ignorant or careless. Use the editing checklist below to check your paper for these problems; then use the editing checklists in each section to help you correct specific errors. Concentrate on any problems likely to reappear in your writing.

■ For editing and proof-reading strategies, see pp. 384–87.

EDITING CHECKLIST

Common and Serious Problems in College Writing

Grammar Problems

___ Have you avoided writing sentence fragments?	**A1**
___ Have you avoided writing comma splices or fused sentences?	**A2**
___ Have you used the correct form for all verbs in the past tense?	**A3**
___ Do all verbs agree with their subjects?	**A4**
___ Have you used the correct case for all pronouns?	**A5**
___ Do all pronouns agree with their antecedents?	**A6**
___ Have you used adjectives and adverbs correctly?	**A7**

Sentence Problems

___ Does each modifier clearly modify the appropriate sentence element?	**B1**
___ Have you used parallel structure where needed?	**B2**

Punctuation Problems

___ Have you used commas correctly?	**C1**
___ Have you used apostrophes correctly?	**C2**
___ Have you punctuated quotations correctly?	**C3**

Mechanics and Format Problems

___ Have you used capital letters correctly?	**D1**
___ Have you spelled all words correctly?	**D2**
___ Have you used correct manuscript form?	**D3**

A   *Editing for Common Grammar Problems*

A1   Check for any sentence fragments.

A complete sentence is one that has a subject, has a predicate, and can stand on its own. A *sentence fragment* lacks a subject, a predicate, or both, or for some other reason fails to convey a complete thought. It cannot stand on its own as a sentence.

Although they are common in advertising and fiction, fragments are usually ineffective in college writing because they do not communicate coherent thoughts. To edit for fragments, examine each sentence carefully to make sure that it has a subject and a verb and that it expresses a complete thought. To correct a fragment, you can make it into a complete sentence by adding a missing part, dropping an unnecessary subordinating conjunction, or joining it to a complete sentence nearby, if that would make more sense.

FRAGMENT	Roberto has two sisters. Maya and Leeza.
CORRECT	Roberto has two sisters, Maya and Leeza.
FRAGMENT	The children going to the zoo.
CORRECT	The children were going to the zoo.
CORRECT	The children going to the zoo were caught in a traffic jam.
FRAGMENT	Last night when we saw Cameron Diaz's most recent movie.
CORRECT	Last night we saw Cameron Diaz's most recent movie.

subject: The part of a sentence that names something—a person, an object, an idea, a situation—about which the predicate makes an assertion: The *king* lives.

predicate: The part of a sentence that makes an assertion about the subject involving an action (Birds *fly*), a relationship (Birds *have feathers*), or a state of being (Birds *are warm-blooded*)

subordinating conjunction: A word (such as *because, although, if, when*) used to make one clause dependent on, or subordinate to, another: *Unless* you have a key, we are locked out.

EDITING CHECKLIST

Fragments

___ Does the sentence have a subject?
___ Does the sentence have a complete verb?
___ If the sentence contains a subordinate clause, does it contain a clause that is a complete sentence too?
___ If you find a fragment, can you link it to an adjoining sentence, eliminate its subordinating conjunction, or add any missing element?

■ For exercises on fragments, visit <bedfordstmartins.com/ bedguide> and do a keyword search:

    fragments

A2   Check for any comma splices or fused sentences.

A complete sentence has a subject and a predicate and can stand on its own. When two sentences are joined together to form one sentence, each sentence within the larger one is called a *main clause*. However, there are rules for joining main clauses, and when writers fail to follow these rules, they create

main clause: A group of words that has both a subject and a verb and can stand alone as a complete sentence: *My sister has a friend.*

coordinating conjunction: A one-syllable linking word (*and, but, for, or, nor, so, yet*) that joins elements with equal or near-equal importance: Jack *and* Jill, sink *or* swim

subordinating conjunction: A word (such as *because, although, if, when*) used to make one clause dependent on, or subordinate to, another: *Unless* you have a key, we are locked out.

serious sentence errors — comma splices or fused sentences, also called run-on sentences. A *comma splice* is two main clauses joined with only a comma. A *fused sentence* is two main clauses joined with no punctuation at all.

COMMA SPLICE	I went to the mall, I bought a new coat.
FUSED SENTENCE	I went to the mall I bought a new coat.

To find comma splices and fused sentences, examine each sentence to be sure it is complete. If it has two main clauses, make sure they are joined correctly. If you find a comma splice or fused sentence, correct it in one of these four ways, depending on which makes the best sense:

ADD A PERIOD	I went to the mall. I bought a new coat.
ADD A COMMA AND A COORDINATING CONJUNCTION	I went to the mall, and I bought a new coat.
ADD A SEMICOLON	I went to the mall; I bought a new coat.
ADD A SUBORDINATING CONJUNCTION	I went to the mall where I bought a new coat.

■ For exercises on comma splices and fused sentences, visit <bedfordstmartins.com/bedguide> and do a keyword search:

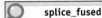 splice_fused

EDITING CHECKLIST

Comma Splices and Fused Sentences

___ Can you make each main clause a separate sentence?

___ Can you link the two main clauses with a comma and a coordinating conjunction?

___ Can you link the two main clauses with a semicolon or, if appropriate, a colon?

___ Can you subordinate one clause to the other?

verb: A word that shows action (The cow *jumped* over the moon) or a state of being (The cow *is* brown)

A3 Check for correct past tense verb forms.

The *form* of a verb, the way it is spelled and pronounced, can change to show its *tense* — the time when its action did, does, or will occur (in the past, present, or future). A verb about something in the present will often be spelled and pronounced differently than a verb about something in the past.

PRESENT	Right now, I *watch* only a few minutes of television each day.
PAST	Last month, I *watched* television shows every evening.

Many writers fail to use the correct form for past tense verbs for two different reasons, depending on whether the verb is regular or irregular.

Regular verbs are verbs whose forms follow standard rules; they form the past tense by adding *-ed* or *-d* to the end of the present tense form: *watch/watched, look/looked, hope/hoped.* Check all regular verbs in the past tense to be sure you have used one of these endings.

FAULTY   I *ask* my brother for a loan yesterday.

CORRECT   I *asked* my brother for a loan yesterday.

FAULTY   Nicole *race* in the track meet last week.

CORRECT   Nicole *raced* in the track meet last week.

TIP: If you say the final *-d* sound when you talk, you may find it easier to add the final *-d* or *-ed* when you write past tense regular verbs.

Irregular verbs do not follow standard rules to make their forms. Their unpredictable past tense forms have to be memorized: *eat/ate, see/saw, get/got.* In addition, the past tense form may differ from the past participle: "She *ate* the whole pie; she *has eaten* two pies this week." The most troublesome irregular verbs are actually very common, so if you make the effort to learn the correct forms, you will quickly improve your writing.

FAULTY   My cat *laid* on the tile floor to take her nap.

CORRECT   My cat *lay* on the tile floor to take her nap.

FAULTY   I *have swam* twenty laps every day this month.

CORRECT   I *have swum* twenty laps every day this month.

■ For a chart showing the forms of many irregular verbs, see pp. A-30–A-31.

participle: A form of a verb that cannot function alone as a main verb, including present participles ending in *-ing* (*dancing*) and past participles often ending in *-ed* or *-d* (*danced*)

TIP: In college papers, follow convention by using the present tense, not the past, to describe the work of an author or the events in a literary work.

FAULTY   In "The Lottery," Shirley Jackson *revealed* the power of tradition. As the story *opened*, the villagers *gathered* in the square.

CORRECT   In "The Lottery," Shirley Jackson *reveals* the power of tradition. As the story *opens*, the villagers *gather* in the square.

EDITING CHECKLIST

Past Tense Verb Forms

____ Have you identified the main verb in the sentence?

____ Is the sentence about the past, the present, or the future? Does the verb reflect this sense of time?

____ Is the verb regular or irregular?

____ Have you used the correct form to express your meaning?

■ For exercises on verbs, visit <bedfordstmartins.com/bedguide> and do a keyword search:

verbs

Principal Parts of Common Irregular Verbs

INFINITIVE (BASE)	PAST TENSE	PAST PARTICIPLE
be	was	been
become	became	become
begin	began	begun
blow	blew	blown
break	broke	broken
bring	brought	brought
burst	burst	burst
catch	caught	caught
choose	chose	chosen
come	came	come
do	did	done
draw	drew	drawn
drink	drank	drunk
drive	drove	driven
eat	ate	eaten
fall	fell	fallen
fight	fought	fought
freeze	froze	frozen
get	got	got, gotten
give	gave	given
go	went	gone
grow	grew	grown
have	had	had
hear	heard	heard
hide	hid	hidden
know	knew	known
lay	laid	laid
lead	led	led
let	let	let
lie	lay	lain
make	made	made
raise	raised	raised
ride	rode	ridden
ring	rang	rung
rise	rose	risen
run	ran	run
say	said	said
see	saw	seen
set	set	set
sing	sang	sung
sit	sat	sat
slay	slew	slain
slide	slid	slid
speak	spoke	spoken

INFINITIVE (BASE)	PAST TENSE	PAST PARTICIPLE
spin	spun	spun
stand	stood	stood
steal	stole	stolen
swim	swam	swum
swing	swung	swung
teach	taught	taught
tear	tore	torn
think	thought	thought
throw	threw	thrown
wake	woke, waked	woken, waked
write	wrote	written

For the forms of irregular verbs not on this list, consult your dictionary. (Some dictionaries list principal parts for all verbs, some just for irregular verbs.)

A4   Check for correct subject-verb agreement.

The *form* of a verb, the way it is spelled and pronounced, can change to show *number* — whether the subject is singular (one) or plural (more than one). It can also show *person* — whether the subject is *you* or *she*, for example.

SINGULAR	Our instructor *grades* every paper carefully.
PLURAL	Most instructors *grade* tests using a standard scale.
SECOND PERSON	You *write* well-documented research papers.
THIRD PERSON	She *writes* good research papers, too.

A verb must match (or *agree with*) its subject in terms of number and person. Regular verbs (those that follow a standard rule to make the different forms) are problems only in the present tense, where they have two forms: one that ends in *-s* or *-es* and one that does not. Only the subjects *he, she, it,* and singular nouns use the verb form that ends in *-s* or *-es.*

I like	we like	Dan likes
you like	you like	the child likes
he/she/it likes	they like	the children like

The verbs *be* and *have* do not follow the *-s/no -s* pattern to form the present tense; they are irregular verbs, so their forms must be memorized. The verb *be* is also irregular in the past tense.

Problems in agreement often occur when the subject is difficult to find, is an indefinite pronoun, or is confusing for some other reason. In particular, make sure that you have not left off any *-s* or *-es* endings and that you have used the correct form for irregular verbs.

verb: A word that shows action (The cow *jumped* over the moon) or a state of being (The cow *is* brown)

subject: The part of a sentence that names something—a person, an object, an idea, a situation—about which the predicate makes an assertion: The *king* lives.

indefinite pronoun: A pronoun standing for an unspecified person or thing, including singular forms (*each, everyone, no one*) and plural forms (*both, few*): *Everyone* is soaking wet.

For a chart showing the forms of many irregular verbs, see pp. A-30–A-31.

Forms of Be and Have at a Glance

THE PRESENT TENSE OF BE

I am	we are
you are	you are
he/she/it is	they are

THE PAST TENSE OF BE

I was	we were
you were	you were
he/she/it was	they were

THE PRESENT TENSE OF HAVE

I have	we have
you have	you have
he/she/it has	they have

THE PAST TENSE OF HAVE

I had	we had
you had	you had
he/she/it had	they had

For exercises on subject-verb agreement, visit <bedfordstmartins.com/bedguide> and do a keyword search:

🔍 **sv agreement**

FAULTY	Jim *write* at least fifty e-mails a day.
CORRECT	Jim *writes* at least fifty e-mails a day.
FAULTY	The students *has* difficulty with the assignment.
CORRECT	The students *have* difficulty with the assignment.
FAULTY	Every one of the cakes *were* sold at the fundraiser.
CORRECT	Every one of the cakes *was* sold at the fundraiser.

EDITING CHECKLIST

Subject-Verb Agreement

___ Have you correctly identified the subject and the verb in the sentence?
___ Is the subject singular or plural? Does the verb match?
___ Have you used the correct form of the verb?

---

pronoun: A word that stands in place of a noun (*he, him,* or *his* for *Nate*)

subject: The part of a sentence that names something—a person, an object, an idea, a situation—about which the predicate makes an assertion: The *king* lives.

subject complement: A noun, an adjective, or a group of words that follows a linking verb (*is, become, feel, seem,* or another verb that shows a state of being) and that renames or describes the subject: This plum tastes *ripe.*

object: The target or recipient of the action of a verb: Some geese bite *people.*

A5 Check for correct pronoun case.

Depending on the role a pronoun plays in a sentence, it is said to be in the *subjective case, objective case,* or *possessive case.* Use the subjective case if the pronoun is the subject of a sentence, the subject of a subordinate clause, or a subject complement (after a linking verb). Use the objective case if the pronoun is a direct or indirect object of a verb or the object of a preposition. Use the possessive case to show possession.

SUBJECTIVE	*I* will argue that our campus needs more parking.
OBJECTIVE	This issue is important to *me.*
POSSESSIVE	*My* argument will be quite persuasive.

There are many types of pronouns, but only some change form to show case. The personal pronouns *I, you, he, she, it, we,* and *they* and the relative pronoun *who* each have at least two forms.

Pronoun Cases at a Glance

SUBJECTIVE	OBJECTIVE	POSSESSIVE
I	me	my, mine
you	you	your, yours
he	him	his
she	her	hers
it	it	its
we	us	our, ours
they	them	their, theirs
who	whom	whose

There are two common errors in pronoun case. First, writers often use the subjective case when they should use the objective case — sometimes because they are trying to sound formal and correct. Instead, choose the correct form for a personal pronoun based on its function in the sentence. If the sentence pairs a noun and a pronoun, try the sentence with the pronoun alone.

FAULTY	My company gave my husband and *I* a trip to Hawaii.
PRONOUN ONLY	My company gave *I* a trip?
CORRECT	My company gave my husband and *me* a trip to Hawaii.

FAULTY	The argument occurred because my uncle and *me* had different expectations.
PRONOUN ONLY	*Me* had different expectations?
CORRECT	The argument occurred because my uncle and *I* had different expectations.

FAULTY	Jack ran faster than *me*.
PRONOUN ONLY	Jack ran faster than *me* ran?
CORRECT	Jack ran faster than *I*.

A second common error with pronoun case involves gerunds. Whenever you need a pronoun to modify a gerund, use the possessive case.

FAULTY	Our supervisor disapproves of *us* talking in the hallway.
CORRECT	Our supervisor disapproves of *our* talking in the hallway.

gerund: A form of a verb, ending in *-ing*, that functions as a noun: Lacey likes *playing* in the steel band.

EDITING CHECKLIST

Pronoun Case

____ Have you identified all the pronouns in the sentence?

____ Does each one function as a subject, an object, or a possessive?

____ Given the function of each, have you used the correct form?

■ For exercises on pronoun case, visit <bedfordstmartins.com/bedguide> and do a keyword search:

case

pronoun: A word that stands in place of a noun (*he, him,* or *his* for *Nate*)

A6 Check for correct pronoun-antecedent agreement.

The *form* of a pronoun, the way it is spelled and pronounced, changes depending on its use in a particular sentence. The form can change to show **number** — whether the subject is singular (one) or plural (more than one). It can change to show **gender** — masculine or feminine, for example — or **person**: first (*I, we*), second (*you*), or third (*he, she, it, they*).

SINGULAR   My brother took *his* coat and left.

PLURAL   My brothers took *their* coats and left.

MASCULINE   I talked to Steven before *he* had a chance to leave.

FEMININE   I talked to Stephanie before *she* had a chance to leave.

In most cases, a pronoun refers to a specific noun or pronoun mentioned nearby; that word is called the pronoun's **antecedent**. The connection between the pronoun and the antecedent must be clear so that readers know what the pronoun means in the sentence. One way to make this connection clear is to ensure that the pronoun and the antecedent match (or *agree*) in number and gender.

A common error in pronoun agreement is using a plural pronoun to refer to a singular antecedent. This error often crops up when the antecedent is difficult to find, when the antecedent is an indefinite pronoun, or when the antecedent is confusing for some other reason. When editing for pronoun-antecedent agreement, look carefully to find the correct antecedent, and make sure you know whether it is singular or plural. Then make the pronoun match its antecedent.

FAULTY   Each of the boys in the Classic Club has *their* own rebuilt car.

CORRECT   Each of the boys in the Classic Club has *his* own rebuilt car.

[The word *each,* not *boys,* is the antecedent. *Each* is an indefinite pronoun and is always singular, so any pronoun referring to it must be singular as well.]

indefinite pronoun: A pronoun standing for an unspecified person or thing, including singular forms (*each, everyone, no one*) and plural forms (*both, few*): *Everyone* is soaking wet.

FAULTY   Everyone in the meeting had *their* own cell phone.

CORRECT   Everyone in the meeting had *his or her* own cell phone.

[*Everyone* is an indefinite pronoun that is always singular, so any pronoun referring to it must be singular as well.]

Indefinite Pronouns at a Glance

ALWAYS SINGULAR			ALWAYS PLURAL
anybody	everyone	nothing	both
anyone	everything	one (of)	few
anything	much	somebody	many
each (of)	neither (of)	someone	several
either (of)	nobody	something	
everybody	no one		

FAULTY   Neither Luz nor Pam has received approval of *their* financial aid yet.

CORRECT   Neither Luz nor Pam has received approval of *her* financial aid yet.

[*Neither Luz nor Pam* is a compound subject joined by *nor*. Any pronoun referring to it must agree with only the nearer part of the compound. In other words, *her* needs to agree with *Pam*, which is singular.]

Indefinite pronouns as antecedents are troublesome when they are grammatically singular but create a plural image in the writer's mind. Fortunately, most indefinite pronouns are either always singular or always plural.

EDITING CHECKLIST

Pronoun-Antecedent Agreement

—— Have you identified the antecedent for each pronoun?
—— Is the antecedent singular or plural? Does the pronoun match?
—— Is the antecedent masculine, feminine, or neuter? Does the pronoun match?
—— Is the antecedent first, second, or third person? Does the pronoun match?

■ For exercises on pronoun-antecedent agreement, visit <bedfordstmartins.com/bedguide> and do a key-word search:

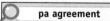

    pa agreement

A7 Check for correct adjectives and adverbs.

Adjectives and *adverbs* describe or give more information about (*modify*) other words in a sentence. Many adverbs are formed by adding *-ly* to adjectives: *simple, simply; quiet, quietly.* Because adjectives and adverbs resemble one another, writers sometimes mistakenly use one instead of the other. To edit, find the word that the adjective or adverb modifies. If that word is a noun or pronoun, use an adjective. (An adjective typically describes which or what kind.) If that word is a verb, adjective, or another adverb, use an adverb. (An adverb typically describes how, when, where, or why.)

modifier: A word (such as an adjective or adverb), phrase, or clause that provides more information about other parts of a sentence: Plays *staged by the drama class* are *always successful.*

FAULTY   Kelly ran into the house *quick*.

CORRECT   Kelly ran into the house *quickly.*

Comparison of Irregular Adjectives and Adverbs

	POSITIVE	COMPARATIVE	SUPERLATIVE
ADJECTIVES	good	better	best
	bad	worse	worst
	little	less, littler	least, littlest
	many, some, much	more	most
ADVERBS	well	better	best
	badly	worse	worst
	little	less	least

| FAULTY | Gabriela looked *terribly* after her bout with the flu. |
| CORRECT | Gabriela looked *terrible* after her bout with the flu. |

Adjectives and adverbs that have similar comparative and superlative forms can also cause trouble. Always ask whether you need an adjective or an adverb in the sentence, and then use the correct word.

| FAULTY | His scar healed so *good* that it was barely visible. |
| CORRECT | His scar healed so *well* that it was barely visible. |

Good is an adjective; it describes a noun or pronoun. *Well* is an adverb; it modifies or adds to a verb (*heal,* in this case) or an adjective.

EDITING CHECKLIST

Adjectives and Adverbs

____ Have you identified which word the adjective or adverb modifies?
____ If the word modified is a noun or pronoun, have you used an adjective?
____ If the word modified is a verb, adjective, or adverb, have you used an adverb?
____ Have you used the correct comparative or superlative form?

■ For exercises on adjectives and adverbs, visit <bedfordstmartins.com/bedguide> and do a keyword search:

🔍   **adj_adv**

Check your sentences to make sure that they are grammatically correct, especially that they are complete (see A1) with parts that agree (see A4). Use the Draft Doctor (pp. A-38–A-39) to help you figure out how to improve your problem sentences. Skim down the left column to identify questions you might ask about your draft. When you answer a question with "Yes" or "Maybe," move straight across the row to the Diagnose column next to that question. Use the diagnostic activities to identify gaps or weaknesses, and then move straight across the row again to the Treat column on the right. Use the advice that suits your problem, and review the relevant section in this guide.

B   *Editing to Ensure Effective Sentences*

B1   Check for any misplaced or dangling modifiers.

modifier: A word (such as an adjective or adverb), phrase, or clause that provides more information about other parts of a sentence: Plays *staged by the drama class* are *always successful.*

For a sentence to be clear, the connection between a modifier and the thing it modifies must be obvious. Usually, a modifier should be placed right before or right after the sentence element it modifies. If the modifier is placed too close to some other sentence element, it is a *misplaced modifier.* If there is nothing in the sentence that the modifier can logically modify, it is a *dangling modifier.* Both of these errors cause confusion for readers — and they sometimes create unintentionally humorous images. As you edit, be sure that a modifier is placed directly before or after the word modified and that the connection between the two is clear.

MISPLACED	George found the leftovers when he visited in the refrigerator.
CORRECT	George found the leftovers in the refrigerator when he visited.
	[In the faulty sentence, *in the refrigerator* seems to modify George's visit. Obviously the leftovers are in the refrigerator, not George.]
DANGLING	Looking out the window, the clouds were beautiful.
CORRECT	Looking out the window, I saw that the clouds were beautiful.
CORRECT	When I looked out the window, the clouds were beautiful.
	[In the faulty sentence, *looking out the window* should modify *I*, but *I* is not in the sentence. The modifier is left without anything logical to modify—a dangling modifier. To correct this, the writer has to edit so that *I* is in the sentence.]

EDITING CHECKLIST

Misplaced and Dangling Modifiers

___ What is each modifier meant to modify? Is the modifier as close as possible to that sentence element? Is any misreading possible?

___ If a modifier is misplaced, can you move it to clarify the meaning?

___ What noun or pronoun is a dangling modifier meant to modify? Can you make that word or phrase the subject of the main clause? Or can you turn the dangling modifier into a clause that includes the missing noun or pronoun?

■ For exercises on misplaced and dangling modifiers, visit <bedfordstmartins.com/bedguide> and do a keyword search:

  modifiers

B2 **Check for parallel structure.**

A series of words, phrases, clauses, or sentences with the same grammatical form is said to be *parallel*. Using parallel form for elements that are parallel in meaning or function helps readers grasp the meaning of a sentence more easily. A lack of parallelism can distract, annoy, or even confuse readers.

To use parallelism, put nouns with nouns, verbs with verbs, and phrases with phrases. Parallelism is particularly important in a series, with correlative conjunctions, and in comparisons using *than* or *as*.

correlative conjunction: A pair of linking words (such as *either/or, not only/but also*) that appear separately but work together to join elements of a sentence: *Neither* his friends *nor* hers like pizza.

FAULTY	I like to go to Estes Park for skiing, ice skating, and to meet interesting people.
CORRECT	I like to go to Estes Park to ski, to ice skate, and to meet interesting people.
FAULTY	The proposal is neither practical, nor is it innovative.
CORRECT	The proposal is neither practical nor innovative.
FAULTY	A parent should have a few firm rules rather than having many flimsy ones.
CORRECT	A parent should have a few firm rules rather than many flimsy ones.

Draft Doctor: Correcting Major Sentence Errors

If you sense a problem, ASK	If you answer Yes/Maybe, DIAGNOSE	If you diagnose a problem, TREAT
Incomplete Sentences or Fragments? Have I written any sentences that actually might be incomplete?	• Check the parts of short or choppy sentences carefully. Put an * by any word group that does not state a verb. FRAGMENT (NO VERB): The fish in Trio Lake.* • Put an X by any word group that does not state a subject. FRAGMENT (NO SUBJECT): Suffer from illnesses and strange growth patterns. X • Underline any word group that begins with a subordinating word such as *because, although,* or *unless.* FRAGMENT: Unless state regulations change.	• Complete any sentence you have marked with an * or an X by adding the missing element (subject or verb) or by joining the incomplete part to a nearby complete sentence (see A1). COMPLETE (MISSING WORDS ADDED, IN ITALICS): The fish in Trio Lake *suffer from illnesses and strange growth patterns.* OR The fish in Trio Lake *are unhealthy. They* suffer from illnesses and strange growth patterns. • Connect any word group you have underlined to a nearby complete sentence, or drop the subordinating word and supply any missing words so that the word group can stand alone. COMPLETE: Unless state regulations change, *chemical run-off will continue to damage Trio Lake.* • Complete each sentence (see A1). Edit until it reads smoothly.
Sentences Fused or Spliced Together? Have I run together several sentences that might be incorrectly fused or spliced?	• Check any long sentences that might contain two or more complete sentences spliced together with a comma or simply fused together without any punctuation. • Underline or color code each separate sentence contained in the long sentence. • Mark any comma used to splice the sentences or any unpunctuated fusion. COMMA SPLICE: Organic crops are grown without chemical fertilizers or pesticides, farmers rely on traditional methods.	• Divide separate sentences with a period and a capital letter. DIVIDED: Organic crops are grown without chemical fertilizers or pesticides. Farmers rely on traditional methods. • Connect separate sentences in one of these ways: (1) with a comma and a coordinating conjunction (*and, but, for, or, nor, so, yet*), (2) with a colon or a semicolon, or (3) with a semicolon and a conjunctive adverb (such as *also, however, namely, therefore, finally*) (see A2). CONNECTED: Organic crops are grown without chemical fertilizers

If you sense a problem, ASK	If you answer *Yes/Maybe,* DIAGNOSE	If you diagnose a problem, TREAT
Sentences Fused or Spliced Together? (continued)		or pesticides, *and* farmers rely on traditional methods.
		• Connect the less important sentence with a subordinating word (for example, *because, despite, although, if, unless* or a relative pronoun such as *who, which, that*).
		CONNECTED: *Because* organic crops are grown without chemical fertilizers or pesticides, farmers rely on traditional methods.
		• Experiment and edit to find the version that presents what you mean (see A2).
Agreement Problems? Have I written any sentences whose parts do not match?	• Underline the subject, and note its form (first person *I,* second person *you,* or third person *he, she, it, they*). Double underline the verb, and see whether its form corresponds. • Underline the subject, and note its number (singular for one, plural for more). Double underline the verb or the related pronoun, and see whether it matches the subject.	• Correct any mismatched sentence by changing the subject to match the verb or by changing the verb to match the subject. • Watch for words between subject and verb that mislead you into picking the wrong form or number. • When the subject is a collective noun that refers to a group (such as *jury, committee, family*), treat the word as singular if the group acts as a single unit: The board <u>votes</u> <u>its</u> conscience today. Treat it as plural if the members act individually: The board <u>vote</u> as <u>their</u> consciences dictate.
	DRAFT: The <u>students</u> who filled out the survey form <u>agrees</u> strongly about the need to expand the studio.	REVISED: The <u>students</u> who filled out the survey form <u>agree</u> strongly about the need to expand the studio. • Rewrite an awkward or misaligned sentence (see A4).
Any Other Sentence Errors? After a final look at the sentences in my draft, should I do anything else to correct them?	• Read your draft out loud to yourself, marking any other sentence errors. • Ask your peer editors whether they see other sentences you should correct.	• Return to each mark to complete, divide, connect, align, or otherwise correct any sentence errors. • Consider advice from your peers. • Edit until your sentences are correct and clear (see the Editing Checklist, p. A-26).

Take special care to reinforce parallel structures by repeating articles, conjunctions, prepositions, or lead-in words as needed.

AWKWARD His dream was that he would never have to give up his routine but he would still find time to explore new frontiers.

PARALLEL His dream was that he would never have to give up his routine but *that* he would still find time to explore new frontiers.

EDITING CHECKLIST

Parallel Structure

____ Are all the elements in a series in the same grammatical form?

____ Are the elements in a comparison parallel in form?

____ Are the articles, conjunctions, or prepositions between elements repeated rather than mixed or omitted?

____ Are lead-in words repeated as needed?

 For exercises on parallel structure, visit <bedfordstmartins.com/bedguide> and do a keyword search:

parallel

Check your sentences to figure out how to construct or express them more effectively. Use the Draft Doctor (pp. A-41–A-43) to help you spot sentences with too much passive voice, faulty parallelism, or dull, repetitive, or wordy passages. Skim down the left column to identify questions you might ask about sentences in your draft. When you answer a question with "Yes" or "Maybe," move straight across the row to the Diagnose column next to that question. Use the diagnostic activities to identify gaps or weaknesses, and then move straight across the row again to the Treat column on the right. Use the advice that suits your problem, and review relevant sections of the book as needed.

C *Editing for Common Punctuation Problems*

C1 Check for correct use of commas.

The *comma* is a punctuation mark indicating a pause. By setting some words apart from others, commas help clarify relationships; they prevent the words on a page and the ideas they represent from becoming a jumble. Here are some of the most important conventional uses of commas.

1. Use a comma before a coordinating conjunction (*and, but, for, or, so, yet, nor*) joining two main clauses in a compound sentence.

   The discussion was brief, *so* the meeting was adjourned early.

2. Use a comma after an introductory word or word group unless it is short and cannot be misread.

   After the war, the North's economy developed rapidly.

3. Use commas to separate the items in a series of three or more items.

    The chief advantages will be *speed, durability,* and *longevity.*

4. Use commas to set off a modifying clause or phrase if it is nonrestrictive — that is, if it can be taken out of the sentence without significantly changing the essential meaning of the sentence.

    Good childcare, *which is difficult to find,* should be provided by the employer.

    Good childcare *that is reliable and inexpensive* is the right of every employee.

5. Use commas to set off a nonrestrictive appositive, an expression that comes directly after a noun or pronoun and renames it.

    Sheri, my sister, has a new job as an events coordinator.

6. Use commas to set off parenthetical expressions, conjunctive adverbs, and other interrupters.

    The proposal from the mayor's commission, however, is not feasible.

appositive: A word or group of words that adds information about a subject or object by identifying it in a different way: my dog *Rover,* Hal's brother *Fred*

parenthetical expression: An aside to readers or a transitional expression such as *for example* or *in contrast*

conjunctive adverb: A linking word that can connect independent clauses and show a relationship between two ideas: Armando is a serious student; *therefore,* he studies every day.

EDITING CHECKLIST

Commas

—— Have you added a comma between two main clauses joined by a coordinating conjunction?

—— Have you added commas needed after introductory words or word groups?

—— Have you separated items in a series with commas?

—— Have you avoided putting commas before the first item in a series or after the last?

—— Have you used commas before and after each nonrestrictive word, phrase, or clause?

—— Have you avoided using commas around a restrictive word, phrase, or clause?

—— Have you used commas to set off appositives, parenthetical expressions, conjunctive adverbs, and other interrupters?

■ For exercises on commas, visit <bedfordstmartins.com/bedguide> and do a keyword search:

🔍   comma

C2   Check for correct use of apostrophes.

An *apostrophe* is a punctuation mark that either shows possession (*Sylvia's*) or indicates that one or more letters have intentionally been left out to form a contraction (*didn't*). Because apostrophes are easy to overlook, writers often omit a necessary apostrophe, use one where it is not needed, or put one in the wrong place. An apostrophe is never used to create the possessive form of a pronoun; use the possessive pronoun form instead.

FAULTY   *Mikes* car was totaled in the accident.

CORRECT   *Mike's* car was totaled in the accident.

FAULTY   *Womens'* pay is often less than *mens'.*

CORRECT   *Women's* pay is often less than *men's.*

Draft Doctor: Improving Sentence Style

If you sense a problem, ASK	If you answer *Yes/Maybe*, DIAGNOSE	If you diagnose a problem, TREAT
Passive Voice? Have I relied on sentences in the passive voice instead of the active voice? Could I change a sentence like *The ball was thrown by John* (passive) to *John threw the ball* (active)?	• Reread your sentence. If its subject also performs the action, your sentence is in the active voice. (You might underline the performer and double underline the action.) • If the sentence subject does not perform the action, your sentence is in the passive voice. You have either not identified the performer of the action or tucked the performer into a *by* phrase.	• Consider changing passive voice to active. Make the performer of the action the sentence subject (which reduces extra words by dropping the *by* phrase). PASSIVE: The primate play area <u>was arranged</u> by the zookeeper. (nine words; emphasizes object of the action) ACTIVE: The zookeeper <u>arranged</u> the primate play area. (seven words; emphasizes zookeeper, who performed the action)
Faulty Parallelism? Have I missed opportunities to emphasize comparable ideas by stating them in comparable ways?	• Read your sentences, looking for lists or comparable items. • Underline items in a series to compare the ways you present them (see B2). DRAFT: Observing primates can reveal how they <u>cooperate, their</u> <u>tool use</u>, and <u>building</u> secure nests.	• Rework so that items in a series all follow the same grammatical pattern. • Select the common pattern based on the clarity and emphasis it adds to your sentence. PARALLEL: Observing primates can reveal how they <u>cooperate</u>, <u>use</u> tools, and <u>build</u> secure nests.
Repetitive Sentence Openings? Do I begin too many sentences the same way so that they all sound alike?	• Add a line break at the end of every sentence in a passage to compare your sentence openings. • Highlight any opening patterns that seem repetitive and dull.	• Rewrite for variety if you repeat opening expressions (*During, After, Then, And, Because*). • Rewrite for directness if you repeat indirect openings (*There are, There is, It is*).
Repetitive Sentence Patterns? Have I written sentences that are boring because they are the same length and follow the same pattern?	• Add a line break at the end of every sentence in a passage so you can easily compare their patterns. With software (or on your own), count the words in each sentence. • Search for variations such as colons (:) and semicolons (;) to see how often you use them.	• Vary sentence lengths if they are all about the same. Tuck in a few short, direct sentences. Combine short, choppy sentences. Add an occasional complicated sentence to elaborate on or build up to your point. • If you rarely use colons or semicolons, try adding some for variety.

If you sense a problem, ASK	If you answer *Yes/Maybe,* DIAGNOSE	If you diagnose a problem, TREAT
Dull Sentences? Have I written correct but boring sentences that will not motivate my audience to keep reading?	• Read the sentences in a passage, and highlight the key words or ideas you want to emphasize. • Read a dull passage, and circle the boring, uninteresting, or overused words.	• Rewrite so highlighted words play major roles as active subjects and lively verbs. Position them for emphasis—beginning or ending, not lost in the middle. • Replace circled words with concrete nouns, energetic verbs, or precise adjectives or adverbs.
Disconnected or Scattered Ideas? Have I tended to toss out my ideas without weighting or relating them?	• Highlight the transitional words (*First, second; for example; however*) in your sentences (see pp. 346–49). • Check all the sentences or sentence parts in a passage that seem to be of equal weight.	• Review passages with little highlighting; add more transitions to relate ideas. • In your checked sentences, introduce less significant parts with subordinating words (*because, although*). Use *and* or *but* to coordinate equal parts.
Wordy Sentences? Have I used more words than needed to say what I mean?	• Read your draft out loud. Check anything that sounds long-winded, repetitive, chatty, or clichéd. • Use past papers to help you list your favorite wordy expressions (such as *a large number of* for *many*) or extra words (such as *very* or *really*).	• At each check, rephrase with simpler expressions or more exact words (see pp. 379–81). • Search with your software for wordy expressions; replace or trim them. • Highlight a passage; use the Tools menu to count its words. See how many extra words you can drop.
Any Other Improvements in Sentence Style? After a final look at the sentences in my draft, should I do anything else to improve them?	• Read your draft out loud. Mark any sentences that sound awkward, confusing, or lifeless. • Ask your peer editors how you might make your sentences stronger and more stylish.	• Return to each mark to make weak sentences clear, emphatic, and lively. • Consider the useful suggestions of your peers. • Refer to Section B of this guide as you edit until your sentences express your ideas as you wish them to.

Possessive Personal Pronouns at a Glance

PERSONAL PRONOUN	POSSESSIVE CASE
I	my, mine
you	your, yours (*not* your's)
he	his
she	her, hers (*not* her's)
it	its (*not* it's)
we	our, ours (*not* our's)
they	their, theirs (*not* their's)
who	whose (*not* who's)

FAULTY   Che *did'nt* want to stay at home and study.

CORRECT   Che *didn't* want to stay at home and study.

FAULTY   The dog wagged *it's* tail happily.

CORRECT   The dog wagged *its* tail happily.

FAULTY   *Its* raining.

CORRECT   *It's* raining. [it's = it is]

EDITING CHECKLIST

■ For exercises on apostrophes, visit <bedfordstmartins.com/bedguide> and do a keyword search:

🔍   **apostrophe**

Apostrophes

___ Have you used an apostrophe when letters are left out in a contraction?

___ Have you used an apostrophe to create the possessive form of a noun?

___ Have you used the possessive case — rather than an apostrophe — to show that a pronoun is possessive?

___ Have you used *it's* correctly (to mean *it is*)?

C3 Check for correct punctuation of quotations.

When you quote the exact words of a person you have interviewed or a source you have read, be sure to enclose those words in quotation marks. Notice how student Betsy Buffo presents the words of her subject in this passage from her essay "Interview with an Artist":

> Derek is straightforward when asked about how his work is received in the local community: "My work is outside the mainstream. Because it's controversial, it's not easy for me to get exposure."

She might have expressed and punctuated this passage in other ways:

> Derek says that "it's not easy" for him to find an audience.

> Derek struggles for recognition because his art falls "outside the mainstream."

If your source is quoting someone else (a quotation within a quotation), put your subject's words in quotation marks and the words he or she is quoting in single quotation marks. Always put commas and periods inside the quotation marks; put semicolons and colons outside.

> As Betsy Buffo explains, "Derek struggles for recognition because his art falls 'outside the mainstream.'"

Substitute an ellipsis mark (. . .) — three spaced dots — for any words you have omitted from the middle of a direct quotation. If you are following MLA style, you may place the ellipses inside brackets ([. . .]) when necessary to avoid confusing your ellipsis marks with those of the original writer. If the ellipses come at the end of a sentence, add another period to conclude the sentence. You don't need an ellipsis mark to show the beginning or ending of a quotation that is clearly incomplete.

In this selection from "Playing Games with Women's Sports," student Kelly Grecian identifies both quotations and an omission:

> "The importance of what women athletes wear can't be underestimated," Rounds claims. "Beach volleyball, which is played . . . by bikini-clad women, rates network coverage" (44).

> For more about quotations from sources, see D3 in the Quick Research Guide (the dark-red-edged pages).

Common errors in punctuating quotations include leaving out necessary punctuation marks or putting them in the incorrect place or sequence.

EDITING CHECKLIST

Punctuation with Quotations

—— Are the exact words quoted from your source enclosed in quotation marks?

—— Are commas and periods placed inside closing quotation marks?

—— Are colons and semicolons placed outside closing quotation marks?

—— Have you used ellipses to show where any words are omitted from the middle of a quotation?

> For exercises on using and punctuating quotation marks, visit <bedfordstmartins.com/bedguide> and do a keyword search:
>
> 🔍   quotation

D   *Editing for Common Mechanics and Format Problems*

D1   Check for correct use of capital letters.

Capital letters are used in three general situations: to begin a new sentence; to begin names of specific people, nationalities, places, dates, and things (proper nouns); and to begin main words in titles. Writers sometimes use capital letters where they are not needed, such as for emphasis, or fail to use them where they are needed.

FAULTY   During my Sophomore year in College, I took World Literature, Biology, History, Psychology, and French — courses required for a Humanities Major.

CORRECT   During my sophomore year in college, I took world literature, biology, history, psychology, and French — courses required for a humanities major.

EDITING CHECKLIST

For exercises on using capital letters, visit <bedfordstmartins.com/bedguide> and do a keyword search:

capitals

Capitalization

____ Have you used a capital letter at the beginning of each complete sentence, including sentences that are quoted?

____ Have you used capital letters for proper nouns and pronouns?

Capitalization at a Glance

Capitalize the following:

THE FIRST LETTER OF A SENTENCE, INCLUDING A QUOTED SENTENCE
She called out, "Come in! The water's warm."

PROPER NAMES AND ADJECTIVES MADE FROM THEM
Marie Curie   Cranberry Island
Smithsonian Institution   a Freudian reading

RANK OR TITLE BEFORE A PROPER NAME
Ms. Olson   Professor Santocolon

FAMILY RELATIONSHIP ONLY WHEN IT SUBSTITUTES FOR OR IS PART OF A PROPER NAME
Grandma Jones   Father Time

RELIGIONS, THEIR FOLLOWERS, AND DEITIES
Islam   Orthodox Jew   Buddha

PLACES, REGIONS, GEOGRAPHIC FEATURES, AND NATIONALITIES
Palo Alto   the Berkshire Mountains   Egyptians

DAYS OF THE WEEK, MONTHS, AND HOLIDAYS
Wednesday   July   Labor Day

HISTORICAL EVENTS, PERIODS, AND DOCUMENTS
the Boston Tea Party   the Middle Ages   the Constitution

SCHOOLS, COLLEGES, UNIVERSITIES, AND SPECIFIC COURSES
Temple University   Introduction to Clinical Psychology

FIRST, LAST, AND MAIN WORDS IN TITLES OF PAPERS, BOOKS, ARTICLES, WORKS OF ART, TELEVISION SHOWS, POEMS, AND PERFORMANCES
The Decline and Fall of the Roman Empire   "The Lottery"

—— Have you avoided using capital letters for emphasis?

—— Have you used a capital letter for each main word in a title, including the first word and the last word? (Prepositions, coordinating conjunctions, and articles are not considered main words.)

D2 Check spelling.

Misspelled words are difficult to spot in your own writing. You usually see what you think you wrote, and often pronunciation or faulty memory may interfere with correct spelling. When you proofread for spelling, check for words that sound alike but are spelled differently (*accept* and *except*, for example), words that are spelled differently than they are pronounced, words that do not follow the basic rules for spelling English words (*judgment*, for example), and words that you habitually confuse and misspell.

EDITING CHECKLIST

Spelling

—— Have you checked for the words you habitually misspell?

—— Have you checked for commonly confused or misspelled words?

—— Have you applied the standard spelling rules, including their exceptions?

—— Have you checked a dictionary for any words you are unsure about?

—— Have you run your spell checker? Have you read your paper carefully for errors that it would miss?

preposition: A transitional word (such as *in, on, at, of, from*) that leads into a phrase

coordinating conjunction: A one-syllable linking word (*and, but, for, or, nor, so, yet*) that joins elements with equal or near-equal importance

article: The word *a, an,* or *the*

▪ For a list of commonly confused words, see p. A-48. For a list of commonly misspelled words, see pp. A-49–A-51.

▪ For spelling exercises, visit <bedfordstmartins.com/bedguide> and do a keyword search:

🔍   **spelling**

Checking Your Spelling

If you know the words you habitually misspell, you can use your software's Search or Find functions to locate all instances and check the spelling. Consider keeping track of misspelled words in your papers for a few weeks so you can take advantage of this feature to simplify your editing.

Spell checkers offer a handy alternative to the dictionary, but you need to be aware of their limitations. A spell checker compares the words in your text with the words listed in its dictionary, and it highlights words that do not appear there. (The size of computer spelling dictionaries varies greatly, but most contain fewer entries than a typical college-level dictionary in book form.) A spell checker cannot help you spell words that its dictionary does not contain, including most proper nouns. Spell checkers ignore one-letter words; for example, they will not flag a typographical error such as *s truck* for *a truck*. Nor will they highlight words that are misspelled as different words, such as *except* for *accept, to* for *too,* or *own* for *won*. Always check the spelling in your text by eye *after* you've used your spell checker.

Grammar checkers may note some commonly confused words, but they often do this even when you have used the correct form. Use a dictionary to decide whether to accept the grammar checker's suggestion.

FOR E-WRITERS

COMMONLY CONFUSED HOMONYMS

accept (v., receive willingly); **except** (prep., other than)

Mimi could *accept* all of Lefty's gifts *except* his ring.

affect (v., influence); **effect** (n., result)

If the new rules *affect* us, what will be their *effect*?

allusion (n., reference); **illusion** (n., fantasy)

Any *allusion* to Norman's mother may revive his *illusion* that she is upstairs, alive, in her rocking chair.

capital (adj., uppercase; n., seat of government); **capitol** (n., government building)

The *Capitol* building in our nation's *capital* is spelled with a *capital* C.

cite (v., refer to); **sight** (n., vision or tourist attraction); **site** (n., place)

Did you *cite* Aunt Peg as your authority on which *sites* feature the most interesting *sights*?

complement (v., complete; n., counterpart); **compliment** (v. or n., praise)

For Lee to say that Sheila's beauty *complements* her intelligence may or may not be a *compliment*.

desert (v., abandon; n., hot, dry region); **dessert** (n., end-of-meal sweet)

Don't *desert* us by leaving for the *desert* before *dessert*.

elicit (v., bring out); **illicit** (adj., illegal)

By going undercover, Sonny should *elicit* some offers of *illicit* drugs.

formally (adv., officially); **formerly** (adv., in the past)

Jane and John Doe-Smith, *formerly* Jane Doe and John Smith, sent cards *formally* announcing their marriage.

led (v., past tense of *lead*); **lead** (n., a metal)

Gil's heart was heavy as *lead* when he *led* the mourners to the grave.

principal (n. or adj., chief); **principle** (n., rule or standard)

The *principal* problem is convincing the media that our school *principal* is a person of high *principles*.

stationary (adj., motionless); **stationery** (n., writing paper)

Hubert's *stationery* shop stood *stationary* until a flood swept it away.

their (pron., belonging to them); **there** (adv., in that place); **they're** (contraction of *they are*)

Sue said *they're* going over *there* to visit *their* aunt.

to (prep., toward); **too** (adv., also or excessively); **two** (n. or adj., numeral: one more than one)

Let's not take *two* cars *to* town — that's *too* many unless Hal comes *too*.

who's (contraction of *who is*); **whose** (pron., belonging to whom)

Who's going to tell me *whose* dog this is?

your (pron., belonging to you); **you're** (contraction of *you are*)

You're not getting *your* own way this time!

COMMONLY MISSPELLED WORDS

absence
academic
acceptable
accessible
accidentally
accommodate
achievement
acknowledgment
acquaintance
acquire
address
advertisement
advice
advise
aggravate
aggressive
aging
allege
all right
all together (all in
    one group)
a lot
already
although
altogether (entirely)
amateur
analysis
analyze
answer
anxiety
appearance
appetite
appreciate
appropriate
arctic
argument
ascent
assassinate
assistance
association
athlete
athletics
attendance
audience
average
awkward
basically
beginning

believe
beneficial
benefited
breath (noun)
breathe (verb)
bureaucracy
business
calendar
careful
casualties
category
cemetery
certain
changeable
changing
characteristic
chief
choose (present tense)
chose (past tense)
climbed
column
coming
commitment
committed
comparative
competition
conceive
condemn
congratulate
conscience
conscientious
conscious
consistent
controlled
criticism
criticize
curiosity
curious
deceive
decision
defendant
deficient
definite
dependent
descendant
describe
description
desirable

despair
desperate
develop
development
device (noun)
devise (verb)
diary
difference
dilemma
dining
disappear
disappoint
disastrous
discipline
discussion
disease
dissatisfied
divide
doesn't
dominant
don't
drunkenness
efficiency
eighth
either
embarrass
entirety
environment
equipped
especially
exaggerate
exceed
excel
excellence
exercise
exhaust
existence
experience
explanation
extremely
familiar
fascinate
February
fiery
financial
foreign
foresee
forth

(continued)

COMMONLY MISSPELLED WORDS *(continued)*

forty
forward
fourth (number four)
frantically
fraternities
friend
fulfill
gaiety
genealogy
generally
genuine
government
grammar
grief
guarantee
guard
guidance
harass
height
heroes
herring
humorous
illiterate
illogical
imitation
immediately
incredible
indefinite
independence
indispensable
infinite
influential
intelligence
intentionally
interest
interpret
interrupt
irrelevant
irresistible
irritable
island
its (possessive)
it's (it is, it has)
jealousy
judgment
knowledge
laboratory
led (past tense of *lead*)
library

license
lightning
literature
loneliness
loose (adjective)
lose (verb)
lying
magazine
maintenance
marriage
mathematics
medicine
miniature
mischievous
misspell
muscle
mysterious
necessary
neither
niece
ninety
ninth
noticeable
notorious
nuclear
nucleus
numerous
obstacle
occasionally
occur
occurrence
official
omission
omitted
opinion
opportunity
originally
outrageous
paid
pamphlet
panicky
parallel
particularly
pastime
peaceable
perceive
performance
permanent
permissible

persistence
personnel
persuade
physical
playwright
possession
possibly
practically
precede
predominant
preferred
prejudice
prevalent
privilege
probably
procedure
proceed
professor
prominent
pronounce
pronunciation
pursue
quantity
quiet
quite
quizzes
realize
rebelled
recede
receipt
receive
recipe
recommend
reference
referring
regrettable
relevance
relief
relieve
religious
remembrance
reminisce
reminiscence
repetition
representative
resistance
restaurant
review
rhythm

ridiculous	supersede	unnoticed
roommate	suppress	until
sacrifice	surprise	useful
safety	suspicious	usually
scarcely	technical	valuable
schedule	technique	vengeance
secretary	temperature	vicious
seize	tendency	view
separate	therefore	villain
siege	thorough	warrant
similar	thoroughbred	weather
sincerely	though	Wednesday
sophomore	thought	weird
source	throughout	whether
specifically	tragedy	who's (who is)
sponsor	transferred	whose (possessive
strategy	traveling	of *who*)
strength	truly	withhold
stretch	twelfth	woman
succeed	tyranny	women
successful	unanimous	
suddenness	unnecessary	

D3 ## Check for correct manuscript form.

In case you have received no particular instructions for the form of your paper, here are some general, all-purpose specifications.

GENERAL MANUSCRIPT STYLE FOR COLLEGE ESSAYS, ARTICLES, AND REPORTS

1. Pick a conventional, easy-to-read typeface such as Courier, Times New Roman, or Palatino. Make sure you have a fresh cartridge in your printer. If you handwrite your paper, keep your handwriting legible.

2. Print in black ink. Use dark blue or black ink if you write by hand.

3. Write or print on just one side of standard letter-size bond paper (8½ inches by 11 inches). If you handwrite your paper, use 8½-by-11-inch paper with smooth edges (not torn from a spiral-bound notebook).

4. For a paper without a separate title page, place your name, your instructor's name, the number and section of the course, and the date in the upper left or right corner of the first page, each item on a new line. (Ask whether your instructor has a preference for which side.) Double-space and center your title. Don't underline the title, don't put it in quotation marks or use all capital letters, and don't put a period after it. Capitalize the first and last words, the first word after a colon or semicolon, and all other words except prepositions, coordinating conjunctions, and articles. Double-space between the title and the first line of your text. (Most instructors do not

For more on document design, see Ch. 21. For an example of MLA-style paper format, see p. 391.

preposition: A transitional word (such as *in, on, at, of, from*) that leads into a phrase

coordinating conjunction: A one-syllable linking word (*and, but, for, or, nor, so, yet*) that joins elements with equal or near-equal importance

article: The word *a, an,* or *the*

require a title page for short college papers. If your instructor requests one but doesn't give you any guidelines, see number 1 under Additional Suggestions for Research Papers, below.)

5. Number your pages consecutively, including the first. For a paper of two or more pages, use a running header to put your last name in the upper right corner of each sheet along with the page number. (Use the heading option under View or Edit.) Do not type the word *page* or the letter *p* before the number, and do not follow it with a period or parenthesis.

6. Leave ample margins — at least an inch — left, right, top, and bottom.

7. If you use a word processor, double-space your manuscript; if you handwrite, use wide-ruled paper or skip every other line.

8. Indent each new paragraph five spaces or one-half inch.

■ For more about citing sources, see D6 and E1 in the Quick Research Guide (the dark-red-edged pages).

9. Long quotations should be double-spaced like the rest of your paper but indented from the left margin — ten spaces (one inch) if you're following MLA (Modern Language Association) guidelines, five spaces (one-half inch) if you're using APA (American Psychological Association) guidelines. Put the source citation in parentheses immediately after the final punctuation mark of the block quotation.

10. Label all illustrations. Make sure any insertions are bound securely to the paper.

11. Staple the paper in the top left corner, or use a paper clip as MLA advises. Don't use any other method to secure the pages unless one is recommended by your instructor.

12. For safety's sake and peace of mind, make a copy of your paper, and back up your file.

ADDITIONAL SUGGESTIONS FOR RESEARCH PAPERS

For research papers, the format is the same as recommended in the previous section, with the following additional specifications.

1. The MLA guidelines do not recommend a title page. If your instructor wants one, type the title of your paper, centered and double-spaced, about a third of the way down the page. Go down two to four more lines and type your name, the instructor's name, the number and section of the course, and the date, each on a separate line and double-spaced.

2. Do not number your title page; number your outline, if you submit one with your paper, with small roman numerals (i, ii, iii, and so on). Number consecutively all subsequent pages in the essay, including your "Works Cited" or "References" pages, using arabic numerals (1, 2, 3, and so on) in the upper right corner of the page.

■ For examples of MLA and APA documentation style, see E1 and E2 in the Quick Research Guide (the dark-red-edged pages).

3. Double-space your list of works cited or references.

HOW TO MAKE A CORRECTION

Before you produce your final copy, make any large changes in your draft, edit and proofread carefully, and run your spell checker. When you give your paper a last once-over, however, don't be afraid to make small corrections in pen. In making such corrections, you may find it handy to use certain symbols used by printers and proofreaders.

A transposition mark (⌒) reverses two words or two letters:

The nearby star Tau Ceti closely resmebles our sun.

Close-up marks (⌒) bring together the parts of a word accidentally split. A separation mark (|) inserts a space where one is needed:

The nearby star Tau Ceti closely re sembles our|sun.

To delete a letter or punctuation mark, draw a line with a curlicue through it:

The nearby star Tau Ceti closely ressembles our sun.

Use a caret (∧) to indicate where to insert a word or letter:

The nearby star Tau Ceti closely reᵊembles our sun.

The symbol ⁋ before a word or a line means "start a new paragraph":

Recently, astronomers have reduced their efforts to study dark nebulae. ⁋ That other solar systems may also support life makes for another fascinating speculation.

To make a letter lowercase, draw a slanted line through it. To make a letter uppercase, put three short lines under it:

i̲ read it for my Ⱨistory class.

You can always cross out a word neatly, with a single horizontal line, and write a better one over it.

                                    closely
The nearby star Tau Ceti ~~somewhat~~ resembles our sun.

Finally, if a page has many corrections on it, print or write it over again.

▪ See the back inside pages of this book for a list of correction symbols.

ACKNOWLEDGMENTS (continued from p. iv)

Joe Brooks, excerpts from "How to Catch More Trout." First published in *Outdoor Life*, May 2006. Copyright © 2006 by Time4 Media, Inc. Reprinted with the permission of the publishers. All rights reserved. Reproduction in any medium is strictly prohibited without permission from Time4 Media, Inc. Such permission may be requested from *Outdoor Life* magazine.

Jonathan Burns, "The Hidden Truth: An Analysis of Shirley Jackson's 'The Lottery'" and "A Synopsis of 'The Lottery.'" Reprinted with the permission of the author.

David Callahan, "A Question of Character" from *The Cheating Culture: Why More Americans Are Doing Wrong to Get Ahead*. Copyright © 2004 by David Callahan. Reprinted with the permission of Harcourt, Inc., and the Stuart Agency. This material may not be reproduced in any form or by any means without the prior written permission of the publisher.

Tim Chabot, "Take Me Out to the Ball Game, but Which One?" Reprinted with the permission of the author.

Yun Yung Choi, "Invisible Women." Reprinted with the permission of the author.

Michael Coil, "Communications." Reprinted with the permission of the author.

Heather Colbenson, from "Missed Opportunities." Reprinted with the permission of the author.

Annie Dillard, from *An American Childhood* by Annie Dillard. Copyright © 1987 by Annie Dillard. Reprinted with the permission of HarperCollins Publishers, Inc.

Tamara Draut, "What's a Diploma Worth, Anyway?" First posted on <www.AlterNet.org>, September 7, 2006. Reprinted with the permission of the author.

Freeman Dyson, from *Infinite in All Directions* by Freeman Dyson. Copyright © 1988 by Freeman Dyson. Reprinted with the permission of HarperCollins Publishers, Inc.

David Edmonds and John Eidinow, from "Fear and Flight" in *Rousseau's Dog*. Copyright © 2006 by David Edmonds and John Eidinow. Reprinted with the permission of HarperCollins Publishers, Inc., and David Higham Associates, Ltd.

Barbara Ehrenreich, "Guys Just Want to Have Fun." First published in *Time*, July 31, 2006. Copyright © 2006 by Barbara Ehrenreich. Reprinted by permission of International Creative Management, Inc.

Robert Frost, "Putting in the Seed" and "The Road Not Taken" from *The Poetry of Robert Frost*, edited by Edward Connery Lathem. Copyright 1916, 1969 by Henry Holt and Company. Reprinted with the permission of Henry Holt and Company, LLC.

David Gelernter, "Computers Cannot Teach Children Basic Skills" from "Unplugged" in the *New Republic*, September 19 and 25, 1994. Copyright © 1994. Reprinted by permission of the New Republic, LLC.

Nancy Gibbs, "Free the Children." Originally published in *Time*, July 14, 2003: 80. Copyright © 2003 by Time, Inc. Reprinted with permission.

Sarah E. Goers, from "Is Inclusion the Answer?" Reprinted with the permission of the author.

Terry Golway, "A Nation of Idol-Worshipers." First published in *America Magazine* 195.3, July 31, 2006: 9. Copyright © 2006. Reprinted with the permission of American Press, Inc. All rights reserved. For more information, visit <www.americamagazine.org>.

Suzan Shown Harjo, "Last Rites for Indian Dead." First published in the *Los Angeles Times*, September 16, 1989. Copyright © 1989 by Suzan Shown Harjo. Reprinted with the permission of the author.

Harvard Magazine, "Creating Community, Online and Off." First published in *Harvard Magazine*, January–February 2004. Copyright © 2004 by the President and Fellows of Harvard College. Reprinted with the permission of the publisher.

Shirley Jackson, "The Lottery" from *The Lottery and Other Stories* by Shirley Jackson. Copyright © 1948, 1949 by Shirley Jackson. Copyright renewed © 1976, 1977 by Laurence Hyman, Barry Hyman, Mrs. Sarah Webster, and Mrs. Joanne Schnurer. Reprinted with the permission of Farrar, Straus and Giroux, LLC.

Robert Jensen, "The High Cost of Manliness." Originally posted on <www.AlterNet.org>, September 8, 2006. Copyright © 2006 Independent Media Institute. Reprinted with permission. All rights reserved.

Stephen King, "Why We Crave Horror Movies." First published in *Playboy*, 1982. Copyright © by Stephen King. Reprinted with permission. All rights reserved.

Jeffrey Kluger, "The New Science of Siblings" from *Time*, July 10, 2006: 47-48. Copyright © 2006 by Time, Inc. Reprinted with permission.

Al Knight, "Perhaps We Should Move to Save Dogs from Their Owners" from the *Denver Post*, November 21, 2006. Reprinted with the permission of the author.

Susan Brady Konig, "They've Got to Be Carefully Taught" from *National Review*, September 15, 1997. Copyright © 1997 by National Review Inc. Reprinted with the permission of *National Review*, 215 Lexington Avenue, New York, NY 10016.

Alex Koppelman, "MySpace or OurSpace?" Posted on <www.Salon.com>, June 8, 2006. An online version remains in the Salon archives. Reprinted with permission.

Dawn Kortz, "Listen." Reprinted with the permission of the author.

William Severini Kowinski, "Kids in the Mall: Growing Up Controlled" from *The Malling of America: An Inside Look at the Great Consumer Paradise* by William Severini Kowinski. Published by New York: William Morrow, 1985. Copyright © 1985 by William Severini Kowinski. Reprinted with the permission of the author.

Ruth La Ferla, "Latino Style Is Cool. Oh, All Right: It's Hot" from the *New York Times*, April 15, 2001. Copyright © 2001 by the New York Times Company. Reprinted with permission.

Melissa Lamberth, "Overworked!" Reprinted with the permission of the author.

Jeffery M. Leving and Glenn Sacks, "Women Don't Want Men? Ha!" from the *Chicago Tribune*, January 21, 2007. Reprinted with the permission of the authors.

Steven Levy, from *The Perfect Thing: How the iPod Shuffles Commerce, Culture, and Coolness* by Steven Levy. Copyright © 2006 by Steven Levy. Reprinted with the permission of Simon & Schuster Adult Publishing Group.

Eric Liu, "The Chinatown Idea" from *The Accidental Asian: Notes of a Native Speaker*. Copyright © 1998 by Eric Liu. Reprinted with the permission of Random House, Inc.

Charles C. Mann and Mark L. Plummer, "The Butterfly Problem." First published in the *Atlantic Monthly* 269, No. 1, January 1992. Copyright © 1992 by Charles C. Mann and Mark L. Plummer. Reprinted with the permission of the authors.

Merrill Markoe, "Who Am I?" First published in *ON: Time Digital Online Magazine*, March 2001. Copyright © 2001 by Merrill Markoe. Reprinted with the permission of the Melanie Jackson Agency, LLC.

Daniel Matthews, from "Taps." Reprinted with the permission of the author.

John McCain, adapted from "The Virtues of the Quiet Hero" in *This I Believe*. Copyright © 2005 by John McCain. Copyright © 2006 by

This I Believe, Inc. Reprinted by permission of Henry Holt and Company, LLC.

Christy De'on Miller, "Give Me Five More Minutes" from *Operation Homecoming: Iraq, Afghanistan, and the Home Front in the Words of U.S. Troops and Their Families*, edited by Andrew Carroll. Copyright © 2006. Reprinted with the permission of Random House, Inc.

Evelyn F. Murphy with E. J. Graff, "Why Not a Dollar?" from *Getting Even: Why Women Don't Get Paid Like Men — and What to Do about It.* Copyright © 2005 by Evelyn F. Murphy with E. J. Graff. Reprinted with the permission of Simon & Schuster Adult Publishing Group.

Madeleine J. Nash, from "The Case for Cloning" in *Time*, February 9, 1998. Copyright © 1998 by Time, Inc. Reprinted by permission.

Dennis O'Neil, "Katrina Documentary Gives Voice to Survivors" from the *Louisville Cardinal*, September 12, 2006. Copyright © 2006. Reprinted with permission.

Tara Parker-Pope, "Custom-Made" from the *Wall Street Journal Europe*, September 30, 1996. Reprinted with permission.

Noel Perrin, "A Part-Time Marriage" from the *New York Times Magazine*, September 9, 1984. Copyright © 1984 by the New York Times Company. Reprinted with permission.

James Poniewozik, "Why Reality TV Is Good for Us" from *Time*, February 17, 2003. Copyright © 2003 by Time, Inc. Reprinted with permission.

Anna Quindlen, "Evan's Two Moms" from *Thinking Out Loud: On the Personal, the Political, the Public and the Private.* Copyright © 1993 by Anna Quindlen. Reprinted with the permission of Random House, Inc.

Anjula Razdan, "What's Love Got to Do with It?" from the *Utne Reader*, June 2003. Copyright © 2003. Reprinted with the permission of the author. This essay includes Emily Dickinson, "Split the Lark — and You'll Find the Music—" from *The Poems of Emily Dickinson*, edited by Thomas H. Johnson. Copyright © 1951, 1955, 1979 by the President and Fellows of Harvard College. Reprinted by permission of the Belknap Press of Harvard University Press.

Elaina Richardson, "Bono-Fire: U2's Brilliant Front Man Rocks Convention" from *O, The Oprah Magazine*, February 1, 2002. Copyright © 2002 Hearst Communications, Inc. All rights reserved. Reprinted with the permission of Hearst Communications, Inc. This essay includes W. B. Yeats, "The Second Coming" (1 line) from *The Collected Works of W. B. Yeats, Volume 1: The Poems*, Revised, edited by Richard J. Finneran. Copyright © 1924 by Macmillan Publishing Company. Copyright renewed 1952 by Bertha Georgie Yeats. Reprinted with permission from Scribner, an imprint of Simon & Schuster Adult Publishing Group.

Wilbert Rideau, "Why Prisons Don't Work." First published in *Time*, March 21, 1994. Copyright © 1994. Reprinted with the permission of the author.

Richard Rodriguez, "Public and Private Language" from "Aria: Memory of a Bilingual Childhood" in *Hunger of Memory: The Education of Richard Rodriguez: An Autobiography.* Copyright © 1980, 1982 by Richard Rodriguez. Reprinted with the permission of Georges Borchardt, Inc., for the author.

Carl T. Rowan, "Unforgettable Miss Bessie" from *Reader's Digest*, March 1985. Copyright © 1985 by the Reader's Digest Association, Inc. Reprinted with the permission of *Reader's Digest*.

William Saletan, from "Please Do Not Feed the Humans." First published in *Slate*, September 2, 2006. Copyright © 2006. Reprinted with the permission of United Media.

Lindsey Schendel, from "How to Heal a Broken Heart (in One Day)." Reprinted with the permission of the author.

Robert G. Schreiner, "What Is a Hunter?" Reprinted with the permission of the author.

Danzy Senna, "The Color of Love." First published in *O, The Oprah Magazine*, 2000. Copyright © 2000 by Danzy Senna. Reprinted with the permission of International Creative Management, Inc.

Brent Staples, "Black Men and Public Space." First published in *Ms.* magazine, September 1986. Copyright © 1986 by Brent Staples. Reprinted with the permission of the author.

Seth Stevenson, "Wham! Bam! Buy a VW, Ma'am!" First published in *Slate*, May 8, 2006. Copyright © 2006 by Seth Stevenson. Reprinted with the permission of PFD, New York.

Amy Tan, "The Mother Tongue." First appeared in *The Threepenny Review*. Copyright © 1990 by Amy Tan. Reprinted by permission of the author and the Sandra Dijkstra Literary Agency.

Lillian Tsu, from "A Woman in the White House." First published in *Cornell Political Forum*, 1997. Copyright © 1997 by Lillian Tsu. Reprinted with the permission of the author.

Sherry Turkle, "How Computers Change the Way We Think." First published in the *Chronicle of Higher Education*, 2004. Copyright © 2004 by Sherry Turkle. Reprinted with the permission of the author.

Anne Underwood, from "The Good Heart" in *Newsweek*, October 3, 2005. Copyright © 2005 by Newsweek, Inc. Reprinted with permission.

E. B. White, "Once More to the Lake" from *One Man's Meat* by E. B. White. Text copyright 1941 by E. B. White. Copyright renewed. Reprinted with the permission of Tilbury House, Publishers, Gardiner, Maine, and Allene White.

Carrie Williamson, from "Rainforest Destruction." Reprinted with the permission of the author.

Yangfeng Wu, "Overweight and Obesity in China" from <www.bmj.com>, August 19, 2006. Print version published in *BMJ* 333, 362–63. Copyright © 2006 by BMJ. Reprinted with the permission of the publisher.

William Zinsser, "The Right to Fail" from *The Lunacy Boon*, New York: Harper & Row, 1970. Copyright © 1969, 1970 by William K. Zinsser. Reprinted by permission of the author.

Art Credits (in order of appearance):

Page 17: *Atlantic Monthly* subscription advertisement. Copyright © the Atlantic Monthly Group. Reprinted by permission. All rights reserved.

Page 26: Graphic of literal and analytical reading skills adapted from *Taxonomy of Educational Objectives, Handbook I: Cognitive Domain* by Benjamin S. Bloom et al. © 1956 McKay.

Page 55: Photo collage of recalled experiences © Lawrence Migdale/Photo Researchers, Inc.; © H. Armstrong Roberts/Aurora Photos, Inc.; © Michael Schwarz/The Image Works; and © Mario Tama/Getty Images, Inc.

Page 65: Photo of soccer game courtesy of Dan Jahn for Photofiler.com.

Page 70: Career day photo © Sarah Gilbert/*Iowa State Daily*.

Page 71: Photo of bungee jumper © John Storey/Getty Images, Inc.

Page 79: Photo of band practice © Ben Ailes Photography.

Page 86: Bar chart © LabWrite /Miriam Ferzli, Ph.D., North Carolina State University. Used with permission.

Page 86: Photo of destroyed fraternity house © Steve Bittner/*Cumberland* (Maryland) *Times-News.*

Page 87: Photo collage of famous people © AP Images/Martin Meissner; © AP Images/Stephen Chemin; and © Bob Daemmrich/The Image Works.

Page 95: Experts database courtesy of Northwestern University.

Page 103: Photo of woman surveying pedestrians © Jeff Greenberg/The Image Works.

Page 104: Photo of Chicago housing development © Jason Reblando.

Page 120: Bar chart of employment data courtesy of the Bureau of Labor Statistics.

Page 120: Camera ratings chart copyright 2003 by Consumers Union of U.S., Inc., Yonkers, NY 10703-1057, a nonprofit organization. Reprinted with permission from the October 2003 issue of *Consumer Reports* for educational purposes only. No commercial use or reproduction permitted. www.ConsumerReports.org.

Page 121: Photo of smokestack under the sun © D. Nunuk/Photo Researchers, Inc.

Page 132: Chart of projected global temperature change courtesy of the Intergovernmental Panel on Climate Change.

Page 138: Graphic on workforce changes from *Business 2.0*. Copyright © 2003 Xplanations TM by xplane.com.

Page 139: Photo of student protest against sweatshops © Jeff Greenberg/The Image Works.

Page 148: Photo of student war protest © Andrew J. Scott/*The Chronicle*.

Page 164: Map showing tuition increases courtesy of the National Center for Public Policy and Higher Education.

Page 165: Poster against consumerism © Jaivin Anzalota.

Page 166: "Riders wanted" advertisement courtesy of <www.adbusters.org>.

Page 173: Ford Foundation grants database reprinted with the permission of The Ford Foundation.

Page 181: Photo of workers reviewing construction plans © Syracuse Newspapers/The Image Works.

Page 182: Poster promoting reading courtesy of Christina Beck. Reprinted with permission.

Page 183: Photo of woman with traffic sign on her head © Lou Beach.

Page 190: Photo of Belhaven College Theatre Department production of *Romeo and Juliet* by Dr. Lou Campbell.

Page 198: Web page from George Mason University Career Services created by Career Services staff.

Page 198: Graphic on video game ratings © AP Images.

Page 199: Photo collage of source usage © John Birdsall/The Image Works; © Sonda Dawes/The Image Works; © Jeff Greenberg/The Image Works; and courtesy of the Trustees of the Boston Public Library.

Page 212: Google search results courtesy of google.com. Used by permission.

Page 232: Photo of police officer filling out report © Bob Daemmrich/The Image Works.

Figure 21.1: *USA Today* front page copyright 2007, USA TODAY. Reprinted with permission. *Wall Street Journal* front page reprinted with permission of the *Wall Street Journal*. Copyright © 2007 Dow Jones & Company, Inc. All rights reserved worldwide.

Figure 21.3: *Utne Reader* spread © Hannah Lobel/Reprinted from the *Utne Reader*. Used by permission. Photo courtesy NASA. *Parenting* magazine spread © the Parenting Group, Inc. Photo © Gabe Palmer/Corbis.

Figure 21.4: Brochure design showing prominent elements by Studio InFlux/The Art Institute of Boston at Lesley University: Jenny Barrett, ManChing Cheng, Lisa Goode, and Yehudit Massouda-Winiarz.

Figure 21.12: Web page illustrating heading usage © 2007 National Service-Learning Partnership at the Academy for Educational Development.

Figure 21.17: Web page illustrating use of color © Smithsonian Institution.

Figure 21.18: Diagram of wastewater treatment courtesy of King County, Washington, Wastewater Treatment Division.

Figure 21.19: Illustration of work at an archaeological dig © DK Images.

Figure 21.20: Weekly album sales © *Billboard*.

Figure 21.22: Bar chart of numerical comparisons courtesy of *Technology Review*. Copyright 2008 by MIT *Technology Review*. Reproduced with permission of MIT *Technology Review* via Copyright Clearance Center. Research by Jason Hill, Erik Nelson, David Tilman, Stephen Polasky, and Douglas Tiffany/University of Minnesota.

Figure 21.23: Table illustrating food portions by Sara Weeks © Copyright 2002, *Health* magazine. For subscriptions please call 1-800-274-2522.

Figure 22.1: Public-service announcement with one prominent element copyright © 2005 by the American Psychological Association. <actagainstviolence.apa.org/materials/psa/ADCA04B0113-Driver.pdf>. Date retrieved: May 29, 2007. Used by permission.

Figures 22.2–22.5: Photo of four children (Kodak Picture of the Day) © Merrilee A. Giegerich.

Figure 22.6: Volkswagen advertisement courtesy Volkswagen of America, Inc.

Figure 22.7: Oldsmobile advertisement courtesy of Leo Burnett.

Figure 22.8: "Stairway" type design © Hyunmee Kum, Samsung Art and Design Institute.

Figure 22.9: "Type as cultural cliché" from Roy Paul Nelson, *Publication Design* © 1990. Reprinted with permission of the McGraw-Hill Companies.

Figure 22.10: Photograph conveying a mood © Jonathan Nourok/PhotoEdit.

Figure 22.11: Photograph with missing element courtesy of the National Park Service. Reprinted with permission.

Figure 22.12: Public-service advertisement showing wordplay © D. Reed Monroe.

Figure 22.13: Billboard showing wordplay © Bill Aron/PhotoEdit.

Figure 22.14: Public-service advertisement using symbolism courtesy of the Ad Council and Project Safe Neighborhoods.

Figure 22.15: Poster conveying a theme courtesy of the Ad Council and the U.S. Department of Transportation.

Page 440: Photo of family gathered for a meal © Tom McCarthy/PhotoEdit.

Page 474: Photo of man and woman at a café © Mary Kate Denny/PhotoEdit.

Page 501: "Sign Language" cartoon © Carol Lay.

Page 529: Man and woman talking on cell phones © Bill Aron/PhotoEdit.

Page 560: Cartoon of basketball game © the New Yorker Collection 2002, Edward Koren from <cartoonbank.com>. All rights reserved.

Icons used for boxed features throughout text: "Draft Doctor" photo © Photodisc/Getty Images, Inc.; "For E-Writers" photo © Photodisc/Getty Images, Inc.; and "For Group Learning" photo © Digital Vision/Getty Images, Inc.

Index